ROMANCE OF THE THREE KINGDOMS

LO KUAN-CHUNG'S

Romance of the Three Kingdoms

« SAN KUO CHIH YEN-I »

translated by
C. H. BREWITT-TAYLOR

VOLUME TWO

CHARLES E. TUTTLE CO.: PUBLISHERS
Rutland, Vermont & Tokyo, Japan

Representatives
Continental Europe: BOXERBOOKS, INC., *Zurich*
British Isles: PRENTICE-HALL INTERNATIONAL, INC., *London*
Australasia: PAUL FLESCH & CO., PTY. LTD., *Melbourne*
Canada: M. G. HURTIG LTD., *Edmonton*

Published by the Charles E. Tuttle Company, Inc.
of Rutland, Vermont & Tokyo, Japan
with editorial offices at
Suido 1-chome, 2-6, Bunkyo-ku, Tokyo, Japan

© 1959 by Charles E. Tuttle Co., Inc.

Library of Congress Catalog Card No. 79-94950

Standard Book No. 8048 0728-0

First published in 1925
by Kelly & Walsh, Ltd., Shanghai

First Tuttle edition, 1959
Third printing, 1970

PRINTED IN JAPAN

TABLE OF CONTENTS.

VOLUME II.

86184

ROMANCE OF THE THREE KINGDOMS

VOLUME TWO

CHAPTER LXI.

In spite of the persuasion of P'ang T'ung and Fa Chêng, Liu Pei steadily refused to sanction the assassination of his host, even if thereby he was to gain possession of the land of Shu.

The next day there was another banquet, this time in the city, whereat host and guest unbosomed themselves freely to each other and became exceedingly friendly and affectionate. All were mellow with wine, and P'ang T'ung, talking with Fa Chêng said, "Since our master will have nothing to do with our scheme we had better set Wei Yen's sword-play to work and take advantage of the confusion to kill Liu Chang."

Wei Yen came in shortly afterward, with his sword drawn, and said, "There being no other distraction at this banquet, may I show you a little fencing to amuse you?"

Thereupon P'ang T'ung called up some of the armed men and ranged them along the lower part of the hall till Wei should fall on. At these preparations the officers of Liu Chang stared with questioning eyes toward the chief seats at the upper end, and one of them, Chang Jên, drew his sword, saying, "An opponent is needed to make fencing a succees, so he and I will display our skill at the same time."

So they began. Presently, at a glance from Wei Yen, Liu Fêng came up and took position at his side. At once three of the officers of Shu followed suit, saying, "And we three will come in too; it may add to your amusement and help to raise a laugh."

But to Liu Pei matters began to take on a serious look. Drawing the two swords he wore, one on the right side and the other on the left, he stood out in the banquet hall and cried, "We brothers have perhaps honoured our meeting with a little too much wine; there is nothing to say against that, but this is no Hung-mên Gathering, where murder was done. Put up your swords or I will slay you!"

"Why wear swords at all at a meeting of two brothers?" cried Liu Chang, at the same time telling his servants to surround his officers and take away their weapons.

Disarmed, they sulkily withdrew, and then Liu Pei called all the captains to the upper end of the banquet hall, gave them wine and said, "You need have no doubts; we two brothers, of the same bone and blood, have talked over the great design and we are one in purpose."

The officers bowed and retired. Liu Chang took his guest by the hand, saying, "Brother, I shall never forget your kindness."

They sat drinking till late, both feeling very happy. When at length Liu Pei reached his camp he blamed his strategist for having caused the confusion.

"Why did you endeavour to force me into committing a great wrong?" said Liu. "There must be no repetition of this."

P'ang T'ung retired, sighing. When Liu Chang reached his own camp his captains waited on him and said, "Sir, you saw the real meaning of that occurrence at the banquet, we suppose. We think it prudent for you to retire at once into the city."

"My brother is different from ordinary men," replied Liu Chang.

"He may not incline toward murder himself, but those about him have but one desire—that is to exploit this land of ours to their own advantage."

"Do not try to sow dissension between us and make us quarrel," said their chief.

And he took no heed of their remonstrance. One day, when he and Liu Pei were enjoying together relaxation from cares of state, the news came that Chang Lu was about to invade Shu at the Chiaming Pass. Thereupon the Prefect begged Liu Pei to go and defend it. He consented and left immediately with his own especial band. At once Liu Chang's officers took advantage of the guest's departure to urge the Prefect to place his own trusty men in command at various strategic points, so as to guard against any attempts of the visitors to seize the land. At first Liu Chang was unwilling and refused, but as they prayed him most earnestly to do this he yielded and consented to take some steps to safeguard himself. He sent Yang Huai, the commander at Paishui, and Kao P'ei to garrison Foushui Pass.

So Liu Chang returned to Ch'êngtu and his guest, Liu Pei, went away to the point where invasion threatened. Arrived there, he soon won the hearts of the people by the strict discipline he maintained over his men and by his gracious manner.

News of these doings in Shu duly reached Wu, and the Marquis summoned his counsellors as to his countermove. Then Ku Yung spoke, saying, "I have an infallible plan to propose. Liu Pei and his army are now far away and separated from us by difficult country. Therefore he cannot return quickly, and my advice is to occupy the passes so that he cannot get through. Then send all your force against Chingchou and Hsiangyang and they will surely fall to you."

" The plan seems excellent," said Sun Ch'üan.

But just then a voice was heard from behind the screen crying, " You may just put to death the man who proposed that scheme for trying to compass the death of my daughter."

Every one started with surprise. It was the Dowager's voice. Further, she looked very angry as she entered, saying, "What is to become of my only daughter, who is the wife of Liu Pei?"

She turned her wrathful eyes to Sun and said, "You were heir to your father and brother and obtained possession of all this district without the least effort. Yet you are dissatisfied, and would forget the claims of your own flesh and blood and sacrifice my daughter for the sake of adding a little to your lands."

"No, no!" murmured Sun, ashamed. "I would never think of going contrary to my mother's wishes and orders."

He abruptly dismissed the assembly, and when they had gone the old lady, still nursing her wrath, retired to her own apartments.

Left alone beneath the portico, Sun Ch'üan sighed sadly. "This chance missed! When will those provinces be mine?" thought he.

While still deep in reverie, Chang came up, saying, "What grieves my lord?"

"No great matter; only this last failure to gain my ends."

"The difficulty may be easily removed," said Chang. "Choose some trusty man and charge him with a secret letter to the Princess saying that her mother is dangerously ill. Give him a half company as escort and tell him to make his way privily into Chingchou and deliver the letter. Hearing her mother wants her she will rush home at once, and she might bring with her the only son of Yüan-tê. He will be glad enough to exchange Chingchou for his son. If he will not, you can still send the army."

"That sounds like a good plan," said Sun. "Further, I have the man to carry it out successfully. He is that Chou Shan, who was a burglar when he was younger and a bold one. He used to accompany my brother. He is the man to go."

"Keep it a secret, then," said Chang, "and let him start quickly."

It was decided that Chou Shan should take with him about half a company of soldiers disguised as ordinary traders. He had five vessels and distributed his men among them, while weapons were hidden in the holds. A letter was forged to look like a veritable letter from the court of Wu.

Chou Shan set out along the river route for Chingchou and was not long on the way. He anchored his ships under the bank, landed and went into the city to the residence, where he bade the doorkeepers announce him. He was admitted and led into the presence of the Lady Sun and presently gave her the secret letter. When she read that her mother was in danger of death she began to weep bitterly and questioned the messenger closely. Chou invented a long story that the Dowager was really fretting for a sight of her daughter and if she did not go quickly it would be too late. He added that she was to take little O-tou with her that her mother might see him once before she died.

The Lady Sun replied, "You know that the Imperial Uncle is far away on military service and I ought to inform the chief of the army before returning home."

"But what will you do if he says he must inform your husband and await his consent?" said Chou.

"If I went without asking permission—but I fear that is impossible."

"My ships are all ready in the river and you have only to drive through the city," said Chou.

Naturally the news of her mother's illness greatly disturbed the young wife. In a short time her carriage was ready and she mounted, taking O-tou with her. She took an escort of thirty men, all armed, and was soon at the river side and had embarked before the palace people could report what she was doing. But just as the ships were starting, a voice was heard, shouting, "Do not start yet; let me bid my lady farewell."

The voice was Chao Yün's; he had just returned from an inspection trip and they had at once told him of Lady Sun's sudden departure. As soon as he had recovered from his surprise he dashed down to the river bank like a whirlwind, with only half a dozen followers. He arrived only just in time; the boat was starting and Chou Shan stood in the prow, a long spear in his hand.

"Who are you that you dare hinder the movements of your mistress?" cried Chou.

Chou bade his men cast off and get under way, and also to prepare their weapons to fight. The ship moved off with a fair wind and a strong current beneath her keel.   .

But Chao Yün followed along the bank. "My lady may go or not as she pleases," cried he, "but I have one word to say to her."

Chou Shan turned a deaf ear and only urged his men to get greater speed on the ship. Chao Yün followed down the bank for some ten or more *li*. Then he saw a fishing boat made fast to the bank. He at once dismounted, cast off the rope, took his spear and leaped into the boat. Then he made the two men row him toward the vessel in which sat Lady Sun. As he approached, the men of Wu threatened him with their spears. Thereupon he threw his spear into the bottom of the boat, drew the glittering steel blade he wore, dashed aside the opposing spears and leaped upon the larger vessel. The men of Wu fell back in surprise and fear, and Chao went down into the body of the ship. There sat the Lady Sun with little O-tou in her arms.

"Why this rude intrusion?" said she angrily.

The warrior sheathed his sword and said humbly, "Whither may my mistress be going, and why goes she privily?"

"My mother is ill and on the point of death; I had no time to inform any person of my departure," said the Lady Sun.

"But why take the young master if you are going merely to see a sick person?" said Chao.

"O-tou is my son and I would not leave him behind to be neglected."

"Mistress, you have acted wrongly. My lord has but this one son of his body and I rescued him from among many legions in the great battle at Ch'angpan Slope. There is no reason for you to take him away."

The Lady Sun took refuge in anger. "You leave my family affairs alone, you common soldier," cried she.

"My lady, if you will go, then go, but leave the young master behind."

"You are a rebel, jumping on board the ship like that!" shrieked the Lady Sun.

"If you will not leave the young lord behind I refuse to let you go, come what may," said Chao.

The Lady Sun called in her maids to seize him, but he just pushed them off. Then he took the boy from her arms and ran out to the prow of the ship. He tried to get the vessel in to the bank, but no one would aid him, and he thought it would be wrong to begin to slay indiscriminately. He knew not what to do in such a quandary. And the Lady Sun was screaming to her maids to take the boy away from Chao. But he kept too firm a grip on the child, and the good sword in his other hand kept every one at bay.

Chou Shan was at the helm, giving all his attention to getting the ship out into the current and away down the river. He steered for the middle of the stream, where the wind was strong. Chao Yün, one hand taken up with holding the boy, was quite unable to get the vessel in toward the shore.

Just as things looked most desperate, Chao saw a string of ships filing out from a creek lower down the stream, flags fluttering and drums beating. He thought that certainly all was over and he was about to fall a victim to a stratagem of Wu, when he noticed a mighty warrior standing in the prow of the leading craft. He was armed with a long spear, and it was Chang Fei. He also shouted to his sister-in-law to leave the child.

Chang Fei had been out scouting when he heard the news of his sister-in-law's sudden departure, and he at once made for the Yu River with the intention of intercepting her flight.

He had arrived just in the nick of time to cut off the ships of Wu. Very soon, sword in hand, he had boarded the vessel. As he came on board Chou drew his sword and advanced toward him, but one sweep of Chang's blade laid him on the deck dead. And the grim warrior flung his head at the feet of the Lady Sun.

"Why this very unseemly behaviour?" cried the Lady Sun, now quite frightened.

"Sister," said Chang, "you thought very little of my brother when you set out on this mad journey. That was behaving rudely."

"My mother is very ill; it is a matter of life and death," cried she. "If I had waited for your brother's permission to go I should have been too late. If you do not let me go now I will throw myself into the river."

The two soldiers took counsel together. It was hardly the correct thing for servants to force their lord's wife into committing suicide. Suppose they kept the child and let the vessel go.

Then they said, "O Lady, we cannot allow the wife of our exalted brother to die a death of shame and so we will take our leave. We trust you will not forget our brother and that you will return quickly."

Taking the child with them they left the vessel, and the five ships of Wu continued their voyage down stream. One poet has praised the conduct of Chao Yün:—

> Some years before, Chao saved O-tou,
> What time his mother died;
> Again like service he performs,
> Upon the Yangtse's tide.
> The men of Wu all in the ship,
> Were stricken down with fear,
> Search all the world, you never find
> Of bold Chao Yün the peer.

Another has eulogised Chang Fei:—

> At Long Slope Bridge,
> With rage Fei boiled,
> Like wild beast roared,
> And men recoiled.
> From danger now
> His prince is saved.
> On history's page
> His name is graved.

Quite satisfied with their success the two warriors sailed homeward. Before they had gone far they met K'ung-ming with a squadron of ships. He was very pleased to find they had recovered the child and they three joyfully returned to Chingchou, whence an account of the whole adventure was written to Liu Pei.

When the Lady Sun reached her home she related the story
of the death of Chou Shan and the carrying off of the child.
Naturally Sun Ch'üan was very wrath at the miscarriage of
his scheme and he resolved to attack Chingchou in revenge
for his messenger's murder.

"Now that my sister has returned home there is no longer
any family tie to prevent the attack, and I will take full
measure of revenge for the death of my henchman," said Sun.
So he called the council to consider the expedition.

But before they could decide upon any plan their delibera-
tions were suddenly cut short by the news that Ts'ao Ts'ao was
coming down upon the south with forty legions, burning to
avenge his defeat at Ch'ihpi (Red Wall). All thoughts now
turned toward repelling his attack.

The Recorder Chang Hung, who had retired to his home
ill, had just died and his testament was sent to his lord to read.
Therein he advised Sun Ch'üan to remove the seat of government to Moling, where the scenery seemed to bear the impress
of kingly dignity, befitting a man who cherished the ambition
of founding an enduring dynasty. Sun read this document
out to his councillors at this meeting, not without some tears
in memory of the writer. He told them he could not withstand
such advice, and he at once gave orders to surround with a wall
the city which he intended henceforth to make his capital.

As a protection against Ts'ao the Admiral Lu Mêng proposed
building a rampart at Port Juhsü. Some other officers opposed
this, saying, "When the enemy appears you will have to land
in order to attack him, and after that you will return to your
ships. What is the use of a rampart?"

Lü Mêng replied, "One must prepare against possibilities.
Soldiers vary in keenness and sometimes lose battles. If an
urgent occasion arises the men may be unable to reach the
water's edge, and how then are they to embark? They will
then need shelter."

Sun Ch'üan said, "Provision against eventualities, such as
he proposes, is good. Against a distant risk provide, and
sorrow walks not by your side."

So they sent many legions of men to build ramparts at Juhsü,
and as the work ceased not day or night the wall was soon
completed.

In the capital Ts'ao Ts'ao's influence and glory waxed daily
greater. Tung Chao proposed that the title of *Kung* (Duke)
should be conferred upon him. He said, "In all history no one
has rendered such services as you have, O Minister, not even
Duke Chou or Lü Wang. These thirty years you have exposed
yourself to all risks, been ' combed by the wind and bathed by
the rain ' and you have swept evil from the land, succoured the
distressed and restored the Hans. Who of all statesmen can
rank with you? It would be fitting for you to become the

Duke of Wei and receive the Nine Gifts, that your merit and virtue be known to all."

Now the Nine Gifts, or signs of honour, were:—

Chariots and Horses (gilt chariots and war chariots drawn by eight horses);
Court Dress;
Music at Banquets, etc.;
Red Doors;
Steps to the Daïs;
Guards (300 at the gates);
Axes;
Bow and Arrows (red-lacquered bow with 100 arrows);
Libation Vessels.

However, all the courtiers were not of one mind. Said Hsün Yü, "This should not be done, O Minister. You raised a force by an appeal to the innate sense of righteousness of the people, and with that force you restored the Han authority. Now you should remain loyal and humble. The virtuous man loves men with a virtuous love and would not act in this way."

Ts'ao Ts'ao did not take this opposition kindly. Tung Chao said, "How can we disappoint the hopes of many because of the words of one?"

So a memorial went to the Throne and Ts'ao's ambitions and desires were gratified with the title of Duke of Wei. The Nine Gifts were added.

"I did not think to see this day," said Hsün, sighing.

This remark was repeated to the newly created Duke and angered him. He took it to mean that Hsün Yü would no longer aid him or favour his designs.

In the winter of the seventeenth year, Ts'ao decided to send an army to conquer Wu, and he ordered Hsün Yü to go with it. Hsün Yü understood from this that Ts'ao wished his death, so he declined the appointment on the plea of illness. While he was at home he received one day a box such as one sent with presents of dainties. It was addressed in Ts'ao's own handwriting. Opening it he found therein nothing. He understood; he took poison and died. He was fifty-two years of age.

> Wên-jo's talents were to all men known,
> 'Twas sad that at the door of power he tripped.
> Posterity is wrong to class him with the noble Liu,
> For, nearing death, he dared not face his lord of Han.

News of his death came to Ts'ao in the form of the ordinary letter of mourning. Then he was sorry and gave orders for an imposing funeral. He also obtained for the dead man the posthumous title of Marquis.

The northern army reached Juhsü, whence he sent a reconnaisance of three legions down to the river. On the river he saw displayed a fleet of ships all arranged in admirable order, the divisions being marked by distinctive flags. The equipment glittered in the sunlight. In the centre was a large ship whereon was a huge umbrella, and beneath the shade sat Sun Ch'üan in the midst of his staff.

"That is the sort of son to have;" said Ts'ao in admiration, "not such piglets and puppies as Liu Piao's."

Suddenly, at the explosion of a bomb, the ships got under way and came flying toward him, while a force moved out of Juhsü. Ts'ao's men at once retired in great haste. A company led by the grey-eyed, red-bearded Sun Ch'üan made straight for Ts'ao, who hastily retreated. But he was sore pressed by other captains and it had gone hard with him but that Hsü Chu came to his rescue and fought with the men of Wu till his master could escape. Hsü Chu fought some score bouts before he could draw off and return to his own side.

When Ts'ao returned to camp he conferred rich rewards upon his henchman who had saved him and he reprimanded his other captains for their too hasty retirement. "You blunt the keen spirits of the men, and if you do such a thing again I will put you to death," said he.

About midnight that night there arose great commotion at the gates of the camp, and when Ts'ao went outside he found that the enemy had crept up secretly and started a conflagration. They forced their way into the stockade and went hither and thither, slaying till morning broke. Then Ts'ao and his army retired.

Ts'ao Ts'ao was greatly distressed by this misfortune. He was sitting in his tent poring over the Book of War when Ch'êng Yü came in to see him.

"O Minister," said Ch'êng, "you who know so thoroughly the art of war, have you forgotten the maxim to strike quickly? You had your army ready, but you postponed action and allowed your enemies to build them ramparts at Juhsü. Now you will find it hard to capture the place. It would be better now to retreat on the capital and await a more propitious moment."

Ts'ao listened, but said nothing; after a time Ch'êng went away. Ts'ao remained seated in his tent, leaning on a small table by his side. And he fell asleep. Suddenly he heard a sound as of a rushing stream or galloping squadrons of horse, and out of the river in front of him arose a huge red sun, so bright that his eyes were dazzled by it. Looking up at the sky he saw two other suns as if reflections of this one. And as he wondered the first sun suddenly flew up and then dropped among the hills in front of his camp with a roar like thunder.

This woke him. He was in his tent and had been dreaming, and the sentry at his tent door was just reporting noon.

Soon he had his horse saddled and rode out, with a small escort, toward the spot he had seen in his dream. As he stood gazing around him a troop of horse came along with Sun Ch'üan at their head. He wore a glittering helmet and was clad in silver armour. Seeing his chief enemy he showed no sign of haste or dismay, but reined in his steed on a rise and, pointing with his whip at Ts'ao, said, "Behold the all-powerful Minister who holds the capital in the hollow of his hand. He has reached the acme of wealth and good fortune and yet he is not content, but must needs come to encroach upon our southern country."

Ts'ao replied, "You are disobedient, and the command of the Emperor is to exterminate you."

"What words!" cried Sun with a laugh. "Are you not ashamed? Every one knows that you control every act of the Emperor and you tyrannise over the nobles. I am no rebel against the dynasty, but I do desire to capture you and reform the government."

Ts'ao grew angry at this speech and bade his captains go over and take Sun prisoner. But before they could obey, two troops of soldiers marched out to the sound of beating drums, and arrows and crossbow bolts began to fall like raindrops around Ts'ao Ts'ao. He turned to retire, and the archers and bowmen followed him. However, presently appeared Hsü Chu, with the Tiger Guard, who rescued Ts'ao and took him back to his camp. The men of Wu had scored a victory and they marched back to Juhsü.

Alone in his camp, Ts'ao thought, "This Sun Ch'üan certainly is no ordinary man, and by the presage of the sun in my dream he will become an emperor."

He began to think it would be well to retire from the expedition, only that he feared the men of Wu would exult over him. So the two armies remained facing each other a whole month, fighting occasional skirmishes and battles in which victory fell sometimes to the one and sometimes to the other.

And so it went on till the new year and the spring rains filled the watercourses to overflowing and the soldiers were wading in deep mud. Their sufferings were extreme and Ts'ao became sad at heart. At the council board his officers were divided, some being for retirement and others anxious to hold on till the warm weather. Their chief could not make up his mind.

Then there came a messenger from Wu bearing a letter, which read: "You and I, O Minister, are both servants of Han, but you are careless for the tranquillity of the people and think only of battle, thereby causing great suffering. Is this conduct worthy of a kindly man?

"But spring with its heavy rains is at hand and you would be wise to retire while you can. If not, you may expect a repetition of the misfortune at Red Wall. It would be well to consider this."

And on the back of the letter was a note in two lines running thus: "No tranquillity for me while you live."

Ts'ao read the letter and laughed. "Chung-mou, you cannot beguile me!" said he.

He rewarded the messenger and issued orders to retreat. The Prefect of Luchiang was left to guard Huanch'êng; the army marched for the capital.

Sun Ch'üan returned to Moling. At a meeting of his advisers he said, "Ts'ao Ts'ao has marched north, Liu Pei is at Chiaming: why should I not lead the army that has just repulsed the northern men to take Chingchou?"

Thereupon Chang Chao offered another plan saying, "Do not move a man; I know how to keep Liu Pei from returning to Chingchou."

> Mêng-tê's army march away,
> Chung-mou's thoughts then southward stray.

The scheme proposed by Chang will be unfolded in the next chapter.

CHAPTER LXII.

TAKING OF FOU PASS; YANG AND KAO SLAIN;
SIEGE OF LO CITY; HUANG AND WEI RIVALS.

Chang Chao proceeded to unfold his device. "If you undertake any expedition farther west Ts'ao Ts'ao will undoubtedly return to the attack. Rather write two letters, one to Liu Chang saying that Liu Pei has leagued himself with you against the west, which will raise suspicions in the mind of Liu Chang and cause him to attack his guest, and another persuading Chang Lu to march upon Chingchou, which will embarrass Liu Pei. Between these two conflicting matters Chingchou will be neglected and we can march against it."

Sun Ch'üan approved, wrote the two letters and sent them by two messengers.

In the meantime, Liu Pei had been winning the hearts of the peoples about Chiaming Pass, where his army lay. When he received the news of his wife's flight and of Ts'ao's threatened attack, he called in P'ang T'ung and laid the matter before him. "The victor, whichever it is, will assuredly possess himself of our city of Chingchou," said Liu Pei at the close.

"You need not trouble about that city," said P'ang. "I do not think Wu will try to take it so long as K'ung-ming is there. But, my lord, write to Liu Chang telling him you wish to return on account of this threatening danger. It will be a plausible excuse. You may say that on account of Ts'ao's attack, Sun has sent to you for help and that as his country and yours are neighbours and dependent upon each other for safety you cannot refuse. Further, you will assure him that there is no danger of any invasion by Chang Lu. However, we have too few men for our purpose and insufficient grain, so you must also urge your relative to send you three or four legions of veterans and a plentiful supply of food. He will not refuse, and with more men and provisions we can do as we please."

Liu Pei agreed to this and sent a messenger to Ch'êngtu. When his messenger reached the Pass, Yang Huai and Kao P'o, who commanded the garrison, already knew of the design, and the former of the two captains went with him to the city. After reading the letter the Prefect asked Yang why he had come.

"Only because of that letter," he replied. "This Liu Pei, from the day he first entered the province, has been trying to win over the hearts of your people by a display of kindness and virtue. He certainly intends no good, and I think you should refuse both the men and the supplies he asks. To help him is like adding fuel to a fire."

"We are affectionate brothers and I must help him," said the Prefect."

"Liu Pei is nothing but a vagabond swashbuckler," some one cried, "and if you keep him here in Shu you are loosing a tiger in your household. If you give him the men and supplies he asks you are adding wings to your tiger."

Turning whence the voice proceeded they recognised the speaker as one Liu Pa, a native of Ch'êngyang. His words threw the Prefect into a state of doubt and hesitation. Huang Ch'üan also dissuaded him most earnestly, and finally Liu Chang actually decided to send only four companies of wornout men and a paltry supply of grain. At the same time fresh orders enjoining a diligent watchfulness were sent to the guardians of the Pass.

When Yüan-tê read the letter that accompanied the Prefect's miserable contribution to his strength he was furious and cried, "I have been spending myself in your defence and this is my reward! You are mean and greedy enough to stint my supplies. How can you expect generous service?"

He tore the letter to fragments and execrated the writer thereof. The bearer of the letter fled back to the capital.

Then said P'ang T'ung, "You have hitherto laid too much stress on humanity and righteousness. However, that is all over now and all affection between you two is at an end, now that you have torn up that letter."

"Yes. And since that is so, what next?" asked Yüan-tê.

"I have three schemes ready in my mind. You may choose which pleases you."

"What are your three schemes?"

"The first, and best, is to send an army forthwith and seize Ch'êngtu. The second is to capture and put to death the two captains of the Pass. They are the two most famous fighting men in this land. If you give out that you are returning to Chingchou they will assuredly come to say farewell. Seize and put them to death, and the Pass and Fouch'êng are both yours. Ch'êngtu will follow soon. The third plan is to drop this rôle you have been playing, go back to Chingchou and make a regular invasion. But if you ponder these schemes too long you will get into such straits that nothing can save you."

Yüan-tê replied, "Of your three schemes, O Commander, I find the first too summary and the last too slow. I choose the second scheme, which is neither."

So a letter was written to Liu Chang saying that Ts'ao Ts'ao was sending an army against Chingchou, the captains there were unequal to the defence and Liu Pei had to go to help.

As the matter was pressing there could be no personal leave-taking.

"I knew that the real desire of Liu Pei was to return to Chingchou," said Chang Sung, when he heard of the letter.

Chang Sung then also composed a letter to Liu Pei. While he was looking about for a trusty person to take it, his brother Su, who was the Prefect of a country district, came to see him. He hid the letter in his sleeve while he talked with his brother. Brother Su noticed his anxious inquietude, which he could not explain. Wine was brought in and, as the two brothers chatted over it, the letter dropped to the floor unnoticed by Chang Sung. One of brother Su's men saw it, picked it up and gave it to his master, who opened and read it.

This is about how it ran:—"What I said to you lately was not mere meaningless talk. Why, then, postpone action? The ancients valued the man who took by force and held by conciliation. If you act at once the whole matter is in your hand. Why abandon all and return to Chingchou? Surely I do not hear aright! When you get this, attack without a moment's delay and remember that I am your ally on the inside. Above all, no delay!"

"This plot of my brother's will end in the destruction of the whole family," said Chang Su. "I must get in the first word."

So at once he went in and laid the whole matter before the Prefect.

"I have always treated your brother so well!" said Liu Chang, very angry.

He issued orders to arrest Chang Sung and behead him and all his household in the market place.

> Chang was quick of comprehension, such as he have been but few,
>   Little thought he that a letter would betray
> When he plotted for another. But success he never knew,
>   For himself there opened out a gory way.

Having thus learned of a real conspiracy to deprive him of his heritage, Liu Chang assembled his officers and asked their advice. Huang Ch'üan spoke out saying, "Prompt action is needed. Send to every strategic point telling them to increase the garrisons and keep careful guard and, above all, prevent the entrance of any person from Chingchou."

Such orders were sent to all points of vantage where were garrisons.

In the meantime, carrying out P'ang T'ung's scheme, Liu Pei had marched down to Fouch'êng, where he halted and sent in a messenger to invite the two captains to come forth and say farewell. But they did not respond at once to this invitation.

"What is the real meaning of this retirement?" said one to the other.

"This Yüan-tê ought to die," said Kao P'o. "Let us hide daggers under our dress and stab him at the place of farewell. That will end all our lord's troubles."

"A most excellent plan," said his colleague.

So they two, taking only a small escort, went down out of the Pass to say good-bye. Most of their men were left in the camp.

On the way down to Fou River, P'ang T'ung had said to his master, "You have need to be on your guard against those two if they come to bid you farewell. If they do not come, then the Pass must be attacked without delay."

Just as he said this a violent gust of wind overthrew the leading flag of the army, and Liu Pei asked what this portended.

"That means a surprise; those two intend to assassinate you, so be on your guard."

Accordingly, Liu Pei put on double armour and girded on his sword in readiness. When the two captains arrived the army halted while the captains should pay the farewell visit.

Then P'ang T'ung said to his two captains, Wei Yen and Huang Chang, "However many soldiers come down from the Pass see to it that none return."

The two captains of Shu, armed with hidden daggers, came up, their escort bearing gifts of sheep and wine. They marked no precautions being taken against an attack and began to think their task of murder would be an easy one. They were led in to where Liu Pei sat under a tent, his adviser with him.

They said, "We hear, O Imperial Uncle, that you contemplate a long march and therefore we come to offer a few poor gifts to speed you on your way."

The cups of farewell were duly filled. Then Yüan-tê replied, "You have a heavy responsibility to defend the Pass, Captains. I pray you drink first."

They drank. Then Liu Pei said, "I have a secret matter to talk over with you."

So all but the two captains were sent away with the escort and were led to the midst of the camp. As soon as they had gone, Liu Pei shouted, "My people, lay hands upon these two rebels!"

Thereupon Liu Fêng and Kuan P'ing rushed out from behind the tent. The two captains of the Pass were taken aback, but began to struggle. However, each of the two seized his man and held him.

"Your lord and I are of the same house," said Liu Pei, "why then have you plotted against me and conspired to sow enmity between us?"

P'ang T'ung bade his men search the captives, and the hidden daggers were found. So both were ordered to immediate execution. However, Liu Pei hesitated and was unwilling to confirm the sentence and put them to death. But his adviser insisted that they were worthy of death for the assassination they had panned, and bade the executioners fall on. So the two men were beheaded. Of their following not one had been allowed to slip away.

Liu Pei summoned the soldiers of the escort to his tent, gave them wine to comfort them and said, "Your leaders conspired to sow dissension between brothers and were found with daggers hidden beneath their clothing. They were assassins in intent and have met the fate they merited. You have committed no crime and need feel no alarm."

The soldiers thanked him for his clemency with low obeisance.

Then said P'ang T'ung, "If you will now show the way so that our men may capture the Pass, you shall even be rewarded."

They consented. That same night the army set out, with the men of the renegade escort leading the way. When they reached the Pass they hailed the gate, saying, "Open the gate quickly: the captains have returned earlier than they expected because of important business."

Hearing the voices of their comrades, the gate guards had no suspicion of treachery and threw open the gates. In rushed the enemy soldiers and so gained possession of Foukuan without shedding a drop of blood. The defenders came over to the side of Liu Pei and were liberally rewarded. This done, the army was posted so as to guard the approaches and maintain what they had captured.

The next few days were spent in banquets and feasts in celebration of success. At one of these feasts Liu Pei turned to his adviser, saying, "This is what one might call a joyful occasion."

"To employ warlike weapons in making an attack upon the possession of another is not using them in the best way." replied P'ang T'ung. "Nor is such attack the most proper occasion for rejoicing."

Liu Pei replied, "The success of King Wu against Chou was celebrated with music; I suppose weapons were not well used on that occasion either. Why do you talk so wide of reason? You had better retire."

P'ang T'ung laughed and withdrew from the table, while the attendants supported Liu Pei to his own chamber, where he had a long sleep. About midnight he awoke from his wine and then the servants told him that he had driven away his adviser from the feast. He was at once filled with remorse. Next day, having dressed early in full costume of ceremony, he took his seat in the great hall, summoned his adviser and apologised handsomely for his rude behaviour the night before.

"I drank too much last night and spoke rudely; pray forget it."

P'ang, who had taken the whole episode in very good part from the first, laughed and talked as usual. But Yüan-tê went on, "Really I was the only one to blame yesterday."

"We both slipped up; it was not only you, my lord," said P'ang.

Then Yüan-tê laughed too and the two were as good friends again as ever.

When the Prefect Liu Chang heard of the doings of his relative and guest he said, "I did not think that such things would come to pass."

The officers of Shu met to consider how to oppose the further advance of Liu Pei, and Huang Ch'üan said, "Let us send without delay a force to hold Lohsien, which is the very throat of the road he must take. He may have veteran soldiers and fiery captains but he will not be able to pass."

So the four ablest captains were told off for this duty and they led five legions. As they marched, one of them, Liu Kuei by name, said, "In the Chinp'ing Hills there is a wonderful Taoist who calls himself 'The Superman of the Dark Void.' He has the gift of second sight, so let us visit him as we pass and enquire what our fortunes are to be."

"What should one seek of a hermit when one is out to repulse an enemy?" said his colleague, Chang Jên, contemptuously.

"Your view is wrong," said Liu. "The Sage has said that it is characteristic of the most entire sincerity to be able to foreknow. So let us enquire of this man of high intelligence that we may know what to do and what to avoid."

Whereupon they went up into the hills and sought the hermit's retreat. They were a small party, on horseback. Meeting a wood-cutter they enquired the whereabouts of the dwelling of the wise man, and he pointed to one of the highest hills, saying that the Sage lived on the very summit. They climbed up to the spot he had told them of and found a small hut. At their summons a lad in Taoist garb came out to speak with them. He asked their names and led them into the presence of the Superman, who received them seated on a rush cushion. They made a low obeisance, told him the reason of their coming and asked of the future.

"How can a poor Taoist recluse know aught of fortunes, good or evil?" said he.

However, after a time, as Liu Kuei repeated his request again and again and comported himself most humbly, the hermit bade the lad bring paper and ink and he wrote eight lines, which he handed to his questioner.

"Supported by dragon and phœnix,
So flies he westward.
But the Phœnix Fledgling shall fall to the earth,
And the Sleeping Dragon shall soar to the sky;

There shall be successes and failures,
For such is the eternal law.
See that ye act when occasion offers,
Lest ye descend to the Nine Springs."

Having read the oracle they pressed the seer to reveal them their individual fortunes, but he replied, "Why ask these things? None can escape his fate." Liu Kuei ventured to question the Sage further, but his eyelids dropped as if he slumbered. Nor would he vouchsafe a word more, and the four captains took leave and descended the hill.

"One must have faith in such as he says," said Liu.

"What is to be gained by listening to the sayings of a daft old man?" replied Chang.

So they continued their road to Lohsien. When they arrived they settled that two of them should guard the ramparts while the other two should station themselves in front of the city, where was a point of vantage sheltered by some hills. Here they established two camps in two stockades, hoping to be able to keep the foe away from the city.

The Pass being captured, Yüan-tê took counsel with his adviser as to the next point to be attempted. This was Lohsien. Scouts had reported the arrival of the four captains sent by Liu Chang and said that a camp had been established sixty *li* from the city. Then Yüan-tê assembled his officers and asked who would go to attack the camps. The veteran Huang Chung offered himself.

"Veteran captain, take your own men and go," said Liu Pei. "A goodly reward shall be yours if you capture the two camps."

Huang thanked his lord and was just leading away his men when suddenly up spake a youthful leader, saying, "The General is old to go on such an expedition; I am of poor ability, but I wish to take his place."

The speaker was Wei Yen. Huang replied, "I already have my commission; why should you wish to supplant me?"

"Because the task is beyond an old man's strength," said Wei. "The two men in those camps we know are the best and boldest in the country. They are strong, and, veteran as you are, I fear you will be unable to overcome them. If you fail, our lord's great design will be hindered. Therefore I ask that I may replace you, and my intent is kindly."

This reminder of his age angered the old man. "Old, am I? Dare you compete with me in the use of warlike weapons?" said he.

"Yes; I dare. And our lord shall be the judge. The winner shall undertake this expedition. Do you agree?"

Huang ran down the steps and called to his men to bring his small sword.

But Yüan-tê would stop this contest and said, "I have need of both of you in the task that lies before me. When two tigers fight one is sure to lose, and the loss of either of you is more than I could bear. Be reconciled and quarrel no more."

"You two must not quarrel," said P'ang T'ung. "But as there are two camps to be taken and two captains to fight, take one each and let each lead his own men. The first to capture his camp shall be held to have rendered the greater service and to have acquired the greater merit."

This decision pacified them and it was settled that Huang the veteran should go against Lêng Pao, and Wei, the younger leader, should attack Têng Hsien. But after they had marched away P'ang recommended Liu Pei to follow them lest they should quarrel on the way. So leaving the city in care of his adviser, Liu also marched, taking with him Fêng, his adopted son, and P'ing, his nephew by adoption. They took five companies.

After having received the command to take one of the camps, Huang went to his own camp and issued orders for the morning meal to be ready very early, and for every one to be in marching order by daybreak. When the time arrived, his little army set out, taking the road through a gully to the left of the hills.

But early as he started, his rival had stolen a march on him. Wei had sent over the night before to find out the hour fixed for the start and had arranged his own departure a watch earlier, by which he would be able to reach his objective at dawn. After his men had taken their early meal they removed the bells from the horses and put gags in their own mouths to prevent talking, and all-silently the army stole out of the camp just as the other party were eating their breakfast. The ensigns were furled and weapons covered lest the glint of steel should betray their movement.

Thus far successful in getting the start of his rival, Wei thought as he rode along what a fine score he would make if he anticipated him also in his attack and captured the camp before he could get there. He at once deviated from his own line and marched toward the camp defended by Lêng Pao, of which the capture had been assigned to Huang.

Just before arrival he halted his men and bade them prepare the drums and ensigns and their weapons.

Early as it was, yet the camp commander was on the alert, for the advancing force had been observed by his scouts. At the first sign of attack the defenders poured out in full force. Wei galloped up and made straight for Lêng. These two fought a score or so of bouts and then the men of Shu came up and joined in the battle. The men of Han, as the force under Wei may be called, having marched a long distance, were fatigued and could not withstand this onslaught, so they fell back. Wei heard the confused sound of hoofs behind him and, giving up all thought of finishing his encounter with Lêng, turned his horse and fled. The men of Shu kept up the pursuit and the attackers were defeated and retired.

They had gone about five *li* when another body of Ssŭch'uan men appeared from behind some hills. They advanced with beating drums. Their leader, Têng Hsien, shouted to Wei to surrender, but Wei heeded him not; whipping up his steed he fled the faster. However, the tired horse tripped and fell on his knees, throwing his rider to the ground. Têng's men came galloping up, and he himself set his spear to thrust and slay Wei. Before the spear could get home, twang! went a bowstring, and Têng lay prone upon the earth.

Lêng, his colleague, rode up quickly to his rescue, but just then a body of horse came dashing down the hill, and their leader shouted, "The veteran captain Huang Chung is here."

With uplifted sword Huang rode toward Lêng, who turned his steed and galloped off to the rear. Huang pursued, and the men of Ssŭch'uan were thrown into confusion. So Huang was able to rescue his colleague Wei. He had thus slain Têng Hsien and forced his way up to the gate of the camp. Once again Lêng came on and engaged Huang. The two had fought a half score bouts when appeared another body of soldiers. Thereupon Lêng fled again and this time he made for the other camp, abandoning his own to the men of Han.

But when he drew near he saw no longer the familiar flags of his own side. Instead, alien banners fluttered in the breeze. He checked his steed and stared at the new force. The leader was a general wearing a silver breastplate and clad in a silken robe, no other than Liu Pei himself. On his left was his son and on his right rode his nephew.

"Whither would you?" cried Liu Pei. "The camp is ours; I have captured it."

Now Liu Pei had led his men in the track of the other two armies ready to help either in case of need. He had come across the empty and undefended camp and taken possession.

Left with no place of refuge, Lêng set off along a by-way to try to get back to Lohsien. He had not gone far when he fell into an ambush and was taken prisoner. Bound with cords he was taken to the camp of Yüan-tê.

Here it is necessary to record that the ambush had been prepared by Wei Yen, who, knowing he had committed a fault that could in no wise be explained away, had collected as many of his men as he could find and made some of the captured men of Shu guide him to a spot suitable for laying an ambush.

Yüan-tê had hoisted the flag of pardon for his enemies, and whenever any man of Shu laid down his weapons and stripped off his armour he was spared. Also all the wounded were granted life. Liu Pei told his enemies that they had liberty of choice. "You men have parents and wives and little ones at home, and those who wish to return to them are free to go. If any wish to join my army they also will be received."

At this proof of generosity the sound of rejoicing filled the land.

Having made his camp, Huang came to Yüan-tê and said, "Wei Yen should be put to death for disobedience."

The culprit was summoned and came, bringing with him his prisoner. Yüan-tê decided that the merit of capturing an enemy should be set against his fault and bade him thank his rescuer, enjoining upon them both to quarrel no more. Wei Yen bowed his head and confessed his fault and Huang Chung was handsomely rewarded.

The prisoner was then taken before Yüan-tê to decide upon his fate. His bonds were loosened and he was given the cup of consolation. After he had drunk he was asked if he was willing to surrender.

"Since you give me my life I can do no other," said he. "Moreover, I and my two companions, Liu Kuei and Chang Jên, are sworn to live or die together. If you will release me I will return and bring them also to you and therewith you will get possession of Loch'êng."

Yüan-tê gladly accepted the offer. He gave Lêng clothing and a horse and bade him go to the city to carry out his plan.

"Do not let him go," said Wei. "If you do, you will never see him again."

Liu Pei replied, "If I treat men with kindness and justice they will not betray my trust."

So the prisoner was set free. When he reached the city and saw his two friends he told them he had slain many of the enemy and had escaped by mounting the steed of one of his victims. He said no word of having been captured. Messengers were sent in haste to Ch'êngtu for help.

The loss of his captain, Têng Hsien, disturbed the Prefect greatly. He called his advisers together to consult. Then his eldest son said, "Father, let me go to defend the city."

"You may go, my son, but who is there to go with you?"

One Wu I at once offered himself. He was uncle to Liu Chang, who said, "It is well that you go, my uncle, but who will second you?"

Wu I at once recommended two men, Wu Lan and Lei Tung, who were appointed to assist in the command. Two legions were given them and they set out for Loch'êng. The two captains came out to welcome them and told them what had happened.

Wu I said, "If the enemy draw near to the walls it will be hard to drive them off again. What do you two think should be done?"

Lêng Pao replied, "The city lies along the river and the current is strong. The enemy camp lies low at the foot of the hills and with half a legion I can cut the river banks, flood their camp and drown Liu Pei and his army with him."

The plan was approved, and Lêng went away to carry it out. Wu and Lan were told off to guard the workers. They began to prepare the tools for cutting the bank.

Leaving Huang and Wei in command of the two camps, Yüan-tê went away to Fouch'êng to consult with P'ang, the army chief. Intelligence had been received that Sun Ch'üan had sent a messenger to seek to make a league with Chang Lu to make a joint attack upon the Chiaming Pass, and Yüan-tê was alarmed lest it should come to pass. "If they do that I am taken in the rear and helpless," said he. "What do you counsel?"

P'ang turned to Wêng Ta, saying, "You are a native of Shu and well skilled ,in its topography; what can be done to make the Pass secure?"

"Let me take a certain man with me and I will defend it myself and answer for its safety."

"Who is he?" asked Yüan-tê.

"He was formerly an officer under Liu Piao. His name is Ho Hsün and he is a native of Chihchiang in the south."

This offer was accepted, and the two men departed.

After the council, when P'ang returned to his lodging, the doorkeeper told him that a visitor had arrived. When P'ang went out to receive him he saw a huge tall fellow eight cubits in stature and of noble countenance. His hair had been cut short and hung upon his neck. He was poorly dressed.

"Who may you be, master?" asked P'ang.

The visitor made no reply, but went at once straight up the room and lay upon the couch. P'ang felt very suspicious of the man and repeated his question. Pressed again, the visitor said, "Do let me rest a little; then I will talk with you about everything in the world."

This answer only added to the mystery and increased the host's suspicion, but he had wine and food brought in, of which the guest partook ravenously. Having eaten, he lay down and fell asleep.

P'ang was greatly puzzled and thought the man must be a spy. He sent for Fa Chêng, met him in the courtyard and told him about the strange visitor.

"Surely it can be no other than P'êng Jung-yen," said Fa.

He went inside and looked. Immediately the visitor jumped up saying, "I hope you have been well since we parted last."

Because two old friends meet again,
A river's fatal flood is checked.

The next chapter will explain who the stranger was.

CHAPTER LXIII.

CHUKO LIANG MOURNS FOR P'ANG T'UNG;
CHANG FEI RELEASES YEN YEN.

Fa Chêng and the new comer met with every sign of joy, clapping their hands and laughing with pleasure.

"This is P'êng Yang of Kuanghan, one of our heroes. His blunt speech, however, offended Prefect Liu, who put him to shame by shaving his head, loading him with fetters and forcing him into a monastery. That is why his hair is short."

The introduction made, P'ang treated the stranger with all the courtesy due to a guest and asked why he had come.

"To save a myriad of your men's lives. I will explain fully when I see General Liu."

A message was sent to Liu Pei, who came over to see the visitor. "How many men have you, General?" asked P'êng, when he arrived.

Yüan-tê told him.

"As a leader you cannot be ignorant of the lie of the land. Your camps over there are on the Fou River; if the river be diverted and armies hold your men in front and rear, not a man can escape."

Liu Pei realised that this was true. P'êng continued, "The bowl of the Dipper lies toward the west and Venus stands over against us. The aspect is ominous of evil, and some misfortune threatens. It must be warded off."

In order to retain his services, Liu Pei gave P'êng an appointment as a secretary. Then he sent messages to the captains at the camps telling them to keep most vigilant look-out to guard against the cutting of the river bank. When this message came the two captains agreed together to take duty day and day about and maintain the strict watch necessary in the presence of an enemy near at hand. They arranged means of communication in case either met with a body of the enemy.

One very stormy night Lêng Pao ventured out with a strong reconnoitring party and went along the river bank to seek a suitable place for the breach. But a sudden shouting in his rear told him that the men of Han were on the alert, and he at once retired. Wei Yen came in pursuit and, as he pressed nearer, Lêng's men hurried forward, trampling each other down in their haste. Suddenly Lêng and Wei ran against each other, and they engaged. The fight was very short, for Wei soon took his opponent prisoner. Those who came to his rescue were easily beaten off, and Lêng was carried away. When he reached the Pass, Yüan-tê saw him and greatly blamed him for his base ingratitude.

"I treated you generously and set you free; you repaid me with ingratitude. I cannot forgive again."

So the prisoner was beheaded and his captor was rewarded. A banquet was given in honour of P'êng.

Soon after this came a letter from K'ung-ming, by the hand of Ma Liang, who reported all calm in Chingchin and told Yüan-tê that he need feel no anxiety. Opening the letter, Yüan-tê read: "I have been making some astrological calculations. This is the last year of the cycle, the bowl of the Dipper is in the western quarter and the planet Venus approaches Loch'êng. The configuration is inimical to leaders and the utmost caution is necessary."

Having read this and sent Ma away, Yüan-tê said he would return himself to Chingchou and discuss the matter. But P'ang, who thought in his heart that K'ung-ming's warning was due to a jealous desire to prevent him from winning the glory of conducting a victorious campaign, opposed this, saying, "I also have made calculations, and I read the signs to mean that the time is favourable for you to get possession of this land, and no evil is foreshown. Therefore be not of doubtful heart, my lord, but advance boldly."

Yüan-tê was won over and decided to follow P'ang's advice. He ordered the two captains Huang Chung and Wei Yen to lead.

P'ang asked of Fa Chêng what roads there were to follow, and the latter drew a map, which was found to agree exactly with that left by Chang Sung.

Fa said, "North of the mountains is a high road leading to the west gate. Both these roads are suitable for the advance of an army."

So P'ang said to Liu Pei, "With Wei to lead the way, I will go along the southern road, while you, my lord, will advance along the high road, with Huang in the van. We will attack at the same time."

Yüan-tê replied, "I was trained as a mounted archer and am accustomed to by-roads, wherefore, O Commander, I think you should take the high road and let me take the other."

"There will be opposition on the high road and you are the best to deal with it. Let me take the by-road."

"No; this does not suit me," replied Yüan-tê. "A spirit bearing a massive iron club appeared to me in a dream and struck my right arm, so that I suffered great pain. I feel sure this expedition will turn out badly."

P'ang replied, "When a soldier goes into battle he may be killed, or he may be wounded; he accepts whichever is his fate. But should one hesitate because of a dream?"

"The real reason of my hesitation is the letter from K'ung-ming. Wherefore I wish you to remain and guard the Pass. Do you agree to that?"

P'ang smiled, saying, "K'ung-ming has indeed filled your mind with doubts. The real thing is that he is unwilling to let me have the merit of accomplishing a great undertaking alone. That is why he has written this. And your doubts and hesitations have produced the dream. But I see nothing ill-omened, and I am prepared for any sacrifice and mean just what I say. Pray, my lord, say no more, but prepare to set forth."

So the order went forth that the morning meal was to be taken early and the army was to march at dawn. Huang and Wei were to take the lead, one along each road. These two set out first, and in due time Liu Pei and P'ang T'ung mounted and followed. Suddenly P'ang's horse shied and stumbled, throwing him off. Yüan-tê jumped down and seized the horse by the bridle, saying, "Why do you ride this wretched beast?"

"I have ridden him a long time and he has never done this before," was the reply.

"A shying steed risks a man's life," said Yüan-tê. "Ride my horse, which is thoroughly trained and will never fail you. Give me yours."

They exchanged horses. "I am deeply affected by your kindness," said P'ang. "I could never repay you if I suffered death a thousand times."

Soon their ways diverged. After his adviser had left, Yüan-tê felt ill at ease and rode gloomily.

When the news of Lêng Pao's capture and death reached Loch'êng the two commanders there took counsel together. Their colleague, Chang Jên, said, "I know a by-road on the east which is of great importance, and I pray you to let me guard it while you two hold the city."

So as soon as the news of the advancing armies came, Chang led three companies to this road and placed them in ambush. They remained hidden while Wei Yen passed and made no attack. The main body under P'ang T'ung soon followed. The soldiers in ambush saw a rider on a fine white horse and pointed him out to one another, saying, "That surely is Liu Pei on the white horse." Their leader rejoiced too, and he gave certain orders, which need not be recorded here.

P'ang hastened forward. By and by the mountain road narrowed to a defile with dense thickets on either hand, and as the season was when summer changes into autumn, the foliage was thick and impenetrable. His heart misgave him, and presently he reined in his steed and asked if any knew the name of that place. One of the Shu soldiers who had joined his army said, "This is called ' The Slope of the Fallen Phœnix.' "

P'ang shuddered. "An evil omen for me, since 'Phœnix Fledgeling' is my Taoist name. There is no luck for me here."

He decided to retire. But as he gave the order the roar of a bomb rent the air and arrows began to fly toward him thick as swarming locusts. All the hidden men were shooting at the rider of the white horse. And there, wounded by many arrows, poor P'ang T'ung died at the age of thirty-six.

A poem says:—

Deep in the blue recesses of the hills
Lay hid the modest cot of Shih-yüan.
But now each village urchin knows his story,
And any village rustic tells his exploits.
He knew the empire must be triply rent,
And far he travelled lonely, to and fro.
None knew that Heaven would cast down his star,
Forbidding his return in glory clad.

A song was also written referring to P'ang T'ung:—

They were two, the Phœnix and the Dragon,
And they would travel far to Shu;
But on the road thither
The Phœnix died on the mountain slope.
The wind drives off the rain,
The rain sends off the wind.
It was the day of the Han restoration,
When Shu was attained,
But in the attainment
The Dragon was alone.

Not only was the leader of the expedition slain, but more than half the soldiers fell in the narrow road that fatal day. Some of the men in the van escaped and ran off to tell Wei of the mishap to the army, and he halted and turned back to help. However, it was difficult to march back and he could not hack a way through, for the road was held by Chang, and archers and crossbowmen occupied all the heights.

Then one of the renegades proposed that they should try to return along the high road, and they started for Loch'êng this way. But in front of them arose a great cloud of dust, betraying the approach of an enemy. The defenders of the city were moving toward them, and Wei Yen was between the two armies closed in like the kernel of a nut. Wei fought hard to get through. When his case seemed most desperate and hopeless, he observed signs of confusion in the army that lay between him and the city. Soon that army turned and faced the other way. He pressed forward and presently saw men of his own side, led by the veteran Huang Chung.

"I will rescue you, Wên-chang," shouted he, as he came near.

Now the defenders of Loch'êng found themselves between two enemies, and they were smitten heavily. They could not check Wei and Huang, who got through to the very walls of

Loch'êng. Seeing them near, Liu Kuei, who had been left to defend the city, came out against them. Thereupon Huang and Wei, in spite of the nearness of the army of Liu Pei, refused battle and turned away from the city. Yüan-tê's army made a dash for two stockades, but when Chang came along a by-road and the other three defenders of the city came on, the stockades could not be held and Yüan-tê's army had to retire. Now fighting and now marching, the army of Liu Pei strove hard to reach Fou Pass, but Chang pressed close. However, Liu Pei's adopted son and nephew came up, and not only drove back the pursuers but chased them some twenty *li*. Finally, Liu Pei and his men reached the Pass, weary and dispirited. His son and nephew returned from the pursuit with many horses they had captured from the flying enemy. However, nothing had been gained and the victory lay rather with the army of Shu.

One of the fugitives from the army finally reached Fou Pass and told Yüan-tê of the sad news of the death of his adviser, man and horse wounded to death. He turned his face to the west and mourned bitterly.

Although the body of the slain leader lay far away they instituted sacrifice to call the spirit, and all the captains keened for him.

Then said Huang, "Now that our leader is no more, certainly the enemy will return to attack the Pass. What is to be done? I think we had better send to Chingchou for Chuko Liang and get him to lay plans for getting possession of the country."

And even then came in one to say that the enemy under Chang Jên had come and were now offering a challenge at the rampart. Huang and Wei wished to go forth to fight, but Liu Pei disapproved, saying, "We have suffered a severe check and the men are low-spirited. Let us rather remain on the defensive until the great adviser can arrive."

Huang and Wei made no objection, but set themselves to guard the Pass most vigilantly, while a letter was written to K'ung-ming and sent by the hand of Kuan P'ing. He set forth at once and Yüan-tê gave himself up to holding the Pass.

It was the seventh day of the seventh moon, and in the evening K'ung-ming invited his officers to a banquet. Conversation turned toward the enterprise in Ssŭch'uan. Suddenly a large and brilliant meteor appeared in the west, illuminating the whole sky. It so disturbed the host that he dashed his wine cup to the ground, covered his face and burst into tears.

"Alas! Alas!"

The guests eagerly asked him why he wept. He replied, "I knew by my calculations that the bowl of the Dipper would be in the west at this season and that the auspices would be unfavourable to leaders of armies, and lo! the Heavens have gone against our men. When Venus was about to stand over Loch'êng I wrote to our lord warning him to be very cautious. I never contemplated the falling of the star this evening. Now P'ang T'ung is no more."

Again he fell to weeping. "My lord has lost an arm!" moaned he.

The guests were rather disturbed, but they only half believed that such a misfortune had happened.

"We shall hear the sad news in a very few days," said K'ung-ming.

The banquet ended sadly enough, and the guests went their ways. A few days later, while K'ung-ming was sitting with Kuan Yü and a few others, they reported the arrival of Kuan P'ing with letters from the west. When the letters were opened they knew that P'ang T'ung had fallen the same evening that the meteor had appeared.

K'ung-ming wailed and the others wept with him.

Then K'ung-ming said, "I must go to help our lord; he is hemmed in at the Pass and cannot move."

"If you go away, who will guard this city?" asked Kuan Yü. "It is of very great importance."

"Our lord has not written plainly, but I know what was in his mind." Then he showed the letter to the others and said, "Provision for the defence of this city is laid upon me and I am to find one equal to the task. I read the letter to mean that he desires Kuan Yü to undertake the defence, and I know that he will do it for the sake of the pledge taken long ago in the Peach Garden. The task is no light one."

Kuan accepted without hesitation or thought of excuse. A special banquet was prepared at which the seal was to be handed over to him.

"All the future rests with you, General," said K'ung-ming as he raised the symbol of office to place it in the hands of the veteran warrior.

"When a man of honour accepts such a task he is only released by death," replied Kuan.

But that ill-omened word "death" displeased K'ung-ming, and even then he would have retracted but that his word had gone forth. He went on. "Now if Ts'ao Ts'ao attack what is to be done?"

"Repel him with all my strength."

"But if Ts'ao Ts'ao and Sun Ch'üan attack you together, what then?"

"Fight both; half my force against each."

K'ung-ming said, "In that case, Chingchou would be in danger. I will give you my advice in a few words, and if you remember them the city is safe."

"What are these few words?" asked Kuan.

"North, fight Ts'ao; south, ally with Sun."

"These words, O Commander, are engraven on my heart."

Thereupon the seal was placed in his hands. K'ung-ming also appointed tried and worthy men to assist the new commander.

This done, K'ung-ming began to prepare for his departure. Chang Fei, with a legion, was sent to fight his way into the country west of Pachou and Loch'êng and he was to go with all speed. The earlier he got through the greater merit would be his. Chao Yün was to lead a force up the river and make a junction at Loch'êng. K'ung-ming, with his own body of men, would follow.

Among those who followed K'ung-ming was one Chiang Wan, a noted scholar from Linghsiang. He went as Recorder.

K'ung-ming and Chang Fei set out the same day. Just before leaving, the great strategist said to Chang, "Do not think lightly of the men of Ssŭch'uan, for there are many mighty men among them. On the march restrain your men from plunder and licence lest the ordinary people be against us. Wherever you halt be compassionate and kindly and do not give way to anger and flog your men. I shall expect you to reach Loch'êng very soon."

Chang joyously mounted and left. He marched rapidly, and on the way all places that surrendered suffered nothing whatever.

When they drew near the Pachou district the scouts of Shu sent out by the Prefect of that place informed their master, Yen Yen. This Yen was one of the famous captains of Shu, and even then, although he was rather old, he had lost none of his boldness and could still pull the stiffest bow and wield the heaviest sword.

Being so famous, Yen was not the man to surrender at the first approach of an enemy. So when Chang came near he cautiously encamped about ten *li* from the city. Thence he sent a messenger to summon the Prefect to surrender. "Tell the old fool to give in, or I will trample down his walls and leave no soul alive."

Yen had never favoured inviting Liu Pei into Shu. When he had first heard of the Prefect's intention, he said, "This is like calling a tiger to protect one when one is alone on a bare hill side." When he heard of the seizure of Fou Pass he was very angry and offered again and again to lead an army and drive out the aggressors. He had feared that his city would be attacked along this very road, so he had prepared his men, and when Chang's message came he mustered them, five companies or so, to oppose him.

Then a certain man said to him, "You must be careful how you oppose a man who by the mere sound of his voice scared the many legions of Ts'ao Ts'ao at Tangyang Slope. Even Ts'ao himself was careful to keep out of his way. Your safety is in defence, lying behind your ramparts and within your deep moats till hunger shall have vanquished your enemies. This Chang has a very violent temper, and if he is provoked he vents his anger in flogging his men. If you avoid battle he will be irritated and his cruelty to his men will cause them to mutiny. Then you can attack and will succeed."

Yen thought the advice good. He therefore resolved only to defend, and he set all his men on the walls. When one of Chang's soldiers came up to the gate and shouted for them to open, Yen gave orders to open the gate and admit the man. When he had come within he gave the message as has been related before. But the Prefect was exceedingly angry and said, "Fool that you are! How dare you speak thus to me? Think you that I, General Yen, will surrender to such as he? By your mouth indeed will I send a message."

Then he bade the executioner cut off the man's ears and nose. And thus mutilated he returned to Chang. When Chang heard of it his wrath boiled up and he cursed the defender of the city. Grinding his teeth and glaring with rage, he put on his armour, mounted his steed and went up close to the walls, with a few mounted men, and challenged those on the ramparts to fight him. But the men on the walls only replied with shameful abuse and none accepted the challenge. Chang galloped again and again to the drawbridge, only to be driven off each time with flights of arrows. But not a man came outside the walls. As the day closed in, the warrior, still fuming with wrath, returned to his own camp.

Next day Chang again led his men to the foot of the wall and challenged; again the challenge was refused. But Yen shot an arrow from the tower that struck Chang's helmet. This angered him still more, and pointing the finger of disdain at his enemy, Chang cried, "I will capture you yet, you old fool, and then I will devour your flesh."

So again at eventide the men of Han returned to camp baulked of their desire. On the third day Chang and his men made the circuit of the city along the edge of the moat, hurling insults at their enemies.

It so happened that the city was set on a hill with rugged heights all round, so that going around it the assailants were sometimes on hill tops and sometimes on the level. While standing on one of the hills, Chang noticed that he could see clear down into the city. There stood the defenders in their ranks, all readly for battle although none of them came out. And the common people went to and fro carrying bricks and bringing stones to strengthen the defences. Then he ordered his horsemen to dismount and his footmen to sit down so that they could not be seen from the city. He hoped thus to cheat the defenders into thinking that there were none to attack and so induce them to come out. But this also was vain, for still they declined battle and another day was lost. The army once more returned to camp.

That night Chang sat in his tent trying to think out some means to overcome an enemy that steadily refused to come out from behind the walls. Presently, however, the brain behind the knitted brow conceived a plan. So next day, instead of sending all the men to offer a challenge from the foot of the wall, he kept most of them in camp and sent only a few to howl insults and hurl abuse. He hoped by this means to inveigle Yen out to attack the small number of men. But this also failed, and he was left all day rubbing his hands with impatience. Never a man appeared without the wall.

Foiled again, another ruse grew up behind the knitted brows above his bushy eyebrows. He set his men to cut firewood and seek out and explore the tracks that lay about the city. No longer did they challenge the wall. After some days of this, Yen began to wonder what mischief was brewing, and he sent out spies, dressed as were the firewood cutters, to mingle with them and try to discover what was afoot.

That day, when the men returned to camp, Chang sat in his tent stamping his foot with rage and execrating his enemy. "The old fool! Assuredly I shall die of disappointed wrath," cried he.

Just then he noticed three or four men lurking about his tent door as if they wished to speak with him. And one of them said, "General, do not let your heart be hot within you. These last few days we have discovered a narrow road by which we can sneak past this city."

"Why did you not come and tell me before?" cried he.

"Because we have only lately discovered it," said they.

"I will lose no time then," said he. "This very night let food be ready at the second watch and we will break camp and steal away as silently as possible. I will lead the way and you shall go with me as guides."

The requisite orders were given. Having made sure that the preparations for the march were really being made, the three spies, for such were they, returned into the city.

"I guessed right, then," said Yen Yen gleefully when the three spies reported their success. "I cannot bear the old fool. He will now try to sneak past with his commissariat following and I will cut off his rear. How can he get through? He is very stupid to fall thus into my trap."

Orders were given to prepare for battle, to have the food ready at the second watch and move out at the third. The force was to hide in the woods and thickets till the greater part of the army had passed and Chang Fei had arrived in the very throat of the road. Then the blow would be struck.

They waited till night had fallen. In due time the late meal was taken, the men donned their armour, stole silently out of the city and hid as they had been told. The Prefect himself, with a few of his captains, went out also, dismounted and hid in a wood. They waited till after the third watch. Then Chang came along, urging his men to the top of their speed. His spear lay ready to thrust. He looked very handsome as he rode at the head of his men. The carts were three or four *li* in the rear.

When the soldiers had got well past, Yen gave the signal. The drums rolled out, up sprang the hidden men and fell on the baggage train.

They began to plunder. But suddenly a gong clanged and along came a company of soldiers Yen had not seen. At the same time a voice was heard shouting, "Old rebel, do not flee; I have been waiting for this chance a long time."

Yen turned his head. The leader of this band was a tall man with a leopard-like bullet head, round eyes, a sharp chin and bristling tiger moustache. He was armed with a long spear and rode a jet-black steed. In a word, it was Chang Fei.

All around the gongs were clanging, and many captains were rushing toward Yen, already too frightened to be able to defend himself. However, the two leaders engaged. Very soon Chang purposely gave his opponent an opening and Yen rushed in to cut down his enemy with his sword. But Chang evaded the blow, made a sudden rush, seized Yen by the lace of his armour and flung him on the ground. He was a prisoner, and in a moment was fast bound with cords.

The handsome leader who had passed first had not been Chang Fei at all, but someone dressed and made up to resemble him. To add to the confusion, Chang had exchanged the signals, making the gong the signal for his men to fall on instead of the usual drum.

As the gongs clanged, more and more of the men of Han came into the fray. The men of Shu could make no fight, and most of them dropped their weapons and surrendered. To reach the walls of the city was now easy. After entering the gates the leader ordered his men not to hurt the people, and he put out proclamations to pacify the citizens.

By and by a party of executioners brought in the prisoner.

Chang Fei took his seat in the great hall, and the late commander of the city was brought before him by a party of executioners. Yen refused to kneel before his captor.

"Why did you not surrender at first?" cried Chang, angrily grinding his teeth. "How dared you try to oppose me?"

"Because you are a lot of unrighteous and lawless invaders," replied Yen without the least sign of fear. "You may behead me an you will, but I will not surrender to you."

Chang angrily gave the order for his execution.

"Strike, if you want to, fool; why be angry?" said Yen.

This bold defiance was not lost upon Chang. Rising from his seat he went down the steps, put aside the lictors and began to loosen the prisoner's bonds. Then he dressed him in new garments, led him to the high place, and, when he was seated, made a low bow, saying, "I have always known you were a hero. Now I pray you not to remember against me the roughness of my speech."

Yen Yen was overcome with this kindness and forthwith surrendered.

> A graybeard ruled in western Shu,
> Clear fame is his the whole world through,
> As radiant sun his loyalty,
> Unmatched his soul's nobility.
> When captive taken rather he
> Would suffer death than crook his knee.
> Pachou he ruled for many a year,
> The world cannot produce his peer.

A poet has also written concerning Chang Fei:—

> Yen Yen made prisoner, then the matchless one
> Exchanged the sword for reason, and so won
> The place he holds among the sacred ones
> Of Shu, to whom they sacrifice to-day.

Then Chang asked him to suggest the means of overcoming Shu. Yen replied, "I am but the defeated leader of a defeated force, indebted to the victor for my life. I have nothing but my humble services to offer, but I can tell you how to get possession of Ch'êngtu without drawing a bow or shooting an arrow."

> Cities yield in quick succession
> Because of one old man's secession.

The proposal will be unfolded in the next chapter.

CHAPTER LXIV.

PLAN FOR THE CAPTURE OF CHANG JÊN;
BORROWING SOLDIERS TO DESTROY MA CH'AO.

As stated in the last chapter, Chang Fei asked Yen Yen to tell him how he might conquer the whole of Shu. This was the reply: "All the fortified posts between this and Loch'êng are under my control and the commanders of all the garrisons owe to me their commissions. The only way for me to prove my gratitude is to make them all yield, as I myself have done. Let me lead the advance and I will summon them one by one to surrender."

Chang thanked him again and again, and the march on this plan began. Whenever the army arrived at a post, Yen summoned the commander and there it ended. Occasionally, one would hesitate, when Yen would say, "You see I have submitted; how much more ought you to do so?"

These bloodless victories followed each other day after day, supporters rallying to the invaders without question. They simply came.

In the meantime, K'ung-ming was preparing. Having decided upon the date of departure, he wrote to inform Yüan-tê and he made Loch'êng the rendezvous for the various armies. On receipt of this letter, Yüan-tê assembled his officers and explained to them its purport. He bade them be ready to march on the twenty-second day of the seventh month. Both river and land forces were to set out the same day.

But the fiery old man Huang Chung was dissatisfied that there should be no local victory. He said, "Day after day the enemy has come to challenge us and day after day we have refused. They must have grown lax, and I propose a night raid on their camp. We shall catch them unprepared and shall score a victory."

Yüan-tê agreed to try. He arranged for a night raid, Huang on the right, Wei on the left, of the centre force under his own command. They set out at the second watch and soon arrived. They found their opponents unprepared, rushed the camp and set it on fire. The flames were very fierce, and the men of Shu fled in confusion and sought shelter in Loch'êng. They were admitted. After pursuing them for some distance Yüan-tê made a camp.

Next day Yüan-tê marched right up to the city to besiege it. Chang Jên kept quiet within and made no attempt to beat off the besiegers. On the fourth day Liu Pei led an attack on the west gate, sending his two lieutenants to attack the east. The south gate was left to give the besieged a chance to escape if they would.

Now, outside the south gate of Loch'êng the country was rough and hilly, while the swift Fou River ran past the north. For this reason the city could not be surrounded. From the city wall Chang Jên watched the progress of the attack and saw Yüan-tê the whole day indefatigably going to and fro directing the assault. He also saw that as the sun dropped toward the west the attacking force showed signs of weariness. Wherefore he sent his two captains, Wu Lan and Lei T'ung, out of the city by the north gate with orders to make their way around and attack Liu Pei's two lieutenants. He said he himself would go out by the south gate and steal round to attack Liu Pei. Lest the withdrawal of men from the ramparts should discover his plans, he sent the populace up on the walls to make a show and bade them shout loudly to reinforce the rolling of the drums.

At sundown Yüan-tê ordered the retirement of his army, and the rearmost company turned about to march back to camp. At this moment arose still louder shouting from the ramparts, and out at the south gate burst Chang Jên and his force. Chang made straight for Yüan-tê, who was in the middle of his army. His men were thrown into confusion. As his two lieutenants on the east side were also attacked, they could render no help, and Yüan-tê fled to the hills. Chang followed and soon got very near. They were a whole company pursuing one solitary man, and as Yüan-tê plied his whip he felt that the odds were much against him. Just then he saw another company of soldiers ahead, emerging from a hill path.

"An ambush in front; pursuers in rear! Surely Heaven wishes to destroy me!" cried he.

But all was not lost. As they drew nearer he recognised his own men, and the leader who dashed to meet him was his brother Chang Fei.

Chang Fei and Yen Yen had happened to take that road and Chang Fei had hastened forward when he saw the dust of conflict.

The two Changs soon came up with each other and they fought a half score bouts. By this time Yen Yen with the main body had come up and Chang Jên turned and fled. Chang Fei followed and chased him as far as the city wall. The gate was opened to allow Chang Jên to enter and at once shut. The drawbridge was raised.

Then Chang Fei returned to his elder brother to report his arrival and the incidents of the way. Hearing that K'ungming had not yet arrived, he rejoiced, saying, "So I have the credit of first arrival although he is travelling by river."

Yüan-tê said, "But how is it you have come so quickly seeing the precipitous road you had to travel? Did you meet no opposition?"

Chang replied, "The fact is I have taken the forty-five places on the way by making use of the veteran general Yen, whom I captured. It was not my own merit at all. I have come all the way without the least effort."

He told the story of Yen's capture and services from beginning to end, and then presented the man himself.

Yüan-tê said, "General, my brother's speedy arrival is certainly owing to your help." Whereupon he took off the golden chain mantlet he was wearing and gave it to his new ally.

Orders were given for a banquet. While it was being prepared a messenger came to say that Huang and Wei had been fighting with the two captains Wu and Lei and had held their own till enemy reinforcements had arrived. They had then gone away eastward. Chang Fei at once asked his brother to go with him to rescue them. Both went. When Wu and Lei saw the men of Han coming they retired into the city. The other two continued the pursuit.

The coming of Yüan-tê and Chang Fei threatened their rear and the fugitives turned and recommenced the battle. The two captains were thus between two fires and helpless. They offered to surrender and were received. Yüan-tê returned to his own camp near the city.

The loss of his two captains grieved Chang Jên sorely. He called his remaining two and asked advice. They proposed to risk all in one desperate battle while they sent to Ch'êngtu to tell their master of their sorry plight.

Chang Jên agreed. Said he, "To-morrow I will go and challenge them. If they accept and come out to fight, I will feign retreat and inveigle them round to the north side of the city. As they follow me, a sortie must be made when they pass the gate so as to cut their army in two. We ought to overcome them in this way."

"Let me lead the sortie," said Wu I. "General Liu can stay to help our lord's son guard the city."

This also was agreed to. Next morning Chang Jên went out to offer the challenge, his men waving flags and shouting lustily. At once Chang Fei took up the challenge and rode out. He stayed not to parley, but galloped up to Chang Jên and engaged him. After half a score of bouts Chang Jên seemed to be getting worsted, so he turned and fled, taking the way around the north of the city. Chang Fei pursued him with all speed. Then as he passed the gate the sortie was made so that Chang Fei was between two forces and unable to get clear. Chang Jên turned back to attack.

Chang Fei seemed in a parlous state. But at this very moment a body of soldiers came up from the river-side and a fierce warrior rode straight for Wu I, and in the first bout made him prisoner. His men were then easily forced back and Chang Fei was free. It was Chao Yün who had so opportunely appeared.

"Where is the Commander-in-chief?" asked Chang Fei.

"He has arrived; I think he has already seen our lord," replied Chao.

The prisoner was carried to the camp where K'ung-ming was. Fei dismounted and went in to greet him. K'ung-ming was surprised, and said, "How comes it that you arrived before me?"

Yüan-tê told the story of Fei's prudence and sagacity in dealing with Yen. K'ung-ming congratulated him and said, "When Chang Fei behaves with such skill my lord's good fortune is indeed ample."

When the prisoner was taken in, Yüan-tê asked him if he would surrender.

He replied, "Why not, seeing I am a prisoner?"

Thereupon Yüan-tê himself loosed his bonds. K'ung-ming began to question him upon the defence. Wu told him the names of the officers, adding, "Liu Kuei does not count for much, but Chang Jên is a man to be avoided."

"Then before we can get the city we must capture Chang," said K'ung-ming.

"There is a bridge on the east; what is it called?"

"It is known as the ' Bridge of the Golden Goose.' "

K'ung-ming rode over to the bridge and scrutinised the neighbourhood.

After his return to camp he summoned Huang and Wei for orders. To them he said, "On the east of the city is a bridge called the 'Bridge of the Golden Goose' and about five *li* south of this I saw a dense growth of reed and sedge which would afford excellent shelter. Wei is to lead a company of men to the left and attack, but only attack horsemen. Huang will lead a company of swordsmen who are to hough the horses. When Chang Jên has lost most of his men and horses he will flee by the hill road, where he will fall into an ambush.

Next Chao Yün was called and sent to lie in ambush close to the bridge, which he was to destroy as soon as the enemy had crossed. That done, Chao was to take up a position beyond the bridge to prevent the enemy from getting away to the north. Forced to the south, their destruction was inevitable.

These arrangements made, K'ung-ming himself went to challenge the enemy and try to bring them to battle.

The Prefect had sent two captains to reinforce Chang Jên. He sent one of them to the help of Liu Kuei in the city, while the other, Cho Ying by name, was to march second with Chang himself. K'ung-ming guilefully led out a mob of disorderly looking soldiers, all in disarray, whom he drew up as if they were a fighting force. He himself, dressed in a simple robe and toying with a fan, took his seat in a small four-wheeled carriage. A few horsemen caracolling gaily to and fro formed his escort.

Having crossed the bridge, K'ung-ming halted and pointed to Chang Jên, saying, "Dare you withstand me and not surrender when Ts'ao Ts'ao's hundred legions fled at my name?"

But the enemy leader was rather occupied with inspecting the disorderly lot of soldiers he saw in front, all standing anyhow and not drawn up into "fives" at all. With a cynical smile, he said, "People talk of Chuko Liang's superhuman military genius; I say his reputation is false."

With that he whirled his spear about his head and he dashed forward with all his men. As he came, K'ung-ming left his carriage, mounted a horse and retired to the far side of the bridge. Chang impetuously pursued and rushed over the Bridge of the Golden Goose. It was only when he had reached the other side that he saw a body of soldiers on either hand. Then he knew that he had been led into a trap.

As soon as he had got across the bridge the two bodies of soldiers came to the attack. Chang turned to re-cross to the north, but Chao Yün had done his work and the bridge was in ruins. He made to turn away north, but Chao's men stopped the way. So he had to turn southward and followed the course of the river. He presently reached the place where grew the reeds and sedges. Out came Wei and his company of spearmen, who attacked fiercely while Huang, with his swordsmen, houghed the horses. Men and horses were soon lying on the ground. The few survivors were quickly made prisoners and bound with cords.

No footman escaped. But a few lucky horsemen followed Chang and got away to the hills. There they met Chang Fei, who fell upon them with a mighty roar, scattered the few men and captured the leader. Seeing Chang Jên a prisoner, his second in command turned toward Chao Yün and surrendered. Victorious, they returned to camp. Yüan-tê rewarded Cho Ying.

When the leader Chang Jên was led in by Chang Fei, K'ung-ming was seated beside his lord.

"Why have you held out so long after all the other captains of Shu have yielded?" said Yüan-tê.

"Can a loyal servant take a second master?" cried Chang fiercely, his eyes glaring with hate.

"You do not know the times; submission means life."

"I might submit to-day, but it would not endure. I should repent it. You had better slay me."

Yüan-tê was inclined to mercy, but the prisoner was irreconcilable and kept up a stream of furious abuse. So at last the order was given for his execution, thus giving him a right to fame.

A poem says:—

> No second lord the heroic servant knows,
> The way of death Chang Jên contented goes.
> Clear shines his fame as doth the heavenly moon
> That nightly lights the ramparts of Lo Town.

Yüan-tê grieved for him although he had been an enemy, for he was a brave man. He was given honourable burial, sepulture beside the Bridge of the Golden Goose, where all the passers-by would be reminded of his loyalty.

Next day the army moved on to Loch'êng, Yen Yen and the other captains who had submitted leading the way. At the gate they hailed the wardens and called upon them to surrender, whereby the city should be saved from utter destruction. From the wall, Liu Kuei abused the treacherous Yen and took his bow to shoot, but just as he was fitting the arrow to the string another man cut him down. Soon the gates were thrown open and the city had yielded.

As Yüan-tê entered the city by one gate, Liu Hsün, who had shared the command of the city, escaped by another gate and set off for Ch'êngtu.

Yüan-tê put forth proclamations to allay the fears of the inhabitants of the city. He enquired who had been on his side in cutting down Liu Kuei and was told it was one Chang I, of Wuyang. He and all who had helped in the capture were amply rewarded.

"Our next city is Ch'êngtu." said K'ung-ming. "However, in the meantime there may be some trouble in pacifying the outlying districts, and hence it will be well for you to send Chao Yün and Chang Fei, with a certain number of those who have joined us, into the country around to reassure the people and to repress any risings that may take place. There will be no need for any especial precautions in the neighbourhood of Ch'êngtu."

The two warriors went their ways, and then K'ung-ming began to make careful enquiries concerning the road to Ch'êngtu. Certain of those who had given in their allegiance to the invaders said that the only place where they could expect any serious defence was Mienchu. Once they had passed this the capital lay at their mercy.

Then Fa Chêng was consulted. Said he, "With the fall of Loch'êng the land of Shu passed to you. Let our lord only deal with the people kindly and justly and there will be no need of weapons. I can write such a letter to the Prefect Liu Chang as shall make him surrender at call."

"That would be most excellent," said K'ung-ming.

The letter was written and sent by the hand of a messenger.

Liu Hsün, son of the Prefect, presently reached Ch'êngtu and told his father of the loss of Loch'êng. The Prefect at once called his counsellors together, and the Secretary Ch'êng Tu said, "Although Liu Pei has been successful and captured cities and towns, yet his army is but small, his hosts are not near him, he depends upon chance for his grain and has no proper supplies. Therefore our best plan is to remove the people of Pahsi and Tzŭchang to the farther side of the River Fou, burn all the granaries, fortify the city and let starvation defeat him. Let us reject all challenges to battle and in a hundred days his men will go off of their own accord. Then we can do with him as we will."

"I like not the plan," said Liu Chang. "Oppose invaders in order that tranquillity may prevail," is a well-worn maxim, but till now I have never heard of disturbing the people in order to oppose the march of an enemy. Your words are not such as mean safety."

Just at the moment the letter from Fa Chêng arrived. It was opened and the Prefect read: "I was sent to Chingchou to negotiate an alliance, but the opposition of those about you to its lord has resulted in the present situation. However, the ruler of Chingchou still remembers old friendship and is mindful of the ties of relationship. If you, my master, could reverse your policy and lend your support to your relative, I think you would be generously treated. I hope you will consider this carefully."

Liu Chang flew into a passion. He tore the letter to fragments and began to abuse its writer as a traitor, an ingrate, a renegade, and drove the bearer of the letter from his presence. He then sent an army under the leadership of Fei Kuan, his wife's brother, to reinforce Mienchu.

Fei Kuan at once recommended as his assistant one Li Yen and the two mustered their men, three legions, and set out for the city. At this juncture the Prefect of Ichou wrote advising to borrow aid from Hanchung, but Liu Chang rejected this plan, saying it would be useless to try to obtain help from a district under the influence of his relentless enemy Chang Lu. Tung Ho, of Ichou, replied, "He may be an enemy, but Liu Pei is in possession of Loch'êng and the situation is extremely dangerous. When the lips are gone the teeth are cold. If you clearly indicate the dangers to him he must come to our help."

So a letter was written.

Two years had elapsed since Ma Ch'ao had been defeated and gone over to the *Ch'iang* tribes of Tangut. He had made friends with them and with their aid had conquered portions of Shênsi. His expeditions had been very successful, the people opening their gates at the first summons. Only Chichou had stood out, but ever this was on the point of yielding. The Governor of the district had sent many urgent appeals for help

to Hsiahou Yüan, who, however, would do nothing without
his master's order. Wei K'ang, the Governor, was in despair,
and at a council his officers advised him to yield. However,
one of them, Yang Fou, earnestly opposed yielding, saying
they could not surrender to a lot of rebels such as were Ma and
his colleagues.

"What is there to hope for?" asked Wei K'ang despairingly.

Although Yang Fou besought him with bitterness to hold
out, it was useless; K'ang rejected his advice, opened the city
gates and bowed his head in submission.

"You only yield now as the last resource," cried Ma, angry
at the delay he had suffered. "This is no real submission."

Whereupon he put to death Wei K'ang and all his to the
number of two score.

But when one told him that Yang had been really responsible
for the long delay, in that he had urged his master to hold out,
Ma did not put him to death but praised him and said Yang
had but done his duty. He further showed his approval by
employing Yang and two of his friends in his own army.
These two friends were named Liang K'uan and Chao Ch'ü.

One day Yang went to his new chief and said, "My wife has
died in Lint'ao; I wish to take leave for two months to bury
her."

Wherefore he was granted leave and went away from the
army. On the way, he went to his maternal cousin, one Chiang
Hsü, the general in command at Tungch'êng. The general's
mother, then an old lady of eighty-two, was Yang's aunt.
When Yang saw her he wept before her, saying, "Behold an
unfortunate man! The city I had to defend is lost; my master
is dead; and I have survived him. I am ashamed to look you
in the face. Now this Ma Ch'ao ravages the country-side,
and every man hates him. Yet my cousin sits still and
does nothing against him. Is this fitting conduct for a state
servant?"

He wept bitterly. The old lady was moved by his grief,
called in her son and said to him reproachfully, "You are the
cause of the evil that has come upon the noble Wei." Then
turning once more toward Yang she said, "But what can now
be done? You have surrendered and, more than that, you
have accepted service under your late enemy."

"It is true," replied Yang. "I have surrendered and I have
accepted service, but it is with the desire to preserve my
miserable life till I can avenge my master."

"A bold man is Ma Ch'ao, and difficult to destroy," said
Chiang.

"Not very difficult," replied Yang, "for though he is bold yet
he is unskilful. Already I have two friends by his side, and
they would help against him if you, my brother, would only
supply a force."

"What is to be gained by delay?" then said the old lady. "Is there any who will not have to die? To perish in the way of loyalty and righteousness is to die in the right path. Do not think of me, for if you do, and heed not the call of your cousin, then will I die at once so that you may be free to make up your mind."

There was now no excuse for delay, and Chiang had to act. He summoned two of his officers, Ying Fêng and Chao Ang, and took counsel with them.

Now the latter of these had a son, Yueh, who was an officer in the army of Ma Ch'ao. When Ch'ao had to consent to take part against his son's chief he became very unhappy and went home to talk over it with his wife. He said, "I have to-day been led into a scheme to destroy Ma Ch'ao and avenge Wei K'ang. But there is our son there in Ma's service, and Ma will certainly put him to death as soon as he hears that we are arming against him. What is to be done?"

But his wife replied angrily, "Should any grudge even his life to avenge his liege lord or his father? How much less a son? My lord, if you let the thought of your son stay your hand then will I die forthwith."

This decided the matter, and without further parley Chao decided to share the expedition and set about preparations. The army was soon on the way. Chiang and Yang went and camped at Lich'êng; the other two, Yin and Chao, camped at Ch'ishan. The wife of Chao Ang sold her ornaments and went in person to her husband's camp to feast his soldiers.

The fears of Chao Ang concerning the fate of his son were only too soon justified. At the first news of the march of an army against him, Ma beheaded the young man. A force was sent to Lich'êng, and the men under Chiang and Yang went out to oppose it. The two leaders on the avenging side went to battle dressed in mourning white. They railed at Ma, calling him traitor and wicked and rebellious.

Ma Ch'ao angrily dashed across toward them, and the fight began. From the very first it was seen that the defenders of the city could not hope to beat off the attack, and they turned to flee. Ma pursued them. But soon he heard the shouting of soldiers behind him and found the other army was attacking his rear. Wherefore he was between two armies and had a double battle to fight. As he turned toward that in his rear those he had been pursuing returned again to the attack. And while engaged with these two, there suddenly appeared a third force under Hsiahou Yüan, who had just received orders from Ts'ao to come against Ma.

Three attacks at once were too much for Ma, and he fled, his force in utter confusion. He retreated all that night and at dawn reached his own city of Chich'êng. He hailed the gate, but a flight of arrows was the response. Soon after, Liang

K'uan and Chao Ch'ü appeared and reviled him from the
ramparts above. More than this, they dragged his wife up
upon the wall, murdered her before his face and threw the
bloody body at his feet. They followed up this by the murder
in like manner of his three sons and other members of his
family to the number of half a score and more. And all their
dead bodies were flung from the wall.

Rage and despair filled Ma's bosom; he almost fell from
his steed. But little time was allowed to grieve, for Hsiahou
Yüan was nearly upon him. Knowing that he could not oppose
this force with any chance of victory, he made no battle line,
but set off with two of his captains to cut his way through such
parties of the enemy as they might meet. Their sole object
was escape, so when they fell upon Yang and Chiang they only
fought to get through, and in the same way they forced a road
through the small army under Yin and Chao. However, they
lost most of their few followers, and at the end had only some
three score left.

About the fourth watch they came to Lich'êng. In the darkness the gate guards, thinking only of the return of their own
men, opened the gates and unwittingly let in the enemy. Once
in the city the slaughter began, and every one, soldier or common person, was slain, till the city was swept clear from the
south gate to the very centre.

Presently they came to the residence of Chiang Hsü and
dragged forth his aged mother. She showed no sign of fear,
but reviled Ma Ch'ao till in his anger he slew her with his own
sword. Thence they went to the house of Yin and Chao and
slew all they found therein. The only person who escaped the
massacre was the wife of Chao Ang, who had accompanied her
husband.

But the city proved no place of safety. Hsiahou with his
army appeared the following day, and Ma fled before him to
the west. But ere he had gone twenty *li* he came face to
face with another army drawn up in battle array. Yang Fou
was the leader. Grinding his teeth with rage, Ma set his spear
and rode at Yang, while his two captains, Ma Tai and P'ang
Tê, attacked the rear. Yang was overcome, and his seven
brothers who had gone with him into the battle were slain.
Yang himself was wounded in five places, but still fought on
till he was made prisoner.

However, Hsiahou had not left pursuing Ma. He came up
to the city, and Ma fled before him to the west. His army was
now reduced to the two captains and about half a score of
horsemen, and these few were left to go their way.

Ts'ao Ts'ao's general, Hsiahou Yüan, set himself to restore
order and tranquillity in the district, after which he appor-
tioned its defence among Chiang Hsü and certain other trustworthy men. The captive leader Yang Fou was sent to the

capital in a cart. When he arrived he saw Ts'ao, who offered
him the title of Marquis. But Yang declined the honour,
saying, "I have neither the credit of a successful defence nor
the merit of death in the attempt. Death should be my portion
rather than honours. How could I accept the offer?"

Ts'ao praised him and did not insist.

Having escaped from their pursuers, Ma Ch'ao and his few
followers decided to make for Hanchung and offer their services to Chang Lu. He received them gladly, for he thought
with such help he could certainly get possession of Ichou on
the west as well as repel Ts'ao on the east. More than this, he
thought to cement the friendship by giving Ma a daughter to
wife. But this displeased one of his captains, Yang Po.

"The misfortune that befell Ma Ch'ao's wife and family was
entirely the fault of his own misconduct. Would you give
your daughter to such as he to wife?" said Yang.

Chang Lu again considered the matter and abandoned his
intention. But a certain busybody told Ma what had been
proposed and that Yang had defeated the scheme. Whereupon Ma was very annoyed and sought to compass the death of
Yang. Yang and his brother Sung on the other side conspired
to destroy Ma.

At this time a messenger arrived in Hanchung begging for
assistance against the invader Liu Pei. Chang Lu refused
help. But then Huang Ch'üan came on the same errand. He
first saw Yang Sung and talked to him and brought him to
favour the scheme, pointing out the inter-dependence of the
eastern and western countries, which stood next each other as
the lips are close to the teeth. So he won over Yang Sung,
who led him to see his master. To him again Huang spoke
forcibly and laid the matter before him so cogently that Chang
promised his help.

One of Chang's officers tried to dissuade him by pointing out
the old enmity between him and Liu Chang, but another suddenly interjected, saying, "Useless I may be, but if you will
give me troops I will capture this Liu Pei and you will retain
all your land."

> The land's true lord goes west and then
> Hanchung sends forth its bravest men.

Who made this bold offer? The next chapter will tell.

CHAPTER LXV.

GREAT BATTLE AT CHIAMING PASS;
LIU PEI TAKES THE GOVERNORSHIP OF ICHOU.

It was Yen Pu who thus opposed sending help to Liu Chang. Then Ma Ch'ao rose and said, "I have been the recipient of much kindness from my lord, which I feel I can never repay adequately. Now let me lead an army to take Chiaming Pass and capture Liu Pei. Then, my lord, Liu Chang will surely lose his twenty districts, and they shall be yours."

This offer rejoiced Chang Lu, who sent away Huang Ch'üan without an answer and told off two legions for Ma Ch'ao to lead. As P'ang Tê was too ill to take part in the expedition, Yang Po was sent in his place. The day to march was chosen.

Meanwhile, the messenger sent by Fa Chêng had returned to Fouch'êng to say Chêng Tu had advised his master to set fire to all the plains and valleys between the capital and the invaders, as well as the granaries, to move away the people and to stand solely on the defensive. This news caused Liu Pei and K'ung-ming great anxiety, for it would be a grave danger to them. However, Fa Chêng was more sanguine.

"Do not be anxious," said he, "the plan would be extremely harmful, but it will not be carried out. Liu Chang will not do that."

Surely enough, very soon they heard that Liu Chang had not adopted the suggestion; he would not remove the people. It was a great relief to Yüan-tê.

Then said K'ung-ming, "Now let us capture Mienchu quickly, for, that done, Ch'êngtu is as good as ours."

He therefore told off Huang Chung and Wei Yen to advance first. When Fei Kuan heard of their advance he ordered Li Yen to go out to stop them, and Li led out his three companies. The two sides being arrayed, Huang Chung rode out and fought some half hundred bouts with Li Yen. Neither was able to claim a victory, and so K'ung-ming from the midst of the host ordered them to beat the gongs to cease from battle. When Huang Chung had got back to his side again he said, "O Commander, why did you sound the retirement just as I was getting the better of my opponent?"

"Because I saw that he was not to be overcome by mere force. To-morrow you shall fight again, and then you shall lead him into the hills by the ruse of pretended defeat. There will be a surprise awaiting him."

Huang Chung agreed to try this ruse, and so on the morrow accepted Li Yen's challenge when it was offered. After about the tenth bout he and his men pretended to be worsted and ran. Li pursued and was quickly lured into the mountains. Suddenly his danger flashed into his mind, and he turned to go back. But he found Wei Yen's men drawn up across his path, while K'ung-ming from a hill top near by cried, "You had better yield; if not, there are bows and crossbows on both sides of you all ready to avenge the death of our P'ang T'ung."

Li dropped off his horse, threw aside his armour and offered submission. Not a man of his had been hurt. The prisoner was conducted to Yüan-tê, who was very affable and so won his heart that he offered to try to seduce Fei Kuan from his allegiance.

"Though he is related to Liu Chang, yet Fei and I are very close friends. Let me go and persuade him."

Wherefore Li was sent back to the city to induce his chief to come over to Liu Pei's side. He talked to such effect of the kindness and virtues of Liu Pei that Fei was won over, opened the city gates and admitted the invaders.

As soon as Yüan-tê had entered Mienchu he set out his men to take the capital. While thus engaged, a hasty messenger came to tell of the doings at Chiaming Pass, whereat had suddenly appeared an army from the east under Ma Ch'ao and his captains. They had attacked, and the Pass would certainly be lost if help was not sent quickly.

"We need both Chang Fei and Chao Yün for this," remarked K'ung-ming. "Then we could oppose successfully."

"But Tzŭ-lung is away," said Yüan-tê. "However, I-tê is here. Let us send him quickly."

"Do not say anything, my lord," said K'ung-ming. "Let me stir him to fight his noblest."

But as soon as Chang Fei heard of the danger he came rushing in, shouting, "I must say farewell, brother. I am off to fight Ma Ch'ao."

However, K'ung-ming made as if he heard not and said to Yüan-tê, "That Ma Ch'ao has invaded the Pass and we have no one to drive him back. Nobody can stand up to him— unless we can get Kuan Yü from Chingchou. He could do it."

"Why do you despise me, O Commander?" cried Chang Fei. "Did I not once drive back a whole army? Think you that I mind a stupid fool like Ma Ch'ao."

K'ung-ming said, "Yes, I-tê; but when you forced back the waters and broke the bridge you succeeded because your enemies were doubtful. If they had known, General, you would not have come off so easily. All the world knows this Ma Ch'ao and has heard about his six battles at the Wei Bridge; and how he made Ts'ao Ts'ao cut off his beard and throw away his robe. He very nearly slew him too. This is no lightsome task like that, and even your brother might fail."

"All I care for is to go, and if I do not overcome this fellow, I will take the consequences."

"Well, if you will put that in writing, you may lead the attack. And I will ask our lord to lead another army to back you up this time. He can leave the defence of this town to me till Chao Yün returns."

"I also want to go," said Wei Yen.

Wei Yen was allowed to go with a half company of light horse in advance of Chang Fei. Yüan-tê marched third. Wei Yen and his scouts soon arrived at the Pass and there fell in with Yang Po. They engaged; but after a few bouts Yang fled.

At this success Wei Yen was seized with ambition to rival it and try to snatch the credit that would fall to Chang Fei. So he pursued. But he presently came across a line of battle all drawn up, the commander being Ma Tai. Wei Yen, thinking it was the redoubtable Ma Ch'ao, rode toward him whirling his sword. Soon Ma Tai turned and ran away, and Wei Yen followed him. However, Ma Tai presently turned back and shot an arrow, which wounded his pursuer in the left arm, so that he left the pursuit and turned his face the other way. Then Ma Tai came after him and chased Wei Yen nearly up to the Pass.

Here Ma Tai was suddenly confronted by a fierce thunder-roaring leader who dashed down from the Pass as on a flying steed.

It was Chang Fei, who had just arrived. Hearing the noise of battle below the Pass he had come to learn what it meant and saw the arrow wound Wei Yen. Soon he was in the saddle and off to the rescue, but before he engaged he would ascertain if the foeman was worthy of his steel.

"Who are you? Tell your name," cried Chang Fei, "then I may fight with you."

"I am Ma Tai of Hsiliang."

"As you are not Ma Ch'ao go away quickly, for you are no match for me. You may bid Ma Ch'ao himself come, and tell him that Chang I-tê of the north is here.

"How dare you treat me with contempt?" cried Ma Tai in hot anger, and he came galloping up with his spear set ready to thrust. But after a half score bouts he fled. Chang Fei was about to pursue when a rider came up to him hastily, crying, "Do not pursue, my brother."

The rider was Yüan-tê, and Chang Fei stopped. The two returned together to the Pass.

"I knew your impulsive temper, and so I followed you. Since you have got the better of him you may well rest and recuperate for the fight to-morrow with Ma Ch'ao."

The rolling of drums at dawn next day declared the arrival of Ma Ch'ao. Yüan-tê looked at the array from a point of vantage and saw Ma Ch'ao emerge from the shadow of his great standard. He wore a lion helmet and his belt was clasped with the shaggy head of a wild beast. His breastplate was silver and his robe of white. As his dress and bearing were not as other men's so were his abilities superior. And Yüan-tê looked at him admiringly.

"He justifies what people say," said Liu Pei. "Handsome Ma Ch'ao."

Chang Fei was for going down at once, but his brother once more checked him, saying, "No; not yet. Avoid the first keenness of his fighting ardour."

Thus below was Ma Ch'ao challenging Chang Fei, while, above, Chang Fei was fretting at being unable to settle Ma Ch'ao. Time after time Fei was setting out, but each time his brother checked him. And so it continued till past midday, when Yüan-tê, noticing signs of fatigue and weariness among Ma Ch'ao's men, decided that it was time to let Chang Fei try his fortune. Whereupon he chose out a half company of horsemen to accompany his brother and let the party go.

Ma Ch'ao seeing Chang Fei coming with so small a force, signalled with his spear to his array to retire a bowshot, and Chang Fei's men halted. When all his men had taken their places, Fei set his spear and rode out.

"Do you know who I am?" shouted Fei, "I am Chang Fei of Yen."

Ma Ch'ao replied, "My family having been noble for many generations I am not likely to know any rustic dolts."

This reply upset Chang Fei, and in a moment the two steeds were rushing toward each other, both men with poised spears. The fight began and continued for a hundred bouts. Neither had the advantage.

"A veritable tiger of a leader," sighed Yüan-tê. But he felt that Chang Fei was running a risk, wherefore he sounded the gong as a signal to cease the fight. And each drew off to his own side. Chang Fei rested his steed for a time, then, leaving his helmet, he wound a turban about his head, mounted and rode out to renew the fight. Ma Ch'ao also came out, and the duel continued.

Presently Yüan-tê thought his brother in danger. So he girded on his armour and went down into the plain. He watched till they had fought another hundred bouts, and then as both seemed to wax fiercer than ever he gave the signal again to cease the battle.

Both drew off and returned each to his own side. It was then getting late, and Yüan-tê said to his brother, "You had better retire for to-day; he is a terrible opponent. Try him again to-morrow."

But Chang Fei's spirit was roused, and was it likely that such advice would be palatable?

"No," shouted he, "I will die and not come back."

"But it is late; you cannot go on fighting," said Yüan-tê.

"Let them bring torches, and we will have a night battle," said Fei.

Ma Ch'ao having mounted a fresh steed, now rode out and shouted, "Dare you try a night battle, Chang Fei?"

Chang Fei's excitement rose higher. He hastily changed horses with his brother and rode forth.

"If I do not capture you, I will not go back to the Pass," said Fei.

"And if I do not overcome you I will not return to the camp," said Ma.

Both sides cheered. They lit many torches till it seemed as light as day, and the two great captains went to the front to fight. At the twentieth bout Ma Ch'ao turned his steed and fled.

"Whither are you going?" called out Fei.

The fact was that Ma Ch'ao had begun to see he could not win in direct and simple combat, so he thought to try a ruse. By a false flight, as though he knew he had lost, he would inveigle Chang Fei into pursuit. He picked up a copper hammer secretly and kept a careful watch on his opponent for the most favourable moment to strike. But his enemy's flight only put Chang Fei upon his guard, and when the moment came for the blow with the hammer he dodged, so that the weapon flew harmlessly past his ear. Then Fei turned his horse. Whereupon Ma Ch'ao began to pursue. Then Fei pulled up, took his bow, fitted an arrow to the string and let fly at Ma. But Ma also dodged, and the arrow flew by. Then each returned to his own side.

Then Yüan-tê came out to the front of his battle line and called out, "Note well, O Ma Ch'ao, that I, who have never treated men other than with kindness and justice and truth and sincerity, swear that I will not take advantage of your period of repose to pursue or attack. Wherefore you may rest awhile in peace."

Ma Ch'ao, hearing these words, withdrew to the rear, and the other captains one by one returned, while Yüan-tê drew off his army toward the Pass.

Early next day Chang Fei was once more going down out of the Pass to fight, when they told him that the Commander-in-chief, Chuko Liang, had arrived. Yüan-tê went to receive him, and K'ung-ming at once began to speak of Ma Ch'ao.

"He is the most terrible leader of the age; if he fights a desperate battle with Chang Fei loss will ensue. So I have come as quickly as I could. I left Mienchu in safe hands. I think I have a little ruse left that will bring Ma over to our side."

"Now I have seen the man. I greatly admire him," said Yüan-tê. "If we could only win him over!"

"Then listen" said K'ung-ming. "Chang Lu greatly desires the title of "Prince of Hanning" and among his most intimate subordinates I know one open to bribery. So we will send a person secretly to see him and give him gold and silver and so win his support. This done, we will write to Chang and tell him that you are set upon taking Hsich'üan from its present ruler, which will give an opportunity to wipe out the enmity he has so long nourished against Liu Chang, and that the reward of his remaining firmly on our side to the end will be that you will memorialise the Throne for the coveted title for him. This will make him order Ma to return, and, when that is done, I shall find a means of winning him over."

Yüan-tê wrote a letter and sent it by the hand of Sun Ch'ien together with gold and pearls. Sun went by secret roads to give these to Yang Sung. And when he found Yang and explained his mission in private, he was quickly led into the presence of Chang Lu.

"How can Yüan-tê memorialise the Throne to confer on me the rank of prince when he is but a simple General himself?" asked Chang Lu, when he understood the offer and its conditions.

"He is an Imperial Uncle;" said Yang Sung, "with such a rank he could present such a memorial."

Chang Lu assented. He sent orders to Ma Ch'ao to cease fighting, and Sun Ch'ien remained as the guest of Yang Sung till he should see whether Ma Ch'ao would obey the command. Before long the messenger returned with a word from Ma that he could not cease fighting till he had been successful. A second messenger returned with a similar response.

"This Ma is untrustworthy," said Yang Sung. "He will not withdraw his soldiers because he contemplates rebellion. That is the real reason."

He set stories afloat that Ma Ch'ao desired to make himself the ruler of Shu and had said that he would no longer be content with subordinate rank. And he meant to avenge the death of his father. The rumours came to the ear of Chang Lu, and he asked Yang Sung what should be done. Yang proposed that he should give Ma Ch'ao a limit of a month in order to accomplish his task, provided he consented to three conditions. And if he would not agree he would have to be put to death.

So a messenger was sent to declare the three conditions, which were: the capture of Hsich'üan, the head of Liu Chang and the repulse of the Chingchou troops.

"If he fails in any one of these just bring his head," said Chang.

While the messenger went to carry these orders Chang Wei was sent as guard at one of the strategic points which would control Ma's army in case of rebellion.

When Ma Ch'ao heard the three demands made on him he was greatly troubled, saying, "What can such a charge mean?"

After taking counsel with his son it seemed best to suspend fighting, and the army rested. But Yang had not yet attained his end, so he dropped another hint that Ma Ch'ao's return with an army would be a danger, and hence all the points of vantage on the homeward road were guarded so that he should not return. Thus Ma Ch'ao was helpless and could see no way out of the difficulty.

Then K'ung-ming said to his lord, "Now is my chance to use my little three inches of unworn tongue; Ma Ch'ao is in a fix. I am going to his camp to persuade him to come over to your side."

"But I do not like you to run such a risk, my Master. You are my most necessary support, and if anything happened to you, what should I do?"

K'ung-ming was set upon going and persisted in his request. Yüan-tê again and again refused. At this juncture a messenger came with letters from Chao Yün. Yüan-tê called him in and questioned him. He was Li Hui of Chienning, the man who had formerly remonstrated so earnestly with Liu Chang.

"You once pleaded with your master to keep me out; why are you here now?"

"Because the prudent bird chooses its perch and the wise man his master. I did attempt to dissuade Liu of Ichou from a course which I felt to be disastrous, and thereby fulfilled my duty as his servant. He rejected my counsel and I knew he would fail. Your liberality, O General, has won over all the province, and success must be yours. I wish to serve under your banner."

"Your services will surely be of great advantage to me, Sir," said Yüan-tê.

Then Li began to talk of Ma Ch'ao. "I knew him when we were in Shênsi together. He is now in great straits, and I may be able to talk him over. What say you?"

"Just the man to go instead of me," interjected K'ung-ming. "But what arguments will you use?"

Li Hui leaned over and whispered in his ear thus—and thus —What he said seemed to please K'ung-ming mightily, and he was bidden to go forthwith.

Arrived at the camp, he sent in his name, at which Ma Ch'ao remarked, "Yes; I know him; a glib and specious talker. I know what he has come for too."

So he placed a score of armed ruffians in hiding about his tent and told them to cut the visitor to pieces if the signal was given.

Then the guest was led in and came walking proudly. His host remained seated stiff and upright. He spoke roughly, saying, "What are you come for?"

"I am here as bearer of a message."

"This sword here in the scabbard is newly ground. You may try me by words, but if the words do not penetrate I shall ask you to try the sword."

Li Hui smiled, saying, "O, General, evil is not far off. However, I am thinking the newly ground sword will not be tried on my head. You will want to try it on your own."

"What evil were you talking about?"

"The worst vilification could not hide the beauty of Hsi-tzŭ nor could the most fulsome praise gloze over the ugliness of Wu-yen. The sun rises to the meridian and then declines; the moon waxes to the full and then wanes. All things obey the one law. Now, Sir, you are at enmity with Ts'ao Ts'ao for your father's death, but Shênsi hates you with a stubborn, grinding hate. You can neither rescue Liu Chang by repulsing the army from Chingchou, nor can you settle Yang Sung by getting an interview with Chang Lu. The whole world now holds no place for a man without a lord, and if you experience further defeats, like that one on the Wei River, or the loss of Chich'êng, will you not be too shamed to look any man in the face?"

Ma Ch'ao bowed his head. "You speak well, Sir. But I am helpless."

"Now that you listen to me I would ask why those fearsome ruffians are in hiding by your tent?" continued Li Hui.

Ma, suddenly stricken with shame, ordered them to retire. Li Hui continued his speech.

"Liu, the Imperial Uncle, is considerate to his subordinates, and I am certain he will succeed, and so I have forsaken Liu Chang to cleave to him. Your honoured father joined him in destroying rebels. Why do you not flee from darkness into the light? Thereby you would avenge your father and become famous."

Ma, convinced of the wisdom of the course thus recommended, proved his conversion by sending for Yang Sung and slaying him forthwith. Taking with him the head of his victim, he accompanied Li Hui to the Pass and tendered his submission. Yüan-tê welcomed him warmly and treated him as a highly honoured guest.

Ma Ch'ao bowed his head, saying, "Meeting you, O illustrious lord, is like seeing the clear sky when the clouds have been swept aside."

When Sun Ch'ien returned, Yüan-tê detached certain forces to go to the capture of Ch'êngtu, left two captains to guard the Pass and made a triumphant entry into Mienchu. Two of the Shu captains came to oppose Yüan-tê, but Chao Yün went out against them while Yüan-tê was entertaining Ma Ch'ao at a banquet on the city wall. Ere it had concluded, Chao Yün slew both the captains and brought their heads to the banquet chamber. This exploit put Ma Ch'ao on his mettle and doubled his respect for the conquerors.

"Let not my lord attack," said he. "I will make Liu Chang surrender of his own accord. Should he resist, my son and I will take the city and offer it to you with both hands."

Yüan-tê was very pleased with the course of events; the day was indeed one of rejoicing. But Liu Chang was greatly distressed at the news of his fresh misfortunes, which reached him with the return of his defeated soldiers. He barred the gates and stopped all exit. Before long came news of the approach of Ma Ch'ao with an army of rescue. The Governor then ventured to mount the walls, and soon Ma Chao and Ma Tai rode up and stood below the ramparts. And the former called out, "I wish to speak with Liu Chi-yü."

Then Liu Chang showed himself, and Ma Ch'ao plunged into the matter without more ado.

"I took the leadership of Chang Lu's army to rescue Ichou, little thinking that, under the calumnious advice of Yang Sung, he would try to slay me. However, now I have gone over to the side of Liu, the Imperial Uncle, and advise you, Sir, to do the same, you and all your officers. Thereby you will all escape harm. If any one holds on a misguided course I shall take the city."

Such words came as a shock, and Liu Chang paled. His feelings overcame him and he swooned. When he came to his senses he muttered, "I am stupid and I am sorry. Better open the gates and end it. The city will be saved."

"No, no," cried Yung Ho. "There are three legions of good soldiers in the city and ample money and stores for a year to come. Hold out."

But Liu was broken. "My father and I have ruled here for twenty years and have done no particular good for the people. If we fight for three years the grass will be stained with the blood of my people and the fault will be mine. I could not bear it, and so I see no better way than to surrender, whereby I may bring peace to the people."

Those about him wept. One man spoke, saying, "You speak as Heaven guides you."

Turning toward him they recognised a man of Pahsi named Ch'iao Chou, who had the reputation of being an astrologer.

"I have studied the aspect of the heavens and a multitude of stars gathered over Shu, one of which shone as the full moon; a right royal star. And I recall a popular couplet of last year:—

> "When comes the ruler from the east,
> Then may you on new rice feast."

This is a sort of presage. None can withstand the decree of the Most High."

Huang and Liu, who heard these words, were very angry at such a speech and rose up to smite the speaker. But Liu Chang stayed them.

Next came news that Hsü Ching, Prefect of the metropolitan district, had gone over to the invaders. This was the last blow. Liu Chang went home weeping.

Next day they reported that Liu Pei, the Imperial Uncle, had sent a secretary to visit Liu Chang and he was even then at the city gate. He was admitted, and Chien Yung entered, riding in a carriage and looking about him most haughtily. Suddenly he was hailed from the street by a man with a sword in his hand, who cried, "You have got your wish, wretched creature, and you seem to think there is no one to compare with you. But do not look so contemptuously at us of Shu."

Chien quickly got out of his carriage to speak to the speaker, who was a man of Mienchu named Ts'in Mi.

"Worthy brother," said he, "I did not recognise you. I pray you not to be angry."

Both then went to visit Liu Chang, and they spoke of the liberality and broad-mindedness of Liu Pei, said he had no intention to harm any one, and praised him to such effect that Liu Chang then and there made up his mind finally that he would give up the struggle. So he treated Chien very honourably that day. And the next day, taking his seal and insignia of office and his archives, he accompanied Chien out of the city and went to Yüan-tê's camp. Yüan-tê came out in person to receive him. Taking Liu Chang by the hand, he wept, saying, "It is not that I wish to act cruelly or wrongly; I am the victim of circumstances and cannot help it."

They entered the camp together, where the seal of office and the documents changed hands. Afterwards they rode into the city side by side. The people gave Yüan-tê a cordial welcome, burning incense and illuminating the city. The victor went to the residence of the chief of the province, where he took his seat and was saluted by all the subordinate officials.

However, Huang Ch'üan and Liu Pa stayed away from the ceremony. This annoyed the more violent of Yüan-tê's supporters, and they wished to kill the delinquents. But Yüan-tê would not allow violence and threatened condign punishment to any one who might interfere with these two. When the reception was over he went to visit the two recalcitrants, whereupon both came out and made their obeisance.

Said K'ung-ming, "We have vanquished, and all opposition is at an end. But there cannot be two rulers, so you must remove Liu Chang to Chingchou."

"But I do not wish to exile him," said Yüan-tê.

"He lost his prestige through weakness. If you are effeminately weak and undecided you also will not last long."

Yüan-tê saw his advice was good, and so he gave a great banquet whereat he begged Liu Chang to pack up his treasures and prepare to move. He gave the dispossessed Prefect the title *Chên-wei Chiang-chün* (Captain of Wide-spread Prestige). Liu Chang went away to Chingchou, taking with him his family and all his possessions.

Yüan-tê thus became Governor of Ichou. He conferred gifts on the inferior officers who joined him, confirming their ranks and titles. Yen Yen was given a high rank in the army. Fa Chêng became Prefect of the District of Shu. Others of the Shu officers whose aid had been conspicuous were given high ranks and finer titles under the new rule, while the services of minor men to the number of three score or more were well rewarded.

Naturally, honours were distributed freely to Yüan-tê's immediate helpers, to whose efforts he owed his position. Chuko Liang became Master of the Forces; Kuan Yü, *Tang-k'ou Chiang-chün* (General, Destroyer of Rebels) and a Marquis; Chang Fei, General, Assailant of the West, and a Marquis; Chao Yün, General, Guardian of the Distant; Huang Chung, General, Guardian of the West; Wei Yen, General, Wager of Successful War; Ma Ch'ao, General, Pacificator of the West. All the others, many of whom had come to Yüan-tê from Chingchou and Hsiangjang, received promotion and rewards.

In addition, a special gift of five hundred "axes" (catties) of gold, a thousand "axes" of silver, much copper money and a thousand rolls of Ssŭch'uan silk, was sent to Kuan Yü. And all the military men were given appointments. Huge numbers of oxen and horses were slaughtered for banquets to the army, and the contents of the granaries were given to the common people. So that there were great rejoicings.

Ichou being settled, Yüan-tê next desired to confiscate the lands of the more famous of the inhabitants about the capital and divide them among his officers. But here Chao Yün and others dissuaded him, saying that the sufferings of the people had been severe and losses great; it would be wise policy to let them settle down to their occupations as soon as possible. "It would be wrong to reward his own men at the expense of these persons." Yüan-tê listened and gave in with good grace.

To Chuko Liang he assigned the revision of the laws, the punishments to be made, on the whole, heavy. Then Fa Chêng spoke up, "The founder of the Hans drew up three chapters of law, and the people were all profoundly affected by his virtue. I would rather that the laws be few and liberal that people may be comforted."

K'ung-ming replied, "You only look at one side. The laws of Ts'in were fiercely cruel and provoked resentment among the people; it was fitting that Kao Tsu should temper them with kindness. Under the weak administration of the late ruler there has never been an efficient government and there is a lack of respect for the law. The proper relationship between ruler and minister has been gradually obscured. Favour has been the means of rising, and the highest in rank have been the basest: kindness has been extended into licence and the most benefited have been the most contemptuous. And thereby have crept in many evils. Now I mean to inculcate respect for the dignity of the law, and kindness shall follow its attainment: there shall be moderation in conferring rank, but honour shall really follow on such promotion. In the mutual co-operation of kindness and honour and in proper distinction between superiors and inferiors lies the efficiency of a government."

Fa Chêng had no argument to oppose. In due time all became perfectly tranquil, and all the forty-and-one districts, with their respective garrisons, were peaceful and contented.

As Prefect of the metropolitan district, Fa Chêng earned much hatred, caring for no one but himself, and one man told of the complaints to K'ung-ming, urging his dismissal.

But K'ung-ming referred to his meritorious services. "When my lord was in Chingchou, fearful of his enemy on the north and trembling lest he be attacked from the east, Fa Chêng was his sure support. In these prosperous days one can hardly begin to discipline him. Could we reasonably forbid him following somewhat his own way?"

So no investigation was made, but Fa Chêng heard of the complaints and corrected his faults.

One day, when Yüan-tê and K'ung-ming were resting and at leisure, Kuan P'ing arrived with a letter from his father, thanking his elder brother for the handsome gifts. Handing in his letter, the son said his father was anxious to come into Ch'üan to try conclusions with Ma Ch'ao.

Said Yüan-tê, "If he were to come and fight I fear they would not both survive."

"There is nothing to be anxious about," said K'ung-ming. "I will write to Kuan Yü."

Yüan-tê feared that his brother's impulsive temperament might lead to trouble, so he told K'ung-ming to compose a letter and send back by Kuan P'ing.

When Kuan P'ing came again to his father the first question was about the contest with Ma Ch'ao. Then the letter was produced, and this is what it said: "I hear you are anxious to decide whether of the twain, Ma Ch'ao and yourself is the better man. Now I can measure Ma Ch'ao. He may be unusually brave and bold, but he is only of the class of Ching

Pu and P'êng Yüeh. He might be a worthy rival of your younger brother, but he is far from the standard set by you, O Duke of the Beautiful Beard. You have a most important charge. If you come into Ssŭch'uan, and Chingchou should be lost, would you not be guilty of a terrible failure? I think you will see this."

Kuan Yü stroked his long beard and smiled as he read the letter. "He knows me thoroughly," said he to himself.

He showed the letter to his clients and friends and thought no more of going westward.

The successes of Liu Pei in the west had been duly noted by Sun Ch'üan, who thought he was surely now going to obtain the much-coveted Chingchou. So he called in Chang Chao and Ku Yung to ask advice.

Chang Chao was ready with a scheme that would need no fighting: Yüan-tê would offer the place with both hands.

> In Shu there shine new sun and moon,
> Wu dreams Chingchou will be his soon.

We shall see in the next chapter the scheme to recover the much-desired district.

CHAPTER LXVI.

Kuan Yü Goes to a Feast Alone, but Armed;
Fu Huang-hou Dies for the State.

The scheme which Chang Chao had in mind he laid before his master thus: "The one man upon whom Liu Pei relies most is Chuko Liang. Now his brother is in your service and in your power. All you have to do is to seize his family and send him west to see his brother and make him persuade Liu Pei to return Chingchou. If he refuse, the family will suffer, and Liang will not be able to resist the claims of brotherhood."

"But Chuko Chin is a loyal and true gentleman. I could not lay hands upon his family," said Sun Ch'üan.

"Explain the ruse to him; that will set his mind at rest," said Chang.

Sun Ch'üan consented and issued the command to confine the family of his retainer in the palace but not really imprison them. Then he wrote a letter for Chuko Chin to take with him on his mission. Before many days Chin reached Ch'êngtu and sent to inform Yüan-tê of his arrival. He at once sought the advice of his able counseller.

"Why think you your brother has come?"

"He has come to force the return of Chingchou."

"How shall I answer him?"

"You must do so and so," said K'ung-ming.

The plan of action being prepared, K'ung-ming went out of the city to welcome his brother, but instead of taking him to his own residence he took him to the guest-house. When the greetings were over, the visitor suddenly lifted up his voice and wept.

"If you have any trouble, my brother, tell; why do you weep thus?" asked K'ung-ming.

"Alas! my family are lost," cried he.

"I suppose it is in the matter of the return of Chingchou? If your family have been seized on my account, how can I bear it calmly? But do not be anxious, my brother. I shall certainly find some way out of the difficulty."

This reply pleased Chuko Chin, and the two brothers went to visit Yüan-tê. The letter was presented, but when Yüan-tê had read it he said, angrily, "He is related to me by marriage and he has profited by my absence from Chingchou to steal away his sister. That is a sort of kindliness I find it hard to bear. When I am just going to lead my army to take vengeance is it likely he will get Chingchou out of me?"

At this point K'ung-ming prostrated himself weeping at his lord's feet and said, "The Marquis of Wu has seized my brother's family, and he will put them all to death if the land be not given up. Can I remain alive if such a fate befall them? I pray my lord for my sake to give back the district and prevent any breach between my brother and me."

But Yüan-tê refused. He seemed obdurate, but K'ung-ming persisted in his entreaty. Finally Yüan-tê reluctantly consented.

"Since things are so, and the Commander-in-chief pleads for it, I will return half," said he. "I will give up Changsha, Lingling and Kueiyang."

"Then, as you have consented, prepare letters ordering Kuan Yü to yield these three districts," said Chin.

Yüan-tê said, "When you see my brother you must use most gracious words to him, for his nature is as a fierce fire, and I fear what he may do. So be very careful."

Chuko Chin, having got the letter, took his leave and went straightway to Chingchou. He asked for an interview, and was received in the grand reception hall. When both were seated in their respective places, the emissary produced his letter, saying, "The Imperial Uncle has promised to return three districts to my master, and I hope, General, you will hand them over at once and let me return."

Kuan Yü's countenance changed, and he said, "The oath sworn in the Peach Garden bound me and my brother to support the Dynasty of Han. Chingchou is a portion of their domain, and how can any part be given to another? When a leader is in the field he receives no orders, not even those of his prince. Although you have brought letters from my brother, yet will I not yield the territory."

"But the Marquis of Wu has laid hands upon my family, and they will be slain if the land be not given up. I crave your pity, O General."

"This is but a ruse on his part, but it does not deceive me."

"Why are you so pitiless?"

Kuan Yü drew his sword, saying, "Let us have no more. This sword is pitiless."

"It will put the Commander-in-chief to shame," said Kuan P'ing. "I pray you not to be angry, my father."

"Were it not for my respect for the Commander-in-chief, you would never go back to Wu," said Kuan Yü.

Chuko Chin, overwhelmed with shame, took his leave, sought his ship and hastily returned to see his brother. But K'ung-ming had gone away upon a journey. However, he saw Yüan-tê and related what had happened, and said that Kuan Yü was going to slay him.

"My brother is hasty," said Yüan-tê. "It is difficult to argue with him. But return home for the present, and when I have finished my conquest I will transfer Kuan Yü to another post, and then I may be able to return Chingchou."

Chuko Chin had no choice but to accept this reply and carry the unsatisfactory news to his master, who was greatly annoyed and said, "This running to and fro was nothing more than one of your brother's tricks."

The unhappy messenger denied this and told how his brother had interceded with tears and obtained the promise to return three districts. It was the obstinacy of Kuan Yü that spoiled all."

"Since Yüan-tê said he would return three districts, we may send officials to take over their administration. Think you that might be done?" said Sun.

"What you say, my lord, seems most proper."

The family of Chuko Chin were restored to liberty and officers were sent to take charge of the three districts that had been named. But they quickly returned, saying that Kuan Yü would have none of them, but had chased them away at once with threats to kill them if they did not hasten.

Sun Ch'üan then summoned Lu Su and laid the blame on him.

"You are Yüan-tê's guarantor in this matter; how can you sit quietly looking on while he fails to perform his contract?" said Sun.

"I have thought out a plan and was just going to impart it to you," said Lu Su.

"And what is your plan?"

Lu Su said, "There is a camp at Luk'ou; invite Kuan Yü to a banquet there and try to persuade him. If he still remain obstinate, have some assassins ready to slay him. Should he refuse the banquet, then we must try conclusions with an army."

"This suits me," said Sun, "and it shall be done."

"It should not be done," interrupted K'an Tsê. "The man is too bold and not at all like common men. The plan will fail and result in more harm."

"Then when may I expect to get my Chingchou?" asked Sun, angrily.

He ordered Lu Su to carry out his plan, and Su went to Luk'ou forthwith and settled the preliminaries of the banquet. The place selected was by the river. Then he wrote a letter and found a persuasive person to deliver it. The messenger set out and sailed across the river to the post, where he was received by Kuan P'ing, who conducted him to his father.

"As Lu Su invites me, I will come to-morrow; you may return," was Kuan Yü's reply.

After the messenger had gone, Kuan P'ing said to his father, "Why did you promise to go? I think Lu Su means you no good."

"Do you think I do not know? This has all come out of my refusal to yield those three districts. They are going to try coercion at this banquet. If I refuse they will think I fear them. I will go to-morrow in a small ship with just my personal guard of half a score, and we shall see whether Lu Su will dare to come near me."

"But, father, why risk your priceless self in the very den of a tiger? I think you are not giving due importance to my uncle's charge."

"I have been in the midst of many and imminent dangers all alone and have been careless of them; think you that I shall begin to show fear of a few such rats as those?"

Nor was the son alone in remonstrance. Ma Liang also warned his chief.

"Although Lu Su has a great repute, yet now he is pushed hard. He certainly is badly disposed toward you, and you must be careful, General."

Kuan Yü replied, "I have given my word, and shall I withdraw from it? In the days of the warring states Lin Hsiang-ju of the State of Chao had not the force even to bind a chicken, yet in the assembly at Shêngch'ih he regarded not the Prince of Ts'in, but did his duty without fear of consequences. Have I not learned to face any number of foes? I cannot break my promise."

"If you must go," said Ma Liang, "at least go prepared."

"Tell my son to choose out half a score of fast ships and a half company of good marines and be in readiness to help me at need. And when he sees a red flag waved he can come over to my aid."

The order was given and the little squadron was got ready.

The messenger returned to his master and told him that Kuan Yü had boldly accepted the invitation, and Lu Su and Lü Mêng took counsel together.

"What do you think of this?" asked Lu Su.

"If he comes with a force, Kan Ning and I will be in readiness for him by the river-side. And you will hear our bomb as a signal that we are attacking. If he has no force with him the assassins can set on during the banquet."

Next day a look-out was kept on the bank, and early in the day a single ship came along. It was manned by very few men, and a simple red flag flew out on the breeze showing but one character, the name of the great warrior. Presently they could see him, a handsome figure in a green robe and black turban. Beside him stood Chou Ts'ang, his sword-bearer, and near him were eight or nine fine-looking men each with a sword at his side.

He landed and was received by the trembling Lu Su, who conducted him to the hall, bowed his greetings and led him to the banquet chamber. When he drank to his host Lu Su dared not raise his eyes, but Kuan Yü was perfectly composed.

When they had become mellow with wine, Lu Su said, "I have a word to say to you, Sir, if haply I may have your attention. You know that your illustrious brother, the Imperial Uncle, made me surety with my master that Chingchou would be returned after Ssŭch'uan had been taken. Well, now that country is in his possession, but Chingchou is still unreturned. Is not this a breach of good faith?"

"This is a government affair," said Kuan Yü. "Such matters should not be introduced at a banquet."

"My master only has petty possessions in the east, and he allowed the temporary loan of Chingchou out of consideration for the need in which you then were. But now you have Ichou, and Chingchou should be given up. The Imperial Uncle has even yielded three districts, but you, Sir, seem unwilling to let them go. This seems hard to explain on reasonable grounds."

Kuan Yü replied, "I braved the arrows and the stones in the battle at Wuling and with all my strength drove back the enemy: did I get a single foot of land for all my efforts? Now you come to force this place out of me."

"No; I do not," said Lu Su. "But at the time that you and your brother suffered defeat at Ch'angpan, when you were helpless and in the greatest straits, fugitives you knew not whither, then my master was moved with pity and did not grudge the land. So he gave your brother a foothold whence he might be able to accomplish other ends. But your brother has presumed upon long-suffering. He has attained his end, the country of his desire, and still he occupies Chingchou. Such greed and such treachery will make the whole world laugh him to shame, as you know quite well."

"All that is no affair of mine; it is my brother's. I cannot yield the land."

"I know that by the oath in the Peach Garden you three were to live or die together. But your brother is now a ruler; how are you going to get out of that?"

Kuan Yü was at a loss to reply. However, Chou Ts'ang burst into the conversation, roaring out, "Only the virtuous get hold of territory, does that mean only you people of East Wu?"

Kuan Yü's anger now showed itself. His face changed; he rose in his place, took his sword from his sword-bearer and said fiercely, "How dare you talk like this at a discussion of state matters? Go! And go quickly."

Chou understood. He left the hall, made his way to the river and waved the red call-flag. The ships darted across like arrows and were ready for action.

The mighty sword in his right hand, Kuan Yü laid hold of his false host with his left and, simulating intoxication, said, "You have kindly invited me to-day, Sir, but do not say anything about Chingchou, for I am so drunk that I may forget our old friendship. Some other day I hope to invite you to Chingchou, and then we will talk about that matter."

Poor Lu Su's soul almost left his body with fright as he was led down to the river bank in the grip of his guest. The two friends he had placed in ambush dared not face the terrible Kuan Yü and so made no move lest they should bring about the evil they feared. When they got to the bank, Kuan Yü released his host, got on board and then said farewell. Lu Su stood stupidly staring at the ship while a fair breeze bore it quickly out of sight.

This episode has been commemorated in verse:—

> He showed his contempt for the men of the east
> By going alone to their traitor feast;
>   He met contempt with disdain.
> To gain his end his pride he controlled,
> As Hsiang-ju of old he was also bold;
>   'Twas the Mien Lake game played again.

Kuan Yü took his homeward way, while Lu Su and his two confederates talked over what had occurred.

"What can be done now?" said Lu Su.

"The only thing is to tell our master and let him send an army," replied Lü Mêng.

Lu Su sent a messenger to Sun Ch'üan, who, in his wrath, was for sending every available soldier at once against Chingchou. But at this crisis there came news that Ts'ao Ts'ao was raising a huge army with the intention of attacking the south. So hasty orders were sent to Lu to make no move, but to send all the men he could toward the north to repel Ts'ao Ts'ao.

However, Ts'ao Ts'ao did not march south. One of his officers, Chuan Kan, sent in a memorial against the scheme.

"I, Chuan Kan, understand that inspiring fear is the chief consideration in war, as inculcating virtue is in government. These two combined in one man fit him to be a prince. Formerly, in the days of disturbance, you, illustrious Sir, attacked the rebels and restored tranquillity almost everywhere, the only districts unsubdued and not under your control being Wu and Shu. The former of these is protected by the great river, the latter secured by its mountains, and both difficult to conquer by force of arms. My humble opinion is that it is more fitting to increase the authority of civil government, to lay aside arms and rest weapons, to cease from war and train your soldiers until the times shall be favourable. If your mighty legions be now sent to camp on the river bank and the rebels should take refuge behind their natural defences, your men will be unable to prove their prowess, and should unforeseen combinations appear their force will not be available. In such a case your high prestige would be impaired. I trust, illustrious Sir, you will deign to examine this."

After reading this, Ts'ao Ts'ao ceased to think of an expedition against the south. Instead, he established schools and set himself to attract men of ability.

About the same time four of his officers conceived the idea of getting for Ts'ao Ts'ao the honour of "Prince of Wei." But another, Hsün Yu, opposed this course, saying, "The minister's rank is already that of "Duke," and he has received the additional honour of the Nine Gifts, so that his position is extremely high. If he advances to the rank of prince it will be inconsistent with reasonableness."

But Ts'ao Ts'ao was annoyed at this opposition and said, "Does the man wish to emulate Hsün Yü?"

When Hsün Yü heard of his anger he was grieved and fell ill, so that in a few days he died. He was fifty-eight years of age. Ts'ao Ts'ao had his remains interred honourably, and he stayed his ambition for princely rank.

But there came a day when he entered the palace wearing his sword and made his way to the apartment where the Emperor and Empress were seated. The Empress rose in a fright and the Emperor gazed at his minister in terror.

"Sun Ch'üan and Liu Pei have each seized a portion of the empire and no longer respect the court; what is to be done?"

To this abrupt speech the Emperor replied, "The matter lies within your province."

Ts'ao Ts'ao answered, angrily, "If such a remark be known outside they will say I treat my prince without respect."

"If you will help me I shall be most happy;" said His Majesty, "if not, then I trust to your kindness to let me alone."

At this Ts'ao Ts'ao glared at the Emperor and went out full of resentment.

The courtiers said, "It is said that Duke Wei desires to become a prince and soon he will aspire to the Throne."

Both the Emperor and his consort wept. Presently Her Majesty said, "My father, Fu Wan, has long nourished a desire to slay this man. Now I will indite a secret letter to my father to accomplish his end."

"Remember the former attempt with Tung Ch'êng. The plot was discovered and great misery ensued. I fear that this will leak out also and both of us will be undone."

Said the Empress, "We pass our days in constant discomfort, like sitting on a rug full of needles. If life is to be like this one were better dead. But I know one loyal man among the attendants to whom I may entrust the letter. That one is Mu Shun, and he will deliver it."

Thereupon she summoned Mu Shun within, and having sent away all others, they told their distress to the faithful one.

"That fellow Ts'ao desires the dignity of prince and soon he will aspire to the throne itself. I, the Emperor, wish to order the father of my consort to make away with the man, but the difficulty is that all the courtiers are his creatures and there is none whom I can trust save yourself. I desire you to convey this secret letter to Fu Wan. I know your loyalty and am sure you will prove no betrayer."

"I am the recipient of much graciousness for which not even death would prove my gratitude. Thy servant prays that he may be allowed to undertake this."

The letter was given to Mu Shun, who hid it in his hair, made his way out of the precincts and handed it to its owner. Fu Wan recognised the handwriting of his daughter and read it. Turning to the messenger he said, "You know the fellow's creatures are many, and one must act with extreme caution against him. Unless we have the aid of Sun Ch'üan and Liu Pei's armies, Ts'ao Ts'ao will certainly attain his ends. In this matter we must gain the support of every loyal and faithful one in the court so that within and without there may be a simultaneous attack."

"Then, O father of the Empress, write a letter in reply asking for a secret edict, so that we may send to Wu and Shu to join in the attack."

So Fu Wan composed a reply, which he gave to Mu Shun to take into the palace. This time also the letter was concealed in his hair and was safely taken in.

But there was a traitor, and Ts'ao heard of the letters. So he waited at the palace gate for Mu Shun to come out.

"Where are you going?" asked Ts'ao Ts'ao, when Mu appeared.

"The Empress is indisposed and has bidden me call a physician."

"Where is the summons for the physician?"

"There is no summons."

Ts'ao Ts'ao bade his men search Mu Shun, but they did not find the letter.

So he was allowed to go. But just then a gust of wind blew off his hat, and it struck Ts'ao that that had not been examined. So Mu Shun was called back. Nothing was found in the hat, but when it was given back Mu Shun put it on with both hands. There was something suspicious about the movement and Ts'ao bade the searchers examine his hair.

Therein the letter was found. Ts'ao Ts'ao read it; it said that Sun and Liu were to be induced to help. The unhappy Mu was taken away into a secret place and interrogated, but he would confess nothing.

That night three companies of soldiers surrounded the dwelling of Fu Wan, who was arrested with all his family. Searching the house they found the first letter in the handwriting of the Empress. Fu Wan and his family were then consigned to a gaol.

At dawn, a party of the Foresters, under Ch'i Lü, bearing ensigns of authority, entered the palace with orders to take away the seal of the Empress. On the way they met the Emperor, who asked the reason for a company of armed men being in the palace.

"I have orders from Duke Wei to get the Empress's seal," said Ch'i Lü.

As soon as the Empress knew of this she recognised her danger and hid herself in the hollow walls of her private apartments behind one of the ceremonial halls. She had not been long in hiding when one Hua Hsin, a president of a Board, with a company of men appeared and asked where she was. The palace people said they did not know. The red doors of the hall were burst open and Hua looked in, but he saw no lady there. It occurred to him where she might be hidden, and he ordered his men to break open the wall. With his own hands he laid hold of the lady's hair and dragged her forth.

"Spare my life!" pleaded she.

"You may say what you have to say to the Duke," cried he surlily.

She pulled down her hair and kicked off her shoes, but a couple of soldiers pushed her along in front of them outside.

It may be said here that this Hua had some reputation for learning. He and two others, Ping Yüan and Kuan Ning, all good friends, made a little coterie which was known as "The Dragon." Hua Hsin was the "head"; his two friends the "belly" and the "tail" respectively. One day Hua and Kuan were hoeing in their garden, when they turned up an ingot of silver. Kuan went on with his labours without giving a second glance at the find, but Hua picked it up. After regarding it a moment he threw it away again.

Another day Kuan and Hua were reading together when there arose a great shouting outside the window of the study. A lady from the palace was passing. Kuan took no notice, but kept his eyes on his book; Hua rose and went to the window. For this, Kuan Ning despised his companion and the two parted for good. Sometime after, Kuan Ning fled into Liaotung, where he led the life of hermit. He wore a white cap and lived in the upper part of a house, never touching the ground with his feet. He would have nothing to do with Ts'ao Ts'ao and would not enter his service.

But the unstable and inconstant Hua Hsin led a totally different life. For a time he was with Sun Ch'üan; then he went over to Ts'ao Ts'ao and served him. And here he is found actually laying hands upon the Empress.

His conduct in this particular is the subject of a poem:—

> 'Twas a dastardly thing that Hua Hsin did,
> When he broke down the wall where the Empress hid
> And dragged her forth by the hair.

He lent his aid to a foul, foul crime
And execrations throughout all time,
Have been, and shall be, his share.

A poet also wrote concerning Kuan Ning:—

East of the Liao, so stories tell't
Is Kuan Ning's tower, where long he dwelt.
Ignoble wealth was Hua Hsin's quest,
The hermit's simple life was best.

As Hua Hsin hurried the unhappy woman out of the hall the Emperor saw her. He went over and clasped her to his bosom, weeping. Hua Hsin tried to force her onward, saying he had orders from Duke Wei.

"My doom is sealed," wept the Empress.

"And I know not when my turn will come," sighed the Emperor.

The soldiers hustled the Empress onward, leaving His Majesty beating his breast in despair.

"Can it be that such things happen in the world?" cried the Emperor to Ch'i Lü, who stood by.

And he swooned. Ch'i Lü made the courtiers pick him up, and they bore him into the palace.

Meanwhile, the unhappy Empress had been taken before Ts'ao Ts'ao.

"I have dealt well with you and yours," said he angrily, "and you requited me by plotting my murder. It is the death of one of us, I see."

He ordered the executioners to beat her till she died. After this, he went into the palace, seized her two sons and had them poisoned. In the evening of the same day the whole household of Mu Shun were put to death publicly. Such terrible deeds spread terror everywhere. They happened in the late autumn of the year 211 A.D.

As Ts'ao stands first in cruelty,
So stands Fu Wan in loyalty.
A married pair of low estate,
Had not been torn apart by fate.

The Emperor grieved bitterly over the loss of his consort, and in his despair refused all food. Ts'ao Ts'ao did not wish him to die of starvation and loneliness, so he proposed his own daughter as consort.

"Be not sad," said he, "thy servant is no rebel. My daughter is already in your palace as a secondary lady. She is wise and dutiful, fit to be your consort and occupy the first rank."

The Emperor Hsien dared not refuse, and therefore at the new year, in the time of the festivities, her name was inscribed on the dynastic rolls as Empress. And no one of the courtiers dared protest.

Wherefore Ts'ao Ts'ao became even more powerful. But it pleased him not to have rivals in the land, so he again thought of subduing Liu Pei and Sun Ch'üan. Chia Hsü proposed that Hsiahou Tun and Ts'ao Jên, who had served on the frontiers, should be called to give their advice. They were sent for, and Ts'ao Jên was the first to arrive. As a relative he felt he had the right to see the great minister without delay and went direct to the palace.

But it happened that Ts'ao Ts'ao had been drinking heavily, and his faithful henchman, Hsü Ch'u, would not admit the new arrival.

"I am of the family," said Ts'ao Jên, angry at the hindrance. "Dare you stop me?"

"General, you may be a relative, but here you are but an officer from the frontier. I am of little account, but a duty lies on me here in the palace. Our lord is overcome with wine and asleep, and I dare not allow you to enter."

The refusal came to Ts'ao Ts'ao's knowledge, and he commended the loyalty of his servant.

Soon after, Hsiahou Tun came and was called to the council, and gave his opinion that the two rivals should be left until Chang Lu of Hanchung had been subdued. The army that could overcome him would be in condition to attack Shu, and it would be conquered without difficulty. The advice coincided with Ts'ao Ts'ao's own idea, and so he prepared an expedition for the west.

> By a dastard crime he showed his power over a feeble king;
> This done, at once he hastened to destroy his neighbour.

What happened will be told in later chapters.

CHAPTER LXVII.

Ts'ao Ts'ao Conquers Hanchung;
Chang Liao Spreads Terror at Chaoyao Ford.

The expedition against Hanchung went out in three divisions, with Hsiahou Yüan as leader of the van, Ts'ao Ts'ao in command of the centre and Ts'ao Jên bringing up the rear. Hsiahou Tun was in charge of the commissariat. The spies soon carried the news into Hanchung, and Chang Lu called in his brother Wei to consult how to meet the attack.

Said Wei, "The strategical point to hold is Yangp'ing Pass, and there should be half a score of stockades there with the forest to support them. You, my brother, should make your dépôt of supplies at Hanning."

Thereupon two captains, Yang Ang and Yang Jên, were sent with Chang Wei to the Pass, and they built the stockades. Soon the vanguard of the enemy arrived and camped at a point fifteen *li* away. The soldiers were fatigued after the long march, and all lay down to rest without placing proper guards. Suddenly the camp was attacked in the rear by the two Yangs from different points. Hsiahou Yüan and Chang Ho mounted quickly and tried to beat off the attackers, but the enemy poured in all round, and Ts'ao's men suffered great loss. They returned to the main body to tell of their defeat, and their chief abused them for their want of care.

"Old soldiers like you should have known better and taken precautions against a raid of the camp when the enemy knew your men were exhausted by a long march."

He even desired to put them to death as a warning, but their fellow-officers interceded and he spared them. Soon Ts'ao himself marched in the van. Then he saw the dangerous and evil nature of the place, with its thick growth of trees, and as he knew nothing of the roads and was fearful of an ambush he returned to his camp.

Calling up his two henchmen, Hsü Ch'u and Hsü Huang, he said, "Had I known the dangerous nature of the place I would never have come."

Hsü Ch'u replied, "The soldiers are here now, my lord, and you cannot recoil before the hardships."

Next day Ts'ao Ts'ao with only his two guards rode out to reconnoitre the enemy's camp. As they rode over the hills Ts'ao Ts'ao pointed out the position with his whip and said, "It will be very difficult to reduce a place as strong as this."

Just then there arose a shout in their rear and a shower of arrows fell about them. The two Yangs were attacking and the danger became great.

"Friend Hsü, you look after our lord;" cried Hsü Ch'u, "I can hold the enemy."

He galloped out and the two leaders took to flight, while their men scattered. In the meantime Hsü Huang led his master over the hills. Soon he met a troop of soldiers led by Hsiahou Yüan and Chang Ho, who had heard the sound of fighting and had come to the rescue, and Ts'ao Ts'ao got back safely to camp. The four captains were rewarded.

For fifty days the two armies held each other at bay without coming to a fight. At the end of this time, orders were given to retire.

"We have not tried the strength of the enemy," said Chia Hsü. "You should not retire, my lord."

"I see that they are always on the alert," said Ts'ao Ts'ao. "I am only retiring to put them off their guard. By and by I will send some light horse to attack their rear. I shall defeat them then."

"Ah! your skill is unfathomable!" cried Chia Hsü.

Two parties were then sent to get round behind the Pass by unfrequented roads, while Ts'ao Ts'ao broke up his camp and led his main body backward.

When Yang Ang heard of the retreat he thought it would be a good chance to attack, but Yang Jên, remembering the cunning of their opponent, opposed it. Yang Ang was wilful and said, "I shall go; you may come or not, as you wish."

In spite of the protestations of his colleague, Yang Ang marched, taking with him the men of five camps and leaving only a few defenders. The day he set out was very foggy, so that one could hardly see his neighbour's face, and soon the force got into difficulties and could not advance. They bivouacked on the road.

Now, Hsiahou Yüan was out with a reconnoitring force behind the hills when they heard the voices of men and the neighing of horses. In the dense fog they could see nothing, but fearing an ambush they hastened to retire. They lost their way and presently stumbled on the deserted camp. The few defenders thought their comrades had returned, so they threw open the gates to let them in. One camp was empty and there they raised a great blaze, which frightened those in the other camps so that they fled. As soon as the fog cleared, Yang Jên came to the rescue, but as more of Ts'ao's men came up, the force was too strong for him and he quickly fled toward Nanch'êng. By and by, when Yang Ang returned, he found his camp in the possession of Ts'ao Ts'ao's men.

Soon Ts'ao Ts'ao's main army came up, and Yang was between two forces. There seemed no other way but to make a dash for it. Falling in with Ho, the two engaged and Yang Ang fell. Those who escaped carried the news of the disaster to Chang Wei, who abandoned the Pass and fled.

So the invaders took possession of the Pass, and its late defenders, Chang Wei and Yang Jên, had to go back and report failure. Chang Wei laid the blame on his companion, saying the Pass could not be held after its supporting positions had been lost. Chang Lu threatened to behead Yang Jên for his failure. Yang said he had tried to prevent the rashness of his brother and begged to be allowed to make another attack. If he failed he would abide by the consequences without protest.

Chang Lu took his formal pledge to succeed, gave him two legions and sent him away. He marched to Nanch'êng and made a stockade.

Before Ts'ao Ts'ao made any further advance he sent Hsiahou Yüan, with half a legion, to reconnoitre the road and they fell in with the force led by Yang Jên. Both sides drew up their battle array. From Yang's side went out Ch'ang Ch'i to engage Hsiahou Yüan, who disposed of him in the third bout. Then Yang Jên set his spear and rode to the front. They two fought near two score bouts and neither could claim victory. Then Hsiahou Yüan pretended defeat and fled. The other rushed in pursuit. The fugitive suddenly employed the Parthian stab and killed his pursuer. His men ran away.

As soon as Ts'ao Ts'ao knew of the death of this leader of the other side he brought up his army, marched straightway to Nanch'êng and camped.

Chang Lu became alarmed and called a council.

"I can propose a man able to stand against the best leader of the enemy," said Yen Pu.

"Who is he?" asked Chang Lu.

"P'ang Tê, of Nanan. He surrendered at the same time as Ma Ch'ao, but could not go with him into Ssŭch'uan as he was ill. If you treated him generously he would save you."

P'ang Tê was summoned. He came, was loaded with gifts and given a force of one legion, with which he marched and camped ten *li* from the city, near the besieging force.

His camp made, P'ang Tê rode out and challenged. Now Ts'ao Ts'ao, remembering his boldness at the battle of the bridge over the Wei, was desirous of winning his help for himself, so he told his captains to try to weary him by prolonging the fights, and so make him captive.

Wherefore first rode out Chang Ho to answer the challenge. He fought a few bouts and returned. Then Hsiahou Yüan did the same thing. So did Hsü Huang. Lastly went Hsü Ch'u, who kept up the fight to half a hundred bouts before he retired. Still P'ang Tê showed no signs of fatigue nor of fear, and all those who had fought with him praised his prowess and skill.

"If only I could win him over to my side!" said Ts'ao Ts'ao longingly.

Said Chia Hsü, "I know one of his subordinates, Yang Sung. He is avaricious and open to a bribe. You might send him secret presents and get him to slander P'ang Tê to his master so as to weaken his position."

"But how can one get at this man? He is in Nanch'eng."

"In the next battle pretend defeat, flee and let P'ang take possession of this camp. Return in the night in force and drive him out, and he must retreat into the city. Let one of your own people with a persuasive tongue mingle with his men, disguised as one of his soldiers, and so gain entrance into the city."

A subtle agent was found, and goodly gifts were his in advance, and he was entrusted with a golden breastplate as a bribe. He put it on and over it put on the dress of an ordinary soldier of Hanchung. And he made his way quietly to a point on the road along which the soldiers of Hanchung would retreat into the city. There he waited.

Next, two parties were sent to lie in ambush and Hsü Huang was sent to challenge, but with orders to be defeated. The scheme went well, and as P'ang Tê came on to smite, Ts'ao Ts'ao's men retired before him till he found himself at their very camp. And therein he entered and was exceedingly pleased to find fodder and forage in great quantities.

Having sent off a messenger to his chief, he spread a feast in celebration of the victory; and when night came on they slept. But about the second watch there was an alarm from three directions, and the camp was threatened by three forces. It was the night-attack arranged by Ts'ao Ts'ao, and P'ang Tê could not make any defence. He got to horse, cut his way through and made for the city. With the attackers in close pursuit he reached the gate, got it opened and rushed in.

And the traitor got in in the confusion. He made his way quickly to Yang Sung's residence and saw him. He told him that the great minister, Duke Wei, knew him by reputation and held him in great esteem and as a token thereof had sent him his golden breastplate and a confidential letter as well. Yang took it all in, read the letter and said, "I will reply by and by, and the duke need feel no anxiety for I shall find a means of proving my gratitude. You may return."

Soon after, he went to see Chang Lu and told him that P'ang Tê had been defeated because he had been bribed. Forthwith Chang Lu summoned his general, abused him and threatened to put him to death. Yen Pu, however, protested and proposed to test P'ang in another encounter. If he lost that, he might be put to death.

P'ang Tê retired full of resentment. The next day Ts'ao Ts'ao attacked, and P'ang went out to repel him. Ts'ao sent out his favourite Hsü Ch'u, but bade him pretend defeat. When P'ang pursued, Ts'ao rode toward the hills, where he halted and presently got speech with P'ang. He proposed surrender.

But P'ang thought within himself that to capture Ts'ao would be a fine exploit, so he boldly faced his escort and rode up the hill. But there arose a great shouting as if heaven and earth were clashing together and he and his followers went headlong into ditches and pits that had been dug. Out flew men with ropes and hooks, and P'ang was a prisoner.

When he was taken to Ts'ao he was received with the greatest kindness. Ts'ao himself dismounted, loosed the captive's bonds and asked him if he would surrender. P'ang thought of the ill-treatment he had just received at the hands of his master and of his injustice, and gave in. At once he was helped to mount a horse by Ts'ao himself and led to the great camp.

Men placed for the purpose on the city wall saw what happened and told Chang Lu that his leader had ridden off on friendly terms with Ts'ao Ts'ao, whereby Chang Lu was persuaded that Yang Sung had spoken truly.

Soon after, scaling ladders were set against the city walls and catapults threw in great stones. The danger being imminent, Chang Wei counselled the destruction of all supplies and flight to Nanshan, where they might be able to defend Pachung. On the other hand, Yang Sung said the best course was to throw open the gates and surrender. Chang Lu could not decide which to do. His brother, Wei, maintained that burning everything and flight was the only course.

Chang Lu said, "I have been always loyal at heart and desired to return to allegiance when circumstances would permit. I have been unable to attain my desire, but now fight seems the only course open to me. However, the granaries and treasures, the public offices and the government property of all kinds must be kept safe."

So the public buildings were all carefully barred and sealed. The same night, in the late evening, Chang and his family went out through the south gate and found their way through. Ts'ao Ts'ao let them go unpursued. When Ts'ao entered the city and saw the proofs of Chang Lu's care of the government property he compassionated the man's misfortunes. He then sent a messenger into Pachung to induce him to surrender. Chang Lu was disposed to do so, but his brother would not hear of it. Nor would Yang Sung, who wrote a secret letter to Ts'ao Ts'ao urging him to attack and promising treacherous aid.

Ts'ao presently attacked, and Chang Wei came out to meet him. But his opponent was the mighty Hsü Ch'u, who made short work of him. The beaten soldiers went back into the city, which Chang Lu then decided to defend. As this would not give Yang Sung the chance to carry out his treacherous scheme, he persuaded his master to go out and fight, leaving him to defend the city. Chang Lu took this advice, although it was opposed by Yen Pu, and went out. But before his van got near the enemy, his rear ranks began to desert, and Chang retreated. Ts'ao pursued him to the city walls, where Chang found the gates shut against him. There being now no way open, Chang dismounted, prostrated himself and gave in. Because of this and his care of the public property, Ts'ao treated him with great kindness and consoled him with the title of General, "Guardian of the South." Yen Pu and many others also were enrolled among the nobles. To each district was appointed a military officer styled *Tu-yü*, in addition to the Prefect. All the soldiers were feasted and rewarded.

Then the traitor Yang Sung, who had sold his master, came and sued for honours. He was condemned to public execution and exposure.

> To harm the wise and compass the death of one's lord may
>   appear signal service,
> But the gains thereof are vanity;
> No glory clings to the house of him who dies a shameful death;
> Wherefore Yang Sung is an object of contempt forever.

When the eastern Ch'üan was quite subdued the Recorder Ssŭma I said, "The men of Shu are against Liu Pei because of his treatment of the late ruler, Liu Chang, and if on the strength of your present success you press forward, Liu Pei will become as a shattered tile. The wise man takes the occasion when it serves and this should not be missed."

Ts'ao Ts'ao sighed. "There is no end; now that I have Shênsi I am forced into taking Shu."

Liu Hua supported Ssŭma I, saying he spoke well. "If you delay, Chuko Liang will have become minister, while Kuan Yü, Chang Fei and the other bold warriors will be at the head of the army. If the man of Shu once settle down, and the points of vantage are held, you will not be able to overcome them."

Ts'ao replied, "My men have marched far and suffered much; beside we must show pity."

Wherefore he rested his army for a time. Meanwhile the populace of West Shu, having heard of Ts'ao's success, concluded that they would suffer next, and fear spread among them. Whereupon Yüan-tê called in the Commander-in-chief and asked his advice. He replied that he could make Ts'ao Ts'ao retreat of his own accord.

"A part of Ts'ao Ts'ao's army is camped at Hofei because of the fear of Sun Ch'üan. If now we restore those three districts they desire so greatly, and send a specious person to talk, we can make Sun Ch'üan attack Hofei, which will lead to Ts'ao going southward."

"Who is a fit person for the messenger?" said Yüan-tê.

And I Chi replied, "I will go."

Yüan-tê, well satisfied, wrote letters and prepared gifts, with which I Chi went, calling in at Chingchou on the way to tell Kuan Yü. Then he went on to Moling and saw Sun Ch'üan. After the greetings, Sun Ch'üan asked on what business he had come.

I Chi replied, "On a former occasion Chuko Chin would have had the three districts but for the absence of the Commander-in-chief, which prevented the actual transfer. Now I am the bearer of letters giving them back to you. Chingchou, Nanchün and Moling were meant to be restored, and now that Ts'ao Ts'ao has got possession of Eastern Ch'uan they are no place for General Kuan. Hofei is empty and we hope you will attack it so as to make Ts'ao Ts'ao withdraw to the south and let my master take East Ch'uan, when he will restore the whole of the Chingchou district."

"Go back to the guest-house and let me take counsel in this matter," said Sun Ch'üan.

As soon as I Chi had gone, the marquis turned to his officers and asked what should be done.

Chang Chao said, "All this is because Liu Pei fears that Ts'ao Ts'ao will attack him. However, since Ts'ao is absent in Hanchung it would be well to seize the opportunity and attack Hofei."

Sun Ch'üan accepted the advice. After he had sent the messenger away he began to prepare for the expedition. He left Lu Su in command over the three districts of Changsha, Chianghsia and Kueiyang. Then he encamped at Luk'ou, and withdrew Lü Mêng and Kan Ning and sent to Hangchou (Yühang) for Ling T'ung.

Very soon, Lü Mêng and Kan Ning returned, and the former suggested a plan, saying, "Ts'ao Ts'ao has sent Chu Kuang, Prefect of Luchiang, to camp at Huanch'êng and plant grain for the supply of Hofei. Let us first take Huanch'êng and then attack Hofei."

"This scheme is just after my own heart," said Sun Ch'üan.

So he made dispositions accordingly, he himself with several generals, commanding the centre. But the famous warriors Ch'êng P'u, Huang Kai and Han Tang were not called to take part in this expedition as they were guarding certain especial places.

The army crossed the river and captured Hochou on the way. The Prefect of Huanchou sent an urgent message to Hofei for help and set himself to strengthen his fortifications for a siege. Sun Ch'üan went very near the city to observe its defence, and a flight of arrows greeted him, some striking his great official parasol. He went back to camp and asked his officers to offer plans of attack.

Then Tung Hsi said, "Pile up great hills of earth and attack from the summits."

Said Hsü Shêng, "Set up long ladders and construct platforms whence you can look over the city walls and thus attack."

But Lü Mêng said, "All such plans need a long time to prepare, and in the meantime the soldiers will arrive from Hofei. Do not try such long-drawn-out schemes, but take advantage of the fine, fresh spirit of our newly arrived men and attack impetuously. Their *élan* will carry the wall. If you attack to-morrow at dawn the city will fall before noon."

So the early meal was taken at the fifth watch and the army went to the attack. The defenders sent down showers of arrows and stones. Kan Ning took an iron chain in his hand and climbed up the wall. They shot at him with bows and crossbows, but he turned aside the arrows and bolts and he threw the chain round the Prefect Chu Kuang to pull him down. Lü Mêng beat the drum for the attack. The soldiers made a rush forward to climb the wall, and they slew Chu Kuang. His officers and soldiers gave in, and so the city fell to Sun Ch'üan. It was still a long time to noon.

In the meantime Chang Liao was marching to the aid of the city. Half-way he heard that the city had fallen, and so he returned to Hofei.

Soon after the conqueror's entry into Huanch'êng, Ling T'ung came there with his army. The next few days were devoted to feasting the army. Especial rewards were given to the two captains who had done such good work at the capture, and at the banquet to the officers Kan Ning was seated in the seat of honour, which his colleague, Lü Mêng, readily yielded to him for his late prowess.

But as the cup of felicitation was passing round, Ling T'ung's thoughts turned to the enmity he bore Kan Ning for having slain his father, and the praises which Lü Mêng now heaped upon him filled Ling's heart with bitterness. For some time he glared savagely at Kan Ning, and then he determined on revenge. Drawing his sword, he suddenly rose to his feet and cried, "There is nothing to amuse the assembly. I will give them a display of swordsmanship."

Kan Ning quickly saw his real intention. He pushed back his table and laid hold of a *ch'i* (halberd) in each hand, crying, "And you may also watch an adept in the use of this weapon."

Lü Mêng saw the evil meaning of both, and assuming his sword and shield he hastily stepped between the two warriors, saying, "Neither of you gentlemen is so dexterous as I."

So he forced the two combatants asunder, while some one ran to tell Sun Ch'üan. He hastily jumped into the saddle and rode to the banquet hall. At sight of their lord they all three lowered their weapons.

"I have bidden you two to forget this old enmity," said Sun Ch'üan. "Why do you revive it to-day?"

Ling T'ung prostrated himself in tears. Sun Ch'üan exhorted him to forget his quarrel, and once again there was peace.

The next day the army set out for Hofei.

Because of the loss of Huanch'êng, Chang Liao grieved greatly. Ts'ao Ts'ao had sent a small casket sealed with his own seal and bearing outside the words, "If rebels come, open this."

So when he received the news of the coming of a powerful army Chang Liao opened the casket and read the letter therein, which said, "If Sun Ch'üan comes to attack Hofei the two captains Chang and Li are to go out to oppose him and Yüeh is to be left to guard the walls." Chang Liao sent the letter to the two men named therein.

"What do you think to do?" said Yüeh Chin.

Chang Liao replied, "Our lord is away and Wu is coming to attack for certain. We must go out to repel them and exert ourselves to the utmost to inflict defeat upon their advanced guard. Thus we shall appease the fears of the populace and then we can hold as best we may."

But Li Tien was silent, for he was ever unfriendly to Chang Liao. Then seeing his colleague inclined to hold off, Yüeh Chin said, "I am for remaining on the defensive since the enemy is so much more numerous than we."

"Gentlemen, it seems you are selfish and not devoted to the common weal," said Chang Liao. "You may have your private reasons for what you do, but I intend to go out and try to repel the enemy. I will fight them to the death."

Thereupon he bade his servants saddle his steed. At this, Li Tien's better feelings were aroused, and he rose saying, "How can I be careless of the common weal and indulge my private feelings? I am ready to follow you and do as you command."

Chang Liao was elated at this moral victory, and said, "Since I can depend upon your help, my friend, then I would ask you to lie in ambush on the north of the Ch'aoyao Ford in order to destroy the bridge there as soon as the army of Wu has crossed. I, with my friend Yüeh Chin, will smite the enemy."

Li Tien went away to muster his men and prepare the ambush.

As has been recorded, the leaders of the advance guard of the Wu army were the veterans Lü Mêng and Kan Ning. Sun Ch'üan and Ling T'ung were in the centre; the other captains followed them. The leaders of the van met Yüeh Chin first, and Kan Ning rode out and challenged him. After a few bouts Yüeh pretended to be defeated and fled. Kan Ning called to his colleague to join in the pursuit.

When Sun Ch'üan heard that this advance guard had been successful he hastened his men to the Ford. But then there came a series of explosions, and up came Chang Liao and Li Tien, one on each flank. Sun Ch'üan was unprepared for this and sent messengers to call off the pursuit and ask for help. Before it could arrived, Chang Liao had come up.

Manifestly, Ling T'ung, who had with him only a small troop of horse, could not long withstand the army of Ts'ao Ts'ao, but he faced them and fought bravely while his lord galloped for the bridge. The southern end had been already broken down and there was a wide breach between the end of the bridge and the shore. Not a single plank was there by which to cross. What could be done? Sun Ch'üan was in a quandary, and helpless.

"Go back and jump for it!" yelled one of the petty officers, Ku Li by name.

He did so. Backing his horse some thirty feet or so, he then gave him his head and lashed him with his whip.

The good beast leaped, cleared the chasm and his master was safe on the southern shore.

> Once Tilu leapt across T'an Torrent wide,
> And when defeat did Sun of Wu betide,
> And death came threateningly at Ch'aoyao Ford,
> His steed too leapt, and saved him from the sword.

Having reached the farther shore, Sun Ch'üan embarked on a boat and was rowed to a place of safety, while Chang Liao's army was held at bay. Kan Ning and Lü Mêng, coming to his aid, were pursued by Yüeh Chin, and Li Tien also stayed their progress. But the men of Wu fought bravely, and Ling T'ung's troop of horse perished to a man. While Ling himself was wounded, but found his way to the bridge. Finding it destroyed, he fled along the stream. Presently he was seen by Sun Ch'üan from the boat and taken on board. Kan Ning and Lü Mêng fled into Honan.

The terrible slaughter at this battle put such fear into the minds of the men from Chiangnan that the name of Chang Liao kept the very children quiet at night.

When Sun Ch'üan reached his camp he richly rewarded Ling T'ung and the petty officer Ku Li. Then he led his army back to Juhsü and began to put his ships in order so that the army and navy might act in unison. He also sent home for reinforcements.

Chang Liao reflected that he had insufficient force to meet another attack if it should be supported by the navy of Wu, so he sent an urgent message to his master in Hanchung. When the messenger arrived, Ts'ao Ts'ao saw that his western expedition would have to yield to the urgency of home defence. However, he called in his counsellors and put a direct question to them.

"Can we take Western Shu now, or not?"

"The country is too well prepared; we cannot," replied Liu Hua. "It is better to go to the succour of Hofei and then go down the river."

Wherefore, leaving Hsiahou Yüan to guard what he had taken of Hanchung, and other reliable captains at other points of vantage, Ts'ao broke up his camp and went toward Juhsü.

> The armoured horsemen would have conquered Shên,
> The ensigns toward the south were turned again.

The subsequent course of the war will be unfolded in later chapters.

CHAPTER LXVIII.

Sun Ch'üan was occupied in ordering his army at Juhsük'ou when he heard of the coming of Ts'ao Ts'ao with forty legions to the relief of Hofei. He told off a fleet of fifty large ships to lie in the port while Ch'ên Wu went up and down the river banks on the look-out.

"It would be well to inflict a defeat upon Ts'ao's men before they recover from the long march; it would dishearten them," said Chang Chao.

Looking around at the officers in his tent, Sun Ch'üan said, "Who is bold enough to go forth and fight this Ts'ao Ts'ao and so take the keen edge off the spirit of his army?"

And Ling T'ung offered. "I will go," said he.

"How many men do you require?"

"Three companies will suffice," replied Ling.

But Kan Ning struck in, saying, "Only a hundred horse would be needed; why send three companies?"

Ling T'ung was angry, and he and Kan Ning began to wrangle even in the presence of their chief.

"Ts'ao Ts'ao's army is too strong to be attacked recklessly," said Sun Ch'üan.

Finally he gave the commission to Ling T'ung with his three companies, bidding him reconnoitre just outside Juhsük'ou, and fight the enemy if he met him.

Marching out, they very soon saw a great cloud of dust, which marked the approach of an army. As soon as they came near enough, Chang Liao, who led the van, engaged with Ling T'ung, and they fought half a hundred bouts without sign of victory for either. Then Sun Ch'üan began to fear for his champion, so he sent Lu Mêng to extricate him from the battle and escort him home. When Ling had come back, his rival went to Sun Ch'üan and said, "Now let me have the hundred horsemen and I will raid the enemy's camp this night. If I lose a man or a mount I will claim no merit."

Sun Ch'üan commended his courage and chose a hundred of his best veterans, whom he placed under Kan Ning's command for the raid. He also gave him as a feast for the soldiers fifty flasks of wine and fifty catties of mutton.

Returning to the tents, Kan Ning drew up his little force and made them sit down in rows. Then he filled two silver goblets with wine, solemnly drank to them and said, "Comrades, to-night our orders are to raid the camp of the enemy. Where-fore fill your goblets and call up all your strength for the task."

But the men did not welcome his words; instead they looked one at another uncertain. Seeing them in this mood, Kan Ning adopted a fierce tone, drew his sword and cried, "What are you waiting for? If I, a leader of rank, can risk my life, cannot you?"

Moved by the angry face of the leader, the men rose, bowed their heads and said they would fight to the last.

Then the wine and meat were distributed to them and each one ate his fill. The second watch was chosen as the hour to start, and each man stuck a white goose plume in his cap where-by they could recognise each other in the darkness.

At the time appointed they buckled on their armour, mounted and, galloping away, quickly came to Ts'ao Ts'ao's camp. Hastily throwing aside the "deer-horns," they burst in with a yell that rose to the very heavens. They made straight for the centre, hoping to slay Ts'ao himself. But the men of the leader's brigade had made a rampart of their carts within which they were sheltered as if in an iron tun, so that the raiders failed to find a way in.

However, the leader and his small force dashed hither and thither, cutting and slashing, till Ts'ao Ts'ao's men were quite bewildered and frightened.

They had no notion of the number of their assailants. All their efforts only increased the confusion. Wherefore the hundred men had it all their own way and rushed from point to point slaying whomever they met. But soon the drums beat in every camp and torches were lit and shouts arose, and it was time for the raiders to get away.

Kan Ning led his little body of men out through the south gate with never a man trying to stop him, and rode for his own camp. He met Chou T'ai, who had been sent to help him in case of need; but the need had not arisen, and the hundred heroes with their leader rode back in triumph. There was no pursuit.

A poem was written praising this exploit:—

> The drums of war make earth to shake
> When Wu comes near e'en devils quake
> Men long will tell of that night raid,
> That Kan Ning's goose-plumed warriors made.

On his return, Kan Ning took the tale of his men at the camp gate, not a man nor a horse was missing. He entered to the sound of drum and fife and the shouting of his men.

"*Wan Shui!* Long Life!" shouted they, as Sun Ch'üan came to welcome them. Kan Ning dismounted and prostrated himself. His lord raised him, and took him by the hand, saying, "This expedition of yours must have given those rebels a shaking. I had not yielded to your desire only I wished to give you the opportunity to manifest your valour. I did not wish to let you be sacrificed."

Kan Ning's exploit was rewarded with gifts, a thousand rolls of silk and a hundred good swords, all of which he distributed among his soldiers. Sun Ch'üan was very proud of his subordinate's doughty deed, and said, "Mêng-tê may have his Chang Liao, but I can match him with my friend Kan Ning."

Soon Chang Liao came to proffer another challenge, and Ling T'ung, impatient at being excelled by his rival and enemy, begged that he might go out to fight. His request was granted, and he marched out a short distance from Juhsü with half a legion. Sun Ch'üan, with Kan Ning in his train, went out to look on at the encounter.

When both armies had come out on the plain and were arrayed, Chang Liao, with Li Tien and Yüeh Chin, one on either side, advanced to the front. Ling T'ung, sword in hand, galloped out towards him and, at his chief's command, Yüeh Chin took the challenge and went to open the combat. They fought half a hundred bouts and neither seemed to have the better of the other. Then Ts'ao Ts'ao, hearing of the great contest going on, rode up to the battlefield and took position under the great standard, whence he could see the fighting. Seeing both combatants were waxing desperate, he thought to decide the struggle by an unfair blow. He bade Ts'ao Hsiu let fly a secret arrow, which he did by creeping up under cover of Chang Liao. It struck Ling T'ung's steed, which reared and threw its rider. Yüeh Chin dashed forward to thrust at the fallen warrior with his spear, but before the blow could be given the twang of another bow was heard and an arrow speeding by hit Yüeh Chin full in the face. He fell from his horse.

Then both sides rushed forward to rescue their champions; the gongs clanged, and the combat ceased. Ling T'ung returned to his camp and reported himself to his master.

"The arrow that saved you was shot by Kan Ning," said Sun Ch'üan.

Ling T'ung turned to his rival and bowed low.

"I could not have supposed you would have rendered me such a service, Sir," said he to Kan Ning.

This episode ended the strife and enmity between the two men, who thereafter swore perpetual friendship.

On the other side Ts'ao saw to it that his captain's wound was dressed, and next day he launched an attack against Juhsü along five different lines. He himself led one army; the other armies were led by Chang Liao, Li Tien, Hsü Huang and P'ang Tê. Each army was one legion strong, and they marched to give battle on the river bank. The crews and fighting men of the Wu naval squadron were greatly frightened by the approach of these armies.

"You have eaten of the bread of your prince and you must give loyal service; why fear?" said Hsü Huang.

Thereupon he put some hundreds of his best men into small boats, went along the bank and broke into the legion under Li Tien. Meanwhile their comrades on the ships beat drums and cheered them on. But a great storm came on, lashing the river to fury, and the waves rolled mountains high. The larger ships rolled as if they would overturn, and the men were frightened. They started to get down into the bulkier cargo-boats to save their lives. But Tung Hsi threatened them with his sword, cutting down some half score of the mutineers.

"My orders are to hold this point against the enemy;" shouted he, "we dare not abandon the ships."

However, the wind increased, and presently the bold Tung Hsi was thrown into the river by the rolling of his ship and was drowned.

Hsü Huang dashed hither and thither among Li Tien's men, slaying right and left. Ch'ên Wu, hearing the noise of battle, set out for the river bank. On his way he met P'ang Tê and the legion under him. A *mêlée* ensued. Then Sun Ch'üan with Chou T'ai and his men joined in.

The small force from the ships that had attacked Li Tien was now surrounded. So Sun Ch'üan gave the signal for an onslaught that should rescue them. This failed, and Sun Ch'üan was himself surrounded in turn and soon in desperate straits. From a height, Ts'ao saw his difficulties and sent in Hsü Ch'u to cut Sun Ch'üan's column in halves so that neither half could aid the other.

When Chou T'ai had cut his way out of the press and reached the river-side he looked for his master. But he was nowhere visible, so he dashed once again into the battle. Coming to his own men, he asked where Sun Ch'üan was. They pointed to where the press was most dense. Chou T'ai stiffened and dashed in. Presently he reached his lord's side and cried out, "My lord, follow me and I will hack a way out."

Chou T'ai fought his way out to the river bank. Then he turned to look, and Sun Ch'üan was not behind him. So he turned back, forced his way in and once again found his way to his master's side.

"I cannot get out; the arrows are too thick," said Sun Ch'üan.

"Then go first, my lord, and I will follow."

Sun Ch'üan then urged his steed as fast as he could go and Chou T'ai kept off all pursuit. He sustained many wounds and the arrows rattled on his helmet, but he got clear at last and Sun Ch'üan was safe. As they neared the river bank, Lü Mêng came up with some of the naval force and escorted Sun Ch'üan down to the ships.

"I owe my safety to Chou T'ai, who thrice came to my aid," said Sun Ch'üan. "But Hsü Shêng is still in the thick of the fight, and how can we save him?"

"I will go to his rescue," cried Chou.

Whirling his spear, Chou again plunged into the battle and presently brought his colleague safely out of the press. Both were severely wounded.

Lü Mêng ordered his men to keep up a rapid flight of arrows so as to command the bank, and in this way the two leaders were enabled to get on board the ships.

Now Ch'ên Wu had engaged the legion under P'ang Tê. Being inferior in force and no aid being forthcoming, Ch'ên Wu was forced into a valley where the trees and undergrowth were very dense. He tried to turn, but was caught by the branches and while so entangled he was killed.

When Ts'ao saw that Sun had escaped from the battle to the river bank he urged his steed forward in pursuit. He sent flights of arrows toward the fugitives. By this time Lü Mêng's men had emptied their quivers, and he began to be very anxious. But just then a fleet of ships sailed up led by Lu Hsün, the son-in-law of Sun Ts'ê, who came with ten legions and drove back Ts'ao's men. Then he landed to pursue. He captured many thousands of horses and slew many men, so that Ts'ao Ts'ao was quite defeated and retired.

Then they sought and found the body of Ch'ên Wu among the slain. Sun Ch'üan was much grieved when he came to know that Ch'ên Wu had been slain and Tung Hsi drowned, and wept sore. Men were sent to seek for Tung Hsi's body, which at last was found. Both captains were buried with great honours.

As a recompense for Chou T'ai's services in his rescue, Sun Ch'üan prepared in his honour a great banquet, where he himself offered Chou a goblet of wine and complimented and embraced him while the tears coursed down his cheeks.

"Twice you saved my life, careless of your own," cried he, "and you have received many wounds. It is as if your skin had been engraved and painted. What sort of a man should I be if I did not treat you as one of my own flesh and blood? Can I regard you, noble Sir, merely as a unit in my army? You are my meritorious minister. I share the glory you have won and mine are your joys and sorrows."

Then he bade Chou T'ai open his dress and exhibit his wounds for all the assembly to see. The skin was gashed all over as if his body had been scored with a knife. Sun Ch'üan pointed to the wounds one after another and asked how each one had been received. And, as Chou told him, for every wound Sun Ch'üan made him drink off a goblet of wine till he became thoroughly intoxicated. Sun Ch'üan then presented him with a black silk parasol and bade him use it on all occasions as a sign of the glory that was his.

But Sun Ch'üan found his opponents too much for him; at the end of a month the two armies were both at Juhsü and neither had won a victory.

Then said Chang Chao and Ku Yung, "Ts'ao Ts'ao is too strong and we cannot overcome him by mere force. If the struggle continue longer you will only lose more men. You had better seek to make peace."

Sun Ch'üan followed this advice and despatched Pu Chih on a peace mission to Ts'ao Ts'ao's camp. He was ordered to offer a yearly tribute. Ts'ao also saw that Chiangnan was too strong to be overcome, and consented. He insisted that Sun Ch'üan should first send away his army and then he would retire. The messenger returned with this message and Sun Ch'üan sent away the greater part, leaving only Chou T'ai and Chiang Ch'in to hold Juhsü. The army returned to Moling. Ts'ao left Ts'ao Jên and Chang Liao in charge of Hofei and marched to Hsüch'ang.

On arrival, all Ts'ao Ts'ao's officers persuaded him to become Prince of Wei. Only the president of a Board, Ts'ui Yen, spoke strongly against the scheme.

"You are, then, the only man who knows not the fate of Hsün Wên-yo," said his colleagues.

"Such times! Such deeds!" cried Ts'ui Yen. "You are guilty of rebellion, but you may commit it yourselves. I will bear no part in it."

Certain enemies told Ts'ao Ts'ao, and Ts'ui Yen was thrown into prison. At his trial he glared like a tiger and his very beard curled with contempt; he raged and cursed at Ts'ao Ts'ao for a betrayer of his prince, and a rebel. The interrogating magistrate reported his conduct to Ts'ao, who ordered Ts'ui to be beaten to death in prison.

> Ts'ui Yen was born in Ch'ingho.
> Firm and unyielding was he,
> With beard crisp curling and gleaming eyes,
> Which showed the man of stone and iron within.
> He drave the evil from his presence,
> And his glory is fair and high.
> For loyalty to his lord of Han,
> His fame shall increase as the ages roll.

In the twenty-first year of the period "Established Tranquillity," in the fifth month of that year, a great memorial signed by many officers went up to the Emperor Hsien, praying that Ts'ao Ts'ao be granted the title of prince for his manifest merits and signal services to the state, exceeding those rendered by any minister before him. The memorial was approved, and a draft Edict was prepared by the famous Chung Yu. Thrice Ts'ao Ts'ao with seeming modesty pretended to decline the honour, but thrice was his refusal rejected. Finally he made his obeisance and was enrolled as "Prince of Wei" with the usual insignia and privileges, a head-dress (or coronet) with twelve strings of beads and a chariot with gilt shafts, drawn by six steeds. But he arrogantly used an imperial chariot with bells and had the roads cleared when he passed along. He built himself a palace at Yehchün.

Then he began to discuss the appointment of an heir-apparent. His real wife, of the Ting family, was without issue, but a concubine had borne him a son, Ts'ao Ang, who had been killed in battle at the siege of Wanch'êng. A second concubine, of the P'ien family, had borne him four sons, P'ei, Chang, Chih and Hsiung. Wherefore he elevated her to the rank of princess-consort in place of the Lady Ting. The third son, Chih, also known as Tzŭ-chien, was very clever and a ready master of composition. Ts'ao Ts'ao wished him to be named the heir. Then the eldest son sought from the high officer Chia Hsü a plan to secure his rights of primogeniture, and Hsü told him to do so-and-so. Thereafter, whenever the father went out on any military expedition, Ts'ao Chih wrote fulsome panegyrics, but Ts'ao Chih wept so copiously at bidding his father farewell that the courtiers were deeply affected and remarked that though the one son was crafty and clever he was not so sincerely filial as the other. Ts'ao P'ei also bought over his father's immediate attendants, who then rang the praises of his virtues so loud that Ts'ao Ts'ao was strongly disposed to name him as the heir after all.

After hesitating a long time, the matter was referred to Chia Hsü.

"I wish to name my heir; who shall it be?"

Chia Hsü would not say, and Ts'ao Ts'ao asked why.

"I was just recalling the past in my mind and could not reply at once," said Chia.

"What were you recalling?"

"I was thinking of two fathers: Yüan Pên-ch'u (Yüan Shao) and Liu Chinghsing (Liu Piao) and their sons."

Ts'ao Ts'ao smiled. Soon after this he declared his eldest son his heir.

In the tenth month the building of the palace of the new Prince of Wei was completed and the furnishing begun. From all parts were collected rare flowers and uncommon trees to beautify the gardens. One agent went into Wu and saw Sun Ch'üan, to whom he presented a letter from Ts'ao Ts'ao asking that he might be allowed to proceed to Wênchow to get some oranges. At that period Sun Ch'üan was in a most complaisant mood toward Ts'ao Ts'ao, so from the orange trees in his own city he picked forty very fine fruits and sent them immediately to Yehchün.

On the way, one of the bearers of the oranges fell ill and they had to stop at the foot of a certain hill. There came along an elderly man, blind of one eye and lame of one leg, who wore a white rattan head-dress and a black loose robe. He saluted the bearers and stayed to talk.

Presently he said, "Your burdens are heavy, O porters; may this old Taoist lend you a shoulder? What do you say?"

Naturally they were pleased enough, and the amiable wayfarer bore each load for five *li*. When they resumed their burdens they noticed that they seemed lighter than before, and they felt rather suspicious. When the Taoist was taking his leave of the officer in charge of the party, he said, "I am an old friend from the same village as Prince Wei. My name is Tso Tz'ŭ, my commoner name being Yüan-fang. Among Taoists I bear the appellation of ' Blackhorn.' When you get to the end of your journey you may say that I was enquiring after your lord."

He shook down his sleeves and left. In due course the orange bearers reached the new palace and the oranges were presented. But when Ts'ao cut one open it was but an empty shell of a thing; there was no pulp beneath the rind. Ts'ao Ts'ao was rather puzzled and called in the porters, who told him of their falling in with the mysterious Taoist on the way. But Ts'ao scouted the idea of that being the reason.

But just then the warden of the gate sent to say that a certain Taoist was at the gate and wished to see the prince.

"Send him in," said Ts'ao Ts'ao.

"He is the man we met on the way," said the porters when he appeared.

Ts'ao Ts'ao said curtly, "What sorcery have you been exercising on my beautiful fruit?"

"How could such a thing happen?" said the Taoist.

Thereupon he cut open an orange and showed it full of pulp, most delicious to the taste. But when Ts'ao cut open another that again was empty, nothing but rind.

Ts'ao Ts'ao was more than ever perplexed. He bade his visitor be seated, and, as Tso Tz'ŭ asked for refreshment, wine and food were brought in. The Taoist ate ravenously, consuming a whole sheep, and drank in proportion. Yet he showed no sign of intoxication or repletion.

"By what magic are you here?" said Ts'ao Ts'ao.

"I am but a poor Taoist. I went into Hsich'uan (Ssŭch'uan) and on Mount Omi I studied the Way for thirty long years. One day I heard my name called from out the rocky wall of my cell. I looked, but could see nothing. The same thing happened next day, and so on for many days. Then suddenly, with a roar like thunder, the rock split asunder and I saw a sacred book in three volumes called "The Supreme Book of Magic." From the first volume I learned to ascend to the clouds astride the wind, to sail up into the great void itself; from the second to pass through mountains and penetrate rocks; from the third, to float light as vapour, over the seas, to become invisible at will or change my shape, to fling swords and project daggers so as to decapitate a man from a distance. You, O Prince, have reached the acme of glory; why not now withdraw and, like me, become a disciple of the Taoists? Why not travel to Mount Omi and there mend your ways so that I may bequeath my three volumes to you?"

"Oft have I reflected upon this course and struggled against my fate, but what can I do? There is no one to maintain the government," replied Ts'ao.

"There is Liu Yüan-tê, a scion of the dynastic family; could you not make way for him? If you do not, I may have to send one of my flying swords after your head one day."

"You are one of his secret agents," said Ts'ao Ts'ao, suddenly enraged. "Seize him!" cried he to his lictors.

They did so, while the Taoist laughed. And he continued to laugh as they dragged him down to the dungeons, where they beat him cruelly. And when they had finished, the Taoist lay there gently respiring in a sound sleep, just as if he felt nothing whatever.

This enraged Ts'ao Ts'ao still more, and he bade them put the priest into the large wooden collar and nail it securely and then chain him in a cell. And he set guards over him, and the guards saw the collar and chains just fall off while the victim lay fast asleep not injured in the least.

The Taoist lay in prison seven days without food or water, and when they went to look at him he was sitting upright on the ground, quite well and rosy looking.

The gaolers reported these things to Ts'ao Ts'ao, who had the prisoner brought in.

"I do not mind going without food for years," said the victim, when Ts'ao Ts'ao questioned him, "yet I could eat a thousand sheep in a day."

Ts'ao Ts'ao was at the end of his resources, he could prevail nothing against such a man.

That day there was to be a great banquet at the new palace, and guests came in crowds. When the banquet was in progress and the wine cup passing freely, suddenly the same Taoist appeared. He had wooden clogs on his feet. All faces turned in his direction and not a few were afraid; others wondered. Standing there in front of the great assembly, the Taoist said, "O powerful Prince, here to-day you have every delicacy on the table and a glorious company of guests. You have rare and beautiful objects from all parts of the world. Is there anything lacking? If there be anything you would like, name it and I will get it for you."

Ts'ao replied, "Then I want a dragon's liver to make soup: can you get that?"

"Where's the difficulty?" replied Tso Tz'ŭ.

With a pencil the Taoist immediately sketched a dragon on the whitewashed wall of the banquet hall. Then he flicked his sleeve over it, the dragon's belly opened of itself and therefrom Tso took the liver all fresh and bloody.

"You had the liver hidden in your sleeve," said Ts'ao Ts'ao, incredulous.

"Then there shall be another test," said the Taoist. "It is winter and every plant outside is dead. What flower would you like, O Prince. Name any one you will."

"I want a peony," said Ts'ao Ts'ao.

"Easy," said the Taoist.

At this request they brought out a flower-pot, which was placed in full view of the guests. Then he spurted some water over it, and in a very short time up came a peony with two fully expanded flowers.

The guests were astonished, and they asked the Taoist to be seated and gave him wine and food. The cook sent in some minced fish.

"The best mince is made from the perch of the Sung River," said the Taoist.

"How can you get fish a thousand *li* away?" said Ts'ao Ts'ao.

"Not at all difficult. Tell someone to get a rod and hook, and fish in the pond just below this banquet hall."

They did so, and very soon several beautiful perch lay on the steps.

"I have always kept some of these in my ponds, of course," said Ts'ao Ts'ao.

"O Prince, do you think to deceive me? All perch have two gills except the Sung perch, which has two pairs. That is the distinguishing feature."

The guests crowded round to look, and, surely enough, the fish had four gills.

"To cook this perch one needs purple sprout ginger though," said the Taoist.

"Can you also produce that?" asked Ts'ao Ts'ao.

"Easily."

He told them to bring in a silver bowl, which the magician filled with water. Very soon the ginger filled the bowl, and he presented it to the host. Ts'ao put out his hand to pick some, when suddenly a book appeared in the bowl and the title was "Mêngtê's New Treatise (on the Art of War)." He took it out and read it over. Not a word of his treatise was missing.

Ts'ao Ts'ao became more and mystified. Tso Tz'ŭ took up a jade cup that stood on the table, filled it with fine wine and presented it to Ts'ao Ts'ao.

"Drink this, O Prince, and you will live a thousand years."

"Drink of it first yourself," said Ts'ao Ts'ao.

The Taoist took the jade pin from his head-dress and drew it across the cup as if dividing the wine into two portions.

Then he drank one half and handed the cup with the other half to Ts'ao Ts'ao. But he angrily refused it. The Taoist then threw the cup into the air, where it was transformed into a white dove which circled round the banquet hall and then flew away.

All faces were turned upward following the flight of the dove, and so no one had noticed the going of the Taoist. But he was gone; and soon the gate warden reported that he had left the palace.

Said Ts'ao Ts'ao, "A magician like this ought to be put to death or he will do some mischief."

The redoubtable Hsü Ch'u and a company of armed men were sent to arrest the Taoist. They saw the Taoist, still wearing his wooden clogs, not far ahead but striding along quickly. Hsü Ch'u rode after him, but in spite of all his horse could do, he could not come up with him. He kept up the chase right to the hills, when he met a shepherd lad with a flock of sheep. And there walked the Taoist among the sheep. The Taoist disappeared. The angry warrior slew the whole flock of sheep, while the shepherd lad looked on weeping.

Suddenly the boy heard a voice from one of the severed heads, telling him to replace the heads on the bodies of his sheep. Instead of doing so, he fled in terror, covering his face. Then he heard a voice calling to him, "Do not run away; you shall have your sheep again."

He turned, and lo! the sheep were all alive again and Tso Tz'ŭ was driving them along. The boy began to question him, but the Taoist made no reply. With a flick of his sleeves he was gone.

The shepherd lad went home and told all these marvels to his master. He could not conceal such a story, and it reached Ts'ao Ts'ao. Then sketches of the Taoist were sent everywhere with orders to arrest him. Within three days were arrested in the city and outside three or four hundred persons all blind of one eye, lame of one leg, and wearing a rattan head-dress, a black loose robe and wooden clogs. They were all alike and all answered to the description of the missing Taoist.

There was a great hubbub in the street. Ts'ao Ts'ao ordered his officer to sprinkle the crowd of Taoists with the blood of pigs and dogs in order to exorcise the witchcraft and take them away to the drill ground on the south of the city. Thither he followed them with his guards, who surrounded the crowd of arrested persons and slew every one. But from the neck of each one, after the head was severed, there floated up into the air a wreath of black vapour, and all these wreaths drifted toward a centre where they joined up into the image of another Tso Tz'ŭ, who presently beckoned to him a white crane out of the sky, mounted it and sat as on a horse.

Clapping his hands, the Taoist cried merrily, "The rats of the earth follow the golden tiger, and one morning the doer of evil shall be no more."

The soldiers shot arrows at both bird and man. At this a tremendous storm burst over the city. Stones were driven along, sand was whirled about and all the corpses arose from the ground, each holding his own head in his hands. They rushed toward Ts'ao Ts'ao as if to strike him. The officials covered their eyes, and none dared to look another in the face.

> The power of a bold, bad man will overturn a State,
> The art of a necromancer produces wonders great.

Read the next chapter and you will know the fate of Ts'ao Ts'ao.

CHAPTER LXIX.

KUAN LU TAKES THE *Sortes* BY THE "BOOK OF CHANGES;" LOYAL SUBJECTS DIE FOR THEIR COUNTRY.

The sight of the corpses of his victims rising to their feet in the storm and running toward him was too much for Ts'ao Ts'ao, and he swooned. However, the wind quickly fell and the corpses disappeared. His followers assisted Ts'ao to his palace, but he was very ill.

A poet celebrated the episode of the murdered Taoist:—

> He studied his magical books,
> He was learned in mystical lore,
> And with magical fleetness of foot
> He could travel the wide world o'er.
> The magical arts that he knew,
> He employed in an earnest essay
> To reform the bad heart of Ts'ao Man,
> But in vain; Ts'ao held on his way.

Ts'ao Ts'ao's illness seemed beyond the art of the leech and drugs seemed of no avail. It happened that T'aishih Ch'êng and Hsü Chih came from the capital to visit the prince, who bade the latter take the *sortes* from the "Book of Changes."

"Have you ever heard of Kuan Lu? He is more than human in his skill at divination," said Hsü.

"I have heard a lot about him, but I do not know how clever he is; you tell me about him," replied Ts'ao.

"He is from P'ingyüan; his other name is Kung-ming. His face is ugly and coarse; he drinks to excess and is rather dissipated. His father was chief of the aborigines of the Langya districts. From a lad Kuan Lu loved to study the stars, staying up all night to watch them, in spite of the prohibition of his father and mother. He used to say that if domestic fowls and wild geese knew the seasons naturally how much more should a man. He often used to play with other boys at drawing pictures of the sky on the ground, putting in the sun, moon and stars. When he grew older he studied the 'Book of Changes' very deeply and observed the winds. He was a marvellous calculator and excellent physiognomist.

"His fame reached the ears of the Prefect Tan Tzŭ-ch'un, who called him to his residence for an interview. There were present some hundred or so other guests, every one of whom could be called able of speech.

"'I am young and not over-bold,' said Kuan Lu to the Prefect. 'I pray you give me three stoups of wine to loosen my tongue.'

"The request was astonishing, but the wine was brought in, and when he had drunk it, Kuan Lu, looking contemptuously at the other guests, said, 'Now I am ready; are these the sort of opponents you have got together for me to contend with? Are these gentlemen sitting around me disputants?'

"'I myself am anxious for a match with you,' said Tan.

"Then they began upon the meaning of the 'Book of Changes.' Kuan Lu's words poured forth like a torrent, and his ideas were most recondite. The Prefect replied, stating difficulties; Kuan swept them away in a stream of eloquence. So it went on the whole day without a pause even for refreshment. Neither Tan nor his other guests could help praising him and agreeing with him.

"His fame spread wide after this encounter, and people spoke of him as the 'Supernatural Boy.'

"After this he became famous in another way. There was a certain Kuo En, a man of the people, who had two brothers. All three became lame and they called in Kuan Lu to cast lots and discover the reason. Kuan Lu said, 'By the lots there is a female demon in your family tomb, an aunt, the wife of one of your father's brothers. Some years ago, in a time of dearth, for the sake of a few measures of grain, she was pushed into a well and a great stone was thrown in on her, crushing her head so that she suffered intensely. She complained to the Most High, and your lameness is the retribution for that crime. No prayers will avert the evil.

"The three brothers wept and acknowledged their guilt.

"The Prefect Wang Chi, of Anp'ing, heard of the diviner's fame and invited him to come on a visit, and he went. It happened that the wife of the magistrate of Hsintu suffered from headaches and his son from pains in the heart. Kuan Lu was asked to discover the reason. He cast lots and said that at the west corner of the main hall there were buried two corpses, one of a man who held a spear, the other of a man who had a bow and arrows. The wall was built across them. The spearman's master had gashed his head and so his head pained. The archer's master had stabbed him in the heart and so his heart suffered anguish. They dug where he indicated and, about eight feet down, found two coffins, one with a spear inside and the other with a strung bow and wooden arrows. All were much decayed. Kuan Lu bade them remove the bones and bury them ten *li* outside the walls. Thereafter the woman and her son suffered no more.

"A certain Chuko Yüan, magistrate of Kuant'ao, newly promoted to Prefect, was leaving for his new post, and Kuan Lu went to see him off. One of the guests mentioned that Kuan Lu could divine what was hidden from sight. The Prefect doubted such powers and said he would put a test. He got a swallow's egg, a wasp's nest and a spider and concealed them in three separate boxes. He asked Kuan to guess the contents. The divination made, he wrote three quatrains:—

> ' The latent life will declare itself;
> It will cling to your lordly hall,
> Or male or female, flung into space,
> Wide wings will prevent its fall.

'This seems to indicate a swallow's egg.

> ' A many-chambered dwelling
> Is hanging to your eaves,
> Each room has a poisonous tenant;
> Who'll be flying when he leaves.

'This answers to a wasp's nest.

> ' Therein 's a long-shanked, trembling thing,
> Who spins a thread from his inside
> And spreads a fine spun net for flies;
> He profits most at eventide.

'And this it a spider.'
"The guests were amazed.

"An old woman in his village having lost a cow, came to consult him. After the divination he told her that seven men had taken away the cow and were cooking and eating it on the bank of a certain mountain stream. She had better go there quickly and see who they were. If she went with all speed she would find the skin and the flesh. She went and found the seven men hidden behind a small shanty, boiling beef. Most of the cow's flesh was still there. She told the Prefect, who arrested the seven men and punished them. Then he asked the old lady how she got to know exactly who the offenders were, and she told him.

"He was dubious, too. He sent for Kuan Lu and put him to the following test. He placed his seal and a pheasant feather in a box and asked what were the contents. The reply was:—

> ' Square within, without so round,
> Beauteous colours here abound;
> The jewel within is held secure
> And what it witnesses is sure.

'Is not this a seal in its bag?'
"With regard to the other thing, Kuan Lu said:—

> ' There's a bird on the precipice steep,
> Its body with flame seems aglow,
> Its wings are barred yellow and black,
> At sunrise it ne'er fails to crow.

'And I think this hints at a pheasant feather.

"The Prefect Liu treated the marvellous diviner with great honour.

"One day Kuan Lu saw a youth ploughing a field. After watching him for a long time, Kuan Lu suddenly asked his name and age.

"'My name is Chao Yen, and I am nineteen,' said the young man. 'Pray, who may you be, Sir?'

"'I am Kuan Lu; you may have heard of me. I see an air of early death about you, and you will be done with life in three days. It is a pity that one so handsome should die so young.'

"Chao Yen forsook his plough, hurried home and told his father. The father at once set out to find Kuan Lu, and, having found him, threw himself on the ground and besought him to save his son.

"'How can I avert the doom? It is fate,' said Kuan Lu.

"'Alas! I have but this one son, I pray you to save him.'

"And the son added his tears and prayers to those of his father. Kuan Lu was deeply touched. Then he turned to the lad and said, 'You get ready some good wine and some venison. To-morrow go into the forest on the south there, and underneath a lofty tree you will see two men seated on boulders playing wei-ch'i. One of them will be dressed in white, and he will be facing the south. He is very evil looking. The other will be seated opposite, dressed in red. He is very hand-home. They will be deeply absorbed in their game and will not notice who offers them food and wine, which you will humbly present on your knees. When they have eaten and drunk, you will prostrate yourself and with tears pray them to grant you length of days. You will gain an increased span of life, but, above all things, do not mention that I told you what to do.'

"The father kept Kuan Lu as a guest, and the next day the son followed out his instructions. He entered the forest and soon came upon the two men seated beneath a pine, playing wei-ch'i. They seemed oblivious to all around them. Chao Yen presented the wine and the food, and the two men ate absent-mindedly, for the game went on.

"But when Chao Yen threw himself on the ground and implored the gift of long life, they seemed startled.

"'This must be some of Kuan Lu's doing,' said Red Robe. 'Still, as we have accepted a gift at his hand we must have pity on him.'

"He who was dressed in white then lifted up a book that hung at his side and looked therein.

"'You are nineteen this year,' said he to Chao Yen. 'You ought to die. But we will insert a 'nine' over the 'ten' and so make it read ninety and nine, and that is the age you will attain. But when you go back, tell Kuan Lu he is not to betray the secrets of fate, or Heaven will surely punish him.'

"Then Red Robe took out a pen and added the figure. A gust of wind passed, and the two old men were transformed into two cranes that rose into the sky and flew away.

"Chao Yen came back home and told what he had seen. Kuan Lu told him the red-robed man was the Southern Dipper Constellation, and the white-robed, the Northern Dipper.

" 'But the Northern Dipper consists of nine stars, and there was only one man,' objected the lad.

" 'Separately they are nine, but they combine to form one. The Northern Dipper records deaths; the Southern Dipper, births. Now the extra figure has been added you need have no anxiety; you will live long.'

"Father and son both thanked him most sincerely, but thereafter Kuan Lu was very careful how he divined for people lest he should betray celestial secrets.

"Now, this man is at P'ingyüan, and you, O Prince, can seek your fate of him. Why not call him?"

Kuan Lu was sent for and came. As soon as the salutations were over, Ts'ao Ts'ao asked him to cast lots for him.

Kuan Lu at once found that the illness was only due to magical machinations, and said so; at which Ts'ao Ts'ao was much relieved in his mind, and his health began to improve.

Next Ts'ao Ts'ao wished to know about the conditions in the world's affairs. After the necessary calculations the prophet said, "Three-eight crosswise; the yellow boar meets the tiger: stop the southern expedition with the loss of one limb."

Then Ts'ao Ts'ao asked him to enquire whether his life should be long or not.

He replied, "Lion in the Palace to preserve the talents of ancestors: the Prince's way is securely renewed and his son and grandson shall come to high honour."

Then Ts'ao Ts'ao asked concerning himself.

"Divinations concerning the fate of the universe may not be foreknown; wait a time and I will look into it."

Ts'ao Ts'ao was pleased and would like to keep such a man near him, so he offered him the post of historiographer (who was also soothsayer) at his court, but it was declined.

"My destiny is mean, my luck despicable; I am not equal to such an office and dare not undertake it."

"Why not?" said Ts'ao Ts'ao.

"My forehead has no lofty fullness; my eyes no steady expression; my nose no bridge; my feet no round, solid heels; my back lacks the triple armour (of shoulder blades and intervening muscles); and my breast the three marks (like the character jên, which indicates wealth). I can only control evil spirits securely; I cannot rule living men."

"What think you of my physiognomy?"

"What can a minister of extremely exalted rank like yourself desire further?" said Kuan Lu.

Ts'ao Ts'ao pressed him to say: the soothsayer only laughed. Then Ts'ao asked him to look at the many officers of all kinds standing around.

"Every one of them is a servant equal to the administration of the world," said Kuan Lu.

But when Ts'ao Ts'ao asked whether good or bad fortune was to be his, the soothsayer would not give a clear and full reply.

A poem says:—

> Kuan Lu was a seer of old,
> Stars to him their secrets told.
> Mysteries, occult and dim,
> Were as daylight unto him.
> His so subtle intellect
> Could the shade of death detect,
> But the secrets of his skill
> Died with him,—are secrets still.

Again Ts'ao Ts'ao asked him to divine concerning his rivals Wu and Shu. He said the former had just lost a famous leader and the latter had encroached on his territory. Ts'ao's doubts as to the accuracy of one of these events were soon set at rest, for a messenger came from Hofei to say that Lu Su had died. Then Ts'ao sent hurriedly into Hanchung, and the scout returned to say that Chang Fei and Ma Ch'ao had taken the Pass at Hsiapien. Ts'ao Ts'ao was angry and inclined to march at once against the invaders; but he consulted the great soothsayer, who advised him not to move.

"In the coming spring there will be a conflagration in Hsütu," said he.

Having been witness of the verification of Kuan Lu's words, Ts'ao Ts'ao was in no mood to neglect the warning. He stayed on in his palace, but he sent Ts'ao Hung with five legions to assist in the defence of East Ch'uan, while Hsiahou Tun, with three legions, went to Hsütu to keep careful watch and be ready against any surprises. He placed Chang Shih and Wang Pi in command of the Imperial Guard.

Ssŭma I warned him against this Wang Pi. Said he, "The man is given to wine, and slack. He is not a fit man for such a post."

Ts'ao Ts'ao replied, "He is very fit. He has followed me through all difficulties and dangers. He is loyal and diligent, solid as stone or iron."

Wang Pi was appointed and led the guard into camp at the capital, outside the *Tung-hua* Gate of the Imperial Palace.

Now there was a certain Kêng Chi, a Loyang man, who had long been employed in the minister's palace in a subordinate capacity and afterward had been promoted to a rather better post. He, Ssuma Chih and Wei Huang were close friends.

These three were greatly distressed at Ts'ao Ts'ao's advance to princely rank, and more especially at his use of the imperial

chariots. In the early months of the twenty-third year **Kêng**
and Wei came to a secret exchange of views on Ts'ao's conduct.

Kêng Chi said, "The man is a rebel and wicked, every day
behaving worse. He intends to go farther, and how can we,
as servants of the dynasty, help him in his wickedness? I
have a friend named Chin I, who also is a servant of Han and
an enemy of Ts'ao Ts'ao's. He is a descendant of Chin Jih-ti,
one-time minister. Beside, he is friendly with **Wang Pi**. If
we all tried our best we ought to succeed."

"But if he is friendly with Wang Pi he will not assist us!"
said Kêng.

"Let us go and sound him," said Wei Huang.

So the two went to see Chin I, who received them in his
private rooms. There they talked.

Said Wei Huang, "O virtuous I, we know you are on most
friendly terms with Commander Wang Pi, and so have come
to beg a favour."

"What is it you ask?"

"The Prince of Wei will soon receive the abdication of the
Emperor and himself ascend to the seat of the mighty. Then
you and your friend Wang will advance to places of great
honour; and when that day comes, we pray you not to forget us,
but to recommend us for employment. We should feel no
shallow gratitude for your kindness."

Chin I flicked down his sleeves and arose looking very angry.
At that instant arrived the tea for the visitors. He snatched
it away from the serving-man and emptied it on the floor.

Wei Huang started up in feigned alarm.

"How have I offended you, my good old friend?" cried he.

"I have been friends with you because you are descendants
of men who have served Han faithfully. Now, if instead of
trying to repay the debt of gratitude you ought to feel, you
turn aside to assist one who is their enemy, think you that I
can regard you as friends? How could I look the world in the
face?"

"But if it be destiny, one cannot help it," said Kêng. "One
must accept it."

Chin grew still more angry, so that the two visitors were
convinced that at heart he was still loyal to the dynasty. Then
they began to tell him the true state of the case.

"Our real desire is to destroy this rebel, and we have come
to ask your help in that. What we said at first was only a test
to find out what you thought."

"Think you, with my ancestry, generation after generation
in the confidence and service of the Hans, that I would willingly
follow a rebel? If you, Sirs, really think of restoring the
dynasty, pray tell me your plans."

"Though we have the desire to prove our gratitude, yet we
lack the means to destroy the enemy," said Wei.

Said Chin, "We desire helpers within and supporters without. If we could slay Wang Pi we could use his name and troops to help the Emperor. With the help of Liu, the Imperial Uncle, we should be able to destroy the rebel Ts'ao."

Hearing Chin I's plan, the others clapped their hands in approval.

"And I have two friends who will go with us,". said Chin. "Both of them have the murder of a father to avenge. They are sons of the great physician Chi P'ing and are called Chi Miao and Chi Mu. Ts'ao Ts'ao put their father to death for his connection with the plot organised by Tung Ch'êng when he received the secret edict conveyed in the robe and girdle that was conferred upon him by the Emperor. The two sons escaped that time by flight, but they have since secretly returned to the capital. With their help all will go well."

The two conspirators rejoiced at the prospect of further help, and a messenger was sent to call in the two Chi. Soon they arrived, and the plot was laid before them. They were deeply affected and shed copious tears. Their wrath rose to the sky and they swore to aid in the destruction of the rebel.

"On the fifteenth day of the first month there will be grand illuminations in the city," said Chin I, "and felicitations will be going on on every side. Kêng Chi and Wei Huang will each lead out their retainers and make their way quickly to Wang Pi's camp to wait till they see the fire begin. Then they will dash in, slay Wang Pi and follow me inside the palace. We will then request the Emperor to ascend the Tower of the Five Phœnixes, assemble his officers and issue orders to destroy the rebels. The two brothers Chi will make their way into the city and set fires going. Then all will raise their voices and summon the populace to their aid. They are to hold up any rescue force in the city till the Emperor has issued the edict and disturbance is allayed, when they will rush toward Yeh-chün and seize Ts'ao Ts'ao. Then a messenger will be despatched with a summons for Liu, the Imperial Uncle. We will begin our work this night at the second watch and we will escape the ill success that attended Tung Ch'êng's attempt."

All five swore before Heaven to be true, and they smeared their lips with blood in earnest of their oath. After this, each returned to his own home to prepare arms and call up their men.

Both Kêng Chi and Wei Huang had a large number of retainers, whom they armed. The brothers Chi also got together some hundreds of men. They gave out a story of a hunting party to explain the gathering.

When the preparations were complete, and before the time fixed for the rising, Chin I went to see Wang Pi and said, "Everything in the world seems now tranquil, and the power of the Prince of Wei extends over all the land. It is a season of joy and felicitation, and everyone is hanging out lanterns and putting up decorations for the occasion."

The night of full moon was very clear, moon and stars most brilliant. The people of the capital took advantage of the night and thronged the "six streets and the three market places." The lanterns were hung out in profusion, and all went merrily. No official interfered with the crowd, no one thought of the flight of time; all was simple gaiety.

That night Wang Pi and his officers of the guards had a feast in their camp. Just after the second watch had begun they heard a great shouting in the camp, and someone came in to say that a fire had started in the rear. Wang Pi hurriedly left the table and went outside. He saw flames leaping up and rolling by and heard shouts of "Kill!" rising on every side and echoing to the very sky. He thought the camp had certainly mutinied, and, jumping on his horse, went out at the south gate. Just outside he ran against Kêng Chi, who loosed an arrow which struck him in the shoulder. He nearly fell with the shock, but he got away toward the west gate. He found he was pursued by armed men, so he got flurried, dismounted and went on foot. Presently he came to the house of Chin Wei and hammered at the door.

Now the fire that had created such a scare had been raised by Chin's own men sent for that purpose, and he had followed them to fight when the time came. Hence there was no one but the women folk left in his house. When the women heard the clamour at the door they thought Chin I had come back, and his wife, from the door of the women's quarter, called out, "Have you killed Wang Pi?"

This was a shock, but it told Wang Pi that his quondam friend was now an enemy. Wherefore he fled further to the house of Ts'ao Hsiu and told him that Kêng Chi and Chin I had raised a disturbance. Ts'ao Hsiu immediately armed himself, got to horse and led a company into the city. He found fires on all sides, and the Tower of the Five Phœnixes was in flames. The Emperor had fled into the recesses of the palace, but Ts'ao Ts'ao's friends and partizans were defending the palace gate like grim death.

In the city the crowd was shouting one to another to slay Ts'ao Ts'ao and restore the Hans.

When Hsiahou Tun had received the command to keep watch and ward over the capital, he had gone into camp five *li* from the city. When he saw the conflagration start he set the army in motion and surrounded the city. He also sent reinforcements to Ts'ao Hsiu within.

Inside the city the fighting went on all night. No one joined the conspirators; the small band were left to their own efforts. Soon it was reported that Chin I and the brothers Chi were slain. Kêng and Wei found their way to one of the gates, but there they met Hsiahou Tun's main force and were made prisoners. The handful of men with them were cut to pieces.

When the fighting subsided, Hsiahou Tun went into the city and set his men to put out the fires. He also laid hands on the whole households of the five conspirators. Then he sent a report to Ts'ao Ts'ao, who sent back orders to execute the two conspirators and put to death in public all the members of the five families. He was also to arrest every official and send the whole batch to Yehchün.

Hsiahou Tun sent his two chief prisoners to the place of execution. They shouted against Ts'ao Ts'ao.

"Living we have failed to slay you, Ts'ao A-man; dead we will be malicious spirits smiting rebels in all places."

The executioner smote Kêng on the mouth with his sword, so that the blood gushed out, but he continued to shout as long as he could. Wei Huang, his fellow-conspirator, dashed his temples on the ground crying, "How I hate him!" and ground his teeth till he broke them to fragments. And he died.

> Who can with outstretched hands uphold the sky
> Or thrones maintain by simple loyalty?
> Han's day was done; two would avert the doom,
> But failed, and carried anger to the tomb.

Hsiahou Tun carried out his chief's orders and sent the officials he had arrested to Yehchün. There Ts'ao Ts'ao set up two flags, one red and one white, in the drill ground and sent all the officials thither. Then he addressed them.

"In this late rebellion some of you went out to extinguish the fire, some of you stayed within doors. Let those who went forth to put out the fire take their stand by the red flag and those who remained in their houses go to the white flag."

The officials thought within themselves, "Certainly there can be nothing wrong in trying to put out a fire," so they nearly all placed themselves under the red flag; only about a third went to the white.

Then the order was given to seize all those by the red flag. They protested. "We are guiltless!" cried they.

Ts'ao Ts'ao said, "At that time you intended not to put out the flames but to aid the rebels."

He sent them all down to the Chang River and had them put to death on the bank. There were more than three hundred victims. He rewarded those who were under the white flag and sent them to their homes in the capital.

Wang Pi died from his wound and was buried with great honour.

Ts'ao Hsiu was placed over the guards; Chung Yu was dreated Prime Minister, Hua Hsin became a Chief Censor. The occasion was taken to create six grades of the title of "Marquis" with three divisions each, eighteen in all. There were seventeen grades of marquis under the name *Kuan-hsi*, or

"West of the Pass." And all these had golden seals of office with purple ribbons. There were also sixteen ranks of marquis called *Kuan-nei*, "Interior," and *Kuan-wai*, "Exterior". They had silver seals with tortoise ornaments on the back and black ribbons. There were five classes of *T'ai-fu* with three grades in each class. These had brass seals, with chain ornaments and ribbons. And with all these various gradations of ranks and nobility reorganised, the Court was entirely transformed. There were new ranks and new men in office.

Ts'ao Ts'ao then remembered the warning about a conflagration in the capital and wished to reward Kuan Lu for his prescience, but he would receive nothing.

Ts'ao Hung with an army went into Hanchung. He placed Hsiahou Yüan and Chang Ho in command at points of importance, while he went on to the attack. At that time Chang Fei with Lei T'ung were holding Pahsi. Ma Ch'ao marched to Hsiapan and sent Wu Lan out as van leader to reconnoitre. He fell in with Ts'ao Hung, and Wu Lan was going to retire. But a petty officer, Jên K'uei, advised against this.

"They are newly arrived, why not fight and take the keen edge off their pride? If we do not fight, how can we look our chief in the face when we return?"

So it was decided to offer battle, and Jên K'uei rode out and challenged Ts'ao Hung. The challenge was accepted, and the warriors advanced. Jên K'uei fell in the third encounter. Ts'ao Hung pressed the advantage, and Wu Lan was driven off. When he returned and told Ma Ch'ao, he was blamed.

"Why did you attack without orders and bring about this defeat?"

"It was the fault of Jên K'uei, who disobeyed orders."

"Defend most carefully; do not engage," said Ma Ch'ao.

Ma Ch'ao sent a report to Ch'êngtu and awaited orders for a further action. Ts'ao Hung suspected some ruse when Ma Ch'ao remained so long inactive, and retired to Nanchün. Here he was visited by Chang Ho, who asked why he had retired after the successful attack and slaughter of one of the enemy leaders.

"Seeing that Ma Ch'ao declined to come out to fight I suspected some ruse," replied he. "Beside, when I was at Yehtu that wonderful soothsayer, Kuan Lu, foretold the loss of a leader here. I heeded what he said and so was careful."

Chang Ho laughed, "You have been a leader of soldiers for half your life and yet you heed the sayings of a soothsayer! I may be of small wit, but I would take Pahsi with my own troop, and the possession of Pahsi would be the key to the whole of Shu."

"The defender of Pahsi is Chang Fei," said Ts'ao Hung. "He is no ordinary man to meet. One must be careful."

"All of you fear this Chang Fei, but I do not; I look upon him as a mere nobody.   I shall have to capture him this time."

"But if you fail, what then?"

"Then I shall be content to pay the penalty according to military rules."

Ts'ao Hung made him put his undertaking in writing, and then Chang Ho marched to the attack.

> The proud are often defeated,
> Lightsome attacks oft fail.

The following chapter will tell how Chang Ho fared.

CHAPTER LXX.

FIERCE CHANG FEI TAKES A POSITION BY GUILE;
AGED HUANG CHUNG CAPTURES A HILL BY STRATAGEM.

Chang Ho's army, with which he felt so sure of victory, consisted of three legions, and they were in three camps protected by some hills. They were named "Yench'ü Camp," "Mêngt'ou Camp" and "Tangshih Camp." When he marched he left half the men in each camp as defenders.

The news soon reached Pahsi, and Chang Fei called in his colleague Lei T'ung to give his opinion. Lei said, "The country is bad and the hills full of danger in Langchung; let us lay an ambush. You, O General, go out to give battle and I will help you by some sudden and unexpected attack. We ought to get Chang Ho."

Whereupon Chang Fei gave half a legion to Lei T'ung and himself led out a legion to a point thirty *li* from Langchung. Having set them in order, he rode out and challenged Chang Ho to single combat. Chang galloped out to meet him.

After the thirtieth or so bout Chang Ho's men suddenly began to shout and soon showed signs of confusion. The reason was the appearance of the banners of Shu from the cover of some hills. Chang Ho dared not continue to fight after this, and he fled. Chang Fei pursued him. Lei T'ung also appeared in his road and attacked, and so, with enemies on both sides, Chang Ho lost the day. Both Chang Fei and Lei T'ung continued to smite him, even into the night, till he got back to his camp at Yench'ü Hill.

Chang Ho reverted to his old plan of defending the three camps, rolling down logs and hurling stones. But he remained behind his defences. Chang Fei made a camp ten *li* off.

Next day he went forth and offered battle, but Chang Ho took no notice. He ascended to the summit of the hill and drank wine to the accompaniment of trumpets and drums, but he would not fight. Chang Fei bade his soldiers shout insults, but these had no effect. Lei T'ung was sent up the hill, but the rolling logs and hurtling stones forced him to retire. Then the men of the other two camps came out to the attack and Lei was discomfited.

Next day Chang Fei again offered battle, but there was no response. Again the soldiers yelled every form of insult, but Chang Ho from the hill top only replied by similar abuse.

Chang Fei was at his wits' ends; and this game was played for more than fifty days.

Then Chang Fei made a strong stockade just in front of the hill, and therein he sat day after day drinking till he became half drunk. And when he was so, he reviled his opponent.

About this time Liu Pei sent gifts to the army, and when the messenger went back he told Liu that his brother was giving himself over to wine. This made Liu Pei anxious, so he lost no time in asking advice from K'ung-ming.

K'ung-ming was jocular, saying, "Since that is so let us send him fifty vessels of the best brew of Ch'êngtu. He probably has but poor stuff in the camp."

"But he has always had a weakness for wine, and he has failed because of it. Yet you would encourage him to drink by sending him more wine?"

"My lord, is it that you do not understand your brother even after all these years? He is brave and steady, yet when we first invaded Shu he released Yen Yen, which was not what a mere bravo would have done. He is face to face with Chang Ho, and has been for nearly two months, and day after day he drinks and rages and insults his enemy openly. He treats him with most perfect contempt. But this is not only the wine-cup; it is a deep plan to get the better of Chang Ho."

"This may be so," replied Liu Pei, "but let us not rely upon it too much. Let Wei Yen go to help him."

K'ung-ming sent Wei Yen with the wine, and the carts set out, each flying a yellow flag with a writing in large characters that it was fine wine for the general use of the army in the field.

When Wei Yen reached the army he handed over the wine, which he said was a gift from the lord of Shu. And Chang Fei received it with due respect.

He told Wei Yen and Lei T'ung each to take a company and move out on the two wings, ready to act when they saw a red flag displayed. And then he had the wine laid out and called up some soldiers to drink with a great display of flags and a rolling of drums.

The spies reported all these doings on the hill-top, and Chang Ho came out to look for himself. There he saw his opponent drinking, and two of the soldiers were boxing before him for his amusement.

"He despises me too much," said Chang Ho, and he gave orders to prepare for a night attack on the enemy camp. His own men should do the raiding and the other two camps were to support them.

There was little moon that night, and Chang Ho took advantage of the obscurity to steal down the side of the hill. He got guite close to the enemy camp and stood for a time looking at Chang Fei sitting amid a blaze of lamps and drinking. Suddenly he dashed forward with a yell, and at the same moment his drums on the hill-top rolled out their defiance. Chang Fei never stirred. Chang Ho rushed at him and delivered a mighty thrust with his spear. Chang Fei toppled over—it was a Chang Fei of straw. Ho checked and turned his steed. At that moment he heard a string of detonations and a warrior appeared before him barring his way. It was the real Chang Fei, as the round head and thundering voice speedily made manifest.

With spear set, he rode toward Chang Ho. The two warriors fought many bouts under the gleaming lights. No help came to Chang Ho. In vain he yearned for the assistance which the two camps were to bring him. How could he know that his reinforcements had been driven back by Wei Yen and Lei T'ung? And that the two camps were now in possession of his enemies? As the help did not come he was powerless; and, to add to his discomfiture, the glare of fire out on the hill told him of the seizure of his third camp. Nothing could be done, and he fled to Wak'ou Pass. The victory was all to Chang Fei

The news of the success delighted Liu Pei, and he knew then that Chang Fei's drinking had been part of a stratagem to entice his enemy into the open and defeat him

Chang Ho reached the Pass, but with the loss of more than half his army. He stood on defence and sent urgent messages to his colleague to come to his rescue.

Ts'ao Hung angrily replied, "He disobeyed my orders and marched; he has lost an important point and now he sends to me for help."

While refusing aid, he sent to urge his colleague to go out and fight. But Chang Ho too greatly feared. At length he decided upon a plan of action. He sent out two parties into ambush and said to them, "I will pretend defeat and fly. They will follow and you can cut off their retreat."

When he did march out he met Lei T'ung. The two engaged in battle and Chang presently ran away. Lei pursued and fell into the ambush. Then Chang Ho returned and slew Lei T'ung. His men went back and told Chang Fei, who came up to provoke another fight. Chang Ho again tried his stratagem, but Chang Fei did not pursue. Again and again the ruse was tried, but Chang Fei knew it was only a ruse and simply retired to his own camp.

He said to Wei Yen, "Chang Ho has compassed the death of Lei T'ung by leading him into an ambush, and he wants to inveigle me into another. What say you to meeting trick with trick?"

"But how?" said Wei Yen.

"To-morrow I will lead the army forward, you following me with some reliable soldiers. When his men come out from their ambush you can smite them, sending half your men against each party. We will secretly fill the by-roads with loads of combustibles, entice the enemy among them and start a fire. In the confusion I shall try to capture Chang Ho. So will we avenge our comrade's death."

So Chang Fei went out, and Chang Ho's men came and began to fight. After a half score bouts, Chang Ho ran away, and this time Chang Fei pursued. Ho, now fleeing, now stopping to exchange a blow or two, led Fei through the hills to a valley. Here, suddenly changing front, he halted, made a camp and offered battle.

It was now the time when he expected his hidden men to appear and surround Chang Fei. But none appeared. He knew not that his ambush had been broken up by Wei Yen's brave men and driven into the valley where the road was filled with cart-loads of combustibles, and that the valley even then was all aflame.

Then Chang Fei came to the attack, and the rout was complete. Chang Ho, fighting desperately, got through to the Wak'ou Pass and there mustered the remnant of his men. He strengthened the position and remained behind his ramparts.

Chang Fei and Wei Yen then tried to take the Pass, but day after day they failed. Chang Fei, seeing no hope of success, retired twenty li and bivouacked. From this point he sent out scouts under Wei Yen to explore the country. While going along they observed some burden-bearers, men and women, going up a very retired path, pulling down the creepers and pushing aside the grasses.

"That is the way to take Wak'ou Pass," cried Chang Fei, pointing with his whip to the wayfarers.

He ordered his soldiers not to scare the people, but to call a few gently and bring them to him. They soon had several standing before their leader, who spoke to them kindly and put them at ease.

"Whence come you?" asked Fei.

"We belong to Hanchung and are going home. We heard that you were out fighting and the high road to Langchung was blockaded, and so we have come across the Ts'angchi Torrent and Tzŭchang Mountain and down Kueichin River. We are going to our homes in Hanchung."

"Can one reach Wak'ou Pass by this road? And how far is it?"

The country people replied, "A small road leads past to the rear of the Pass from Tzŭchang Mountain."

For this piece of information Chang Fei rewarded them by taking them into his camp and giving them a good meal, and he sent off Wei Yen to make a frontal attack on the Pass while he himself with some light horse attacked it from the rear by way of Tzŭchang Mount.

Chang Ho was grieved and disappointed that his colleague sent no help, and the news of Wei Yen's attack only added to his sorrow. But he girded on his armour and was about to ride out when they told him that fires had started at half a dozen places behind the Pass. They most likely indicated soldiers. However, he went out to meet them, and, to his horror, when the flags opened out, his eyes fell on the figure of Chang Fei. Away he ran along a by-road.

But his steed was not fast, and as Chang Fei pressed him close, Chang Ho dismounted and ran up the mountain side. So he saved his life. He had, however, very few followers, and it was a small and dejected party that presently found its way into Nanch'êng. He saw Ts'ao Hung, and Ts'ao was very angry at his plight.

"I told you not to go, but you were wilful. And you gave in your written pledge. You have lost all your men, yet you do not commit suicide. What will you do next?"

Ts'ao Hung ordered the lictors to put him to death. But the Commissary General interceded.

"An army is easily raised; a leader is hard to find. Though Chang Ho is guilt, he is a great favourite with our prince. I think you should spare him. Rather give him command of another army and send him to take Chiaming Pass and so hold up the soldiers at all the stations. Hanchung will be tranquil of its own accord. If he fail a second time you can punish him for both faults."

Ts'ao Hung was satisfied to do this, and instead of dealing with his fault gave Chang Ho half a legion and told him to take the Pass.

The captains of the Pass he was to capture were Mêng Ta and Ho Hsün. They were at variance—the former desiring to go out to meet Chang Ho, the letter being in favour of defence. Mêng Ta being set on having his way went out, gave battle and was defeated. Ho Hsün reported this to the capital, where Yüan-tê at once called in the Commander-in-chief to ask advice. K'ung-ming assembled all the chief captains into the hall.

"Chiaming Pass is in danger; we must get Chang Fei from Langchung to drive off Chang Ho," said he.

Fa Chêng replied, "Chang Fei is encamped at Wak'ou, and Langchung is no less important than Chiaming. I do not think he should be recalled. Choose one among the captains to go and defeat Chang Ho."

K'ung-ming laughed, "Chang Ho is renowned in Wei; no ordinary leader will avail. Chang Fei is the only man to send, the only one equal to the task."

Then among the captains one started up crying angrily, "O Commander, why do you thus despise us? I will use what little skill I have in slaying our enemy and I will lay his head at the foot of our standard."

The speaker was the veteran Huang Chung, and all eyes centred on him.

"Friend Huang, you are bold enough, but what about your age? I fear you are no match for Chang Ho."

Huang Chung's white beard bristled, and he said, "I know I am old. But these two arms can still pull the three hundred catty bow, and the vigour of my body is not yet departed. Am I not strong enough to meet such a poor thing as Chang Ho?"

"General, you are nearly seventy; can you still hold you are not aged?"

Huang tore down the hall. Seizing one of the great swords off the rack he whirled it as if it flew. And the stiffest bow that hung on the wall he pulled till it snapped.

"Well, if you will go, who will second you?" said K'ung-ming.

"I would prefer Yen Yen. And if there is the least anxiety, —well, here is this hoary head."

Yüan-tê was pleased to let these two go to fight Chang Ho. However, Chao Yün put in a protest.

"Chang Ho has already got through Chiaming Pass, so that the fighting will be no child's play, and the loss of that Pass endangers the whole of Ichou. It is no task to set to a couple of old men."

Replied K'ung-ming, "You regard the two as too old and stupid to succeed, but I think the attainment of Hanchung depends upon these two."

Chao Yün and many others sniggered as they went from the hall; they did not agree with K'ung-ming.

In due course the veteran captain and his chosen colleague arrived at the Pass. At sight of them the defenders laughed in their hearts, thinking that in sending such a pair of dotards on such a mission K'ung-ming had slipped up in his calculations.

Huang Chung said to his colleague, "You see the behaviour of these people? They are laughing at us because we are old. Now we will do something that will win admiration from all the world."

"I should be glad to hear your orders," replied Yen Yen.

The two captains came to a decision how to act. Huang Chung led his men down below to meet Chang Ho in the open plain. Both drew up their array. When Chang Ho rode out and saw his venerable opponent he laughed in his face.

"You must be very old, and yet you are unashamed to go into the battle, eh?" said Chang Ho.

"You menial!" replied the veteran. "Do you despise me for my age? You will find my good sword, however, young enough."

So he urged forward his steed and rode at Chang Ho. The two chargers met and a score of bouts were fought. Then suddenly a great shouting came from the rear. Yen had come up and fallen upon the rear portion of Chang Ho's army Thus attacked on two sides, Chang Ho was defeated. The pursuit did not cease with nightfall, and Chang Ho was driven back near a hundred *li*. Contented with this success, Huang and his colleague went into their camp, where they rested their men for a time.

When Ts'ao Hung heard of Chang Ho's new defeat, he was going to exact the penalty. But Kuo Chun persuaded him to forbear.

"If he is pressed too hard he may take refuge in Shu," said he. "Rather send him help. You will thus keep a hold over him and prevent his desertion."

Wherefore Hsiahou Shang was sent with reinforcements. This Shang was a nephew of Hsiahou Tun. The brother of Han Yüan, Han Hao by name, was also sent. They had half a legion.

The two captains soon reached Chang Ho, and asked how now the war was going.

"That old man Huang is really a hero," said Chang; "and with Yen Yen's help he is very formidable."

"When I was at Changsha I heard the old man was very fierce. He and Wei Yen yielded the city and killed my own brother. Now that I shall meet him I can have my revenge," said Han Hao.

So he and Hsiahou Shang led out the new army.

Now, by means of spies Huang had got a thorough knowledge of the country, and Yen said, "Hereabout there is a mountain named "T'ientang" wherein Ts'ao Ts'ao has stored his supplies. If we can gain possession we shall reduce the enemy to want and we shall get Hanchung."

Huang replied, "I think so, too, and so let us do so-and-so."

Yen agreed with him and marched off with a body of men to carry out his part in the stratagem.

At news of the coming of new armies, Huang Chung marched out to meet them. He found Han Hao in front of his array, and Han began to abuse the veteran as a disgraceful old ruffian. Then he whipped up his steed and set his spear at Huang. Hsiahou Shang also rode out and took part in the combat. The veteran held them both at bay for some half score bouts and then fled. They pursued him for twenty *li*, when they reached and seized his camp. Huang, however, quickly made another defence of brushwood. Next day they renewed the pursuit, which ended with the capture of the temporary camp of the day before. And they had advanced twenty *li* further. Then they called upon Chang Ho to protect the rear camp. When Chang Ho came up he dissuaded them from continuing.

"Huang Chung has retreated before you for two days; there is some deep stratagem behind this," said Chang Ho.

Hsiahou Shang scoffed at him. "You are such a coward that you have been defeated many times. Now say no more, but let us accomplish something."

Chang Ho retired much mortified and shamed. Next day the two captains again went out to battle, and again Huang fled from them for twenty *li*. The two captains pursued as quickly as they could. The day after, Huang fled without any pretence of showing fight, except at short intervals. He got to the Pass and went on the defensive. The pursuers knocked at the very gate of the Pass and made a camp close by.

Then Mêng Ta secretly wrote to Yüan-tê that Huang Chung had been repeatedly defeated and now was in the Pass and unable to go out. Yüan-tê became alarmed and consulted K'ung-ming, who said, "The old captain is making the enemy over-confident,—to their ultimate destruction. But Chao Yün did not share this opinion, nor did many others, and Yüan-tê decided to send Liu Fêng to reinforce his aged captain. The young man came to the Pass and saw Huang, who asked him bluntly why he had come to help.

"My father heard that you have sustained several defeats, and he has sent me," said Liu Fêng.

"But I am only employing the ruse of leading on the enemy," said Huang Chung, smiling. "You will see to-night that in one battle I shall regain all the camps and capture their supplies and many horses. I have only lent the camps to them to store their supplies. To-night I shall leave Ho Hsün to guard the Pass, while General Mêng will gather up the spoils for us. Now, young Sir, you shall see the destruction of the enemy."

That same night, at the second watch, Huang left the Pass with half a legion. But now Hsiahou Shang and Han Hao, seeing no move from the Pass for many days, had become careless and so their camps were unable to resist. Their men had no time to don their armour or to saddle their horses. All the leaders did was to flee for their lives, while their men trampled each other down and were killed in great numbers. All three camps were recovered by dawn, and in them were found all sorts of military equipment. Horses and their caparisons also fell to the victors, and all the booty was carried off by Mêng Ta and stored in the Pass.

Huang Chung pressed on his victory. Liu Fêng ventured to say that the men needed repose.

"Can you seize the tiger's whelps without going into the tiger's den?" cried Huang. And he urged on his steed.

The soldiers also were eager. Chang Ho's own army was thrown into confusion by the flying men from the other armies, and he could not maintain his station, but was forced to retreat. They abandoned all their stockades and rushed to the bank of the Han Waters.

Then Chang Ho sought the two captains who had brought about the misfortune and said to them, "This is T'ientang Mountain, where our stores are. Close by is Mits'ang Mountain, where the grain is stored. They are the very source of life of the Hanchung army. Lose them and Hanchung is gone too. We must see to their security."

Hsiahou Shang said, "My uncle, Hsiahou Yüan, will look out for the defence of the mountain where the granaries are: there need be no anxiety about that as it is hard by Tingchün Mount and my brother, Hsiahou Tê, guards T'ientang Mountain. Let us go to him and help to protect that."

Chang Ho and the two captains set out at once. They reached the mountain and told Hsiahou Tê all that had happened.

"I have ten legions in camp here," replied he. "You may take some of them and recover your lost camps."

"No," replied Chang Ho. "The only proper course to defend."

Almost as they spoke the rolling of drums and the clang of gongs were heard, and the look-outs came to say that Huang Chung was near.

"The old ruffian does not know much of the art of war, after all," said Hsiahou Tê with a laugh; "he is only a brave."

"Be not mistaken; he is crafty and not only bold," said Chang Ho.

"This move is against the rules and not at all crafty. He is fresh from a long march and his men are fatigued and they are deep in an enemy's country."

"Nevertheless, be careful how you attack," said Chang Ho. "You would still do well to depend upon defence only."

"Give me three companies of good men and I will cut him to pieces," cried Han Hao.

They told off the three companies for him, and down he went into the plain. As he approached, Huang Chung arrayed his men. Liu Fêng put in a note of warning that it was late in the day to fight and the men were weary, but Huang paid little attention.

"I do not hold with your objections. This is the one God-given opportunity to make good, and it would be a sin not to take it."

So saying, the drums rolled for a great attack. Han Hao came forward with his men and the aged captain went toward him whirling his sword. In the first encounter Han Hao fell. At this the men of Shu gave a yell and went away up the hill, whereupon Chang Ho and Hsiahou Shang hastily moved out to withstand them. But a great red glare sprang into the sky from behind the hill, and a shouting arose. Hastily Hsiahou Tê led off his men to meet the danger there and went straight into the arms of Yen Yen. His arm rose, the sword fell and Hsiahou Tê dropped from his steed to rise no more.

This ambush, into which the dead captain had rushed, had been carefully prepared by Huang, who had sent Yen away before he marched himself and given him orders what to do. It was the brushwood that his men had spent the time in collecting that now sent forth the flames reaching up to the heavens and filling the valleys.

Yen Yen, after slaying Hsiahou Tê, came round the hill to aid in the attack, so that the defenders were taken both in front and rear. They could do nothing and presently left the battle-field and rushed toward Tingchun Mount to seek refuge with Hsiahou Yüan.

Meanwhile the victors took steps to hold the position they had won and sent the good news of victory to Ch'êngtu. And when the news arrived, Yüan-tê called together all his officers to rejoice.

Then said Fa Chêng, "Not long ago Chang Lu submitted to Ts'ao Ts'ao, and thereby he got possession of Hanchung quite easily. Instead of following up this by an advance on the west he left two captains to guard it and went north. That was a mistake. Now, my lord, do not make a mistake yourself, but take advantage of the present favourable position, with Chang Ho newly defeated and T'ientang captured, to attack Hanchung and you will have it at once. Once that is yours, you can train your army and amass supplies ready for a stroke against the arch-rebel himself. This God-given advantage will be confirmed to you and you should not miss it."

Both Yüan-tê and K'ung-ming saw the wisdom of this scheme and prepared to act. Chao Yün and Chang Fei were to lead the van, while Yüan-tê with K'ung-ming commanded the main army of ten legions. A day was chosen to set out, and orders were sent to everyone to keep careful guard.

It was a certain auspicious day in the seventh month of the twenty-third year that the army marched. Reaching Chiaming Pass, Huang Chung and Yen Yen were summoned and well rewarded for their services.

"People said you were old, General, but the army know you better than they, and you have rendered amazing service. Still, Tingchün Mountain is yet to be captured and Paochang is a great central store of supplies. If we could get Tingchün Mount we could be quite easy about the whole district of Yangp'ing. Think you that you are equal to taking Tingchün Mountain?"

To this harangue of Liu Pei the veteran nobly answered that he was willing to try and was ready to start when they would.

Said K'ung-ming hastily, "Do not be hasty. You are brave enough, General, but Hsiahou Yüan is a man of different stamp from Chang Ho. Hsiahou is a real strategist and tactician;

so much so that Ts'ao Ts'ao relies upon him as his defence against Hsiliang. He it was who was set to defend the capital when threatened by Ma Ch'ao. Now he is in Hanchung and Ts'ao Ts'ao puts his whole confidence in him and his skill as a leader. You have overcome Chang Ho, but it is not certain you will conquer this man. I think I must send down to Chingchou for Kuan Yü for this task."

Huang hotly replied, "Old Lien P'o was four score and yet he ate a measure of rice and ten catties of flesh, so that his vigour frightened the nobles and not one dared encroach upon the borders of Chao. I am not yet seventy. You call me old, O Commander; then I will not take any helper, but go out simply with my own three companies and we will lay Hsiahou Yüan's head at your feet."

K'ung-ming refused to allow him to go; Huang Chung insisted. At last K'ung-ming consented, but said he would send an overseer.

> They put upon his mettle the man who was to go,
> Youth's vigour may be lesser worth than age's powers, we know.

The next chapter will tell who the overseer was.

CHAPTER LXXI.

At the Capture of Tui Hill Huang Chung
Scores a Success;
on the Han Waters Chao Yun Conquers a Host.

"If you are really determined to undertake this expedition, I shall send Fa Chêng with you," said K'ung-ming to the veteran leader. "You will have to discuss everything with him. I shall also despatch supports and reinforcements."

The expedition set out. Then K'ung-ming explained to Yüan-tê that he had purposely tried to spur on the old captain that he should really exert himself, else he feared he would not do much. After this, he ordered Chao Yün to march after the first army and help, if help was needed. So long as the old man was victorious, Chao Yün was to do nothing; if he was in difficulties then he was to be rescued. Three companies also were sent out among the hills to take position at strategical points and set up many banners and make a brave show in order to spread the impression of huge forces, and so frighten and perplex the enemy. In addition, he sent to Hsiapan to tell Ma Ch'ao what part to play in the campaign; Yen Yen was to hold Langchung in place of Chang Fei.

The refugees, Chang Ho and Hsiahou Shang, reached Hsiahou Yüan's camp and told their doleful tale of the loss of T'ientang Mountain and the death of their colleague and the threatened attack. The news was sent to Ts'ao Hung, who bore it quickly to the capital.

Ts'ao Ts'ao lost no time in calling a council. Then the Historian Liu Hua said, "The loss of Hanchung would shake the whole country. You, O Prince, must not shrink from toil and hardship, but must yourself go to lead the army."

"This state of things comes of my not heeding your words before, gentle Sir," said Ts'ao Ts'ao, then repentant.

However, he hastily prepared and issued an edict to raise an army of forty legions which he would lead. The army was ready in the seventh month, the early autumn, and marched in three divisions. The leading division was under Hsiahou Tun, Ts'ao Ts'ao commanded the centre and Ts'ao Hsiu was the rear guard.

Ts'ao Ts'ao rode a white horse, beautifully caparisoned. His guards were clad in embroidered silk. They carried the huge red parasol woven of silk and gold threads. Beside him in two lines were the symbols of princely dignity, the golden melons, silver axes, stirrups, clubs, spears and lances; bannerols embroidered with the sun and moon, dragon and phœnix, were borne aloft. His escort of twenty-five thousand stout warriors led by bold officers, marched in five columns of five thousand each, under banners of the five colours, blue, yellow, red, white and black. The five companies made a brave show as they marched, each column under its own flag with men in armour and horses in caparisons all of one colour and all glittering in the sun.

As they debouched through Chang Pass, Ts'ao Ts'ao noticed in the distance a thick wood, very luxuriant, and asked those near him what it was called.

"This place is Lant'ien, the Indigo Fields," they replied. "And in that wood is the estate of the late Ts'ai Yung. His daughter, Ts'ai Yen, and her present husband, Tung Chi, live there."

Now Ts'ao Ts'ao and Ts'ai Yung had been excellent friends at one time. His daughter had been first married to Wei Taochieh. Then she was abducted and taken away to the north, where she had borne two sons. She had composed a ballad called, "Eighteen Stanzas for the Mongol Flageolet," which is well known. Ts'ao Ts'ao had been moved by pity for her sorrows and sent a messenger with a thousand tales to ransom her. The Prince of Tsohsien, overawed by Ts'ao Ts'ao's strength, had restored her to Ts'ai Yung.

Ordering his escort to march on, Ts'ao went up to the gate with only a few attendants, dismounted and enquired after the lady of the house. At this time Tung Chi was absent at his post and the lady was alone. As soon as she heard who her visitor was she hastened to welcome him and led him into the reception room. When he was seated and she had performed the proper salutations, she stood respectfully at his side. Glancing round the room, he saw a rubbing of a tablet hanging on the wall. So he got up to read it, and asked his hostess about it.

"It is a tablet of Ts'ao Ê, or the fair lady Ts'ao. In the time of the Emperor Ho (*circ.* 100 A.D.), in Shangyü there was a certain magician named Ts'ao Hsü, who could dance and sing like the very Spirit of Music. On the fifth of the fifth month he was out in a boat, and being intoxicated, fell overboard and was drowned. He had a daughter then fourteen years of age. She was greatly distressed and sought the body of her father for seven days and nights, weeping all the while. Then she threw herself into the waves, and five days later she floated to the surface with her father's body in her arms. The villagers buried them on the bank, and the magistrate reported the occurrence to the Emperor as a worthy instance of daughterly affection and remarkable piety. A later magistrate had the story inscribed by Hantan Shun in memory of the event. At that time Hantan Shun was only thirteen, but the composition of the inscription was so perfect that neither jot nor tittle could be added, and yet he had written it *currente calamo*. The stone was set up beside the grave, and both inscription and story were the admiration of all the men of that day. My father went to see it. It was evening, but in the obscurity he felt out the inscription with his fingers. He got hold of a pencil and wrote eight large characters on the reverse of the stone and, later, some person recutting the stone engraved these eight words as well.

Ts'ao Ts'ao then read the eight words; they formed an enigma. Literally they read, "yellow silk, young wife, a daughter's child, pestle and mortar."

"Can you explain?" asked Ts'ao Ts'ao of his hostess.

"No; although it is a writing of my father's, thy handmaid cannot interpret it," she replied.

Turning to the strategists of his staff, Ts'ao Ts'ao said, "Can any one of you explain it?"

All but one made no reply. The man who said he had fathomed the meaning was a Recorder named Yang Hsiu.

"Do not tell me yet; let me think it out," said Ts'ao Ts'ao.

Soon after they took leave of the lady, went out of the farm and rode on. About three *li* from the farm the meaning suddenly dawned upon Ts'ao Ts'ao, and he laughingly turned to Yang Hsiu saying, "Now, you may try."

"This is the solution of the enigma," said Yang. "Yellow silk" is silk threads of natural colour, and the character for "silk" placed beside that for "colour" forms a word meaning "finally, decidedly"; the "young wife" is a "little female," and the character for "female" with "little," or "few," placed beside it forms a word meaning "admirable, fine,"; the "daughter's child" is "daughter" and "child," which side by side make the word "good;" and a "pestle and mortar" suggest pounding together the five bitter herbs in a receptacle: the character for "receptacle" and "bitter" form a word meaning "to tell." So the four words are "Decidedly fine and well told."

Ts'ao Ts'ao was astonished at his cleverness, and said, "Just what I made it."

Those around greatly wondered at Yang's ingenuity and knowledge.

In less than a day they reached Nanchün, where Ts'ao Hung welcomed them. He told the tale of Chang Ho's misfortunes.

"To suffer defeat is no crime;" said Ts'ao Ts'ao, "that and victory are things that happen constantly in war."

"Liu Pei has sent Huang Chung to take Tingchün Mount," said Ts'ao Hung. "Hsiahou Yüan, hearing you were coming, O Prince, has been defending the position and not going out to give battle."

"But standing always on the defensive is showing weakness," said Ts'ao Ts'ao.

Thereupon he bade a man carry a *chieh*, simple authority to act, to the mountain commander and so order him to attack the enemy.

"Hsiahou Yüan is very stern and inflexible, and he may be carried too far and fall victim to some vile ruse," said Liu Hua.

Wherefore the prince wrote a letter to him to accompany the *chieh*. And when the messenger arrived and the letter was opened it read: "Every leader must exercise a combination of inflexibility and yielding. Boldness is not the only thing that counts; if he make it so, then is he a mere creature to fight. Now I am camped at Nanchün ready to watch the deeds of your admirable prowess and capacity, and all I have to say is, 'Do not disgrace your previous reputation.'"

The letter pleased the commander mightily. Having sent away the bearer, he called in Chang Ho to consult.

"The prince has a great army at Nanchün ready to destroy Liu Pei. We have been on the defence here long enough, and it is time we rendered some solid service. To-morrow I am going out to battle, and hope to capture Huang Chung."

"Your opponent combines ready resource with boldness and prevision," said Chang Ho. "Beside, he has Fa Chêng to aid him; and you must be cautious, for the country is very difficult and dangerous. You had better keep on the defensive."

"How shall we be able to look our prince in the face when other men render good service? However, you just keep the hill, and I will go out to battle."

Then an order was issued asking who would go out to reconnoitre and provoke a battle. His brother Hsiahou Shang volunteered. He was told that he was not to make a real stand, but merely to begin the fight. He was to lose and not win, for a grand ruse was ready for the enemy. He explained his plans, and Hsiahou Shang went away with a small column.

Now Huang Chung and his helper, Fa Chêng, were camped quite close to the Tingchün Mountain. They had endeavoured to entice Hsiahou Yüan out into the field to fight, but failed; to attack him as he stood in that country was very difficult. So thus far no advance had been made. But as soon as Ts'ao's men appeared and seemed to offer battle, Huang Chung was ready to march out to meet them at once. But a certain minor captain named Ch'ên Shih offered his services.

"Do not trouble yourself to move, O General," said Ch'ên Shih, "for I will go out to fight them."

Huang Chung consented, and placed three companies under Ch'ên Shih, who went out of the valley and set his army in array. And when Hsiahou Shang came up and, as arranged, merely fought a few bouts and ran away, Ch'ên Shih followed to take advantage of his success. But he was soon brought to a standstill by the rolling of logs and hurling of stones on the part of his opponents. As he turned to retire, Hsiahou Yüan brought out his men and attacked. Ch'ên Shih had no chance against them and was quickly made prisoner. Many of his men joined the enemy, but a few escaped to their own side and told Huang Chung of the misfortune.

Huang Chung at once asked advice from Fa Chêng, who said, "This Hsiahou Yüan is easily provoked to anger, and being angry he is bold without discretion. Your way now is to work up the enthusiasm of your men, then break camp and advance. Do this in a series of marches, and you will excite your enemy up to the point of giving battle, when you can capture him. They call this the 'Ruse of the Interchange of Host and Guest.'"

So Huang Chung collected all the things his men liked, and made them presents, till the sound of rejoicing filled the whole valley and the men were hot to fight. Then camp was broken, and the army marched forward a certain distance. Then they encamped. After some days' rest the manœuvre was repeated; and then again.

When tidings of the advance reached Hsiahou Yüan, he proposed to go out and fight.

"No, no," said the prudent Chang Ho. "This is a well-known ruse, and you should remain on the defensive. You will lose if you fight."

Hsiahou was not the man to stomach this moderate advice, so he sent out Hsiahou Shang to give battle. As soon as this force reached the camp of Huang Chung, he mounted and rode out to fight. In the very first bout he captured Hsiahou Shang. Those who escaped told how their leader had been captured, and Hsiahou Yüan at once sent to offer an exchange of prisoners. This was agreed to, to be effected the following day in front of both armies.

So next day both sides were arrayed in a spot where the valley widened, the two leaders on horseback beneath their respective standards. Beside each stood his prisoner. Neither was encumbered with robe or helmet, but each wore thin, simple dress. At the first beat of the drum each started to race over to his own side. Just as Hsiahou Shang reached the ranks of his own side, Huang Chung shot an arrow and wounded him in the back. The wounded man did not fall, but went on.

But Hsiahou Yüan, mad with rage, could contain himself no longer. He galloped straight at Huang Chung, which was exactly what the latter wanted to irritate him into doing. The fight that then ensued went on for a score of bouts, when suddenly the gongs clanged out from Hsiahou Yüan's side and he drew off, losing some men while doing so. When he reached his own side he asked why the gong had sounded.

"Because we saw the banners of Shu through openings in the hills in several places and we feared an ambush."

The leader believed them, and did not return to the battlefield; he simply remained defensive. Before long, Huang Chung had got quite near to the Ts'ao camp, and then he asked further advice from his colleague.

Fa Chêng pointed over to the hills, and said, "There rises a steep hill on the west of Tingchün Mountain, difficult of access, but from its summit one has a complete view of the defences of the enemy. If you can take this hill, the mountain lies in the hollow of your hand."

Huang looked up and saw the top of the hill was a small tableland and there were very few men there. So that evening he left his camp, dashed up the hill, drove out the small host there and took it. It was just opposite Tingchün Mount.

Then said Fa Chêng, "Now take up position half way up the hill, while I go to the top. When the enemy appears I will show a white flag. But you will remain quiet till the enemy become tired and remiss, when I will hoist a red flag. That will be the signal for attack.

Huang cheerfully prepared to act on this plan. In the meantime Tu Hsi, who had been driven from the hill-top, had run back and reported the loss of the hill to Hsiahou Yüan.

"With Huang Chung in occupation of that hill I simply must give battle," said he.

Chang Ho strongly dissuaded him, saying the whole thing was but a ruse of Fa Chêng's, but Hsiahou Yüan was obstinate.

"From the top of that hill the whole of our position is visible, our strength and our weakness; I must fight."

In vain were the remonstrances repeated. Hsiahou Yüan set out his men to surround the hill and then began to vent his rage at his enemy so as to incite him to give battle.

Then the white flag was hoisted. However, Hsiahou Yüan was allowed to fume and rage in vain. He tried every form of insult, but no one appeared. In the afternoon the men became weary and dispirited. Plainly their eagerness had gone; and Fa Chêng unfurled the red flag.

Then the drums rolled out, and the men shouted till the earth seemed to shake as the hoary old leader rode out and led his men down the slope with a roar as of an earthquake. Hsiahou Yüan was too surprised to defend himself. His chief enemy rushed straight to his standard and with a thundering shout raised his sword and cleft Hsiahou Yüan through between the head and shoulders so that he fell in two pieces.

> Hoary headed is he, but he goes up to battle;
> Gray haired, yet recklessly mighty;
> With his strong arms he bends the bow,

The arrows fly.
With the swiftness of the wind he rides,
The white sword gleams.
The sound of his voice is as the roar of a tiger,
His steed is fleet as a dragon in flight.
Victory is his and its rich rewards,
For he extends the domain of his lord.

At the death of their captain, the soldiers fled for their lives, and Huang captured the mount. Chang Ho came out to oppose him, but, attacked at two points by Huang Chung and Ch'ên Shih, he could not stand. He lost the day and fled. However, before he had gone far, another cohort flashed out from the hills and barred his way. And the leader was Chao Yün. Confused and uncertain what to do, he led his men toward Tingchün Mount. But a body of soldiers came out to stop him and said that the mount was in the hands of the enemy. So he and Tu Hsi joined their forces and went to the Han Waters, where they camped.

Thence they sent to tell Ts'ao Ts'ao of their defeat. At the news of the death of his favourite, he uttered a great cry and then he understood the prediction of the soothsayer, Kuan Lu, that the *sortes* showed opposition. It was the twenty-fourth year of the period, the yellow boar had met the tiger and the year of the cycle was the thirty-sixth. The expedition had suffered a loss indeed by the death of a general, and the death had taken place at the mount known as "Army Halt." The affection between Ts'ao Ts'ao and his captain had been very close.

Ts'ao Ts'ao sent to enquire the whereabouts of Kuan Lu, but no one knew.

Ts'ao nourished feelings of resentment against the slayer of his friend, and he led his army out against Tingchün Mount to avenge his death. Hsü Huang led the van. When the army reached the Han Waters, Chang Ho and Tu Hsi joined them.

They said to Ts'ao Ts'ao, "This mount is lost. Before marching farther, the stores in Granary Hill should be moved north."

And Ts'ao Ts'ao agreed.

Huang Chung cut off the head of Hsiahou Yüan and took it to Yüan-tê when he reported his victory. For his services he was rewarded with the title "Conqueror of the West," and great banquets were given in his honour.

While these were going on, his colleague, Ch'ên Shih, brought the news of Ts'ao Ts'ao's army of twenty legions on the way to avenge his friend's loss; and the supplies on Granary Hill were being moved north.

Then said K'ung-ming, "Ts'ao Ts'ao is certainly short of supplies. If we can burn what he has and destroy his baggage train he will have but little spirit left to fight."

"I am willing to undertake the task," said Huang Chung.

"Remember Ts'ao Ts'ao is a different sort of man from your latest victim."

Yüan-tê said, "After all, Hsiahou Yüan was but a bold warrior. It would have been ten times better to have killed Chang Ho."

"I will go and kill him," said the aged one, firing up.

"Then go with Chao Yün," said K'ung-ming; "act in concert and see who can do best."

Huang Chung agreed to this condition, and Chang Cho was sent as second.

Soon after the army had marched out, Chao Yün asked of his colleague what plan he had prepared against Ts'ao Ts'ao's army of twenty legions in their ten camps, and how the stores of grain and forage were to be destroyed.

"I am going to lead," said Huang Chung.

"No wait; I am going first," said Chao Yün.

"But I am the senior leader; you are only my second," said Huang Chung.

"No; you and I are equal in responsibility and both anxious to render good service. We are no rivals. Let us cast lots for who is to lead the way."

They did so, and the aged one gained precedence.

"Since you have won the right to make the first attempt, you must let me help you," said Chao Yün. "Now let us decide upon a fixed time, and if you have returned by that time I shall not need to stir. But if at that time you have not come back then I shall come to reinforce you."

"That suits me admirably," said Huang Chung.

So they decided upon noon as the time; and Chao Yün went back to his own camp, where he called in his next in command and said, "My friend Huang is going to try to burn the stores to-morrow. If he has not returned at noon I am to go to aid him. You are to guard our camp, which is in a dangerous place by the river, but you are not to move out unless compelled."

Huang Chung went back to his camp and said to his senior captain, Chang, "I have slain one leader and cowed another. I am going to destroy the enemy's store of grain to-morrow, taking with me most of the men. You are to come and assist me. A meal for the men is to be ready about midnight to-night, and we shall move at the fourth watch. We shall march to the foot of their hill, capture Chang Ho and then start the fire."

All being ready, they set out—Huang Chung leading—and stole across the Han Waters to the foot of the hills. As the sun got up out of the east, they saw before them mountains of grain and only a few men on watch. These fled at first sight of the men of Shu. The horsemen dismounted and began to collect brushwood and pile it round the grain heaps. Just as they were starting the fire, there appeared a cohort led by Chang Ho, who at once began a fight with Huang Chung. Then Ts'ao Ts'ao heard of the fight and sent Hsü Huang to help. He came up in the rear, and Huang Chung was surrounded. Chang Cho with a small company tried to get away to their camp, but they were intercepted by Wên P'ing, and more men coming up by the rear he also was surrounded. Both were in difficulties.

Meanwhile, time passed and noon came with no news of Huang Chung. Wherefore Chao Yün girded on his armour, took three companies with him and went to his aid. Just as he was leaving he again warned Chang I to keep good watch.

"Guard the camp most carefully; see that you have archers and crossbow men on both sides."

"Yes, yes," said Chang.

Chao Yün rode off, spear in hand, and went out to give battle where he could find the enemy. Soon he fell in with one of Wên P'ing's companies: these were easily disposed of. Then he came to the real press. A cohort barred his way, led by Chiao Ping of Wei.

"Where are the soldiers of Shu?" cried Chao Yün.

"All killed," cried Chiao Ping.

Chao Yün angrily dashed forward and thrust Chiao Ping through so that he died. The cohort scattered, and Chao Yün went on to the foot of the north hills, where he found Huang Chung surrounded. With a yell he dashed at the encircling ring, thrusting this way and shoving that, so that every one shrank and recoiled before him. The mighty spear laid low his opponents as the whirlwind scatters the petals of the wild pear tree till they lie on the bosom of the earth like snowflakes. Panic seized Chang Ho and Hsü Huang, so that they dared not stand in his way, and thus Chao Yün fought his way through and rescued his fellow warrior. Then they fought their way out and none could withstand them.

Ts'ao Ts'ao had been watching the course of the fighting from a high place, and when he saw a doughty warrior forcing his way into the press and all going down before him he asked of his officers if they knew who the hero was.

"That is Chao Yün of Ch'angshan," replied one who knew him.

"So the hero of Tangyang is still alive," said Ts'ao Ts'ao.

He gave general orders to his men not to attack Chao Yün without being sure of success, no matter where they met him.

Having rescued his colleague and got clear of the battle, some-one pointed out Chang Cho hemmed in on a hill not far off. Wherefore Chao Yün went to his relief before going back to his own camp. He had little need to fight, for Ts'ao Ts'ao's soldiers no sooner saw the name emblazoned on the banners than they fled without more ado.

But it filled Ts'ao Ts'ao with rage to see his men falling away before Chao Yün, who marched on as though no one would think of standing in his way, and he went in pursuit himself with his officers.

Chao Yün reached his own camp, where he was welcomed by Chang I. But a cloud of dust was seen in the distance, and they knew Ts'ao Ts'ao was in that cloud and coming upon them.

"Let us bar the gates while we make preparation," said Chang I.

"Do not bar the gates," said Chao Yün. "Have you never heard of my exploit at Tangyang, when I laughed at Ts'ao's many legions? Now that I have an army at my back and captains to help, what is there to fear?"

Then he placed the archers and the bowmen in a covered position outside, while he threw down all the weapons and flags within. And no drums beat. But he himself, alone, stood outside the gate of the camp.

It was dusk when Chang Ho and Hsü Huang neared the camp of the men of Shu. They saw that the ensigns and weapons had been overthrown, and no drums beat at their approach. They also saw the one figure of the doughty warrior at the gate, and then they halted and dared advance no farther. While they hesitated, Ts'ao Ts'ao arrived and urged his army to march quicker. They answered with a shout and made a dash forward—but they saw the one figure at the gate, and every man stood still. And before long, man by man they turned about and went away. Then Chao Yün beckoned to his men to come out of the moat, and the archers and bowmen began to shoot. The men of Ts'ao knew not in the dusk how many their enemies were, but terror seized upon them and they ran, each trying to be first. And as they ran the drums rolled and the men shouted and pursued, till the flight became a perfect rout and a confused mass of men reached the banks of the Han Waters. The press continuing, many were forced into the river and were drowned.

The three captains of Shu followed close on the heels of the routed army, and while Ts'ao Ts'ao was making off with all speed, two other captains of Shu came along and set fire to all the army stores of food and forage. Then Ts'ao Ts'ao abandoned the northern hill stores and set out hastily for Nanchün. Chang Ho and Hsü Huang could make no stand, and they also abandoned their camps, which Chao Yün at once occupied. Beside the stores of food, the victors collected countless weapons along the banks of the river.

They sent news of the victory to Liu Pei, who came with K'ung-ming to the scene of the victory, and there they heard the full story of Chao Yün's prowess. And Yüan-tê was glad, and when he had seen the steepness and difficulties of the surrounding hills and understood the fine deeds of valour that had been done, he turned to K'ung-ming and said, "Truly, the man is brave all through."

> Behold Chao Yün, the warrior of Ch'angshan,
> Whose whole body is valour;
> Formerly he fought at Ch'angpan,
> And his courage to-day is no less.
> He rushes into the array to manifest his heroism;
> Surrounded by his enemies,
> He is dauntless and daring.
> Devils howl and spirits cry,
> The sky is afaid and earth trembles.
> Such is Chao Yün, the brave,
> Whose whole body is valour.

For his services Yüan-tê gave Chao Yün the title of "Tiger Terror." And the men of his army were rewarded and there was banqueting to a late hour.

Soon it was reported that Ts'ao Ts'ao was coming again down through Hsieh Valley to try to capture the Han Waters. But Yüan-tê laughed, saying, "He will not succeed, for I think that we shall gain command of the river."

Then he led his army west of the river to oppose him. When Ts'ao Ts'ao drew near he sent out Hsü Huang to lead the van and open the battle. A certain Wang P'ing, who said he knew the country, offered to go as well, and he was sent as second in command.

Ts'ao Ts'ao camped on the no h of Tingchün Mount, and his advanced guard marched away making for the River Han. And when they reached the bank, Hsü Huang gave orders to cross to the other side.

"To cross the river is well," said his second, "but what if you have to retreat?"

"When Han Hsin made his array with a river in his rear, he said that out of the place of death one could return to life."

"You are mistaken now. The cases are not the same, for then Han Hsin knew his opponents were unskilful. Have you reckoned upon the skill of our opponents, Chao Yün and Huang Chung?"

"You may lead the footmen to hold the enemy while I destroy them with the horsemen," said Hsü Huang.

Then bridges were built and the army crossed.

> A man of Wei blindly quotes Han Hsin,
> In a minister of Shu who whould recognise another Chang Liang?

Who won the victory will next be revealed.

CHAPTER LXXII.

CHUKO LIANG'S WIT TAKES HANCHUNG;
TS'AO A-MAN'S ARMY RETIRES UP HSIEHKU.

In spite of the most earnest dissuasion, Hsü Huang crossed the river and camped. Huang Chung and Chao Yün asked to be allowed to go against the host of Ts'ao Ts'ao, and Yüan-tê gave his consent.

Then said Huang Chung, "Hsü Huang has been bold enough to come; we will not go out against him till evening, when his men are fatigued. Then we will fall upon him one on either side."

Chao Yün consented, and each retired to a stockade. Hsü Huang appeared and for a long time tried to draw them into a fight, but they refused to go forth. Then Hsü ordered his bowmen to begin to shoot straight before them, and the arrows and bolts fell in the Shu camp.

Huang said, "He must be thinking of retreat or he would not shoot thus. Now is our time to smite him."

Then the scouts reported that the rearmost bodies of the enemy had begun to retreat. The drums of Shu rolled a deafening peal and the armies came to the attack, one on either side, and the double fight began. Defeated, the flying soldiers were forced to the Han Waters, where many were drowned. But their leader escaped, and when he got back to camp he blamed his colleague Wang P'ing for not having come to his aid

"Had I done so, the camps would have been left unguarded," said Wang P'ing. "I tried to dissuade you from going, but you would not hear me, and you brought about this reverse yourself."

Hsü Huang in his wrath tried to slay Wang, but he escaped to his own camp. In the night a fire broke out and great confusion reigned in the lines. Hsü ran away, but Wang crossed the river and surrendered to Chao Yün, who led him to Yüan-tê. He told Yüan-tê all about the Han Waters and the country near by.

"I shall surely capture Hanchung now that you are here to help me, friend Wang," said Yüan-tê.

He gave Wang P'ing an appointment as a supernumerary leader and guide.

Wang P'ing's defection, when Hsü Huang told him, made Ts'ao Ts'ao very angry. He placed himself at the head of a force and tried to retake the bank of the river. Chao Yün, thinking his men too few, retired to the west side, and the two armies lay on opposite sides of the stream. Yüan-tê and his adviser came down to view the position. The latter saw in the upper course of the stream a hill which might well screen a thousand men, so he returned to camp, called in Chao Yün and bade him lead half that number, with drums and horns, and place them in ambush behind the hill, to await certain orders which would come some time during the night or at dawn. When he heard a detonation he was not to appear, only give a long roll of the drums at every report.

Chao Yün departed to play his part in the drama, while K'ung-ming went to a hill whence he could overlook the scene.

When next the men of Ts'ao approached the camp of Shu and offered battle not a man came out, nor was an arrow or a bolt shot. They retired without any result. But in the depths of the night, when all the lights in the camp were extinguished and all appeared tranquil and restful, K'ung-ming exploded a bomb, and at once Chao Yün beat his drums and blared his trumpets. Ts'ao Ts'ao's men awoke in alarm, thinking it was a night raid. They rushed out, but there was no enemy, and as the hubbub ceased they went back to sleep. Soon after there was another bomb, and again the drums and the trumpets seeming to shake the earth itself, and the fearsome roar echoing along the valleys and from the hills again scared Ts'ao's soldiers. Thus the night passed in constant alarms. The next night was the same, and the next. On the fourth day Ts'ao broke up his camp, marched his men thirty *li* to the rear and pitched his camp in a clear, wide space among the hills.

K'ung-ming was pleased at the result of his ruse. Said he, smiling, "Ts'ao is skilled in war, but still he is not proof against all deceitful tricks."

The men of Shu then crossed the river and camped with the stream behind them. When Yüan-tê asked the next move he was told, but also told to keep the plan a secret.

Seeing his enemy thus encamped, Ts'ao Ts'ao became doubtful and anxious, and, to bring things to a decision, he sent a written declaration of war, to which K'ung-ming replied that they would fight a battle on the morrow.

On the morrow the armies faced each other half way between the two camps in front of The Hill of Five Frontiers, and there they arrayed. Ts'ao Ts'ao presently rode up and stood beside his banner; with his officers right and left and the dragon and phœnix banners fluttering in the wind. His drums rolled thrice, and then he summoned Liu Pei to a parley. Yüan-tê rode out supported by his officers. Then Ts'ao insolently flourished his whip and vilified his opponent.

"Liu Pei, you have forgotten kindness and lost the sense of right; you are a rebel against the government."

Yüan-tê answered, "I am related to the imperial family, and I hold an edict authorising me to seize all rebels. You have dared to lift up your hand against the Empress, made yourself a prince and arrogantly presume to an imperial chariot. If you are not a rebel, what are you?"

Then Ts'ao ordered Hsü Huang out to give battle, and Liu Fêng went to meet him. As the combat began, Yüan-tê retired within the ranks of his array. Liu Fêng was no match for his opponent, and fled. Ts'ao Ts'ao issued an order to capture Liu Pei. At this the army of the king of the west country uttered one great roar of rage. Then Ts'ao's men came surging on. The men of Shu fled toward the river abandoning everything, even throwing aside their weapons, which littered the road. But as Ts'ao's men pressed forward, he suddenly clanged the gongs, called a halt and drew off.

"Why did you call us off, O Prince, just as we were on the point of success?"

"Because I saw the enemy had encamped with the river in their rear, which was very suspicious. They also abandoned their steeds and weapons, which made me doubt. Wherefore I could only retire. But retain your armour. Let not a man take off his harness on pain of death. Now retire as quickly as you can march."

As Ts'ao Ts'ao turned about to retire, K'ung-ming hoisted the signal to attack, and the retreating soldiers were harassed on every side both night and day till they were all disordered. Ts'ao Ts'ao ordered his army to take refuge in Nanch'êng.

Presently they saw flames rising all around, and soon it was known that their city of refuge was in the hands of their enemies. Disappointed and saddened, Ts'ao Ts'ao bade them march to Yangp'ing Pass. But Yüan-tê with the main army followed them to Paochou in the Nanch'êng district and there pacified the people and restored confidence.

"Ts'ao Ts'ao was exceedingly quickly overcome this time," said Liu Pei; "how was that?"

"He has always been of a suspicious nature," said K'ung-ming, "and that has led to many failures although he is a good leader of men. I have defeated him by playing upon his doubts."

"He is rather weakened now," said Liu Pei. "Can you not devise a plan to drive him away finally?"

"That is all thought out."

"Next Chang Fei and Wei Yen were sent along two different roads to cut off Ts'ao Ts'ao's supplies. Two other cohorts were bidden to go and fire the hills. All these four had natives of the place to act as guides and show the way.

The scouts sent out from Yangp'ing Pass returned to report that the roads far and near were blocked by the men of Shu and every place seemed to be burning. They had not seen any soldiers. Ts'ao Ts'ao knew not what to do. Then they told him that his stores were being plundered by Chang Fei and Wei Yen. At this, he called for a volunteer to drive off the plunderers; and Hsü Ch'u offered. He was given a company of veterans, and went up to act as escort of the grain wagons. The officers in charge of the transport were very glad to get a guard of such renown.

"Except for you, O General, the grain could never reach Yangp'ing."

They entertained Hsü Ch'u with the wine and food on the carts; and he ate and drank copiously, so that he became very intoxicated. And in that state he insisted on marching, urging the convoy to start at once.

"The sun has nearly set," said the transport officers, "and the road near Paochou is bad and dangerous, so that we cannot pass there at night."

"I can face any danger," boasted the drunken captain; "I am brave as a myriad men put together. What do you think I fear? Beside, there is a good moon to-night, just the sort of thing to take grain carts along by."

Hsü Ch'u took the lead, sword in hand. By the second watch they were passing Paochou. About half the train had passed when the rolling drums and the blare of horns came down to them through a rift in the hills. It was soon followed by the appearance of a cohort led by Chang Fei. With spear ready, he came racing down straight for Hsü Ch'u, who, whirling his sword, dashed to the front to meet him.

But Hsü Ch'u was too drunk to stand against such a warrior. After a few bouts he received a spear thrust in the shoulder, turned round in his saddle and fell from his horse. His men rushed to his help, and they carried him away as they retreated, while Chang Fei took the whole transport train of fodder and forage away to his own camp.

The defeated escort carried their wounded leader back to Ts'ao's camp, where he was placed in the care of physicians. Then Ts'ao himself led out his army to fight a decisive battle with the men of Shu. Yüan-tê went out to meet him, and, when both sides were arrayed, Liu Fêng went out to challenge. Ts'ao at once let loose a torrent of taunts and reproaches.

"Seller of shoes, you are always sending out this pretended son of yours to fight for you. If I only call my youngster, your so-called son will be chopped to mincemeat."

These words enraged Liu Fêng, who raised his spear and galloped toward Ts'ao. Ts'ao bade Hsü Huang do battle with the young man, and Fêng at once ran away. Ts'ao led on his legions, but he was harassed by the explosion of bombs, the beating of drums and the blare of trumpets that came from every side. He concluded that he was being led into an ambush, and he hastened to retire. The retreat was unfortunate, for the soldiers trampled upon each other and many were killed. Anon they all ran off to Yangp'ing Pass as quickly as they could.

But the men of Shu came right up to the walls of the city, and some burned the east gate while others shouted at the west. Others, again, burned the north gate while drums rolled at the south. Leader and led were alike harassed and frightened, and presently they left the Pass and ran away. They were pursued and sore smitten.

The road to safety was not easy. In one direction Chang Fei barred the way, while Chao Yün and Huang Chung came and attacked from different points. Ts'ao's army lost many men, and he was severely defeated. His officers gathered about him and took him off toward Hsiehku. Here a great cloud of dust was seen in the distance.

"If that is an ambush it is the last of me," sighed Ts'ao.

The soldiers came nearer, and then Ts'ao recognised not a enemy but his second son, Chang. As a lad Chang was a good horseman and an expert archer. He was more powerful than most men and could overcome a wild beast with his bare hands. Ts'ao did not approve of the young man's bent, and often warned him to study instead.

"You do not study, but only love your bow and your horse; this is the courage of a mere person. Think you that this makes for an honourable career?"

But Chang replied, "The really noble man ought to imitate such grand men as Wei Ching and Ho Ch'u-ping. They won their reputation in the Shamo Desert, where they led a mighty host able to overrun the whole world and go anywhere. What have I to do with scholarship?"

Ts'ao Ts'ao used to ask his sons what career they found admirable, and Chang always replied that he would be a leader of armies.

"But what should a leader be like?" asked Ts'ao.

"He should be inbued with firmness and courage; never turn aside from a difficulty, but be in the van of his officers and men. Rewards should be certain; and so should punishments."

Ts'ao Ts'ao smiled with pleasure.

In the twenty-third year of the period, Wu Huan of Taichün revolted, and Ts'ao Ts'ao sent this son with five legions to suppress him. Just as he was leaving, his father read him a homily on his duty.

"At home we are father and son, but when a task is given you you have to consider your duty as a servant of your ruler. The law knows no kindness, and you must beware."

When the expedition reached the north of Tai he led the array and smote as far as Sangkan, and peace was restored. He had lately heard that his father was at Yangp'ing Pass, and had come to help him to fight.

His coming greatly pleased his father, who said, "Now that my callow-bearded son has arrived, we can destroy Liu Pei for certain."

Then the army was marched back again and pitched camp at Hsiehku.

Someone told Yüan-tê of the arrival of Ts'ao Chang, and he asked for a volunteer to go out against him. Liu Fêng offered. Mêng Ta also desired to go, and Yüan-tê decided to let both go.

"Vie with each other," said he.

Each captain had half a legion, and Liu Fêng led the way. Ts'ao Chang rode out and engaged him, and in the third bout Fêng was overcome and ran off. Then Mêng Ta advanced, and a battle was just beginning when he saw that Ts'ao's men were in confusion. The cause was the sudden coming of Ma Ch'ao and Wu Lan. Before the enemy had recovered from the panic, Mêng Ta attacked on another side. Ma Ch'ao's men, who had been nursing their courage for a long time, fought brilliantly, so that none could withstand their onslaught, and they won the day. But in combat with Ts'ao Chang, Wu Lan received a spear thrust and fell.

After a great fight, Ts'ao Ts'ao's army was led off and went into camp at Hsiehku. Here Ts'ao remained many days, prevented from advancing by Ma Ch'ao and fearing ridicule if he should retreat. One day, while he was anxiously trying to decide what to do, his cook sent in some chicken broth. He noticed in the broth some chicken tendons, and this simple fact led him into a train of reflection. He was still deep in thought when Hsiahou Tun entered his tent to ask the watchword for that night. Ts'ao Ts'ao at once involuntarily replied, "Chicken tendon."

The word was passed on in orders. When the Recorder Yang Hsiu saw the order that the watchword was "chicken tendon" he told all his men to pack up their belongings ready for the march. One who saw this went and told Hsiahou Tun, who sent for Yang Hsiu and asked why he had packed up.

He replied, "By to-night's orders I see that the prince is soon going to retire. 'Chicken tendons' are tasteless things to eat, and yet it is a pity to waste them. Now if we advance we cannot conquer, and if we retire we fear we shall look ridiculous. There being no advantage here, the best course is to retire. You will certainly see the Prince of Wei retreat before long. I have made my preparations so as not to be hurried and confused at the last moment."

"You seem to know the prince's inmost heart," said Hsiahou Tun, and he bade his servants pack. The other captains seeing this, also made preparations for departure.

Ts'ao Ts'ao's mind was too perturbed for sleep. In the night he got up, took a steel battle-axe in his hand and wandered privily through the camp. When he got to Hsiahou Tun's tents he saw everything packed and ready for a move. Much surprised, he made his way back to his own tent and sent for that officer.

"Why is everything in your camp packed as if ready for the march?"

"Yang Hsiu, the Recorder, seems to have private knowledge of the Prince's design to retire," said he.

Ts'ao Ts'ao summoned Yang Hsiu and questioned him, and Yang replied with the chicken tendon incident.

"How dare you invent such a story and disturb the hearts of my army?"

Ts'ao called in his lictors and told them to take the man away and behead him and hang his head at the camp gate.

The victim was a man of acute and ingenious mind, but inclined to show off. His lack of restraint over his tongue had often wounded Ts'ao Ts'ao's susceptibilities. Once Ts'ao Ts'ao was having a pleasance laid out, and when it was completed he went to inspect the work. He uttered no word of praise or blame; he just wrote the word "alive" on the gate and left. Nobody could guess what he meant till Yang Hsiu heard of it.

"Gate" with "alive" inside it makes the word for "wide," said he. "The minister thinks the gates are too wide."

Thereupon they rebuilt the outer walls on an altered plan. When complete, Ts'ao Ts'ao was asked to go and see it. And he was then delighted.

"But who guessed what I meant?" said he.

"Yang Hsiu," replied his men.

Ts'ao Ts'ao thereafter lauded Yang's ingenuity, but in his heart he feared.

Another time Ts'ao Ts'ao received a box of cream cheese from Saipei (Mongolia). Ts'ao Ts'ao just scribbled three words on the top and left it on the table. The words seemed to have no meaning. But Yang Hsiu happened to come in, saw the box and at once handed a spoonful of the contents to each guest in the room. When Ts'ao asked why he did this, he explained that that was the interpretation of the words on the box, which, resolved into primary symbols, read, "Each man a mouthful."

"Could I possibly disobey your orders?" said he.

Ts'ao Ts'ao laughed with the others, but hatred was in his heart.

Ts'ao lived in constant fear of assassination, and said to his attendants, "Let none of you come near me when I am sleeping, for I am like to slay people in my dreams."

One day he was enjoying a siesta, and his quilt fell off. One of the attendants saw it and hastened to cover him again. Ts'ao Ts'ao suddenly leaped from the couch, cut down the intruder with his sword and lay down again to sleep. Some time after he awoke, simulated surprise and asked who had killed his attendant. When they told him, he wept aloud for the dead man and had him buried in a fine grave. Most people thought that Ts'ao Ts'ao had slain the man while asleep, but Yang Hsiu knew better, and at the funeral of the victim he remarked, "The minister was in no dream, but the gentleman in him was asleep."

This only increased the hatred.

Ts'ao Ts'ao's third son, Chih, took great delight in Yang Hsiu's cleverness and often invited him, when they would talk the whole night.

When Ts'ao Ts'ao was considering the nomination of his heir and desired to name Chih, Ts'ao P'ei got to hear of the proposal to set him aside in favour of his younger brother, so he secretly requested the Master of the Court Singers, Wu Chih, to come and discuss this matter. Then fearing that someone might see his visitor, he got a large basket made, in which his friend was smuggled into the palace. He gave out that the basket contained rolls of silk. Yang Hsiu heard the truth and informed Ts'ao Ts'ao, who sent men to watch at the gates. Ts'ao P'ei, in alarm, told Wu Chih, who told him not to be afraid but to fill a basket actually with rolls of silk on the morrow and have it carried in as before. The searchers peeped into the basket and found the rolls of silk. They told Ts'ao Ts'ao the result of their search, and he began to think Yang Hsiu was plotting against his son. This also added to his hatred.

Another time Ts'ao, wishing to compare the abilities of his two sons P'ei and Chih, told them both to go out of the city, at the same time ordering the gate wardens to forbid their exit. Ts'ao P'ei first came to the gate, was stopped by the wardens and returned to his palace. But his brother Chih consulted Yang Hsiu, who said, "You have received orders from the prince to go out; simply cut down any who may try to prevent you."

When Ts'ao Chih went to the gate and was stopped, he shouted out to the wardens, "I have the prince's order to go out; dare you stop me?"

He slew the man who would have prevented him. Wherefore Ts'ao Ts'ao considered his younger son the more able. But when some other person told him that the device came from Yang Hsiu, he was angry and took a dislike to his son Chih.

Yang Hsiu also used to coach Chih in preparing replies to likely questions, which were learned by heart and quoted when necessary. Ts'ao Ts'ao was always asking this son his opinion on military matters, and Chih always had a fluent reply ready. His father was not without suspicions, which were turned into certainties when the eldest son gave his father the written replies which he had bribed a servant to filch from his brother's apartments. Ts'ao Ts'ao was quite angry.

"How dare he throw dust in my eyes like this?" said Ts'ao Ts'ao.

Yang Hsiu very nearly lost his life for his share in that business. Now sending him to execution on the charge of destroying the morale of the soldiers was only a subterfuge. Yang Hsiu was but thirty-four when he met his end.

> Talented was Yang Hsiu,
> Born of an illustrious stock,
> His pen traced wonderful characters,
> In his breast were beautiful words.
> When he talked, his hearers were astonished,
> His alert responses overpast every one.
> He died because of misdirected genius
> And not because he foretold retreat.

Ts'ao Ts'ao thus put to death the prime mover and simulated anger against Hsiahou Tun. He threatened to execute him, but listened to those who begged him to show mercy.

"Get out of this!" said he.

Next he issued an order to advance on the morrow. The army moved out of the valley and came face to face with the men of Shu led by Wei Yen. He summoned Wei to surrender, but received abuse and contumely in return.

P'ang Tê went out to fight Wei Yen, but while the combat was in progress fires broke out in Ts'ao Ts'ao's camp and a soldier came flying to say that the rear and centre camps had been seized by Ma Ch'ao. Fearing lest this should lead to a rout, he drew his sword and stood before the army crying out, "Death for any officer who flinches!"

Wherefore they pressed forward valiantly, and Wei Yen, pretending defeat, retreated. Having driven back this army, Ts'ao Ts'ao gave the signal to turn toward camp and fight with Ma Ch'ao. He took up his station on the top of a hill whence he could survey the field. Suddenly a cohort appeared just below him, and the leader cried, "Wei Yen is here!" Wei fitted an arrow to his bow, shot and wounded Ts'ao Ts'ao just in the raphe of his lip. He turned and fell. Wei Yen threw aside his bow, seized his sword and came charging up the hill to finish his enemy. But with a shout P'ang Tê flashed in.

"Spare my lord!" cried he.

He rushed up and drove Wei Yen backward. Then they took Ts'ao Ts'ao away. Ma Ch'ao also retired, and the wounded prince slowly returned to his own camp.

As has been said, Ts'ao Ts'ao was wounded full in the face, and the arrow knocked out two of his front teeth. When in the hands of the physicians he lay thinking over Yang Hsiu's words. In a repentant mood he had the remains decently interred.

· Then he gave the order to retreat. P'ang Tê was the rear guard. Ts'ao Ts'ao set out homeward in a padded carriage, escorted by his Tiger Guard.

Before they had gone far, there was an alarm of fire and ambush. The soldiers were all fear-stricken.

'Twas something like the danger once at T'ung Kuan met,
Or like the fight at Red Cliff which Ts'ao could n'er forget.

How Ts'ao Ts'ao fared will next be told.

CHAPTER LXXIII.

Yüan-tê Becomes Prince of Hanchung;
Yün-ch'ang Attacks and Occupies Hsiangyang.

When Ts'ao Ts'ao retired to Hsiehku, K'ung-ming considered it to mean the abandonment of his attempt to acquire possession of Hanchung, and he sent out several parties to harass and hasten his retreat by guerilla attacks. For this reason the retreating army had to keep on the move. Beside, he was suffering from his wound, and marched as hurriedly as possible. But it was a dejected army. The leading legions once encountered fire on both flanks, which had been raised by men placed in ambush while Ma Ch'ao's main force kept driving the army before it. Every man in the Ts'ao army was dispirited, and there was no more courage in them. They pressed forward day and night alike without halting to rest. It was only after reaching Chingchao that they had some repose.

Then Yüan-tê sent Liu Fêng, Mêng Ta and Wang P'ing to take Shangyung. Shên T'ang and his colleagues, knowing that Ts'ao Ts'ao had retreated, offered their submission. After confidence had been restored among the people, Yüan-tê rewarded his army generously, and they were all joyful.

It was after this that the general body of the officers decided to urge Yüan-tê to assume the title of "Emperor," but they dared not tell him so. However, they sent up a petition to K'ung-ming, who replied that he had already decided on this course. So he and Fa Chêng headed a deputation that went in to see their lord.

They said, "Now that Ts'ao Ts'ao really holds the reins of authority the people are without a king. Our lord, your kindness and sense of justice have spread throughout the empire. You have restored peace over this 'Land of Streams,' and your becoming Emperor would be according to God's will and the desire of the people. Then by right and title you could destroy rebels. This matter should not be delayed and we pray you to choose the auspicious day."

But Yüan-tê evinced great surprise, and replied, "Your words, O Commander of the Army, are wrong. Although I am of the imperial house, yet I am but a minister; and to do this thing would be rebellion against Han."

K'ung-ming replied, "Not so. To-day the empire is riven and many of the bolder spirits have seized upon, and claim

the rule of, various portions. The talented of the empire
and the virtuous among officers, who have risked death and
lost their lives in serving those above them, all desire to have
the opportunity of serving an Emperor and doing service for
a Throne. Now, if you insist on modestly maintaining your
righteous way I fear that you will lose popular support My
lord, I would that you should reflect upon this."

"But you desire me to usurp a place of great honour in the
state, and I dare not. Let there be more delay and discussion."

But with one voice they said, "Our lord, if you reject this
the hearts of the people will turn from you."

"My lord," said K'ung-ming, "you have made rectitude
your motto all your life. If you really object to the most
honoured title, then, since you have Chingchou and Hsiangyang, take the title temporarily of 'Prince of Hanchung.'"

"Gentlemen, though you may desire to honour me by the
title of 'Prince,' yet, without an edict from the Emperor, such
action would be usurpation."

Said K'ung-ming, "The time demands recognition of the
actual state of authority, and not a rigid adherence to all the
rules of propriety."

And Chang Fei roared out, "All sorts of people with all
sorts of names are making themselves rulers; how much more
ought you, O Brother, who are of the dynastic stock? It ought
not to be 'Prince of Hanchung' but 'Emperor.' What
prevents it?"

"Brother, say no more," said Yüan-tê, roughly.

"My lord," said K'ung-ming, "it is fitting to follow political
changes and suit one's conduct to circumstances. Wherefore
first take the princedom and then memorialise the Throne."

As there seemed no option, Yüan-tê listened and complied.
In the twenty-fourth year (219 A.D.), in the seventh month,
an altar was set up at Mienyang (in Hupeh), square and nine
li about, which was set around with the proper flags and
banners and symbols, and thereon, in the presence of all his
officers assembled according to their rank, and at the request
of the two ministers Hsü Ching and Fa Chêng, Yüan-tê received
the head dress and seal of a prince. Then he took his seat,
facing the south as a ruler should, and received the salutes
and felicitations of all his officers as Prince of Hanchung.

And his son Liu Ch'an was nominated his heir-apparent.

Hsü Ching was given the title of Royal Preceptor; Fa
Chêng that of a president of a Board. Chuko Liang was reappointed Commander-in-chief of the Forces, with the additional powers of control over the whole state policy. The
two brothers, with Chao Yün, Huang Chung and Ma Ch'ao,
were the Five Tiger Leaders. Wei Yen was made Governor
of Hanchung, and all the others who had assisted were given
ranks and offices.

As soon as the investiture was completed, Liu Pei composed a memorial and sent it to the capital. This is the document:—

"I, Pei, have but ordinary talents, yet was I made a general of high rank and led a great army. Though I received a commission to purge the empire of rebels I was unable to cleanse it and so renew the tranquillity to Your Majesty's house and restore the dynasty. Too long have I delayed to spread Your Majesty's sacred governance. The world is evil and not in good case, and as I sorrowfully think it over and over I am distressed as one in severe pain.

"Rebellion began with Tung Cho, and all kinds of evils have spread abroad; cruelty and ferocity have become rife. Strong in faith in Your Majesty's sacred virtue and inspiring presence, many banded together to help. The loyal exerted themselves to destroy the rebels, but others of them were smitten of heaven. The fierce and the contumacious have been exterminated, and gradually rebellion has melted away.

"Only Ts'ao Ts'ao now remains, too long unpunished. He has arrogated to himself the authority of the state. His wicked heart is very rebellious. Once I, with the officer of high rank Tung Ch'êng, conspired against him, but the plot was discovered and my fellow conspirator suffered. Thenceforward I was a wanderer and my loyalty availed nothing. It only allowed Ts'ao further licence and liberty to do evil, till he dared even to accomplish the death of the Empress and the destruction of her sons. Although we might band together and form associations, yet, with all our energy, we had to recognise that we were too weak for war. Wherefore the years passed and nothing was accomplished. In constant fear of destruction, we even forgot our duty to the state. Waking and sleeping we sighed, and our nights were times of anxiety.

"Now my fellows consider that history has repeated itself. They attach the utmost importance to the family and would manifest it with all their might. Hereditary succession of rulers is still a principle. The Rulers of Chou, taking the two preceding dynasties as models, strengthened its position through all the states, and it reinforced itself with the support of Chin and Chêng. When the great Founder of the Hans came into his own he ennobled his whole family. Later, the dynasty had to issue a general command throughout the whole of the nine divisions in order to destroy the widespread family of Lu.

"Now Ts'ao is an enemy of all rectitude, and his followers are all evil. His treachery is manifest. Since the members of the imperial clan are few and weak the clan is not honoured. Having reflected upon the ancient models and being desirous of temporary alleviation, my fellows have made me assume the title of 'Prince of Hanchung' with the addition of *Ta-ssŭ-ma*.

I have deeply considered these things. If one receive kindness from the Throne and accept the responsibility for a portion of the state and fail, then such a fault would only be made the more serious by holding high rank and thereby increasing the burden of reproach. But my fellows have urged me, and they have convinced me that it would be right; and, should I refuse, the wicked will not be destroyed and the danger to the state will not be removed. The temple of your ancestors is in danger, the imperial prerogatives are failing. A faithful servant, who in the day of tribulation can undertake a suitable policy whereby to preserve the dynasty, should not refuse his help at any cost. Wherefore I have yielded and accepted the position for the glory of the state.

"Humbly I think of such a title and its exalted position and the favour vouchsafed me, and I would endeavour to show true gratitude. My anxiety is deep, for the responsibility is heavy. I am as one on the brink of a great gulf. I must surely exert myself to the utmost and encourage my armies and lead all disciples of rectitude, in accordance with the will of heaven and as occasion serves, to smite rebellion so as to restore the dynasty."

When this memorial reached the capital, Ts'ao Ts'ao was in his palace at Puyeh and it annoyed him greatly.

"How dare this mean weaver of straw shoes behave thus?" said he. "Now I swear that I will destroy him."

So he issued orders for the whole force of the state to go out against Hsich'uan to wage fierce war with the new Prince of Hanchung.

But a remonstrance came from the mouth of Ssŭma I.

"Let not the great Prince trouble himself to go on a distant expedition because of a temporary annoyance. I can propose a plan of which the execution will need not the bending of a single bow, and yet it will make Liu Pei bring down disaster upon his own head. When his army shall have become exhausted, it will only be necessary to send one single captain against him and victory will be ours."

"What is your exalted view, my friend?" said Ts'ao Ts'ao.

"Sun Ch'üan's sister is wife to Liu Pei, but Sun has found an occasion to steal away the bride. Liu Pei is in possession of Chingchou still, and he and Sun are bitter enemies. Therefore send some able speaker with a letter to Wu to persuade him to send an army to recover Chingchou. That will draw thither all the armies of Hsich'uan, when you can send your army to Han and Ch'uan. Liu Pei will be helpless and his strength will be wasted."

The scheme pleased Ts'ao Ts'ao. He at once drew up a letter and sent it by the hand of Man Ch'ung, who soon arrived in Chiangtung. As soon as Sun Ch'üan knew of the mission, he summoned his advisers to consult.

Chang Chao said, "Wei and Wu are primarily enemies because of the dissension fomented by the words of Chuko. They have been fighting for several years and many lives have been lost. Now this messenger has surely come to discuss terms of friendship, and he should be welcomed."

On the strength of this, Man Ch'ung was well received and conducted into the city and into the presence of Sun Ch'üan. He presented his letters at the conclusion of the ceremonies of reception and declared his mission.

"Wu and Wei have no fundamental quarrel, and their dissension has been brought about by Liu Pei. My master sends me to covenant with you for an attack on Chingchou, while he goes against Han and Ch'uan. This double attack being successful, the conquered country can be divided between you two and you can both swear to respect each other's territory."

Having read the letter, Sun Ch'üan prepared a banquet in honour of Man Ch'ung and then sent him to the guest-house to rest while he discussed the matter with his council of advisers.

Said Ku Yung, "Although the messenger's speech was all special pleading it was correct in form. I propose that the messenger be allowed to return and that a covenant be made with Ts'ao Ts'ao for joint attack. In addition, let spies be sent over the river to find out Kuan Yü's movements, and then we may act."

Chuko Chin said, "I hear that since Kuan Yü has been in Chingchou, Liu Pei has found him a wife, who has borne him a son and a daughter. The daughter is too young to have been betrothed, wherefore let me go to ask her in marriage with your heir. If Kuan Yü agree, then we can arrange with him to attack Ts'ao. If Kuan Yü refuse, then let us aid Ts'ao in an attack on Chingchou."

Sun took this advice. So he sent Man Ch'ung away and sent Chuko Chin to Chingchou to try to arrange the betrothal. Chuko Chin was received; and when the time came to state the reason for his coming, Kuan Yü asked him bluntly what he had come for.

"I have come seeking to ally the two houses. My master, the Marquis of Wu, has a son who is quite clever. Hearing that you have a daughter, General, I ask her in marriage, whereby the two houses may join in an attack on Ts'ao Ts'ao. This would be an admirable result and I pray you to consider the proposal."

But the warrior flared up. "How can my tiger daughter marry with a dog's whelp? Were it not for your brother I would take your head. Say no more!"

Kuan Yü called his servants to hustle forth the hapless messenger, who ran away with his hands over his head too astonished to look any one in the face. And reaching his own place he dared not hide the manner of his reception, but told the whole truth.

"What ruffianism!" exclaimed the marquis.

Thereupon he ordered the council again to consider an attack on Chingchou.

Pu Chih rose and said, "It has been long manifest that Ts'ao Ts'ao wishes to usurp the Throne, but he is afraid of Liu Pei. Now we are to attack Shu with an army. The marriage has brought us misfortune indeed."

"But I also want the place," said Sun Ch'üan.

Said Pu Chih, "Ts'ao Jên is already camped at Fanch'êng in Hsiangyang and in no danger from the river. If Ts'ao can take Chingchou by land why does he not take it? However, he wants you, my lord, to send your army, and you can judge his real intention from this. Send to Ts'ao and tell him to make Ts'ao Jên attack by land. Then Kuan Yü must take the army from Chingchou to Fanch'êng. When he has left Chingchou you can send an army to seize it."

Sun Ch'üan thought the scheme good and sent letters with these proposals to Ts'ao Ts'ao. Ts'ao adopted the plan, and having sent the messenger back to Wu, he next sent Man Ch'ung to help Ts'ao Jên at Fanch'êng as assistant adviser in the matter of attack. He also sent despatches to Wu to ask for the assistance of Sun Ch'üan's marine force.

Having laid on Wei Yen the task of holding eastern Ch'uan, the Prince of Hanchung, with his officers, returned to Ch'êngtu and began to set his new house in order. A palace was begun and public guest-houses were built, and between Ch'êngtu and Paishui, at selected places, they built four hundred rest-houses and post stations. The prince also set himself to accumulate great stores of grain and forage and to fill his arsenals with weapons with the design of mastering the capital and the whole country.

Then his spies told him of the treaty between Ts'ao and Wu, with designs upon Chingchou, and he hastily called in K'ung-ming to ask what should be done.

"I felt that Ts'ao Ts'ao would try to do this," said K'ung-ming, "and most of the advisers in Wu will persuade Ts'ao to order Ts'ao Jên to begin the campaign."

"But what am I to do?" asked the prince.

"First send a special messenger to Kuan Yü with his new title, telling him to capture Fanch'êng, which will so damp the ardour of the enemy that he will break off himself."

Therefore the prince sent Fei Shih, a high official from his Board of War, to take the patent of his new title to Kuan Yü, who received the delegate with great deference and conducted him into the city. After they had arrived at the official residence, Kuan Yü enquired what new title had been conferred upon him.

"Chief of the Five Tiger Generals," replied the delegate.

"And who are the five?"

"Their names are Kuan, Chang, Chao, Ma and Huang."

"The second is my brother," said Kuan Yü discontentedly. "Ma comes of a famous family and Chao Yün has been with my elder brother so long that he is as a brother. It is right for him to be put on a level with me. But what sort of a man is this Huang Chung that he is ranked with us? The really great man does not stand shoulder to shoulder with any old soldier that comes along."

And he refused both title and seal.

"You do wrong to refuse," said Fei Shih. "Of old, Hsiao Ho and Ts'ao Ts'an helped the Founder of the Han Dynasty in his great enterprise and were very dear friends, while Han Hsin was but a runaway leader from Ch'u. Yet Han Hsin became a prince, and so was placed over the heads of the other two. I have never heard that these two resented it. The prince has his Five Tiger Generals, but he is still your brother and all that that means. As his brother you are he and he is you. Is there any comparison with any other? The prince has always treated you with the greatest kindness. You are one in sorrow and joy, sharers of disaster and good fortune. No such question as that of a mere title ought to reckon at all. I pray you, Sir, to reflect."

Kuan Yü understood, and thanked the messenger for having prevented him from making a great mistake. He then received the seal with all humility.

Next Fei Shih produced the edict ordering the capture of Fanch'êng. Kuan Yü lost no time in obeying its command. He appointed Fushih Jên and Mi Fang leaders of the van to take the first army out of the city into camp. This done, a banquet was prepared for the messenger, and they sat late at their wine. While still at table there was an alarm of fire in the new camp, and Kuan Yü hastened out of the city to see. He found that the two captains had also been feasting and the fire had started behind their tent, a spark having fallen into some explosives, whence it spread and destroyed the whole camp and all that was in it. Kuan Yü and his men did what they could to put out the fire and then re-entered the city. There he summoned the two captains before him, abused them for their lack of care and sentenced them to death.

However, Fei Shih interceded for them, saying, "It is not well to put two leaders to death at the beginning of a campaign, before even the army has marched. You might reprieve them at least."

Kuan Yü's anger had by no means subsided, but he recalled the two peccant captains and said, "Were it not that I have the greatest regard for the President Fei here I had let the sentence take its course. Now I will only flog you."

So the two officers received forty blows each and were degraded from leading the van. Their seals were taken away and one was sent to Nanchün, the other to Kungan.

"Now be warned," said Kuan Yü. "If, when I return from my victories, there is the least sign of disorder on your part, you will suffer for both faults."

The two men flushed crimson and went out.

Then two new officers were appointed, Liao Hua and Kuan P'ing. Next Kuan Yü took command of the main army, and he had two advisers. Then it was that Hu Hua's son, Hu Pan, came to Chingchou and joined Kuan, who loved him for the sake of his father and the good service he had rendered. Kuan Yü sent him to the Prince of Hanchung in the train of Fei Shih.

The day that Kuan Yü sacrificed to his standard before starting, he was lying in his tent resting when suddenly there dashed into his tent a huge boar, very large, as big as a bullock and quite black. It bit his foot. He jumped up to kill the creature, when it squealed with the sound of tearing cloth—and he awoke. But he had a pain in his foot.

The dream perplexed him, and he could not explain it. He related it to his son, who interpreted it happily, saying that the boar was something of a royal beast, like the dragon, and coming to his feet meant a rise for his adopted father. When the dream got noised abroad, for he told his officers, some interpreted it as auspicious and some the reverse.

"When a man nears sixty he ought not to be greatly disturbed by the thought of death," said Kuan Yü. "After all, I am a man."

Just about that time came an edict from the Prince of Hanchung making him Chief General, with honourable insignia of rank and control over the nine districts in Chingchou and Hsiàngyang. When the officers congratulated him on his new honours they did not forget the dream.

"This shows what a dream of boars means."

This new distinction pleased Kuan Yü greatly and he had no more perplexing doubts. Soon he marched away along the great road to the point of danger.

Ts'ao Jên was in the city when he heard that the great warrior was coming against him. He was much put about, and inclined to trust solely to defence. But his next command, Chai Yüan, did not support this course and argued against it.

"Our prince has ordered you to act in concert with Wu and take Chingchou. For the other side to come against such a combination is to walk in the way of death; certainly we have no occasion to avoid a conflict."

On the other hand the newly sent adviser inculcated caution. Said he, "Kuan is brave and cunning and one not to be met lightly. I think defence is best."

Then Hsiahou Ts'un said contemptuously, "This is all the talk of a lot of book-folk. When the flood approaches bank up to keep it out. Let the enemy come and we shall only have to sit still and receive our reward, for we are sure of victory."

Ts'ao Jên was won over to the side of the men of action. He placed Man Ch'ung in command of the defences while he went outside to beat off Kuan Yü. When the two forces met, Kuan Yü called to his side Kuan P'ing and Liao Hua, to whom he gave certain orders. These two advanced, settled their array and Liao Hua then rode out and offered a challenge. Chai Yüan accepted it; but soon after the combat began Liao Hua made as if he was defeated and turned to leave the field. Chai Yüan went after him. The Chingchou men retired twenty *li* or so.

Soon the Chingchou soldiers came again and offered battle, when Hsiahou Ts'un and Chai Yüan both went out. The manœuvre of the preceding day was repeated. But suddenly there was a detonation behind the men of Ts'ao and the rolling of drums as for attack. Ts'ao Jên hastily called upon his men to return. They did so; but Kuan P'ing and Liao Hua then turned and followed on their heels so that the men of Ts'ao were thrown into confusion.

Ts'ao Jên by this time had seen that a trap had been laid and he had fallen therein, so he hastily marched with one army to Hsiangyang. He got to within a short distance of the city when he saw before him a handsome banner waving in the wind, and out came the great warrior with his sword ready to slay. Ts'ao Jên was powerless from fear, and, fighting being impossible, he turned off in a diagonal direction for Hsiangyang. Nor was he pursued.

Shortly after, Hsiahou Ts'un came. He fell into a rage at the sight of the old warrior and went to fight him. He was slain in the first encounter. His colleague fled, but Kuan P'ing captured and slew him. Then the pursuit was continued, and the loss on Ts'ao's side was very heavy. Many were drowned in the Hsiang River. This phase ended with Ts'ao Jên defending Fanch'êng and Kuan in possession of Hsiangyang. His was the victory.

"You have obtained this city very easily," said the Transport Officer Wang Fu, "but the task is not ended. Ts'ao's men have been beaten and their courage broken, but there is danger from the side of Wu. Lü Mêng is at Luk'ou, and he has long cherished the desire to lay hands on Chingchou. Suppose he now attacks; what will happen?"

"I was e'en thinking of that myself. You may go and attend to this matter. You will certainly be able to find certain elevated spots on the river bank, not too far apart, suitable for alarm beacons, whence could be signalled any attempt of the men of Wu to cross the river. Fifty men could guard each station. Let there be a flame by night and a smoke by day. If they cross the river I must go and smite them."

Wang Fu replied, "Fushih Jên and Mi Fang are defending important places and doing it well. But there ought to be a commander-in-chief over Chingchou."

"There is no need for anxiety; P'an Chün is guarding the city."

"The objection is the character of P'an Chün. He is jealous and selfish and not a fit man for the task. I think you would do well to replace him by Chao Lei, now of the commissariat. He is loyal, trusty, clean-handed and straight, a much more desirable man for the post."

"I know P'an Chün very well, but I have delegated him for that duty and cannot change now. The work your friend has to do in the supplies is also most important. I do not think you need be anxious. Just get along with those beacons for me."

Wang Fu, annoyed, took his leave. Then Kuan P'ing was bidden to prepare ships ready to cross the river and attack Fanch'êng, whither Ts'ao Jên had retired after his defeat.

Now Ts'ao Jên said to Man Ch'ung, "Neglecting your advice I lost my men, my two captains and the city of Hsiangyang. What am I to do now?"

"Kuan Yü is very dangerous, too brave and skilful for you to try to defeat. You had better remain on the defensive," replied Man Ch'ung.

Just about this time came the tidings that Kuan Yü was crossing the river on the way to attack. Man maintained his policy, that of defence. But the subordinate leader Lu Ch'ang was for going out to meet the enemy.

"I ask for a few companies," said Lu, "and I will meet the enemy on the way."

"You cannot do any good," said Man.

"According to the advice of you and the other bookish officials there is only one thing to do. But will defence drive off the enemy? The proper way is to attack your enemy while he is crossing a river, and as Kuan Yü is doing that now, why not attack now? It will be quite another matter if you let him reach the walls and get possession of the moat."

As a result of his arguments and protest, Lu got command of two companies, whom he led to the river. And there he found Kuan Yü already arrayed for battle. Kuan Yü at once rode out, and the bold Lu was going to attack him. But his men were panic-stricken at the sight of Kuan Yü's fierce countenance and ran away. Lu Ch'ang called them to come back, but they would not stop, and as Kuan Yü came on with a rush, the army of Ts'ao again lost the day. Many were slain, and the remainder ran into Fanch'êng. Ts'ao Jên sent off a hasty messenger for help and a letter to Ch'angan to tell what

Kuan Yü had done and how Fanch'êng was in imminent danger of falling.

The letter reached Ts'ao, who chose a certain one among his officers and asked if he could relieve Fanch'êng. The man at once stepped out and said he could.

The man was Yü Chin.

"Let me have some captain to lead the van," said he.

"Who volunteers?" asked Ts'ao, looking around.

"I do," cried a man; "I will give my poor services for what they are worth. And I will capture this fellow Kuan and bring him as an offering before your standard."

> The men of Wei began the war
> E'er Wu had sent out spies.

But who was the man bold enough to say he would capture Kuan Yü? For his name see the next chapter.

CHAPTER LXXIV.

P'ANG TÊ TAKES HIS COFFIN ON A CAMPAIGN; KUAN YÜ DROWNS HIS ENEMIES.

The bold and self-confident officer of Ts'ao's army who promised to make an end of Kuan Yü was P'ang Tê. Ts'ao was glad to find such a man.

"That fellow Kuan has a great reputation, and in the whole country he has no rival. He has not met his match yet, but now you are going he will find all his work cut out."

So spake Ts'ao Ts'ao. He conferred on Yü Chin the title of "Corrector of the South" and on P'ang Tê that of "Corrector of the West and Leader of the Van," and they two marched out with their seven armies to Fanch'êng.

These seven armies were composed of sturdy fellows from the north, led by two of their own chiefs named Tung Hêng and Tung Ch'ao. Hearing who was to command them, these two, supported by their chiefs, went to see Yü Chin and represented that the leader of the van was unsuitable.

Tung Hêng spoke, and said, "Sir General, the expedition you lead is for the relief of Fanch'êng and it can confidently expect victory, but is it not unwise to place such as P'ang Tê in command of the van?"

"Why?" said Yü Chin, surprised.

"Because he was once under the command of Ma Ch'ao. He had no alternative but to surrender and fight for Wei. But his former chief is now in high honour in Shu, one of the Five Tiger Generals, and his own brother is there, too, as an officer. To send him as leader of the van just now seems like trying to extinguish a fire with oil. Would it not be well to inform the Prince of Wei and ask him to exchange this man for another?"

Without further argument or delay Yü Chin went to see the prince and laid before him the objections to P'ang's appointment. As soon as Ts'ao understood, he summoned P'ang Tê to the steps and bade him yield his seal as "Leader of the Van."

"O Prince, why do you reject my services? I was just about to do my best for you."

"I do not doubt you, but Ma Ch'ao is now in Hsich'uan and your brother also, both in the service of Liu Pei. I myself have no doubts, but it is what all the crowd are saying. What can I do?"

P'ang Tê took off his head-dress and prostrated himself, bitter tears rolling down his cheeks.

"Since I surrendered to you, O Prince, I have experienced much kindness, so that I would undergo any sufferings to show my gratitude. I hope you will trust me. When my brother and I were at home together his wife was a wicked woman and I slew her, pretending I was drunk. My brother has never forgiven me, but is permeated with hate for me. He swears never to see me again, and we are enemies. For my old master, Ma Ch'ao, I have profound contempt. He is bold, but only that, and was in a pitiable and dejected state when he found his way to the west. Now, like me, he serves his own master, but our friendship is at an end. How could I think of another after your kindness to me?"

Ts'ao Ts'ao raised him from the ground and soothed him, saying, "I have always known what a noble man you are, and what I said just now was to satisfy the feelings of other people. Now you can strive to win fame, and if you do not turn your back on me I shall not on you."

Then P'ang took his leave and returned to his house, where he ordered the artificers to make him a coffin. Next he invited all his friends to a banquet, and the coffin was set out in the reception room for all to see. And they asked one another what that inauspicious thing could mean put out on the eve of a campaign. By and by, drinking to them, P'ang Tê said, "The Prince of Wei has been generous to me, and I am pledged to show my gratitude to the death. I am about to go out against this Kuan, and I have to kill him or he must kill me. If he does not kill me I must commit suicide, and so I have prepared what is necessary. I will not return leaving my task unachieved."

The terrible omen saddened the guests, and they fell to sighing. Then he called in his wife and bade her bring their son Hui, whom he commended to her care.

"I have been appointed leader of the van of this new expedition against Kuan Yü, and my duty bids me seek death or glory on the battle-field. If I die, our son is in your special care. Alas, the child has been born ill-starred, and when he grows up he will have to avenge a father."

Both mother and son wept as they bade him farewell. When the army marched, the coffin was carried in its train. He bade his officers place his body therein if he fell in combat with Kuan Yü.

"And if I slay him, then will I bring his head in this coffin as an offering to our prince."

Then outspake a captain of five hundred men and said, "If you are like this, O General, then we also will follow you to the end."

The vanguard then marched away. A certain man told the story of these happenings to Ts'ao Ts'ao, who was very pleased, saying he had no anxiety with such a captain to lead his men.

But Chia Hsü said, "I am anxious for P'ang Tê's safety. He is over-bold and imprudent to fight with Kuan Yü to the death."

Ts'ao Ts'ao thought such an act would be unwise, and he hastily sent a messenger with an edict warning P'ang Tê against his antagonist.

"This Kuan lacks neither cunning nor valour. You are to be most cautious in engaging him. If you can conquer, then conquer; but if there be any doubt remain on the defensive."

"How highly does our prince regard this fellow Kuan!" said the captain to his officers when he heard this new command. "But I think I shall be able to take the keen edge off his thirty-year reputation."

"The command of the prince is to be obeyed," said Yü Chin.

P'ang Tê hastened to Fanch'êng in all the pomp and panoply of war, his gongs clanging, his drums rolling as he marched.

Kuan Yü was sitting in his tent when his spies came to tell him of the approach of the men from the north, seven cohorts of them, all bold fighting men. And they were thirty *li* away. Rage took possession of him. His face changed colour, his beard shook and he roared out, "There is never a fighting man in all the world who has heard my name without trembling. Does this fellow dare disdain me?"

Then he ordered Kuan P'ing to attack the city while he went out to stay the impudent boaster who dared him.

"Father," said Kuan P'ing, "Mount T'ai in its majesty does not quarrel with a pebble. Let me go and fight this P'ang Tê."

"Well, my son, go and try; I will support you."

So Kuan P'ing took his sword, mounted his steed and went out with his men. Both sides being drawn up for battle. On the side of Wei there flew a single black flag on which was inscribed, "P'ang Tê, 'Pacificator of the South,' " in white. The leader himself wore a blue robe with a silver helmet and rode a white charger. He stood out in front backed by his five hundred faithfuls, and a few foot soldiers were there too, bearing the gruesome coffin.

Kuan P'ing was startled at the crowd behind his opponent.

"Who is that?" asked P'ang Tê of his followers.

A certain one replied, "That is Kuan's adopted son, Kuan P'ing."

P'ang cried, "I have an edict from the Prince of Wei to take your father's head. You are but a weakling and I will spare you. But call your father."

Kuan P'ing dashed forward flourishing his sword. P'ang Tê went to meet him, and there followed thirty odd bouts with no advantage to either.

Both sides then drew off to rest. Soon the news of this combat reached Kuan Yü, and he was not pleased. He sent Liao Hua to assault the city while he went to do battle with P'ang Tê   Kuan P'ing met his father and related the story of the indecisive fight. So Kuan Yü rode out with his great sword ready, and he shouted to P'ang Tê, "Come quickly and be slain."

The drums re-echoed as P'ang Tê rode out and replied, "The edict from the Prince of Wei tells me to take your head. In case you disbelieve it, here is the coffin ready to receive it. If you fear death, down from your horse and surrender."

"I hold you for a simple fool" cried Kuan Yü.. "What can you do? It is a pity to stain my Black Dragon sword with the blood of such a rat."

Then he galloped out toward P'ang Tê, flourishing the sword. P'ang Tê whirled his blade and came to meet him, and they two fought a hundred bouts. And as they fought the lust of battle seemed to grow and both armies were lost in amazement.

But the army of Wei began to fear for their champion, and the gongs sounded the retirement. At the same time Kuan P'ing began to think of his father's fatigue, and his gongs clanged too. So that both armies drew off at the same time.

"Kuan Yü is really a mighty man of war," said P'ang Tê, when he had got back among his own men.

Then his chief, Yü Chin, came to see him and spoke of the great combat of a hundred bouts which had ended indecisively.

"I think it would be prudent to retire out of his way," said Yü Chin at the close.

But P'ang Tê replied haughtily, "What makes you so soft? Yet the prince gave you the command! But to-morrow I will fight again and that to the death. I swear I will never give way."

Yü Chin could not overcome his decision, so he went back to his own camp.

When Kuan Yü had got back to his camp he extolled the swordsmanship of his opponent and acknowledged him a worthy enemy.

"The new-born calf fears not the tiger," said Kuan P'ing, "But if you slay this fellow, my father, you have only killed a barbarian of the tribes beyond the frontier. If any accident occur, then you will have the reproach of not having considered your brother's charge."

"How can my resentment be assuaged save by the death of this man?" returned Kuan. "I have decided to fight, so say no more."

Next day Kuan took the field first, but P'ang quickly came out. Both arrayed their men and then went to the front at the same moment. This time neither spoke, but the combat began forthwith. It went on for fifty bouts and then P'ang pulled his horse, sheathed his sword and fled. Kuan went in pursuit, and Kuan P'ing followed lest there should be need of him. Kuan Yü roared out revilings to his flying foe and that he wanted to get the chance for an unfair blow. But he was not afraid.

But the fact was that P'ang Tê had only pretended to try for a foul stroke in order to cover a resort to his bow. He pulled in his horse, fitted an arrow to the string and was just on the point of shooting when Kuan P'ing, who was sharp-eyed, shouted out a warning.

"The bandit is going to shoot!"

Kuan Yü saw it, but the bowstring sang and the arrow came flying. He was not nimble enough to avoid it and it wounded his left arm. Kuan P'ing at once went to his father's assistance and led him away to the camp. P'ang wished to follow up this advantage and came back whirling his sword, but, ere he could strike, the gongs of his own side rang out. He thought there was something amiss in the rear and stopped.

The signal for retreat had been sounded by Yü Chin out of jealousy, for he had seen that Kuan Yü had been wounded and he grudged his colleague the glory which would eclipse his own. P'ang obeyed, but when he got back he wanted to know why retreat had been sounded on the very verge of a great success.

"Why did the gongs clang?" asked he.

"Because of our prince's warning. Though he was wounded I feared some trick on his part. He is very cunning."

"I should have killed him if you had not done that," said P'ang.

"Haste makes slow going; you can postpone your fight with him," said Yü Chin.

P'ang Tê, though ignorant of the real reason why he was made to miss success at the critical moment, was still very vexed.

Kuan Yü went back to camp, and the arrow-head was puled out of the wound. Happily it had not penetrated very deeply, and the usual remedies against injuries by metal were applied. Kuan Yü was very bitter against his enemy and declared that he would have his revenge for his wound.

"Never mind anything but recovering now," said his officers. "Rest and get well; then you may fight again."

Before long, P'ang Tê renewed his challenge, and Kuan Yü was for going out to fight; however, he yielded to the entreaties of his officers. And when P'ang set his men to reviling the hero, Kuan P'ing saw to it that his father never heard it. After ten days of challenges hurled uselessly at an army that ignored them, P'ang took council with Yü Chin.

Evidently Kuan Yü is helpless from the effects of that arrow-wound. We ought to advance all our seven armies against him while he is ill and destroy his camp. Thereby we shall relieve Fanch'êng."

Thus spake P'ang, but jealousy of the glory that might accrue to his next in command again made Yü Chin urge caution and obedience to the command of the prince. He refused to move his men in spite of P'ang's repeated persuasion; still more, he led the army to a new camping ground behind the hills some distance north of Fanch'êng. There his own army stopped communication by the main road, while he sent P'ang into a valley in the rear so that he could do nothing.

To the son's great joy Kuan Yü's wound soon healed. Soon after they heard of Yü Chin's new camp, and as Kuan P'ing could assign no reason for the change, and suspected some ruse, he told his father, who went up to a high place to reconnoitre. Looking round, he noted that there seemed much slackness about everything in Fanch'êng that horse and foot were camped in a valley to the north and that the Hsiang River seemed to run very swiftly. After impressing the topography on his mind he called the guides and asked the name of the gully about ten *li* north of the city.

"Tsêngk'ouch'üan," was the reply.

He chuckled. "I shall capture Yü Chin," said he.

Those with him asked how he knew that. He replied, "Why, how can anyone last long in such a place?"

Those in his train gave but little weight to what he said, and presently he went back to his own tent. It was just then the time for the autumn rains, and a heavy downpour came on, lasting several days. Orders were given to get ready boats and rafts and such things. Kuan P'ing could not think what such preparations meant in a dry land campaign. So he asked his father.

"Do you not know even?" replied his father. "Our enemies have camped in difficult ground instead of the open country and are crowded in the dangerous valley there. After some days of this rain the Hsiang River will swell, and I shall send men to dam up all the outlets and so let the water rise very high. When at its highest I shall open the dams and let the water out over Fanch'êng. That valley will be flooded too, and all the soldiers will become aquatic animals."

It is time to return to the Wei armies. They had camped in the gully, and after several days of heavy rain the captain Ch'êng Ho ventured to speak to his general.

He said, "The army is camped near the mouth of a stream in a depression. There are hills around us, but they are too far off to keep the water away. Our men are already suffering from these heavy rains, and, moreover, they say the Chingchou men have moved to higher ground. More than that, at Hanshuik'ow they are preparing boats and rafts so that they can take advantage of the floods if there are any. Our men will be in great danger, and something should be done."

But the general scoffed at his words, called him a fool and blamed him for injuring the spirit of his men. So Ch'êng Ho went away greatly ashamed.

Then he went to P'ang Tê, who saw the force of his words and promised that if Yü Chin would not move camp the next day he himself would do so. So Ch'êng Ho left it at that.

That night there came a great storm. As P'ang Tê sat in his tent he heard the sound as of ten thousand horses in stampede and a roar as of the drums of war seeming to shake the earth. He was alarmed, left his tent and mounted his charger to go and see what it meant. Then he saw the rolling waters coming in from every side and the seven armies flying from the flood, which speedily rose to the height of ten feet. Yü Chin and P'ang Tê, with many other officers, sought safety by rushing up the hills.

As day dawned, Kuan Yü and his men came along in large boats with flags flying and drums beating. Yü Chin saw no way of escape, and his following was reduced to about three score. They all said they must surrender. Kuan Yü made them strip and then took them on board.

After that he went to capture P'ang Tê, who was standing on a hillock with the two Tungs, Ch'êng Ho and the faithful five hundred, all unarmed. P'êng Tê saw his arch enemy approach without a sign of fear, and even went boldly to meet him. Kuan Yü surrounded the party with his boats, and the archers began to shoot. When more than half the men had been struck down, the survivors became desperate. The two Tungs pressed their chief to give in. But P'ang Tê only raged.

"I have received great kindness from the prince; think you that I will bow the head to any other?"

He cut down the two Tungs and then shouted, "Anyone who says surrender shall be as these two."

So the survivors made a desperate effort to beat off their enemies, and they held their own up to mid-day. Then Kuan Yü's men redoubled their efforts, and the arrows and stones rained down upon the defenders, who fought desperately hand to hand with their assailants.

"The valorous leader fears death less than desertion; the brave warrior does not break faith to save his life," cried P'ang Tê. "This is the day of my death, but I will fight on to the last."

So Ch'êng Ho pressed on till he fell into the water wounded, and then the soldiers yielded.

P'ang Tê fought on. Then one of the boats happened to close in to the bank. With a tremendous leap P'ang Tê lighted on it and slashed at the occupants, killing several. The others

jumped overboard and swam away. Then P'ang Tê, one
hand still holding his sword, tried to manœuver the boat across
the river to the city. Then there came drifting down a raft,
which collided with and upset his boat so that he was struggling in the water. But a captain on the raft jumped into the
water, gripped him and put him on the boat again.

The captor was Chou Ts'ang, a skilful waterman who,
having lived in Chingchou for many years, was thoroughly
expert in boat navigation. Beside, he was very powerful and
so was able to make P'ang Tê a prisoner.

In this flood perished the whole of the seven armies, except
the few that saved themselves by swimming; these latter,
having no way of escape, surrendered to the victors.

> In the depth of night rolled the war drums,
> Summonding the warriors as to battle:
> But the enemy was no man,
> For the waters had risen and the flood came.
> This was the plan of Kuan Yü, the crafty,
> To drown his enemies. More than human
> was he in cunning. The ages hand on his fame
> As his glory was told in his own day.

Kuan Yü then returned to the higher ground, where his tent
was pitched and therein took his seat to receive his prisoners.
The lictors brought up Yü Chin, who prostrated himself
humbly and begged his life.

"How dared you think to oppose me?"

"I was sent; I came not of my own will. I crave my lord's
pity, and one day I will requite."

"To execute you would be like killing a dog or a hog. It
would be soiling weapons for nothing," said Kuan Yü, stroking
his beard.

Yü Chin was bound and sent to the great prison in
Chingchou.

"I will decide your fate when I return," said Kuan Yü.

The general having thus dealt with his chief, P'ang Tê was
sent for. He came, pride and anger flashing from his eyes;
he did not kneel but stood boldly erect.

"You have a brother in Hanchung and your old chief was
Ma Ch'ao, also in high honour in Shu. Had you not better
join them?"

"Rather than surrender to you I would perish beneath the
sword," cried P'ang.

He reviled his captors without ceasing till, losing patience
at last, Kuan Yü sent him to his death. He was beheaded.
He stretched out his neck for the headsman's sword. Out of
pity he was honourably buried.

The floods were still out, and taking advantage of them
they boarded the boats to move toward Fanch'êng, which now

stood out as a mere island with waves breaking against the walls. The force of the waters being great, the city wall was beginning to give way, and the whole population, male and female, were carrying mud and bricks to strengthen it. Their efforts seemed vain, and the leaders of Ts'ao Ts'ao's army were very desperate. Some of the captains went to see Ts'ao Jên, who said, "No ordinary man's strength can fend off to-day's danger. If we can hold out till nightfall we may escape by boat. We shall lose the city, but we shall save our skins."

But Man Ch'ung interposed before the boats could be got ready. He pointed out that the force of the waters was too great for any boats to live, while they only had to wait ten days or so and the flood would have passed.

"Though Kuan Yü has not assaulted the city, yet he has sent another army to Chiahsia, and he dares not abvance lest we should fall upon his rear. Remember, too, that to retire from this city means the abandonment of everything south of the Yellow River. Therefore I decide that you defend this place, which is strong."

Ts'ao Jên saluted Man Ch'ung as he concluded his harangue, saying, "What a tremendous error I should have committed had it not been for you, Sir!"

Then riding his white charger he went up on the city walls, gathered his officers around him and pledged himself not to surrender.

"The prince's command being to defend this city, I shall defend it to the last. And I shall put to death anyone who even mentions abandonment," said he.

"And we desire to defend it to out last gasp," chimed in his officers.

Then they saw to it that the means of offence were good. Many hundreds of archers and crossbowmen were stationed on the wall and kept watch night and day. The old and the young of ordinary people were made to carry earth and stones to strengthen the wall.

After some ten days the flood was at an end. Then the news of Kuan Yü's success got abroad, and the terror of his name spread wider and wider. About the same time, too, his second son, Hsing, came to visit his father in camp. Kuan Yü thought this a good opportunity to send his report of success to Ch'êngtu and entrusted to Hsing a despatch mentioning each officer's services and requesting promotion for them. Kuan Hsing accordingly took leave of his father and left.

After his departure the army was divided into two halves, one under Kuan Yü to attack the city and the other to go to Chiahsia. One day Kuan Yü rode over to the north gate. Halting his steed, he pointed with his whip toward the defenders on the wall, and called out, "You lot of rats will not give in then! What are you waiting for?"

156

Ts'ao Jên, who was among his men on the wall, saw that
Kuan Yü had no armour on, so he ordered his men to shoot.
The archers and bowmen at once sent a great flight of arrows
and bolts that way. Kuan Yü hastily pulled the reins to
retire, but an arrow struck him in the arm. The shock of
the blow made him turn in the saddle and he fell from his
horse.

Just now a mighty army perished
By the river's overflow;
A crossbow bolt from the city wall
Lays a valiant warrior low.

What further befell Kuan Yü will be told in the next chapter.

CHAPTER LXXV

Surgery on a Wounded Arm;
Lü Mêng in a White Robe Crosses the River.

At the sight of Kuan Yü falling from his charger, Ts'ao Jên led his men out of the city to follow up with an attack, but Kuan P'ing drove him off and escorted his father back to camp. There the arrow was extracted, but the head had been poisoned. The wound was deep, and the poison had penetrated to the bone. The right arm was discoloured and swollen and useless.

Kuan P'ing consulted with the other leaders and proposed that, as fighting was impossible for the moment, they should withdraw to Chingchou, where his father's wound could be treated. Having decided upon this, they went to see the wounded warrior.

"What have you come for?" asked Kuan Yü when they entered.

"Considering that you, Sir, have been wounded in the right arm, we fear the result of the excitement of battle. Moreover, you can hardly take part in a fight just now and we therefore propose that the army retire till you are recovered."

Kuan Yü replied angrily, "I am on the point of taking the city, and if I succeed I must press forward to the capital, Hsütu, and destroy that brigand Ts'ao Ts'ao, so that the Hans may be restored to their own. Think you that I can vitiate the whole campaign because of a slight wound? Would you dishearten the army?"

Kuan P'ing and his colleagues said no more, but somewhat unwillingly withdrew.

Seeing that their leader would not retire and the wound showed no signs of healing, the various captains enquired far and near for a good surgeon to attend their general.

One day a person arrived in a small ship and, having landed and come up to the gate of the camp, was led in to see Kuan P'ing. The visitor wore a square-cut cap and a loose robe. In his hand he carried a small black bag. He said his name was Hua T'o and he belonged to Ch'iaochun. He had heard of the wound sustained by the famous hero and had come to heal it.

"Surely you must be the physician who treated Chou T'ai," said Kuan P'ing.

"I am."

Taking with him the other captains, Kuan P'ing went in to see his father. He found him engaged in a game of *wei-ch'i*, although his arm was very painful. But he kept up appearances so as not to discourage the men. When they told him that a physician had come, he consented to see him.

So Hua T'o was introduced, asked to take a seat and, after the tea of ceremony, was shown the injured arm.

"This was caused by an arrow," said the doctor. "There is some 'blackhead' poison in the wound, and it has penetrated to the bone. Unless the wound is soon treated the arm will become useless."

"What do you propose to do?" asked Kuan.

"I know how to cure the wound, but I think you will be afraid of the remedy."

"Am I likely to be afraid of that when I am not even afraid of death? Death is only a return home after all."

Then Hua said, "This is what I shall do. In a private room I shall erect a post with a ring attached. I shall ask you, Sir, to insert your arm in the ring, and I shall bind it firmly to the post. Then I shall cover your head with a quilt so that you cannot see, and with a scalpel I shall open up the flesh right down to the bone. Then I shall scrape away the poison. This done, I shall dress the wound with a certain preparation, sew it up with a thread, and there will be no further trouble. But I think you may quail at the severity of the treatment."

Kuan Yü smiled. "It all sounds easy enough," said he; "but why the post and the ring?"

Refreshments were then served, and after a few cups of wine the warrior extended his arm for the operation. With his other hand he went on with his game. Meanwhile the surgeon prepared his knife and called a lad to hold a basin beneath the limb.

"I am just going to cut; do not start," said Hua T'o.

"When I consented to undergo the treatment did you think I was like the generality of people, afraid of pain?"

The surgeon then performed the operation as he had predescribed. He found the bone much discoloured, but he scraped it clean. "*Hsi, hsi,*" went the knife over the surface, and all those near covered their eyes and turned pale. But Kuan Yü went on with his game, only drinking a cup of wine now and again, and his face betrayed no sign of pain. When the wound had been cleansed, sewn up and dressed, the patient stood up smiling and said, "This arm is now as good as it ever was; there is no pain. Indeed, Master Leech, you are a marvel."

"I have spent my life in the art," said Hua T'o; "but I have never seen such a patient as you, Sir. You are the real marvel."

Here as surgeons, there physicians, leeches boast their skill;
Bitter few are those that cure one when one's really ill.
As for superhuman valour rivals Kuan had none,
So for holy touch in healing Hua T'o stood alone.

When the cure was well advanced, Kuan Yü gave a fine banquet in honour of Hua T'o and offered him a fee of a hundred taels. But he declined it. He had come to treat his patient from admiration of his great virtue and not for money.

"Noble Marquis, although your wound is cured you must be careful of your health, and especially avoid all excitement for a hundred days, when you will be as well as ever you were."

Then Hua T'o, having prepared dressings for the wound, took his leave, refusing fees to the very last.

Having captured Yü Chin and accomplished the death of P'ang Tê, Kuan Yü became more famous and more fear-inspiring through the whole country than even before. Ts'ao Ts'ao called together his advisers to help him decide upon what he should do.

Said Ts'ao, "I must acknowledge this Kuan Yün-ch'ang as the one man who, in skill and valour, overtops the whole world. Lately he has obtained possession of Chingchou and the district near it, and has so become very terrible. He is a tiger with wings added. P'ang Tê is no more; Yü Chin is his prisoner; the armies of Wei have lost their morale; and if he led his armies here we should be helpless. I can only think of avoiding the peril by removal of the capital. What think you?"

"No; do not take that step," said Ssŭma I, rising to reply. "Yü Chin and all the others you lost were victims of the flood and slain in battle. These losses do no harm at all to your great plan. The Suns and Lius are no longer friends since Kuan Yü has accomplished his desire. You may send a messenger into Wu to foment the quarrel and cause Sun Ch'üan to send his armies to attack the army of Kuan Yü from the rear, promising that, when things are tranquil, you will reward Sun with a slice of Chiangnan. In this way you will relieve Fanch'êng."

Here the Recorder Chiang Chi said, "Ssŭma I speaks well, and the messenger should lose no time. Do not move the capital or send an army."

Ts'ao Ts'ao therefore did not carry out his first proposal. But he was sad at the loss of Yü Chin, and spoke of him affectionately. "Yü Chin had followed me faithfully for thirty years, and I did not think I was sending him into danger. P'ang Tê was not on the same footing as he."

It was necessary to send someone with the letters to Wu and also to find another leader willing to face Kuan Yü. Ts'ao had not long to wait for the latter, as an officer stepped out from the ranks of those in waiting and offered himself. It was Hsü Huang.

His offer was accepted, and he was given five legions of veterans. Lü Chien was sent as his second, and the army marched to Yanglingp'o, where they halted to see if any support was coming from the south-east.

Sun Ch'üan fell in with the scheme of Ts'ao Ts'ao as soon as he had read his letter. He at once prepared a reply for the messenger to take back, and then gathered his officers, civil and military, to consult. Chang Chao was the first speaker.

"We know Kuan Yü has captured one leader and slain another. This has added greatly to his fame and reputation. Ts'ao was going to move the capital rather than risk an attack. We also know that Fanch'êng is in imminent danger. Ts'ao has asked for our help, but when he has gained his end I doubt whether he will hold to his promise."

Before Sun Ch'üan had replied they announced the arrival of Lü Mêng, who had come in a small ship from Luk'ou with a special message. He was at once called in and asked what it was.

Said Lü, "The armies of Kuan Yü being absent at Fanch'êng, the opportunity should be taken to attack Chingchou."

"But I wish to attack Hsüchou in the north; what of this plan?" said Sun Ch'üan.

"It would be better to attack Chingchou, and so get control of the Long River (Yangtse Kiang.). Ts'ao Ts'ao is far away to the north and too occupied to regard the east. Hsüchou is weakly held and could be taken easily, but the lie of the land favours the use of an army rather than a navy. If you capture it, it will not be easy to hold, but once you hold Chingchou you can evolve other schemes."

"Really, my desire was to attack Chingchou, but I wished to hear what you would say to the other plan. Now, Sir, make me a plan speedily and I will act upon it."

So Lü Mêng took his leave and went back to Luk'ou. But soon they heard that beacon towers were being erected at short distances all along the river, and that the Chingchou army was being put into most efficient condition.

"If this is so, it is hard to make a plan that will ensure success," said Lü Mêng. "I have already advised my master to attack Chingchou, but I am unable to meet this complication."

Therefore he made illness an excuse to stay at home, and sent to inform Sun Ch'üan, who was very distressed at the news.

Then said Lu Hsün, "The illness is feigned; he is quite well."

"If you know that so well, go and see," said Sun.

Away went Lu Hsün and speedily arrived at Luk'ou, where he saw Lü Mêng, who indeed appeared to be in perfect health. Nor did his face bear any signs of recent illness.

"The marquis has sent me to enquire after your honourable complaint," said Lu Hsün.

How distressed I am that the state of my wretched carcase has caused anyone the inconvenience of enquiring!" replied Lü Mêng.

"The marquis placed a very heavy responsibility on your shoulders, but you are not making the best use of the opportunity. However, what is the real origin of your distress?"

Lü sat gazing at his visitor a long time without replying.

"I have a little remedy," said Lu Hsün. "Do you think I might use it?"

Lü dismissed the servants, and when the two were alone he said, "This remedy, my friend, please tell me what it is."

"Your ailment is due simply to the efficiency of the Chingchou soldiers; and I know how to keep the beacons from flaring, and I can make the Chingchou defenders come to you with their hands tied. Would that cure you?"

"My friend, you speak as if you saw into my inmost heart. Pray unfold your good scheme."

"Kuan Yü thinks himself too much of a hero for anyone to dare to face him, and his only anxiety is yourself. Now you must take advantage of this excuse you have made of illness actually to resign this post so that the farce may be kept up and another man be appointed. Let this man, your successor, humbly praise Kuan Yü till he becomes so conceited that he will withdraw all the troops from Chingchou to send them against Fanch'êng. When Chingchou is left undefended then is our chance, and the city will fall into our hands."

"The plan seems most excellent," said Lü Mêng.

Wherefore Lü Mêng's malady waxed worse, so that he was confined to bed; and he gave Lu Hsün his letter of resignation to carry back to Sun Ch'üan. The messenger hastened back and explained the ruse to his master, who soon after issued a command for Lü Mêng to retire and attend to the recovery of his health.

But Lü Mêng came to Sun Ch'üan to discuss the matter of a successor. Sun Ch'üan said to him, "As to the appintment at Luk'ou, you know Chou Yü recommended Lu Su, who in turn proposed you. Now you ought to be able to mention some other talented and well-known officer to succeed you."

"If you choose a well-known man, Kuan Yü will certainly be on his guard against him. Now Lu Hsün is deep and far-seeing, but he has no widespread fame. Hence no particular notice would be taken of his appointment and no counter-measures taken. So he is the most suitable person to send."

"Sun Ch'üan agreed and thereupon promoted Lu Hsün to the rank of "General and Commander-in-chief of the Right," and sent him to defend the port.

"I am very young," said Lu Hsün, "and feel unequal to such a post."

"Lü Mêng has proposed you, and you will not make any mistakes. Pray do not decline," said Sun.

So the appointment was made, and Lu Hsün set out at once. When he had assumed charge of the cavalry, the infantry and the marines, he set about drawing up a letter to Kuan Yü, and he selected fine horses and beautiful silks and good wines and delicacies suitable for gifts to go with the letter. He sent all by the hand of a trusty messenger to Fanch'êng.

The news of the change of command reached Kuan Yü when he lay ill from the effects of his wound and unable to conduct any military operations. Close upon the news came the letter and the gifts from Lu Hsün, and the bearer was called in to see the great warrior.

"Friend Sun was not very prudent when he made a general out of a mere scholar," said Kuan, pointing to the messenger.

The messenger said, "General Lu sends this letter and some presents, which he hopes you will accept. He also sends his felicitations, and would rejoice if the two houses could become friends."

Kuan Yü read the letter, which was couched in most modest language, and then threw back his head and laughed loud. He bade the attendants receive the various gifts, and sent the bearer away. The messenger forthwith returned to Luk'ou and said the old warrior had seemed very gratified and would henceforward feel no anxiety that danger might threaten from their direction. Spies were sent out to report on proceedings, and they returned to say that half the troops had been sent to assist in the siege of Fanch'êng. That city was to be seriously assaulted as soon as Kuan Yü had recovered.

This news was promptly sent on to Sun Ch'üan, who at once called in Lü Mêng to decide upon the next move.

"Now is the favourable moment to get possession of Ching-chou," said Sun. "I propose to send you and my brother, Sun Chiao, to lead the army."

This Sun Chiao was really only a cousin, as he was the second son of Sun Ch'üan's uncle. His secondary name was Shu-ming.

But Lü Mêng objected. "My lord, if you think to employ me, then employ me only; if Shu-ming, then Shu-ming only. You cannot have forgotten that Chou Yü and Ch'êng P'u were associate commanders, and although the final decision lay with Chou Yü, yet the other presumed upon his seniority and there was some unfriendliness between the two. All ended well because Ch'êng P'u recognised the ability of his colleague and so supported him. I know I am not so clever as Chou Yü, but Shu-ming's consanguinity will be a greater obstacle than mere length of service, and I fear he may not be wholly with me."

Sun Ch'üan saw the force of the contention, and appointed Lü Mêng to sole command with Sun Chiao to help him in the commissariat. Lü Mêng thanked his lord for his commission, soon got his three legions together and assembled four score ships for the expedition.

He dressed a number of sailors in the plain costumes of ordinary merchants and put them on board to work his vessels. He concealed his veterans in the holds of the *kolu* ships (shallow-draught transports). He selected seven captains to serve under him and settled the order of their successive movements. The remainder of the forces was left with Sun Ch'üan as supports and reserves. Letters were also written to Ts'ao Ts'ao that he might co-operate by sending his army to attack Kuan Yü in the rear.

The sailors in plain dress navigated the ships to Hsünyang-chiang as quickly as possible, and then crossed to the north bank. When the beacon-keepers came down to question them, the men of Wu said they were traders forced into the bank by contrary winds. And they offered gifts to the beacon-keepers, who accepted them and let the ships come to an anchor close to the shore.

At about the second watch the soldiers came out of hiding in the holds of the transports, suddenly fell upon the beacon-keepers and made them prisoners, officers and men. Next the signal for a general landing was given, and all the soldiers from the eighty ships went ashore. The guard stations were attacked, and all the men captured and carried off to the ships, not a man being allowed to escape. Then the whole force hurried off to Chingchou, having so far carried out their plans that no one knew of their coming.

Nearing Chingchou, Lü Mêng spoke kindly to his captives, and gave them gifts and comforted them in order to induce them to get the gates opened for him to enter the city. He won them over to his side, and they promised to aid him. They would show a flare as a signal that the gates were free. So they went in advance and arrived at the gates about midnight. They called the watch; and the wardens of the gate, recognising their voices, opened for them. Once within, they shouted and lit the flares. Immediately the men of Wu came in with a rush and were soon in possession.

The first order issued by Lü Mêng was to spare the people. Instant death should be the punishment for any murder or robbery. The various officials over the people were retained in their offices and continued their functions. Special guards were set over Kuan Yü's family dwelling, and none dared break open any other house. A messenger was sent with tidings to Sun Ch'üan.

One very wet day Lü Mêng, with a few horsemen as escort, was going round the walls and visiting the gates. One of the soldiers took from a passer-by his broad-brimmed hat and put it on over his helmet to keep his armour dry. Lü Mêng saw it, and the offender was seized. He was a fellow-villager of Lü Mêng's, but that did not save him.

"You are an old acquaintance, but you knew my order; why did you disobey it?"

"I thought the rain would spoil my uniform, and I took the hat to protect it. I did not take it for my own advantage, but to protect official property. Spare me, O General, for the sake of our common dwelling-place."

"I know you were protecting your armour, but still it was disobedience to the order against taking anything from the people."

The soldier was beheaded, and his head exposed as a warning. But when all was over, Lü Mêng had the body buried decently and wept at the grave for the loss of his friend. Never after this was there the least laxity of discipline.

When Sun Ch'üan visited the city, Lü Mêng met him at the boundary and led him to the official residence, where he issued rewards and commendations. This done, he ordered P'an Chün to take charge of the new possession. Yü Chin, who was in prison, was freed and sent back to his master. When the people had been comforted and the soldiers rewarded, there was a great banquet in honour of the success of the expedition.

Then said Sun Ch'üan to his general, "We have got this place, but now we want Kungan and Nanchün. How can we get them?"

Suddenly one Yü Fan started up and offered his services. "You will need neither bows nor arrows," said he, "unless my little tongue is worn out. I can persuade Fu Shih-yen to surrender."

"Friend Yü, how will you do it?" asked Sun Ch'üan.

"He and I are very old friends, ever since we were boys, and if I explain the matter to him I am sure he will come over to this side."

So Yü Fan, with an escort, left quickly for Kungan, where his friend was in command.

Now when Fu heard of the capture of Chingchou he closed his gates. Yü Fan arrived, but was refused entrance. So he wrote a letter, attached it to an arrow and shot it over the city wall. A soldier picked it up and took it to his commander, who found therein much-persuasion to surrender. Having read all this, he thought within himself, "I think I should do well, for the other day Kuan Yü was very bitter against me."

163

165

Without further ado he bade the wardens open the gate, and his friend came in. After their greetings they talked of old times, and Yü Fan praised Sun Ch'üan's magnanimity and liberality and greatness generally. So finally Fu Shih-yen decided to exchange masters and went away, taking with him his seal of office. He was presented to Sun Ch'üan, who reappointed him to the command of Kungan under its new lord. Lü Mêng thought the appointment imprudent while Kuan Yü was yet unconquered, and proposed instead to send him to Nanchün to induce his former colleague and fellow in disgrace to join him in desertion to the enemy. His advice was followed, and Fu was recalled.

"Go to Nanchün and win over Mi Fang, and I will reward you richly," said Sun Ch'üan.

Fu Shih-yen accepted the mission and duly left for Nanchün.

Kungan's defender failed when tried,
So Wang Fu's words were justified.

For the events of the journey see the next chapter.

CHAPTER LXXVI

HSÜ FIGHTS ON THE MIEN RIVER;
KUAN RETREATS TO MAICH'ÊNG.

The fall of Chingchou put Mi Fang in a quandary, and before he could decide upon any course his ancient colleague Fu Shih-jên came to see him. He was admitted, and when asked why he had come he blurted out his business without beating about the bush.

"I am faithful enough, but I got into difficulties and danger and could not hold on, so I have surrendered to Wu. And I advise you to do the same."

"You and I have both fed on the bounty of the Prince of Hanchung, and I cannot understand how you can turn against him."

"Kuan Yü went away hating both of us intensely, and even if he comes back victorious I do not think he will forgive us. Just think it over."

"My brother and I have followed the prince these many years, and I do not like leaving him like this."

Mi Fang hesitated. Before he could make up his mind, there came a messenger to say that the army was short of grain and he had been sent to demand white rice for the soldiers. Nanchün and Kungan were to send ten myriad *tan* at once. Delay would be most severely punished.

This sudden demand was a shock to Mi Fang. "Where am I to get the rice?" said he despairingly to his friend and tempter. "Chingchou is now in the hands of Wu."

"Do not dilly-dally," said Fu Shih-jên. Thereupon he drew his sword and slew the messenger as he stood in the hall.

"What have you done?" cried Mi Fang.

"Kuan wanted to slay us two and has forced me to this. Are we to fold our hands and await death? Either you give in at once and go over to Wu, or you will be put to death by Kuan Yü."

Just then they heard that Lü Mêng's men had actually reached the city wall. Mi Fang saw that nothing could save his life but desertion, so he went out with Fu and gave in his allegiance to Lü Mêng, by whom he was led to Sun Ch'üan. Sun Ch'üan gave both of them presents, after which he proceeded to restore order and to reward his army for their services.

At the time that great discussion about Chingchou was going on in the capital, a messenger arrived with a letter from Sun Ch'üan. It told the tale of the acquisition of Chingchou and begged Ts'ao Ts'ao to send an army to attack Kuan Yü in the rear, enjoining the utmost secrecy.

At the meeting of advisers that Ts'ao Ts'ao summoned to consultation, Tung Chao said, "Now that the relief of Fanch'êng is contemplated it would be well to let the besieged know, so that they may not yield to depression. Moreover, if Kuan Yü hears that Chingchou is in the hands of Wu he will come back to try to recover it. Then let Hsü Huang take the chance to attack, and our victory will be complete."

Ts'ao Ts'ao agreed that the plan was good, and so he sent a messenger to urge Hsü Huang to attack. Ts'ao himself led a large force to Yanglup'o, south of Loyang, to rescue Ts'ao Jên.

Hsü Huang was sitting in his tent when they told him that a messenger from the Prince of Wei had arrived. The messenger was called in and said. "The prince has led an army to Loyang, and he wishes you to hasten to attack Kuan Yü in order to relieve Fanch'êng."

Just then the scouts came to report that Kuan Yü had encamped at Yench'êng and Liao Hua at Ssüchung. The enemy had built a line of twelve stockades. Hsü Huang ordered two of his lieutenants to Yench'êng to masquerade as if he himself was in command, by showing his ensigns. Hsü himself, at the head of a few veterans, went along the Mien River to attack Yench'êng in the rear.

When Kuan P'ing heard of the approach of Hsü Huang he prepared his own division to meet him. When both sides were arrayed, Kuan P'ing rode out and engaged one Hsü Shang. After three encounters Hsü Shang had the worst of it and fled. Then the other lieutenant, Lü Chien, went out. He fought half a dozen bouts and also ran away. Thereupon Kuan P'ing went in pursuit and smote the flying enemy for twenty *li*. But then there was an alarm of fire within the city, and Kuan P'ing knew that he had been inveigled into the pursuit and was a victim. So he turned and set out for the city again. On his way he met a body of troops and standing under the great standard was Hsü Huang.

Hsü Huang shouted out, "Kuan P'ing, my worthy nephew, it is strange that you do not recognise death when it stares you in the face. Your Chingchou has fallen into the hands of Wu and yet you act so madly."

Kuan P'ing, whirling his sword, just rode hard at Hsü Huang, and they engaged. But after the third bout there was a tremendous shouting among the soldiers, for the flames within the city burst up higher than before. Kuan P'ing could not follow up his desire to continue the fight, but cut his way out and made a dash for Ssŭchung, where Liao Hua received him with the news of the disaster to Chingchou

"People say that Chingchou has fallen to Lü Mêng, and the news has frightened the whole army; what is to be done?" said he.

"It is only a malicious rumour; do not let it spread. If any one repeats it, put him to death."

Just then a man came running in to say that Hsü Huang was attacking the first stockade on the north.

"If that goes," said Kuan P'ing, "the remainder will follow. But as we have the river at our back, they will not dare attack this. Let us go to the rescue."

So Liao Hua summoned his subordinate leaders and gave them orders to hold the camp and make a signal if the enemy came.

"There is no danger here" said they. "The camp is defended by a tenfold line of 'deer-horns' (*chevaux de frise*): even a bird could not get in."

Kuan P'ing and Liao Hua mustered all the veterans they had and went away to the first stockade. Seeing the Wei soldiers camped on a low hill, Kuan P'ing said to his colleague, "Those men are stationed in an unsafe place; let us raid their camp to-night."

"You take half the force, General, and I will remain to keep the camp," said Liao Hua.

When night fell, the attacking force went out. But on reaching the camp not a man opposed them. The camp was empty. Then Kuan P'ing knew he had been deceived, and turned to retreat. He was at once attacked on two sides by Hsü Shang and Lü Chien. Unable to stand, his men ran for the camp. The men of Wei followed, and presently the camp was surrounded. They were compelled to abandon the position and set off for Ssŭchung. As they drew near they saw torches, and presently knew by the ensigns displayed that the camp had also fallen to the enemy. Retiring, they hastened along the high road toward Fanch'êng, but presently their way was barred by a force under Hsü Huang himself. By dint of hard fighting they got away and returned to their main camp, and Kuan P'ing went to his father.

"Hsü Huang has got possession of Yench'êng. Ts'ao's main army is on the way in three divisions, and many say that Chingchou is in the enemy's hands."

Kuan Yü bade him be silent. "This is a fabrication of the enemy," said he, "but it may dishearten the soldiers. We know Lü Mêng is ill, and they have appointed that impractical fellow Lu Hsün to succeed him at Luk'ou. There is nothing to fear."

He was soon undeceived. The news came that Hsü Huang had arrived . At once Kuan Yü bade them saddle his charger.

"Father, you are not strong enough to go into the battle," said Kuan P'ing.

"Hsü Huang and I were once friends, and I know what he can do and not do. I will give him the chance to retire, and if he does not take it then I shall just slay him as a warning to the others."

Mounting his charger, Kuan Yü rode out as impetuously as of yore, and the sight of the old warrior made to quake the hearts of the men of Wei. When he came close enough to his enemy, Kuan checked his steed and said, "Where is my friend Hsü?"

As a reply, the gate of the camp opened and Hsü Huang appeared under the standard. With a low bow he said, "Some years have passed since I met you, most excellent Marquis, but I had not expected to see you so grey. I have not forgotten the old brave days, when we were together and you taught me so much, and I am very grateful. New your fame has spread throughout the whole of China, and your old friends cannot but praise you. I am indeed glad that I have the happiness to see you."

Kuan Yü replied, "We have been excellent friends, Ming-kung; better than most. But why have you pressed my son so hardly of late?"

Hsü Huang suddenly turned to the officers about him and cried fiercely, "I would give a thousand for this Yün-ch'ang's head."

Kuan Yü, greatly shocked, said, "What did you say that for?"

"Because to-day I am on state business, and I have no inclination to let private friendship over-ride my public duty."

As he said this, he whirled his battle-axe and rode at Kuan Yü, who, greatly enraged, threw up his great sword to strike. They fought a half score bouts, but although his skill lacked nothing of its pristine vigour and excelled all the world, the old warrior's right arm was still weak from the wound. Kuan P'ing saw that his father failed somewhat, and so hastily beat the gong for retreat. Kuan Yü rode back.

Suddenly the noise of a great shouting was heard; it came from the troops of the city, for Ts'ao Jên, having heard of the arrival of men of his own side, had made a sortie and was about to attack to help Hsü Huang. His men fell on, and the army of Chingchou were routed. Kuan Yü, with as many of his officers as could, fled away along the banks of the Hsiang River, hotly pursued by the army of Wei. Crossing the river, he made for Hsiangyang. Thence he marched for Kungan. But the scouts told him that that city was in the hands of Wu. Then some of the men he had despatched for supplies came in and reported the murder of their officer and the further treachery of Mi Fang. The story filled him with boundless rage. It was too much. The wound re-opened, and he fell in a swoon.

"Wang Fu, you were right," said he when he recovered con sciousness. "How I regret that I did not heed what you said! And now——."

"But why were the beacon fires not lighted?" continued he presently.

"Lü Mêng's men in the guise of traders came over the river. There were soldiers hidden in the *koulu* ships, and they seized the beacon guards, so preventing them from kindling the fires."

Kuan Yü sighed. Beating the ground with his foot, he said, "Indeed I have fallen into their trap. How shall I look my brother in the face?"

Then outspake the commissariat officer Chao Lei, saying, "We are in straits. Send to Ch'êngtu for help, and let us take the land road to Chingchou to try to recover it."

So three messengers were sent by different routes to ask for help, while the army set out to return to Chingchou, Kuan Yü leading and Liao Hua with Kuan P'ing keeping the rear.

The siege of Fanch'êng being thus raised, Ts'ao Jên went to see his master. With tears he acknowledged his fault and asked pardon.

"It was the will of heaven, and no fault of yours," said Ts'ao Ts'ao; and he rewarded the armies.

When he visited Ssǔchung and had inspected the captured stockades, he remarked on the defences. "Hsü Huang was very clever to overcome these. With my thirty years of war I should not have dared to penetrate such opposition. He is valiant and wise, and both in a high degree."

"Aye," said they with him, for they could not but agree.

Ts'ao's army marched back to Mop'o and there camped. When Hsü Huang returned, Ts'ao went out of the stockade to meet him, and noted with joy the excellent order and discipline that his army showed. Every man was in his place, the ranks perfectly kept, all without a trace of disorder.

"He has the spirit of Chou A-fu," said Ts'ao, and on the spot conferred on his captain the title of "Pacificator of the South." Hsü was sent soon after to share in the defence of Hsiangyang to meet Kuan Yü's army.

Chingchou being still in turmoil, Ts'ao remained at Mop'o waiting for news.

Kuan Yü found himself at a standstill on the road to Chingchou with the army of Wu in front and the men of Wei coming up behind. What was to be done? He discussed the position with Chao Lei, who proposed a halt to try to shame Lü Mêng into aiding him.

Said he, "When Lü Mêng was at Luk'ou he used to write to you often, and you agreed to join hands in the destruction of Ts'ao Ts'ao. Now he is a traitor and fighting on the other

side. Send a letter and reproach him. Perhaps we may get
a satisfactory reply."

So the letter was written and sent. Meanwhile, by Lü
Mêng's special command, the most complete protection was
given to the families of all the officers who were serving under
Kuan Yü, and they were kept supplied with all they required.
Even the ailing members of their households were treated by
physicians free of charge. The result was that they were
quite won over to the new order of things, and there was no
attempt to disturb it. When Kuan Yü's letter came, the
messenger was led into the city and well treated. When Lü
read the letter, he said to the bearer thereof, "You must
understand the different circumstances. When your general
and I were leagued together it was a personal matter between
us two. Now things have changed. I am sent here with
certain orders and am not my own master. I would trouble
you, O Messenger, to return and explain thus to your master
and in good words."

The bearer of the letter was entertained at a banquet and
sent to repose himself in the guest-house, where the families
of the absent officers sought him to have news of their
husbands and fathers. Moreover, they brought him letters
and gave him messages for the officers, and the whole tenor
of these letters and messages was that they were all in good
health, all their needs were supplied and they lacked nothing.
When he left the city, Lü Mêng himself escorted him to the
outskirts and set him on his way.

On his return to the army, he gave to Kuan Yü the message
of Lü Mêng and told him that the family were all well and
safe and well cared for. This, however, did not greatly please
Kuan Yü, for he saw in this merely a plan to gain favour and
popularity.

"The brigand! If I cannot slay him while I live, I will
after I am dead. My hate shall not go unappeased."

He roughly dismissed the messenger, who went out and
was at once surrounded by those whose families were in the
city and who desired to have news of them. And when he
gave them the letters and messages and told them all were
well, there was great rejoicing among the men in the camp,
and kindly feelings for Lü Mêng prevailed. And therewith
died down the spirit of fighting.

Kuan Yü led the army to attack Chingchou, but day by
day the men deserted and ran away to the very city they were
moving to attack. So day by day Kuan's bitterness and anger
increased, and he advanced in angry haste. One day there
was a great shouting and the noise of drums, and he found
his way blocked.

"Why do you not surrender, friend Kuan?" said the leader
of this body, Chiang Ch'in by name.

"Could I give in to a rebel, I, a servant of the Hans and a leader of their troops?" roared Kuan Yü in a passion.

Thereupon he whipped his horse forward and swung up his sword to strike. However, Chiang Ch'in would not fight. The two exchanged a few blows, and Chiang fled. Kuan Yü followed. When he had gone a long way, there suddenly appeared from a gully near him Han Tang, while Chou T'ai came out from the other side. Thereupon Chiang Ch'in wheeled round and once more came to do battle, so that three forces were opposed to Kuan Yü. Unable to withstand these, he retreated.

Before he had gone very far he saw signs of many people bivouacking among the hills, and presently made out, on a huge white banner that flapped in the breeze, the words, "Natives of Chingchou," and the people about were calling out, "All the inhabitants of this place have surrendered." Kuan Yü felt like rushing up and cutting these people to pieces, but just then two other cohorts appeared led by Ting Fêng and Hsü Shêng, who supported Chiang Ch'in. The three bodies of men then set on with shouting and loud beating of drums that seemed to make the very earth tremble. And Kuan Yü was like the kernel in a nut, quite surrounded.

This was not all. He saw the number of his followers diminishing every moment. He fought on till dusk, and looking about him he saw all the hills crowded with Chingchou folk and heard them calling brother for brother and son for father, till his soldiers' hearts had melted within them. One by one they ran to their relatives, heedless of their leader and his voice. Presently he had but three hundred left, but with them he kept up the battle till the third watch. Then there was another shouting in another note, for his faithful leaders, Kuan P'ing, his son, and Liao Hua, came to his help. And they rescued him.

"The soldiers' hearts are all melted," said Kuan P'ing. "We must find some place wherein to camp till help can arrive. There is Maich'êng, small, but sufficient; let us camp there."

Kuan Yü consented, and the exhausted army hurried thither as quickly as they could.

The small force was divided among the four gates. Here it seemed as though they could find safety till help could be obtained from Shangyung, which was near.

But disappointments dogged them. Very soon the army of Wu came up and laid siege to the city.

"Who will try to break through and go away to Shangyung for assistance?" asked Kuan Yü.

"I will go," said Liao Hua.

"And I will escort you past the danger zone," said Kuan P'ing.

Kuan Yü wrote his letter, which Liao Hua concealed next his skin, and having eaten a full meal, he rode out at the gate. A certain leader of the enemy, Ting Fêng, tried to check him, but Kuan P'ing fought vigorously and drove him away. So Liao reached the city, while Kuan P'ing returned. Then they barred the gates and went not forth again.

Now, having captured Shangyung, Liu Fêng and Mêng Ta had remained to guard it, and the Prefect had surrendered. Liu Fêng had been created an assistant general with Mêng Ta to aid him. When they heard of the defeat of Kuan Yü they took counsel what to do. When Liao Hua came, he was admitted into the city. He told the tale of Kuan Yü's straits, and asked for help.

"Kuan Yü is closely besieged in Maich'êng. Help from the west will be a long time in coming, so I have been sent to beg your assistance. I hope you will march the Shangyung troops thither as quickly as possible, for any delay will be fatal."

Liu Fêng replied, "Sir, go to the rest-house for a time till we can decide."

So he went, and the two leaders talked over the matter.

Liu Fêng said, "This is bad news; what is to be done?"

"Wu is very powerful," replied his colleague. "Now they have control over the whole district save this small clod of earth called Maich'êng. Ts'ao Ts'ao is at hand with half a hundred legions, and we cannot stand against the two mighty houses. I say we must not move."

"I know all this. But Kuan Yü is my uncle, and I cannot bear to sit still and not try to save him."

"So you hold him as an uncle!" said Mêng Ta with a smile. "Yet I do not think he holds you much as a nephew. When the Prince of Hanchung created him a generalissimo he was greatly annoyed. And after the prince had accepted his new dignity and was nominating his heir, I hear he consulted K'ung-ming, who said the affair was one to be decided within the family and declined to advise. Then the prince sent to ask Kuan Yü's advice. Did he name you? Not at all. You were only a son by adoption and could have no place in the succession. Further, he advised that you be sent to a distance lest you might cause trouble. This is common knowledge, and I am surprised that you are ignorant of it. Yet to-day you make capital out of the relationship and are willing to run a great risk to support it."

"Granted that what you say is true, still what reply can we give?"

"Simply say that this city is still unsettled and you dare not move lest it be lost."

Liu Fêng took his colleague's view, sent for the messenger and told him. Liao Hua was greatly disappointed. He threw himself on the ground and knocked his head, imploring assistance.

"If you act thus, there is an end of Kuan Yü," cried he.

"Will a cup of water extinguish a waggon load of blazing wood?" said Mêng Ta. "Hasten back and await patiently for the coming of help from the west."

Liao Hua renewed his entreaties. The two commanders simply rose, shook out their sleeves and left him. Liao Hua saw that things had gone against him and thought his best course would be to go at once to Ch'êngtu. He rode out of the city cursing its defenders and went away west.

Kuan Yü from his fortress looked anxiously, but vainly, for the coming of the expected aid. He was in a sorry plight. His men numbered but a few hundred, many wounded; there was no food.

The someone came to the foot of the wall and, calling out to the men on the wall not to shoot, said he had a message for the commander. He was allowed to enter; it was Chuko Chin. When he had made his salutations and taken tea, he began his harangue.

"I come at the command of my master, Marquis Wu, to persuade you to a wise course. From of old it has always been recognised that the hero must bow to circumstances. The districts that you ruled have come under another, with the exception of this single city. Within, there is no food, without, no help, so that it must fall quickly. Wherefore, O General, why not hear me and join your fortunes to those of Wu? You shall be restored to your governorship and you will preserve your family. If haply, Sir, you would reflect thereon."

Kuan Yü replied, quite calmly, "I am a simple soldier of Chiehliang. I am the 'hands and feet' of my lord, his brother. How can I betray him? The city may fall, and then I can but die. Jade may be shattered, but its whiteness remains; bamboo may be burned, but its joints stand out. My body may be broken, but my fame shall live in history. Say no more, but leave the city, I beg. I will fight Sun Ch'üan to the death."

"My master desires to enter into such a league with you as did Ts'in and Chin in former days, that you may mutually assist to destroy Ts'ao Ts'ao and restore the Hans. That is his idea, and why do you persist in this wrong course?"

As he finished this speech, Kuan P'ing, who was by, drew his sword to slay him. But his father checked him.

"Remember his brother is in Shu, helping your uncle. If you hurt him you will injure the principle of fraternity."

He then bade his servants lead Chuko Chin away. He went, his face covered with shame, and left the city. When he reached his master he told of Kuan Yü's obduracy and rejection of all argument.

"He is indeed a loyal servant!" said Sun Ch'üan. "Still, what is to be done next?"

"Take the *sortes*," said Lü Fan.

So the lots were taken and explained to mean that the lord's enemies should flee to a distance.

Then Sun Ch'üan asked Lü Mêng, saying, "If he fly to a distance, how can he be captured?"

"The divination exactly fits in with my schemes," replied he, "and though Kuan had wings to soar to the skies he would not escape my net."

> The dragon in a puddle is the sport of shrimps,
> The phœnix in a cage is mocked of small birds.

The scheme of Lü Mêng will be unfolded in the next chapter.

CHAPTER LXXVII.

Kuan Yü Manifests his Sacred Character at the
Jade Fount Hill;
Ts'ao Ts'ao is Possessed at Loyang.

Sun Ch'üan having asked Lü Mêng for a plan, Lü replied, "This man Kuan has very few men left, and he will not venture along the high road. North of Maich'êng is a risky path, and he will try to escape along that. Therefore you must lay an ambush for him twenty *li* away from the city, but do not stop him. Let him go by, and then harass his rear. Thus he will be forced into Linchü. Set another small ambush near there, and you will capture your enemy. For the present, attack the city vigorously on all sides but one, leaving the north gate for escape."

Before carrying out this plan, Sun bade Lü Fan consult the auspices. He did so, announcing that the enemy would flee toward the northwest, but would be caught that night before midnight.

So Chu Jan was sent in command of the first ambush, five companies, and P'an Chang with a cohort was the second. The men were all veterans.

When Kuan Yü mustered his fighting men in the city, he had but three hundred, all told. The food was done. That night many men of Wu came to the city walls and called to their friends by name, and many of these slipped over the wall and deserted, reducing the small force still further. No rescue force appeared, and Kuan was at the end of his resources. Again he bewailed to Wang Fu the obstinacy that had led him to neglect his wise warning.

"I think even if Tzǔ-ya (Lü Shang) could come to life again he would be helpless in this case," replied Wang Fu, sadly.

Said Chao Lei, "Liu Fêng and Mêng Ta have surely decided not to send help from Shangyung. Let us abandon this miserable place and try to regain Hsich'uan. We may then tempt our fortune once more."

"I agree with you that that is the best plan," said Kuan Yü.

Then he ascended the walls and surveyed the country. Noting that the weakest side was the north, he called in some of the inhabitants and enquired the nature of the country on that side.

They replied, "There are only paths there, but by them one may get into Hsich'uan."

"We will go that way to-night," said Kuan.

Wang Fu opposed it, pointing out that they would surely fall into an ambush. The main road would be safer.

"There may be an ambush, but do I fear that?" said the old warrior.

Orders were given to be ready to march.

"At least be very cautious," said Wang Fu. "I will defend this city to the very last; I only need a few men. Never will we surrender. Only I hope, most noble Marquis, that you will send me speedy help."

The two parted in tears; Wang Fu and Chou Ts'ang remaining to guard Maich'êng. Kuan Yü, Kuan P'ing and Chao Lei marched with their weak force out of the north gate. Kuan Yü, his great sword ready to hand, went first. About the time of watch-setting, a score of *li* lay between them and the city. There they saw a deep cleft in the hills wherefrom rolled the sound of beaten drums. And men were shouting.

Soon appeared a large force with Chu Jan at their head. He came dashing forward, and summoned the small party to surrender if they would save their lives. But Kuan Yü whipped his steed to a gallop and bore down on the leader with anger in his eyes. Then Chu Jan ran away. Kuan Yü followed him till there came the loud boom of a large drum, and out sprang men from all sides. Kuan Yü dared not engage such a number, and fled in the direction of Linchü. Chu Jan came up behind and attacked the flying soldiers, so that Kuan's following gradually became smaller and smaller.

Still he struggled on. A few *li* farther the drums rolled again, and torches lit up all round. This was P'an Chang's ambush, and he appeared flourishing his sword. Kuan Yü whirled his blade and went to meet him, but P'an ran away after a couple of bouts. However, Kuan Yü saw they were too many for him, and sought refuge among the mountains. His son followed, and when he got within speaking distance he gave him the mournful tidings that Chao Lei had fallen. Kuan Yü was very sad, and bade his son try to protect the rear while he should force his way forward.

With a half score men he reached Chüehshih, a place with mountains on both sides. At their foot was a thick mass of reeds and dried grass. The trees grew very close. It was then the fifth watch. Presently the small party stumbled into another ambush, and the men thrust forth hooks and threw ropes. Entangled in these, Kuan Yü's horse fell, and Kuan Yü reeled out of the saddle. In a moment he was a prisoner. Kuan P'ing dashed to his rescue, but before he could do anything he also was surrounded and held. Father and son were both captives.

With great joy Sun Ch'üan heard of the success of his plans. He assembled all his officers in his tent to await the arrival of the prisoners. Before long, Ma Chung, who had actually caught Kuan Yü, came hustling his prisoner before him.

"I have long had a friendly feeling for you," said Sun Ch'üan to Kuan Yü, "on account of your great virtues. Now I would have made a covenant and alliance with you, if you would. You and your son have long held yourselves to be invincible, but you see you are my prisoners to-day. Yet I hope to win you over to my side."

But Kuan Yü only answered roughly, "You green-eyed boy! You red-bearded rat! I made a covenant in the Peach Garden with my brothers to uphold the Hans. Think you that I will stand side by side with a rebel such as you are? I am a victim of your vile schemes, but I can only die once. And there is no need of many words."

"He is a real hero, and I love him," said Sun Ch'üan to those standing near. "I will treat him well and endeavour to win him over. Do you think it well?"

Said one of them, "When Ts'ao Ts'ao had hold of this man he treated him lavishly well. He created him a marquis; he feasted him day after day at public and private banquets; he gave him gold and presented him with silver; all this, hoping to retain him at his side. But he failed. The man broke through his gates, slew his captains and went away. To-day Ts'ao Ts'ao fears him, and almost moved the capital for dread of him. Now he is in your power destroy him, or you will rue the day. Evil will come if you spare him."

Sun Ch'üan reflected for some time.

"You are right," said he presently, and gave the order for execution.

So father and son met their fate together in the twenty-fourth year (219 A.D.) in the tenth month. Kuan *Kung* was fifty-eight.

A poem says:—

> Peerless indeed was our lord Kuan, of the latter days,
> Head and shoulders stood he out among the best;
> Godlike and terrible in war, elegant and refined in peace,
> Resplendent as the noonday sun in the heavens,
> Haloed as are the noblest of those early days,
> He stands, the brightest model for all ages,
> And not only for the strenuous days he lived in.

And another:—

> Seek ye a noble one? Then take ye the way of Chiehliang,
> Watch ye how all men revere Yün-ch'ang,
> Each excelling others to honour him,
> Him, one of the three brothers of the Peach Garden Oath,
> Of whom two have won sacrifices, as Emperor and prince.
> Incomparable, their aura spreads through the world;
> They are resplendent as the great lights of the firmament;
> Temples to our lord Kuan abound, no village lacks one,
> Their venerable trees at sundown are the resting places for birds.

So the great warrior ended his life. His famous steed, also captured with his master, was sent to Sun Ch'üan, who gave him as a reward to his captor, Ma Chung. But "Red Hare" survived his master only a short time; he refused to feed, and soon died.

Forebodings of misfortune came to Wang Fu within the city of Mai. His bones felt cold; his flesh crept; and he said to his colleague, "I have had a terrible dream in which I saw our lord all dripping with gore. I would question him, but I was overcome with dread. May it augur no evil tidings!"

Just then the men of Wu came up to the city wall and displayed the gory heads of the two, father and son. Wang Fu and Chou Ts'ang went up on the wall to see if the dread tokens were real. There was no doubt. Wang Fu with a despairing cry threw himself over the wall and perished, Chou Ts'ang died by his own hand. Thus the city fell to Wu.

Now the spirit of Kuan the Noble did not dissipate into space, but wandered through the void till it came to a certain spot in Tangyanghsien on a famous hill known as the Mount of the Jade Spring. There lived a venerable Buddhist priest whose name in the faith was P'u-ching. He was originally of Ssŭshui Kuan and abbot of a state guardian temple. In the course of roaming about the world he had reached this place. Entranced with its natural beauty, he had built himself a shelter of boughs and grass, where he sat in meditation on The Way. He had a novice with him to beg food and to attend to his simple wants.

This night, about the third watch, the moon was bright and the air serene. P'u-ching sat in his usual attitude in the silence of the mountains. Suddenly he heard a great voice calling in the upper air, "Give back my head; give back my head."

Gazing upward he saw the shape of a man mounted on a horse. In the hand he saw a shining blade like unto the Black Dragon. Two military figures were with him, one on either side. He on the left had a white face; he on the right was swarthy of countenance with a curly beard. And they followed the figure with the shining blade. They floated along on a cloud which came to rest on the summit of the mountain.

The recluse recognised the figure as that of Kuan the Noble, so with his yak's tail flagellum he smote the lintel of his hut and cried, "Where is Yün-ch'ang?"

The spirit understood, and the figure dismounted, glided down and came to rest at the door of the hut. Interlacing its fingers, it stood in a reverential attitude and said, "Who is my teacher, and what is his name in the faith?"

"In the state guardian temple in Ssŭshui Kuan I once saw you, O noble Marquis, and I was not likely to forget your face," replied the priest.

"I am deeply grateful for the help you gave me. Misfortune has befallen me, and I have ceased to live. I would seek the pure instruction and beg you to indicate the obscure way."

"Let us not discuss former wrongdoings nor present correct actions. Later events are the inevitable result of former causes. I know that Lü Mêng has injured you. You call aloud for the return of your head; who will also return the heads of your several victims—Yen Liang, Wên Ch'ou and the guardians of the five passes?"

Thereupon Kuan the Noble seemed suddenly to comprehend, bowed in token of assent and disappeared. After this appearance to the recluse his spirit wandered hither and thither about the mountain, manifesting its sacred character and guarding the people.

Impressed by his virtue, the inhabitants builded a temple on the Mountain of the Jade Spring, wherein they sacrificed at the four seasons. In later days, one wrote a couplet for the temple, the first member reading, "Ruddy faced, reflecting the honest heart within, out-riding the wind on the Red Hare steed, mindful of the Red Emperor"; and the second, "In the light of clear lamp, reading the histories, resting on the Black Dragon Blade curved as the young moon, heart pure as the azure heaven."

The execution of Kuan gave Sun Ch'üan undisputed possession of the whole of the Chingchou district. He rewarded his soldiers and spread a great feast at which Lü Mêng was in the seat of honour. He made a speech, saying, "After long waiting, the desire of my heart has come to me very easily through the magnificent efforts of my friend Lü Mêng."

Lü Mêng bowed and bowed deprecatingly, but Sun Ch'üan continued, "My good Chou Yü was superior to most men, and he defeated Ts'ao Ts'ao at Red Wall. Alas! he died too soon. My good Lu Su succeeded him. His first appearance inaugurated the general policy of creating a state. That was the first instance of his keen insight. When Ts'ao Ts'ao descended upon my country, and everyone counselled me to yield, he advised me to summon my good Chou Yü to oppose and smite him. That was the second instance of his keen insight. He made only one fault; he advised me to let Liu Pei occupy this district. Now to-day my good Lü Mêng has succeeded, and in that he far surpasses both his predecessors."

Then he filled a goblet and in person presented it to the guest of the evening. Lü took the cup, but as he raised it a sudden change came over him. Dashing the cup to the ground, he seized Sun Ch'üan, crying, "O green-eyed boy! O red-bearded rat! Do you know me?"

Consternation seized the whole assembly, but some rushed to the rescue of their lord, who had been thrown to the floor by the guest he had so lately complimented. Rushing forward over his body, Lü Mêng sat himself in the host's seat, his eyebrows staring stiff and his eyes glaring.

"After I quelled the Yellow Turbans, I went hither and thither for thirty years. Now I have fallen victim to your base plots and you have overcome me. If living I have been unable to gorge upon the flesh of mine enemy, dead I will pursue the spirit of this bandit Lü. I am the Marquis of Hanshout'ing, Kuan Yün-ch'ang."

Terror-stricken, Sun Ch'üan was the first to fall prostrate, and all his officers followed him.

Thereupon Lü Mêng fell over dead, with blood gushing from the seven orifices of his body.

In due time the body was coffined and interred. He was created posthumously "Prefect of Nanchün and Marquis of Ch'uanling." His son was given hereditary nobility.

After this visitation Sun Ch'üan lived in constant terror. Soon Chang Chao came in from Chienyeh to see him and blame him for the murder.

"My lord, by the slaughter of Kuan Yü you have brought misfortune very near to your state. You know the oath sworn in the Peach Garden. Now Liu Pei has the force of Hsich'uan at his back, Chuko Liang as adviser, and those heroes Chang Fei, Huang and Ma Ch'ao to carry out his behests. When Liu Pei hears of the death of both father and son he will set in motion the whole force he has to avenge them, and I fear you cannot stand such an onslaught."

Sun Ch'üan started up in a fright. "Yes; I have made a little mistake," said he. "But seeing it is so, what shall I do?"

"You need have no fear," replied Chang. "I have a plan to fend off the armies of Hsich'uan from our borders and keep Chingchou quite safe."

"What is your plan?" asked Sun Ch'üan.

"Ts'ao Ts'ao with his many legions is greedily aiming at the whole country. Liu Pei, eager for revenge, will ally himself with him, and, should they combine against this country, we should be in great danger. Therefore I advise you to send Kuan Yü's head to Ts'ao Ts'ao to make it appear that Ts'ao Ts'ao was the prime cause of his destruction. This should divert Liu Pei's extreme hatred toward him and send the armies of Western Shu against Wei instead of toward Wu. After carefully considering the whole matter, I counsel this as the best course of action."

Sun Ch'üan thought the move worth making, and so the head of the great warrior was placed in a box and sent off as quickly as possible to Ts'ao Ts'ao.

At this time Ts'ao's army had marched back from Mopei to Loyang. When he heard of the coming of the gruesome gift he was glad at heart and said, "So Yün-ch'ang is dead; now I can stick to my mat and sleep soundly at night."

But Ssŭma I saw through the ruse and said from his place by the steps, "This is a trick to divert evil from Wu."

"What do you mean? How?" said Ts'ao Ts'ao.

"The Peach Garden Oath bound the three brothers to live and die together. Now Wu is fearful of revenge for the execution of one of the three and sends the head to you to cause Liu Pei's wrath to fasten on you, O Prince. He wishes Liu to attack you instead of himself, the real perpetrator of the crime. Then he will find a way of accomplishing his ends while you two are quarreling."

"You are right, friend," said Ts'ao; "and now how can we escape?"

"I think escape is easy. You have the head of Kuan Yü; make a wooden image of the remainder of the body and bury the whole with the rites suitable to a minister of state. When Liu Pei hears of this he will turn his hate toward Sun Ch'üan and raise all his forces to attack him. If you will think it out you will see that whichever is victor the other will be smitten, and if we get one of the two the other will follow before very long."

Ts'ao Ts'ao was pleased with the solution. Then he ordered the messenger to come in with the box, which was opened, and he looked upon the face of the dead. The features had not changed; the face bore the same appearance as of old. Ts'ao Ts'ao smiled.

"I hope you have been well since our last meeting, Yün-ch'ang," said Ts'ao.

To his horror, the mouth opened, the eyes rolled and the long beard and hair stiffened. Ts'ao Ts'ao fell to the ground in a swoon.

They rushed to him, but it was a long time before he recovered consciousness.

"General Kuan is indeed a spirit," he said.

Suddenly the messenger who had brought the dead warrior's head became also possessed by the spirit of Kuan Yü, and fell to cursing and reviling his master, Sun Ch'üan, and he told the story of what had befallen Lü Mêng.

Ts'ao Ts'ao, filled with dread, prepared sacrifices and performed the rites for the honoured dead. An effigy was carved out of heavy "fragrant" wood and buried outside the south gate with all the rites of a princely noble, a huge concourse of officials of all grades following in the procession. At the funeral Ts'ao Ts'ao himself bowed before the coffin and poured a libation. He also conferred on the dead the posthumous title of "Prince Ching," and appointed guardians of the tomb. The messenger was sent back to Wu.

The Prince of Hanchung returned to his capital. Fa Chêng memorialised, saying. "O Prince, thy consort has passed away and the Lady Sun has returned to her maiden home, perhaps never to come again. Human relations should not be set at nought, wherefore a secondary consort should be sought, so that all things may be correctly ordered within the palace."

The prince having signified his acceptance of the principle, Fa Chêng continued, "There is the sister of Wu I, comely and good, and declared by the physiognomist as destined to high honour. She was betrothed to Liu Pao, son of Liu Yen, but he died in youth, and she has remained unwedded. Take her as a wife."

"It is incompatible with propriety; Liu Mao and I are of the same ancestry."

"As to the degree of relationship, would it differ from the marriage of Wên of Chin and Huaiying?"

Upon this precedent the prince gave his consent and wedded the lady, and she bore to him two sons, the elder of whom was named Jung and the younger Li.

Meanwhile, the whole land of Shu was prospering, the people were tranquil, and the state was becoming wealthy. The fields yielded bountiful harvests. Suddenly there came one who told of the attempt of Sun Ch'üan to ally himself with Kuan Yü by marriage, and the indignant rejection of the proposal.

"Chingchou is in danger," said K'ung-ming. "Recall and replace Kuan Yü."

Then began to arrive a series of messengers from Chingchou, bearers of news of the moves in the game. At first they brought good tidings, then evil. Kuan Hsing came first to tell of the drowning of the seven armies. Then one reported the installation of beacon towers along the river bank, and other preparations which seemed as near perfect as any could be. And Liu Pei's anxiety ceased.

But evil tidings were on the way. Liu Pei was ill at ease and felt a creepiness of the skin that boded evil. He was restless by day and sleepless by night. One night he rose from his couch and was reading by the light of a candle when drowsiness overcame him and he fell asleep over the low table by his side. He dreamed. A cold gust of wind swept through the chamber, almost putting out the candle flame. When it brightened again he glanced up and saw a figure standing near the light.

"Who are you, who thus come by night to my chamber?" asked he.

The figure made no reply, and Yüan-tê got up to go over and see who it was. Then the figure took the shape of his brother. But it avoided him, retreating as he advanced.

"Brother, there is nothing wrong, I hope. But surely something of great importance brings you here thus in the dead of the night. And why do you avoid me thus; your brother, who loves you as himself?"

Then the figure wept and said, "Brother, send your armies to avenge me."

As Kuan Yü said that, a chilly blast went through the room, and the figure disappeared. Just then Yüan-tê awoke and knew that he had dreamed.

The drums were beating the third watch as he awoke. He felt greatly worried and disturbed. So he went into the front portion of the palace and sent for K'ung-ming. Soon he came, and Yüan-tê told him of the vision.

"You have been thinking too deeply of Kuan Yü lately, my lord," said K'ung-ming. "There is no need to be distressed."

But Yüan-tê could not find comfort, and K'ung-ming was long in calming his feelings and arguing away his fancies.

As K'ung-ming left the palace he met Hsü Ching, who said, "I have a very secret piece of news to tell you, so I came on here."

"What is your secret?"

"There is a report about that Wu has got possession of Chingchou; Lü Mêng has taken it. And more than that, Kuan Yü is dead. I had to come to tell you."

"I saw it in the sky. A large star fell over against Chingchou, and I knew some evil had befallen Kuan Yü. But I feared the effect upon our master and I forbore to say anything."

They did not know that Yüan-tê was standing just within the door. Suddenly he rushed out, seized K'ung-ming by the sleeve and said, "Why did you deceive me? Why, when you had such terrible news?"

"Because it is only a rumour," replied they. "It is too improbable for belief. We pray you not to be distressed."

"By our oath we live or die together; how can I go on living if he is lost?"

The two men soothed their lord as best they could, but even as they spoke to him one of the private attendants said that Ma Liang and I Chi had arrived. Yüan-tê called them in and questioned them eagerly. They said Chingchou was indeed lost, and Kuan Yü begged for instant help.

The letters they brought had not been read before Liao Hua was ushered in. He prostrated himself and, weeping, told the story of the refusal of help on the part of Liu Fêng and Mêng Ta.

"Then is my brother lost!" cried Yüan-tê.

"If those two have really behaved so badly, the offence is even too great for death," said K'ung-ming. "But calm yourself, O Prince. I will see about an army and lead it to the rescue."

"If Yün-ch'ang is gone, I cannot live," moaned Yüan-tê. "To-morrow I will set out with an army to rescue him."

Yüan-tê sent off a messenger to Chang Fei and gave orders to muster horse and foot for instant departure.

Before day dawned other messengers arrived, giving step
by step the sequence of the tragedy, the last relating Kuan
Yü's capture, haughty refusal to bend, and his death.

When he heard of the final catastrophe, Yüan-tê uttered a
great cry and fell swooning.

> His mind went back to the pledge of days gone by;
> Could he live still and let his brother die?

What happened will be told in the next chapter.

CHAPTER LXXVIII

HUA T‘O, TREATING TS‘AO TS‘AO, HIMSELF DIES;
TS‘AO TS‘AO'S LAST WORDS AND DEATH.

As has been said, the Prince of Hanchung swooned on hearing the terrible news of the death of the two Kuans, father and son. His officers went to his help, and when he had recovered sufficiently they led him to his private apartments.

"My lord, control your grief," said K‘ung-ming. "Life and death are fixed by fate. Kuan Yü brought the evil upon himself by his harshness and haughtiness. You must now take care of your health and mature your vengeance."

"When we swore brotherhood in the Peach Garden we pledged ourselves to live or die together. What enjoyment of riches and honours is there for me now that my brother is gone?"

Just then he saw Kuan Yü's son, Hsing, coming in in deep distress. At sight of the youth, Liu Pei uttered a great cry and again sank to the earth. By and by he came to, and spent the whole day weeping and swooning at intervals. For three days he refused all nourishment, and he wept so bitterly that his garments were wetted, and there were spots of blood. K‘ung-ming and the others tried every means to soothe him, but he was inconsolable.

"I swear I will not live under the same heaven as Sun Ch‘üan," cried he.

"It is said that the head of your brother has been sent to Ts‘ao Ts‘ao, but Ts‘ao has buried the remains with the rites of a princely noble," said K‘ung-ming.

"Why did he do that?" asked Yüan-tê.

"Because he thought thereby to bring evil upon Ts‘ao. But Ts‘ao saw through the subterfuge and has buried your brother with great honour so that your anger may burn against Wu."

"I want to send my armies to punish Wu and appease my wrath," said Yüan-tê.

"No; you may not do that. Wu wishes to move you to smite Wei, and Wei wishes you to attack Wu, each harbouring the malevolent design of taking advantage of the quarrel. You would do well, my lord, to keep your armies at home. Put on mourning for Kuan Yü, and wait till Wei and Wu are at war. That will be your time."

The other officers supported K‘ung-ming, and Yüan-tê listened. Presently his grief spent itself, and he began to take food again. An edict was promulgated enjoining mourning dress upon all officials. The prince went outside the south gate to summon the spirit home, and sacrificed and wailed a whole day for the dead warrior, his brother.

Although Ts'ao Ts'ao had given honourable burial to the remains of Kuan Yü, yet he was continually haunted by the dead man's spirit. Every night when he closed his eyes he saw Kuan the Noble as he knew him so well in the flesh. These visions made him nervous, and he sought the advice of his officers. Some suggested the building of new rooms for his own use.

"There is much witchcraft and malign influence in this old palace at Loyang; build new rooms for your own occupation," said they.

"I would, and it should be called 'Chienshih,' or 'The Firm Foundation,'" said he. "But where is the architect?"

They told him there was one Su Yüeh, a very cunning artificer. He was called and set to work on the plans for a nine *chien* pavilion for Ts'ao Ts'ao's own use. It had verandahs and upper rooms as well. His plans pleased Ts'ao greatly.

"You have planned just such a place as I wished, only where will you find the main beam for such a building?"

"I know a certain tree that will serve," said the architect. "About thirty *li* from the city there is the Pool of the Leaping Dragon. Near it is a shrine, and beside that grows a fine pear tree. It is over a hundred feet high, and that will serve for the roof tree.

Ts'ao Ts'ao at once sent men to fell the tree. But after one whole day's labour the men came back to say they could make no impression on it neither with saw nor axe. Ts'ao, doubting their word, went to see. When he had dismounted and stood by the tree he could not but admire its size and proportions, as it rose above him tall, straight and unbranched till the wide-spreading and symmetrical top reached into the clouds. But he bade the men attack it again. Then a few aged men of the village came and said, "The tree has stood here some centuries and is the haunt of a spirit. We think it should not be cut down."

Ts'ao grew annoyed. "I have gone to and fro in the world now some forty years, and there is no one, from the Emperor to the commoner, who does not fear me. What spirit is there who dares oppose my wish?"

Drawing the sword he was wearing, he went up to the tree and slashed at the trunk. The tree groaned as he struck, and blood stains spattered his dress. Terror-stricken, he threw down the sword, mounted his horse and galloped off.

But that evening when he retired to rest he could not sleep. He rose, went into the outer room and sat there leaning on a

low table. Suddenly a man appeared with his hair unbound,
dressed in black and carrying a naked sword. The visitor
came straight toward Ts'ao stopped in front of him and,
pointing, cried out, "Behold the Spirit of the pear tree. You
may desire to build your *chien-shih* pavilion and you may
contemplate rebellion, but when you began to attack my sacred
tree the number of your days was accomplished. I am come
now to slay you."

"Where are the guards?" shouted Ts'ao in terror.

The figure struck at him with the sword. Ts'ao cried out
and then awoke. His head was aching unbearably.

They sought the best physicians for him, but they failed to
relieve the terrible pain.

Sympathy for their lord was universal among Ts'ao's
subordinates. Hua Hsin one day said to his master, "My lord,
have you heard of Hua T'o?"

"Do you mean him of Chiangtung who cured Chou T'ai?"

"Yes; that is he," replied Hua Hsin.

"I have heard something of his fame, but I know nothing of
his capabilities in his art."

"He is very clever; there are few so skilful. If one is ill
and calls him in he knows immediately whether to use drugs,
or the needle, or the cautery, and the patient finds relief at
once. Let one suffer from an internal complaint and drugs
are ineffectual, with a dose of hashish he throws the patient
into a state of perfect insensibility and then opens the
abdomen and washes the affected organs with a medicament.
The patient feels no pain. When the cleansing is complete,
he sews up the wound with thread, dresses it, and in a month
or less the patient is well. This shows you how skilful he is.

"One day Hua was travelling, when he heard a man by the
wayside groaning with pain.

"'That is dyspepsia,' said he. And further questions confirmed the diagnosis. He prescribed long draughts of the
juice of garlic as an emetic, and the man vomited a worm;
after this he was quite well. One Ch'ên Têng, the Prefect of
Kuangling, suffered from a heavy feeling at the heart. His
face was red and congested, and he had no appetite. Hua
gave him a drug, and he threw up many internal wriggling
parasites with red heads. The Prefect asked what had caused
the trouble, and Hua told him that he ate too much strong-
smelling fish. He could cure him this once, but in three years
the disease would recur, and then nothing could save him.
Three years later Ch'ên died. Another man had a tumour
between the eyes, and it itched intolerably. Hua examined
it and said there was a bird in it. The tumour was opened,
and, surely enough, a canary flew out. The patient was
relieved. A dog bit a man's toe, and two tumourous growths
ensued, one of which itched intolerably and the other pained

severely. Hua said the painful one contained several needles, and the other a couple of *wei-ch'i* pips. He opened the two swellings, and the contents were as he had said. Really he is of the same class of leech as Pien Ch'iao and Ts'ang Kung. He lives at Chinch'êng, not far away, and could be here very soon."

Ts'ao Ts'ao summoned him, and as soon as he arrived Hua T'o felt the pulse and made careful examination.

"Prince, your headaches are due to a malignant humour within the brain case. The humour is too thick to get out. Swallowing drugs will do no good. But I propose to administer a dose of hashish, then open the brain case and remove the thickened humour. That will be a radical cure."

"You mean you want to kill me," cried Ts'ao angrily.

"O Prince, you have heard how I cured Kuan Yü of the poison that had got into his bones? I scraped them, and he did not hesitate a moment. Your malady is trifling, and why do you mistrust me?"

"A painful arm may be scraped, but how can you cut open a man's head? The fact is you have conspired with some of Kuan's friends to take this opportunity to make away with me in revenge for his death."

He told his lictors to hale Hua T'o to gaol, and there he was tortured to try to find who were his accomplices. Chia Hsü pleaded for him on account of his rare skill, but his intervention was of no avail.

"The man wants to get a chance to kill me; he is the same sort of scoundrel as Chi P'ing."

The wretched physician was subjected to worse sufferings. His gaoler was a certain Wu, nicknamed "The Gaoler" by nearly everybody. He was kindly disposed to Hua and saw that he was well fed. Hua T'o conceived a liking for his gaoler and said to him one day, "I am doomed, I know. The pity is that my Black Bag treatise on medicine may be lost. You have been most kind to me, and as I have no other way of recompensing you I will give you a letter to my wife telling her to send the Black Bag, and I will give it to you that you may carry on my art."

Wu rejoiced greatly, thinking that he would throw up the menial position of gaoler and travel about the country healing sick folk, and so he told Hua T'o to write the letter and promised to carry on his work.

The letter was written and given to Wu "The Gaoler," who lost no time in sending a man to Hua T'o's house for the Black Bag. After Hua T'o had read through the book carefully, he presented it to Wu, who took it home and hid it away.

Not many days after this, Hua T'o died in prison. "The Gaoler" bought a coffin and had him buried. This done, he quitted the prison and went home. But when he asked for the book he found that his wife had discovered it and was using it to light the fire. He snatched away what was left of it, but a whole volume was missing, and what was left amounted only to a few pages. He vented his anger in cursing his wife, and she retorted, saying, "If you become such a learned person as Hua T'o you will only die in prison like him. What good did it all do him?"

It struck Wu that there was something in what she said, and he ceased grumbling at her. But the upshot of all this was that the learning in the "Treatise of the Black Bag" was finally lost to the world, for what was left only contained a few recipes relating to domestic animals.

> Hua T'o was the ablest of leeches
> Like Chang Sung, who overtopped all,
> He saw what diseases were lurking
> Within a man's outermost wall.
> Alas! that he died, and his writings
> Passed beyond any man's ken,
> With the famous Black Bag that contained them,
> For he was a healer of men.

Meanwhile, Ts'ao Ts'ao became worse, the uncertainty of the intentions of his rivals aggravating his disease not a little. Then they said an envoy had come with letters from Wu, the gist of which was satisfactory, as it ran like this:—

"Thy servant, Sun Ch'üan, has long seen whom destiny indicates as master of all, and looks forward with confidence to his early accession to the dignity. If he will send his armies to destroy Liu Pei and sweep rebellion from the west, his servant at the head of his armies will submit and accept his land as a fief."

Ts'ao Ts'ao laughed as he read this, and he said to his officers, "Is this youth trying to put me on a furnace?"

But his attendants seriously replied, "O Prince, the Hans have been feeble too long, while your virtues and merits are like the mountains. All the people look to you, and when Sun Ch'üan acknowledges himself as your minister he is but responsive to the will of God and the desire of men. It is wrong that you oppose when such contrary influences work to a common end, and you must soon ascend to the high place."

Ts'ao Ts'ao smiled. "I have served the Hans for many years; and if I have acquired some merit, yet I have been rewarded with a princedom and high rank. I dare not aspire to greater things. If the finger of heaven points to me, then shall I be as Wên *Wang* of Chou."

"As Sun Ch'üan acknowledges himself your servant and promises obedience, you, my lord, can confer a title upon him and assign to him the duty of attacking Liu Pei," said Ssŭma I.

Approving of the suggestion, Ts'ao Ts'ao gave Sun Ch'üan the title of *"P'iao-ch'i,* General of Cavalry, and Marquis of

Nanch'ang," and appointed him to the governorship of Chingchou.   Forthwith this command was sent away to Sun Ch'üan.

Ts'ao Ts'ao's condition grew worse daily.   One night he
had a dream of three horses feeding out of the same manger.
Next day he told it to Chia Hsü, adding that he thought it
betokened some evil through the Ma family.   How did he
interpret the dream?

"It is auspicious to dream of *lu* (pay) and *ma* (horses),"
replied Chia Hsü.   "And naturally such things come to the
ts'ao (a manger, eating place).   I do not think you need feel
any misgivings."

Ts'ao Ts'ao was comforted.

> Ts'ao dreamed three steeds together fed,
> The vision seers could not explain,
> None guessed how soon, when Ts'ao was dead,
> One dynasty would rule again.
> Ah, yes; Ts'ao Ts'ao had vainly wrought;
> Of none avail each wicked wile,
> For, later, in Wei court, there fought
> Against him one with equal guile.

That night Ts'ao Ts'ao became worse.   As he lay on his
couch he felt dizzy and could not see, so he rose and sat by a
table, upon which he leaned.   It seemed to him that someone
shrieked, and, peering into the darkness, he perceived the
forms of many of his victims.   And all were bloodstained.
They stood in the obscurity and whispered, demanding his
life.   He rose, lifted his sword and threw it wildly into the
air.   Just then there was a loud crash, and the south-west
corner of the new building came down.   And Ts'ao Ts'ao
fell with it.   His attendants raised him and bore him to
another palace, where he might lie at peace.

But he found no peace.   The next night was disturbed by
the ceaseless wailing of women's voices.   When day dawned,
Ts'ao sent for his officers, and said to them:

"Thirty years have I spent in the turmoil of war and have
always refused belief in the supernatural.   But what does
all this mean?"

"O Prince, you should summon the Taoists to offer
sacrifices and prayers," said they.

Ts'ao Ts'ao sighed.   "The wise man said, 'He who offends
against heaven has no one to pray to.'   I feel that my fate is
accomplished, my days have run and there is no help."

But he would not consent to call in the priests.   Next day
his symptoms were worse.   He was panting and could no
longer see distinctly.   He sent hastily for Hsiahou Tun, who
came at once.   But as he drew near the doors he too saw the
shadowy forms of the slain Empress and her children and
many other victims of Ts'ao Ts'ao's cruelty.   He was overcome with fear and fell to the ground.   The servants raised
him and led him away, very ill.

Then Ts'ao called in four of his trusty advisers, Ts'ao Hung, Ch'ên Chün. Chia Hsü and Ssūma I, that they might hear his last wishes. Ts'ao Hung, speaking for the four, said, "Take good care of your precious self, O Prince, that you may quickly recover."

But Ts'ao Ts'ao said, "Thirty and more years have I gone up and down, and many a bold man has fallen before me. The only ones that remain are Sun Ch'üan and Liu Pei. I have not yet slain them. Now I am very ill, and I shall never again stand before you; wherefore my family affairs must be settled. My first born fell in battle, when he was young. The Lady P'ien bore four sons to me, as you know. The third, Chih, was my favourite, but he was vain and unreliable, fond of wine and lax in morals. Therefore he is not my heir. My second son, Chang, is valiant, but imprudent. The fourth is weakly and may not live long. My eldest, P'ei, is steady and serious; he is fit to succeed me, and I look to you to support him."

Ts'ao Hung and the others wept as they heard these words, and they left the chamber. Then Ts'ao Ts'ao bade his servants bring some of the Tibetan incense that he burned every day, and he handed out sticks to his handmaids. And he said to them, "After my death you must diligently attend to your womanly labours. You can make silken shoes for sale, and so earn your own living."

He also bade them go on living in the Bronze Bird Pavilion and celebrate a daily sacrifice for him, with music by the singing women, and presentation of the eatables laid before his tablet.

Next he commanded that seventy-two sites for a tomb should be selected near Wuch'êng in the Changtê Prefecture, that no one should know his actual burying place, lest his remains should be digged up.

And when these final orders had been given he sighed a few times shed some tears and died. He was sixty-six, and passed away in the first month of the twenty-fifth year (210 A.D.).

A certain poet composed a song on Yehch'êng expressing sympathy for Ts'ao Ts'ao, which is given here:—

I stood in Yeh and saw the River Chang
Go gliding by. Methought no common man
E'er rose from such a place. Or he was great
In war, a poet, or an artist skilled.
  Perchance a model minister, or son,
Or famous for fraternal duty shown.
The thoughts of heroes are not ours to judge,
Nor are their actions for our eyes to see.
A man may stand the first in merit; then
His crimes may brand him chief of criminals.
And so his reputation's fair and foul;
His literary gifts may bear the mark
Of genius; he may be a ruler born;

But this is certain; he will stand above
His fellows, herding not with common men.
Takes he the field, then is he bold in fight;
Would he a mansion build, a palace springs.
In all things great, his genius masters him.
And such was Ts'ao Ts'ao.   He could never be
Obedient; he a rebel was, foredoomed.
He seized and ruled, but hungered for more power;
Became a prince, and still was not content.
   And yet this man of glorious career
When gripped by sickness, wept as might a child.
Full well he knew, when on the bed of death,
That all is vanity and nothing worth.
His latest acts were kindly.   Simple gifts
Of fragrant incense gave he to the maids.
Ah me!
   The ancients' splendid deeds or secret thoughts
We may not measure with our puny rule.
But criticise them, pedants, as ye may
The mighty dead will smile at what you say.

As Ts'ao Ts'ao breathed his last the whole of those present raised a great wailing and lamentation.   The news was sent to the members of the family, the heir, Ts'ao Pei, the Marquis of Yenling, Ts'ao Chang, the Marquis of Lintzŭ, Ts'ao Chih, and the Marquis of Hsiaohuai, Ts'ao Hsiung.   They wrapped the body in its shroud, enclosed it in a silver shell and laid it in a golden coffin, which was sent at once home to Yehchün.

The eldest son wept aloud at the tidings and went out with all his following to meet the procession and escort the body of his father into his home.   The coffin was laid in a great hall beside the main building, and all the officials in deep mourning wailed in the hall.

Suddenly one stood out from the ranks of the mourners and said, "I would request the heir to cease lamentation for the dead and devote himself to the present needs of state."

It was Ssŭma Fu, and he continued, "The death of the prince will cause an upheaval in the empire, and it is essential that the heir should assume his dignity without loss of time. There is not mourning alone to be seen to."

The others replied.   "The succession is settled, but the investiture can hardly proceed without the necessary edict. That must be secured."

Said Ch'ên Chiao, who was President of the Board of War, "As the prince died away from home it may be that his favourite son will presume to succeed, and dangerous disputes will ensue."

He slashed off the sleeves of his robe with a sword and shouted fiercely, "We will invest the prince forthwith, and any who do not agree let him be treated as this robe."

Still fear held most of the assembly.   Then arrived Hua Hsin post haste from the capital.   They wondered what his sudden arrival meant.   Soon he entered the hall and said,

"The Prince of Wei is dead and the world is in commotion; why do you not invest his successor quickly?"

"We await the command," cried they in chorus, "and also the princess-consort's order concerning the heirship."

"I have procured the Imperial edict here," cried he, pulling it out from his breast.

They all began to congratulate him. And he read the edict.

Hua Hsin had always been devoted to Wei, and so he drafted this edict and got it sealed by the Emperor Hsien almost by force. However, there it was; and therein Ts'ao P'ei was named as "Prince of Wei, First Minister of State and Governor of Ichou."

Ts'ao P'ei thereupon took his seat in the princely place and received the congratulations of all the officers. This was followed by a banquet.

However, all was not to pass too smoothly. While the banquet was in progress the news came that Ts'ao Chang, with an army of ten legions, was approaching.

In a state of consternation the new prince turned to his courtiers, saying "What shall I do? This young brother of mine, always obstinate and determined and with no little military skill, is marching hither with an army to contest my inheritance."

"Let me go to see the marquis; I can make him desist," said one of the guests.

The others cried, "Only yourself, O Exalted One, can save us in this peril!"

> Quarrel 'tween two sons of Ts'ao
> Just as in the House of Shao.

If you would know who proposed himself as envoy, read the next chapter.

CHAPTER LXXIX.

A Cruel Brother; a Poem;
An Undutiful Nephew: Punishment.

All eyes turned toward the speaker, the high officer of state Chia K'uei, and the young prince commanded him to undertake the mission. So he went out of the city and sought to speak with Ts'ao Chang. Ts'ao Chang came quickly to the point.

"Who has the late prince's seal?" asked he.

Chia K'uei replied calmly, "There is an eldest son to a house, and an heir-apparent to a state. Such a question from you is unbecoming, O Marquis."

The marquis held his peace, and the two proceeded into the city to the gates of the palace. There Chia K'uei suddenly asked him whether he came as a mourner or as a rival claimant.

"I am come as a mourner; I never had any ulterior motive."

"That being so, why bring in your soldiers?"

Whereupon Ts'ao Chang ordered his escort to retire, and entered the city alone. When the brothers met they fell into each other's arms and wept. Then the younger brother yielded command of all his following, and he was directed to go back to Yenling and guard it. He obediently withdrew.

Ts'ao P'ei, being now firmly established, changed the name of the period of his rule to *Yen-K'ang,* "Prolonged Repose." He gave high rank to Chia Hsü, Hua Hsin and Wang Lang, and made many promotions. To the late prince he gave the posthumous title of *Wu Wang,* "Prince of War," and buried him in Kaoling. To the superintendence of the building of his tomb he nominated Yü Chin, but with malevolent intent. For when Yü Chin reached his post he found the walls of the rooms decorated with chalk sketches depicting the drowning of his army and the capture of himself by Kuan Yü. Kuan Yü was looking very dignified and severe. P'ang Tê was refusing to bow to the victor, while he himself was lying in the dust pleading for his life.

Ts'ao P'ei had chosen this method of putting Yü to open shame because he had not preferred death to the dishonour of capture, and had sent an artist on purpose to depict the shameful scenes. When Yü Chin saw them, shame and rage alternately took possession of him till he fell ill. Soon after he died.

War waged he for many a year,
Yet fell prey to craven fear.
None can know another's heart,
Drawing tigers, with bones start.

Soon after the accession, Hua Hsin memorialised, saying, "The Marquis of Yenling has cut himself loose from his army and gone quietly to his post, but your other two brothers did not attend the funeral of their father. Their conduct should be enquired into and punished."

Ts'ao P'ei took up the suggestion and sent a commissioner to each. He who was sent to the younger quickly returned to say that the Marquis of Hsiaohuai had committed suicide rather than suffer for his fault. P'ei ordered honourable burial for him and gave him the posthumous title of "Prince."

Soon after, the envoy to Lintzǔ returned to report that the marquis was spending his time in dissipation, his especial boon companions being two brothers named Ting. They had been very rude. When the envoy had presented himself, the marquis had sat bolt upright, but would not say a word. Ting I had used insulting words.

"The late prince intended our lord to succeed, but was turned therefrom by the slanderous tongues of certain among you. As soon as he is dead your master begins to think of punishment for his own flesh and blood."

The other brother said, "In intellect our lord leads the age, and he ought to have been heir to his father. Now, not only does he not succeed, but he is treated in this harsh way by a lot of court persons of your sort, ignorant of what genius means."

And then the marquis, in a fit of anger, had ordered his lictors to beat the envoy and turn him out.

This treatment of his messenger annoyed Ts'ao P'ei greatly, and he despatched a force under Hsü Chu to arrest his brother and all his immediate surroundings. When Hsü Chu arrived he found the marquis and all his companions dead drunk; so he bound them, put them into carts and sent them to court. He also arrested all the officers of the palace.

Ts'ao P'ei's first order was to put to death the two brothers Ting. The two brothers were not wholly base; they had a reputation for learning, and many were sorry for them.

Ts'ao P'ei's mother, the Lady P'ien, was alarmed at the severity of the new rule, and the suicide of her youngest son wounded her deeply. When she heard that Ts'ao Chih had been arrested and his comrades put to death, she left her palace and went to see her eldest son. As soon as he saw her, the prince hastened to meet her. She began to weep.

"Your brother has always had that weakness for wine, but we let him go his way out of consideration for his undoubted ability. I hope you will not forget he is your brother and that I bore you both. Spare his life that I may close my eyes in peace when I set out for the deep springs."

"I also admire his ability, mother, and have no intention to hurt him. But I would reform him. Have no anxiety as to his fate."

So the mother was comforted and withdrew. The prince then went to a private room and bade them call his brother.

Said Hua Hsin, "Surely the princess-mother has just been interceding for your brother; is it not so?"

"It is so," replied the prince.

"Then let me say that he is too clever to be content to remain in a humble station. If you do not remove him he will do you harm."

"I must obey my mother's command."

"People say your brother simply talks in literature. I do not believe it myself, but he might be put to the test. If he bears a false reputation you can slay him; if what they say is true, then degrade him, lest the scholars of the land should babble."

Soon Ts'ao Chih came, and in a state of great trepidation bowed low before his elder brother, confessing his fault.

The prince addressed him, saying, "Though we are brothers, yet the proper relation between us of prince and minister must not be overlooked. Why then did you behave indecorously? While the late prince lived you made a boast of your literary powers, but I am disposed to think you may have made use of another's pen. Now I require you to compose a poem within the time taken to walk seven paces, and I will spare your life if you succeed. If you fail, then I shall punish you with rigour."

"Will you suggest a theme?" asked Chih.

Now there was hanging in the hall a black and white sketch of two bulls that had been fighting at the foot of a wall, and one of them had just fallen dead into a well. Ts'ao P'ei pointed to the sketch and said, "Take that as the subject. But you are forbidden to use the words 'two bulls, one bull, fighting, wall's foot, falling, well and dead.'"

Ts'ao Chih took seven paces and then recited this poem:—

> Two butcher's victims lowing walked along,
>   Each head bore curving bones, a sturdy pair,
> They met just by a hillock, both were strong,
>   Each would avoid a pit new digged there.
> They fought unequal battle, for at length
>   One lay below a gory mass, inert.
> 'Twas not that they were of unequal strength—
>   Though wrathful both, one did not strength exert.

This exhibition of skill amazed the prince and the whole court. Ts'ao P'ei thought he would use another test, so he bade his brother improvise on the theme of their fraternal

relationship, the words "brotherhood" or "brother" being
barred. Without seeming to reflect, Ts'ao Chih rattled off
this rhyme:—

> They were boiling beans on a beanstalk fire;
> Came a plaintive voice from the pot,
> "O why, since we sprang from the selfsame root,
> Should you kill me with anger hot?"

The allusion in these verses to the cruel treatment of one
member of a family by another was not lost upon Ts'ao P'ei,
and he dropped a few silent tears.

The mother of both men came out at this moment from
her abiding place and said, "Should the elder brother thus
oppress the younger?"

The prince jumped from his seat, saying, "My mother, the
laws of the state cannot be nullified."

Ts'ao Chih was degraded to the rank of "Marquis of
Anhsiang." He accepted the decision without a murmur and
at once left his brother's court.

Ts'ao P'ei's accession was the signal for a set of new laws
and new commands. His behaviour toward the Emperor
was more intemperate than his father's had ever been.

The stories of his harshness reached Ch'êngtu and almost
frightened Liu Pei, who summoned his counsellors to discuss
what he should do.

Said he, "Since the death of Ts'ao Ts'ao and the accession
of his son the position of the Emperor has changed for the
worse. Sun Ch'üan acknowledges the lordship of Wei, and its
influence is becoming too great. I am disposed to destroy
Sun Ch'üan in revenge for the death of my brother. That
done, I will proceed to the capital and its district and purge
the whole land of rebellion. What think you?"

Then Liao Hua stood out from the ranks of officers and
threw himself upon the earth, saying with tears, "Liu Fêng
and Mêng Ta were the true cause of the death of your brother
and his adopted son; both these renegades deserve death."

Yüan-tê was of the same opinion and was going to send and
arrest them forthwith, but here K'ung-ming intervened and
gave wiser advice.

"That is not the way; go slowly or you may stir up strife.
Promote these two and separate them. After that you may
arrest."

The prince saw the prudence of this procedure and stayed
his hand. He raised Liu Fêng to the Prefectship of Mienchu,
and so separated the two delinquents.

Now P'êng Yang and Mêng Ta were old friends. Hearing
what was afoot, the former hastened home and wrote warning
his friend. The letter was confided to a trusty messenger to
bear to Mêng Ta. The messenger was caught as he went out
of the city and carried before Ma Ch'ao, who thus got wind of

the business. He then went to P'êng's house, where, nothing being suspected, he was received kindly and wine was brought in. The two drank for some time. When Ma Ch'ao thought his host sufficiently off his guard, he said, "The Prince of Hanchung used to look on you with great favour; why does he do so 'no longer?"

The host began to rave against his master.

"The obstinate old leather-belly! But I will find some way to pay him out."

In order to see to what lengths he would go, Ma Ch'ao led him on, saying, "Truth to tell, I have long hated the man too."

"Then you join Mêng Ta and attck, while I will win over the Hsich'uan men. That will make it easy enough," said P'êng Yang.

"What you propose is very feasible, but we will talk it over again tomorrow," said Ma Ch'ao, and took leave.

Taking with him the captured man and the letter he carried, he then proceeded to see the prince, to whom he related the whole story. Yüan-tê was very angry and at once had the intended traitor arrested and put in prison, where he was examined under torture to get at full details.

While P'êng Yang lay in prison, bitterly but vainly repentant, Yüan-tê consulted his adviser.

"That fellow P'êng meant to turn traitor: what shall I do with him?"

"The fellow is something of a scholar, but irresponsible," replied K'ung-ming. "He is too dangerous to be left alive."

Thereupon orders were given that he should be put to death in gaol. The news that he had been made away with frightened his sympathiser and friend, Mêng Ta, and put him in a quandary. What had he better do? On the top of this, Liu Fêng's promotion and transfer to Mienchu arrived, and frightened him still more. So he sought advice from two friends, brothers, who lived in Shangyung.

"My friend Fa Chêng and I did much for the prince. But now Fa is dead and I am forgotten. More than that, he wishes to put me to death. What can I do?" said Mêng.

Shên Tan, one of the two, replied, "I think I can find a plan that will secure your safety."

"What is it?" asked Mêng Ta, feeling happier.

"Desertion. My brother I and I have long desired to go over to Wei. You just write the prince a memorial resigning your service and betake yourself to the Prince of Wei, who will certainly employ you in some honourable way. Then we two will follow."

Mêng Ta saw that this was his best course, so he wrote a memorandum, which he gave to the messenger who had brought the recent despatches to take back with him. That night he left his post and went to Wei.

The messenger returned to Ch'êngtu, handed in Mêng Ta's memorial and told the story of his desertion. The king was angry. He tore open the letter and read:—

"In the humble opinion of thy servant, O Prince, you have set out to accomplish a task comparable with that of I Yin and Lu Shang, and to walk in the meritorious footsteps of Huan Kung and Wên Kung. When the great design was rough-hewn you had the support of Wu and Ch'u, wherefore many men of ability incontinently joined you. Since I entered your service I have committed many faults; and if I recognise them, how much more do you see them! Now, O Prince, you are surrounded by famous men, while I, useless as a helper at home and inept as a leader abroad, should be shamed were I to take a place among them.

"It is well known that when Fan Li saw certain eventualities he went sailing on the lakes, and Chiu Fan acknowledged his faults and stayed by the river. Inasmuch as one cannot take means of safeguarding one's self at the critical and dangerous moment, I desire—as is my duty—to go away as I came, untainted. Moreover, I am stupid and without use or merit, merely born in these days as the sport of circumstances. In the days of old, Shên Shêng, though perfectly filial, incurred the suspicions of his father and died; Tzǔ-hsü (Wu Yüan), though perfectly loyal, was put to death. Mêng T'ien, though he extended the borders, suffered the extreme penalty; and Yüeh I, though he destroyed the might of Ch'i, was the victim of calumny. Whenever I have read of these men I have been moved to tears, and now I am in like case and the more mortified. Lately Chingchou was overwhelmed and many officers of rank failed in their duty, not one in a hundred behaving as he should. Only I remained in Fangling and Shangyung and sought service abroad. Now I desire you, O Prince, graciously to understand, to sympathise with thy servant and to condone the step he is about to take. Really I am but a mean man, incapable of great deeds. I know what I am doing, and I dare to say it is no fault. They say that dissolution of bonds should not occasion recrimination and the dismissed servant should take leave without heartburnings. I have taken your orders many times, and now, O Prince, you must act yourself. I write this with extreme trepidation."

But the reading gave rise to great anger in the breast of the prince.

"The stupid fellow!" said he "He turns traitor and dares to insult me by sending a letter of farewell."

He was just giving orders to send a force to seize the deserter, when K'ung-ming interposed, saying, "You had better send Liu Fêng to capture him and let the two tigers worry each other to weakness. Whether Liu Fêng succeeds or fails, he will have to come to the capital, and you can kill him. Thus will you cut off two evils."

Yüan-tê took his advice. Orders were sent to Mienchu, and Liu Fêng obediently led out his men.

Now Mêng Ta arrived when Ts'ao P'ei was holding a great council. When the attendants told him that Mêng Ta of Shu had come, Ts'ao P'ei summoned him to enter and said to him, "Is not this an insincere surrender?"

Mêng Ta replied, "I was in fear of death for not having relieved Kuan Yü. That is my only reason for coming."

However, Ts'ao P'ei did not trust him. When they reported that Liu Fêng was coming to arrest him, with a large army, and had attacked Hsiangyang and was challenging Mêng Ta to battle, Ts'ao P'ei said, "You seem to be true. Go then to Hsiangyang and take Liu Fêng. If you bring me his head I shall no longer doubt."

Mêng Ta replied, "I will convince him by argument; no soldiers will be needed. I will bring him to surrender too."

So Mêng Ta was given rank and honours and sent to guard Hsiangyang. Now there were two generals there already, Hsiahou Shang and Hsü Huang engaged in reducing the surrounding district. Mêng Ta arrived, met his two colleagues and was told that Liu Fêng was fifty *li* from the city. Whereupon he wrote him a letter urging him to surrender. But Liu Fêng was in no mood to surrender; instead he tore up the letter and put the messenger to death.

"The renegade has already made me offend against my duty to my uncle, and now would sever me from my father so that I shall be reproached as disloyal and unfilial," said Liu Fêng.

Mêng Ta went out with his army to give battle. Liu Fêng rode to the front, pointed with his sword at his opponent and railed against him.

"Death is very near you," replied Mêng Ta, "yet you continue blindly in the way of foolishness and will not understand."

Liu Fêng rode out flourishing his sword. He engaged Mêng Ta, who ran away before the conflict had well begun. Liu Fêng pursued hotly to a long distance. Then he fell into an ambush and found himself attacked on two sides. Also Mêng Ta returned to the attack. Liu Fêng was forced to fly. He made straight for Shangyung, pursued all the way. When he reached the city and hailed the gate he was met by a volley of arrows.

"I have surrendered to Wei," cried Shên Tan from the city tower.

It was impossible to attack the city, as the army of Wei was close behind, and having no resting place he set off for Fangling. He arrived there to find the banners of Wei set out along the walls. Then he saw Shên I wave a signal from the tower, and at once there appeared from the shelter of the wall a body of men led by Hsü Huang.

Then Liu Fêng made for home. But he was pursued, and only a handful of his men remained to him when he regained Ch'êngtu.

Seeking an interview with his adopted father, he found but scant sympathy, for in reponse to his petition, made prostrate and weeping, Yüan-tê said, "Shameful son! How are you come to see me at all?"

"My uncle's mishap was not due to my refusal of help, but because Mêng Ta thwarted me."

"You eat as a man, you dress as a man; but you have no more the instincts of a man than an image of clay or wood. What mean you by saying another wretch thwarted you?"

Yüan-tê bade his executioners expel him and put him to death. But he felt some compunction later when he heard of the treatment meted out to the messenger who had brought Mêng Ta's letter inviting him to become a traitor. And he gave way to grief for the death of his brother until he fell ill. So no military movements were made.

It may be stated here that after he had succeeded to the princedom, Ts'ao P'ei raised all his officers to high rank and had an army prepared of thirty legions, and manœuvred them over the southern districts and made great feasts. And the aged villagers lined the roads offering gifts of wine, just as when the Founder of the Hans returned home to P'ei.

When it was announced that the faithful warrior Hsiahou Tun was near death, Ts'ao P'ei hastened back to Yeh, but arrived too late to see him. He put on mourning for the great leader and instituted magnificent funeral ceremonies.

In the late summer of this same year it was reported that a phœnix had been seen to bow at Shihihsien and a *ch'i-ling* had appeared at Lintzǔ, while a yellow dragon was observed in Yeh. Whereupon certain high officers discussed these appearances, and putting them all together concluded that they presaged that Wei was about to supplant Han and the altar of abdication should be set up. Presently a deputation of two score officers went into the palace and proposed to the Emperor Hsien that he should abdicate and yield to the Prince of Wei.

> It is time to set up the throne of Wei,
> And steal the land from the Hans.

The next chapter will record the Emperor's reply.

CHAPTER LXXX.

Deposition of the Emperor;
The Prince of Han Chung Claims to be the True
Successor.

Hua Hsin was the spokesman of the deputation of officers that went into the palace, and he spake thus: "Since the inauguration of the Prince of Wei virtue has spread to the four corners of the empire and humanity has permeated all the earth to a degree unexcelled in all the ages, even in the days of the ancient rulers T'ang and Yü. We, your servants, have taken account of these things and have reached the conclusion that the race of Han is worn out, wherefore we trust Your Majesty, in imitation of the great prototypes Yao and Shun, will yield the empire to a more able guardian and high priest of the sacrifices in the person of the Prince of Wei, thereby pleasing Heaven and satisfying the hearts of men, and enabling Your Majesty to enjoy the happiness of freedom and repose from the exacting duties of the chief ruler. The happiness of your ancestors and of humanity at large would thereby be enhanced. Having thoroughly debated this matter, we have come to lay it before you."

The Emperor listened in amazement, and for a time could not reply. Then, looking at the assembly, he said sadly, "How can I abandon my empire for the sake of repose; the empire won by my Great Ancestor, its Founder, when he slew the Snake and restored Right, and consolidated when he reduced Ts'in and overwhelmed Ch'u; the empire which has been handed down for four centuries? Though I possess not brilliant talents, yet I have done no wrong. Go back and debate this again in a just and moderate spirit."

Then Hua Hsin led forward Li Fu and Hsü Chih nearer the throne, saying, "If Your Majesty thinks we may be mistaken, pray ask these two, who will explain."

Said Li Fu, "Since the Prince of Wei has taken his seat the Ch'i-ling has descended, the Phœnix has appeared, a yellow Dragon has come forth, the Grain of Felicity has flourished and Sweet Dew has watered the earth. All these things augur that Heaven decrees a change and Wei must replace Han."

Hsü Chih continued, "The astrologers, watching the aspect of the skies at night, have seen the blazing light of the star of Han gradually fade away and Your Majesty's own star become dim. On the other hand, the aspect of the sky and the attitude of the earth have been wholly in favour of Wei to a degree hard to state in words. Moreover, the lots have been cast and they gave the word 'devil' at the side of 'sent,' and there must be an inroad upon Han. Another lot, 'words and east of noon,' gave two words which, joined, compose Hsü. A third gave 'two suns, one on the other,' which is *chang*. These signs are unmistakeable, for when put together the whole reads, 'Wei at Hsüchang is to receive the abdication of Han.' If you consider, Your Majesty must admit this."

"All empty words and madness, this talk of auguries and lots! Is it reasonable that I should suddenly abandon the great heritage for such nonsense?"

Then Wang Lang said, "Wax and wane has been the law of all things from the beginning; every period of glory is followed by one of obscurity. Has any rule endured for ever or any House never failed? The Rule of Han, handed down through four centuries to Yourself, has lost its vigour and the time has come to yield. Retirement may not be delayed or confusion will ensue."

The Emperor wept aloud and retired to his private chamber, while the officers left the hall laughing.

Next morning they assembled in the court, but the Emperor did not appear. So they sent the palace officers to request his presence. Still he feared to show himself. The Empress Ts'ao asked him why he did not hold the court as usual, especially when he was requested to go out.

"Because your brother wishes to depose me and become Emperor himself. He has set the whole host of officers against me to force me to abdicate, and I will not expose myself to this compulsion."

"But what can have induced my brother to do such a dreadfully rebellious thing?" said she.

Just as she spoke, Ts'ao Hung and Ts'ao Hsiu, both armed, forced their way into the inner apartments and requested His Majesty to come to the Hall of Audience.

The Empress broke out into abuse. "So you are two of the disorderly rebels who, for the sake of your own ends, have conspired to upset all the good service of my father. Though he overshadowed the whole land, yet he never dared to aspire to the sacred Throne. But my brother, who has only just succeeded him, sets no bounds to his ambition and temerity and would usurp the Throne. Heaven will surely cut off his offspring!"

She wept bitterly as she went away, and the attendants sobbed and wept too. But Ts'ao Hsiu and Ts'ao Hung still urged the Emperor to go to the Hall of Audience, and at last he had to yield. There Hua Hsin took up the question again.

"Your Majesty should act as was advised yesterday and so avoid any misfortune."

The Emperor sobbed, "All of you have eaten of the bounty of Han for years, and among you are many whose fathers and grandfathers were conspicuous for merit. How can you bring yourselves to act thus improperly toward me?"

"If Your Majesty refuses to follow advice I fear that there will soon be trouble in the family. Really we are not disloyal."

"Who would dare to murder me?" cried the Emperor.

"Everyone knows that Your Majesty lacks the happy attributes of a successful ruler and that is why there is so much confusion in the country. If it was not for the presence of the Prince of Wei in your court many a man would murder you. Your Majesty has never yet learned how to treat men; is your sole desire to set men against you?"

The Emperor, alarmed at the violence of his language, shook out his sleeves and rose to go away. Then Wang Lang glanced at Hua Hsin, who rushed forward and seized the Emperor by the sleeve.

"Is it consent or not?" cried he angrily. "One word!"

The Emperor was dumb with terror.

"Where is the Keeper of the Seal?" shouted Ts'ao Hung and Ts'ao Hsiu, drawing their swords.

"The Keeper of the Seal is here," said Tsu Pi, stepping calmly to the front.

They tried to force the seal from him, but he said it belonged to the Emperor and he would not yield it. Ts'ao Hung called up the executioners and told them to behead him, which they did. He abused the ruffians to the last breath.

> Dethroned by wicked traitors was the ruling House of Han,
> They falsely claimed as precedent the deeds of Yü and T'ang.
> The crowd of officers at court were all on Ts'ao P'ei's side
> Save one, the Keeper of the Seal, and loyally he died.

The Emperor was in a state of abject terror, and when he saw the whole court filling up with armed men, all the soldiers of Wei and so enemies, he burst into tears.

"Yes; I will give up the throne to the prince, if haply I may be spared to live out the few years Heaven has assigned me," wailed he.

"The prince will always take care of Your Majesty," said Chia Hsü. "It would be as well to prepare the abdication manifesto quickly so as to preserve tranquillity."

Such a hint could not be missed, and Ch'ên Chün was directed to draft the document. As soon as it was finished, Hua Hsin followed by a host of officers, took it off to the palace and presented it, with the seal, in the name of the Emperor. Very joyfully, Ts'ao P'ei read this writing:—

"During the whole of my thirty-two years of reign the land has been in a state of turmoil, but the spirits of my ancestors have preserved me in the midst of danger. Now from the signs of the heavens and the hearts of the people I see that the virtue of the Hans is exhausted and happy fortune has devolved upon the House of Wei, as may be seen from the success in war enjoyed by the late prince and the resplendent virtue of the present prince, which answers to the times.

"By all noble principles the empire is no private possession, but a public trust. Wherefore the Great Yao, to his eternal glory, passed over his own son. How I admire this deed! Now in imitation thereof I have resolved to abdicate in favour of my Prime Minister, the Prince of Wei, who will not, I hope, disappoint my wishes."

Ts'ao P'ei heard this and was going to accept it as final. But Ssŭma I said no. Although the declaration and the seal had been sent, yet decorum demanded refusal at first so as to silence men's criticism. Then Wang Lang drafted a memorial modestly declining the proposal of succession on the ground of unfitness and asking that some other be sought. When this reached the Emperor he was much perturbed and asked what was to be done next.

Replied Hua Hsin, "When his father was offered a princedom he declined thrice; but he finally accepted. Wherefore Your Majesty should renew the offer. The prince will end by acceptance."

There was no help for it, and so Huan K'ai was bidden to draft another declaration of offer, which was sent by the hand of the officer of the Dynastic Temple, Chang Yin, together with the emblems and the seal.

This new declaration read thus:—

"To the Prince of Wei. You have sent your modest refusal of Our offer to abdicate. But I have long since seen that the virtue of Han is passing and I could only rely upon the late prince, your father, who virtuously undertook the great task of removing the evil oppressors and purging the land. Now his son P'ei has succeeded. His perfect virtue is resplendent, his fame universal and his benevolence is wafted to all parts. The divine choice rests upon him. In the days of old, Shun, after his twenty labours, would abdicate, and did so in favour of Yü the Great, who possessed merit. The House of Han succeeded in the course of ages to the work of Yao and now passes on the sacred trust, to promote the repose of the Earth and manifest the command of Heaven.

"By the hand of the Censor Chang Yin this is sent with the emblems and the seal."

Greatly rejoicing, Ts'ao P'ei received this. But he said to Chia Hsü, "Although I have received two such declarations, yet I fear that I may not escape being branded as a usurper by posterity."

"That is easily arranged," replied Chia Hsu. "Direct Chang Yin to take the seal back again and tell Hua Hsin to cause the Emperor to set up a Terrace of Abdication and select an auspicious day for the ceremony. Then assemble all the officers at the terrace and cause the Emperor to offer the seal with his own hands and surrender the empire to you. Thus can you dissipate all doubts and prevent any cavillings."

So the seal was once more rejected with a memorial to say so. Chang Yin returned and the Emperor enquired of the courtiers how he was to understand this act. Then Hua Hsin said, "Your Majesty can set up a Terrace of Abdication and assemble nobles, officers and common people to witness the act of abdication. Thereafter the descendants of your House shall receive favour at the hands of Wei."

The Emperor consented and sent officers to select a site at Fanyang. And there they built a terrace of three storeys, and they chose the day *keng-wu* of the tenth month for the act of abdication. On the appointed day the Emperor Hsien requested Ts'ao P'ei to ascend the terrace and receive his abdication. At the foot of the terrace stood the officials, more than four hundred, and the Imperial Guards and the Tiger Guards, and soldiers to the number of thirty legions. Thereupon the Emperor presented the seal, which Ts'ao P'ei received into his hands. Then all those about the terrace knelt to listen to the reading of the manifesto.

"To the Prince of Wei. In days of old, Yao yielded the empire to Shun, and Shun in turn gave it to Yü. The will of Heaven does not follow the way of mortals, but seeks the virtuous. The rule of Han has lost its virility and the times are out of joint. When my turn came to rule, great disorder arose, and evils stalked abroad till the empire was in danger of subversion. I trusted to the military genius of the late Prince of Wei to restore order and purge away the evil, whereby to ensure tranquillity to my House. What could my single hand do to correct this and ensure peace for my Nine Domains?

"The present prince has succeeded to his father; he is also resplendent in virtue, capable as Wên and Wu of the great task, brilliant in the glory of his father. The spirit of empire is upon him; gods and men declare his worth. To him be the bright reward, and let him accept this mandate. For all say his capabilities fit him to stand beside Shun.

"As did my great predecessor, I respectfully retire that you may be set up. The revolution of Heaven brings the glory upon your person, and you will accept the high office and comfort all men by reverently obeying the decree of Heaven."

The reading finished the Prince of Wei, Ts'ao P'ei, proceeded to the terrace and ascended to the place of the Emperor. Then Chia Hsü, at the head of the great concourse of officers, came to the foot of the terrace, and a court was held. The year of reign was changed to the style *Huang-Ch'u* and the government became that of *Ta Wei.* An edict was then published proclaiming a general amnesty, and the title of "Founder of the Dynasty" was conferred upon the late Prince Ts'ao Ts'ao.

Then said Hua Hsin, "As heaven has but one sun, so the people can have but one ruler. The Hans have abdicated, and it is fitting that they withdraw to a distance. I pray for an edict naming the place of residence of the Liu family."

Taking the late Emperor by the arm, he led him forward and made him kneel below the terrace to hear the command. Then the new Emperor conferred upon him the title of "Duke of Shanyang," bidding him depart forthwith. Tnereupon Hua Hsin drew his sword and in a harsh voice said, "It is an old rule that the setting up of one Emperor means the degradation of another. Now, through the gracious kindness of His Majesty you are spared personal injury and created a duke. Proceed at once and return not to court without express command."

The late Emperor controlled his emotion, thanked the Emperor for his clemency and left. But those who saw the departure could not help a feeling of pity for him.

Said Ts'ao P'ei to his courtiers, "I understand the relation of Shun and Yü."

Then they all shouted *"Wan-sui;* O Ruler, may thy life be eternal."

> The ruling policy of Han had failed them,
> Dangers pressed in upon the House,
> And the land they had held so long
> Passed from them for ever.
> Little thought he, who then snatched their sceptre,
> That the precedent he then claimed
> Would be used in due time by another
> To justify the destruction of his own House.

The officials then requested Ts'ao P'ei to make a solemn declaration to Heaven and Earth, which he did with humble obeisance.

But at this moment a sudden storm burst, whirling up the dust and rolling along stones till no man could see the face of his neighbour. All the lights on the terrace were extinguished. The newly enthroned Emperor was terrified and fell prostrate. He was borne away unconscious. When he revived he was assisted into the palace, but for many days he was too ill to hold a court.

When he had somewhat recovered, he met his courtiers and received their felicitations. He rewarded Hua Hsin, who had taken so active and prominent a part in the late scenes, with the post of Minister of Instruction, and Wang Lang with that of Minister of Works. All the officers were advanced in rank. But as his recovery was slow, he began to think there was too much witchcraft about the palace at Hsüch'ang and left it for Loyang, where he erected a large palace.

The tale of these doings reached Ch'êngtu and caused great grief to the Prince of Hanchung, for it was told him the late Emperor had been put to death. He issued an order for mourning to be worn and instituted sacrifices, and he conferred the posthumous title of *Hsiao-mên* on the late Emperor. This worry brought on an illness, so that he could not transact the business of the court, which was left in the hands of K'ung-ming.

Then K'ung-ming and some of his colleagues took counsel one with another, saying, "The empire cannot be one single day without its ruler, wherefore we desire that our prince should be honoured with the title of ' Emperor.' "

Chiao Chou said, "There have been auspicious indications. A yellow vapour has been seen in the northwest rising to the clouds, and the Emperor's star has greatly increased in splendour. These signs mean that our prince is to become Emperor in succession to the House of Han. There can be no doubt."

Whereupon K'ung-ming and Hsü Ching, at the head of a large number of officers, presented a memorial requesting the prince to assume the title of "Emperor." But he objected.

"O Nobles, do you desire to set my feet in the way of disloyalty and wrong-doing?"

"Not so," said K'ung-ming. "But Ts'ao P'ei has usurped the Throne, while you are a scion of the House. It is right and proper that you succeed and prolong the line."

But the prince suddenly showed anger, saying, "Can I imitate the deeds of such a rebel?"

He rose and left the chamber, going to his own apartments. So the officials dispersed. But three days later K'ung-ming again led a deputation to the court, and they requested that the prince should come forth and hear them. He came, and they all prostrated themselves.

Hsü Ching spoke. "The late Emperor of the Hans has been slain by Ts'ao P'ei. You, O Prince, will fail both in loyalty and rectitude if you do not assume the succession and destroy the wrong-doers. The whole empire requests you to rule that you may avenge the death of the late Emperor, and the people will be disappointed if you do not accede to their wishes."

The prince replied, "Although I am descended from the grandson of an emperor I have not been of the least advantage, and if I assumed the title of 'Emperor,' how would that act differ from usurpation?"

K'ung-ming pleaded with him again and again, but the prince remained obdurate. Then K'ung-ming bethought that where argument failed a ruse might succeed. So having arranged the parts his several colleagues were to play, he pleaded illness and remained at home. Presently it was told the prince that his adviser's condition was becoming serious, wherefore he went to see him as he lay on his couch.

"What illness affects you, my Commander-in-chief?" asked he.

"My heart is sad like unto burning, and I shall soon die."

"What is it that causes you such grief?"

But K'ung-ming did not reply. And when the question was repeated again and again he said nothing, but just lay with his eyes closed as if he was too ill to speak. The prince, however, pressed him to reply, and then with a deep sigh he said, "Great Prince, from the day I left my humble cottage to follow you you have always listened to my words and accepted my advice, and now this western district, the whole of the Two Ch'uan is yours just as I said it would be. But this usurpation of Ts'ao P'ei means the annihilation of the Hans and the cessation of their sacrifices, wherefore I and my colleagues desired you to become Emperor in order to crush this upstart Wei and restore the Lius. We all worked for this end, never thinking that you would refuse so obstinately to accede to our wishes. Now the officers are all annoyed, and they will drift away before very long. If you are left alone and Wu and Wei come to attack, it will be difficult for you to hold on to what you have. Do you not think this sufficient reason for me to feel grieved?"

"Unless I refused, the whole land would blame me; and I am afraid," replied the prince.

Quoting the Holy One, K'ung-ming replied, " 'If names be not correct, language is not in accordance with the truth of things.' In other words, if one be not really straight, people will not speak of one favourably. O Prince, you are straight and people speak of you favourably. What more is there to say? You know when Heaven offers and you refuse, you are certainly to blame."

"When you have recovered it shall be done," said the prince.

Up leapt K'ung-ming from his bed, tapped at the screen in front of a doorway and in rushed a number of high officers, who prostrated themselves, crying, "So you have consented, O Prince! Then choose the day for the ceremony."

They were all the most trusted of his court: Hsü Ching, the Grand Tutor; Mi Chu the General; Shang Chu, Marquis of Ch'ingi; Liu Pao, Marquis of Yangch'üan; Chao Tsu, the General; and many others. The prince was greatly startled, and again said they were committing him to doing what was wrong.

But K'ung-ming said, "Since consent has been given, let a terrace be built and a day chosen for the great ceremony."

The prince was escorted back to his palace, and officers were told off to see to the building of the terrace near Ch'êngtu, south of Wutan. And when all was ready a great concourse of officers solemnly escorted the prince, seated in a carriage of the imperial pattern, to the ground prepared, and he went up to the altar and performed the appointed sacrifice.

This done, the solemn announcement was read in a loud voice:—

"On this twefth day of the fourth month of the year of 'Established Tranquillity' period, Pei, the Emperor, makes this solemn announcement to Heaven and Earth. The Dynasty of Han has possessed the empire for years without end. Formerly Wang Mang rebelled against his sovereign, and the Emperor Kuang-Wu rose in his wrath and put him to death, thus restoring the prerogatives of the great sacrifices to him who rightly exercised them. Lately Ts'ao Ts'ao, powerful and cruel, slew the Empress, and his crimes cry aloud to Heaven for vengeance. His son, Ts'ao P'ei, carrying evils into every quarter, then seized the sceptre. My subordinates, regarding the dynasty as having been overthrown, think it fitting that I, Pei, would continue the line. As successor to my two warrior ancestors, Kao-Tsu and Kuang-Wu, I will punish as Heaven decrees. Fearing lest my virtue be inadequate to the Imperial Throne, I consulted the voices of the people, and all, even the most distant, have said that the mandate of Heaven may not be disobeyed and the great task of my ancestors may not continue in the hands of another; the land must have a lord and they aver the cynosure of all eyes is myself. Now I, respecting the mandate of Heaven and fearing lest the great achievements of Kao-Tsu and Kuang-Wu may be overthrown, have reverently selected this auspicious day to ascend the altar, sacrifice and announce my assumption of the imperial seal in order to comfort all the people, rejoice the ancestors of the Dynastic House and bring eternal tranquillity to all the domains."

When the reading was ended, and the sacrifice and the prayer, K'ung-ming, in the name of all those assembled, presented the imperial seal. The prince received it in both hands, laid it upon the altar and again declined acceptance, saying, "I, Pei, am unfitted; I pray that another, more able, may be chosen."

But K'ung-ming said, "Our lord has settled the empire, and his merits are manifest to the whole world. Moreover, he is of the Dynastic Family and it is fitting that he succeed. Now that the great announcement has been made such self-abnegation is impossible."

So all the officers shouted, "Eternal life to the Emperor!" and did obeisance. And then the style of the reign was announced to be *Wu-Yüan.*

The Lady Wu was declared Empress-Consort and the eldest son, Ch'an, was declared Heir-Apparent. The second son was made Prince of Lu and the third, Prince of Liang. Chuko Liang became Prime Minister, and Hsü Ching, Minister of Instruction. Many others were promoted, and a general amnesty was proclaimed, so that there was great rejoicing throughout all the length and breadth of the Two Ch'uan.

Next day the first court was held, and after the ceremonial prostrations, and when they were all arranged in due order, the First Ruler made a pronouncement.

"In the Peach Garden I and my brothers Kuan and Chang pledged ourselves to live and die together. Unhappily my brother Yün-chang came to his end at the hands of Sun Ch'üan of Wu, and I must avenge him lest I fail to fulfil the oath. Therefore will I devote the whole force of my kingdom to the destruction of Wu and the capture of its rebellious chief, whereby to wipe away my reproach."

But just as he closed this oration an officer threw himself down at the foot of the throne, crying, "It may not be so."

All eyes turned to this man; he was Chao Yün.

> "Dire vengeance will I wreak!" so cried the King,
> His minister replied, "Do no such thing."

What arguments were used will appear in the next chapter.

CHAPTER LXXXI.

CHANG FEI IS ASSASSINATED;
THE FIRST RULER GOES TO WAR.

Chao Yün was opposed to the attempt to fight Wu, and spoke against the plan.

"The real rebel was not Sun Ch'üan, but Ts'ao Ts'ao; and now it is his son who has usurped the Imperial Throne and called forth the anger of gods and men. You should first aim at the inside by camping on the River Wei, from which to attack the rebel. After that the right-thinking sort on the east of the Passes will do their utmost to help you. If you leave Wei out of consideration in order to fight Wu, your military force will be engaged, and could you disengage it quickly in case of necessity? It is worth reflection."

The First Ruler replied, "Sun Ch'üan slew my brother. Many of my officers hate him so that they could eat his flesh with gusto and devour his relatives, whereby I should have my vengeance. Why, Noble Sir, do you obstruct me?"

"Because the enmity against Ts'ao is a public matter; vengeance for the manner of your brother's end is private. The empire should be placed first."

"What care I for myriads of *li* of territory as long as my brother is unavenged?"

So Chao Yün's remonstrance was disregarded, and orders went forth to prepare an army against Wu. The king also sent into The Five Valleys to borrow the aid of five legions of barbarians. He sent a messenger to Langchung conferring on Chang Fei the rank of General of Cavalry and the titles of *"Hsiao-yü"* and "Marquis." He became also Governor of Langchung.

When Chang Fei heard the tidings of his brother's death at the hands of Sun Ch'üan he wept very bitterly day and night, so that his raiment was soaked with his tears. His subordinates tried to cheer him with wine, but he over-drank and this increased his ill-humour, which he vented on any offender in his camp. Some of his men even died under the lash. Every day he gazed southward, grinding his teeth with rage and glaring. He wept and groaned without ceasing.

Then a messenger was announced. He was summoned immediately, and Chang Fei at once tore open and read his despatches. When he read the edict he accepted his new rank in all humility, bowing northward toward the imperial mandate. Then he gave a banquet to the messenger.

He said, "My enmity for the death of my brother is deep as the sea. Why do not the officers at the court propose an avenging expedition?"

The messenger replied, "Most of them favour first the destruction of Wei; Wu is to follow."

"What sort of talk is this?" cried Chang angrily. "When we three swore brotherhood in the Peach Garden we pledged ourselves to die together. Now, alas! my brother has perished by the way, and can we enjoy wealth or honours without him? I must see the Son of Heaven and pray to be allowed to lead the van. I will wear mourning, and in that garb I will smite Wu and capture the bandit that rules there. He shall be sacrificed to my brother's manes in virtue of our oath."

He accompanied the messenger on his return. In the meantime the First Ruler had been training his armies. Day after day he went to the drill ground, and he decided upon a day to start, and he would accompany the expedition. Thereupon a number of courtiers went to the palace of the Prime Minister to try to get this intention modified.

They said, "It is not in accordance with the importance due to the Emperor's position that he should go in personal command of this army, particularly as he has but lately assumed his throne. You, Sir, hold the weighty post of adviser in such a matter, and why do you not dissuade him?"

"I have done so, most sincerely and repeatedly, but he will not listen. But now you all come with me to the drill ground, and we will try once more."

So they proceeded thither, with K'ung-ming at their head, and he said, "Your Majesty has but lately taken the imperial seat. If the expedition was one to march northward to destroy the rebels against Han and in the interest of rectitude, it would be perfectly correct for the Emperor to lead the army, but an officer of high rank should more properly be sent against Wu. Why should Your Majesty expose yourself to such fatigues?"

The First Ruler was touched by the depth of his minister's concern and the sincerity of his counsel, and was on the point of yielding when the arrival of Chang Fei was announced. Fei was immediately summoned and came to the pavilion on the drill ground, where he threw himself on the ground and clasped the king's feet, weeping bitterly. The king joined in the lamentation.

Your Majesty is now ruler and too quickly forgets the oath in the Peach Garden; why is our brother's death not avenged?"

The king replied, "Many officers dissuade me from such a course; I cannot act rashly."

"What do others know of our oath? If Your Majesty will not go, then let me sacrifice myself to avenge our brother. If I cannot, then would I rather die and see your face no more."

"Then will I go with you," said the king. "Bring your own troops from Langchou and I will bring my veterans to meet you at Chiangchou. We will both attack Wu and wipe out the reproach."

As Fei rose to take leave, the king said to him, "I know that your weakness for wine leads you astray, and you become very cruel in your cups and flog your men and the beaten men are kept near you. They may be dangerous, and it is certainly the road to misfortune. Now you must be more kindly and not give way to passion as before."

Thus admonished, Chang Fei said farewell and left. Soon after, when the king was preparing to march out, Ch'in Mi, a high officer, memorialised, saying, "That Your Majesty, the Lord of a Myriad Chariots, should risk his person in what is not the way of perfect rectitude is not what the ancients would have done. I pray that this may be reflected upon."

But the king replied, "Yüan-chang and I were as one body, and the way of perfect rectitude is here. Have you forgotten?"

But the officer remained at his feet and said, "I fear disaster if Your Majesty disregards your servant's words."

The king replied angrily, "Why do you use such bad words when I desire to march?"

He bade the executioners thrust forth and put to death the bold speaker. Still Ch'in's face showed no sign of fear. He only smiled, saying, "I die without regret. It is a pity that this newly established state should be overturned ere it be well begun."

Others interceding, the death punishment was remitted, but the faithful officer was committed to prison. His fate was to be decided when the army of vengeance should return. K'ung-ming sent up a memorial in favour of Ch'in Mi, saying, "I, Chuko Liang, address Your Majesty in my own name and those of my colleagues; we regard as most grievous the recent events, Wu's perfidy, by which Chingchou was lost and the star of a great general was brought down, and we shall never forget. But it is to be remembered that the crime of overturning the Throne of Han rests on Ts'ao Ts'ao and the fault of driving away the Liu Family lies not on Sun Ch'üan. We venture to think that the destruction of Wei would involve the submission of Wu, wherefore we beg consideration of the valuable words of Ch'in Mi. Thus the army will be spared needless exertion and occasion given to make other plans for the prosperity of the Throne and the happiness of the people."

But the memorial was not well received. The king threw it to the floor, saying that he had decided and would listen to no remonstrances. Then he appointed the Prime Minister Regent and Guardian of his son, and the two Mas and Wei Yen were ordered to guard Hanchung. Chao Yün was to be in reserve and to control the supplies. Many old leaders were appointed to the expedition, the veteran Huang Chung being leader of the van, and some new ones. The whole army, including the borrowed foreign troops, numbered seventy-five legions. And the *ping-wu* day of the seventh month was selected as the most propitious day for the start.

As soon as Chang Fei had got back to his post he issued orders that his men should be ready to march in three days and the whole body was to be in mourning, white flags and whitened arms. Just after the order appeared, two officers named Fan Chiang and Chang Ta came to their chief saying that the time allowed was insufficient and asked for some delay.

"I am hot to avenge my brother," said Chang Fei. "My only regret is that I cannot reach the miserable wretch's country to-morrow. Do you dare to disobey my order?"

He called in the lictors, had the two officers bound to trees and ordered each to receive fifty lashes, and at the close of the flogging he said, "Now you will be ready to-morrow; if you are not, I will put you to death as an example."

The two officers returned to their place, spitting blood and hot with anger, and they said one to another, "We have been beaten to-day; what about to-morrow? This man's temper is unbearable, and if things are not ready we shall suffer death."

"Suppose we slay him," suddenly said Chang Ta, "since if we do not he will kill us."

"But how can we get near him?"

"If we are to have a chance to live, he will get drunk and go to bed; if we are to die, he will remain sober."

They made all their arrangements for the crime. Chang Fei was greatly disturbed in his mind and restless. He told some of his subordinates that he was nervous and felt creepy and shivery and could not rest. What did it mean?"

"This is due to too much brooding over the loss of your brother," said they.

Then Chang Fei bade them bring in wine, and he drank with his officers. Presently he became quite intoxicated and lay down on a couch in his tent.

Meanwhile the two assassins had followed all his doings, and when they knew he was lying on his couch intoxicated and incapable, they went into the tent, each armed with a dagger. They got rid of the attendants by saying they had confidential matters to talk about and so got into the inner rooms.

But even then they dared do nothing, for Chang Fei slept always with open eyelids, and he lay on his couch as if still awake. However, huge snores soon convinced them that their victim really slept, and they crept to the side of the couch. Then both stabbed simultaneously deep into the body. Chang Fei uttered one cry and lay still.

So he died at the hand of assassins at the age of fifty-and-five years.

> He who whipped th' inspector years agone,
> Who swept vile rebels from the land of Han,
> And thereby won great glory for the Lius,
> Whose valour shone at Tiger Corral Pass,
> Who turned the tide of victory at the bridge,
> Who freed a captive and thus won a friend
> That helped him and his brothers conquer Shu,
> Whose wisdom to a district brought repose,
> Is dead, the victim of assassins' blows.
> Not his t'avenge his brother's death on Wu,
> Langti will grieve him all the ages through.

Having done their victim to death, the two murderers hacked off his head and made off for the country of Wu without loss of time, and when the deed was known they had got too far for capture. The assassination was reported in a memorial by a minor officer named Chang Pan, who had left Chingchou to see the king and then had been sent to serve under Chang Fei. He bade the eldest son, Chang Pao, prepare a coffin for the remains and, leaving the younger brother, Chang Shao, to hold the Langchung Pass, went to see the Emperor.

The day of departure had already come, and the First Ruler had left the capital. K'ung-ming and many officers had escorted him out of the city for ten *li* and taken leave. But K'ung-ming felt ill at ease, and he remarked to his colleagues, "If Fa Chêng had been alive he would have been able to interdict this expedition."

One night the First Ruler felt nervous and shuddered from time to time. He could not sleep so he went out of his tent and looked up at the stars. Suddenly he saw a bright meteor fall in the north-west, and began to wonder what the portent meant. He sent at once to ask K'ung-ming to tell him. K'ung-ming sent back the reply that it meant the loss of a great leader and there would be bad news in a few days.

So the army was halted and did not march. Then the arrival of a message from Chang Pan of Langchung was announced. The king's forebodings increased, and he stamped his foot, saying, "My other brother is gone."

Opening the letter he found it was indeed so. As he read the news of the assassination he uttered a loud cry and fell in a swoon. He was raised and presently they brought him back to life.

Next day they reported a body of horsemen coming. The king went out of the camp to look at them and presently recognised Chang Pao, dressed all in white. As soon as he reached the king's presence he dismounted and bowed to the earth weeping, "My father has been killed by the two ruffians Fan Chiang and Chang Ta. They have gone over to Wu, taking my father's head with them."

The news was very grievous, and the king refused food. His officers remonstrated, saying, "Now Your Majesty has the loss of two brothers to avenge, and you must not destroy yourself."

So after a time he began to eat and drink, and he then offered the leadership of the van to Chang Pao, so that he might have the satisfaction of avenging his father and uncle.

"For my country or for my father, I would shrink from no sacrifice," said the young man.

Just as the force for the young man's leadership was being organised, another party of horsemen approached, also dressed in white. This was a small force under Kuan Hsin, son of Kuan the Noble. The youth also threw himself to the ground and wept.

At sight of him thoughts stirred in the king's breast, and he burst into tears. Neither reason nor persuasion could stop them.

"I think of the plain and simple days of long ago when we pledged ourselves one to the other. Now I am Emperor. How I should rejoice to share my good fortune with them! But they have met violent deaths, and the sight of these two youths wrings my heart to the very core."

"Young gentlemen, please retire," said the officers to the two youthful captains, "and let our sacred one repose his 'dragon body.'"

They went. Said the attendants, "Your Majesty is no longer young; you are over sixty, remember, and it is not fitting that you give way to such extreme sorrow."

"But my brothers,—dead," wailed the First Ruler. "How can I live without them?"

He broke into a fresh paroxysm and beat his head on the ground.

"What can be done?" asked the officers one to another. "He is in such trouble! How can we comfort him?"

Ma Lang said, "Sire, it is bad for the army to spend whole days in wailing and tears when leading against the enemy."

And then Ch'ên Chên said, "There is a certain hermit living among the Ch'ingch'êng Hills, near Ch'êngtu, who is said to be three hundred years old. He is called Li I and people say he is a seer. Let us tell His Majesty and let him send for this old man that he may know what the future may have in store. It will have more weight than anything we can say."

They went to the king and told him; he agreed to summon the seer and sent Ch'ên Chên with the command. Soon the messenger reached the town near the hills and asked the people where the prophet dwelt. They led him far into a secluded valley like a fairy village, very unlike any ordinary spot. Soon a lad came to receive the visitor.

"You are surely Ch'ên Hsiao-ch'i."

Ch'ên Chên was startled that the lad knew him, and still more so at the familiar address, and said, "O superhuman boy, how do you know my name so well?"

"Last evening my master told me that a messenger with an imperial command would come to-day and mentioned your name."

"Truly he is more than wise," said Ch'ên Chên; "and men have not believed him."

So the two proceeded to the old man's abode, and Ch'ên declared his errand. The old man said he was too aged to travel.

"But the Emperor anxiously desires to see you face to face if haply you would not mind making the effort."

In the end, and after much persuasion, the old fellow consented and went. The First Ruler received him affably, surprised at the contrast between his hoary head and fresh boyish complexion. The venerable one had blue eyes, with square and sparkling pupils. His carriage was erect and he stood straight as a pine tree.

"This is no common man," thought he, and he treated him with distinguished courtesy.

The seer said, "I am but an old man of the barren hill country, without learning or wisdom; you shame me, O Emperor, by calling me, and I know not why."

"I and my two brothers, both now deceased, swore a mutual oath some thirty years ago. Both have gone, both by violent death. I would lead a great army to avenge them and wish to know how the expedition will end. Hearing that you, Venerable Sir, are learned in the deeper mysteries, I sent for you and beg you to tell me."

"But this is fate; it is not for an old man like me to know."

But the First Ruler pressed him to say. However, the aged one got paper and a brush and wrote, "Soldiers, horses, weapons" again and again on many sheets of paper. Having done this, he suddenly tore them into fragments. Further, he drew a picture of a tall man lying supine and another above him digging a grave. And over all he wrote, "white."

After this he bowed and departed, leaving the First Ruler annoyed.

"This is only a demented old man; what he says is not worthy of confidence," said the First Ruler. And he burned the paper.

Then he ordered an advance at full speed. Chang Fei's son, Pao, came in saying, "Wu Pan and his men have come; I pray that I may be appointed to lead the van."

The First Ruler admired his noble intent and gave him a van-leader's seal. But just as he was attaching the seal to his girdle another youth boldly stepped forth and said, "Leave that seal to me!"

It was Kuan Hsing, son of Kuan Yü.

"I have already received my commission," said Chang Pao.

"What abilities have you for such a task?" cried Hsing.

"That I have been training as a soldier since my boyhood. I can shoot and never miss."

"I should like to see your prowess," said the First Ruler, "that I may decide who is the better."

Chang Pao ordered some of his men to set up a flag at a hundred paces, and on the flag he drew a heart in red. Then he took his bow and shot three arrows, each of which went through the "heart". Those present commended the performance. Then Kuan Hsing seized his bow, saying, "What is it to hit such a mark?"

Just as he said this a flock of wild geese flew over his head. "I will hit the third of the flying geese," said he.

He shot; and the third fell.

"Fine!" cried all the assembly as one voice.

But Chang Pao was enraged. Leaping on his steed he seized the long spear left him by his father, crying, "Dare you try a real combat?"

Kuan Hsing took up the challenge at once. He sprang into the saddle, took his father's great sword and galloped out.

"You can use the spear, think you that I cannot wield a sword?" cried he.

The two impetuous youths were on the point of a battle when the First Ruler bade them hold.

"Do not behave so badly!" cried he.

Both dropped out of the saddle, threw aside their weapons, ran to his feet and begged pardon.

"Young men, from the time I left my native place and swore brotherhood with your fathers they were as my own flesh and blood. You two are also brothers and you should help each other in vengeance rather than quarrel and dispute. You have lost the sense of rectitude while your fathers' deaths are still recent and what will happen in future?"

Both fell at his feet and implored forgiveness.

"Which of you two is the elder?" asked the First Ruler.

"I am the elder by a year," said Chang Pao.

The ruler then bade Kuan Hsing bow to Chang Pao as to an elder brother, and there, in front of all, they broke an arrow as a pledge that each would always succour the other.

Then the First Ruler issued a mandate appointing Wu Pan leader of the van, and the two young men were enrolled as his own escort.

The advance began on land and on water, and they made a brave show as they moved against the land of Wu.

In the meantime the two assassins, with the grim evidence of their crime, duly reached Wu and told their story to the marquis who received them.

Then he said to his assembled officers, "Liu Pei has declared himself Emperor and is leading against us in person a great host. What shall we do, for the danger is imminent?"

They all turned pale and looked one at another. Then Chuko Chin spoke out.

"I have been in your service these many years and have never justified the favour you have shown me. I will risk my life and go to this Liu Pei of Shu that I may talk to him plainly and prove to him the advantages of friendship and alliance against Ts'ao P'ei."

This offer pleased Sun Ch'üan, who then appointed Chuko Chin as his messenger to try to induce the First Ruler to keep the peace.

> Messengers pass when states are at wrangle;
> May this one succeed and unravel this tangle!

What fortune attended this messenger will be related in the next chapter.

CHAPTER LXXXII.

Sun Ch'uan Submits to Wei and is Rewarded;
The First Ruler Attacks Wu and Rewards His Army.

In the eighth month of the year *Chang-wu* (221 A.D.) the
First Ruler marched at the head of his army and camped at
Paitich'êng (City of the White Emperor), through the K'uei
Pass. His advanced guard had reached Ch'uank'ou when his
attendants told him that Chuko Chin had come as a messenger
from Wu. He told them not to admit him. But Huang
Ch'üan said, "His brother being your Prime Minister he is
certainly come on some important mission. Your Majesty
ought to see him and hear what he says. If his proposals are
admissible, then agree; if not, he can be made use of to take
knowledge of your intentions to Sun Ch'üan and let him know
that you intend to punish his crime."

Then the First Ruler gave way, and the messenger was
brought in. He bowed down to the earth.

"Sir, you have come a long journey; what is its object?"
said the First Ruler.

"My brother has long served Your Majesty; I have come
at the risk of my life to discuss Chingchou affairs. When
Kuan the Noble was at Chingchou my master repeatedly
sought to ally the two families by marriage, but was refused.
When he attacked Hsiangyang, Ts'ao Ts'ao wrote again and
again urging my master to attack Chingchou. But he was
unwilling, and it was the enmity between your brother and
Lü Mêng that led to the attack and the unfortunate success.
My master is now very sorry for it, but it was Lü Mêng's
doing. However, Lü Mêng is now dead and his enmity has
died with him Moreover, the Lady Sun is always thinking
over returning to you. My master now proposes to send back
the lady, to hand over to you those officers who surrendered
and to restore Chingchou. If the two houses swear perpetual
amity then they may join forces against Ts'ao P'ei and punish
his usurpation."

To this harangue the First Ruler only replied, "You of East
Wu killed my brother; yet you dare to come with your artful
talk!"

Chuko Chin said, "I only wish to discuss the relative
importance of the issues. Your Majesty is an Imperial Uncle,
and Ts'ao P'ei has seized the throne of your House. Yet you

do not think of destroying the usurper, but on the other hand you disregard the most honourable position in the world for the sake of a so-called brother, a connection of another name. Surely this is rejecting the chief for the subordinate, the main issue for a detail. The country concerned is a part of the empire, and the two capitals, Loyang and Ch'angan, are both famous as places whence the two, one the founder, the other the restorer, of the Hans, initiated their mighty task. Your Majesty takes no thought of these, but would dispute over Chingchou; in other words, the important is adandoned for the worthless. All the world knows of your assumption of the dignity of Emperor and that you will assuredly restore the Hans and rescue their territory; only now you do not try to deal with Ts'ao, you only desire to attack Wu. I venture to think you have made a bad choice."

All this argument only added fuel to the fire.

"The slayer of my brother shall not live in the same world as I. You ask me not to fight. I will cease when I have slain your master. Were it not for the sake of your brother I would behead you at once. As it is, you may go; and you may tell your master to cleanse his neck ready for the blade of the executioner."

Chuko Chin saw that the position was hopeless and took his leave.

But while he had been absent, calumny had not been idle. Chang Chao, one day when he was with Sun Ch'üan, insinuated doubts of Chuko's honesty.

"He knows something of the strength of the armies of Shu, and he made this mission of his an excuse to get out of danger. He will not return."

The marquis replied, "I and he are sworn friends; friends to the death. I shall not wrong him nor will he betray me. When he was at Ch'aisang and his famous brother paid him a visit, I wanted my friend Chuko to persuade his brother to remain with me. His reply was that his brother would not remain any more than he himself would go: each would be faithful to his salt. That was quite clear enough. How could he desert me after that? Our friendship has something of the divine in it, and no talk from outside can sow dissension between us."

Even as he spoke the servants told him that Chuko Chin had returned.

"What do you think now?" said Sun Ch'üan.

Chang Chao retired overwhelmed with shame. The luckless messenger unfolded his tale of failure.

"Then the south is in great danger," said Sun Ch'üan, as he heard the story.

But a certain man here interposed saying he could find a way out of the difficulty. He was Chao Tsŭ.

"What good scheme do you propose, friend Chao?" said Sun Ch'üan.

"Let my lord draw up a document, which I will take to Ts'ao P'ei in Wei, making a full statement of the case, and get him to attack Hanchung and so draw off the danger from our land."

"Though the suggestion is good, yet shall we not lose something of our dignity by that?" said Sun Ch'üan.

"If there is any such thing I will simply jump into the river: I could not look our people in the face again."

Sun Ch'üan was satisfied and composed the memorial, styling himself "Minister." Therein Chao was duly appointed messenger. He took the document and soon reached the capital, where he first sought out the *T'ai-yü*, Chia Hsü, and then saw certain others.

Soon after, Chia Hsü stood forth one day at court and said, "Eastern Wu has sent a high officer, Chao Tzŭ, with a memorial."

"Because he wants the Shu armies driven off," said Ts'ao P'ei, smiling, and as if completing the sentence. But he summoned Chao, who, having prostrated himself in the outer court handed in his memorial. After reading it, P'ei said, "What sort of an over-lord is the marquis?"

"Intelligent, clear-sighted, wise, brave and perspicacious," was the reply.

P'ei laughed, "Your praise is none too enthusiastic."

"I do not wish to overstate," replied Chao Tzŭ, "but my master has shown various qualities at different times. He made use of Lu Su at all times, which shows he is intelligent. He chose Lü Mêng as leader of an army, which showed his clear-sightedness. He captured Yü Chin but did not hurt him, which shows his kindliness. He took Chingchou without slaughter, which shows his wisdom. He maintains the three *Chiangs* so as to command the respect of the world, which shows his boldness. Lastly, he bows before Your Majesty, which shows his perspicacity. You see now that my epithets are justifiable."

"Is he at all learned?"

"Sire, remember he commands a large fleet and a huge army. He endeavours to find wise and capable men to heln him, and his mind is full of plans and projects. When he has a little leisure he reads the histories and the annals, for the sake of the general lessons to be learned therefrom. He is no dryas-dust pedant seeking remarkable passages and culling model sentences."

"Do you think I could overcome Wu?"

"If a large state has military force to attack, a small one has also preparations for defence."

"Does Wu fear me?"

"How can you think so, considering our army and the defensive moat we have in the river?"

"How many such persons as yourself does Wu possess?"

"Nearly a hundred, intelligent and specially qualified ministers like your servant; of 'one cart' or 'one bushel' capacity there are too many to reckon up."

Ts'ao P'ei sighed, saying, "You would do credit to your mission wherever you were sent. That is the sort of man you are."

Thereupon he issued the mandate ordering the *T'ai-ch'ang*, Hsing Chên, to be his ambassador to Sun Ch'üan, bearing for him the title of "Prince of Wu" and the "Nine Gifts."

But when the messenger had gone out of the city, Liu Yeh went to remonstrate, saying, "Sun Ch'üan has done this for fear of the armies of Shu. In my opinion, if Shu and Wu fight, heaven will make an end of him. If you will send an army across the river to attack, and Shu attack at the same time, Wu as a state will disappear. If Wu goes, then Shu will be left alone and can be dealt with when you will."

"But I cannot attack him now that he has come over to my side. It would prevent anyone else from doing so. No; I will really accept his submission. It is the best course."

Liu Yeh said, "After all, though talented, he is but *P'iao-chi Chiang-chün* and a marquis of the decadent days of Han. His rank is low and his influence small, and he still fears the central government. If you promote him to princely rank he is only one step below yourself. While doubting the reality of his submission, you give him an exalted rank and increase his influence. Surely this is only giving wings to a tiger."

"Not at all; I am helping neither Wu nor Shu. I am waiting till they are at grips, and if one goes under there will be only one left to destroy. That will be easy. However, say no more, for I have decided."

Whereupon Hsing Chên was bidden to take the mandate with the "Gifts" and accompany Chao Tzŭ to Wu.

Sun Ch'üan assembled his officers to discuss how the armies of Shu could be driven off. Then came the news of princely rank conferred by Wei, and by the rules of courtesy the messenger bearing the edict should be met at a great distance from the capital. Ku Yung was opposed to accepting the rank.

"My lord, you should style yourself 'Superior *Chiang-chün*' and earl of this country; you should not receive any rank from Wei."

"But on one occasion Duke P'ei received rank from Hsiang Yü; it depends upon the times. Why refuse?"

He discussed the matter no more, but went out at the head of a great gathering of officers to welcome the messenger.

Hsing Chên, the bearer of the mandate from Wei, on first arrival comported himself haughtily as the representative of a superior country and an imperial ambassador. And when he entered the city he did not descend from his carriage. Wherefore Chang Chao ventured to rebuke him.

"Everyone must obey the rules of courtesy as everyone must respect the laws. You, Sir, are behaving proudly as if there was no such thing as a sword in the country."

Immediately the messenger descended from his chariot and was presented to Sun Ch'üan. Afterwards they went in side by side.

As the cavalcade proceeded, a loud voice was heard in the rear of the two carriages, crying, "Here we are prevented from risking our lives in smashing Wei and swallowing Shu; and our lord receives a title from another man. Are not such things shameful?"

The man was Hsü Shêng. And the messenger sighed, saying, "If all the leaders and ministers of Chiangtung are like this, the lord of the country will not long be content to obey another."

However, the title was accepted. And when he had received the felicitations of his officers, Sun gave orders to collect beautiful works in jade and brilliant pearls, which were sent as return gifts.

Not long after came tidings of the forces under the ruler of Shu. He led his own army and a large number of barbarians from the east and south, *Mankuo* and *Samoko*, and the Han Dynasty generals of Tunghsi. Tulu and Liu Ning, with their cohorts. They advanced both by land and by water, a mighty host, of which the shouting shook the heavens. The naval force had already come out at Wuk'ou and the land force had reached Tzŭkuei.

Although Sun Ch'üan had been created a prince, yet the King of Wei would not help him.

And when the news came he asked present advice from his officers, but there was none to help him; they only muttered and were silent.

"Ah!" sighed he. "After Chou Yü I had Lu Su, and Lü Mêng succeeded him. But now they have all three gone and there's no one to share my troubles!"

But just then a very youthful captain stepped out from the ranks of the officials and said, with a lowly obeisance, "Though I am young I am not a little versed in the books of war, and with a few legions I could destroy the power of Shu."

Sun Ch'üan recognised Sun Huan, the son of Yü Ho. Sun Ch'üan loved the youth and gave him his own family name of Sun and so made him a member of his own clan. Yü Ho had four sons, of whom Sun Huan was the eldest. He was an expert archer and horseman and had accompanied his protector in several campaigns, where he had distinguished himself right well and had been given a rank. At this time he was twenty-five.

"How do you think you can overcome them?"

"There are two able captains under my command named Li I and Hsieh Ching, both very brave. With a few legions I will capture Liu Pei."

"Though you are brave, nephew, yet you are young and ought to have an assistant."

Thereupon the *Hu-wei Chiang-chün*, Chu Jan, stepped forward with, "Let me go."

Sun Ch'üan consented, and he told off five legions of soldiers and marines, over whom he placed Sun Huan and Chu Jan as joint commanders. They were to start as soon as possible.

The scouts reported that the army of Shu was camped at Itu, and Sun Huan led half his men to the borders of that district and camped.

Now Wu Pan had received his seal as leader of the van. From the day he left the borders of Shuch'uan he had had uninterrupted success. Everyone had submitted at the mere rumour of his coming. He had conducted his campaign with unstained swords as far as Itu. When he heard that Sun Huan was camped there to oppose his progress he sent back rapid messengers to the First Ruler, who was then at Tzǔkuei. He was angry that so young a captain should be sent against him.

"Do they think this youth able to withstand me?"

"Since this son of his has been made a leader," said Kuan Hsing, "it is unnecessary to send a leader of high rank; let me go."

"I was just wishing to see what you could do," said the First Ruler, and he gave him orders to go.

Just as he was leaving, Chang Pao stepped forth and asked permission to go too.

"Then both go, my nephews," said the king. "But you must be prudent and not hasty."

So they took leave, collected their men and advanced. Sun Huan, hearing of the coming of a large army, called out all his men and drew up his array. His two famous captains were placed by the great standard. They watched the men of Shu filing out and noted two leaders in silver helmets and silver mail, riding on white horses. And the flags were white. First came Chang Pao with a long spear, and then Kuan Hsing carrying a great sword.

"Sun Huan, you stupid, your time has come," cried Chang Pao abusively. "How dare you stand against the forces of the Emperor?"

"Your father is a headless devil," cried Sun Huan, no way backward in reviling, "and you are going just now to join him; don't you see?"

Then Chang Pao rode at Sun Huan. From behind his chief, Hsieh Ching dashed out to meet him. They fought nearly two score bouts, and then Hsieh Ching ran away with Chang Pao in pursuit.

When Li I saw his comrade overcome he whipped up his steed and came into the fray, whirling his silvered battle-axe. Chang Pao fought a score of bouts with him, but neither got the better.

Then a certain minor captain named T'an Hsiung, seeing that his two comrades could not overcome Chang Pao, shot a treacherous arrow from the ranks and wounded Chang Pao's steed. Feeling the pang of the wound, the horse bolted back to his own side, but fell before he reached it, throwing his rider sprawling on the ground. Seeing this, Li I turned and rode toward the prostrate leader to slay him with his battle-axe. But just as he was about to deliver his blow, lo! a red flash came between, and his head rolled along the earth.

The red flash was Kuan Hsing's great sword. Seeing the horse fall and Li I coming up, he had rushed in and dealt that fatal blow. And he had saved Chang Pao from death. Then they attacked and lay on so that Sun Huan suffered a great defeat. Then each side beat the retreat and drew off.

Next day Sun Huan came out to offer battle again, and the two cousins went forth together. Kuan Hsing, from horseback by the main standard, challenged his enemy. Sun Huan rode out fiercely, and they two fought near two score bouts. But he was not strong enough and drew off. The two youths followed and reached his camp. Wu Pan and two others fought well. Chang Pao helped them with all his force and was the first to force his way into the ranks of Wu. He came across Hsieh Ching, whom he slew with a spear thrust. The men of Wu scattered and fled, and the victory was on the side of Shu.

But Kuan Hsing was missing. Chang Pao was desperate, saying he would not survive his cousin. So he girded on his huge spear and rode far and wide seeking him. Presently he met Kuan Hsing, bearing his sword in his left hand, while his right held a captive.

"Who is this?" asked Chang Pao.

"In the mêlée I met an enemy," cried Kuan Hsing, "and I took him prisoner."

Then Chang Pao recognised the man who had let fly the treacherous arrow that had brought down his horse. The two returned to camp, where they slew their prisoner and poured a libation of his blood to the dead horse.

After this they drew up a report of the victory for the First Ruler. Sun Huan had lost his two famous captains as well as many other officers and many men. His army was too weakened to continue the campaign, so he halted and sent back to Wu for reinforcements.

Then Chang Nan and Fêng Hsi said to Wu Pan, "The power of Wu is broken; let us raid their encampment."

But Wu Pan said, "Though so many have been lost, there are many left. Chu Jan's marine force is in a strong position on the river and is untouched. If you carry out your plan and the marines land in force and cut off our retreat we shall be in difficulties."

"That is easily met," said Chang Nan. "Let each of the two leaders Kuan and Chang take five companies and go into ambush in the valleys to guard against any such move."

"I think it better to send some persons to pretend to be deserters. Let them tell Chu Jan of the plan to raid the camp, and Chu Jan will come to the rescue as soon as he sees fire. Then the ambushed men can attack him."

They thought this a fine plan, and they made the necessary arrangements.

Hearing of the ill success and losses of his colleague, Chu Jan was already thinking of going to his help, when a few deserters appeared and boarded his ship. He questioned them, and they said they were Fêng Hsi's men, who had deserted because of unfair treatment. They had a secret to tell.

"What secret can you betray?"

"To-night Fêng is going to make an attack upon General Sun's camp; he thinks it is a good chance. They are going to raise a fire as a signal."

Chu Jan saw no reason to doubt the men, and he sent off at once to tell Sun Huan. But the messenger never arrived, as Kuan Hsing intercepted and slew him. Then he deliberated upon going to help.

"You cannot trust what those soldiers said," said Ts'ui Yü, one of the captains. "Both army and navy will be lost if anything goes agley. No, General; rather keep careful watch and let me go."

Chu Jan saw this was the wiser plan, so he gave Ts'ui a legion and he left. But that night an attack was made on Sun Huan's camp, and the men were scattered and fled. Ts'ui Yü saw the flames as he marched and pressed on. Then just as he was passing some hills he came upon the ambush, and the two cousins appeared, one on either side. Taken by surprise, Ts'ui could only try to flee, but he met Chang Pao, who made him prisoner. When Chu Jan heard it he was panic-stricken and dropped down-river some distance.

The remnant of Sun Huan's men ran away. As they went he enquired what places lay on their road. They told him that if he went north he would come to Illing, where they could camp. So they went thither.

Just as they reached the wall, their pursuers came up and the city was besieged. Kuan Hsing and Chang Pao went back to Tzŭkuei and saw the First Ruler, who rejoiced at their success. The prisoner was put to death, and the soldiers were rewarded. The effect of these victories spread far, so that the captains in Wu had no inclination to fight.

When the Prince of Wu received Sun Huan's call for help he was frightened and knew not what to do. So he called a great council, and he said, "Sun Huan is besieged in Illing and Chu Jan has been defeated on the river; what can be done?"

Then Chang Chao said, "Though several of your captains are dead, yet have you some left. Half a score is enough to relieve your anxiety. Send Han Tang, with Chou T'ai as his second, P'an Chang as van-leader, Ling T'ung as rear-guard; Kan Ning in reserve. You want ten legions."

Sun Ch'üan made the appointments as proposed. Kan Ning was very seriously ill just then, but he accepted the task.

Now the First Ruler had made a line of forty camps from Wuhsia and Chien-p'ing to Iling, at distances of seventy *li* apart. He was exceedingly pleased with his two nephews, who had distinguished themselves again and again, and thought how fortunate it was that they could help him at the time his old captains were failing.

When he heard of the coming of Sun Ch'üan's army under newly appointed leaders, he wished to select a captain to oppose the Wu army. Then those near him told him that Huang Chung and a half dozen other officers had run off to Wu.

"Huang is no traitor," said the ruler, smiling; "it is only that he heard what I happened to say about old and useless leaders. He will not confess he is old and wants to prove he is not."

Then he called his two nephews and said to them, "Huang Chung may fail in this enterprise of his, so I hope you two will not mind going to his assistance. As soon as there is some success to report get him to return and do not let him come to grief."

So the two got their men together and went off to assist the aged warrior.

> When young, success is easy, thine at will,
> The aged servant fails, though willing still.

The next chapter will relate the outcome of Huang Chung's expedition.

CHAPTER LXXXIII.

FIGHTING AT HSIAOT'ING; THE FIRST RULER CAPTURES
CERTAIN ENEMIES;
DEFENCE OF CHIANGK'OU; A STUDENT ACCEPTS
SUPREME COMMAND.

As has been said, the veteran warrior Huang Chung was among the officers who followed the First Ruler to war against Wu. When he heard his master talk of old and incapable leaders he girded on his sword and with a few faithful followers made his way to the camps at Iling. He was welcomed by the captains there, but they knew not why he had come.

"For what reason do you come, O Veteran?" asked they.

"I have followed our lord the Emperor ever since he left Changsha, and I have done diligent service. I am now over seventy, but my appetite is good, I can stretch the strongest bow, and I can ride any distance without fatigue. I am not weak or worn out. But our master has been talking of old and stupid leaders, and I am come to take part in the fight with Wu. If I slay one of their leaders he will see I may be old but not worn out."

Just about that time the leading division of the Wu army drew near, and the scouts were close to the camp. Huang Chung hastily rose, went out of the tent and mounted to go into the battle.

"Aged General, be careful," said the captains.

But Huang Chung paid no attention and set off at full speed. However, Fêng Hsi was sent to help him. As soon as he saw the array of the enemy, he pulled up and challenged the leader of the vanguard. The van-leader, P'an Chang, sent out one of his subordinates, Shih Chi, to take the challenge. Shih Chi despised his aged antagonist and rode lightly forth with his spear set, but in the third bout Huang Chung cut him down. This angered P'an, who flourished Black Dragon, the sword of the old warrior Kuan which had passed into his possession, and took up the battle. These two fought several bouts, and neither was victor, for Huang Chung was brimful of energy. His antagonist, seeing that he could not overcome the old man, galloped off. Huang Chung pursued and smote him and scored a full victory.

On his way back he fell in with the two youthful captains, Kuan and Chang, who told him they had come by sacred command to aid him if necessary.

"And now that you have scored so complete a victory we pray you to return to the main camp," said they.

But the veteran would not. Next day P'ang Chang came to challenge again, and Huang Chung at once accepted. Nor would he allow the young men to come with him, or accept assistance from any other.

He led out five companies. Before many bouts had been exchanged P'an Chang made a feint and got away. Huang Chung pursued, shouting to him not to flee.

"Flee not, for now will I avenge the death of Kuan Yü," cried he.

Huang pursued some score *li*, but presently he fell into an ambush and found himself attacked on both flanks and in the rear, and the erstwhile flying enemy turned, so that Huang was surrounded and hemmed in. Suddenly a great storm came on. The wind blew violently, forcing Huang to retreat. And as he was passing some hills an enemy cohort came down the slopes, and one of the arrows wounded the veteran in the armpit. He nearly fell from his horse with the shock. The men of Wu, seeing Huang wounded, came on all together, but soon the two youthful captains, Kuan Hsing and Chang Pao, drove them off and scattered them. Thus they rescued Huang Chung.

He was taken back to the main camp. But he was old and his blood was thin, and the wound gaped wide, so that he was near to die. The First Ruler came to visit him and patted his back and said, "It is my fault, O Veteran, that you have been hurt in the battle."

"I am a soldier," said the old man. "I am glad that I could serve Your Majesty. But now I am seventy-five and I have lived long enough. Be careful of your own safety for the good of the state."

These were his last words. He became unconscious and died that night. A poem was written of him:—

> First among veterans stands Huang Chung,
> Who won great merit in the conquest of Shu.
> Old, he still donned his coat of mail,
> And laid his hand to the curving bow.
> His valour was the talk of all the north,
> Fear of his might maintained the new-won west.
> Tardy he bowed his snow-white head to death,
> Fighting to the end; in very truth a hero.

The First Ruler was very sad when he heard of Huang Chung's death and made him a grave in Ch'êngtu.

"My brave captain is gone," sighed he, "and the third of my brave leaders, and I have been unable to avenge their death; it is very grievous."

Next Liu Pei led the Imperial Guard to Hsiaot'ing, where he summoned a great assembly. He divided his forces into eight parts ready for an attack by land and water. The marines were placed under Huang Ch'üan, and he himself led the land forces. It was then the second month.

When Han Tang and Chou T'ai heard that the army of Shu was approaching, they marched toward it. When near, the two armies were arrayed. The two leaders of Wu rode out and saw the First Ruler standing beneath the great standard with his staff about him. A silken umbrella splashed with gold was over his head; right and left were white banners, golden axes and other insignia of an emperor. Then Han Tang spoke:

"Your Majesty is now Ruler of Shu; why do you risk your life in the battle-field. It would be most regrettable if any untoward event happened."

The First Ruler pointed the finger of scorn at the speaker and said, "You dogs of Wu bereft me of my brother, and I have sworn that you shall not live with me under the same sky."

"Who dares plunge in among the enemy?" asked Han Tang, turning to those in his train.

A certain Hsia Hsün set his spear and rode to the front and as he did so Chang Pao with a roar galloped out to meet him. But this thunderous voice affrighted Hsia, and he sought to flee. Then Chou T'ai's brother, Chou P'ing, seeing that his colleague was panic-stricken, flourished his sword and rode out too. At once Kuan Hsing dashed to the front. Chang Pao roared again, and thrusting at Hsia bore him from his steed. This disconcerted Chou P'ing and enfeebled his defence, so that Kuan speedily slew him. Then the two youths rode furiously at the two leaders. They sought refuge in the rear.

"The tiger fathers have not begotten curs of sons," said the First Ruler with a sigh of satisfaction.

Then he waved his whip as a signal to fall on, and the Wu army suffered a great defeat. The force of the eight divisions was irresistible as a river in flood, and the slaughter was immense.

Kan Ning was in his ship ill, but he roused himself when he heard the armies of Shu had come, and mounted to go into the battle. Soon he met a cohort of the *Man* soldiers. These men wore their hair loose and went barefoot. Their weapons were bows and crossbows and long spears and swords and axes. And they had shields to ward off blows. They were led by their own Prince Shamoko. His face was spotted with red as if splashed with blood, and his eyes were grey. He rushed among Kan Ning's men wielding a spiked iron staff with bone pendants, and he had two bows slung at his belt. He was terrible to look upon. Kan Ning recognised that he had no chance of victory against such a man and did not engage him, but turned his steed to flee. But as he fled Shamoko shot an arrow that pierced Kan Ning's skull. Wounded as he was, he rode on to Fuch'ihk'ou, but there he dismounted and sat under a tree, where he died. On the tree were many hundreds of crows, and they gathered round the corpse. The Prince of Wu was sore grieved at the news of his death, and had the remains buried honourably. Moreover, he raised a temple to his memory.

> Kan Ning was first of warriors in Wu,
> With silken sails he stemmed the Yangtse's tide,
> Right loyally he served his prince, and true,
> He made two ill friends put their hate aside.
> Light horse led he by night a camp to raid,
> And first he warmed his men with generous wine.
> His resting place the solemn birds betrayed,
> And fragrant incense smoulders at his shrine.

This victory gave the First Ruler possession of Hsiaot'ing. But at the muster after the battle Kuan Hsing did not appear. Search parties were sent to find him, and they went far and wide beating the country around.

However, the dashing young soldier was only following in his father's footsteps. When Kuan Hsing had got in among the men of Wu, he had caught sight of P'an Chang, his especial enemy, and galloped in pursuit. In terror, P'an took to the hills and disappeared in one of the valleys. In seeking him Kuan Hsing lost his way and went to and fro till it grew dark without finding a way out. It was clear moonlight. Near midnight he came to a farm, where he dismounted and knocked at the door. A venerable old man appeared and asked who he was.

"I am one of the leaders of the army, and I have lost my way. I beg a meal, for I am starving," said Kuan.

The old man led him into a hall lit by many candles, and there he saw a picture of his dead father. At once he began to wail and bowed before it.

"Why do you wail thus?" asked the old man.

"This is my father," said Kuan.

At this, the old man prostrated himself before his guest.

"Why should you treat my father with such respect?" asked Kuan.

"This place is sacred to his honoured spirit. While he lived the people served him, and now that he is a spirit should they not revere him the more? I have been waiting for the armies of Shu to avenge his death, and it is indeed the great good fortune of the people that you have come."

Then he brought forth wine and food and served his guest. Moreover, he unsaddled and fed his horse.

Some two hours later a knocking came at the door, and when the old man opened it, the visitor was no other than P'an Chang, the Wu General. He also asked shelter.

As he came in Kuan recognised him and drew his sword, crying, "Stay; you ruffian! Do not flee!"

P'an turned and would have gone out, but on the threshold suddenly appeared a figure of ruddy complexion with bright eyes and heavy eyebrows, and a long, flowing beard. And it wore a green robe and golden armour and was armed with a huge sword.

P'an shrank back, for he recognised the noble Kuan in spirit form. He uttered a shriek and became as one distraught, but before he could turn, Kuan Hsing raised his sword; it fell, and P'an lay dead. Taking the heart-blood of his dead enemy Kuan poured it in libation before the picture of his father. After that he took possession of his father's sword, Black Dragon, curved as the young moon.

Having hacked off the head of his fallen enemy he fastened it to his bridle. Then he took leave of his aged host, saddled his enemy's horse and rode away toward his own camp. The old man dragged the corpse of the dead soldier outside and burned it.

Kuan had not gone very far when he heard the neighing of horses and soon met a troop led by Ma Chung, one of P'an Chang's lieutenants, who was looking for his chief. Ma fell into a great rage when he saw the head of his chief swinging at the neck of Kuan Hsing's horse and beheld the famous sword in his hand. He galloped up furiously, and Kuan Hsing, who recognised an enemy of his late father, rushed to meet him. Just as he would strike, however, Ma Chung's men galloped up to support their captain, and Kuan Hsing was surrounded. He was in dire danger, but just opportunely came up a troop of horse led by his cousin Chang. At this, Ma, thinking discretion the better part, drew off his men and rode away.

The two cousins pursued him. Before they had gone far they met another force under Mi Fang and Fushih Jên, who had come out to seek Ma Chung. The two bodies of soldiers met and fought, but the men of Shu were too few for victory and drew off. Thence they made their way to headquarters, where they told their adventures and presented the head of their late enemy.

Ma Chung went back and rejoined Han Tang and Chou T'ai. Many men were wounded. Then they marched to Chiangchu and encamped. The night they arrived many men were groaning with the pain of their wounds. Mi Fang, who was listening unknown to the men, heard one of them say, "We are Chingchou men and victims of Lü Mêng's vile machinations. If we had only remained under Liu Pei! Now he

is Emperor and has set out to destroy Wu, and he will do it
one day. But we have a special grudge against Mi Fang and
Fushih Jên. Why should we not kill these two and go over
to Shu? They will think we have done well." Another said,
"Do not be hasty; we will do it presently when there is a
chance."

Mi Fang did not like this at all. He told his colleague the
men were mutinous and they themselves were in danger.

"Ma Chung is an object of especial hatred to the Ruler of
Shu; suppose we kill him and surrender. We can say we were
compelled to give in to Wu, but as soon as he came near we
wanted to get back."

"It will not do," said Fushih. "If we go they will kill us."

"No; the Ruler of Shu is liberal and kind. And the heir,
Atou, is related to me. They will surely not do any harm
to a connection."

In the end they decided to go. And in the third watch they
made their way into their chief's tent and stabbed him to
death. Then they cut off his head, and with their grisly
trophy and a few followers they set off for the camp of the
Ruler of Shu. They arrived at the outposts and were taken
to see Chang Nan and Fêng Hsi, to whom they told their tale.
Next day they went into the camp and were admitted to the
presence of the First Ruler, to whom they offered their trophy.
And they threw themselves on the ground and wept, saying,
"We are not traitors. We were the victims of Lü Mêng's
wickedness. He said that Kuan Yü was dead and tricked us
into giving up the city. We could not help surrendering.
When we heard the 'sacred chariot' had come we slew this
man to satisfy your vengeance, and we implore forgiveness."

But the First Ruler was angry, and said, "I left Ch'êngtu
a long time ago; why did you not come to confess your fault
before? Now you find yourselves in danger and so you come
with this specious tale to try to save your lives. If I pardon
you, how shall I look my brother in the face when we meet
beneath the Nine Springs?"

Then he bade Kuan Hsing set up an altar to his father in
the camp, and thereon he offered the head they had brought
in sacrifice before the tablet of Kuan Yü. This done, he had
the two deserters stripped and made them kneel before the
altar, and presently with his own hand he hewed them in
pieces as a sacrifice.

Presently Chang Pao came in and wailed before him, saying,
"The two enemies of my uncle have been slain, but when will
vengeance be taken upon those of my father?"

"Do not grieve, my nephew," said the First Ruler, "I am
going to lay waste Chiangnan and slay the whole of the curs
that live there. I will assuredly capture the two murderers of
your father, and you shall hack them to pieces as a sacrifice."

Chang Pao went away, still weeping.

About this time the fear of the First Ruler was very great among the men of Chiangnan, who stood in dread of him so that they grieved night and day. Han Tang and Chou T'ai were rather frightened too, and they sent a report to their master of the assassination of Ma Chung and what had befallen the assassins.

Then Sun Ch'üan was distressed and called together his counsellers. At this meeting Pu Chi proposed submission and self-humiliation for the sake of peace.

Said he, "There were five persons whom Liu Pei had a grudge against, and they are all dead. Now the objects of his hate are the murderers of Chang Fei. Why not send back Chang Fei's head, and these two assassins, and give up Chingchou and restore the Lady Sun and ask for peace and alliance against Wei? This will make the men of Shu retire, and we shall have peace."

This proposal seemed good. So the head of Chang Fei was enclosed in a sandalwood box; Fan Chiang and Chang Ta were bound and put in a cage-cart. All these were sent, with letters, by the band of Ch'êng Ping to the camp at Hsiaot'ing.

The First Ruler was about to march farther east when they told him that a messenger had come from Chiangnan and what he had brought. The Ruler struck his forehead with both hands, saying, "This is the direct gift of Heaven through my youngest brother's spirit."

He bade Chang Pao prepare an altar whereon to sacrifice the heads of his father's assassins. When he opened the box and saw the features of his brother he seemed at first outwardly unmoved, but soon he broke into wailing for the dead. Then the son hewed the two men in pieces and offered them upon the altar.

But this sacrifice did not appease Liu Pei's anger, and he still desired to destroy Wu. Whereupon Ma Liang remonstrated.

"Your enemies are now all dead: you are avenged. Wu has sent a high officer with large concessions and awaits your reply."

But Liu Pei savagely replied, "The one I would grind to pieces is Sun Ch'üan. To act as he proposes and enter into alliance would be treachery to my two brothers and a breach of our oath. Now I will exterminate Wu, and Wei shall follow."

He wished also to put the messenger to death, but relented when his officers interceded; and poor Ch'êng Ping ran off, terrified, glad to escape with life. He went back and told Sun Ch'üan how implacable his enemy seemed.

Sun Ch'üan was frightened and bewildered. Seeing this, K'an Tsê stepped forward and said, "Since there is a sky-supporting pillar, why not use it?"

"Whom do you refer to?" asked Sun Ch'üan.

"You once had perfect confidence in Chou Yü, and he was followed by Lu Su, equally able. Lü Mêng succeeded and you pinned your faith upon him. Though now he is dead, yet there is Lu Hsün. And he is quite near, in Chingchou. He is reputed to be a scholar, but really he is a bold and capable man, no whit inferior to Chou Yü, in my opinion. The plan that broke Kuan Yü was his. If anyone can destoy Shu, it is he. If he fail, then I will stand the same punishment as may be his."

"If you had not spoken thus my whole scheme might have gone amiss," said Sun Ch'üan.

"Lu Hsün is a student," said Chang Chao. "He is no match for Liu Pei. You may not use him."

Ku Yung also said, "He is too young and too inexperienced. I fear he will not be obeyed, and that will be mischievous."

Pu Chi also said, "He is well enough to control a district, but he is not fit for a big matter."

K'an Tsê got desperate. "It is the only hope," shouted he. "I will guarantee him with the lives of all my house."

"I know he is able," said Sun Ch'üan, "and I have now made up my mind he is the man. Gentlemen, that is enough."

Lu Hsün was called home. Lu Hsün was originally named Lu I: his *tzŭ* was Po-yen. He was a native of Wu, son of Lu Chün, who was *Tu-yü* of Kiukiang and grandson of Lu Yü. He was of medium height, with a clear complexion, "like the finest jade."

Having arrived at court and made his bow, Sun Ch'üan said to him, "I wish to send you in supreme command of all the forces against Shu."

"Sir, you have numerous old and tried officers under your command; I am very young and not at all clever," replied Lu.

"K'an Tsê goes bail for you and pledges his whole house. Moreover, I know your abilities. You must be Commander-in-chief and may not refuse the appointment."

"But what will happen if the officers do not support me?"

"Here is authority!" said Sun Ch'üan, taking his own sword from his side. "Slay the disobedient and report afterwards."

"I am grateful for this proof of confidence, but I dare not accept forthwith. I pray you to assemble all the officers and confer the office upon me in their presence."

Said K'an Tsê, "The ancient fashion was to set up a platform and thereon present to the leader-elect a white yak's tail and a golden axe with the seal of office and the *fu* (commission). Thereafter his dignity and the reverence due from others were beyond all question. It would be well, O Prince, to follow the old rule. Choose a good day and appoint Lu Hsün before all the world, and no one will refuse support."

An altar was begun at once. They worked at it day and
night, and as soon as it was finished a great assembly was
called. Then Lu Hsün was requested to ascend and make his
bow on receiving his appointment as "Commander-in-chief,
Leader of the Senior Guardian Army of the West and Marquis
of Fênglou." The sword of authority and the seal of office
were presented. His powers extended over the six districts
and the eighty-one departments (of Chiangnan), over the
forces in Chingchou and Chin.

And in charging him Sun Ch'üan said, "Domestic affairs
belong to me; outer affairs are under your direction."

Lu Hsün then descended. He chose Hsü Shêng and Ting
Fêng as commanders of his guards, and the army lost no time
in taking the field. The various dispositions of horse and foot
were made, and despatches were sent to the outlying commanders.

When the despatch reached Han Tang and Chou T'ai they
were much upset at this appointment of a mere bookish student
to command them. So when the new Commander-in-chief
came they showed their discontent by a lack of hearty support.
Lu Hsün went to his tent to receive the reports, and there the
majority of the officers manifested only sullen respect and
unwilling deference.

Then Lu addressed them, saying, "By order of my superior
I am Commander-in-chief, and my commission is to destroy
Shu. You, gentlemen, all know the ordinary military rules,
and you would do well to obey them. The law is no respecter
of persons, as those who disobey will find out. Do not have to
regret when it is too late."

They nodded in sullen acquiescence. Then Chou T'ai said,
"There is Sun Huan, nephew of our prince; he is surrounded
at Iling and is short of food. I venture to request you to send
relief to him and get him out so that the prince's heart may be
comforted."

"I know all about him. His men are faithful, and he can
easily maintain his position. There is no need to go to his aid.
When Shu is broken he will be free to come out."

They all sniggered as they left the tent, and Han Tang did not
fail to express his contempt for the newly appointed "scholar."

"This will be the end of Wu," said he to his colleague. "Did
you note what he said?"

"I tried him just to see what he would do," said Chou T'ai.
"You see he had no plan ready; he destroy Shu indeed!"

Next day general orders were issued for defence and prohibi-
tions against giving battle, which provoked more laughter at
the incapable pedant, as they thought him, in command, and
secret resolves to disobey. Moreover, the officers showed their
contempt by a general disregard of orders. So once more Lu
Hsun assembled them and said, "You know I am in command;

yet the recent orders for defence have been disregarded. Why?"

Then Han Tang spoke up, "Some of us followed General Sun when he first subdued Chiangnan. Others won fame in destroying rebels, or in following the present prince in his campaigns. All of us have donned our armour and gripped our weapons in many a bloody fight. Now, Sir, you have been placed in supreme command to repulse Shu, and there should be some plan of campaign made for us at once, some dispositions of our forces and some definite advance toward that end. Instead of that we are told to strengthen our defences and are forbidden to fight. What are we to wait for? Will Heaven destroy our opponents for us? We are not afraid to die. Why is our keenness left to be eaten away and our energies wasted in idleness?"

All the others applauded this speech and cried that the speaker had expressed their own ideas.

"General Han Tang just says what we think: let us fight a decisive battle," they cried.

The new general waited till the uproar had subsided. Then drawing his sword, he shouted, "That I am a student is true. But I have been entrusted with a great task, a task for which the prince considers me competent and for the performance of which I am prepared to bear all the responsibilities. As for you, you will do well to act on the defensive as I ordered and not allow yourselves to be led astray into any attacks. And I shall put the disobedient to death."

This speech had little effect, and they dispersed mumping and grumbling.

As has been told, the First Ruler had made a long chain of stations reaching back to his base, and these camps looked very imposing with their fluttering banners by day and their fires at night. Then the spies came in and told him of the new commander of the Wu army and his policy and orders to defend.

"What sort of a man is this Lu Hsün?" said he.

"He is famous as a scholar among the people of Wu, and, though young, he is very talented," replied Ma Liang. "His schemes are very deep. He was the author of the villainous and crafty plan of attack on Chingchou."

"His crafty scheme caused the deaths of my brothers, the blockhead; but now I shall have him," said Liu Pei.

He gave orders to advance. But Ma Liang ventured to remonstrate and dissuade him. "Be very careful," said he; "this Lu Hsün is no whit inferior to Chou Yü."

"I have grown old in the field," said the king. "Don't you think me a match for this callow youth?"

He confirmed the order to go forward, and they attacked pass and ford and redoubt wherever they were. Han Tang notified his chief of the attack, and Lu Hsün, still rather dubious of the strict obedience to his orders, hastened to the point of danger. He found Han Tang on a hill surveying the enemy's force, which advanced like a great wave. Amidst the army they saw a wide yellow umbrella, and Han Tang pointed it out.

"That must be Liu Pei," said he. "I should like to kill him."

"Careful," said Lu Hsün. "So far he has scored victory after victory, and his men are very keen and confident. Maintain a careful defence and do not go out to battle. If you do, you will lose. Impress that upon your officers and men and make them understand the strategy while you follow the enemy's moves. They are hastening into the wide open space of P'ingyüan, and I do not wish to hinder them. Nor will I accept any challenge to battle, but wait till they have moved their camps into the forest and among the trees. Then I shall have a scheme ready."

Han Tang agreed so far as words went, but in his heart he was still mutinous and ill-conditioned. When the Shu army drew near, a small force came to challenge. They shouted all sorts of abuse and hurled reproaches to put their opponents to shame, but Lu Hsün took no notice and bade his men stop their ears. He would not allow them to go out to battle, but he went from fort to redoubt encouraging the soldiers to remain carefully on the defensive.

The First Ruler's heart burned within him at this refusal to come out to battle, and it angered him none the less that Ma Liang dinned into his ears how deep Lu Hsün was and crafty.

"He recognises the disadvantages of Your Majesty's troops in being far from their base, and from spring to autumn he will not come out to fight till some move occurs that he may profit by."

"What ruse can he be contemplating?" said Liu Pei. "The real fact is that he is afraid. Their army has suffered nothing but defeat times and again. They dare not meet us."

One day the leader of the van, Fêng Hsi, memorialised the First Ruler, saying, "The weather is scorching and the troops are camped in the full glare of sun. Beside, water is scarce and hard to get."

Thereupon orders were given to move the camps into the shade of the forest close by and near the streams till the summer heats should have passed. This order given, Fêng Hsi was the first to choose a retired and shady spot for his men.

Ma Liang said, "If our men move, the enemy will rush out on us and we shall be hard set."

"I will provide for that," said the First Ruler. "I will send Wu Pan with a legion of our inferior troops to camp near their lines. But I will choose eight companies of veterans and place them in ambush. Wu Pan will have orders to flee

242

before the men of Wu and lead them into my ambush if they come out, and I will cut off their retreat. We ought to capture this precocious youth."

"A genius in plans, a marvel of prevision!" cried all those about him as this plan was unfolded. "None of us can approach him in cleverness."

So they felicitated their ruler. But Ma Liang said, "They say the Prime Minister is on a tour of inspection of the fastnesses in the eastern portion of Shu, seeing that they are in good order against any attack on the part of Wei. Why not send him a sketch of your present dispositions of troops and ask his opinion?"

"I also am not entirely ignorant of the art of war, and I see no reason to seek advice," was the cold reply.

"There is an old saying about hearing both sides," said Ma Liang.

"Well, then; you go round to all the camps and make a map and take it to the Prime Minister. If he finds any fault you may come and tell me."

So he went while the First Ruler busied himself with getting his men into shelter from the fierce heat of summer. His move was no secret, and the scouts soon told Han and Chou, who rejoiced at the news and soon went to tell Lu Hsün that all the enemies' camps had been moved into the shade.

"Now, Sir, you can attack!" said they.

'Twas not a bad plan, an ambush to set,
Thus thought he his chiefest opponent to get.

Whether Lu Hsün acted upon the suggestion of his subordinates will be seen in the next chapter.

CHAPTER LXXXIV.

Lu Hsün Burns His Enemy's Camps;
K'ung-ming Plans the Eight Arrays.

The last chapter closed with the report that the First Ruler had shifted camp in search of coolth, and the news was very welcome to Lu Hsün. He went forthwith to assure himself of the truth of the report and observe the new position. A level plain lay at his feet, whereon he saw something short of a legion, the greater part of whom appeared invalids. On the banner of their leader he read the name Wu Pan.

"We despise these men," said Chou T'ai. "Let me and General Han go out and smite them. I will give the formal guarantee of victory."

The Commander-in-chief made no reply, but remained gazing out before him. Presently he said, "It seems to me that an air of slaughter is rising over there from that valley; surely there is an ambush there. These poor troops in the foreground are nothing but a bait. No, Gentlemen; do not leave your positions."

Those who heard this took it only as another proof of the imbecility of their pedant commander. Next day Wu Pan's men approached closer and challenged to battle, swaggering about and brandishing their weapons and shouting volleys of abuse without end. They manifested contempt by throwing off their armour and clothing and moving to and fro with the utmost carelessness, bare bodies and naked forms, blatantly unready to fight. Some even sat or lay asleep.

Hsü Shêng and his colleague came to the commander's tent to complain of these insults and ask permission to go out and punish the enemy, but Lu Hsün only smiled.

"You see everything from the point of view of brute courage. You seem not to know the principles of war laid down by Sun and Wu. This display is only meant to entice us into fight. You will see the pretence yourselves in about three days."

"In three days the change of camp will be complete, and the enemy will be too strongly posted for our success," said they.

"I am just letting them move their camp."

These two left the tent also sniggering. But on the third day the officers were assembled at a certain look-out point whence they saw that Wu's men were leaving."

"There is still a deadly look over the valley," said Lu Hsün. "Liu Pei will soon appear."

He was right. Very soon they saw a whole army all well accoutred pass across the field escorting the First Ruler. And the sight took away all their courage.

"That is why I would not listen to those of you who wanted to fight," said Lu. "Now that the ambush has been withdrawn we can settle them in about ten days."

"The proper time to attack was when they began to transfer their camp. Now they are fully established with encampments stretching hundreds of *li*. Having spent seven or eight months in strengthening where they might be attacked, will it not be difficult to destroy them?"

"I see you do not understand how to carry on war. This man Pei is a bad man, but capable and crafty. When he first started on this expedition his methods were of the best, and he kept to them for a long time, so we gave him no chance against us. When his men are worn out and his thoughts cease to be clear that will be our day to attack."

At last they agreed with their chief.

> The general discoursed on war,
> According to the book;
> Right craftily the bait for whales
> Was put upon the hook.
> When kingdoms three were carven out,
> Though famous men were many,
> Commander Lu of Chiangnan
> At least stands high as any.

The truth is, the plan whereby the Shu army was to be crushed was all ready, and at this stage he wrote to the Prince Wu full details, even naming a day for the victory.

"We have found another remarkably able man," said the prince, "and I have no further anxiety. They all said he was a useless pedant, and only I knew better. Reading this letter shows him nothing at all of a pedant."

Then the Prince of Wu mustered the remainder of his soldiers to hold in reserve.

Meanwhile the First Ruler had sent orders to hasten the marines down the river and take up stations along the banks deep in the territory of Wu. However, Huang Ch'üan spoke against this, saying, "It is easy enough for the ships to go down, but how about returning? Let me make the first advance, and Your Majesty may follow. That will make it more than probable that nothing will go wrong."

"Those Wu dogs are afraid," objected the ruler, "and I want to make a dash at them. Where is the difficulty?"

It was only after many others had spoken against the proposal that the First Ruler gave up the notion of going into the forefront of the attack. Then dividing the army into two portions, he placed Huang Ch'üan in command on the north bank, to keep a watch on Wei, while he commanded on the southern bank. They made encampments and stations along the bank.

The spies of Wei duly reported these doings to Ts'ao P'ei, who laughed aloud when he heard the details of the long line of camps and the encampments among the trees and all this.

"Liu Pei is going to be defeated," said he.

"How do you know?" asked his courtiers.

"Because Liu Yüan-tê does not know how to wage war. How can he beat off an enemy along a front of seven hundred *li*? The maxims of war forbid to camp in open plains, among marshes, amid preciptous heights and obstacles. He will be defeated at the hand of Lu Hsün, and we shall hear of it in about ten days."

His officers felt more than doubtful and entreated their master to prepare an army. But the lord of Wei replied, "If successful, Lu Hsün will lead all his force westward into Hsich'uan, and his country will be defenceless. I shall pretend to send an army to help. I shall send them in three divisions, and I shall overcome Wu easily."

They all bowed acquiescence and approval. Then orders went out appointing Ts'ao Jên to lead an army out by Juhsü, Ts'ao Hsiu to take a second out by Tungk'ou and Ts'ao Chên to command a third to go through Nanchün, and the three armies were to combine on a given date for a sudden attack on Wu.

The story of that attack will not be told here; it is necessary to say how Ma Liang fared. Reaching Ch'êngtu, he lost no time in seeing the Prime Minister and presenting the plan of the armies as they were in the field.

"Now the forces are on both sides of the river extending along a front of seven hundred *li*, with forty stations, each beside a mountain stream or in a pleasantly shaded forest. At our lord's command I prepared this map, and he sent me to ask your opinion."

"Who advised such an arrangement? He ought to be put to death, whoever it was," cried K'ung-ming sorrowfully, tapping the table at his side.

"It is entirely our lord's own work; no other had any hand in it," said Ma.

"The life and energy of the Hans are done indeed," said K'ung-ming. "He has committed those very faults which the rules of the 'Art of War' lay down as to be particularly avoided. The camps are made where free movement is impossible, and nothing can save him if the enemy use fire. Beside, what defence is possible along a seven hundred *li* front? Disaster is at hand, and Lu Hsün sees it all, which explains his obstinate refusal to come out into the open. Go back as quickly as you can and tell our lord that this will not do, that it must be changed at once."

"But if I am too late! If Wu has already attacked and won, what then."

"The enemy will not dare to follow up their victory by a march on Ch'êngtu from fear of Wei. So this city is secure. Our lord will be compelled to shelter in Paitich'êng. I have already placed a legion of men in hiding at Fishbelly Creek (Yüfupu).

"Have you? I have been up and down that creek three or four times without seeing a man. I do not see the reason of telling lies to me," said Ma.

"You will see; do not ask so many questions."

With the precious instructions which he had persuaded the great strategist to draw up, Ma Liang hastened back to the imperial camp. while K'ung-ming went to the capital to prepare a relief expedition.

The men of Shu had become slack and idle and no longer maintained adequate defence, wherefore Lu Hsün perceived that his moment had arrived, and called his captains to his tent to receive orders.

"There has been no fighting since I received our lord's command. I have spent the time in acquiring a knowledge of the enemy. As a preliminary operation I want to capture a camp on the south bank. Who volunteers?"

Out stepped Han and Chou and Ling, all three at once, each crying that he wanted to be sent. But they were sent back; the Commander-in-chief did not want any of them. Then he called up the junior captain, Shunyü Tan, and said, "You will take the fourth camp on the south side; you may have half a legion. The commander of the post is Fu T'ung. I shall support you."

When Shunyü had gone, he summoned Hsü Shêng and Ting Fêng and said, "Each of you will take three companies and bivouac five *li* from the camp, so that if your colleague is repulsed and pursued you can rescue him."

Shunyü Tan marched between the lights and reached the camp he was to capture just after the third watch. His drums rolled, and he attacked at once. The defenders came out led by Fu Tung, who, spear ready to thrust, rode straight toward the leader of the attack and forced him back. Suddenly there arose the roll of other drums, and a cohort under Chao Yung barred the way. Shunyü turned off along another road, escaping with loss of many men.

But he was not yet safe. Some distance farther he ran against the barbarian leader Shamoko. However, Shunyü avoided him also and went on his way, pursued now by three parties. Soon he reached the spot five *li* from the camp. and here the two leaders of Shu, who had been placed ready to afford succour, came out and stopped the pursuit. When the enemy had retired, Shunyü Tan was escorted back to camp.

He was wounded, and with the arrow still undrawn he appeared before Lu Hsün and apologised for his failure.

"It was no fault of yours," said the Commander-in-chief. "I wanted to test the force of our enemy. My plan of attack is quite ready."

"The enemy is very strong and will not be easily overcome," said Hsü and Ting. "We have now suffered great loss to no purpose."

"This plan of mine would not hoodwink Chuko Liang, but happily he is not here. His absence will allow me to score a great success."

Then he summoned his captains to receive orders. He sent Chu Jan to lead the marine force. He was to advance next day, after noon, when the south-east wind would serve. His ships were laden with reeds and straw, which were to be used as ordered. Han Tang was directed to attack the north bank, Chou T'ai the south. Each soldier, in addition to his weapons, was to carry a bundle of straw or reeds, with sulphur and nitre hidden therein, and each had a piece of tinder. They were to advance, and, when they reached the Shu camps, they were to start a conflagration. But they were to burn only alternate camps, twenty in all, leaving the others untouched. They were to advance and only stop if they captured Liu Pei. And so they set out.

The First Ruler was in his own camp, pondering over a plan to destroy the armies of Wu, when suddenly the staff that bore the great standard in front of his own tent fell over and lay on the ground. There was no wind to account for this, so he turned to Ch'êng Ch'i and asked what it might portend.

"It means only one thing, that the men of Wu will raid the camp to-night," said Ch'êng.

"They will not dare after the slaughter of yesterday."

"But suppose that was only a reconnaisance; what then?"

Just then a report came in that some men of Wu could be seen, very far off, going along the hills eastward.

"They are soldiers meant to put us off the scent," said the First Ruler. "Tell the captains not to move, but let Kuan Hsing and Chang Pao, with a small mounted force, go out to reconnoitre."

It was dusk when these two returned, and they then reported fire among the camps on the north bank. The king hastily bade Kuan Hsing go to the north camps and Chang Pao to the south to find out what was really happening. And they started.

About the middle of the first watch the wind got up and blew strong from the east. Then fire arose from the camp on the left of the ruler's own. He was starting to extinguish this flame when another fire began in the camp on his right. With the aid of the strong breeze both fires became fierce, and soon the trees caught. A confused roar showed the gathering strength of the fire. The soldiers of the burning camps were rushing into the First Ruler's own camp to escape the fire, and in their confusion they trampled on each other, so that many died.

Behind them came the men of Wu bent on slaughter. Ignorant of how many they might be, the First Ruler mounted and dashed for Fêng Hsi's camp, but that also was in flames, which seemed to rise to the very sky By this time flames were rising from both sides of the river, so that everything was as visible as by day.

Fêng Hsi leaped to his horse and fled, followed by a few of his mounted men. This small force ran against the men of Wu under Hsü Shêng. Thereupon the First Ruler turned and galloped west. Hsü Shêng then left Fêng Hsi and went in pursuit. Presently the king saw a party of soldiers in the way and became greatly alarmed.

This was Ting Fêng's army, and the First Ruler was between two foes. In his terror he saw no possibility of safety, no road was open. Just at this moment another cohort broke through to his side and rescued him. The leader was Chang Pao, and he led the Imperial Guards, who fled, taking the First Ruler with them. As they marched along they fell in with another force; the leader was Fu Tung, and he joined up with them. The Wu army was still following when the fugitives reached Saddle Hill (Ma-an Hill). The two leaders, Chang and Fu, were urging their lord to go to the top of this out of immediate danger. Soon some of Lu Hsün's men arrived and began to surround the hill. Chang and Fu held the road up the hill and kept the enemy from ascending. From the summit could be seen flames all around, and the First Ruler knew the corpses of his men lay about in heaps or floated in the streams.

Soon the men of Wu set themselves to firing the hill. The First Ruler's remaining escort fled for their lives like rats, and their lord was in despair. Suddenly he saw a captain followed by a few horsemen cutting his way through and coming up the hill. As he drew nearer the king recognised Kuan Hsing. Kuan quickly leapt down, prostrated himself and said, "Your Majesty, the fire is gaining all round, and this place is not safe. I request you to try to reach Paiti-ch'êng, and as many as possible will gather there."

"Who will dare stay behind to keep off the enemy?" said the First Ruler.

Fu Tung volunteered for this task. It was dusk when they started. Kuan Hsing led the way. They got their lord safely down the hill and away. As soon as the men of Wu noticed the flight they pressed forward, each anxious to gain kudos by the capture of the king's person. Great armies, blotting out the sky and hiding the earth, went westward in pursuit. The First Ruler ordered the men to make fires of their clothing and other things in the road so as to hinder pursuit.

Chu Jan marched up from the river to try to intercept the flight, and the noise of his drums was terrifying. The king thought there was no possibility of escape from this force, and cried "This is the end!"

His two nephews dashed to the front to cut a road through, but returned wounded and bleeding. And the noise of the pursuers came constantly nearer as they found their way along the valleys. About the first glimpse of dawn the case seemed quite desperate. But just at the worst they saw Chu Jan's men suddenly begin to break up and scatter, tumbling into streams and rolling down precipices. Soon the reason was evident; a fearsome captain was among them leading a cohort.

Once again the king was rescued from pressing danger, and this time the rescuer was the faithful Chao Yün. He had been in Chiangchou, and news of the straits of his lord had reached him there. He had set out forthwith. Then he had seen the glow of the burnings and had marched toward it. And thus he had arrived just at the moment to save his master when danger was most imminent.

As soon as Lu Hsün heard that Chao Yün had appeared, he ordered his men to stop pursuit and retire. Chao Yün happening upon Chu Jan, engaged him forthwith and in the first encounter slew him with a spear thrust. And so the men of Wu were dispersed and retired, and the First Ruler got safely to Paitich'êng.

But on the way thither his thoughts went back to his companions in misfortune, and he enquired after them anxiously.

"The pursuers are close upon us and we cannot wait for anything," said Chao Yün. "I wish Your Majesty to get into the city as quickly as possible, and while you are reposing yourself we may try to rescue some of the leaders."

When the First Ruler reached Paitich'êng he was in sore straits, only having about a hundred men left.

A poet wrote concerning this victory of Lu Hsün:—

He grips the spear, he kindles fire, the camps are swept away.
Liu Pei to Paiti City flees, lonely and sad to-day.
But Lu Hsün's meteoric fame now shoots through Shu and Wei,
For bookish men the Prince of Wu has naught but good to say.

But Fu Tung, who commanded the rear-guard, was surrounded by the enemy. Ting Fêng shouted to him, "You had better surrender. Many of the men of Shu have fallen, more have surrendered and your lord is a prisoner. You have no hope against us with your scanty force."

But Fu replied, "Shall I, a servant of Han, give in to the curs of Wu?"

Undaunted, he rode at his opponents and fought many bouts.
But his strength and valour availed naught; struggle as he
would, he could not make his way out. And so he died among
his enemies.

A poem celebrates his valiancy.

> Wu, at Iling, strove with Shu,
> Flames, not swords, used crafty Lu.
> Worthy of a place among
> Han's bold captains is Fu Tung.

The Libationer Ch'êng Ch'i, having got clear of the battle,
rode swiftly to the river bank and called to the marines to join
in the battle. They landed, but were soon scattered. One of
Ch'êng Ch'i's lieutenants shouted to him to beware, for the
men of Wu were upon him, but he shouted back, "Since I
first followed my lord I have never yet turned my back upon
the foe."

The enemy surrounded him, and, as he could do no more, he
took his sword and slew himself.

> Noble among the warriors of Shu was Ch'êng Ch'i.
> He kept his sword for the service of his prince.
> When danger pressed near he wavered not,
> Wherefore his fame remains forever bright.

Now Wu Pan and Chang Nan had been besieging Iling.
Then came Fêng Hsi and told of the need of their lord, and
they led off their army to rescue him. Whereupon Sun Huan
was set free as Lu Hsün had foretold would happen.

As soon as Sun Huan was free he set off in pursuit of Fêng
and Chang. These two marched until they met an army of
Wu face to face, and so were between two forces. A battle
was fought, and both these captains perished therein.

> Fêng Hsi was loyal without peer.
> Chang Nan was righteous, few have equalled him.
> In battle on the sandy shore they died,
> And the histories record their deeds.

Wu Pan broke through. He was pursued, but he luckily
fell in with Chao Yün and got safely to Paitich'êng.

The barbarian King Shamoko was flying from the battle-
field when he met Chou T'ai, who slew him after a short fight.

The Shu captains T'u Lo and Liu Ning surrendered to Wu,
as did many soldiers. Of the stores and weapons in the camps
of Shu nothing was saved.

When the story of the disaster to Shu reached the south,
and with it the report that the First Ruler had been killed in
battle, the Lady Sun gave way to wild grief. She rode down
to the river bank and, gazing westward, wept and lamented.
Then she threw herself into the stream and was drowned.
Posterity erected a temple on the shore called "The Shrine of
the Bold Beauty," and one who described it wrote a poem:—

> The king, defeated, fled,
>   And rumour said he'd died;
> His consort in remorse
>   Committed suicide.
> A carven stone now showeth where
> And why this heroine died.

There could be no question that this exploit brought tremendous glory to Lu Hsün. Anxious to push his advantage as far as possible, he led his exultant army westward. But as he drew near to K'uei Pass he suddenly pulled up his horse, remarking that he saw an aura of death about the mountain side in front.

"We may not yet advance farther; I suspect an ambush."

So they retreated ten *li* and camped in a wide open space. And the army was arrayed ready against any sudden attack. Meanwhile, scouts were sent out. They returned reporting no soldiers. Lu Hsün doubted and went up to the summit of a hill whence he could see over the country. The aura was still visible to him, and so he despatched other men to spy. But he received the same report; not a man, not a horse.

Still, as the sun got lower and lower in the west he saw the same appearance accentuated, and he began to feel grave doubts. He sent a confidant to look once more. This man came back saying he had not met a single man, but he had noticed on the river bank nearly a hundred heaps of boulders.

The commander, still doubting, called in several of the natives and questioned them about the stones: Who put them there? Why did they look so ghastly?

"We do not know. This place is called Fishbelly Creek. When Chuko Liang was going west into Szŭch'uan he came along here with a lot of soldiers and heaped up the boulders like that above the Sandy Rapid. We have seen vapours rising from the boulders; they seemed to come from inside them."

Lu Hsün decided to go and look at these boulders himself. So he rode off, with a small escort. Looking down at the stones from a declivity they were evidently arranged with a design related to the eight points of the compass. There were doors and door-sills and lintels.

"This looks likely to drive a man out of his senses," he said; "I wonder whether it is any good."

They rode down with intent to examine the mysterious arrangement more closely and went in among the stones. Presently one of the escort called attention to the increasing darkness and said they ought to be returning to camp. But as Lu Hsün glanced round to look for an exit a sudden squall came on and the dust whirled up, obscuring both sky and earth. And in the swirl the stones reared themselves up like steep mountains, pointed like swords, and the dust and sand shaped themselves into waves and hillocks one behind the other. The roar of the boiling river was as the drums before a battle.

"This is some trick of Chuko's," said Lu in a scared voice; "and I have been caught."

He would go out, but he had quite lost his way and could find no exit. As he stopped to consider what he should do, an old man suddenly appeared, who said, "Does the General wish to go out?"

"I greatly desire that you would pilot me out, O Elder," replied he.

Leaning on his staff, the old man led the way and with quiet dignity conducted Lu Hsün outside. He had no difficulty in finding his way and paused not a single instant. When they were once again on the slope Lu asked his aged guide who he was.

"I am Chuko K'ung-ming's father-in-law; my family name is Huang. My son-in-law placed these boulders here as you see them, and he said they represented "The Eight Arrays." They are like eight doors, and according to the scheme are named:—

> The Gate of Rest,
> The Gate of Life,
> The Gate of Injury,
> The Gate of Obstruction,
> The Gate of Prospect,
> The Gate of Death,
> The Gate of Surprise and
> The Gate of Openings.

They are capable of infinite mutations and would be equal to ten legions of soldiers. As he was leaving he told me that if any leader of Wu became mazed in them I was not to conduct him outside. From a precipice near by I saw you, General, enter in at the Gate of Death, and as I guessed you were ignorant of the scheme I knew you would be entangled. But I am of a good disposition and could not bear that you should be entrapped without possibility of escape, so I came to guide you to the Gate of Life."

"Have you studied this matter, Sir?" asked Lu.

"The variations are inexhaustible, and I could not learn them all."

Lu Hsün dismounted, bowed low before the old man and then rode away.

The famous poet Tu Fu wrote some verses which run something like this:—

> Founder of a Kingdom; no small praise
> Is his; Inventor of the Eight Arrays
> And for that famous. On the river's brim,
> Firm set, the boulders stand as placed by him.
> No current rolls them down. Time's waters too
> Drown not regret he did not conquer Wu.

Lu Hsün took his way to his camp in deep thought.

"This K'ung-ming is well named 'Sleeping Dragon,'" said he, "I am not his equal."

Then, to the amazement of all, he gave orders to retire. The officers ventured to remonstrate, seeing that they had been so successful.

"General, you have utterly broken the enemy, and Liu Pei is shut up in one small city; it seems the time to smite, and yet you retire because you have come across a mysterious arrangement of stones."

"I am not afraid of the stones, and it is not on their account that I retire. But I fear Ts'ao P'ei of Wei. He is no less resourceful than his father, and when he hears I am marching into Shu, he will certainly attack us. How could I return then?"

The homeward march began. On the second day the scouts brought word that three armies of Wei had debouched at three different points and were moving toward the borders of Wu.

"Just as I thought," said Lu Hsün. "But I am ready for them."

> "And now the west is mine," the victor thought,
> But danger from the north discretion taught.

The story of the retreat will be told in the next chapter.

CHAPTER LXXXV.

LIU, THE FIRST RULER, CONFIDES HIS SON TO K'UNG-MING'S
CARE;

CHUKO LIANG PEACEFULLY SETTLES THE FIVE ATTACKS.

It was in the sixth month of the second year of *Chang-Wu*
that Lu Hsün destroyed the army of Shu at Iling and forced
the king to seek refuge in Paitich'êng, of which Chao Yün
then undertook the defence. When Ma Liang returned only
to find his lord defeated he was more distressed than he could
say. He announced what K'ung-ming had said concerning the
plans, and the First Ruler sighed, saying, "If I had listened
to the Prime Minister's advice the defeat would not have
happened. Now how can I face a return to my capital?"

So he promulgated a command to change the guest-house
into the "Palace of Eternal Peace." He was deeply grieved
when they told him of the death of so many of his captains.
Next he heard that Huang Ch'üan, who had been given
command of the army on the north bank, had given in to Wei.
They suggested to him that the family of the renegade was
in his power and he could hold them responsible. But he only
said, "The army was quite cut off, and he had no alternative
but to surrender. Really, I betrayed him, not he me. Why
should I take vengeance on his family?"

So he continued the issue of the renegade's pay to his family.

When Huang Ch'üan surrendered he was led into the
presence of the King of Wei, who said, "You have surrendered
to me because you desired to imitate the admirable conduct of
Ch'ên and Han."

But Huang replied, weeping, "The Emperor of Shu has
been very kind to me, and he gave me the leadership of the
army on the north bank. Lu Hsün cut me off so that I could
not return to Shu, and I would not surrender to Wu, wherefore
I have yielded to Your Majesty. Defeated as I am, I should
be only too happy if my life were spared, but I have no claim
to the credit of the virtuous ones of old."

The reply satisfied the King of Wei, and he conferred an
office on Huang, who, however, declined the offer. Then one
of the courtiers said that a spy had reported that all the family
of Huang had been put to death. But the leader replied that
he could not believe it.

"I have the greatest confidence in the clemency of the King of Shu. He knows I would not have surrendered of my own free will, and he would not injure my family."

And the King of Wei agreed with his opinion.

But a poem has been written upbraiding Huang Ch'üan:

'Twas a pity that Huang Ch'üan grudged to die;
Though he yielded to Wei, not Wu,
Yet he crooked the knee in an alien court,
Which the loyal cannot do.
And the judgment calm of history
Condemns such men all through.

Ts'ao P'ei sought advice from Chia Hsü concerning his design of bringing the whole country under his own rule.

"I wish to bring the whole empire under my rule; which shall I first reduce, Shu or Wu?"

"Liu Pei is an able warrior, and Chuko Liang is a most capable administrator; Sun Ch'üan possesses discrimination, and his general, Lu Hsün, occupies all the strategical positions of importance. The natural obstacles, the intervening rivers and spreading lakes, would be hard to overcome. I do not think you have any leader to match either of these two men. Even with the prestige of Your Majesty's own presence, no one could guarantee the result. The better course is to hold on and await the outcome of the struggle between those other two."

"I have already despatched three armies against Wu; can it be that they will fail?"

The President, Liu Yeh, held the same opinion as his colleague. Said he, "Lu Hsün has just won a great victory over the great host of Shu, and all his army is full of confidence. Further, there are the lakes and the rivers, which are natural difficulties hard to cope with. And again, Lu Hsün is resourceful and well prepared."

The king said, "Formerly, Sir, you urged me to attack Wu; why do you now give contrary advice?"

"Because times have changed. When Wu was suffering defeat after defeat the country was depressed and might be smitten. Now this great victory has changed all that and their morale has increased a hundredfold. I say now they may not be attacked."

"Well; but I have decided to attack. So say no more," said the king.

He then led the Imperial Guards out to support his three armies. But the scouts soon brought news justifying the opinion of his advisers. A force had been sent to oppose each of his three armies. Liu Yeh pointed this out and again said that no success could be expected. Still the king was obstinate, and marched.

The Wu leader, Chu Huan, who had been sent against Ts'ao Jên at Juhsü, was a young man of twenty-seven. He was bold and resourceful, and Sun Ch'üan held him in great regard. Hearing that Ts'ao Jên was going to attack Tzŭchi, Chu led the bulk of his men to befend it, leaving only half a legion in Juhsü. Then he heard that the van of the enemy, under Ch'ang Tiao, had made a dash for Juhsü, so he hastened back and found the small garrison a prey to fear. Drawing his sword, he made a speech, "Success depends upon the leader rather than on the number of men. The 'Art of War' says that the value of soldiers who come from afar is doubled; that of those who inhabit a place is halved, yet always those who are in possession overcome those who come from afar. Now the enemy is weary from a long march and I and you, my men, can hold this place together. We have a great river to defend us on the south, and we are backed by the mountains on the north. Success should be ours easily, and we are as hosts at home awaiting the arrival of our weary visitors. This will give us victory in every fight. Even if the great Ts'ao P'ei come, we need feel no anxiety. How much less care we for Ts'ao Jên and his men?"

Then he issued orders to furl all the banners and to silence all the drums as if the city was empty of defenders.

In time, Ch'ang Tiao and his veterans of the van came to the city. Not a man was visible, and he hastened forward with all speed. But as he neared the city, suddenly a bomb went off. Immediately up rose a forest of flags, and out dashed Chu Huan. with his sword drawn. And he made for Ch'ang Tiao. In the third encounter he cut down his enemy, and his men, rushing to the attack, thoroughly routed the invaders, slaying innumerable men. Beside scoring a complete victory, Chu Huan took much spoil of flags and weapons and horses. Ts'ao Jên himself, coming up later, was attacked by the garrison of Tzŭchi and also routed. He fled home to his master with the news of defeat and destruction.

And before the king could decide what course to take in regard to this loss the news came of the defeat of his other two armies.

So all three had failed and were lost, and P'ei sighed and said sadly, "This has come from my wilfulness and neglect of advice."

The summer of that year was very unhealthy, and a pestilence swept away the soldiers in huge numbers. So they were marched home to Loyang. The two countries were at enmity though they were not fighting.

Meanwhile the First Ruler was failing. He remained in his Palace of Eternal Peace and presently was confined to his couch. Gradually he became worse, and in the fourth moon of the third year his condition became serious. He himself felt the end was near, and he was depressed and wept for his two lost brothers till the sight of his eyes suffered. He was morose and ill-tempered: he could not bear any of his court near him, drove away his servants and lay upon his couch sad and solitary.

One evening as thus he lay, a sudden gust of wind came into the chamber, almost extinguishing the candles. As they burned bright again he saw two men standing in the shade behind them.

"I told you I was worried," said the king, "and bade you leave me; why have you come back? Go!"

But they remained and did not go. Wherefore the king rose and went over to look at them. As he drew near he saw one was Yün-ch'ang; the other I-tê.

"Are you still alive, then, brothers?" said he.

"We are not men; we are shades," said Kuan Yü. "The Supreme One has conferred spirithood upon us in consideration of our faithfulness throughout life, and ere long, brother, we three shall be together again."

The king clutched at the figures and burst into tears; then he awoke. The two figures were no longer there. He called in his people and asked the hour: they told him the third watch.

"I am not much longer for this world," said he with a sigh.

Messengers were sent to the capital to summon the Prime Minister and certain other high officers of state to receive the king's last instructions. They came, K'ung-ming bringing the two younger sons. The eldest, the heir-apparent, was left in charge of the capital.

K'ung-ming saw at once that his master was very ill. He bowed to the ground at the foot of the "dragon" couch. The dying king bade him come near and sit beside him, and he patted his faithful minister on the back, saying, "The attainment of emperorship was your work. Little thought you that I should prove so stupid as not to follow your advice and so bring about the late disasters. But I am deeply sorry, and now I shall not live long. My heir is a degenerate, but I must leave him to do the best he can with the great inheritance."

And the tears flowed in streams.

"I trust Your Majesty will fulfil the hopes of the people by a speedy recovery," said K'ung-ming, also in tears.

Turning his head, the king saw Ma Liang's brother at the bedside. He bade him retire. When he had left the chamber, the king said, "Do you think Ma Su is clever?"

"He is one of the ablest men in the world," said K'ung-ming.

"I do not think so. I think his words exceed his deeds. Do not make much use of him. Watch him carefully."

Having said this, he bade them summon the high officers of state to the chamber. Taking paper and pen the First Ruler wrote his testament. He handed it to the Prime

258

Minister with a sigh and said, "I am no great scholar, and I only know the rough outlines of what should be known. But the Holy One has said that a bird's song is sad when death is near and a dying man's words are good. I was waiting that we might aid each other in the destruction of Ts'ao and the restoration of the Hans, but ere the work is complete I am called away, and this last command of mine I confide to you as Prime Minister to be handed to my son and heir, Ch'an. My words are to be taken seriously. I trust that you will instruct and guide my son."

K'ung-ming and all those present wept and prostrated themselves, saying, "We pray Your Majesty to repose yourself. We will do our utmost whereby to prove our gratitude for the kindness we have received."

At the king's command the attendants raised K'ung-ming from the earth. With one hand the dying man brushed away the falling tears, while with the other he grasped K'ung-ming's hand and said, "The end is near; I have something more to say as to a friend."

"What holy command has Your Majesty to give?"

"You are many times more clever than Ts'ao P'ei, and you must safeguard the kingdom and complete the great work. If my son can be helped, help him. But if he prove a fool then take the throne yourself."

Such a speech almost startled K'ung-ming out of his senses. A cold sweat broke out all over his body, and his limbs threatened to cease to support him. He fell on his knees, saying, "I could never do otherwise than wear myself to the bone in the service of your son, whom I will serve till death."

He knocked his head upon the ground. The dying man called K'ung-ming closer, and at the same time making his two sons come near, he said to them, "My sons, remember your father's words. After my death you are to treat the Prime Minister as you would your father and be not remiss, for thereby you will fulfil your father's hopes."

He made the two princes pay to K'ung-ming the obeisance due to a father.

Said K'ung-ming, "Were I destroyed and ground into the earth, I should be unable to repay the kindness I have experienced."

Turning to the assembled officers, the First Ruler said, "As you have seen, I have confided my orphan son to the care of the Prime Minister and bidden my sons treat him as a father. You too, Sirs, are to treat him with deference. This is my dying request and charge to you."

Turning to Chao Yün, he said, "I and you have gone together through many dangers and difficulties. Now comes the parting of our ways. You will not forget our old friendship, and you must see to it that my sons follow my precepts."

"I shall never dare to give other than my best," said Chao Yün. "The fidelity of the dog and horse is mine to give and shall be theirs."

Then he turned to the others, "Noble Sirs, I am unable to speak to you one by one and lay a charge upon each individual; but I say to you, Maintain your self-respect."

These were his last words. He was sixty-three, and he died on the twenty-fourth day of the fourth month (223 A.D.)

A poem was written by Tu Fu on his death:—

The king set out to destroy the land that lay through the gorges,
Failed he and breathed his last in the palace "Eternal Tranquillity,"
The palace fair of his thoughts lay not this side the highlands.
Beautiful chambers are vainly sought in his rural temple,
Now are the pines near his shrine nesting places for herons,
Through the courts aged peasants saunter, enjoying their leisure,
Nearby often is found a shrine to this strategist famous,
Prince and minister's needs are now but offerings in season.

Thus died the First Ruler. All present lifted up their voices and wept.

The Prime Minister led the procession that escorted the coffin to the capital, and the heir, Liu Ch'an, came to the outskirts of the city, as a dutiful son should, to receive the remains with due respect. The coffin was laid in the Great Hall of the palace, wherein they lamented and performed the ceremonies appointed. At the end of these the testament was opened and read.

"I first fell ill from a simple ailment. Other disorders followed, and it became evident that I should not recover. They say that death at fifty cannot be called premature, and as I have passed three score I may not resent the call. But when I think of you and your brothers I regret. Now I say to you, strive and strive again. Do no evil because it is a small evil; do not leave undone a small good because it is a small good. Only with wisdom and virtue men can be won. But your father's virtue was but slender and unequal to the strain.

"After my death you are to conduct the affairs of the state with the Prime Minister. You are to treat him as a father and serve him without remissness. You and your brothers are to seek instruction. This is my final and simple command."

When this had been read, K'ung-ming said, "The state cannot go a single day without a prince, wherefore I beg you to install the heir as successor to the great line of the Hans."

Thereupon the ceremony was performed, and the new Emperor took his place. The style of the reign was changed to *Chien-Hsing*. Chuko Liang became "Marquis of Wuhsiang and Governor of Ichou."

Then they buried the late king at Huiling with the posthumous style of *Chao-Lieh Huang-ti*.

The Empress, of the Wu family, was formally created Empress Dowager. The late consort Kan became *Chao-Lieh* Empress, and the Lady Mi was granted similar, also post-humous, rank. There were promotions in rank and rewards for all, and a general amnesty was proclaimed.

Before long, knowledge of these things came to the army of Wei, and a report was sent to the capital and made known to the Prince of Wei. Ts'ao P'ei felt relieved and was glad of the death of his rival, and his thoughts at once turned toward an attack during the critical moment of a change of ruler.

But Chia Hsü dissuaded him. "Liu Pei is gone, but surely he has confided the care of the state to Chuko Liang, who is indebted to him so deeply. He will exhaust every effort to support his young lord. You may not hastily attack."

As he tendered this remonstrance, a man suddenly stepped out from the serried ranks of courtiers and said fiercely, "If you neglect this moment can you expect a more favourable opportunity?"

All eyes turned to the speaker; it was Ssŭma I.

The interruption greatly pleased P'ei, who at once asked how it was to be done. He propounded his plan in the following speech:—

"It would be very difficult to obtain success with our own resources. Hence we must use five armies and attack all round at the same time, so as to embarrass Chuko Liang."

"Where are the five armies to come from?" said Ts'ao P'ei.

Ssŭma went on, "The first is to be got from Liaotung, from the Hsian-pi country (Inner Mongolia). You must write to Prince K'opinêng and send him presents of gold and silks so that he may send ten legions of the *Ch'iang* (Tanguts) from Liaohsi to attack Hsip'ing Pass. Secondly, the present prince of the *Man* Tribes, Mênghuo, must be persuaded to attack the south of Hsich'üan, the districts of Ichou, Jungch'ang, Tsang-ko and Yüehchien. Thirdly, you must send an ambassador to Wu with fair promises of an increase of territory, and so induce Sun Ch'üan to lead ten legions to the attack, making Fouch'êng his objective. The fourth army can be got from Mêng Ta in Shangyung, who can attack Hanchung. Lastly, our own force may be placed under Ts'ao Chên, who will attack by way of Yangping Pass. With fifty legions making a simultaneous attack along five different directions, it would be hard for Chuko Liang to hold his own even if he had the talent of Lü Wang (T'ai Kung) himself."

The scheme delighted Ts'ao P'ei, who at once cast about for four glib-tongued messengers. He also issued a commission to Ts'ao Chên as Commander-in-chief.

At this time Chang Liao and most others of the veterans who had served Ts'ao Ts'ao were enjoying their leisure in various parts of the country, and as nobles were keeping watch and ward at certain passes and fords and such places. Their appointments were more or less sinecures. They were not summoned for this expedition to the west.

Although all the details of what came to pass in Shu after the accession of the Second King Liu Ch'an need not be told, yet it may be noted that many of those who had served his father died after the decease of their master. The work of the administration of the kingdom, the choice of officials, law-making, taxation, decision of legal cases, was all done by the Prime Minister.

As the new king had no consort, the courtiers, headed by K'ung-ming, proposed a daughter of the late Chang Fei as young and prudent, and she was married to the Emperor and so became Empress.

It was in the autumn of the year of his accession that the Later Ruler heard of the plans and intentions of Wei against his state. The persons who told him gave him full details of the five armies and said they had previously told the Prime Minister.

"But his conduct puzzles us," said the informers. "We do not know why he does not take some action instead of remaining shut up in his palace all the time."

The Later Ruler became really alarmed, and he sent one of his personal attendants to call the Prime Minister to court. The servant was gone a long time, and then returned to say that the servants had told him the Prime Minister was ill and not to be seen.

The young Emperor's distress increased, and he sent two high officers to K'ung-ming, saying they were to see him even if he was on his couch and tell him the dreadful news of invasion. They went; but they got no farther than the gate. The keepers of the gate refused them admission. Then they confided their message in brief to the wardens of the gate, who went inside with it. After keeping them waiting a long time the wardens returned to say that the Prime Minister was rather better and would be at court in the morning.

The two messengers sighed deeply as they wended their way to the Emperor's palace.

Next morning a great crowd of officers assembled at the gate of the Prime Minister's residence to wait for him to appear. But he did not come out. It began to grow late, and many of them were tired of waiting, when at last Tu Ch'iung, one of the two who had been sent to tell K'ung-ming why his presence was desired at council, went again to the Emperor and suggested that His Majesty should go in person and try to get K'ung-ming to say what should be done.

The Emperor then returned to his palace and told his Consort his trouble. She was also alarmed.

"What can he mean?" said she. "This does not look like acting in the spirit of the charge laid upon him by the late Emperor. Let me go myself."

"Oh no," said Tung Yün. "Your Majesty must not go. We think all is well, and the Prime Minister certainly understands and will do something. Beside, you must let His Majesty go first, and if the Prime Minister still shows remissness then Your Majesty can summon him to the Temple of the Dynasty and ask him."

So it was left at that. And the next day the Emperor rode in his chariot to the gate of his minister. When the doorkeepers saw the imperial chariot appear they fell upon their faces to welcome the Emperor.

"Where is the Prime Minister?" asked he.

"We do not know. But we have orders not to let in the crowd of officers."

The Emperor then descended and went on foot right in to the third gate. Then he saw K'ung-ming leaning on a staff beside a fishpond looking at the fish. He approached, and stood behind him for a long time. Presently the king said slowly and with dignity, "Is the Prime Minister really enjoying himself?"

K'ung-ming started and looked round. When he saw who the speaker was he suddenly dropped his staff and prostrated himself.

"I ought to be put to death ten thousand times," said he.

But the Emperor put forth his hand and helped him to rise, saying, "Ts'ao P'ei threatens immediate invasion from five points; why will you not come forth and attend to business?"

K'ung-ming laughed. He conducted the Emperor into an inner room, and, when he was seated, K'ung-ming addressed his king, saying, "Could it be possible that I was ignorant of these five armies? I was not looking at the fish; I was thinking."

"But, this being so, what shall we do?"

"I have already turned back that K'opinêng, of the Tanguts, and Mênghuo of the *Man* and the rebel leader Mêng Ta and the army from Wei. I have also thought out a plan to circumvent the army from Wu, but I need a special sort of man to carry it out. I want an envoy, an able talker, one capable of persuading other people. It was because I have not found such a man yet that I was so deeply in thought. But Your Majesty may set your mind at rest and not be anxious."

The Later Ruler heard this half terrified and half glad.

"Surely your superhuman devices are too deep for mortal man. But may I ask how these armies have been made to turn back."

Since His late Majesty bade me take the best care of your welfare, I dare not be remiss for a single moment. These officers in Ch'êngtu are ignorant of that refinement of war which consists in not allowing the enemy to guess your plans. How could I let them know anything? When I heard that the Tanguts might invade, I remembered that Ma Ch'ao's forefathers were friendly with them and they had a high opinion of Ma Ch'ao, thinking him a leader of supreme prestige. So I sent orders by despatch to Ma Ch'ao to hold the Hsip'ing Pass, and to prepare ambushes in certain places and change them daily so as to keep the *Ch'iang* off. That settled them. I sent hastily to the south to order Wei Yen to move certain bodies of men about through the south-west districts, to be seen and then to disappear, to go in and come out and march to and fro, so that the *Mans* should be perplexed. The *Mans* are brave, but prone to doubts and hesitations, and they would not advance in the face of the unknown. Hence there is nothing to fear in that quarter. I also knew that Mêng Ta and our Li Yen were sworn friends. I had left him in charge of the Palace of Eternal Tranquillity. I then wrote a letter as if from Li to Mêng, so that I know Mêng will feign illness and not move his army. I sent Chao Yün to occupy all the strategical positions on the way by which Ts'ao Chên would march, and bade him defend only and not go out to battle. If our men refuse to come out, Ts'ao Chên will certainly have to retire. So all those four are settled. But for greater security I have sent your two cousins each with three legions to camp at points whence they can quickly help any of the others who may need it. And none of these arrangements are known here.

"Now there is only Wu left to deal with. Had the other four succeeded and Shu been in danger, Sun Ch'üan would have come to the attack. If the others fail I know he will not budge, for he will remember that Ts'ao P'ei has just sent three armies to attack his country. And this being so, I want some man with a ready tongue and ingenious mind to go and talk plainly to Sun Ch'üan. So far I have not found such a man, and I am perplexed. I regret that I have given Your Majesty occasion to make this journey."

"My Consort also wanted to come," said the Emperor. "But now you have spoken, O Minister-Father, I am as one awakened from a dream; I shall grieve no more."

They two drank a few cups of wine together, and the minister escorted his master to his chariot. A ring of courtiers were waiting, and they could not help remarking the happiness that shone in their master's face. The Emperor took his leave and returned to his palace, but the courtiers did not know what to think.

Now K'ung-ming had noted a certain man among the crowd who smiled and looked quite happy. He looked at him intently and then recollected his name, which was Têng Chih, a man of reputable ancestry, who came from Hsinyeh. He sent a man privately to detain Têng, and when all the others had gone, K'ung-ming led him into the library for a chat. Presently he came to the matter near his heart.

"The three states have become a fact," said he. "Now if our state wanted to absorb the other two and restore the condition of one rule, which country should it attack first?"

"Though Wei is the real rebel, yet Wei is strong and would be very difficult to overthrow. Any move against it would have to develop slowly. As our Emperor has but lately succeeded his father and the people are none too decided in his favour, I should propose a treaty of mutual defence with Wu. This would obliterate the enmity of His late Majesty and would have important results. However, you, Sir, may have another opinion. What is it?"

"That is what I have been thinking of this long time, but I had not the man for the task. Now I have found him."

"What do you want a man to do?"

"I want him to go as envoy to Wu to negotiate such a treaty. As you understand the position so well you will surely do honour to your prince's commission as envoy. There is no other who would succeed."

"I fear I am not equal to such a task: I am not clever enough and too ignorant."

I will inform the Emperor to-morrow and beg him to appoint you. Of course you will accept."

Têng Chih consented and then took his leave. As promised, K'ung-ming memorialised, and the Emperor consented that the mission should be entrusted to Têng Chih. And he started.

> The din of war will cease in Wu,
> When Shu's desires are known.

For the success or failure of this mission read the next chapter.

CHAPTER LXXXVI.

A PHILOSOPHICAL ENCOUNTER;
FIRE USED TO DESTROY TS'AO PEI'S ARMY.

After his recent exploits Lu Hsün became the one hero of Wu. He was given the title "Pillar of the State," was ennobled as "Marquis of Chiangling," and received the Governorship of Chingchou. He became commander of all the military forces.

Chang Chao and Ku Yung, thinking the moment opportune for enhancing their lord's dignity, sent in a memorial proposing that his rule should be designated by a distinctive style, and he assumed *Huang-Wu* as his *nien-hao*.

Then arrived a messenger from Wei, and he was called in to an assembly and bidden to state his business. He said, "Recently Shu sent to Wei for help, and, the situation being misunderstood, a force was despatched. Now this action is greatly regretted. In Wei it is thought desirable to set four armies in motion against Shu to capture it, and if Wu will assist, and success crown these efforts, Wei and Wu will share the conquered territory."

Sun Ch'üan listened, but was not prepared to give a decided answer. He betook himself to his counsellors, who suggested that the sapient Lu Hsün should be consulted. So he was called, and his speech ran thus:—

"Ts'ao P'ei is too firmly established in the capital to be upset now, and if this offer of his be refused we shall provoke his enmity. Neither Wei nor Wu, so far as I see, has any man fit to oppose Chuko Liang. We must perforce consent and put our army in order. But we can wait till we see how the four armies speed. If Shu seems likely to fall and Chuko Liang is out-manœuvred, then our army can be despatched and we will take the capital. If the four armies fail we shall have to consider."

So Sun Ch'üan said to the envoy of Wei, "We are not ready at the moment, so we will choose a day to start later." And with this answer the envoy left.

Next they made careful enquiries about the success or failure of the armies against Shu. They heard that the western tribes had turned back when they saw Ma Ch'ao in command at Hsip'ing Pass. The *Mans* had been perplexed at the tactics of Wei Yen and had retreated to their caves. The Shangyung leader, Mêng Ta, had set out, but half way had fallen ill and gone back, and Ts'ao Chên's army had been brought to a halt by the defensive preparations of Chao Yün, who had garrisoned every pass and occupied every point of vantage. They had eventually retreated, after being camped in Hsiehku for some time.

Knowing all this, Sun Ch'üan said to his officials, "Lu Hsün's words were indeed prophetic; he made most perfect deductions. Any rash action on my part would place me on bad terms with Shu."

Just then the coming of an envoy from Shu was announced.

Said Chang Chao, "This mission is also part of Chuko Liang's scheme to divert danger from Shu. Têng Chih has come as envoy."

"That being so, how should I reply?" asked Sun Ch'üan.

"I will tell you. Set up a large cauldron and pour therein a quantity of oil. Light a fire beneath. When the oil is boiling, choose a goodly company of your tallest and brawniest fighting men, arm them and draw them up in lines between the palace gate and your throne room. Then summon the envoy, but before he can say a word upbraid him with being guilty of the same sort of treachery as Li Shê-ch'i and worthy of the same fate of being boiled in oil. Then see what he will say."

Sun Ch'üan followed this advice, and prepared the cauldron of oil and had the strong men ready. Then he bade them introduce the envoy.

Têng Chih came, his ceremonial dress in perfect order, and advanced as far as the gate. Seeing the grim array of fighting men armed, some with gleaming swords, some with great axes, some with long spears and some with short knives, he understood at once what was meant, but he never blenched. He advanced quite steadily and bravely till he reached the door of the hall. Even when he saw the boiling cauldron of oil and the savage executioners glaring at him he only smiled.

He was led to the front of the curtain behind which sat the prince, and he made the ordinary salutation of raising his extended arms, but he did not bow in obeisance.

The prince bade his attendants roll up the curtain, and called out, "Why do you not make an obeisance?"

Têng Chih boldly replied, "The envoy of the superior state does not make an obeisance to the ruler of a smaller country."

"If you do not control that tongue of yours, but will let it wag, you will be like that fellow Li who went to talk to Ch'i. You will soon find yourself in the cauldron."

Then Têng Chih laughed aloud. "People say there are many sages in Wu; no one would believe that they would be frightened of a simple scholar."

This reply only increased Sun Ch'üan's anger, and he said, "Who fears a fool like you?"

"If you fear not the envoy, why so anxious about what he may have to say?"

"Because you come here as spokesman of Chuko Liang and you want me to sever with Wei and turn to your country; is not that your message?"

"I am a simple scholar of Shu, and I am come to explain matters to the state of Wu. But here I find armed men and a boiling cauldron all prepared against a simple envoy. How can I form any other opinion than that you will not allow me to speak?"

As soon as Sun Ch'üan heard these words he bade the soldiers go, and called the envoy into the hall. There he invited him to a seat and said, "What is the real matter between Wei and Wu? I desire that you would inform me."

Then Têng replied, "Do you, great Prince, desire to discuss peace with Wei or with Shu?"

"I really desire to discuss peace with the lord of Shu. But he is young and inexperienced and ignorant, and unable to carry a matter through."

"Prince, you are a valiant warrior, just as Chuko Liang is a great minister. Now Shu has the strength of its geographical difficulties just as Wu has the protection of its three rivers. If these two countries are at peace they are mutually protective. They may swallow up the rest of the empire, or they may stand secure alone. If you send tribute to Wei, and acknowledge yourself one of its ministers, you will be expected to attend at court, and your heir-apparent will become a servant in that court; and if you disobey, an army will be sent to attack you. Shu also will come down the river and invade your country. Then this country will be yours no longer. And if you listen not to these words of mine, and refuse my offer, I shall commit suicide before your face and so justify the post I have as an envoy."

As he spake these last words he gathered up his robes and marched down the hall as though he was just going to jump into the cauldron.

"Stop him!" cried Sun Ch'üan, and they did so. Then he requested Têng to go into an inner apartment, where he treated the envoy as a guest of the highest honour.

"O Master," said Sun Ch'üan; "your words exactly express my thoughts, and I desire to make a league of peace with your country. Are you willing to be the intermediary?"

"Just now it was you, O Prince, who wished to boil this poor servant; now it is also you who wish to use him. How can such a doubtful person be trusted?"

"My mind is made up," replied Sun Ch'üan. "Do not doubt me, Master."

Têng Chih was detained, and a conclave of officers gathered.

Said Sun Ch'üan to the assembly, "Under my hand are all the four score and one districts of the east, and I have the lands of Chingchou and Ch'u to boot, yet I am not so well off as that little country of Shu, for Shu has Têng Chih for an envoy, and he glorifies his lord. I have no one to send to declare my wishes to Shu."

Then one stepped forth and said he would go. The speaker was Chang Wên, of Wu, who held an office of no great rank.

"Sir, I fear that when you reach Shu and are in the presence of Chuko Liang you will not explain my real sentiments," said Sun.

Chang Wên replied, "Think you that I shall fear him? He also is but a man."

Sun Ch'üan conferred great gifts on Chang Wên, and sent him on the return mission to Shu to negotiate the league of peace.

While Têng Chih was absent, K'ung-ming said to his lord, "This mission to Wu will succeed, and of the many wise men in the east one will come as return envoy. Your Majesty should treat him with courtesy, and let him return to Wu to complete the league. For if we have an alliance with Wu, Wei will not dare to send an army against us. And if we are safe from those quarters, I will lead an expedition to subdue the *Mans* in the south country. After that we can deal with Wei. If Wei is reduced, Wu will not last long, and the whole empire will again be under one ruler."

Presently the report reached the capital that Têng Chih and Chang Wên, as envoy of Wu, would soon arrive. The king and court assembled to receive them honourably. The envoy of Wu carried himself as one who had attained his desires, and advanced boldly. Having made his salute, the Later Ruler gave him to sit on a brocaded stool on his left hand. A banquet followed at which Chang Wên was treated with much honour. At the end of the banquet the whole court escorted the envoy to the guest-house where he was to lodge.

On the second day there was a banquet at the Prime Minister's palace, and K'ung-ming broached the real business. He said, "Our late ruler was not on friendly terms with Wu. But that is all changed, as is demonstrated by these banquets, and our present king is disposed to be very friendly. It is hoped that the former enmity may be entirely forgotten and the two countries swear eternal friendship and alliance in their common end, the destruction of Wei. I look to you, Sir, to speak in favour of this league."

Chang Wên said that he would support the plan. The wine went merrily round, and as the envoy became mellow he laughed freely and swaggered and put on a proud demeanour.

The king gave Chang Wên rich presents of gold and stuffs and prepared a parting banquet for him in the south guest-chamber, and all the court assembled to take leave of him. The Prime Minister paid him assiduous attention and pressed him to drink. While this banquet was in progress, a man suddenly came in as if he were already drunk, made a proud sort of salutation to the company and at once took a seat. His conduct seemed strange to Chang Wên, who asked who the new comer was.

"He is a man named Ch'in Fu, a learned education officer of Ichou," replied K'ung-ming.

"He may be that," said Chang with a laugh, "but I wonder if he has any learning at all inside him."

Ch'in Fu listened without changing countenance, and said, "Since our children are all learned, of course I am more so."

"What may have been your special studies, Sir?" said Chang Wên.

"Everything; astronomy on one hand, geography on the other; the three teachings and the nine systems; all the philosophers; history all through and all sacred books and traditions. There is nothing I have not read."

"Since you talk so big," said Chang, "I should like to ask you a few questions on celestial matters. Now has the sky (*t'ien*) a head?"

"Yes; it has a head."

"Where is it?"

"In the western quarter; the Odes say, 'God turned his head kindly toward the west,' and further it follows from this that the head is in the west."

"Well; has the sky ears?"

"O yes. The sky is above and listens to all things below. The Odes say, 'The crane calls from the midst of the marsh, his cry is heard by the sky (*t'ien*).' How could the sky hear without ears?"

"Has the sky feet?"

"It has; the Odes say, '*t'ien* (heaven) treads down difficulties.' If there were no feet how could it tread?"

"Has heaven a name?"

"Why not?"

"Then what is it?"

"Liu."

"How do you know that?"

"Because the Emperor's family name is Liu, and he is the Son of Heaven. That is how I know."

"Does the sun spring from the east?"

"Though it does, yet it disappears in the west."

All this time Ch'in Fu's repartees had flashed back clear and perfect; they came so naturally as to astonish all the guests. Chang Wên had no word to reply to them. Then it became Ch'in's turn.

"You are a famous scholar in your own land, Sir, and since you have asked so many questions about *t'ien* I take it you are well up in all celestial matters. When original chaos resolved into its two elements, *yin* and *yang*, or female and male, the lighter portion, or ether, rose and became *t'ien*, sky, and the grosser sank and solidified into *ti*, earth. When Kung Kung's rebellion was crushed, its head struck the Puchou (Imperfect) Mountain, the supports of heaven were broken and the bonds of earth were destroyed. Heaven fell over to the north-west, and earth sank into the south-east. Since heaven was ethereal and had floated to the top, how could it fall over? Another thing I do not know is what is beyond the ether. I should be glad if you would explain, Master."

Chang Wên had no reply ready, but he rose from his place and bowed his acknowledgements, saying, "I knew not that there was so much ability in this land. I am happy to have heard such a discourse. Now all obstructions have disappeared, and I see quite clearly."

But K'ung-ming, fearing lest the guest should feel mortified, soothed him with fair words, saying, "This is all play upon words, the sort of puzzles one propounds at a merry feast. You, honoured Sir, know that the tranquillity and safety of states are no matters to joke with."

The envoy bowed. Then Têng Chih was ordered to return to Wu and thank its ruler for his courtesy; and he was to accompany Chang Wên. So both, having taken leave of the Prime Minister, set out on their journey to the east.

In the meantime Sun Ch'üan was beginning to feel perplexed at the long delay of his envoy. He had summoned a council to discuss this question, when the report came that his own envoy had returned, and Têng was with him. They were brought in forthwith; and Chang Wên, having made his obeisance, began to discourse upon the virtue of the King of Shu and K'ung-ming and to lay before his lord the proposal for a league of peace. Têng Chih, the President of a Board, was empowered to discuss this matter.

Turning to Têng, Sun Ch'üan said, "Would it not be a happy result if tranquillity should be restored to the empire by the destruction of Wei, and Wu and Shu should share its administration?"

"The sky knows not two suns," replied Têng, "nor can the people recognise two kings. If Wei be destroyed, no one can say upon whom the divine command will devolve. But one who becomes a prince must perfect his virtue, and those who become ministers must be wholly loyal. In this way strife will cease."

Sun Ch'üan smiled, saying, "And your sincerity is like this, eh?"

Têng Chih was dismissed with rich gifts, and after this Wu and Shu were good friends.

The negotiations between his two rivals were reported in the capital without loss of time, and Ts'ao P'ei was very angry.

"If they have made an alliance it can only mean that they cherish the intention of destroying the capital. My best move is to strike first."

He called a great council. This council lacked the presence of Ts'ao Jên and Chia Hsü, who had both died, but Hsin P'i stepped forward and said, "The country is extensive, but the population so sparse that no successful army could be raised just now. My advice is to wait ten years, spending that period in forming an army and in cultivating the land till stores and weapons shall have been accumulated. Then both our rivals may be destroyed."

"This is only the distorted opinion of a perverted pedant. Having made this league, the two countries may fall upon us at any moment. This matter cannot be postponed for ten years," said the king.

An edict appeared commanding the enlistment of soldiers and the formation of an army. Ssŭma I then pointed out that ships were necessary, as Wu was protected by the Great River, and he proposed a plan of campaign.

"Your Majesty must lead. The navy can advance by way of the Huai, taking Shouch'un. When you reach Kuangling, the river is to be crossed and Nanhsü is to be captured."

This plan was accepted, and the construction of dragon ships was put in hand and went on day and night. Ten were built two hundred feet long to carry two companies (of a thousand) each. They also collected three thousand fighting ships.

In the autumn of the fifth year the various captains assembled, and Ts'ao Chên was appointed leader of the first corps. Chang Liao, Chang Ho, Wên P'ing and Hsü Huang were chief leaders. Hsü Ch'u and Lü Wên were guards of the centre, and Ts'ao Ho commanded the rear guard. The strategists were Liu Yeh and Chiang Chi. In all, land and marine forces numbered over thirty legions. When the starting day was decided upon, Ssŭma I was made President of the Board of War with the Lordship of the Archery, and left in the capital with the powers of a regent.

Passing over the story of how the Wei army started, history shifts the scene to Wu, where the spies told the king's attendants of the dangers, and the latter hastened to inform the king. They said Ts'ao P'ei was leading in person and the danger was great.

When Sun Ch'üan met his council, Ku Yung said, "My lord, you can call upon Shu for help according to the treaty. Write to K'ung-ming and get him to send out an army through Hanchung so as to divert part of Wei's army. Also send an army to Nanhsü to oppose them there."

"I shall have to recall Lu Hsün," said the prince. "He is the only man to undertake this great task."

"Do not move him if you can help it; he is necessary for the protection of Chingchou."

"Yes, I know; but there is no other strong enough."

At these words Hsü Shêng advanced, saying, "I know I am not very able, but I desire to be given an army tò meet this danger. If Ts'ao P'ei crosses the river in person I will make him prisoner and present him at the gate of your palace. If he does not come over here I will slay so many of his men that his army shall not dare even to look this way."

Sun Ch'üan was pleased to find a willing volunteer, and replied, "Noble Sir, what anxiety need I feel if I have your protection?"

Hsu was given the title of "Protector of the East" and made Commander-in-chief of all the forces in Nanhsü. As soon as he had received his orders, he retired. He gave command to gather enormous quantities of weapons, and had many flags and banners made for the protection of the river banks.

But another impetuous young leader was anxious to take more vigorous measures, and he stood forth, saying, "My lord has laid upon you, O General, a heavy responsibility, but if you really desire to capture the ruler of Wei you should send an army to meet him on the north side in Huainan. I fear failure if you wait till the northern men have come this far."

The young man was Sun Shao, cousin of the Prince of Wu. He had already the title of "Leader of Wide Prestige," and was in command at Kuangling. Though young and impetuous, he was very valiant.

"Ts'ao P'ei's army is strong and its leaders famous. I hold that we may not cross the river to meet him, but wait the arrival of his ships on the other side. Then I shall carry out my plan," said Hsü.

"I have three companies of my own, and I know the country about Kuangling thoroughly. Let me go across the river and fight a battle. I will willingly undergo the penalty if I fail," said the younger Sun.

However, Hsü Shêng refused, and all the pleadings of his impetuous captain were vain. And when he still persisted, the Commander-in-chief grew angry and said, "What control shall I have if you are allowed to disobey orders?" He ordered the lictors to take him out and put him to death.

They led him away, and forthwith the black flag was hoisted. But one of Sun Shao's captains went off in hot haste to tell Sun Ch'üan, who came immediately to try to save his favourite.

Happily the execution had not been accomplished when the prince appeared on the scene, and he bade the executioners disperse. The youth was saved. He began to press his claim to the prince. "I have been at Kuangling, and if we do not attack the enemy there, but let him get down to the river, there will be an end of Wu."

Sun Ch'üan went into the camp, and Hsü Shêng came to receive him. When the prince was seated in his tent, he said, "O Prince, you placed me in command of the force to repulse Wei. Now this captain of mine, Sun Shao, is disobedient and should suffer death. I would ask why he should be pardoned."

"He is naturally hot and impetuous. He has been guilty of disobedience, but I hope you will overlook his fault."

"The law is none of my making, nor is it yours, O Prince; it is a state penalty, and if relationship is enough to evade it, where is discipline?"

"He has offended, and you have the right to judge and punish. But although his real name was Yü, yet my brother loved him and gave him our family name. He has rendered me good service, and if he should be put to death I should fail in my fraternal duty."

"Since you have intervened, O Prince, I remit the death penalty."

Sun Ch'üan bade his nephew thank his chief, but the youth would not make an obeisance. On the contrary, he loudly maintained the correctness of his view. "I can only lead my men against Ts'ao and so die," cried he. "I cannot consent to the other plan."

Hsü Shêng's countenance changed. The recalcitrant young man was ordered to leave the tent.

"He will not be any loss," said Sun Ch'üan, "and I will not employ him again."

Then the prince left and returned to his own place. That night they reported to Hsü Shêng that Sun Shao had gone secretly over the river with his own force, and the commander, who did not wish him to come to harm, as evidently that would displease the prince, sent a force to support him. Ting Fêng was chosen to command this reinforcement, and he was told what to do.

The Ruler of Wei, in his dragon ships, reached Kuangling, and the van got to the river bank. He came to survey the position.

"How many soldiers are on the other bank?" asked Ts'ao.

Ts'ao Chên replied, "I have not seen a single one; nor are there any flags or encampments."

"That is a ruse; I will go and find out."

So he set out to cross the river in one of the dragon ships. He anchored under the bank. On his boat were displayed the emblems proper to an imperial equipage, and they shone out bravely. Seated in the ship, the prince looked up and down the south bank, but not a man was visible.

"Do you think we should cross?" asked the prince of his strategists.

"If the rules of war mean anything, they ought to be prepared. We think Your Majesty should exercise caution.

Wait a few days and watch. Then perhaps the van might be sent to make a reconnaissance."

"So I think," said the prince. "But as it is now late, we will pass the night on the river."

It was a dark night, and the ship was brilliantly lighted up; it seemed like day on board. But all along the south bank there appeared no glimmer of light.

"What do you think it means?" said Ts'ao.

The courtiers replied, "They heard that Your Majesty's heavenly army was coming, and ran away like so many rats."

The prince laughed to himself. When daylight came there came with it a thick fog, so that nothing on the bank could be seen. After a time a breeze blew off the fog, and then, to their immense surprise, they found that the whole length of the south bank as far as they could see was one battlement, with towers at intervals, while spears and swords glittered in the sun and flags and pennons fluttered in the breeze. Also the scouts began to report a similar wall at Nanhsü. A long stone wall had grown up in a night and stood there with carts and masts of ships lying along it.

This may be explained. The fact was that the wall was an imitation, and the warriors that manned it were bundles of reeds dressed in soldiers' uniforms. But the sight chilled the ardour of the invaders.

"My hosts of men are no use against such warriors; we can do nothing," said Ts'ao.

He thought over this sadly enough. But now the wind had increased in force, and white combers began to heave up in the river, and seas broke over his boat, drenching the dragon robes. The ship seemed as if she would roll right over. So Ts'ao Chên sent out small boats to rescue his master and his men. But they were too affrighted to move. Wherefore Wen P'ing, who was in charge, leaped on board and helped the prince down into one of the smaller craft, which then flew away before the wind and got safely into a creek.

Soon came a hasty messenger from the west to say that Chao Yün had marched out through Hsip'ing Pass and threatened Ch'angan. This frightened Ts'ao P'ei so badly that he decided to retreat, and gave orders to retire. The whole army were in a mood to run away, and moved off toward the north, pursued by the men of Wu. To hasten the march, the Prince of Wei bade his men abandon all the imperial paraphernalia and impediments. The dragon ships withdrew into the Huai River one by one.

As they moved in disorder, suddenly arose the sounds of an enemy force, shouts and the rolling of drums and the blaring of trumpets, and a cohort marched down obliquely on to their line. And at the head was Sun Shao.

The men of Wei could make no effective stand, and many were slain, while large numbers were driven into the river and drowned. By dint of great efforts, the prince was saved and got away up the river. But when they had sailed about thirty *li*, they saw ahead a tract of blazing reeds. The enemy had poured fish oil over the dry reeds and set them alight. The wind was spreading the flames down river toward the men of Wei, and the heat was intense. The dragon ships had to stop.

Ts'ao P'ei was put into a smaller craft and taken on shore; his larger ships were presently set on fire and destroyed. They mounted the prince on a horse and moved along the bank, but soon they fell in with another body of men. This time it was the supports under Ting Fêng.

Chang Liao rode ahead to engage the leader, but was soon wounded by an arrow in the loins. However, he was helped away by Hsü Huang, and the prince was got safely out of the turmoil. The loss of men was heavy, and a huge booty of horses, carts, ships and weapons fell to the victors.

So the Wei armies went away north thoroughly beaten, while Hsü Shêng had scored a great success. He was richly rewarded.

Chang Liao got to Hsüch'ang, but only to die from the effects of his wound He was honourably buried by the prince, but the story of his funeral will not be told.

It has been said that Chao Yün was threatening Ch'angan, but soon after he went through the Pass the Prime Minister of Shu sent a despatch to recall him because the aged General Yung K'ai of Ichou had joined himself with the *Mans* and invaded the four districts. So Chao Yün returned. Meanwhile Ma Ch'ao was put in charge of the Yangp'ing Pass. The Prime Minister was about to go to invade the south. He was then preparing at Ch'êngtu for this expedition.

> First Wu met Wei and drove them north,
> Then Shu against the *Mans* went forth.

The story of this campaign will follow in the next chapters.

CHAPTER LXXXVII.

K'UNG-MING'S SOUTHERN EXPEDITION;
THE KING OF THE *Mans*.

With K'ung-ming's administration of affairs in the Two Ch'üan began a period of happiness and prosperity for the people. Tranquillity prevailed, and the state of society was well nigh perfect, doors unbolted at night, property left by the roadside remaining untouched till the owner returned for it. Moreover, the harvests were rich year after year, and old and young, with fair, round bellies, well lined, simply sang with joy. The people hastened to fulfil their state duties and vied with each other in the performance of any *corvée*. As a natural consequence all military preparations were perfect, the granaries bursting with grain and the treasury full to overflowing.

Such was the state of things when, in the third year, the news came to the capital that a host of *Mans* had invaded the south and were laying waste the country, and that the Prefect of Chienning, a man of an honourable and even noble family, had joined them. Already two districts had yielded to the invaders, but a third was staunchly holding out. The three rebels, who had joined the invaders, were now acting as guides and assisting in the attack on Jungch'ang, which had remained faithful. Wang K'ang, the Prefect of Jungch'ang, ably seconded by Lü K'ai, one of his subordinates, was making a desperate effort to defend the city with only its ordinary inhabitants as fighting men. The position was very desperate.

When this news came, K'ung-ming went into the palace and thus memorialised to his lord, "The contumacy of the *Mans* is a real danger to our state. I feel it incumbent upon me to lead an expedition to reduce the barbarians to obedience."

But the king was afraid, and said, "There are enemies on two sides; if you abandon me and either of them comes, what shall I do?"

"Your Majesty need have no fear. We have just concluded a league of peace with Wu, and I think they will be true to their pledge. Li Yen is quite a match for Lu Hsün. Ts'ao P'ei's recent defeat has taken the keenness out of his men, so that he will not feel inclined to make any expeditions further. Ma Ch'ao is in command at the Pass between Wei and Hanchung. I shall also leave Kuan and Chang with forces to reinforce any point where danger may appear. I can assure

Your Majesty that no untoward event will happen. I am going to sweep clean the *Man* country, so that we may have a free hand to attack Wei when the day comes. Thus I shall be enabled to requite the honour paid me by your father the First Ruler, who came thrice to seek me and who doubled my obligation when he confided to me the care of his son."

"Indeed I am young and ignorant," replied the king, "and can only exist with you to decide for me."

At that moment an officer, Wang Lien by name, a man of Nanyang, stepped forward, crying, "No, no, Sir; you may not go. The south is a desert country reeking with malaria. It is wrong that an officer of state in such an exalted and responsible position should go away on a distant expedition. These rebels and barbarians are but an irritation, not a disease, and an ordinary leader would be enough to send against them. He would not fail."

K'ung-ming replied, "This country of the *Mans* is distant and mostly uncivilised. To reduce them to reasonableness will be difficult, and I feel I ought to go. When to be harsh and when to show leniency are matters to be decided on at the moment, and instructions cannot be easily given to another."

K'ung-ming steadily opposed all Wang's efforts to bring about a change of intention, and he soon took leave of his master and made ready to start.

Chiang Yüan was Councillor of the expedition. Fei Wei was Recorder; Tung Chüeh and Fan Chien were Historians; Chao Yün and Wei Yen were Generals; Wang P'ing and Chang I were Deputy Generals and leaders of the fighting men. Beside these were officers originally belonging to Shu, and the whole force was fifty legions.

Soon after the force marched south, the third son of Kuan the Noble appeared and wished to see K'ung-ming. After the fall of Chiangchou this youth had fled to Paochia, where he had fallen ill. His illness had been long and severe, and he had only just recovered. He was then travelling toward Ch'êngtu. He knew that vengeance had been taken on the murderers of his father. And he asked to take part in this expedition.

K'ung-ming was greatly surprised to see him. However, he sent news of the young man's arrival to the court and gave Kuan So a military appointment.

The army, foot and horse, marched in the best of order, eating when hungry, drinking when thirsty, camping at night and moving by day. No plundering was permitted, and the people suffered not at all.

When Yung K'ai and his fellow rebels heard that the Prime Minister of Shu was marching against them, they called their men together and formed three divisions, Kao Ting in the centre, Yung and Chu on the wings. They mustered about five legions in all, and they went to oppose the march of the Shu army. Kao Ting sent O Huan to lead the van.

This O Huan was tall of stature, but ugly and evil of countenance. His weapon was a sort of halberd. He was very valiant, and no one could face him. He led his own cohort out in advance of the main body and fell in with the leading bodies of the Shu army immediately after they had got into Ichou. The two sides drew up for battle, and, the arrays being complete, Wei Yen rode out and vilified the rebels, calling upon them to surrender. Instead, O Huan galloped out and fought with Wei. After a few bouts Wei seemed to be bested and fled. But this was only a ruse. However, O Huan followed, fell into the ambush as had been arranged, and was captured.

He was taken to the tent of K'ung-ming, who bade his attendants loose his bonds, gave him wine and comforted him. Then he asked who he was.

O Huan replied, "I am one of the captains under Kao Ting."

"I know Kao Ting as a loyal and good sort, but he has been led away by this Yung K'ai. Now I shall release you, but you are to bring Kao to his senses and see to it that he comes to surrender. It will be best for him."

O Huan thanked him and withdrew. He went to his own side and soon saw Kao Ting. He told him what K'ung-ming had said, and K'ung-ming's kindly feeling deeply affected Kao.

Soon after, Yung K'ai came over to Kao Ting's camp to visit him. After the exchange of salutations, Yung asked how it came about that O Huan had been released.

"Chuko Liang released him out of pure kindness," replied Kao Ting.

"This is a ruse of his to separate you from me: he wishes to make us enemies."

Kao Ting almost believed this too, and he was much perplexed.

Just then the watchers reported that the leaders of Shu had come up and were offering battle. So Yung K'ai led out three legions to take up the challenge. But after the third encounter he fled. Wei Yen pursued him and smote for a distance of two score *li*.

Next day Yung K'ai challenged, but the men of Shu refused to fight, and remained within their lines for three days. On the fourth day Yung and Kao divided their men into two parts and came to attack the camp. Now K'ung-ming had told Wei Yen to wait for this double attack, and so when it came to pass both divisions fell into an ambush and suffered great loss, many being killed and more captured.

The prisoners were taken to the camp, and the men belonging to the two divisions were confined separately. Then K'ung-ming told the soldiers to let it be known that only those belonging to Kao Ting would be spared, the others would be put to death. When time had been given for this story to spread among the prisoners, Yung's men were brought up to the commander's tent.

"Whose men were you?" asked he.

"Kao Ting's" cried they all, falsely.

Then they were all pardoned, and, after being given wine and food, they were taken to the frontier and set free.

Next the real Kao Ting's men were brought forward, and the same question was put to them.

"We all really belong to Kao Ting's command," said they.

In like manner they were pardoned and refreshed with wine and food. Then K'ung-ming addressed them, saying, "Yung K'ai has just sent a messenger to ask that he may surrender, and he offers to bring with him the heads of your commander and of Chu Pao as a proof of merit. But I will not receive him, and you, since you are Kao Ting's men, shall be released and allowed to return to him. But let there be no ingratitude and fighting again, for if there is, I certainly will not pardon you next time."

So they thanked their liberator and went away. As soon as they reached their own camp they told the whole story. Then Kao Ting sent a spy to the camp of his colleague to find out what was doing. There he met the men who had been released, and they were all talking about K'ung-ming's kindness, and many of them were inclined to desert their own camp for the other. Although this seemed very satisfactory, yet Kao Ting did not feel convinced, and he sent another man to K'ung-ming's camp to try to verify what had happened. But this man was captured and taken before the Commander-in-chief, who pretended that he thought the spy belonged to Yung K'ai, and said to him, "Why has your leader failed to send me the heads of Kao and Chu as he promised? You lot are not very clever, and what are you come to spy out?"

The soldier muttered and mumbled in confusion. But K'ung-ming gave the man wine and food, and then wrote a letter which he handed to the spy, saying, "You give this letter to your commander, Yung K'ai, and tell him to get the job done quickly."

The spy took the letter and got away. As soon as he reached camp he gave the letter to Kao Ting and also the message.

Kao Ting read the missive and became very angry.

"I have ever been true to him, and yet he wants to kill me. It is hard to be either friendly or reasonable."

Then he decided to take O Huan into his confidence, and called him. O Huan was much prejudiced in favour of K'ung-ming, and said, "K'ung-ming is a most benevolent man, and it would be ill to turn our backs upon him. It is Yung K'ai's fault that we are now rebels, and our best course would be to slay him and betake ourselves to K'ung-ming."

"How could it be done?" asked Kao Ting.

"Invite him to a banquet. If he refuse, it means he is a traitor, and then you can attack him in front while I will lie in wait behind his camp to capture him as he runs away."

They agreed to try this plan; the banquet was prepared and Yung invited. But as his mind was full of suspicion from what his returned men had said, he would not come. That night, as soon as darkness fell, Kao Ting attacked his camp.

Now the men who had been released were imbued with the goodness of Kao Ting and quite ready to help him fight. On the other hand, Yung K'ai's men mutinied against him, and so Yung K'ai mounted his steed and fled. Before he had gone far he found his road blocked by the cohort under O Huan, who galloped out with his halberd and confronted the fugitive. Yung could not defend himself, and was struck down. O Huan decapitated him. As soon as they knew he was dead, his men joined themselves to Kao Ting, who then went and surrendered to K'ung-ming.

K'ung-ming received him sitting in state in his tent, but at once ordered the lictors to decapitate him.

But Kao Ting said, "Influenced by your kindness, Sir, I have brought the head of my colleague as a proof of the sincerity of my surrender: why should I die?"

"You come with false intent; do you think you can hoodwink me?" said K'ung-ming, laughing.

"What proof have you that I am false?"

K'ung-ming drew a letter from his box, and said, "Chu Pao sent this secretly to say he wished to surrender, and he said you and Yung K'ai were sworn friends to death. How could you suddenly change your feelings and slay him? That is how I know your treachery."

"Chu Pao only tried to make trouble," cried Kao, kneeling.

K'ung-ming still refused to believe him, and said, "I cannot believe you without more solid proof. If you would slay Chu I could take that as proving you were sincere in your surrender."

"Do not doubt me. What if I go and capture this man?"

"If you did that my doubts would be set at rest."

Thereupon Kao Ting and his subordinate, O Huan, led away their men to the camp of Chu Pao. When they were about ten *li* from his camp Chu Pao appeared with a cohort. As soon as they recognised each other, Chu Pao hastily came forward to parley. But Kao Ting cried out to him, "Why did you write a letter to the Prime Minister and so intrigue with him to get me killed?"

Chu Pao stared open mouthed and could not reply. Then O Huan rode out from behind his chief and struck Chu with his halberd so that he fell to the ground. Thereupon Kao Ting shouted to the men that they should either yield or be slain, and they yielded in a body.

Kao Ting then went back to K'ung-ming and offered the head of the man just slain. K'ung-ming laughed again.

"I have made you kill both these as a proof of loyalty."

Then he created Kao Prefect of Ichou and chief of three districts, while O Huan was given a junior rank. Thus the three divisions were disposed of and troubled the peace no more.

The Prefect of Jungch'ang then came out of the city and welcomed K'ung-ming, and, when he had made his entry into that city, he called Wang K'ang and asked who had aided him in the defence.

The Prefect said, "The safety of this city is due entirely to Lü K'ai."

So Lü was called. He came and bowed.

K'ung-ming said, "Long since I heard of you as a remarkable man of this district. We are greatly indebted to you for its safety. Now we wish to conquer the *Mans;* have you any advice to offer?"

Lü K'ai then produced a map of the country and presented it, saying, "From the time of my appointment I have felt certain that the southern men would rise against you, and so I sent secret agents to map out the country and find the strategical points. From that information I prepared this map, which I call 'An Easy Scheme to Conquer the *Mans.*' I beg you, Sir, to accept it, as it may be of use."

Then K'ung-ming took Lü K'ai into his service as adviser and guide. With his help he advanced and penetrated deeply into the country.

While the army was advancing, there came a messenger from the Court. When he appeared, K'ung-ming saw it was Ma Su, and he was clothed in white. He was in mourning for his brother, Ma Liang, who had just died. He had come by special command of the Emperor with gifts of wine and silk.

When the ceremonies proper on receipt of a mandate from the Emperor had been performed, and the gifts distributed as instructed, Ma Su was asked to remain to talk over matters.

K'ung-ming said, "I have His Majesty's command to conquer these *Mans.* I hear you have some advice to offer, and I should be pleased if you would instruct me."

"Yes; I have one thing to say that may be worth thinking over. These people refuse to recognise our supremacy because they think their country is distant and difficult. If you should overcome them to-day, to-morrow they would revolt. Wherever your army marches they are overcome and submit, but the day you withdraw the army and attack Ts'ao P'ei they will renew their attack. In arms even it is best to attack hearts rather than cities; to fight with sentiment is better than to fight with weapons. It will be well if you can win them over."

"You read inmost thoughts," said K'ung-ming.

Then Ma Su was retained with the army as adviser, and the army marched on.

When the King of the *Mans*, Mênghuo by name, heard how cleverly K'ung-ming had got rid of Yung K'ai, he called together the leaders of the "Three Ravines" to discuss matters.

The chief of the first Ravine was Chinhuansanchieh, of the second Tung-T'una and of the third Ahuinan. These having come to the king's place, he said to them, "Our country has been invaded, and we must exert our united strength to drive out the invaders. You three must lead your forces, and whoever conquers the enemy shall be chief of chiefs."

It was arranged that Chinhuansanchieh should march in the centre division, with the others on his flanks. Each division was five legions.

When the scouts made out that the *Man* armies were coming, they at once told K'ung-ming, who called Chao Yün and Wei Yen to his side, but gave them no orders. Next he sent for Wang P'ing and Ma Chung, and said to them, "I cannot send Chao Yün and Wei Yen against the *Mans* because they do not know the country. You two are to go, one against each wing, and the two veteran warriors shall support you. Get your men ready and start to-morrow at dawn."

Then the two Changs were sent against the centre army; they were to act with Wang and Ma. And once more K'ung-ming seemed to taunt the two veterans with ignorance.

The two heroes now began to feel hurt. Noticing this, K'ung-ming said, "I have no wish to pass you over, you two, but I fear that if you get too deeply into the country and should fall victims to the *Mans* that it will have an ill effect on the others."

"But what if we did know the geography of the country?" said Chao Yün.

"All I say to you is to be careful how you do anything," replied K'ung-ming.

The two old soldiers left and went together to the camp of Chao Yün.

Chao Yün said, "We are greatly ashamed at being put in the background because we do not know the country. We cannot bear this."

"Then let us ride out and survey," said his colleague. "Let us capture a few natives and make them show us the road, and let us defeat these savages."

They rode off. Before they had gone far they saw a cloud of dust in the distance. Climbing a hill to get a better view, they saw a small party of mounted *Mans* coming toward them. The two waited till they were near and then suddenly burst out. The *Mans*, taken entirely by surprise, ran away all but a few, who yielded themselves prisoners. The two warriors returned to camp.

The prisoners were given wine and food, and when they had satisfied their hunger they were questioned.

Said they, "The camp of the Chief Chinhuansanchieh is just in front, just by the entrance to the mountains. Near the camp, running east and west, is the Ravine of the Five Streams. The camps of the other two chiefs are behind."

The two leaders got together five companies, took the captured men as guides and marched out about the second watch. It was a clear night, and the moon gave light to march by.

The first camp was reached about the fourth watch. The *Man* soldiers were already awake and preparing their morning meal, as they intended to attack at daylight. The vigorous and unexpected attack of the two captains threw the camp into confusion; the chief was slain and his head cut off.

Then Wei Yen took half the force and went west to the second camp. By the time he reached it day had dawned. They also had news of his coming, and drew up the camp to oppose. But when they had got clear, there was a great uproar behind them at the stockade gates, and confusion followed. The reason was the arrival of Wang P'ing. Between the two bodies the *Mans* were beaten. Their chief, Tungt'una, got away. Wei Yen's men followed, but they could not catch him.

When Chao Yün led his men to attack the third camp in the rear, Ma Chung made an attack on the front. They scored a success, but the chief, Ahuinan, escaped.

They returned to headquarters, and K'ung-ming said, "The three parties of *Mans* have fled; where is the head of the first of the three chiefs?"

Chao Yün produced it. At the same time he reported that the other two chiefs had escaped by abandoning their horses and going over the hill. They could not be followed.

"They are already prisoners," said K'ung-ming with a laugh.

The fighting men could not credit it. But soon after the two chiefs were brought in. When some expressed surprise and admiration, K'ung-ming said, "I had studied the map and knew the positions of the camps. I taunted Chao Yün and Wei Yen into making a supreme effort at the same time that I sent other forces, because I knew the first two were the only men for the task. I felt certain the two chiefs would run away along those small roads, and I set men on those roads to wait for them. They also were supported."

They all bowed, saying, "The Prime Minister's calculations are divine and incomprehensible."

The two captive chiefs were then called. As soon as they appeared, K'ung-ming loosed their bonds, gave them refreshments and released them, bidding them offend no more. They thanked him for their liberty, and disappeared along a by-road.

Then K'ung-ming said to his captains, "To-morrow Mênghuo will come in person to make an attack. We shall probably capture him again."

Then he summoned Chao Yün and Wei Yen and gave them orders. They left, each with a half legion. Next he sent Wang P'ing. And then he sat in his tent to wait for the result.

The King of the *Mans* was sitting in his tent when the scouts told him that his three chiefs had been captured and their armies scattered. It made him very angry, and he quickly got his army ready to march. Soon he met Wang P'ing, and, when the armies were arrayed, Wang P'ing rode out to the front. The flaunting banners of his foes then opened out, and he saw their ranks. Many captains were on horseback. In the middle was the king, who advanced to the front. He wore a golden, inlaid head-dress; his belt bore a lion's face as clasp; his boots had pointed toes and were green; he rode a frizzy-haired horse the colour of a hare; he carried at his waist a pair of swords chased with the pine-tree device.

He looked haughtily at his foes, and then, turning to his captains, said, "It has always been said that Chuko Liang is a wonderful soldier, but I see that is false. Look at this array with its banners all in confusion and the ranks in disorder. There is not a weapon among all the swords and spears better than ours. If I had only realised this before I would have fought them long ago. Who dares go out and capture a Shu captain to show them what sort of warriors we are?"

At once a captain rode toward the leader, Wang P'ing. His name was Huanmangyachang; his weapon was a huge headsman's sword, and he rode a dun pony. Riding up to Wang P'ing, the two engaged.

Wang P'ing only fought a short time, and then fled. The king at once ordered his men on in quick pursuit, and the men of Shu retreated a score or so of *li* before the *Mans* were near enough to fight. Just as the *Mans* thought their enemies were in their power, a great shouting arose and two cohorts appeared, one on either flank, and attacked. The *Mans* could not retreat, and as another force under Kuan So also turned upon them, the *Mans* were surrounded and lost the day. Mênghuo and some of his captains fought their way out and made for the Chintai Mountains. The men of Shu followed and forced them forward, and presently there appeared, in front, Chao Yün.

The king hastily changed his route to go deeper into the mountains, but Chao Yün's men spread around, and the *Mans* could not make a stand. Here some were captured. Mênghuo and a few horsemen got away into a valley, which however, soon became too narrow for the horses to advance. The king then left his horse and crawled up the mountains, but very soon he fell upon Wei Yen, who had been sent to lie in wait in that very valley. So he was again prisoner.

The king and his followers were taken to the main camp, where K'ung-ming was waiting with wine and meat ready for the captives. But his tent was now guarded by a seven-deep force of men all well armed with glittering weapons, beside the lictors bearing the golden axes, a present from the Emperor, and other insignia of rank. The feather-hatted drummers and clarion players were in front and behind, and the Imperial Guards were extended on both sides. The whole was very imposing and awe-inspiring.

K'ung-ming was seated at the top of it all and watched the captives as they came forward in crowds. When they were all assembled, he ordered their bonds to be loosed, and then he addressed them.

"You are all simple and well-disposed people who have been led into trouble by Mênghuo. I know your fathers and mothers, your brothers and wives; and your children are anxiously watching from the doorways for your return, and they are cut to the quick now that the news of defeat and capture has reached their ears. They are weeping bitter tears for you. And so I will set you all free to go home and comfort them."

After they had been given food and wine and a present of grain, he sent them all away. They went off grateful for the kindness shown them, but they wept as they thanked K'ung-ming.

Then the guards were told to bring the King before the tent. He came, bound, being hustled forward. He knelt in front of the great leader, who said, "Why did you rebel after the generous treatment you have received from our Emperor?"

"The two Ch'uan belonged to others, and your lord took it from them by force, and gave himself the title of 'Emperor.' My people have lived here for ages, and you and yours invaded my country without the least excuse. How can you talk of rebellion to me?"

"You are my prisoner; will you submit or are you still contumacious?"

"Why should I submit? You happened to find me in a narrow place; that is all."

"If I release you, what then?"

"If you release me I shall return, and when I have set my army in order I shall come to fight you again. However, if you catch me once more I will submit."

286

The king's bonds were loosed; he was clothed and refreshed, given a horse and caparisons and sent with a guide to his own camp.

Once more the captured chieftain is let go,
To yield barbarians are ever slow.

Further results of this war will be related in the next chapter.

CHAPTER LXXXVIII.

CROSSING THE RIVER LU; BINDING OF THE BARBARIAN KING;
RECOGNISING A PRETENDED SURRENDER; CAPTURE OF MENGHUO.

The officers did not approve of the release of the King of the *Mans*, and they came to the tent of K'ung-ming and said, "Mênghuo is the most important personage of all the *Mans*, and his capture is the key to restoring order in the south. Why then, O Minister, did you release him?"

"I can capture him just as easily as I can get something out of my pocket. What I want to do is to overcome and win his heart, so that peace may follow of itself."

They listened, but they had no great confidence in the success of the policy of conciliation.

In the meantime Mênghuo had reached the Lu River, and there he fell in with some of his defeated men, who were trying to get news of their king's fate. They were surprised, but glad, to see him, and asked how he had been able to get back.

The king lied, saying, "They confined me in a tent, and I broke out in the night. I slew a half score of my guards and ran. And then I met one of their spies, killed him, and that is how I got this horse."

They never doubted his word, and very joyfully they hurried him over the river to a camping place. Then all the notables assembled from the various ravines, and the soldiers that had escaped death were mustered and got into shape as a fighting force.

The two leaders in the late campaign, Tungt'una and Ahuinan, were in one of the ravines, and the king sent to ask them to come. They were afraid, but they could not disobey, and they came with an escort. When all had assembled, the king proclaimed as follows:—"I know Chuko Liang is too full of ruses for us to conquer him in a fight; we should only fall victims to other base devices. However, we must remember that his men have marched far and the weather is sultry, which are factors in our favour. Beside, the Lu River is our rampart. We will have boats and rafts on the south side, and we will build a mud wall. With such good defences we can afford to wait and see what the enemy intends."

His speech met with approval, and his plan was carried out. The wall was supported by the hills and strengthened by fighting turrets, upon which were placed large bows and crossbows and balistae. The defences looked as if they were permanent. Moreover, each ravine sent supplies in plenty. And having made these preparations, Mênghuo felt comfortable and safe.

K'ung-ming had advanced, and his leading division was now close to the river. However, no boats or rafts could be found to cross, and the current was too strong to think of fording. Beside, they could see the formidable defences on the farther bank, the mud wall and the turrets all fully manned. The weather was burning hot, for it was the fifth mouth, and the soldiers could not tolerate their armour nor even their clothing.

When K'ung-ming had inspected the river, he returned to his tent and assembled his officers, to whom he read this order: "The enemy is securely established on the south bank ready to repel our attack. Yet, having come so far, we cannot return empty. For the present you will all seek what shelter you can find in the forests, and rest and refresh your men."

Then he sent Lu K'ai to a distance to select a cool spot, and there he made two stockades. Within the stockades he built huts for the men and sheds for the horses, so that they were sheltered from the intense heat.

However, a junior captain, Chiang Wan, was ready to carp at these shelters, and went to K'ung-ming, saying, "These shelters of Lu K'ai's are very unsuitable. He has made the same mistake as that which led to the defeat of our former king at the hands of Wu. He has not taken into account the surroundings of the stockades, and if the *Mans* should come over and start a fire, there could be no rescue."

"Do not anticipate trouble," said the Commander-in-chief, smiling. "I have provided against all such dangers."

The fault-finder did not know what the chief meant to do, but he said no more. Then Ma Tai arrived from Ch'êngtu, and he brought summer medicines and further supplies of grain. He saw K'ung-ming, and then proceeded to distribute the supplies he had brought according to orders.

Then K'ung-ming said, "What force have you brought?"

"Three companies," was the reply.

"My men are weary and worn out; I want to use yours. You have no objections?"

"Of course not; they are equally government troops. They are ready even to die for you if you wish."

"This Mênghuo is established on the river, and we have no means of crossing. But I am anxious to intercept his supplies, so that his men may mutiny."

"How can you do it?"

"Some distance lower down there is a place called Shak'ou, where the current is slow; you could cross there on rafts. I wish you and your men to cross and cut the road of supplies.

After that you are to arrange with the two leaders whose lives I spared to be your allies on the inside, and we shall succeed."

Ma Tai went off gladly enough, and marched his men to Sha'kou, where they set about the crossing at once. And as the water was shallow they did not trouble to make rafts, but just tucked up their clothes and waded in. But half-way across, the men began to fall over; and when they had been rescued and taken to the bank many of them began to bleed from the nose and mouth and died. In great alarm, Ma Tai sent hasty messages to K'ung-ming, who called in the guides and asked what this meant. They told him that it happened so every year. In the hot season, poisonous miasma collected over the waters of the Lu River, especially during the heat of the day. Anyone who drank the water would surely die. Travellers who wished to cross had to wait till night, because the cooler waters did not breathe out the poisonous vapours. Further, the natives said the crossing should be attempted on a full stomach.

K'ung-ming bade the local guides point out the best crossing place. He sent some well-seasoned soldiers to Ma Tai to lash together poles into rafts at Shak'ou, and in the night the crossing was safely accomplished. Further, the guides then led the men of Shu over to where the grain road of the *Mans* led through a narrow valley, called Chiashan Gorge, where, for part of the way, only single file was possible as the road was only wide enough for a man and a horse.

Ma Tai at once occupied this valley and stationed a force there. And a stockade was put up with tents inside. Presently a convoy of grain came along, and it was captured. The men ran off to the king's great camp and told him.

Mênghuo, thinking all was safe during the hot season, was enjoying himself; wine and music were the order of the day, and military matters were far from his thoughts. In his cups he admitted K'ung-ming was ruseful, but said his army had nothing to fear.

"If I attempt to oppose Chuko Liang I shall certainly fall a victim to some wile of his. However, my waiting policy is a safe one. With our defences, and the river to back them, we can wait for the heat to overcome these men of Shu, who cannot stand the hot season. They will have to retreat, and then we can harass them. And we will capture this Chuko."

He lay back and laughed at the thought. However, one chief, more prudent than the others, stood forth and said, "Remember the shallows at Shak'ou; it would be very serious if the men of Shu got across there secretly. It ought to be guarded."

"You belong to these parts. Do you not know that I want the enemy to try to get across there? Why, they will all perish in the water."

"But what if the natives tell them to cross only in the night?"

"Do not be so anxious," said Mênghuo. "Our own people will not help the enemy that far."

It was just then that intelligence came that the men of Shu had crossed the river and, moreover, had seized the Chiashan Gorge. The flags showed that the commander was Ma Tai.

Mênghuo affected indifference. "This sort of fellow is not worth talking about," said he.

He sent a junior officer named Mangyachang with three companies to recapture the gorge and reopen the grain road.

When Ma Tai saw the *Man* soldiers approaching, he placed two companies in front of the hills and drew up the others in formal array. Then Mangyachang rode out to give battle. This was but a small engagement, as the barbarian fell at the first stroke of Ma Tai's sword. The *Mans* ran away at once.

They returned to the king's camp and told him what had happened. Whereupon he called up all his captains and asked for another to go up against Ma Tai.

"I will go," cried Tungt'una.

The king gave him three companies. After he had gone, Mênghuo thought it would be wise to keep others from crossing the river. So he sent a force to guard Shak'ou.

Tungt'una duly arrived at the gorge and made a camp. Ma Tai came out to meet him. Among the men in his cohort were some who recognised the leader of the *Mans* and told Ma Tai certain things about how he had been captured and liberated. So Ma Tai galloped toward him, shouting out reproaches of ingratitude and so on. Tungt'una was very greatly ashamed and turned red in the face, and went away without striking a blow. Ma Tai followed and fell on, slaying many of the *Mans*. Tungt'una went back and told the king that Ma Tai was too strong for him.

But the king was angry, and cried, "You are a traitor! I know Chuko Liang was good to you, and that is why you would not fight."

He ordered Tungt'una out to execution. However, the notables and chiefs interceded, and the death penalty was remitted, but the unhappy leader was severely beaten, one hundred strokes with the heavy staff.

The chiefs were mostly on the side of the beaten captain and against the king's policy.

They said, "Tnough we live in the *Man* country we have never had any thoughts of rebellion against the Central Government, nor has China ever encroached upon our land. We must own that Mênghuo's superior power forced us into this rising, and we could not help ourselves. K'ung-ming is too clever for us, and no one can guess what he may do. Even Ts'ao Ts'ao and Sun Ch'üan fear him; how much more must we? Moreover, we have received kindness at his hands and owe him our lives. We ought to show our gratitude. Now let us at all risks slay this Mênghuo and submit to K'ung-ming so that our people may not suffer."

Tungt'una said, "I do not know your inner sentiments."

At this, all those who had been prisoners and released cried with one voice, "We desire to go to him."

Thereupon Tungt'una took in his hand a sharp sword, placed himself at the head of the malcontents and rushed into the great camp. At that moment Mênghuo was, as usual, intoxicated and lay in his tent. The mutineers rushed in. They found two captains on guard.

"You also received kindness from K'ung-ming and ought to repay it," cried Tungt'una.

They replied, "You may not slay him; let us carry him a prisoner to K'ung-ming."

So they bound the king securely, took him down to the river and crossed in a boat to the northern bank. There they halted while they sent a messenger to K'ung-ming.

Now K'ung-ming knew what had been happening, and he had issued orders for every camp to prepare their weapons. All being ready, he told the chiefs to bring up their prisoner, and bade the others return to their camps. Tungt'una went first and told the matter to K'ung-ming, who praised his zeal and gave him presents. Then he retired to summon the chiefs. When they had arrived, the executioners brought in Mênghuo.

"You said once before that if you were captured again you would give in," said K'ung-ming, smiling. "Now will you yield?"

"This capture is not your work," replied the king. "It is the work of these minions of mine who want to hurt me. I will not yield on this."

"If I free you again, what then?"

"I am only a *Man,* I know, but I am not wholly ignorant of war. If you, O Minister, let me return to my ravines I will muster another army and fight a decisive battle with you. If you capture me again then I will incline my heart and own myself beaten and yield. I will not go back on my promise again."

"If you refuse to yield next time you are captured, I shall hardly pardon you."

At K'ung-ming's orders the cords were loosed and refreshments were brought for the prisoner.

"Remember," said K'ung-ming, "I have never failed yet. I have never failed to win a battle or to take a city I have assaulted. Why do you *Mans* not yield?"

Mênghuo only nodded his head; he said nothing. After the wine, K'ung-ming and Mênghuo rode round the camps together, and the king saw all the arrangements and the piles of stores and heaps of weapons, and after the inspection he said, "You are silly not to yield to me. You see my veteran soldiers, my able captains, my stores of all kinds and war gear; how can you hope to prevail against me? If you will yield I will inform His Majesty, and you shall retain your kingship and your sons and grandsons shall succeed as perpetual guardians of the *Man* country. Do you not think it would be well?"

The king replied, "If I did yield, the men of my valleys would not be content. If you release me once more I will see to it that my own men keep the peace and bring them round to unanimity of feeling, and then they will not oppose any more."

But Mênghuo's first act on his return to his own camp was to assassinate the two leaders Tungt'una and Ahuinan. Their corpses were thrown into a gully. Then he sent his friends to guard the most important strategical points, while he marched to fight a battle with Ma Tai. But when he got near the valley he saw no signs of the enemy, and, on questioning an inhabitant, he heard that the Shu army, with all their stores, had recrossed the river and joined the main body.

Mênghuo then returned to his own ravine and discussed matters with his brother, Mêngyu, and told him that he knew all the details of the enemy's force from what he had seen in their camp, and he gave his brother certain instructions, which he at once began to carry out. He loaded a hundred men with gold and jewels and pearls and ivory and rhinoceros horn, crossed the Lu River and was on his way to the main camp, when he was stopped by a cohort under Ma Tai himself. He did not expect to meet an enemy, and was surprised. But Ma Tai only asked what he had come for. And when he had heard, Mêngyu was detained while a message was sent to K'ung-ming.

The messenger arrived while a council was in progress, the matter under discussion being how to reduce the *Mans*. When the messenger had announced that Mêngyu had come bearing gifts of gold and pearls and such things, K'ung-ming turned to Ma Su, who was there, saying, "Know you why this man has come?"

"I dare not say plainly; but let me write it," said Ma Su.

"Write it, then."

So Ma Su wrote and handed the paper to his chief, who had no sooner read it than he clapped his hands with joy, crying, "What you say is exactly what I think. But you may know I have already made arrangements for the capture of Mênghuo."

Then Chao Yün was called, and some orders were whispered into his ear. Next Wei Yen came, and he also went off with secret orders. Wang P'ing, Ma Chung and Kuan So also came, and left with particular instructions.

All these things done, the bearer of gifts was called. He came and bowed low at the door of the tent, saying, "The brother of my house, Menghuo, having received great kindness at your hands in sparing his life, feels bound to offer a paltry gift. He has presumed to collect a few pearls and some gold and other trifling jewels by way of something to give your soldiers. And hereafter he will send tribute to your Emperor."

"Where is your brother at this moment?" asked K'ung-ming.

"Having been the recipient of your great bounty, he has gone to the Silver Pit Hills (*Yink'êng Shan*) to collect some treasures. He will soon return."

"How many men have you brought?"

"Only about a hundred; I should not dare to bring any large number. They are just porters."

They were brought in for K'ung-ming's inspection. They had blue eyes and swarthy faces, auburn hair and brown beards. They wore earrings. Their hair was fuzzy, and they went barefoot. They were tall and powerful.

K'ung-ming made them sit down, and bade his captains press them to drink and treat them well and compliment them.

The King Mênghuo was anxious about the reception that would be given to his brother and the treatment of his gifts, so he sat in his tent expecting the messenger at any moment. Then two men came, and he questioned them eagerly. They said the presents had been accepted, and even the porters had been invited to drink in the tent and had been regaled with beef and flesh in plenty.

"O King, your brother sent us with the news, and we were to tell you secretly that all would be ready at the second watch."

This was pleasing news, and he prepared his three legions ready to march out to the camp. They were divided into three divisions.

The king called up his chieftains and notables, and said, "Let each army carry the means of making fire, and as soon as they arrive let a light be shown as a signal. I am coming to try to capture Chuko Liang."

With these orders they marched, and they crossed the Lu River in the dusk. The king, with a hundred captains as escort, pressed on at once toward the main camp of Shu. They met with no opposition. They even found the main gate open, and Mênghuo and his party rode straight in. But the camp was a desert; not a man was visible.

Mênghuo rode right up to the large tent and pushed open the flap. It was brilliantly lighted with lamps, and lying about under their light were his brother and all his men, dead drunk. The wine they had been pressed to drink while the plays were going on had been heavily drugged, and the men had fallen down almost as soon as they had swallowed it One or two who had recovered a little could not speak: they only pointed to their mouths.

Mênghuo then saw that he had been the simple victim of another ruse. However, he picked up his brother and the others and started off to return to his main army.

But as he turned, torches began to flash out and drums to beat. The *Mans* were frightened and took to their heels. But they were pursued, and the pursuing cohort was led by Wang P'ing. The king bore away to the left to escape, but again a cohort appeared in front of him; Wei Yen was there. He tried the other side; and was stopped by Chao Yün. He was in a trap; and attacked on three sides and no fourth to escape by, what could he do? He abandoned everything, making one wild rush for the Lu River.

As he reached the river bank he saw a bark on the river with *Man* soldiers on board. Here was safety. He hailed the boat and jumped on board as soon as it touched the bank. No sooner had he embarked than suddenly he was seized and bound. The boat, which Ma Tai had provided and prepared, was part of the general plan, and the *Man* soldiers therein were his men disguised.

Many of Mênghuo's men accepted the chance of surrender held out by K'ung-ming, who soothed them and treated them well and did not injure one of them.

The remains of the conflagration were stamped out, and in a short time Ma Tai brought along his prisoner. At the same time Chao Yün led in his brother, Mêngyu. Each of the other captains had some prisoners too, chiefs or notables.

K'ung-ming looked at the king and laughed. "That was but a shallow ruse of yours to send your brother with presents to pretend to submit to me; did you really think I should not see through it? But here you are once more in my power; now do you yield?"

"I am a prisoner owing to the gluttony of my brother and the power of your poisonous drugs. If I had only played his part myself and left him to support me with soldiers, I should have succeeded. I am the victim of fate and not of my own incapacity. No; I will not yield."

"Remember this is the third time; why not?" said K'ung-ming.

Mênghuo dropped his head and made no answer.

"Ah well; I will let you go once more," said K'ung-ming.

"O Minister, if you will let me and my brother go we will get together our family and clients and fight you once more. If I am caught that time then I will confess myself beaten to the ground, and that shall be the end."

"Certainly I shall scarcely pardon you next time," said K'ung-ming. "You had better be careful. Diligently tackle your Book of Strategy: look over your list of confidants. If you can apply a good plan at the proper moment you will not have any need for late regrets."

The king and his brother and all the chiefs were released from their bonds. They thanked K'ung-ming for his clemency and went away.

By the time the released prisoners had got back to the river the army of Shu had crossed to the farther side and were all in order with their flags fluttering in the breeze. As Mênghuo passed the camp, he saw Ma Tai sitting in state. Ma Tai pointed his sword at the king as he passed, and said, "Next time you are caught you will not escape."

When Mênghuo came to his own camp he found Chao Yün in possession and all in order. Chao Yün was seated beneath the large banner, with his sword drawn, and as the king passed, he also said, "Do not presume on the kindness of the Prime Minister because you have been generously treated."

Mênghuo grunted and passed on. Just as he was going over the frontier hills he saw Wei Yen and a company drawn up on the slopes. Wei Yen shouted, "See to it; we have got into the inmost recesses of your country and have taken all your defensive positions. Yet you are fool enough to hold out. Next time you are caught you will be quite destroyed. There will be no more pardons."

Mênghuo and his companies ran away with their arms over their heads. Each one returned to his own ravine.

In the fifth moon, when the sun is fierce,
Marched the army into the desert land,
Marched to the Lu River, bright and clear,
But deadly with miasma.
K'ung-ming the leader cared not,
Pledged was he to subdue the south
Thereby to repay deference with service.
Wherefore he attacked the *Mans*.
Yet seven times he freed their captured king.

After the crossing of the river the soldiers were feasted. Then he addressed his officers.

"I let Mênghuo see our camp the second time he was our prisoner because I wanted to tempt him into raiding it. He is something of a soldier, and I dangled our supplies and resources before his eyes, knowing he would try to burn them and that he would send his brother to pretend to submit that thereby he could get into our camp and have a chance to betray us. I have captured and released him three times, trying to win him over. I do not wish to do him any harm. I now explain my policy that you may understand I am not wasting your efforts and you are not still to work your best for the government."

They all bowed, and one said, "O Minister, you are indeed perfect in every one of the three gifts: wisdom, benevolence and valor. Not even Chiang Tzŭ-ya or Chang Liang can equal you!"

Said K'ung-ming, "How can I expect to equal our men of old? But my trust is in your strength, and together we shall succeed."

This speech of their leader's pleased them all mightily.

In the meantime Mênghuo, puffed up with pride at getting off three times, hastened home to his own ravine, whence he sent trusted friends with gifts to the Eight Hordes of Barbarians and the Ninety-three Tribes and all the *Man* quarters and clans to borrow shields and swords and *Lao* warriors and braves. He got together ten legions. They all assembled on an appointed day, massing like clouds and sweeping in like mists gathering on the mountains, each and all obeying the commands of the King Mênghuo.

And the scouts knew it all, and they told K'ung-ming, who said, "This is what I was waiting for, that the *Mans* should have an opportunity of knowing our might."

Thereupon he seated himself in a small carriage and went out to watch.

> O let our enemy's courage glow
> That we our greater might may show.

The history of the campaign will be continued in the next chapter.

CHAPTER LXXXIX.

K'UNG-MING'S SUCCESSFUL FOURTH RUSE;
THE KING OF THE *Mans* CAPTURED FOR THE FIFTH TIME.

K'ung-ming's small carriage was escorted by only a few horsemen. Hearing that a sluggish river, the Western Erh, lay in·the way, and having no boat, K'ung-ming bade the escort cut down some trees and make a raft. They did so; but the raft sank. So K'ung-ming turned to Lü K'ai and said, "There is close by a mountain covered with bamboos. I have heard of these bamboos, and some are several spans in girth. We can make a bridge of them for the army to cross."

So three legions were sent to the mountains, where they cut down many thousands of bamboos, and floated them down river. Then at the narrowest point they made a bridge a hundred feet or so in length. Next the main army was brought down to the river and camped in line along the bank. The camp was protected by a moat, crossed by a floating bridge, and a mud rampart. On the south bank they constructed three large stockades so as to prepare for the coming of the *Man* soldiers.

They had not long to wait. King Mênghuo was hot with rage and came quickly. As soon as he got near the river, he led out a legion of fierce warriors and challenged the first stockade.

K'ung-ming went forth in simple state. He wore a silk cap, a white robe and held in his hand a feather fan. He sat in a small quadriga, and his captains rode right and left.

The King of the *Mans* was clad in mail of rhinoceros hide and wore a bright red casque. In his left hand he bore a shield, and his right gripped a sword. He rode an ordinary ox.

As soon as he saw his enemies he opened his mouth and poured forth abuse and insults, while his men darted to and fro brandishing their weapons.

K'ung-ming at once ordered the army to retire within the stockades and bar the gates. The *Mans* came close up to the stockade and pranced about naked, shouting in derision.

Within the stockade the captains grew very angry, and they went in a body to their leader to beg that he would withdraw the order to remain on the defensive. But he would not listen.

Presently he said, "These men are ignorant of our culture and are naturally fierce and turbulent. In that mood we are no match for them. But all we have to do is to remain on guard for a few days till their ferocity has spent itself. Then I have a plan that will overcome them."

Days passed, and the men of Shu made no move; they only maintained the defensive. K'ung-ming watched the besiegers from an eminence, and saw the first vigour of their advance give way to careless idleness. Then K'ung-ming called together his captains and asked if they dared give battle. They all rejoiced at the suggestion; so he called them two by two or one by one and gave them secret orders. Chao Yün and Wei Yen went in first. Wang P'ing and Ma Chung followed.

To Ma Tai he said, "I am going to abandon these stockades and retire north of the river. As soon as we have crossed you are to cut loose the floating bridge and move it down the stream so that Chao and Wei may cross."

Chang I was to remain by the camp and light it up at night as if it was still occupied. When Mênghuo pursued, then he was to cut off his retreat. Last of all, Kuan So was to escort K'ung-ming's carriage.

The soldiers marched out of the camp at evening, and the lamps were hung up as usual. The *Mans* saw this from a distance and dared not attack. But the next morning at dawn Mênghuo led his men to the stockades and found all was quiet. He went close up and saw they were all empty and bare; not a man was there. Grain and fodder lay about among empty carts; all was in confusion, suggesting hasty departure.

"They have abandoned the camp," said Mênghuo. "But this is only a ruse.

"I think that Chuko Liang has important news from the capital that has made him leave without his baggage train like this. Either Wu has invaded or Wei has attacked. They left these lamps burning to make us think the camps were occupied, but they ran away leaving everything behind. If we pursue we cannot go wrong."

So the king urged his army onward, himself heading the leading division. When they reached the Erhho bank they saw on the farther side that the camps were all in order and the banners flying as usual like a brightly tinted cloud of silk. Along the bank stood a wall of cloth. They dared not attack.

Mênghuo said to his brother, "This means that Chuko fears lest we may pursue. That is only a temporary halt, and they will retire in a couple of days."

The *Mans* camped on the river bank while they sent into the mountains to cut bamboos to make rafts. The boldest of the soldiers were placed in front of the camp till the rafts should be ready to cross. Little did Mênghuo suspect that the army of Shu was already within his borders.

One day was very stormy. Then the *Mans* saw great lights spring up around them, and at the same time the rolling of drums heralded an attack. The *Mans* and the *Laos*, instead of going out to meet the enemy, began a fight between themselves. Mênghuo became alarmed and fled with all his clan and dependents. They fought their way through and made a dash for their former camp.

Just as they reached it there appeared a cohort of the enemy led by Chao Yün. Mênghuo turned off west and sought refuge in the mountains. But he was stopped by a cohort under Ma Tai. With a small remnant of his men he got away into a valley. Soon he saw clouds of dust rising on three sides and the glow of torches, so that he was forced to halt. However, the east remained clear, and presently he fled in that direction. As he was crossing the mouth of a gully he noticed a few horsemen outlined against a thick wood and saw they were escorting a small carriage. And in that carriage sat K'ung-ming.

K'ung-ming laughed, and said, "So the defeated king of the *Mans* has got here! I have waited for you a long time, O King."

Mênghuo angrily turned to his followers and said, "Thrice have I been the victim of this man's base wiles and have been put to shame. Now chance has sent him across my path, and you must attack him with all your energy. Let us cut him to pieces and those with him."

A few of the *Man* horsemen, with Mênghuo shouting to encourage them, pushed forward in hot haste toward the wood. But in a few moments they all stumbled and disappeared into some pits that had been dug in the way. And just then Wei Yen emerged from the wood. One by one the *Mans* were pulled out of the pits and bound tight with cords.

K'ung-ming returned to his camp, where he arrived before the captors of the king could bring in their prisoner. He busied himself in soothing the other *Man* prisoners. Many of the notables and chiefs of the tributaries had betaken themselves to their own ravines and villages with their kerns and followers. Many of those who remained came over and yielded to Shu. They were well fed and assured of safety, and allowed to go to their own. They went off gladly enough.

By and by Chang I brought up the king's brother. K'ung-ming reproached him for his brother's behaviour.

"Your brother is a misguided simpleton; you ought to remonstrate with him and persuade him to change his course. Here you are, a captive for the fourth time; are you not ashamed? How can you have the effrontery to look anyone in the face?"

A deep flush of shame passed over his face, and he threw himself to the earth begging forgiveness.

K'ung-ming said, "If I put you to death, it shall not be to-day. This time I pardon you, but you are to talk to your brother."

So Mêngyu was loosed from his bonds and allowed to get up. He went away weeping.

Very soon Wei Yen brought up the king, and to him K'ung-ming simulated great rage, saying, "What can you say now? You see you are in my hands again."

"I am again an unfortunate victim," said the king. "Once more I have blundered into your net, and now I shall die with no one to close my eyes."

K'ung-ming shouted to the lictors to take him away and behead him. Mênghuo never blenched at the sentence, but he turned to his captor and said, "If you freed me only once more I would wipe out the shame of all four captures."

K'ung-ming smiled at the bold reply and bade the lictors loose his bonds, and the attendants served him with wine. Mênghuo was invited to sit in the commander's tent.

Said K'ung-ming, "Four times you have been treated generously and yet you are still defiant. Why?"

"Though I am what you call a barbarian, I would scorn to employ your vile ruses. And that is why I remain defiant."

"I have liberated you four times; think you you can give battle again?"

"If you catch me again I will incline my heart to yield and I will give everything in my ravine to reward your men. I will also take an oath not to cause any further trouble."

K'ung-ming smiled, but let him go. The king thanked him and left. As soon as he was set at liberty the king got together as many of his adherents as he could and went away southward. Before long he fell in with his brother, Mêngyu, who had got together some sort of an army and was on his way to avenge his brother. As soon as they saw each other the brothers fell upon each other's necks and wept. They related their experiences.

Mêngyu said, "We cannot stand against the enemy. We have been defeated several times. Now I think we had better go into the mountains and hide in some dark gully where they cannot find us. Those men of Shu will never stand the summer heat; they must retire."

"Where can we hide?" asked his brother.

"I know a valley away south-west from us called 'T'ulung Ravine,' or 'Bald Dragon Ravine,' and the chief, Tossu, is a friend of mine. Let us take refuge with him."

"Very well; go and arrange it," said Mênghuo.

So Mêngyu went. When he got there, the chief, Prince Tossŭ, lost no time, but came out with his soldiers to welcome

Mênghuo, who then entered the valley. After the exchange of salutations, Mênghuo explained his case.

Tossŭ said, "O King, rest content. If those men from the Land of Streams come here I will see to it that not one goes home. And Chuko Liang will meet his death here too."

Naturally, Mênghuo was pleased; but he wanted to know how his host could feel so secure.

Tossŭ said, "In this ravine there are only two roads, the one you came by and another by the north-west. The road you travelled along is level, soft and the waters are sweet. Men and horses may both use it. But if we close the mouth of the ravine with a barricade no one, however strong, can get in. The other road is precipitous, dangerous and narrow. The only path is beset with venomous serpents and scorpions, and as evening comes on there are malarial exhalations which are dangerous till past noon the next day. The road is only practicable between *shên* (3 p.m.) and *yu* (7 p.m.), for about three watches. Then the water is undrinkable. The road is very difficult.

"Then again there are four wells actually poisonous. One is called 'The Dumb Spring.' Its water is pleasant to the palate, but it makes men dumb and they die in a few days. A second fountain is called ' The Spring of Destruction ' and is hot. But if a man bathe therein his flesh rots till his bones protrude and he dies. The third is 'The Black Spring.' Its waters are greenish. If it be sprinkled on a man's body his extremities turn black and presently he dies. The fourth is 'The Spring of Weak Water,' ice cold. If a man drink of this water his breath is chilled, he becomes weak as a thread and soon dies. Neither birds nor insects are found in this region, and no one but the Han General Ma Yüan, who was styled *'Fu-po'* for this exploit, has ever passed. Now the north-east road shall be blocked, and you may hide here perfectly safe from those men of Shu, for, finding that way blocked, they will try the other road, which is waterless save for the four deadly springs. No matter how many they be, they will perish; and we need no weapons."

"Now indeed I have found a place to live in," cried Mênghuo, striking his forehead. Then looking to the north he said, "Even Chuko Liang's wonderful cunning will be of no avail. The four springs alone will defeat him and avenge my army."

The two brothers settled down comfortably as guests of the Prince Tossŭ, with whom they spent the days in feasting.

In the meantime, as the *Mans* did not appear, K'ung-ming gave orders to leave the West Erh (Hsierh) River and push south. It was then the sixth month, and blazing hot. A poet sang about the bitter heat of the south:—

> The hills are sere, the valleys dry,
> A raging heat fills all the sky,

Throughout the whole wide universe
No spot exists where heat is worse.

Another poem runs:—

The glowing sun darts out fierce rays,
No cloud gives shelter from the blaze,
In parching heat there pants a crane,
The whale swims through the hissing main.
The brook's cool margin now I love,
Or idle stroll through bamboo grove.
I would not march to deserts far
In leathern jerkin donned for war.

Just at the moment of setting out southward, the spies brought news of Mênghuo's retreat into the Bald Dragon Ravine and the barricading of one entrance. They also said that the valley was garrisoned, the hills were precipitous and even impassable. So K'ung-ming called in Lü K'ai and questioned him, but he did not know exactly the conditions.

Then out spoke Chiang Yüan, saying, "Mênghuo's repeated captures have broken his spirit so that he dare not take the field again. The men are exhausted with this intense heat and little is to be gained by prolonging the campaign. The best move would be to return to our own country."

"If we do this we shall fall victims to Mênghuo's scheme," said K'ung-ming. If we retreated he would certainly follow. Beside, having advanced so far, it would be foolish to turn back now."

Wang P'ing was sent on with the advanced guard and some of the *Mans* as guides to seek an entrance on the north-west. They found the road and came to the first spring, of which the thirsty men and horses drank freely.

Wang P'ing returned to report his success, but by the time he reached camp he and all his men were speechless. They could only point to their mouths. K'ung-ming knew they had been poisoned, and was alarmed. He went forward in his light chariot to find out the cause. He came to the spring. The water was very deep and dark green. A mass of vapour hung about the surface rising and falling. The men would not touch the water. K'ung-ming went up the hills to look around, but could see nothing except a rampart of mountains. A deep silence hung over all, unbroken by the cry even of a bird. He was perplexed.

Presently he noticed an old temple away up among the crags. By the aid of the lianas and creepers he managed to clamber up, and in a chamber hewn out of the rock he saw the figure of an officer. Beside it was a tablet saying the temple was dedicated to Ma Yüan, the famous general who had preceded him in that country. The natives had erected it to sacrifice to the leader who had overcome the *Mans*.

K'ung-ming, much impressed, bowed before the image of the great leader, and said, "Your humble servant received a sacred trust, the protection of the son of the First Ruler. That son, the present king, sent him here to subdue the *Mans* that the land might be free from peril when he decided to attack Wei and take possession of Wu and thereby restore the glory of the Hans. But the soldiers are ignorant of the country, and some of them have drunk of a poisonous spring so that they have become dumb. Your servant earnestly prays your honoured spirit, out of regard for the kindness and justice of the present king, to reveal your spiritual character and manifest your holiness by safeguarding and assisting the army."

Having prayed thus, K'ung-ming left the temple. While seeking some native whom he might question, he saw in the distance, on a hill opposite, an aged man leaning on a staff. He approached, and as he drew nearer K'ung-ming noted his extraordinary appearance. When he had reached the temple, he asked the venerable visitor to walk in. After the salutations, the old man sat on the stones, and K'ung-ming opened the conversation with the usual questions. The old gentleman replied, "Sir Minister, I know you well by repute, and am happy to meet you. Many of the *Mans* owe their lives to you, and all have been deeply impressed by your kindness."

Then K'ung-ming returned to the matter nearest his heart, the mystery of the spring. The old man told him the name of that spring and the symptoms its waters produced, and went on to speak of the other three springs and the malarial exhalations, just as has been related.

"In short, the *Mans* cannot be conquered," said K'ung-ming, when the old man had finished. "And Wu cannot be repressed, nor Wei overcome. And the Hans cannot be restored. So, I fail in the task set me by my king. Would that I might die!"

"Be not so cast down, O Minister," said the aged one. "I can lead you to a place where you may counteract all this."

"I would ask for your instruction, Venerable One," said K'ung-ming. "What exalted advice have you to confer upon me? I hope you will instruct me."

"West of this, not far off, is a valley, and twenty *li* from its entrance is a stream called 'Wanan,' near which there lives a recluse known as the Hermit of the Stream. He has not left the valley these twenty years. Behind his hut there gushes out a spring of water, called the 'Spring of the Medicine of Tranquillity.' This is the antidote to your poison. Bathing in its waters is a cure for skin diseases and for malaria. Moreover, near the hut grows a herb called *hsiehyeh yünhsiang,* "the garlic-leaved fragrance." Chewing a leaf of this safeguards one from malaria. You can do no better than go to the hut of the recluse forthwith and get these remedies."

K'ung-ming humbly thanked his aged counsellor, and said, "Venerable Sir, I am profoundly affected by your merciful kindness and compassion. May I ask again by what name I may call you?"

The old man rose and entered the temple, saying, "I am the Spirit of this mountain, sent by *Fu-po Chiang-chün* to guide you."

As he said this he shouted at the solid rock behind the temple, and it opened of itself and let him in."

K'ung-ming's astonishment was beyond words. He made another obeisance to the Spirit of the temple and went down by the way he had come. Then he returned to his camp.

Next day, bearing incense and gifts, Wang P'ing and his stricken men went off to the spot which the old man had indicated. They quickly found the valley and followed its narrow road till they came to a small, farm-like enclosure, where tall pines and lofty cypresses, luxuriant bamboos and gorgeous flowers sheltered a few simple huts. An exquisite perfume pervaded the whole place.

K'ung-ming rejoiced to recognise the spot and at once knocked at the door. A lad answered his knock, and K'ung-ming was telling his name when the host came out quickly, saying, "Surely my visitor is the Prime Minister of the Han Dynasty?"

K'ung-ming saw at the door a man with a bamboo comb holding back his hair, grass shoes on his feet, and a robe of white girded in by a black girdle. He had grey eyes and a reddish beard.

"Great Scholar, how did you know who I was?" said K'ung-ming.

"How could I not have heard of your expedition to the south?"

He invited K'ung-ming to enter, and when they had seated themselves in their relative positions as host and guest, K'ung-ming said, "My former master, the Emperor, confided to me the care of his son and successor. That son, now Emperor, gave me a command to lead an army to this country, get the *Mans* on our side and spread our culture among them. But now to my disappointment Mênghuo, the king, has hidden himself in a certain ravine, and some of my men on the way to seek him drank of a certain fountain and are dumb. But last evening the former leader of an expedition, *Fu-po Chiang-chün*, manifested his sacred presence and told me that you, Exalted Sir, had a remedy for this evil, and I pray you of your pity to give me of the potent fluid whereby my soldiers' lives may be saved."

The recluse replied, "I am only a worthless old man of the wild woods and unworthy of the visit of such as you, O Minister. The water you desire flows out at the back of my cottage and you may take what you will of it."

The serving lad then showed Wang P'ing and his dumb companions to the stream, and he dipped up the waters for them to drink. As soon as they had drunk they coughed up some mucus and could speak. The lad also led the soldiers to a place where they could bathe.

In the cottage the recluse regaled K'ung-ming with tea made of cypress seeds and a conserve of pine flowers. He also told his guest that in the ravines were many serpents and scorpions, and that the lily flowers blown into the springs by the wind made them unfit to drink. However, if he dug wells he would find good water.

Then K'ung-ming begged some of the garlic-leaved *yün-hsiang* as an antidote against malaria. The recluse said the soldiers could pluck as much as they wanted. And so every man put a leaf in his mouth and thus became malaria-proof.

K'ung-ming, with a low bow then begged to be told the name of his benefactor.

"I am Mênghuo's eldest brother," said the recluse, smiling. "My name is Mêngchieh."

K'ung-ming started.

"Do not be afraid," said the recluse. "Let me explain. We were three brothers of the same parents, the eldest being myself. Our parents are both dead. My brother Mênghuo, being headstrong and vicious, has never been amenable to culture. I have talked to him many times, but he kept his own course. Finally, under an assumed name, I retired to this spot. I am ashamed for my brother's rebellion, which has put you, O Minister, to the trouble of making this expedition into a barren country, but it has given me the privilege of seeing you. For my responsibility in this I deserve to die a thousand times, as I own to your face, and I beg your pardon."

K'ung-ming sighed, saying, "Now I believe that story of Robber Chih and Liu Hsia Hui; this is the same thing over again. Men renowned for virtue and villainy may come from the same stock."

Then he said to his host, "Would you wish me to represent your merits to the Emperor and get you created a prince?"

"How can you think I desire honours or wealth when I am here because of my contempt for all such things?"

K'ung-ming then wished to make him certain presents, but the recluse would have none of them.

So taking leave of his host K'ung-ming went back to his camp.

In the southern expedition when the *Mantsz* were subdued,
K'ung-ming found a high-born recluse in a shady solitude.
Up till then the gloomy forests were thought destitute of men,
That no curling smoke wreath ever floated upwards from the glen.

As soon as K'ung-ming reached camp he set the men digging for water. They dug to a great depth but found none; nor

20

were they more successful when they tried other places. They were very discouraged. Then K'ung-ming in the depths of the night burned incense and prayed to God:—"Unworthy as is thy servant Liang, he has received favour from the Great Hans and now has been ordered to subdue the *Mans*. Alas! now our water is spent and my men and animals are parched with thirst. If Thy will be to preserve the line of Han then give, I beseech Thee, sweet water, but if their course is run, then may Thy servant and those with him die in this place."

The morning after this prayer the wells were full of sweet water.

> The *Mantzŭ* must be conquered; Chuko led a great array,
> Though his skill was superhuman, yet he held the righteous way;
> As the wells gave forth sweet water when Kêng Kung's head bowed full low,
> So the reverent prayers of Chuko made the lower springs to flow.

The soldiers' spirits revived with the supply of water, and the army soon advanced by hill paths to the Valley of the Bald Dragon, where they camped.

When Mênghuo heard the news he was greatly taken aback.

"These men do not appear to have suffered either thirst or fever," said he. "Our springs have lost their power."

Tossŭ, the king, heard it, but doubted. He and Mênghuo ascended into a high hill whence they could see their enemies. They saw no signs of illness or distress; all went on calmly and quietly in the camps, water carrying and cooking, eating and attending to the cattle. Tossŭ's hair stood on end as he looked at them.

"These are not human soldiers," said he, shivering.

"We two brothers will fight one fierce battle with these men of Shu and die therein," said Mênghuo, "We cannot wait calmly to be put into bonds."

"But, O King, if your men should be beaten my whole family will also perish. Let us encourage the men of the ravines. Let us kill bullocks and slaughter horses to feed them and urge them to go through fire and water to rush right up to the camp of the enemy and seize upon victory."

So there was great feasting before the *Mans* took the field. Just as this was going on, there arrived one Yang Fêng, lord of twenty-and-one ravines in the west, and he led three legions. Mênghuo rejoiced exceedingly at this unexpected addition to his army and felt sure of victory. So he and Tossŭ went out of their own valley to welcome Yang Fêng, who said, "I have with me three legions of men in iron mail, brave and intrepid men, who can fly over mountains and bound across the peaks; they of themselves are a match for the enemy even if they numbered a hundred legions. And, moreover, my five sons, all trained in arms, are with me, all to help you, O King."

The five sons were brought in and presented. They were handsome young fellows, bold and martial looking. Father and sons were entertained at a banquet. Halfway through the feast Yang Fêng proposed a diversion.

"There is but scanty amusement in the field," said Yang, "and so I have brought along some native singing girls who have been taught fencing and such things. If you care for it, they might give an exhibition."

The feasters hailed the suggestion with joy, and soon the half score maidens came to the front of the tent. Their hair hung about their shoulders, and they were barefooted. They danced and skipped and went through their performance outside. The guests inside clapped their hands and applauded their skill, and the soldiers joined in the choruses.

Presently, at a signal from their father, two of Yang's sons bore a goblet to Mênghuo and two others to his brother. They took the cups and were raising them to their lips when Yang shouted a single word of command, and, instantly, the cup-bearers had the two Mêngs out of their seats and helpless in their hands. At this, Tossŭ jumped up to run away, but Yang Fêng gripped him, and he was a prisoner too. The *Man* maidens ranged themselves in a line along the front of the tent so that none dared approach.

"When the hare dies the fox mourns," said Mênghuo. "One sympathises with one's own as a rule. We are both chiefs and have been friends. I know not why you should injure me."

"I had to repay Chuko Liang the Minister for his compassion on me and mine, and there was no way till you rebelled. Why should I not offer up a rebel in propitiation?"

Leaving Mênghuo and his brother and Tossŭ in the hands of Yang Fêng, the *Man* warriors dispersed, each man returning to his own valley. Liu Fêng then took the prisoners to the camp of Shu, where he bowed at the tent door, saying, "I and my sons and the sons of my brother are grateful to you for much kindness, wherefore we bring to you as an offering the persons of these rebels."

K'ung-ming rewarded Yang and bade them bring forward the king.

"This time are you prepared to yield?" said the minister.

"It is not your ability, but the treachery of my own people that has brought me to this. If you wish to slay, slay; but I will not yield."

"You know you were the cause of my men entering into a waterless land, where there were those four evil fountains, and yet my soldiers were not poisoned and came to no harm. Does it not seem to you like evidence of a superior protecting power? Why will you follow this misguided road and always be obstinate?"

Mênghuo replied, "My fathers have long held the Silver Pit Hills, and the three rivers are their ramparts. If you can take that stronghold then will I and my heirs for ever acknowledge your power and yield."

"I am going to liberate you once more," said K'ung-ming, "and you may put your army in order if you will and fight a decisive battle. But after that, if you are my prisoner and are still refractory and unsubmissive, I shall have to exterminate your whole family."

He ordered the lictors to loose the prisoner's bonds and let him go. After he had gone, the other two, the king's brother and Tossŭ, were led in and they also received their liberty. They were given wine and food, but they were confused and could not look K'ung-ming in the face. They were given horses to travel on.

> The way has been long and now danger is near,
> But faith in their leader banishes fear.

The next chapter will tell how Mênghuo reorganised his army and whose was the victory.

CHAPTER XC.

WILD BEASTS AS WARRIORS; K'UNG-MING'S SIXTH VICTORY;
BURNING OF THE RATTAN ARMY; SEVENTH CAPTURE OF THE
KING.

All the prisoners were released; and Yang Fêng and his
sons were rewarded with ranks, and his men were given
presents. They expressed their gratitude and returned to
their own, while Mênghuo and his hastened home to Silver-pit
Ravine.

Outside this ravine were three rivers, the Lu, the Kannan
Shui, or Sweet South Water, and the Hsich'êng Shui, or West
Water. These three streams united to form one river which
was called the Sanchiang, or Three Rivers. Close to the
ravine on the north was a wide and fruitful plain; on the
west were salt wells. The Lu River flowed about two hundred
li to the south-west, and due south was a valley called the
Liangtu Ravine. There were hills in, as well as surrounding,
the ravine, and in these they found silver; whence the name
"Silver Pit."

A palace had been built in the ravine, which the *Man* kings
had made their stronghold, and there was an ancestral temple,
which they called *Chia-kuei*, or Family Devil, where they
solemnised sacrifices of bulls and horses at the four seasons.
They called these sacrifices "Enquiring of the Demons."
Human sacrifices were offered also, men of Shu or men of
their own people belonging to other villages. Sick persons
swallowed no drugs, but prayed to a chief sorcerer, called Drug
Demon. There was no legal code, the only punishment for
every transgression being death.

When girls are grown and become women they bathe in a
stream. Men and women are kept separate, and they marry
whom they will, the parents having no control in that particular. They call this *hsüeh-i* (Learning the Trade). In good
seasons the country produces grain, but if the harvest fails
they make soup out of serpents and eat boiled elephant flesh.
All over the country the head of the family of greatest local
consideration is termed "Lord of the Ravine," and the next in
importance is called a "Notable." A market is held in the city
of Sanchiang, or Three Rivers, on the first day of every moon,
and another on the fifteenth; goods are brought in and
bartered.

In his own ravine Mênghuo gathered his family and clan to the number of a thousand or more and addressed them: "I have been put to shame by the men of Shu many times, and I have sworn to take revenge for the insults. Has anyone any proposal to make?"

Thereupon a certain one replied, saying, "I can produce a man able to defeat Chuko Liang."

The assembly turned to the speaker, who was a brother of Mênghuo's wife. He was the head of eight tribes of barbarians, and was named Tailai. He was a chief.

"Who is the man?" asked Mênghuo.

Chief Tailai replied, "He is Mulu, Prince and Lord of the Pana Ravine. He is a master of witchcraft who can call up the wind and invoke the rain. He rides upon an elephant and is attended by tigers, leopards, wolves, venomous snakes and scorpions. Beside, he has under his hand three legions of superhuman soldiers. He is very bold. O King, write him a letter and send him presents, which I will deliver. If he will consent to lend his aid, what fear have we of Shu?"

Mênghuo was pleased with the scheme and ordered the "State Uncle" to draft a letter. Then he ordered Tossŭ to defend Sanchiang and make the first line of defence.

K'ung-ming led his men near Sanchiang. Taking a survey of the country, he noted that the city could be reached by a bank on one face, so he sent Wei Yen and Chao Yün to march along the road and attack. But when they reached the rampart they found it well defended by bows and crossbows.

The men of the city were adepts in the use of the bow, and they had one sort which discharged ten arrows at once. Furthermore, the arrows were poisoned, and a wound meant certain death. The two captains saw that they could not succeed, and so retired.

When K'ung-ming heard of the poisoned arrows, he mounted his light chariot and went to see for himself. Having regarded the defences, he returned to his camp and ordered a retirement of ten *li*. This move delighted the *Mans*, who congratulated each other on their success in driving off the besiegers, who, as they concluded, had been frightened away. So they gave themselves up to rejoicing and kept no watch. Nor did they even send out scouts.

The army of Shu made a strong camp in their new halting place and closed the gates for defence. For five days they gave no sign. One evening, just at sunset, a slight breeze began to blow. Then K'ung-ming issued an order that every man should provide himself with a coat by the first watch. If any one lacked he would be put to death. None of the captains knew what was in the wind, but the order was obeyed. Next, each man was ordered to fill his coat with earth. This order appeared equally strange, but it was carried out. When all were ready, the men were told to carry the earth to the foot of the city wall, and the first arrivals would be rewarded. So they ran with all speed with the dry earth and reached the wall. Then with the earth they were ordered to make a raised way, and the first man on the wall was promised a reward.

The whole of the ten legions of Shu, and their native allies, having thrown their burdens of earth near the wall, then quickly rushed up the incline, and with one great shout were on the wall. The archers on the wall were seized and dragged down; those who got clear ran away into the city. Tossŭ was slain in the mêlée that followed on this attack. The men of Shu moved through the city slaying all they met. Thus was the city captured and with it great booty of jewels, which were made over to the army as a reward for their prowess.

The few soldiers who escaped went away and told the king what had happened. He was much distressed. Before he had recovered they told him that the men of Shu had come over and were encamped at the mouth of his own ravine.

Just as he was in the very depths of distress, a laugh came from behind the screen, and a woman appeared, saying, "Though you are brave, how stupid you are! I am only a woman, but I want to go out and fight."

The woman was his wife, Chujung. Her family had lived long among the *Mans*, but she was a descendant of the Chujung family. She was expert in the use of the flying sword and never missed her aim.

Mênghuo rose and bowed to her. The woman thereupon mounted a horse and forthwith marched out at the head of many captains, leading five legions of men of the ravines, and set out to drive off the men of Shu.

Just as the host got clear of the ravine it was stopped by a cohort led by Chang I. At once the *Mans* deployed, and the woman leader armed herself with five swords such as she used. In one hand she held an eighteen-foot signal staff, and she sat a curly-haired, reddish horse.

Chang I was secretly troubled at the sight before him, but he engaged the amazon. After a few passes the lady turned her steed and bolted. Chang I went after her, but a sword came flying through the air directly at him. He tried to fend off with one hand, but it wounded his arm, and he fell to the ground. The *Mans* gave a loud shout; some of them pounced on the unlucky leader and made him prisoner.

Then Ma Chung, hearing his comrade had been taken, rushed out to rescue, but only to be surrounded. He saw the amazon holding up her staff and made a dash forward, but just then his steed went down under him, and he was also a prisoner.

Both captains were taken into the ravine and led before the king. He gave a banquet in honour of his wife's success, and during the feast the lady bade the lictors put the two prisoners to death. They hustled the two captains in and were just going to carry out their orders when Mênghuo checked them.

"No; five times has Chuko Liang set me at liberty. It would be unjust to put these to death. Confine them till we have taken their chief; then we may execute them."

His wife was merry with wine and did not object. So their lives were spared.

The defeated soldiers returned to their camp. K'ung-ming took steps to retrieve the mishap by sending for Ma Tai, Chao Yün and Wei Yen, to each of whom he gave special and private orders.

Next day the *Man* soldiers reported to the king that Chao Yün was offering a challenge. The amazon forthwith mounted and rode out to battle. She engaged Chao Yün, who soon fled. The lady was too prudent to risk pursuit, and rode home. Then Wei Yen repeated the challenge; he also fled as if defeated. But again the lady declined to pursue. Next day Chao Yün repeated his challenge and ran away as before. The amazon signalled no pursuit. But at this Wei Yen rode up and opened a volley of abuse and obloquy. This proved too much, and she gave the signal to go after him and led the way. Wei Yen increased his pace, and the amazon doubled hers, and she and her followers pressed into a narrow road along a valley. Suddenly behind her was heard a noise, and Wei Yen, turning his head, saw the lady tumble out of her saddle.

She had rushed into an ambush prepared by Ma Tai; her horse had been tripped up by ropes. She was captured, bound and carried off to the Shu camp. Some of her people endeavoured to rescue her, but they were driven off.

K'ung-ming seated himself in his tent to see his prisoner, and the amazon was led up. He bade them remove her bonds, and she was conducted to another tent, where wine was laid before her. Then a message was sent to Mênghuo to say that she would be exchanged for the two captive leaders. The king agreed, and they were set free. As soon as they arrived, the lady was escorted by K'ung-ming himself to the mouth of the ravine, where Menghuo welcomed her half gladly, half angrily.

Then they told Mênghuo of the coming of the Lord of the Pana Ravine, and he went out to meet him. He rode up on his white elephant, dressed in silks, and with many gold and pearl ornaments. He wore a double sword at his belt, and he was followed by the motley pack of fighting animals that he fed, gambolling and dancing about him.

Mênghuo made him a lowly obeisance and then poured out his tale of woes. Mulu promised to avenge his wrongs and was led off to a banquet which had been prepared.

Next day the deliverer went out to battle, with his pack of wild creatures in his train. Chao Yün and his colleague quickly made their array of footmen and then took their station in front side by side and studied their opponents. The *Man* banners and weapons were all extraordinary. Most of the men wore no armour and none wore any clothing. Their faces were ugly. They carried four sharp pointed knives in their belts. Signals were not given by drum or trumpet, but by a gong.

King Mulu had two swords in his belt and carried a hand bell. He urged his white elephant forward and emerged from between his flags.

"We have spent all our life in the army, but we have never seen the like of that before," said Chao Yün.

As they talked to one another they noticed that the opposing leader was mumbling something that might be a spell or a curse, and from time to time he rang his bell. Then suddenly the wind got up, stones began to roll and sand to fly, and there was a sound as of a heavy shower of rain. Next a horn rang out, and thereupon the tigers and the leopards, and the wolves and the serpents, and all the other wild beasts came down on the wind snapping and clawing. How could the men stand such a thing as that? So they retreated, and the *Mans* came after them fiercely, chasing their enemies as far as the city.

Chao and Wei mustered their defeated men and went to their leader to confess their failure. The chief, however, was neither angry nor dejected.

"The fault is not yours." he said. "Long ago, when I was still in my forest hut, I knew the *Mans* possessed certain powers over beasts, and I provided against this adventure before we left Shu. You will find a score of small sealed carts in the baggage train. We will use half of them now."

He bade his staff bring forward ten of the red box-carts. They all wondered what would happen. Then the carts were opened, and they turned out to be carved and coloured models of huge wild beasts, with coats of worsted, teeth and claws of steel; each could accommodate half a score of men. Choosing a sufficient number of seasoned warriors, he told off ten companies and bade each company stuff the mouths of the beasts full of inflammables.

Next day the army of Shu marched out to the attack and were arrayed at the entrance to the ravine. The *Man* soldiers went into the ravine and told their lord. Mulu, thinking himself perfectly invincible, did not hesitate, but marched out, taking Menghuo with him. K'ung-ming, dressed in the simple robe of a Taoist, went out in his light chariot. In his hand he held a feather fan. Mênghuo, who recognised his enemy, pointed him out to Mulu.

"That is Chuko Liang in that small chariot. If we can only capture him, our task is done."

Then Mulu began to mutter his spells and to ring his bell. As before, the wind got up and blew with violence, and the wild beasts came on.

But at a wave of the simple feather fan, lo! the wind turned and blew the other way. Then from out of the host of Shu there burst the wonderful wild beasts. The real wild beasts of the *Mans* saw rushing down upon them huge creatures, whose mouths vomited flames and whose nostrils breathed out black smoke. They came along with jingling bells, snapping and clawing, and the real beasts turned tail and fled in among the men of their own side, trampling them down as they sped. K'ung-ming gave the signal for a general onset, and his men rushed forward with beating drums and blaring trumpets. Mulu was killed. Mênghuo's whole clan fled in panic and tore up among the hills out of the way. And thus the Silver Pit Ravine was taken.

Next day, as K'ung-ming was telling off parties to search for and capture the king, it was announced that the brother-in-law of Mênghuo and Chief Tailai, having vainly tried to persuade the king to yield, had made prisoners of him and his wife and all his clan and were bringing them to K'ung-ming.

Hearing this, Chang I and Ma Chung were called and received certain orders, upon which they hid themselves in the wings of the tent with a large body of sturdy warriors. This done, K'ung-ming ordered the keepers to open the gates, and in came Chief Tailai with Mênghuo and his people in custody. As he bowed at the entrance of the hall, K'ung-ming called out, "Let my strong captors appear!" At once out came the hidden men, and every two of them laid hands upon a prisoner and bound him.

"Did you think your paltry ruse would deceive me?" said K'ung-ming. "Here you are a second time captured by your own people and brought before me that you might surrender. I will not hurt you, but I firmly believe this surrender is part of a plot to kill me."

Then he called out to his men to search the prisoners. They did so, and on every man they found a sharp knife.

"Did you not say that if your family were taken prisoners you would yield? How now?" said K'ung-ming.

"We have come of our own will and at the risk of our lives; the credit is not yours. Still I refuse to yield," replied Mênghuo.

"This is the sixth time I have captured you, and yet you are obstinate; what do you expect?"

"If you take me a seventh time, then I will turn to you and never rebel again."

"Well, your stronghold is now destroyed. What have I to fear?" said K'ung-ming.

He ordered the bonds to be loosed, saying, "If you are caught again and lie to me once more I shall certainly not be inclined to let you off."

Mênghuo and his people put their hands over their heads and ran off like rats.

The defeated *Mans* who had fled were many, and most of them were wounded. They fell in with their king, who restored what order was possible and felt glad that he had still some men left. Then he and the Chief Tailai took counsel together.

"Whither can we go?" said Menghuo. "Our stronghold is in the hands of the enemy."

Tailai replied, "There is but one country that can overcome these men; that is the *Wuko* country. It lies seven hundred *li* to the south-east. The king of that state is named Wut'uku. He is a giant. He does not eat grain, but lives on serpents and venomous beasts. He wears scaly armour, which is impenetrable to swords and arrows. His men wear rattan armour. This rattan grows in gullies, climbing over rocks and walls. The inhabitants cut the rattans and steep them in oil for half a year. Then they are dried in the sun. When dry they are steeped again, and so on many times. Then they are plaited into helmets and armour. Clad in this the men float across rivers, and it does not get wet. No weapon can penetrate it. The soldiers are called the Rattan Army. You may seek aid from this king, and with his help you can take Chuko Liang as easily as a sharp knife cleaves a bamboo."

Mênghuo went to the Wuko country and saw the king. The people of this country do not live in houses, but dwell in caves. Mênghuo told the story of his woes and obtained a promise of help, for which he expressed great gratitude. Wut'uku called up two decurions named T'uan and Hsini and gave them three legions of the rattan-armoured soldiers and bade them march north-east.

They came to a river called the Peach-flower Water (*T'ao-hua Shui*), on both banks of which grow many peach trees. Year after year the leaves of these trees fall into the river and render it poisonous to all but the natives. But to the natives it is a stimulant which doubles their vigour. They camped on the bank of this river to await the coming of the army of Shu.

Now K'ungming was informed of the journey of Mênghuo and its results, and he knew when the rattan-clad army camped at the ford. He also knew that Mênghuo had callected all the men of his own that he could to help. He at once marched to the ford. Really, the *Man* soldiers did not seem human; they were so hideous. He questioned the natives, and they told him that the peach leaves were falling and the water of the river was undrinkable. So he retired five *li* and camped.

Next day the *Wuko* men crossed the stream, and, with a rolling of drums, Wei Yen went out to meet them. The Wuko men approached bent double. The men of Shu shot at them, but neither arrows nor bolts penetrated their armour; they rolled off harmless. Nor could swords cut or spears enter. The enemy, thus protected and armed with swords and prongs, were too much for the men of Shu, who had to run away. However, they were not pursued. When, on the retreat, they came to Peach-flower Water ford they saw the *Mans* crossing. Some of them were tired, so they took off their rattan breast-plates, sat upon them and floated to the other side.

When K'ung-ming heard the report of his captain he summoned Lu K'ai and called in some natives. Lu K'ai said he had heard of the Wuku country as perfectly barbarous, the people having no notion of human relations as they were understood in the Central Land. He had heard of this rattan armour and the harmful Peach-flower Waters. He wound up by saying that these people were really untameable and advised retreat.

"No, no," said K'ung-ming merrily; "we have had too much difficulty in getting here to go back so easily. I shall have a counter-plan for these people to-morrow."

Having provided for the defence of his camp and given strict orders to his captains not to go out to fight, K'ung-ming went to reconnoitre. He rode in his light chariot with a few natives as guides. He came to the ford, and from a secluded spot in the mountains on the north bank he looked about him.

The whole country was mountainous and difficult, impassable for any carriage. So he got out and went afoot. Presently, from a hill he saw a long winding valley, like a huge serpent. The sides were very precipitous and bare. However, a road ran through the middle.

"What is the name of the valley?" asked K'ung-ming.

"It is called 'Coiled Serpent Valley,' " said the guides. "At the other end you come into the high road to Sanchiang. The valley was formerly called 'T'alangtien.' "

"The very thing," cried K'ung-ming. "Surely this is providence. I shall score a great success here."

Having seen enough, he retraced his steps, found his chariot and returned to camp. Arrived at the camp, Ma Tai was called and put in charge of the preparations. He was to take the ten black painted carts and get a thousand long bamboo poles. What the carts contained and what was to be done with the contents K'ung-ming told his captain in confidence. Then he was to keep the two ends of the valley. Half a month was allowed to carry out his task, which was to be performed with the most perfect secrecy under pain of severe punishment.

Next Chao Yün was sent to a point on the Sanchiang road; Wei Yen to camp at the ford. If the *Mans* came over the river he was to abandon the camp and march toward a certain white flag he would see. Further, he was warned that in half a month he would have to acknowledge defeat some fifteen times and abandon seven camps. On no account was he to come to interview K'ung-ming even after fourteen defeats.

Wei Yen went off, not a little hipped at the prospect, but prepared to obey. Next, Chang I was sent to make a stockade at a certain indicated point, and others were given other tasks.

Mênghuo had begun to have a real terror of K'ung-ming, and he warned the king of the *Wuko*, saying, "This Chuko is exceedingly crafty. Ambush is one of his favourite ruses, so you should warn your soldiers that on no account should they enter a valley where the trees are thick."

"Great King, you speak with reason," said Wut'uku. "I have always heard that the men of the Central State are full of wiles, and I will see that your advice is followed. I will go in front to fight, and you may remain in the rear to give orders."

Presently the scouts told them of the arrival of the men of Shu on the bank of the Peach-flower Water. Wut'uku sent his two captains to cross the river and engage them. The two sides met, but Wei Yen soon left the field. The *Mans* were afraid to pursue as they dreaded an ambush.

In the meantime, Wei laid out another camp. The *Mans* crossed the river in greater force. Wei came out to meet them, but again fled after a very short fight. This time the *Mans* pursued, but having lost their hold of the enemy and coming then to the late camp of the men of Shu, which seemed quite safe, they occupied it.

Next day the two captains asked their King Wut'uku to come to the camp, and they reported what had happened. He decided to make a general advance to drive the men of Shu before him. They fled, even casting aside their breastplates and throwing away their arms, they were in such haste to flee. And they went toward a white flag that appeared in the distance. They found a camp already made, which they occupied.

Soon, however, King Wut'uku came near, and as he pressed forward Wei Yen abandoned this camp and fled. When the *Mans* reached the camp they took up quarters therein.

Soon after they set out to renew the pursuit, but Wei Yen turned back and checked them. This was only a temporary check, for he fled after three encounters, going toward a white flag in the distance.

To avoid wearisome iteration it may be said that this sort of thing continued daily until the men of Shu had been defeated and driven out of the field fifteen times and had abandoned their camp on seven different occasions.

The *Mans* were now warm in pursuit and pressed on with all their might, the King Wut'uku being in the forefront of the pursuers. But then they came to a thick umbrageous wood; and he halted, for he saw flags moving about behind the sheltering trees.

"Just as you foretold," said Wut'uku to Mênghuo.

"Yes; Chuko Liang is going to be worsted this time. We have beaten off his men now daily for half a month and won fifteen successive victories. His men simply run when they hear the wind. The fact is he has exhausted all his craft and has tried every ruse. Now our task is nearly done."

Wut'uku was greatly cheered and began to feel contempt for his enemy.

The sixteenth day of the long fight found Wei Yen leading his oft-defeated men once more against the rattan-protected foe. King Wut'uku on his white elephant was well in the forefront. He had on a cap with symbols of the sun and moon and streamers of wolf's beard, a fringed garment studded with gems, which allowed the plates or scales of his cuirass to appear, and his eyes seemed to flash fire. He pointed the finger of scorn at Wei Yen and began to revile him.

Wei whipped up his steed and fled. The *Mans* pressed after him. Wei made for the Coiled Serpent Valley, for he saw a white flag calling him thither. Wut'uku followed in hot haste, and as he saw only bare hills without a sign of vegetation, be felt quite confident that no ambush was laid.

So he followed into the valley. There he saw some score of black painted carts in the road. The soldiers said to each other that they must be the commissariat waggons of the enemy, abandoned in their hasty flight. This only urged the king to greater speed, and he went on toward the other mouth of the valley, for the men of Shu had disappeared. However, he saw baulks of timber being tumbled down across the track and great boulders rolled down the hill side into the road.

The pursuers cleared away the obstacles. When they had done so and advanced a little they saw certain wheeled vehicles in the road, some large, some small, laden with wood and straw, which was burning. The king was suddenly frightened and ordered a retreat. But he heard much shouting in the rear, and they told him that the wood-laden carts on being broken open had been found to contain gunpowder, and they were all on fire. However, seeing that the valley was barren and devoid of grass and wood, Wut'uku was not in the least alarmed and merely bade his men search for a way round.

Then he saw torches being hurled down the mountain side. These torches rolled till they came to a certain spot, where they ignited the fuses leading to the powder. Then the ground suddenly heaved with the explosion of bombs beneath. The whole valley was soon full of flames, darting and playing in all directions, and wherever they met with rattan armour the rattan caught fire, and thus the whole army, huddled and crowded together, burned in the midst of the valley.

K'ung-ming looked on from the heights above and saw the *Mans* burning. Many of the dead had been mangled and torn by the explosions of the mines. The air was full of suffocating vapour.

K'ung-ming's tears fell fast as he saw the slaughter, and he sighed, saying, "Though I am rendering great service to my country yet I have sacrificed many lives."

Those who were with him were also deeply affected.

King Mênghuo was in his camp awaiting news of success when he saw a crowd of his men come along, and they bowed before him and told him that King Wuko was fighting a great battle and was about to surround Chuko Liang in the Valley of the Coiled Serpent. But he needed help. They said they themselves had had no alternative when they had yielded to Shu, but now they had returned to their allegiance and were come to help him.

So Mênghuo placed himself at the head of his clansmen and those who had just come to him, and lost no time in marching out. He bade them lead him to the spot. But when he reached the valley and saw the destruction, he knew he had been made a victim again. As he made to retire there appeared a body of his enemies on each side, and they began to attack. He was making what stand he could when a great shouting arose. The *Mans* were nearly all disguised men of Shu, and they quickly surrounded him and his clansmen to make them prisoners.

Mênghuo galloped clear and got into the hills. Presently he fell upon a small chariot, with a few men about it, and therein sat Kung-ming, simply dressed and holding a fan.

"What now, rebel Mênghuo?" cried he.

But Mênghuo had galloped away. He was soon stopped by Ma Tai and lay a helpless prisoner bound hand and foot. His wife, Chujung, and the other members of his family were also taken.

K'ung-ming returned to camp and seated himself in the high place in his own tent. He was still sad at the thought of the sacrifice of life, and he said to his officers, "There was no help for it; I had to use that plan. But it has sadly injured my inner virtue and destroyed my self-satisfaction. Guessing that the enemy would suspect an ambush in every thicket, I sent persons to walk about in wooded places with flags. Really there was no ambush. I bade Wei lose battle after battle just to lead the enemy on and harden their hearts. When I saw the Valley of the Coiled Serpent, with its bare sides of smooth rock and the road in its depths, I recognised what could be done and sent Ma Tai to arrange the contents of the black carts, the mines, which I had prepared long ago for this purpose. In every bomb were nine others, and they were buried thirty paces apart. They were connected by fuses laid in hollow bamboos that they might explode in succession, and the force was enormous. Chao Yün prepared those carts laden with straw and rolled down the baulks of timber and boulders that blocked the mouth. Wei Yen led the king on and on till he had enticed him into the valley, when he took up a position to escape. Then the burning began. They say that what is good for water is not much good for fire, and the oil-soaked rattan, excellent as a protection against swords and arrows, was most inflammable, catching fire at sight. The *Mans* were so stubborn that the only way was to use fire, or we should never have scored a victory. But I much regret that the destruction of the men of Wuko has been so complete."

The officers praised his ability and flattered his craftiness; that need not be said.

Then Mênghuo was summoned. He appeared and fell upon his knees. His limbs were freed from the bonds, and he was sent into a side tent for refreshment. But the officers told off to entertain him received certain secret orders.

The chief prisoners were Mênghuo, his wife, brother and the Chief Tailai. There were many of his clan as well. As they were eating and drinking a messenger apeared in the door of the tent and addressed the king, "The Minister is ashamed and does not wish to see you again, Sir. He has sent me to release you. You may enlist another army if you can and once more try a decisive battle. Now you may go."

But instead of going Mênghuo began to weep.

"Seven times a captive and seven times released!" said the king. "Surely there was never anything like it in the whole world. I know I am a barbarian and beyond the pale, but I am not entirely devoid of a sense of propriety and rectitude. Does he think that I feel no shame?"

Thereupon he and all his fell upon their knees and crawled to the tent of the Commander-in-chief and begged pardon, saying, "O Minister, you are the majesty of Heaven. We men of the south will offer no more opposition."

"Then you yield?" said K'ung-ming.

"I and my sons and grandsons are deeply affected by your all-pervading and life-giving mercy. Now how can we not yield?"

K'ung-ming asked Mênghuo to come up into the tent and be seated, and he prepared a banquet of felicitation. Also he confirmed him in his headship and restored all the places that had been captured. Everyone was overwhelmed with K'ung-ming's generosity, and they all went away rejoicing.

A poem has praised K'ung-ming's action:—

He rode in his chariot green,
In his hand just a feather fan,
Seven times he released a king
As part of his conquering plan.
Having chosen a beautiful spot
Where the valleys debouch on the plain,
Lest his kindness should e'er be forgot,
The vanquished erected a fane.

Chang Shih and Fei Wei ventured to remonstrate with K'ung-ming on his policy. They said, "You, O Minister, have led the army this long journey into the wilds and have reduced the *Man* country, and have brought about the submission of the king; why not appoint officials to share in the administration and hold the land?"

K'ung-ming replied, "There are three difficulties. To leave foreigners implies leaving a guard for them; there is the difficulty of feeding a guard. The *Mans* have lost many of their relatives. To leave foreigners without a guard will invite a calamity; this is the second difficulty. Among the *Mans* dethronements and murders are frequent, and there will be enmities and suspicions. Foreigners and they will be mutually distrustful; this is the third difficulty. If I do not leave men I shall not have to send supplies, which makes for peace and freedom from trouble."

They had to agree that the policy was wise.

The kindness of the conqueror was rewarded by the gratitude of these southern people, and they even erected a shrine in his honour, where they sacrificed at the four seasons. They called him their "Gracious Father" and they sent gifts of jewels, cinnabar, lacquer, medicines, ploughing cattle and chargers for the use of the army. And they pledged themselves not to rebel.

When the feastings to the soldiers were finished, the army marched homeward to Shu. 'Wei Yen was in command of the advanced column. He marched to the Lu waters. But on his arrival the clouds gathered and a gale blew over the face of the waters. Because of the force of the gale the army could not advance. Wei Yen then returned and reported the matter to his chief. K'ung-ming called in Mênghuo to ask what this might mean.

The *Mans* beyond the border have yielded now at last,
The water demons raging mad won't let our men go past.

The next chapter will contain Mênghuo's explanation.

CHAPTER IXC.

Sacrifice at Lu Shui; Homeward March;
Attack on the Capital; Chuko's Memorial.

Mênghuo at the head of the *Man* Chieftains and Notables, with the *Lolos*, attended to do honour to the army of Shu on its departure. They reached the Lu waters in the ninth month. But on trying to cross the river a tremendous storm came and hindered them. The leader having reported his difficulty to K'ung-ming, the king was asked if he knew of any reason for such a storm. He replied, "Wild spirits have always troubled those who would cross this river; it is necessary to propitiate them with sacrifices."

"What is the sacrifice?" asked K'ung-ming.

"In the old days when malicious spirits brought misfortune, they sacrificed men to the number of seven sevens and offered their heads. They also slew a black ox and a white goat. Sacrifice thus; the wind will subside and the waters come to rest. The same used to be done to secure a plenteous harvest."

"How can I slay a single man without good reason now that fighting is done and peace has returned?" said K'ung-ming.

He went down to the river to see for himself. The north wind was blowing hard, and the waves were high. Both men and horses seemed frightened. He himself was perplexed. Then he sought out some of the natives and questioned them. They said they had heard the demons moaning every night since he had crossed. The cries began at dusk and continued till dawn. There were many dark demons in the malarial vapours and no man dared cross.

"The sin is mine," said K'ung-ming, "for many of Ma Tai's men perished in these waters beside the southern men. Their poor distressed souls are not yet freed. Therefore I will come this night and sacrifice to them."

"According to the ancient rule the number of victims ought to be forty-nine; then the spirits will disperse," said the natives.

"As the resentful demons are here because of the deaths of men, where is the sense in slaying more men? But this will I do. I will make balls of flour paste after the manner of human heads and stuff them with the flesh of oxen and goats. These shall be used instead of human heads, for indeed they be (punningly) called *man-t'ou*,* heads of Man."

*Bread is called "*man-tou*"

By nightfall, an altar had been set up on the bank of the river with the sacrificial objects all arranged. There were also forty-nine lamps. Flags were flying to summon the souls. The *man-t'ou* were piled up on the ground. In the middle of the third watch, at midnight, K'ung-ming, dressed in Taoist garb, went to offer the sacrifice in person, and he bade Tung Chüeh read this prayer:—

"On the first day of the ninth month of the third year of the period *Chien-Hsing* of the Han Dynasty, I, Chuko Liang, Prime Minister of Han, Marquis of Wuhsiang, Governor of Ichou, reverently order this sacrifice to appease the shades of those men of Shu who have died in their country's service and those of the southern men who have perished. I now declare to you, O ye shades, the majesty of my master, the Emperor of the mighty Han Dynasty, excelling that of the Five Feudatories and brilliantly continuing the glory of the three ancient kings. Recently, when the distant south rebelliously invaded his territory, contumeliously sent an army, loosed the venom of their sorcery, and gave free rein to their savagery in rebellion, I was commanded to punish their crimes. Wherefore my brave armies marched and utterly destroyed the contemptible creatures. My brave soldiers gathered like the clouds, and the insensate rebels melted away. Hearing of the easy successes I won, they were entirely demoralised. My army consists of heroes from the Nine Provinces and officers and men are famous in the empire; all are expert in war and skilled in the use of arms, they go whither light leads them and serve the king. All have exerted themselves to obey orders and carried out the plans for the seven captures of Mênghuo. They were whole-hearted in their service and vied in loyalty. Who could foresee that you, O Spirits, would be sacrificed in the strategy and be involved in the enemies' wicked wiles? Some of you went down to the deep springs wounded by flying arrows; others went out into the long night hurt by lethal weapons. Living you were valorous, dead you left behind a name.

"Now we are returning home. The victors' song is in our mouths and our prisoners accompany us. Your spirits are with us still and certainly hear our prayers. Follow the banners, come with the host, return to your country, each to his own village, where you may enjoy the savour of the meat offerings and receive the sacrifices of your own families. Do not become wandering ghosts in unfamiliar hamlets of restless shades in strange cities. I will memorialise our Emperor that your wives and little ones may enjoy his gracious bounty, every year gifts of food and clothing, every month donations for sustenance. Comfort yourselves with this provision.

"As for you, Spirits of this place, shades of the departed men of the south, here is the usual sacrifice. You are near home. Living you stood in awe of the celestial majesty, dead you come within the sphere of refining influence. It is right that you should hold your peace and refrain from uttering unseemly cries. With bowed head I pray you to partake of the sweet savour of this sacrifice.

"Alas, ye dead! To you this offering!"

K'ung-ming broke into loud lamentations at the end of this prayer and manifested extreme emotion, and the whole army shed tears. Mênghuo and his also moaned and wept, and amid the sad clouds and angry mists they saw the vague forms of many demons floating away on the wind till they disappeared.

The material portion of the sacrifice was then thrown into the river. Next day the army stood on the south bank with a clear sky over their heads and calm waters at their feet, the clouds gone and the winds hushed; and the crossing was made without misadventure. They continued their way, whips cracking, gongs clanging, spurs jingling, and ever and anon the song of victory rising over all.

Passing through Yungch'ang, Wang K'ang and Lü K'ai were left there in command of the four districts, and then Mênghuo was permitted to leave. He was ordered to be diligent in his administration, maintain good control, and soothe and care for the people left to him to govern and to see to it that agriculture was promoted. He took leave with tears rolling down his cheeks.

When the army neared the capital, the Latter Ruler came out in state to welcome his victorious minister. The king stood by the roadside as K'ung-ming came up, and waited.

K'ung-ming quickly descended from his chariot, prostrated himself and said, "Thy servant has offended in causing his master anxiety; but the conquest of the south was long."

His lord took him kindly by the hand and raised him. Then the chariots of the king and his minister returned to Ch'êngtu side by side. In the capital were great rejoicings with banquets and rewards for the army. Henceforward distant lands sent tribute to the court to the number of two hundred.

As proposed in a memorial, the king provided for the families of the soldiers who had lost their lives in the expedition, and they were made happy. And the whole land enjoyed tranquillity.

The King of Wei, Ts'ao P'ei, had now ruled seven years, and it was the fourth year of the king's reign in Shu. Ts'ao P'ei had taken to wife a lady of the Chên family, formerly the wife of the second son of Yüan Shao. He had discovered her at the sack of Yehch'êng and had married her. Shu bore him a son, Jui, also known as Yüan-chung, who was very clever and a great favourite with his father. Later he took as *kuei-fei* a daughter of one Kua Jung. She was a woman of exceeding beauty whom her father called "Queen of Women," and the name stuck to her. But with her arrival at court the Lady Chên fell from her lord's favour, and the *kuei-fei's* ambition led her to intrigue to replace the Empress. She took Chang T'ao, a minister at the court, into her confidence.

At that time the king was indisposed, and Chang alleged that in the palace of the consort had been dug up a wooden image with the king's date of birth written thereon, so that it represented him. It was meant to exercise a maleficent influence. Ts'ao P'ei in his anger put his consort to death; and he set up the *kuei-fei* in her place.

But she had no issue. Wherefore she nourished Jui as her own. However, loved as Jui was, he was not then named heir. When he was about fifteen Jui, who was an expert archer and a daring rider, accompanied his father to the hunt. In a gully they started a doe and its fawn. The king shot the doe, while the fawn fled. Seeing that the fawn's course led past his son's horse the king called out to him to shoot it. Instead the youth bursts into tears.

"Your Majesty has slain the mother; how can one kill the child as well?"

The words struck the king with remorse. He threw aside his bow, saying, "My son, you would make a benevolent and virtuous ruler."

From this circumstance he decided that Jui should succeed, and conferred upon him the princedom of P'ingyüan. In the fifth month the king fell ill, and medical treatment was of no avail. So the chief officers were summoned to the bedside of the king. They were Ts'ao Ch'ên, Ch'ên Chün, Ssŭma I. When they had come, the king's son was called, and the dying king spake thus: "I am grievously ill, and my end is near. I confide to your care and guidance this son of mine; you must support him out of good feeling for me."

"Why does Your Majesty talk thus?" said they. "We will do our utmost to serve you for a thousand autumns and a myriad years."

"No; I know that I am about to die," said the king. "The sudden fall of the city gates was the omen, as I well knew."

Just then the attendants said that Ts'ao Hsiu had come to ask after the king's health. They were told to call him into the chamber. When he had entered, Ts'ao P'ei said to him, "You and these three are the pillars and cornerstones of the state. If you will only uphold my son I can close my eyes in peace."

These were his last words. A flood of tears gushed forth, and he sank back on the couch dead. He was forty years of age and had reigned seven years.

The four ministers raised the wailing for the dead and forthwith busied themselves with setting up Ts'ao Jui as the

Emperor of Ta Wei. The late king received the posthumous style of "Emperor Wên." The new Emperor's mother, the consort who had suffered death, was styled "Empress Wên-chao."

Honours were distributed freely in celebration of the new reign. Chung Yu was made *T'ai-fu;* Ts'ao Chên, General; Ts'ao Hsiu, Minister of War; Hua Hsin a *T'ai-yu;* Ssǔma I became a Cavalry General; and many others, conspicuous and cbscure, were promoted. A general amnesty was declared throughout all the land.

About this time a vacancy existed in the governorship of Yungchou and Hsiliang. Ssǔma I asked for the post and got it. He left for his new office as soon as he had received the appointment.

In due time the news of all these doings reached K'ung-ming and perturbed him not a little. He was anxious, not because of the death of one ruler and the succession of another, but about Ssǔma I, who was very crafty, and who, in command of such forces as were in his two provinces, might prove a serious danger to Shu. He felt that this man ought to be attacked at once.

Ma Su spoke of this matter. "You, O Minister, have just returned from an arduous and exhausting expedition, and you should take time to recuperate before you undertake such another. However, I have a scheme by which Ts'ao Jui may be brought to work the destruction of Ssǔma I. May I lay it before you?"

"What plan have you?" said he.

"The young king has no confidence in Ssǔma I although he is a high minister of state. Now send someone secretly to Loyang and Yehchün to disseminate reports that Ssǔma is about to rebel. Further, prepare a proclamation in his name and post it up so as to cause Ts'ao Jui to mistrust him and put him to death."

K'ung-ming adopted the suggestion. Whence it came about that a notice suddenly appeared on the city gate of Yehch'êng. The wardens of the gate took it down and sent it to Ts'ao Jui. This is what it said: "I, Ssǔma I, *Piao-chi Ta Chiang-chün,* Commander of the Forces of Yung and Liang, confident in the universal principles of right, now inform the empire, saying, the Founder of this Dynasty, the Emperor Wu, established himself with the design of securing the empire to the son of Prince Ch'ên Ssǔ. Unfortunately, calumny spread abroad, and the Emperor could not manifest himself for many years. His grandson, Ts'ao Jui, does not follow a virtuous course, though sitting in the high place, and has not fulfilled the great intention of his ancestor. Now I, in accordance with the will of Heaven and favouring the desires of the people, have decided upon a day to set my army in motion in order to secure the wish of the people, and when that day arrives I call upon each one to gather to his lord; and I will destroy utterly the family of any who shall disobey. You are hereby informed that you may all know."

This document frightened the young king, and he turned pale. At once he called a council of his lords to consider it.

Hua Hsin said, "That was the reason for his having requested the governorship of the two provinces. Now the Founder of your House frequently said to me that Ssǔma I was ambitious and cruel, and should not be entrusted with military authority lest he harm the state. This is the first beginning of rebellion, and the author should be put to death."

Wang Lang said, "Ssǔma I is a master of strategy and skilled in tactics. Moreover, he is ambitious and will cause mischief if he be allowed to live."

Wherefore Ts'ao Jui wrote a command to raise an army, which he would lead to punish the minister. Suddenly Ts'ao Chên stood forth from the rank of military officers and said, "What you advise is impossible. His late Majesty confided his son to the care of certain officers of state, of whom Ssǔma I is one, wherefore it is certain that he felt sure of his probity. So far nothing is known certainly. If you hastily send an army to repress him, you may force him into rebellion. This may be but one of the base tricks of Shu or Wu to cause dissension in our midst so that occasion be found to further their own aims. As no one knows, I pray Your Majesty to reflect before you do anything."

"Supposing Ssǔma I really contemplates a revolt; what then?"

Ts'ao Chên replied, "If Your Majesty suspects him, then do as did Han Kao-Tsu when, under pretence of taking a trip on the lakes Yün and Mêng he summoned his vassals—and seized Han Hsin, who had been denounced. Go to Ani; Ssǔma I will assuredly come out to meet you, and his actions and demeanour may be watched closely. He can be arrested if need be."

Ts'ao Jui changed his mind. Leaving Ts'ao Chên to regulate the affairs of state, the young king went out with the Imperial Guards, to the number of ten legions, and travelled to Ani. Ignorant of the reason of his coming, and anxious to show off his dignity, Ssǔma I went to welcome his ruler in all the pomp of a commander of a great army. As he approached, the courtiers told the king that Ssǔma I's defection was certain since such a large army could only mean that he was prepared to resist. Whereupon Ts'ao Hsiu, with a large force, was sent in front to meet him. Ssǔma I distrusted this show of force, but he advanced alone and stood humbly by the roadside till Ts'ao Hsiu came up.

Ts'ao Hsiu advanced and said, "Friend, His late Majesty entrusted you with the heavy responsibility of caring for his son; why are you in revolt?"

Ssŭma I turned pale, and a cold sweat broke out all over him as he asked the reason for such a charge. Ts'ao Hsiu told him what had occurred.

"This is a vile plot on the part of our rivals to cause dissension," said he. "It is a design to make the Emperor work evil upon his ministers that thereby another may profit. I must see the Son of Heaven and explain."

Ordering his army to retire, he went forward alone to the Emperor's chariot, bowed low and said, weeping, "His late Majesty gave me charge of his son; could I betray him? This is a wile of the enemy. I crave permission to lead an army, first to destroy Shu and then to attack Wu, whereby to show my gratitude to the late Emperor and Your Majesty and manifest my own true heart."

However, Jui did not feel quite convinced, and Hua Hsin said, "In any case withdraw his military powers and let him go into retirement."

And thus it was decided. Ssŭma I retired to his native village. Ts'ao Hsiu succeeded to his command, and Jui returned to Loyang.

K'ung-ming rejoiced when they told him of the success that had attended the ruse.

"Ssŭma I and the forces he commanded have been the obstacles in my long-wished-for attack on Wei. Now he has fallen I have no more anxiety."

At the first great assembly of officers at court K'ung-ming stepped forth and presented a memorial on the expedition he contemplated.

"The late Emperor had accomplished but half his great task at his death. At this moment the empire is in three parts, and our country is weak; it is a most critical moment for us. Still, ministers are not remiss in the capital, and loyal and devoted soldiers sacrifice their lives abroad, for they still remember the special kindness of the late Emperor and wish to show their gratitude to him by service to Your Majesty. Therefore it would be indeed fitting that you should extend your holy virtue to glorify his virtuous memory in the stimulation of the will of your purposeful officers. Your Majesty should not lose yourself in the pursuit of mean things, quoting phrases to confound the eternal principles of rectitude and so preventing remonstrance from honest men. One rule applies to the palace of the Emperor and the residence of a courtier; there must be one law rewarding the good and punishing the evil. Evil-doers and law-breakers, as also true and good men, should be dealt with according to their deserts by the officers concerned in order to manifest Your Majesty's impartial and enlightened administration. Partiality is wrong, as is one law for the court and another for the provinces.

"The high officers Kuo Yu-chih, Fei I and Tung Yün are honest men, devotedly anxious to be loyal to the last degree; wherefore His late Majesty chose them in his testament. My advice is to consult them in all palace matters, great or small, before taking action. Your Majesty will reap the enormous advantage of having any failings corrected.

"General Hsiang Ch'ung is a man of well-balanced temperament, versed in military matters, to whom, after testing him, the late Emperor applied the epithet 'capable.' The concensus of opinion is that he should be Commander-in-chief. My advice is to consult him in all military matters, great or small, whereby your military forces will yield their maximum, each one being employed to the best advantage.

"Attract worthy men; repel mean men. This policy achieved the glory of the Former Hans, while its reversal ruined the Latter Hans. When the late Emperor was with us he often discussed this with your servant, and he took much to heart the story of Huan and Ling.

"President Ch'ên Chên and Historian Chiang Wan are both incorruptible and enlightened men, honest to the death. I would that Your Majesty should have them near and hold them in confidence. If this be done, then the glory of the House of Han will be quickly consummated.

"I was originally a private person, a farmer in Nanyang, concerned only to secure personal safety in a troubled age and not seeking conversation with the contending nobles. His late Majesty, overlooking the commonness of my origin, condescended to seek me thrice in my humble cot and consult me on the trend of events. His magnanimity affected me deeply, and I consented to do my utmost for him. Then came defeat, and I took office at a moment of darkest outlook and at a most difficult crisis. This is twenty-one years ago. The late Emperor recognised my diligent care, and when dying he confided the great task to me. From that day I have lived a life of anxiety lest I should fail in my trust and so dim his glory. That is why I undertook the expedition to the wastes beyond the Lu River. Now the south has been quelled, and our army is in good condition. I ought to lead it against the north, where I may meet with a measure of success in the removal of the wicked ones, the restoration of Han and a return to the old capital. This is my duty out of gratitude to the late Emperor and loyalty to Your Majesty. As to a discussion of the pros and cons and giving a true version of the whole matter, that belongs to Kuo and Chiang and Tung. I desire Your Majesty to confide to me the task of slaying the rebels and restoring the Hans. If I fail, then punish me by telling the spirit of the late Emperor. If you know not what restoration implies that is the fault of your advisers.

"Your Majesty should take pains to be guided into the right path and examine carefully what is laid before you, carefully remembering the late Emperor's testament.

"I cannot express what would be my delight if you had the goodness to accept and act on my advice.

"Now I am about to depart on a distant expedition I write this with tears and scarce know what I have said."

The king read it through and said, "My Father-Minister, you have only just returned from a distant and fatiguing expedition; you are not yet refreshed, and I fear this march to the north will be almost too much even for you."

K'ung-ming replied, "The heaviest responsibility lies upon me, the well-being of Your Majesty confided to me by the late Emperor. My efforts may not be relaxed night or day. The south is at rest, at home is no anxiety; what better time could be hoped for to destroy the rebels and recover the capital?

Forth from the ranks of courtiers stood Ch'iao Chou and said, "I have studied the aspect of the stars; the northern quarter is brilliant and strong. The scheme will not speed." Then turning toward the Prime Minister, he continued, "You, O Minister, understand the mysteries of the skies; why do you oppose the stars?"

"Because the stars are not in their courses," replied K'ung-ming; "they have been disturbed. One may rely on the stars too much. Moreover, I have already sent the army into Hanchung, where I shall act as soon as I have studied what is afoot."

Ch'iao Chou pleaded in vain; K'ung-ming was too strongly set upon his purpose to yield. So Kuo Yu-chih, Tung Yun and Fei I were ordered to attend to matters in the palace; Hsiang Ch'ung was to control all military affairs and forces. Many special appointments were made; Ch'ên Chên became *Shih-chung;* Chiang Wan became *Ts'an-chün;* Chang I, Controller of the Prime Minister's palace; Tu Ch'iung was created Censor; Tu Wei and Yang Hung, Presidents; Mêng Kuang and Lai Min, Libationers; Yin Mo and Li Chuan, *Po-shih;* Ch'i Chêng and Fei Shih, Private Secretaries; Ch'iao Chou, a *T'ai-shih;* and others to the number of over a hundred, all to control the administration of Shu in the absence of Chuko Liang.

After having received his Emperor's command to lead an expedition against the north, K'ung-ming returned to his palace and summoned the officers of the army to listen to the orders. And they came, and to each was appointed a duty in the great army of Chuko Liang, Commander-in-chief of the North-conquering Expedition, Prime Minister of Shu, Marquis of Wu-hsiang, Governor of Ichou, Director of Internal and External Affairs.

Li Yen was given the task of guarding the country against Wu.

All being ready, a day was chosen for the start, the fifth year, the third month on the day *ping-yen*.

After the appointments had all been made, there came forward a veteran who had listened in vain for the duty assigned him.

"Old I may be," said he, "yet have I still the valour of Lien P'o, the heroism of Ma Yüan. Why am I thought useless any more than these two who refused to acknowledge old age?"

It was Chao Yün.

K'ung-ming said, "I have lost my friend Ma Ch'ao by illness since I returned from the south, and I feel as I had lost an arm. Now, General, you must own that the years are mounting up. Any slight lapse would not only shake the life-long reputation of yourself, but might have a bad effect on the whole army."

Chao replied bitterly, "I have never quailed in the presence of the enemy from the day I first joined the late Emperor; I have ever pressed to the front. It is a happy ending for a man of valour to die on the frontier. Think you that I should resent it? Let me lead the van, I pray."

K'ung-ming used all his skill to dissuade the veteran, but in vain; he was set on it, threatening suicide if this honour was refused him. At last K'ung-ming yielded on the condition that he would accept a colleague.

"I will go to help the veteran leader," cried Têng Chih, without a moment's hesitation. "I am not worth much, but I will help lead the attack on the enemy."

Accordingly five companies of veterans were chosen for the advanced guard, and with them, to assist Chao Yün, went Têng Chih and half a score of lesser captains.

After the vanguard had set out, the main body marched by the north gate, the Emperor himself going to see his minister start. The farewell was taken ten *li* from the gate, in the face of the grand army with its banners and pennons flaunting in the wind, and spears and swords gleaming in the sun. Then they took the road leading to Hanchung.

Naturally, this movement was duly reported in Loyang at a court held by Ts'ao Jui, when a minister said, "A report from the border stations says that Chuko Liang has marched thirty legions into Hanchung. Chao Yün and Têng Chih are leading the advanced guard."

The report alarmed the king, and he asked who could lead an army to repel the advance. At once out spake one, saying, "My father died in Hanchung, and to my bitter resentment his death is unavenged. Now I desire to lead the army against Shu, and I pray that the armies west of the Pass may be given me for this purpose. As well as taking vengeance for my private wrong I shall render a service to the state. I care not what fate may befall me."

The speaker was Hsiahou Yüan's son Mou. He was by nature very impulsive and also very miserly. When young he had been adopted by Hsiahou Tun. When Hsiahou Yüan was killed by Huang Chung, Ts'ao Ts'ao had taken pity on him and married him to one of his daughters, Ching-ho (or Clear River), so that he was an Emperor's son-in-law. As such he enjoyed great deference at court. But although he held a military commission, he had never been with the army. However, as he requested the command he was made Commander-in-chief to get the army ready to march.

The Minister Wang Lang spoke against the appointment, saying, "The appointment is wrong. Hsiahou, the "Son-in-law," has never seen a battle and is unsuitable for this post, especially when his opponent is the clever and crafty Chuko Liang, a man thoroughly versed in strategy."

"I suppose you have arranged with Chuko Liang to be his ally," sneered Hsiahou. "Ever since I was a boy I have studied strategy, and I am well acquainted with army matters. Why do you despise my youth? Unless I capture this Chuko Liang I pledge myself never again to see the Emperor's face."

Wang Lang and his supporters were silenced. Hsiahou took leave of the King of Wei and hastened to Changan to get his army in order. He had a score of legions.

> He would go to battle, take the signal flags in grip,
> But could he play the leader, he a lad with callow lip?

The next chapter will deal with this campaign.

CHAPTER VIIIC.

CHAO YÜN SLAYS FIVE CAPTAINS;
K'UNG-MING CRAFTILY TAKES THREE CITIES.

K'ung-ming's army marched northward, passing through Mienyang, where stood Ma Ch'ao's tomb. In honour of the dead hero, K'ung-ming sacrificed there in person, Ma Ch'ao's brother being chief mourner for the occasion.

After this ceremony, when the Commander-in-chief was discussing his plans, the spies came in to tell him that Ts'ao Jui had put in motion an army under Hsiahou Mou. Then Wei Yen went in to offer a complicated and lengthy ruse, saying, "Hsiahou Mou is a fatling, soft and stupid. Give me five companies, and I will go out by Paochung, follow the line of the Ts'inling east to the Tzŭwu Valley and then turn north. In ten days I can be at Ch'angan. Hearing of my intent, Hsiahou will hasten to get out of my way. He must go by way of Hêngmen and Tiko. I will come in by the east, and you, Sir, can advance by the Hsieh Valley. In this way all west of Hsienyang will be ours."

K'ung-ming smiled at the suggestion. "I do not think the plan quite perfect," said he. "You are misled by thinking there is no one worth considering guarding the capital. If anyone suggest sending a force across by way of Shanpichung we should be lucky if we lost only half a legion, to say nothing of the check to our *élan*. The ruse will not do."

"If you, O Minister, march by the high road they will bring against you the whole host within the Pass and will thus hold you indefinitely; you will never get to the capital."

"But I shall go along the level road on the right of Shênsi. I cannot fail if I keep to the fixed rules of war."

Wei Yen withdrew, gloomy and dissatisfied. Then Chao Yün sent orders to the advanced guard to move.

Hsiahou Mou was at Ch'angan preparing his force. There came to him a certain captain from Hsiliang, named Han Tê, a man of great valour, whose weapon was a mighty battle-axe called "Mountain Splitter." He brought with him eight legions of the *Ch'iang* and offered his services. They were gladly accepted, and his army was made the van of the attack.

This Han Tê had four sons, all very expert in archery and horsemanship. They were named Ying, Yao, Ch'iung and Ch'i, and they came to serve under their father. Han Tê led his sons and the eight legions by the road to Fengming Hill

(The Hill of the Phœnix Song), where they were near the men of Shu, and here they drew up the array.

When the battle line was in order, the father, with his four sons, rode to the front and began to revile their enemy as rebels and raiders. Chao Yün quickly lost his temper, rode forward and challenged. The eldest son, Yin, accepted and galloped out; but he was slain in the third bout. Immediately his brother Yao went out, whirling his sword. But now Chao Yün's blood was up, and the old dash and vigour came upon him so that the young man had no chance. Then the third son, Ch'iung, took his great halberd and dashed out to his brother's aid. Chao Yün had now two opponents; nevertheless he held his own, nor blenched nor failed a stroke. Seeing that his two brothers were nearing defeat, the fourth son went to join in the fray with his pair of swords that he had named "Sun and Moon." And there was the veteran warrior with three against him, and he still kept them at bay.

Presently a spear thrust got home on Han Ch'i, who fell. Another captain then coming out to take his place, Chao Yün lowered his spear and fled. Han Ch'iung then took his bow and shot three arrows at the fugitive, who turned them aside so that they fell harmless. Angry at this, Han Ch'iung again seized his halberd and went in pursuit. But Chao Yün took his bow and shot an arrow that wounded his pursuer in the face. So he fell and died. Han Yao then galloped up and raised his sword to strike, but Chao Yün slipped past, got within his guard and made Yao a prisoner. He quickly galloped into his own array with his captive, dropped him and then, dashing out, recovered his spear, which had fallen when he seized his man.

Han Tê was overwhelmed with the loss of all his sons and went behind the array. His barbarians were too frightened at the prowess of Chao Yün to be of any use in battle, and no one dared to meet the old warrior. So they retired, while Chao Yün rode to and fro among them slaying at his will.

I thought of brave old men, of Chao Tzŭlung,
Who, spite of numbered years three score and ten,
Was marvellous strong in battle; who one day
Slew four opposing captains, greater feat
Than when at Tangyang he had saved his king.

Seeing the successful battle that Chao Yün was waging, Têng Chih led on his men to join in the fight. This completed the discomfiture of the Hsiliang men, and they ran away. Han Tê, seeing the danger of being captured, threw off his armour and went on foot. The men of Shu drew off and returned to their camp.

In camp Têng Chih felicitated his veteran colleague.

"For a man of seventy years you are unique and wonderful," said he. "You are as much the hero as you ever were. It is almost an incomparable feat to have slain four captains in one day."

"Yet the minister thought me too old and did not wish to employ me. I had to give him a proof."

The captive Han Yao was sent to the main body with the messenger who bore an account of the victory.

In the meantime, Han Tê led his defeated army back to his chief, to whom he related his sad story with many tears. Then Hsiahou Mou decided to lead his own army out against Chao Yün.

When the scouts reported his coming, the veteran took his spear and mounted his steed. He led one company out to Fêngming Hill, at the foot of which he made his array. On the day of the battle Hsiahou Mou wore a golden casque, rode a white horse and carried a huge sword. From his place beneath the great standard he saw Chao Yün galloping to and fro. He was going out to give battle, when Han Tê checked him.

"Is it not mine to avenge my four sons?" said he.

He seized his axe, the "Mountain Splitter," and rode directly at the hero, who advanced with fury. The contest was but short, for in the third encounter Chao Yün's spear thrust brought Han Tê to the earth. Without waiting a moment he made for Hsiahou Mou, who hastily dashed in behind his ranks and so escaped. Then Têng Chih led on the main body and completed the victory. The men of Wei retired ten *li* and made a camp.

This first battle having gone against him, Hsiahou called his officers to consult. He said he could now credit the story of Chao Yün's stand at Tangyang and that, alone, he had fought against a whole host and come out victor. But what to be done against such a champion?

Then Ch'êng Wu, an adviser, said, "My opinion is that this Chao, though brave in the field, is lacking in the council chamber. Really he is not greatly to be feared. Give battle again soon, but first prepare an ambush. You can retreat and so draw him into it. Then go up on the hill top and direct the attack from that point of vantage so that he may be hemmed in on all sides and be captured."

The necessary plans for this were made, and two parties of three legions each, led by Tung Hsi and Hsüeh Tsê, went into ambush right and left. The ambush laid, Hsiahou Mou advanced once more to attack, drums rolling and flags flying. As soon as he appeared Chao Yün and Têng Chih went to meet him.

Têng Chih said, "The men of Wei were beaten only yesterday. This renewed attempt must mean that they are trying some trick. You should be cautious, General."

"I do not think this youth, with the smell of mother's milk still on his lips, worth talking about. We shall surely capture him to-day."

Chao Yün pranced out, and P'an Sui came to meet him from the side of Wei. But P'an Sui made no stand and quickly ran away. Chao Yün pursued. Then there came out to stop him no less than eight captains of Wei, all of whom passed in front of Hsiahou. But one by one they too fled. Chao Yün pressed forward at full spead, Têng Chih coming up behind.

When Chao Yün had got deeply involved, with the battle raging all around him, Têng Chih decided to retire. This was the signal for the ambush to come out, and Têng was so hampered that he could not attempt to rescue his colleague. Chao Yün was thus entirely surrounded. However, he struggled on, losing men at every dash, till he had but one company left. He was then at the foot of the hill whence Hsiahou Mou was directing operations, and observing his enemy from this point of vantage, he sent men to check him whithersoever he went. Chao decided to charge up the hill, but was stopped by rolling baulks of timber and tumbling rocks.

The battle had lasted long, and Chao Yün was fatigued. So he halted to rest a time, intending to renew the struggle when the moon should be up. But just as he had taken off his armour the moon rose and, with it, his enemies began to attack with fire as well, and the thunder of the drums was accompanied by showers of stones and arrows. The oncoming host shouted to him to yield. However, he did not think of that, but got upon his steed to strive once more to extricate himself. And his enemies pressed closer and closer, pouring in flights and flights of arrows. No advance was possible, and the end seemed very near.

"I refused the repose of age," sighed he, "and now my end will come to me here."

Just then he heard new shouting from the north-east, and to his joy he saw Chang Pao coming toward him, his father's long spear in his hand and a man's head hanging at his bridle. Soon he reached the old man's side and cried, "The minister feared some misfortune had befallen you, so he sent me to your help I have half a legion here. We heard that you were surrounded. On the way I met Hsüeh Tsê and slew him."

Chao Yün's courage revived, and he and the young captain went on toward the south-west, driving the men of Wei before them in disorder. Soon another cohort came in from the side, the leader wielding a huge curved sword. This was Kuan Hsing, and he used the same words that his cousin had used, only that the enemy he had encountered, and slain, was Tung Hsi.

"Here is his head," cried he, "and the minister is coming up too."

"But why not press on to capture Hsiahou Mou since you have had such wonderful success?" cried Chao Yün.

Chang Pao took the hint and went forward. Kuan Hsing followed.

"They are as my own," said Chao Yün to those who stood near. "And they press on wherever there is merit to be won. I am an old leader and high in rank, but I am not worth so much as these two youths. Yet will I risk my life once more for the sake of my old lord the late Emperor."

So he led the remnant of his men to try to capture Hsiahou Mou.

During that night the army of Wei was smitten till corpses covered the earth and gore ran in rivers. Hsiahou was unskilful, and young, and inexperienced in battle. His army was in utter rout, and he could only flee. At the head of a few survivors he made for Nananchün. His army, leaderless, scattered like rats.

Kuan Hsing and Chang Pao set out for Nananchün. At the news of their coming Hsiahou Mou closed the city gates and urged his men to defend. Chao Yün soon joined the captains, and they attacked on three sides. Têng Chih arrived also, and the city was quite surrounded.

After vain efforts for ten days, they heard that of the main body of the army some had occupied Yangp'ing, others Shih-ch'êng, while K'ung-ming was leading the centre toward them. The four captains went to visit him and told him their ill-success at the city. He got into his light chariot and rode out to view the city, after which he returned and summoned the officers to his tent.

He said, "The moat is deep, the walls are steep; wherefore the city is well defended and difficult to take. My present plan omits this place. If you persist in the attack and the Wei armies march to try for Hanchung our army will be in danger."

"Consider what the capture of Hsiahou Mou would mean," said Têng Chih. "He is a Son-in-law, and worth more than slaying a hundred ordinary leaders. We have begun the siege, and I do not like to raise it."

K'ung-ming said, "I have other plans. West of this lies T'ienshuichün and north Antingchün; does any one know the Prefects of these two places?"

"Ma Sun is the Prefect of T'ienshui; Ts'ui Liang that of Anting," replied a scout.

K'ung-ming then called to him one by one Wei Yen, Chang Pao, Kuan Hsing and two soldiers he could depend upon, and gave each certain instructions. They left to carry out their orders.

Next K'ung-ming ordered the soldiers to pile up beneath the walls heaps of firewood and straw, saying he was going to burn the city. The defenders on the wall derided him.

The Prefect of Anting was much frightened when he heard that Hsiahou Mou was besieged, and began to see to his own defences. He mustered his four companies of soldiers, resolved to defend his city as long as possible. Then there came a man from the south, who said he had secret letters. The Prefect had him brought into the city, and, when questioned, the man replied that he was one of Hsiahou's trusted soldiers named P'ei Hsü, sent to beg for help from T'ienshui and Anting.

"The city is hard pressed; every day they have raised fires to call the attention of your cities to their plight, but their signals have all failed. No one has come. I was ordered to fight my way through the besiegers and come to tell you. You are to give assistance immediately, and our general will open the gates to help you."

"Have you a letter from the general?" asked the Prefect.

A letter was produced from inside the man's dress, all moist with perspiration. After the Prefect had read it the soldier took it back and went on to T'ienshui.

Two days later a mounted messenger came to say that the T'ienshui men had already started for Nanan, and he urged the Anting men to march at once.

Ts'ui Liang took the advice of his officers. Most of them said, "If you do not go, and Nanan is taken, we shall be blamed for giving up the Son-in-law. He must be rescued."

Thereupon the Prefect marched; the civil officers were left in charge of the city. The little army took the high road to Nanan. They saw flames shooting up to the sky all the time. When fifty *li* from the city, there was heard the drums of an attacking force, and the scouts came to say that the road ahead was held by Kuan Hsing, while Chang Pao was coming up quickly in their rear.

At this news the soldiers scattered in all directions. The Prefect had a few men left with whom he tried to cut his way out that he might return to his own city. He got through. But when he came to his own city a flight of arrows greeted him from the wall, and Wei Yen shouted to him, saying, "I have taken the city; you had better yield."

This was what had happened. Wei Yen, disguised as an Anting soldier, in the darkness of the night had beguiled the wardens of the gate into opening it, and the men of Shu had got in.

Ts'ui Liang set off for T'ienshui. But one march away a cohort came out, and beneath the great flag he saw a light chariot. In the chariot sat a man in Taoist robe with a feather fan in his hand. He at once recognised K'ung-ming, but as he turned, up came Kuan and Chang, who summoned him to surrender. As he was entirely surrounded, no other course was open to him, so he gave in. He went to the great camp with K'ung-ming, who treated him with courtesy.

After a time K'ung-ming said, "Is the Prefect of Nanan a friend of yours?"

"He is one Yang Ling, a brother of Yang Fou. Being neighbouring districts we are very good friends.'

"I wish to trouble you to persuade him to capture Hsiahou Mou; can you?"

"If you, O Minister, order me to do this, I would ask you to withdraw your men and let me go into the city to speak with him."

K'ung-ming consented and ordered the besiegers to draw off twenty *li* and camp. Ts'ui Liang himself went to the city and hailed the gate. He entered and went forthwith to his friend's residence. As soon as he had finished the salutations, he related what had happened.

"After the kindness we have received from Wei we cannot be traitors," said Yang Ling. "But we will meet ruse with ruse."

He led Ts'ui Liang to the general and told the whole story. "What ruse do you propose?" asked Hsiahou Mou.

"Let us pretend to offer the city, and let the men of Shu in. Once they are in we can massacre them."

Ts'ui Liang agreed to take a share in this scheme, and went back to K'ung-ming's camp, where he told the necessary tale, adding that Yang Ling's men were too few and he wanted help.

"That is simple enough," replied K'ung-ming. "Your hundred men are here. We can mix with them some of my captains dressed as your officers and so let them get into the city. They can hide in Hsiahou's dwelling and arrange with Yang to open the gates in the night."

Ts'ui Liang thought within himself that not to take the Shu captains would arouse suspicion. So he agreed, determining to kill them as soon as they got within the walls. Then, thought he, he would give the signal and beguile K'ung-ming to enter, and so dispose of him.

So he consented to K'ung-ming's proposal, and K'ung-ming gave him instructions, saying, "I will send my trusty Kuan Hsing and Chang Pao with you. You will pass them off as the rescuers just to set Hsiahou Mou's mind at rest. But when you raise a fire I shall take that as my signal and come in."

At dusk the two trusty captains, having received their secret orders, put on their armour, mounted, took their weapons and got in among the Anting men. Ts'ui Liang led the small force to the gate. Yang Ling was on the wall. The drawbridge was hoisted. He leaned over the guard rail and scanned the men below.

"Who are you?" asked he.

"We are rescuers from Anting."

Now Ts'ui shot an arrow over the wall, to which a secret letter was bound, saying, "Chuko Liang is sending two captains into the city that they may help him to get in, but do nothing till we get inside lest the ruse gets known and the game be spoiled."

Yang went to show this letter to the general, who said, "Then Chuko Liang is going to be our victim. Put a company of axe and bill men in the palace, and as soon as these two captains get inside shut the gates and fall on. Then give the signal. As soon as Chuko gets inside the gate, seize him."

All arrangements being made, Yang Ling went back to the wall and said, "Since you are Anting men you may be allowed in."

The gate was thrown open and, while Kuan followed close after Ts'ui, Chang Pao was a little way behind. Yang Ling came down to the gate to welcome them. As soon as Kuan got near he lifted his sword and smote Yang, who fell headless. Ts'ui Liang was startled and lashed his steed to flee.

Chang Pao cried, "Scoundrel! Did you think your vile plot would be hidden from the eyes of our master?"

With that Ts'ui fell from a spear thrust. Then Kuan went up on the wall and lit the fire. Soon the men of Shu filled the city. Hsiahou Mou could make no defence, so he tried to fight his way through the south gate. There he met Wang P'ing and was captured. Those with him were slain.

K'ung-ming entered the city and at once forbade all plunder. The various captains reported the deeds of valour. The captive general was placed in a prisoner's cart.

Then Têng Chih asked how the treachery of Ts'ui Liang had been discovered.

"I knew the man was unwilling in his heart to yield, so I sent him into the city that he might have a chance to weave a counter plot with Hsiahou Mou. I saw by his manner he was treacherous, and so I sent my two trusty captains with him to give him a feeling of security. Had he been true to me he would have opposed this, but he accepted it gaily and went with them lest I should suspect him. He thought they could slay my two men and entice me in. But my two men already had orders what to do. Everything turned out as I thought, and as they did not expect."

The officers bowed their appreciation of his wonderful insight.

Then K'ung-ming said, "I sent one of my trusty men to pretend he was a certain P'ei Hsü of Wei and so deceive this Ts'ui Liang. I also sent another to T'ienshui to do the same, but nothing has happened yet; I do not know the reason. We will capture the place."

It was decided to take T'ienshui next, and thither they
moved, leaving guards at Anting and Nanan.

When Ma Tsun, Prefect of T'ienshui, heard of Hsiahou
Mou's disaster he called a council at which one party were
strongly of opinion that a rescue should be attempted.

"If anything sinister happens to 'Son-in-law' Hsiahou,
'Golden Branch' and 'Jade Leaf' as he is, we shall be held
guilty of having made no attempt to save him. Wherefore,
Prefect, you must do all you can," said they.

Ma Tsun found decision difficult, and while thinking over
what was best to do the arrival of P'ei Hsü, a messenger from
Hsiahou Mou, was announced. P'ei was taken to the Prefect's
residence and there produced his despatch and asked for aid.
Soon came another man saying that the Anting men had set
out and calling upon Ma Tsun to hasten. This decided him,
and he prepared his men.

Then an cutsider came in and said, "O Prefect, you are the
sport of one of Chuko Liang's wiles."

All looked at him with surprise. He was one Chiang Wei,
son of a former local official who had died in the king's service.
Chiang Wei was well up in books, seeming to have read
everything, and was also skilled in all warlike exercises. He
had studied books on war. He was a very filial son and much
esteemed. He held military rank.

Chiang Wei said to the Prefect, "I hear Chuko Liang has
defeated Hsiahou, who is now in Nanan most closely besieged.
How then can this messenger have got out? P'ei is an
unknown officer whom no one has heard of, and this messenger from Anting bears no despatch. The fact is the men are
imposters sent to beguile you into leaving your city undefended
so that it may be the more easily captured."

The Prefect began to understand. He thanked Chiang for
his caution. Then Chiang said, "But do not be anxious; I
have a scheme by which we can capture Chuko Liang and
relieve Nanan."

> The fates all changing bring the man that's needed,
> And warlike skill comes from a source unheeded.

The next chapter will unfold the ruse proposed by Chiang
Wei.

CHAPTER VIIC.

CHIANG WEI GOES OVER TO K'UNG-MING;
K'UNG-MING REVILES WANG LANG, WHO DIES.

Chiang Wei propounded his scheme of defence, saying, "Chuko Liang will lay an ambush behind the city, induce our soldiers to go out and then take advantage of its undefended state to capture it. Now give me three companies of good men, and I will place them in ambush at a certain critical place. Lead your men out, but go slowly and not too far, and then turn to retire. However, look out for a signal, and if you see one, attack, for the attack will be double. If Chuko is there himself we shall capture him."

The Prefect adopted this plan, gave the needed men to Chiang Wei, who marched at once, and then went forth himself with Liang Ch'ien. Only two civil officials were left to guard the city.

Chao Yün had been sent to lie in ambush in a secret place among the hills till the T'ienshui men left the city, when he was to rush in and capture it. His spies reported the departure of the Prefect, and he sent on the news to those who were acting with him, Chang I and Kao Hsiang, that they might attack Ma Tsun.

Chao Yün and his five companies then quickly marched to the city wall and called out, "I am Chao Tzŭ-lung of Ch'ang-shan; you have fallen into our trap you know, but if you will surrender quickly you will save many lives."

But instead of being alarmed Liang Hsü looked down and said, "On the contrary, you have fallen into our trap; only you do not know it yet."

Chao Yün began his attack on the walls. Soon there was heard a roar, and fire broke out all round, and forth came a youthful leader armed with a spear, riding a curvetting steed.

"Look at me, Chiang of T'ienshui!" cried he.

Chao Yün made at him, but after a few bouts he found Chiang Wei was getting too much for him. He was surprised, and wondered who the youngling could be, for he had never heard that such a man belonged to T'ienshui. As the fight went on along came the other forces under Ma Tsun and his colleague, now returning. As Chao Yün found he could not prevail, he set to cut his way through and lead off his defeated men. He was pursued, but the timely interposition of his colleagues saved him, and he got away safely.

K'ung-ming was surprised when he heard what had happened.

"Who is this," said he, "who has thus seen into the dark depths of my secret plan?"

A man of Nanan, who happened to be there, told him Chiang's name and all about him. Chao Yün also praised his skill with the spear, which was superior to any other's.

K'ung-ming said, "I want to take T'ienshui now; I did not expect to find such a man as this."

The Shu army then advanced in force. Chiang Wei went back to Ma Tsun and said, "Chao Yün's defeat will bring up K'ung-ming with the main body. He will conclude that we shall be in the city, wherefore you had better divide your force into four. I, with one party, will go into hiding on the east so that I may cut off our enemies if they come that way. You, O Prefect, and two other leaders, had better lie in ambush on the other sides of the city. Let Liang Hsü and the common people go up on the wall."

K'ung-ming's general orders were to proceed at once to attack a city from the first moment they reached it, and by the rolling of drums incite and urge the men to advance with a rush. The keenness of the men would be spoiled by any delay.

So this time also the army came straight up to the rampart. But they hesitated and dared not attack when they saw the flags flying in such good order and apparently such thorough preparation.

About the middle of the night, fires started up all around and a great shouting was heard. No one could see whence the soldiers were coming, but there were answering shouts from the wall. The men of Shu grew frightened and ran. K'ung-ming mounted a horse and, with Kuan Hsing and Chang Pao as escort, got out of danger. Looking back, they saw many mounted men with torches winding along like a huge serpent. K'ung-ming bade Kuan Hsing find out what this meant, and when he heard that these were Chiang Wei's men, he remarked that an army owed more to its leading than to its numbers.

"This man Chiang is a true genius," mused he.

He led the army back to camp, and then he thought for a long time. Suddenly he called up one of the Anting men and said, "Where is the mother of this Chiang Wei?"

"She lives in Chihsien," replied he.

Kung-ming called Wei Yen and said to him, "March off with a body of men, giving out that you are going to take Chihsien. If Chiang Wei comes up let him enter the city.

"What is the most important place in connection with this place?" asked K'ung-ming.

The man replied, "The storehouse of T'ienshui is at Shangkuei; if that is taken the supplies are cut off."

This was good news, so Chao Yün was sent to attack Shangkuei while K'ung-ming made a camp some distance south of the city.

The spies took the news of the movements of these three forces into T'ienshui. When Chiang Wei heard that one army was to attack his own place he pleaded with Ma Tsun the Prefect to let him go to its defence, that he might keep the city and do his duty by his mother at the same time. So he received command of three companies and marched toward his home.

When Chiang Wei came near the walls he saw a cohort under Wei Yen. He attacked. After a show of defence Wei Yen retreated, and Chiang entered the city. He closed the gates and prepared to defend the wall. Then he went home to see his mother.

In the same way Liang Ch'ien was allowed to enter Shangkuei.

Then K'ung-ming sent for his prisoner, Hsiahou Mou, and, when he was brought to his tent, said suddenly. "Are you afraid of death?"

Hsiahou prostrated himself and begged for his life.

"Well, Chiang Wei of T'ienshui, who is now gone to guard Chihsien, has sent a letter to say that he would surrender if only that would secure your safety. Now I am going to let you go if you will promise to induce Chiang Wei to come over to me. Do you accept the condition?"

"I am willing to induce him to yield to you," said Hsiahou Mou.

K'ung-ming then gave his prisoner clothing and a horse and let him ride away. Nor did he send anyone to follow him, but let him choose his own road.

Having got outside, Hsiahou wanted to get away, but he was perfectly ignorant of the roads and knew not which to take. Presently he came across some people, apparently in flight, and he questioned them.

"We are Chihsien people," said they. "Chiang Wei has surrendered the city and deserted to Chuko Liang. The men of Shu are looting and burning, and we have escaped. We are going to Shangkuei."

"Do you know who is holding T'ienshui?"

"The Prefect Ma is in there," said they.

Hearing this, Hsiahou rode quickly toward T'ienshui. Presently he met more people, evidently fugitives, leading sons and carrying daughters, who told the same story. By and by he came to the gate of the city, and, as he was recognised, the wardens of the gate admitted him, and the Prefect came to greet him and asked of his adventures. He told all that had happened, that Chiang Wei had surrendered and related what the fugitives had said.

"I did not think Chiang Wei would have gone over to Shu," said the Prefect sadly.

"It seems he thought by this to save you, General," said Liang Hsü. "I am sure he has made only a pretence of surrendering."

"Where is the pretence when it is a fact that he has surrendered?" said Hsiahou.

They were all perplexed. Then at the watch-setting the men of Shu came to begin an attack. The fires round the wall were very bright, and there in the glare was seen Chiang Wei, armed and riding up and down under the ramparts calling out for Hsiahou Mou.

Hsiahou Mou and the Prefect ascended the wall, whence they saw Chiang Wei swaggering to and fro. Seeing the chiefs on the wall, he called out, "I surrendered for the sake of you, General; why have you gone back on your word?"

"Why did you surrender to Shu after enjoying so much of Wei's bounty?" said Hsiahou. "And why do you talk thus?"

"What do you mean talking thus after writing me a letter telling me to surrender? You want to secure your own safety by involving me. But I have surrendered, and as I am a superior captain in their service now, I see no sense in returning to Wei."

So saying, he urged the men on to the attack. The assault continued till dawn, when the besiegers drew off.

Now the appearance of Chiang Wei in this fashion was but a ruse. K'ung-ming had found among his men one who resembled Chiang Wei and had disguised him so that Chiang Wei appeared to be leading the attack on the ramparts. In the smoke and fire during the night no one could penetrate the disguise.

K'ung-ming then led the army to attack Chihsien. The grain in the city was insufficient to feed the people. From the wall Chiang Wei saw waggons of grain and forage being driven into Wei Yen's camp, and he determined to try to secure some. So he led three companies out of the city to attack the train of waggons. As soon as he appeared the convoy abandoned the carts and fled. Chiang Wei seized them, and was taking them into the city, when he was met by a cohort under the command of Chang I. They fought. After a short time Wang P'ing came to reinforce his colleague, so that Chiang Wei was attacked on two sides. All Chiang's efforts were vain, and he had to abandon the spoil and try to re-enter the city.

But as he drew near he saw the walls were decorated with Shu ensigns, for Wei Yen had captured the place and was in possession. By desperate fighting Chiang Wei got clear and set off for T'ienshui. But he only had a few score horsemen left. Presently the small force fell in with Chang Pao, and at the end of this engagement Chiang Wei found himself alone, a single horseman. He reached the city and hailed the gate. The watchers above the gate knew him and went to tell the Prefect.

"This fellow has come to beguile me into opening the gate," said Ma Tsun.

So he ordered the defenders to shoot at him. Chiang Wei turned back, but there were the men of Shu close at hand. He set off as fast as he could for Shangkuei. But when he got there Liang Ch'ien hurled a valley of abuse at him.

"You traitor," cried he. "Dare you come to try to cajole me out of my city? I know you have surrendered to Shu."

His men also began to shoot at the hapless fugitive.

Chiang Wei was helpless. He could not explain the real truth to those who doubted him. Lifting his eyes to heaven, while tears rolled down his cheeks, he whipped up his steed and rode off toward Ch'angan.

Before he had got very far he came to a spot where were many heavy foliaged trees. From among these appeared a company of soldiers, led by Kuan Hsing. Weary as were both horse and rider, there was no chance of successful resistance, and Chiang Wei turned back. But soon appeared a small chariot in which sat K'ung-ming, dressed simply as usual in a white robe and carrying his feather fan.

"Friend Chiang," said he, "is it not time to yield?"

Chiang Wei stopped and pondered. There was K'ung-ming, and Kuan Hsing's men were behind him. There was no way out. So he dismounted and bowed his head in submission. K'ung-ming at once got out of the chariot and bade him welcome, taking him by the hand and saying, "Ever since I left my humble cottage I have been seeking some worthy man to whom I might impart the knowledge that my life has been spent in acquiring. I have found no one till this moment, and now my desire is attained. You are the one."

Chiang Wei bowed and thanked him, and they two returned to camp.

Soon after their arrival the new recruit and K'ung-ming consulted how to capture T'ienshui and Shangkuei. Chiang Wei had a scheme.

"The two civil officers in charge of the city are excellent friends of mine," said he, "and I will write a letter to each, shoot it over the wall tied to an arrow, and ask them to help by raising a revolt within the city."

They decided upon this, and two secret letters were duly written and sent flying over the ramparts, where they were found and taken to the Prefect. Ma Tsun was doubtful what action to take and consulted with Hsiahou Mou, asking him to decide.

"Put both the men to death," he replied.

But Yin Shang heard what was toward and said to his colleague, "The best course for us is to yield the city to Shu and trust to them to treat us well as our recompense."

That evening Hsiahou Mou sent many times to summon the two officers to him, but they thought it too great a risk to answer the call. Instead, they armed themselves and rode at the head of their own soldiers to the gates, opened them and let in the men of Shu. The Prefect and his exalted guest fled by the west gate with a few faithful followers and sought refuge with the *Ch'iang*.

The traitors welcomed K'ung-ming, who entered the city, restored order and calmed the people.

This done, K'ung-ming asked how he might capture Shangkuei. Liang Hsü said, "My brother holds that city, and I will call upon him to yield it."

Thereupon Liang Hsü rode over to Shangkuei and called out his brother to submit. K'ung-ming rewarded him and then made Liang Hsü Prefect of T'ienshui; Yin Shang, magistrate of Chich'êng; and Liang Ch'ien, magistrate of Shangkuei.

Next the army prepared to advance. Some of the officers asked their chief why he did not pursue and capture Hsiahou Mou.

He replied, "I let him go as I would release a duck; in my friend Chiang Wei I recognised a phœnix."

Such awe and fear seized upon the country round when these exploits were heard of that many other cities simply opened their gates without making any resistance. The army then, horse and foot, marched on to Ch'ishan.

When they reached the west bank of the River Wei the scouts reported their movements in Loyang, and, at a court held in the first year of the period *T'ai-Ho* a minister told the king of the threatened invasion. He said, "Hsiahou, the imperial Son-in-law, has lost the three cities and fled to the *Ch'iang*. The enemy has reached Ch'ishan, and their advanced columns are on the west bank of the Wei. I pray that an army be sent to repulse them."

The Emperor Jui was alarmed and asked for some general to go out and drive off the enemy.

The Minister Wang Lang stepped forward and said, "I observed that whenever the General Ts'ao Chên was sent by the late Emperor on any expedition he succeeded; why not send him to drive off these men of Shu?"

Jui approved of the suggestion, whereupon he called up Ts'ao Chên and said to him, "The late Emperor confided me to your guardianship; you cannot sit by while the enemy ravages the country."

Ts'ao Chên replied, "Your Majesty, my talents are but poor and unequal to the task you propose."

348

"You are a trusted minister of state and you may not really refuse this task," said the Emperor.

"I will use the little strength left me to accompany you," said Wang Lang.

"After the bounties I have received I cannot refuse," replied Ts'ao Chên. "But I must ask for an assistant."

"You have only to name him, O noble One," said the Emperor.

So Ts'ao Chên named Kuo Huai, a man of Yangchu, whose official rank was Marquis of Shêt'ing; he was also Governor of Yungchou.

Thereupon Ts'ao Chên was appointed Commander-in-chief, and the ensigns of rank were conferred upon him. Kuo Huai was appointed his second and Wang Lang was created Instructor of the Army. He was then already old, seventy-six.

The army of Ts'ao Chên consisted of twenty legions, the best men from both capitals. His brother, Ts'ao Tsun, was made leader of the van with an assistant, Chu Tsan, "Opposer of Brigands." The army moved out in the eleventh year, and the Emperor went with it to the outside of the west gate.

Ts'ao Chên marched by way of Ch'angan and camped on the west bank of the Wei River. At a council which the Commander-in-chief called to consider the best mode of attack, Wang Lang asked that he might be allowed to parley with the enemy.

"Let the army be drawn up in complete battle order and unfurl all the banners. I will go out and call a parley with Chuko Liang, at which I will make him yield to us without a blow, and the men of Shu shall march home again."

Ts'ao Chên agreed that the aged councellor should try. So orders were given to take the early meal at the fourth watch and have the men fall in in their companies and files at daylight, all in review order. Everything was to be grand and imposing, the flags fluttering and the drums rolling, every man in his place. Just before this display a messenger was to deliver a declaration of war.

Next day, when the armies were drawn up facing each other in front of Ch'ishan, the men of Shu saw that their enemies were fine, bold men, very different from those that Hsiahou Mou had brought against them. Then after three rolls of the drums the Minister Wang Lang mounted his horse and rode out, preceded by the Commander-in-chief and followed by the second in command. The two leaders of the van remained in charge of the army. Then an orderly rode to the front and called out in a loud voice, "We request the leader of the opposing army to come out to a parley."

At this, an opening was made at the main standard, through which came out Kuan Hsing and Chang Pao, who took up their stations right and left. Then followed a guard, and beneath the standard, in the rcentre of the array, was seen a four-wheeled carriage wherein sat K'ung-ming, with turban, white robe and black sash; and the feather fan was in his hand. He advanced with the utmost dignity. Looking up, he saw three commander's umbrellas and flags bearing large white characters. In the middle was an aged figure, the Minister Wang Lang.

"He intends to deliver an oration," thought K'ung-ming, "I must answer as best I may."

His carriage was then pushed to the front beyond the line of battle, and he directed one of his officers to reply, saying, "The Prime Minister of the Hans is willing to speak with the Minister Wang."

Wang Lang advanced. K'ung-ming saluted him from the carriage with raised hands, and Wang replied from horseback with an inclination. Then he began his oration.

"I am happy to meet you, noble Sir; your reputation has been long known to me. Since you recognise the decrees of Heaven and are acquainted with the conditions of the world, why do you, without any excuse, lead out such an army?"

K'ung-ming replied, "How mean you no excuse? I hold an edict to destroy rebels."

Wang Lang replied, "Heaven has its mutations, and changes its instruments from time to time; but the supreme dignity comes at last to the man of virtue. This is the inevitable and immutable law. In the days of Huan and Ling arose the Yellow Turban rebellion, and the whole earth was involved in wrangling and warfare. Later, in the periods *Ch'u-P'ing* and *Chien-An*, Tung Cho arose in revolt, a revolt which Li Ts'ui and Kuo Ssŭ continued after he had been destroyed. Next Yüan Shu usurped the imperial style, and his brother Yüan Shao played the man of might and valour in the land of Yeh. Liu Piao occupied Chingchou, and Lü Pu seized and held Hsü District. Thus rebels have arisen in the land like swarms of wasps and bold spirits have followed their own will, to the danger of the supreme dignity and the peril of the people. Then the founder of our House, the Emperor Wu (Ts'ao Ts'ao), swept away rebellion purged the land and restored order. All hearts turned to him in gratitude, and the people of the four quarters admired his virtue. He gained his position by no manifestation of force; it was simply the will of Heaven. His son and successor, the Emperor Wên, was wise and warlike, adequate to the great heritage and fitted to wield supreme power. Wherefore, in accordance with the will of Heaven and the desires of men, and following the example of the earliest emperors, he took his place as arbiter of the Central Government, whereby the myriad countries are ordered and governed. Can any maintain that it was not the desire of Heaven and the wish of men?

"Noble Sir, you are a man of natural talent and acquired attainments, worthy, you say yourself, to be compared with Kuan and Yo. Why then place yourself in opposition to the decree of Heaven and turn away from the desire of mankind to do this thing? You cannot be ignorant of the wise old saying that he who accords with the Heavens shall flourish, while he who opposes shall be destroyed.

"Now the armies of Wei are countless legions, and their able leaders are beyond number. Can the glow-worm in the parched stubble rival the glorious moon in the sky? If you will turn down your weapons and throw aside your armour and dutifully yield, you shall not lose your rank. The state will have tranquillity and the people rejoice. Is not that a desirable consummation?"

K'ung-ming laughed. Said he, "I regarded you as an old and tried servant of the Han Dynasty and thought you would hold some noble discourse. Could I imagine you would talk so foully? I have a word to say that all the army may hear. In the days of Huan and Ling the rule of Han declined, the officers of state were the authors of evil, the government fell into confusion and misfortune settled on the country. Trouble was rife in every quarter. The three rebels you mentioned arose one after another, deposing the emperor and afflicting the people. Because the household officers were corrupt and foolish, and the court officials were as brute beasts, living only that they might feed; because men, wolfishly cruel in their hearts, currishly mean in their conduct, were in office one after another and slavish flatterers bending slavish knees confounded the administration, therefore the Throne became as a waste heap and the people were trodden into the mire. I know all about you. You came from the eastern sea-shore; you got into office with a low degree; you properly aided your sovereign and supported the state, cared for the tranquillity of Han and magnified the Lius. But could one have imagined that you would turn and assist rebels and enter into a plot to usurp the Throne? Indeed your crime is great and your guilt heavy. Heaven and earth will not suffer you; the inhabitants of this country would devour you. But happily the design of Heaven is to retain the glorious dynasty. The late Emperor Chao-Lieh continued the line in Hsich'uan, and I have been entrusted by the present Emperor with the task of destroying you rebels. Since you are such a false and specious minister you have but to hide your body and cover your head, concern yourself about your belly and your back, but do not come out before the army to rave about the decrees of Heaven. You hoary-headed old fool! you grey-haired rebel! Mark you, to-day is your last day; this day even you descend to the Nine

Springs. How will you stand before the two score and four emperors of Han that you will meet there? Retire, you old rebel! Go tell your rebellious companions to come and fight one battle with me that shall decide the victory."

Fierce wrath filled the old man's breast. With one despairing cry he fell to the earth dead.

This exploit of K'ung-ming's has been lauded in verse:—

In west Ts'in, when the armies met in the field,
He, the bold one, singly faced a myriad warriors,
And with a simple weapon, just his cruel tongue,
He did to death an old and wicked man.

After Wang Lang had fallen, K'ung-ming waved the fan toward Ts'ao Chên and said, "As for you, I leave you alone for this occasion. Go and get your army in order for to-morrow's battle."

The chariot turned and left the ground; both armies retired for that day. To Ts'ao Chên fell the melancholy duty of rendering the last services to the aged counsellor and setting his coffin on its journey to Ch'angan.

Then said the general Kuo Huai, "Chuko Liang will certainly think the army occupied with mourning and make a night attack. Let us anticipate him and set out an ambush about our camp. Let two bodies of our men be hidden outside and two others take the occasion to raid the camp of the enemy."

"I thought of such a scheme myself," said Ts'ao Chên. "It exactly suits my plans."

So the orders were given; the two leaders of the van were to take a legion each, get away by the rear of the mountain and look out for the passing of the men of Shu. When they had gone by, these two were to make for their camp. They were only to attempt a raid if the men of Shu had left. Then the Commander-in-chief arranged with his second each to lead a force and hide outside the camp. A few men only were to be left within to make a fire if the enemy were seen to be coming. And each captain set about his necessary preprations.

When K'ung-ming reached his tent he called to him Chao Yün and Wei Yen, and said to them, "You two are to make a night attack."

"Ts'ao Chên is a man of experience and will be on the lookout," ventured Wei Yen.

"But that is just what I want, I want him to know we shall attack to-night. He will then put some men in hiding in rear of Ch'ishan, who will make for our camp as soon as they see us pass toward theirs. I am sending you to let yourselves be seen passing the hill, but you are to camp behind it and at a distance. When the men of Wei attack this camp you will see a signal. Then Wei Yen will hold the approach to the hill, and Chao Yün will make his way back in fighting order. He will meet the men of Wei returning and will let them pass on to you. You will attack. The enemy will assuredly fall to fighting among themselves, and we shall conquer."

These two having gone away to carry out their portions of the plan, he next called up Kuan Hsing and Chang Pao: "You are to take each a legion and hide in the high road to the mountain. When the men of Wei come, let them pass and then march along the road they came by to the camp they have just left."

These two having left, the plan concluded with placing four bodies of men in ambush about the camp.

Within the camp the tents and shelters were left standing as if the camp was occupied, while wood and straw were heaped up ready to give the signal. This done, K'ung-ming and his officers retired to the rear of the camp to watch proceedings.

On the side of Wei the two van-leaders, Ts'ao Tsun and Chu Tsan, left at dusk and hastened toward the camp of Shu. About the second watch they saw men busily moving about in front of the hill.

Ts'ao Tsun thought to himself, "Commander Kuo Huai is an excellent strategist and of wonderful prevision."

Then he hastened the march, and in the third watch reached the camp of Shu. He at once dashed into the enclosure, but only to find it totally deserted. Not a man was visible. At once he knew he had stumbled into a trap, and began to withdraw. Then the flames sprang up. Chu Tsan arrived ready to fight, and the two bodies of men, thrown into confusion, fought with each other till the two leaders met, when they found out they were fighting their own men.

As they were restoring order, on came the four bodies of men of Shu who had lain in ambush ready for them. The two leaders, with a handful of those nearest to them, ran away to get to the high road. But before long the rolling drums announced another body of their enemy, and their flight was stopped by Chao Yün.

"Whither go ye, O rebel leaders?" cried he. "Stop, for here is death."

But the two leaders of Wei still fled. Then came up a force led by Wei Yen and completed the defeat. The men of Wei were wholly beaten and ran away to their own camp. But the guard left in the camp thought they were the enemy come to raid, so they lit the fires, and at this signal Ts'ao Chên rushed up from one side and Kuo Huai from the other, and a fierce fight with their own men began.

While this was going on, three cohorts of the men of Shu arrived from three points, and a great and confused battle began. The men of Wei were driven off and chased for ten *li*.

In the fight Wei lost many leaders, and K'ung-ming gained a great success. Ts'ao Chên and Kuo Huai got together their beaten men and went back to their own camp.

When they discussed the fight, Ts'ao Chên said, "The enemy are too strong for us. Have you any plan to drive them away?"

Replied Kuo Huai, "Our defeat is one of the ordinary events of war. Let us not be cast down. I have a plan to suggest that will disorder them so that one body cannot help the other and they will all be compelled to flee."

> Wei leaders fail and sadly send
> To pray barbarians help to lend.

The plan will be unfolded in the next chapter.

CHAPTER VIC.

CHUKO SMITES THE BARBARIANS IN A SNOWSTORM;
SSŬMA QUICKLY CAPTURES MÊNG TA.

The scheme by which Kuo Huai proposed to overcome the men of Shu he laid before his colleague, saying, "The *Ch'iang* (Tangut) tribes have paid tribute regularly since the days of the Founder of our House. The Emperor Wên (220-227) regarded them with favour. Now let us hold such points of vantage as we may while we send secret emissaries to engage their help in exchange for kindly treatment. We may get them to attack Shu and engage their attention while we gather a large army to smite them at another place. Thus attacking, how can we help gaining a great victory?"

A messenger was sent forthwith bearing letters to the barbarians.

The prince of the western *Ch'iang* was named Ch'êlichi. He had rendered yearly tribute since the days of Ts'ao Tsao. He had two ministers, one for civil the other for military affairs, named, respectively, Yatan and Yüehchi. The former was termed Prime Minister and the latter Chief Leader.

The letter was accompanied by presents of gold and pearls, and when the messenger arrived he first sought Yatan, to whom he gave gifts and whose help he begged. Thus he gained an interview with the prince, to whom he presented the letter and the gifts. The prince accepted both and called his counsellors to consider the letter.

Yatan said, "We have had regular intercourse with the Wei country. Now that Ts'ao Chên asks our aid and promises an alliance we ought to accede to his request."

The prince agreed that it was so, and he ordered his two chief ministers to raise an army of twenty-five legions of trained soldiers, archers and crossbowmen, spearmen and swordsmen, men who flung caltrops and men who hurled hammers. Beside these various weapons the barbarians used chariots covered with iron plates nailed on. They prepared much grain and fodder and many spare weapons, all of which they loaded upon these iron-clad chariots. The chariots were drawn by camels or teams of horses. The carts or chariots were known as iron chariots.

The two leaders took leave of their prince and went straightway to Hsip'ing Pass. The officer in command, Han Chên, at once sent intelligence to K'ung-ming, who asked who would go to attack the *Ch'iang*. Kuan Hsiang and Chang Pao said they would go.

Then K'ung-ming said, "You shall be sent; but as you are ignorant of the road and the people, Ma Tai shall accompany you."

To Ma Tai he said, "You know the disposition of the *Ch'iang* from your long residence there; you shall go as guide."

They chose out five legions of veterans for the expedition. When they had marched many days and drew near their enemy, Kuan Hsing went in advance with a few horsemen and got first sight of them from a hill. They were marching, the long line of iron chariots one behind another in close order. Then they halted and camped, their weapons piled all along the line of chariots like the ramparts of a moated city. Kuan studied them for a long time quite at a loss to think how to overcome them. He came back to camp and consulted with his two colleagues.

Ma Tai said, "We will see to-morrow what they will do when we make our array, and discuss our plans when we know more."

So the next day they drew up their army in three divisions, Kuan Hsing's division being in the centre. Thus they advanced.

The enemy also drew up in battle order. Their military chief, Yüehchi, had an iron mace in his hand and a carven bow hung at his waist. He rode forward on a curvetting steed boldly enough. Kuan Hsing gave the order for all three divisions to go forward. Then the enemy's ranks opened in the centre and out rolled the iron chariots like a great wave. At the same time the barbarians shot arrows and bolts, and the men of Shu could not stand against them.

The wing divisions retired, and the *Ch'iang* were thus enabled to surround the centre. In spite of every effort, Kuan could not get free, for the iron chariots were like a city wall and no opening could be found. The men of Shu were absolutely helpless, and Kuan Hsing made for the mountains in hope of finding a road through.

As it grew dark a *Ch'iang* leader with a black flag approached, his men like a swarm of wasps about him. Presently Kuan made out the iron mace of Yüehchi, who cried out to him, "Youthful captain, flee not; I am the Chief Leader of the army."

But Kuan Hsing only hastened forward, plying his whip to urge his steed. Then he suddenly came on a deep gully, and there seemed nothing but to turn and fight. But Kuan Hsing's courage turned cold at the sight of Yüehchi, and he leaped into the gully. Yüehchi come close and struck at him with the mace. Kuan avoided the blow but it fell upon his steed and knocked him over into water. Kuan went into the water too.

Presently he heard a great noise again behind him. Yüehchi and his men had found a way down into the gully and were coming at him down the stream. Kuan braced himself for a struggle in the water.

Then he saw someone on the bank fighting with, and driving off, the *Ch'iang*. Kuan Hsing gripped his sword and was waiting to get in a stroke at Yüehchi as he came up when suddenly his enemy jumped out of the water and ran away. At once Kuan Hsing caught the steed he had left, led him up the bank and soon had him ready to mount. Then he girded on his sword, and was just getting on the horse when again appeared the captain he had seen before driving off his enemies.

"Whoever this may be, he has saved my life," thought Kuan Hsing. "I ought to make his acquaintance."

He accordingly pressed forward after his deliverer. As he drew nearer he saw, enveloped in mist, a man, evidently an officer of rank, with a dark red face and heavy eyebrows, wearing a green robe and a golden helmet. He wielded a huge sword such as was Black Dragon and rode a hare-coloured steed. From time to time he stroked a long flowing beard. Then he understood; it was his dead father, Kuan the Noble.

Kuan Hsing was frightened. But his father pointed southeast and said, "My son, go quickly along that road and I will guard you to your camp."

With that the figure disappeared. Kuan took the road he had been shown and hastened along. About midnight he saw a cohort advancing to meet him, and recognised his cousin Chang Pao.

"Have you seen my uncle?" asked Chang.

"How did you know?" asked Kuan.

"I was pursued by the iron chariots when I suddenly saw my uncle coming down from the sky, and he frightened the pursuers away. Then he told me to come along this road and rescue you. So I came."

Thereupon Kuan Hsing related what had happened to him, and they were both astonished.

They quickly gained the camp, where Ma Tai welcomed them.

"I do not know how to overcome these men," said Ma Tai. "Let me protect the camp while you go back and ask the minister what we should do."

The two started at once and made the best of their way back. They told K'ung-ming what had happened. He at once sent off Chao Yün and Wei Yen to go into ambush. After this he went himself with three legions and certain officers and soon came to Ma Tai's camp. The day after, from the summit of a hill, he surveyed the country and the enemy, who were coming on in a ceaseless stream.

"It is not difficult," said K'ung-ming.

He called up Ma Tai and Chang I and gave them certain orders.

They having gone, he turned to Chiang Wei, saying, "My friend, do you know how to overcome them?"

"The *Ch'iang* only depend upon force or courage, not upon fine strategy," was the reply.

"You know," said K'ung-ming, smiling. "Those dark clouds and the strong north wind mean snow. Then I can do what I wish."

The two leaders, Kuan and Chang, were sent into ambush, and Chiang Wei went out to offer battle. But he was to retire before the iron chariots. At the entrance to the camp were displayed many flags, but the men that should serve under them were not there.

It was now full winter, the twelfth month, and the snow had come. The army of Shu went out to offer battle, and when the iron chariots came forward they retired and thus led the *Ch'iang* to the gate of the camp, Chiang Wei going to its rear. The *Ch'iang* came to the gate and stopped to look. They heard the strumming of a lute, but there were no soldiers there; the flags meant nothing. They told Yüehchi, and he suspected some ruse. Instead of entering, he went back to the Minister Yatan and told him.

"It is a ruse," said Yatan. "Chuko Liang's base trick is the pretence of a pretence, and you had better attack."

So Yüehchi led his men again to the camp gate, and there he saw K'ung-ming with a lute just getting into his chariot. With a small escort he went toward the back of the camp. The barbarians rushed into the camp and caught sight of the light chariot again just as it disappeared into a wood.

Then said Yatan, "There may be an ambush, but I think we need not be afraid of these men."

Hence they decided to pursue. Ahead of them they saw the division under Chiang Wei hastening off through the snow. Yüehchi's rage boiled up at this sight, and he urged his men to go faster. The snow had filled in the roads among the hills, making every part look like a level plain.

As they marched, one reported that some of the enemy were appearing from the rear of the hills. Some thought this meant an ambush, but Yatan said it did not matter, and they need not fear. He urged them to hasten.

Shortly after this they heard a roaring as if the hills were rending asunder and the earth falling in, and the pursuers on foot fell one atop of the other into great pits that were invisible in the snow. The iron chariots, being close behind and hurrying along, could not stop, and they went into the pits also. Those still farther in the rear halted, but just as they were facing about, Kuan and Chang came up, one on either side, and attacked. Myriads of bolts flew through the air. Then three other divisions arrived and confusion was worse than ever.

The *Ch'iang* leader, Yüehchi, fled to the rear and was making for the mountains when he met Kuan Hsing, who slew him in the first encounter. The Minister Yutan was captured and taken to the main camp. The soldiers scattered.

Hearing of the capture of one leader, K'ung-ming took his seat in his tent and bade them bring the prisoner. He told the guards to loose his bonds, and he had wine brought to refresh him and soothed him with kindly words. Yatan was grateful for this kindness, and felt more so when K'ung-ming said, "My master, the Emperor of the Great Hans, sent me to destroy those who are in revolt; why are you helping them? But I will release you, and you will return to your master and say that we are neighbours and we will swear an oath of everlasting friendship, and tell him to listen no more to the words of those rebels."

The minister was released and so were all the soldiers that had been captured, and all their stuff was given back to them. They left for their own country.

The *Ch'iang* being thus disposed of, K'ung-ming quickly marched again to Ch'ishan. He sent letters to the capital announcing his success.

Meanwhile Ts'ao Chên anxiously waited for news of his expected allies. Then a scout came in with the news that the men of Shu had broken camp and were marching away.

"That is because the *Ch'iang* have attacked," said Kuo Huai gleefully, and the two made ready to pursue.

Ahead of them the army of Shu seemed to be in confusion. The van-leader Ts'ao Tsun led the pursuit. Suddenly, as he pressed on, there came a roll of drums, followed by the appearance of a cohort led by Wei Yen, who cried, "Stop! you rebels!"

But Ts'ao Tsun did not obey the summons. He dashed forward to meet the attack. He was killed in the third encounter. His colleague Chu Tsan in similar fashion fell in with a cohort under Chao Yün, to whose long spear he soon fell victim. The loss of these two made the Commander-in-chief and his second hesitate, and they made to retire.

But before they could face about they heard the drums of an army in their rear, and Kuan Hsing and Chang Pao came out and surrounded them. They made a stand for a time, but were soon worsted and fled. The army of Shu pursued the beaten enemy to the banks of the River Wei, where they took possession of the enemy's camp.

Ts'ao Chên was greatly chagrined at his defeat and sad at the loss of his captains. He send a repart of his misfortune to his master and asked for reinforcements.

At the court of Wei one of the ministers told the story of defeat of Ts'ao Chên and the allies and asked the king to decide upon the next step. Jui was alarmed and asked for someone to say how to drive off the victorious foe. Thereupon Hua Hsin said, "It will be necessary for Your Majesty to go in person. You should call together all the nobles, and each will have to exert himself. Unless this is done the capital will be lost and the whole country be in danger."

But Chung Yu opposed him. Said he, "The knowledge of every leader must exceed that of those led; then only will he be able to control them. Sun, the military writer, sums it up very briefly: 'Know the enemy, know thyself; and every battle is a victory.' I know Ts'ao Chên has had great experience in the field, but he is no match for Chuko Liang. Still there is such a match, and I will pledge my whole family that he will succeed. But Your Majesty may be unwilling to listen to me."

King Jui replied, "You are a minister of high rank and old. If you know any wise man able to repel these men of Shu, call him without delay and ease my mind."

Then said Chung Yu, "When Chuko Liang decided to invade us he was afraid of the one man I will name. Wherefore he spread calumnies concerning him, raising suspicion in Your Majesty's mind that you might dismiss him. That done, he invaded. Now employ this man again, and the enemy will retire."

"Who is it?" asked Jui.

"I mean the great general Ssŭma I."

"I have long regretted my action," said Jui. "Where now is friend Ssŭma?"

"He is at the city of Wan, idle."

An edict was prepared recalling Ssŭma and restoring him to his rank and titles, and conferring upon him the new title Commander-in-chief, "Pacificator of the West." The troops of Nanyang were set in motion and King Jui led them to *Ch'angan*. At the same time he ordered Ssŭma I to be there to meet him on a certain day. And the orders were sent by a swift messenger to the city of Wan.

At this time K'ung-ming greatly rejoiced at the success he had had. He was at Ch'ishan, busy with plans for other victories, when Li Yen, who was still in command at Jungan, sent his son Li Fêng to the camp. K'ung-ming concluded that such a visit could only mean that Wu had invaded them, and he was in consequence cast down. However, he summoned Li Fêng to his tent, and when asked the object of his mission Li replied that he had joyful news to impart.

"What is your joyful news?" said K'ung-ming.

"Formerly Mêng Ta deserted to Wei, but only because he could do nothing else. Ts'ao P'ei thought much of his capabilities, treated him most generously, kept him at his side, gave him titles and offices and so on. But when P'ei died all was changed. In Ts'ao Jui's court were many who were jealous of his influence and power, so that he enjoyed no peace. He used to talk about being originally one of the Shu leaders and he would be forced to do so-and-so. Lately he has sent several confidants with letters to my father asking that he would state his case to you as to the happenings when the five armies came upon Shu. Now he is at Hsinch'êng, and, hearing you are attacking Wei, he proposes to lead the men of the three districts about Chinch'êng, Hsinch'êng and Shangyung to attack Loyang while you attack Ch'angan, whereby both capitals will be taken. I have brought with me his messenger and his letters."

This was good news, and the bearer was fittingly rewarded. But at that moment came the news that Ts'ao Jui was leading an army to Ch'angan and had recalled the banished Ssŭma I to office. This piece of bad news saddened K'ung-ming not a little. He told Ma Su, who at once proposed the plan to capture Ts'ao Jui on the road, and there would be an end of him.

"Do you think I fear him?" said K'ung-ming bitterly. "But the recall of Ssŭma I is another matter; that troubles me. And Mêng Ta's proposal will avail nothing if he comes across this man. Mêng Ta is no match for him. He will be captured, and, if he should be, there will be no capital for us."

"Why not put Mêng Ta on his guard then?" said Ma Su.

K'ung-ming decided to write, and the letter was despatched immediately. Mêng was then at Hsinch'êng, anxiously expecting the return of his last confidential messenger, when, one day, the man returned and gave him this letter from K'ung-ming himself :—

"Your last letter has convinced me of your loyal rectitude, and I still remember with joy our old friendship. If your plan succeed you will certainly stand in the first rank of most worthy ministers. But I scarcely need impress upon you the extreme necessity for most perfect secrecy. Be very careful whom you trust. Fear everyone, guard against everyone. This news of the recall of Ssŭma I and the proposed junction of armies at Ch'angan is very serious, and if a word reaches Ssŭma he will come to you first. Therefore take every precaution and do not regard this as a matter of unimportance."

"They say K'ung-ming leaves nothing to chance," said Mêng, smiling as he read. "This proves it."

He lost no time in preparing a reply, which he sent also by a trusty messenger. This letter was like this:—"I acknowledge your most valuable advice, but is it possible that I should be remiss? For my part I do not think the Ssŭma affair need cause anxiety, for Wanch'êng is eight hundred *li* from Loyang and twelve hundred *li* from here. Should he hear anything, it would take a month to send a memorial and get a reply. My ramparts here are strong and my forces posted in the best positions. Let him come! I am not afraid of the result, so you, O Minister, need feel no anxiety. You have only to wait for the good news of success."

K'ung-ming read the letter and threw it on the ground, stamping his foot with rage.

"You are a dead man," said he; "a victim of Ssǔma I."

"Why do you say that?" said Ma Su.

"What does the book say? 'Attack before the enemy is prepared; do what he does not expect.' What is the use of reckoning upon a month's delay for sending up a memorial? Ts'ao Jui's commission has already gone and Ssǔma may strike whom he will. He will not have to wait to memorialise. Ten days after he hears of Mêng's defection he will be upon him with an army, and Mêng Ta will be helpless."

The others agreed. However, K'ung-ming sent the messenger back again to say that if the matter had not yet actually started no other person was to be told of it, for if anyone knew it would certainly come to nothing. And the man left for Hsinch'êng.

In his idle retreat in Wan City Ssǔma had heard of his master's ill-success against the armies of Shu, and the news made him very sad. He lifted up his eyes and sighed.

He had two sons, Shih the elder and Chao, both clever and ambitious, and both earnest students of military books. One day they were present when their father seemed very cast down, and the elder asked his father the reason.

"You would not understand," said the father.

"I think you are grieving because the lord of Wei does not use you," replied Ssǔma Shih.

"But they will send for you presently," said the younger son.

The prophecy was not long in fulfilment, for even then the bearer of the command stood at the gate, and the servant announced a messenger from the court bearing a commission.

As soon as he heard its terms, Ssǔma set about ordering the armies of his own city. Soon came a messenger from the Prefect of Chinch'êng with a secret message for Ssǔma I. He was taken into a private chamber, and his message was that Mêng Ta was on the point of rebellion. The authority for this was a confidential fried, Li Fu, and a nephew, Têng Hsien.

Ssǔma I smote his forehead.

"This is the Emperor's great good fortune, high as heaven itself. Chuko Liang's army is at Ch'ishan already, and if he had got these places all men's courage would fail. The Emperor must go to Ch'angan, and if he does not use me soon

Mêng Ta will carry out his plan; his plot will succeed and both capitals will be lost. This fellow is surely in league with the enemy, and if I can seize him before he makes any move, that will damp Chuko's spirits and he will retreat."

His elder son remarked that it would be necessary to memorialise.

"No," replied his father; "that would take a month, and delay would mean failure."

Ssŭma gave orders to prepare to advance by double marches and threatened death to all loiterers. In order to avert suspicion, he sent letters to Mêng Ta in Hsinch'êng to tell him to prepare to join the expedition.

Ssŭma I quickly followed this messenger. After two days' march the general Hsü Huang came over the hills and told Ssŭma that the Emperor had arrived at Ch'angan to lead an expedition against Shu, and he asked whither the Commander-in-chief was then going.

Ssŭma, in a low voice, said to him, "Mêng Ta is on the verge of rebellion, and I am going to seize him."

"Let me go as your van-leader," said Hsü.

So Hsü Huang's men were joined to the expedition and marched in the van. The sons of Ssŭma I brought up the rear.

Two days farther on some of the scouts captured Mêng Ta's confidential messenger, and with him K'ung-ming's reply. Ssŭma promised the man his life if he would tell all he knew. So he told all about the letters and messages he had taken from one to the other. When Ssŭma read the captured letter he remarked that all able people thought the same way.

"Our plan would have been foiled by K'ung-ming's cleverness unless, by the good luck of the Emperor, this man had been captured. Now Mêng Ta will be helpless."

The army pressed on still more rapidly.

Mêng Ta had arranged for his stroke with the Prefects of the other two cities and was awaiting the way he had fixed. But the other two, Shên I and Chên Ch'ên, were only pretending to abet him, although they went on training and drilling their men to keep up appearances till the men of Wei could arrive. To Mêng Ta they pretended delay in their transport as the reason for being unable to start. And he believed them.

Just then Liang Ch'i came, and when he had been ceremoniously received, he produced the order from Ssŭma I and said, "The Commander-in-chief has received the edict of the Emperor to call in all the forces in this district, and he has sent me to direct you to hold your men in readiness to march."

"On what day does the Commander-in-chief start?" asked Mêng Ta.

"He is just about starting now," replied the messenger.

Mêng smiled inwardly, for, this being so, he saw success before him. He gave a banquet to Liang, and after he had set him on his way he sent to his fellow conspirators to say the first step must be taken next day by exchanging the banners of Wei for those of Han and marching to attack Loyang.

Then the watchmen reported a great cloud of dust in the distance as though an army was coming. Mêng Ta was surprised and went up on the ramparts to see for himself. Soon he made out the banner of Hsü Huang leading. He ran down from the wall and in a state of trepidation ordered the raising of the drawbridge. Hsü Huang still came on and in due time stood on the bank of the moat.

Then he called out, "Let the traitor Mêng Ta yield quickly!"

Mêng Ta, in a rage, opened upon him with arrows, and Hsü Huang was wounded in the forehead. He was helped to a place of safety while the arrows flew down in great numbers. When the men of Wei retired, Meng opened the gates and went in pursuit. But the whole of Ssŭma's army soon came up, and the banners stood so thick that they hid the sun.

"This is what K'ung-ming foresaw," said Mêng despairingly. The gates were closed and barred.

Meanwhile the wounded captain, Hsü, had been borne to his tent, where the arrow head was extracted and the physician attended to him. But that night he died. He was fifty-nine. His body was sent to Loyang for burial.

Next day, when Mêng went up on the wall, he saw the city was entirely surrounded as with a girdle of iron. He was greatly perturbed and could not decide what to do. Presently he saw two bodies of troops coming up, their banners bearing the names of his fellow conspirators. He could only conclude that they had come to his help, so he opened the gates to them and went out to fight.

"Rebel, stay!" cried they both as they came up.

Realising that they had been false, he turned and galloped toward the city, but a flight of arrows met him, and the two who had betrayed him, Li Fu and Têng Hsien, began to revile him.

"We have already yielded the city," they cried.

Then Mêng Ta fled. But he was pursued, and as he and his horse were both exhausted he was speedily overtaken and slain. They exposed his head, and his soldiers submitted. Ssŭma was welcomed at the open gates. The people were pacified, the soldiers were rewarded and, this done, a report of their success was sent to Ts'ao Jui.

Ts'ao Jui ordered the body of Mêng Ta to be exposed in the market place of Loyang, and he promoted the two Shêns and gave them posts in the army of Ssŭma. He gave the two betrayers command of the cities of Hsinch'êng and Shangyung.

Then Ssŭma marched to Ch'angan and camped. The leader entered the city to have audience with his master, by whom he was most graciously received.

"Once I doubted you," said Ts'ao Jui; "but then I did not understand, and I listened to mischief-makers. I regret it. You have preserved both capitals by the punishment of this traitor."

Ssŭma replied, "Shên I gave the information of the intended revolt and thought to memorialise Your Majesty. But tnere would have been a long delay, and so I did not await orders, but set forth at once. Delay would have played into Chuko's hands."

Then he handed in K'ung-ming's letter to Mêng Ta, and when the Emperor had read that he said, "You are wiser than both the great strategists."

He conferred upon the successful leader a pair of golden axes and the privilege of taking action in important matters without first obtaining his master's sanction.

When the order was given to advance against the enemy, Ssŭma asked permission to name his leader of the van, and nominated Chang Ho.

"Just the man I wished to send," said Ts'ao Jui, smiling.

And Chang Ho was appointed.

> By strategy the leader shows his skill;
> He needs bold fighting men to work his will.

The result of the campaign will appear in the next chapter.

CHAPTER VC.

MA SU'S WRANGLING LOSES CHIEHT'ING;
K'UNG-MING'S LUTE REPULSES SSUMA.

Beside sending Chang Ho as van-leader, Ts'ao Jui appointed two other captains, Hsin P'i and Sun Li, to assist Ts'ao Chên. Each led five legions. Ssŭma's army was twenty legions strong. They marched out through the pass and made a camp.

When encamped, the Commander-in-chief summoned the leader of the van to his tent and admonished him, saying, "A characteristic of Chuko Liang is his most diligent carefulness; he is never hasty. If I were in his place I should advance through the Tzuwu Valley to capture Ch'angan and so save much time. It is not that he is unskilful, but he fears lest that plan might miscarry, and he will not sport with risk. Therefore he will certainly come through the Hsieh Valley, taking Meich'êng on the way. That place captured, he will divide his force into two, one part to take Chi Valley. I have sent orders to guard Meich'êng strictly and on no account to let its garrison go out to battle. The captains Sun Li and Hsin P'i are to command the Chi Valley entrance, and should the enemy come they are to make a sudden attack."

"By what road will you advance?" asked Chang.

"I know a road west of Ts'inling valley called Chieht'ing, on which stands the city Liehliuch'êng. These two places are the throat of Hanchung. Chuko Liang will take advantage of the unpreparedness of Ts'ao Chên and will certainly come in by this way. I and you will go to Chieht'ing, whence it is a short distance to Yenp'ing Pass, and when K'ung-ming hears that the road through Chieht'ing is blocked and his supplies cut off, he will know that Shênsi is in danger, and will retire without losing a moment into Hanchung. I shall smite him on the march, and I ought to gain a complete victory. If he should not retire, then I shall block all the smaller roads and so stop his supplies. A month's starvation will kill off the men of Shu, and Chuko will be my prisoner."

Chang Ho took in the scheme and expressed his admiration of the prescience of his chief.

Ssŭma continued, "However, it is not to be forgotten that Chuko is quite different from Mêng, and you, as leader of the van, will have to advance with the utmost care. You must impress upon your captains the importance of reconnoitring a long way ahead and only advancing when they are sure there is no ambush. The least remissness will make you the victim of some ruse of the enemy."

Chang Ho, having received his instructions, marched away. Meanwhile a spy had come to K'ung-ming in Ch'ishan with news of the destruction of Mêng Ta and the failure of his conspiracy. Ssŭma, having succeeded there, had gone to Ch'angan when he had marched through the pass.

K'ung-ming was distressed. "Mêng's destruction was certain," said he. "Such a scheme could not remain secret. Now Ssŭma will try for Chieht'ing and block the one road essential to us."

So Chieht'ing had to be defended, and K'ung-ming asked who would go. Ma Su offered himself instantly. K'ung-ming urged upon him the importance of his task. "The place is small, but of very great importance, for its loss would involve the loss of the whole army. You are deeply read in all the rules of strategy, but the defence of this place is difficult, since it has no wall and no natural defences."

"I have studied the books of war since I was a boy, and I may say I know a little of the art of war," Ma replied. "Why alone is Chieht'ing so difficult to hold?"

"Because Ssŭma I is an exceptional man, and also he has a famous second in Chang Ho as leader of the van. I fear you may not be a match for him."

Ma replied, "To say nothing of these two, I would not mind if Ts'ao Jui himself came against me. If I fail, then I beg you to behead my whole family."

"There is no jesting in war," said K'ung-ming.

"I will give a written pledge."

The general agreed, and a written pledge was given and placed on record.

K'ung-ming continued, "I shall give you two legions and a half of veterans and also send an officer of rank to assist you."

Next he summoned Wang P'ing and said to him, "As you are a careful and cautious man I am giving you a very responsible position. You are to hold Chieht'ing with the utmost tenacity. Camp there in the most commanding position so that the enemy cannot steal by. When your arrangements are complete, draw a plan of them and a map of the local topography and let me see it. All my dispositions have been carefully thought out and are not to be changed. If you can hold this successfully it will be of the first service in the capture of Ch'angan. So be very, very careful."

After these two had gone and K'ung-ming had reflected for a long time, it occurred to him that there might be some slip between his two leaders, so he called Kao Hsiang to him and said, "North-east of Chieht'ing is a city named Liehliuch'êng and near it an unfrequented hill path. There you are to camp and make a stockade. I will give you a legion for this task, and if Chieht'ing should be threatened you may go to the rescue."

After Kao Hsiang had left, and as K'ung-ming knew his man was not a match for his opponent Chang Ho, he decided there ought to be additional strength on the west in order to make Chieht'ing safe. So he summoned Wei Yen and bade him lead his troop to the rear of Chieht'ing and camp there.

But Wei Yen thought this rather a slight, and said, "As leader of the van I should go first against the enemy; why am I sent to a place where there is nothing to do?"

"The leadership of the van is really a second-rate task. Now I am sending you to support Chieht'ing and take post on the most dangerous road to Yenp'ing Pass. You are the chief keeper of the throat of Hanchung. It is a very responsible post and not at all an idle one. Do not so regard it and spoil my whole plan. Be particularly careful."

Wei Yen, satisfied now that he was not being slighted, went his way.

K'ung-ming's mind was at rest, and he called up Chao Yün and Têng Chih, to whom he said, "Now that Ssŭma I is in command of the army the whole outlook is different. Each of you will lead a force out by Chi Valley and move about so as to mislead the enemy. Whether you meet and engage them or not you will certainly cause them uneasiness. I am going to lead the main army through Hsieh Valley to Meich'êng. If I can capture that, Ch'angan will fall."

For this march Chiang Wei was appointed leader of the van.

When Ma Su and Wang P'ing had reached Chieht'ing and saw what manner of place it was, Ma Su smiled, saying, "Why was the minister so extremely anxious? How would the Wei armies dare to come to such a hilly place as this?"

Wang P'ing replied, "Though they might not dare to come, we should set our camp at this meeting of many roads."

So Wang ordered his men to fell trees and build a strong stockade as for a permanent stay.

But Ma Su had a different idea. "What sort of a place is a road to make a camp in? Here is a hill standing solitary and well wooded. It is a heaven-created point of vantage, and we will camp on it."

"You are wrong, Sir," replied Wang. "If we camp on the road and build a strong wall the enemy cannot possibly get past. If we abandon this for the hill, and the men of Wei come in force, we shall be surrounded, and how then be safe?"

"You look at the thing like a woman," said Ma Su, laughing. "The rules of war say that when one looks down from a superior position one easily overcomes the enemy. If they come I will see to it that not a breastplate ever goes back again."

"I have followed our general in many a campaign, and always he has carefully thought out his orders. Now I have studied this hill carefully, and it is a critical point. If we camp thereon and the enemy cut off our water supply we shall have a mutiny."

"No such thing," said Ma Su. "Sun Wu says that victory lies in desperate positions. If they cut off our water will not our men be desperate and fight to the death? Then everyone of them will be worth a hundred. I have studied the books, and the minister has always asked my advice. Why do you presume to oppose me?"

"If you are determined to camp on the hill, then give me part of the force to camp there on the west so that I can support you in case the enemy come."

But Ma Su refused. Just then a lot of the inhabitants of the hills came running along saying that the Wei soldiers had come.

Wang was still bent on going his own way, and so Ma said to him, "Since you will not obey me, I will give you half a legion and you can go and make your own camp, but when I report my success to the minister you shall have no share of the merit."

Wang P'ing marched about ten *li* from the hill and made his camp. He drew a plan of the place and sent it quickly to K'ung-ming with a report that Ma Su had camped on the hill.

Before Ssŭma marched, he sent his younger son to reconnoitre the road and to find out whether Chieht'ing had a garrison. He had returned with the information that there was a garrison.

"Chuko Liang is rather more than human," said his father regretfully when the son gave in his report. "He is too much for me."

"Why are you despondent, father? I think Chieht'ing is not so difficult to take."

"How dare you utter such bold words?"

"Because I have seen. There is no camp on the road, but the enemy are camped on the hill."

This was glad news. "If they are on the hill then Heaven means a victory for me," said his father.

Ssŭma changed into another dress, took a small escort and rode out to see for himself. The moon shone brilliantly, and he rode to the hill whereon was the camp and looked all round it, thoroughly reconnoitring the neighbourhood. Ma Su saw him, but only laughed.

"If he has any luck he will not try to surround this hill," said Ma.

He issued an order to his captains that in case the enemy came they were to look to the summit for a signal with a red flag, when they should rush down on all sides.

Ssŭma I returned to his camp and sent out to enquire who commanded in Chieht'ing. They told him Ma Su, brother of Ma Liang.

"A man of false reputation and very ordinary ability," said Ssŭma. "If K'ung-ming uses such as he, he will fail."

Then he asked if there were any other camps near the place, and they told him Wang P'ing was about ten *li* off. Wherefore Chang Ho was ordered to go and check Wang P'ing.

This done, the hill was surrounded and the road to the water supply was blocked. Lack of water would cause a mutiny, and when that occurred it would be time to attack. Chang Ho marched out and placed himself between Wang P'ing and the hill. Then Ssŭma led the main body to attack the hill on all sides.

From the summit of his hill Ma Su could see the banners of his enemy all round, and the country about was full of men. Presently the hemming in was complete, and the men of Shu became dejected. They dared not descend to attack although the red flag signalled for them to move. The captains stood huddled together, no one daring to go first. Ma Su was furious. He cut down two officers, which frightened the others to the point of descending and making one desperate rush. But the men of Wei would not fight with them, and they re-ascended the hill.

Ma Su saw that matters were going ill, so he issued orders to bar the gates and defend till help should come.

When Wang P'ing saw the hill surrounded he started to go to the rescue, but Chang Ho checked him, and after exchanging a half score encounters Wang was compelled to retire whence he had come.

The Wei men kept a close siege. The men in the hill camp, having no water, were unable to prepare food, and disorder broke out. The shouting was audible at the foot of the hill and went on far into the night. The men on the south face got out of hand, opened the gates and surrendered. The men of Wei went round the hill setting fire to the wood, which led to still greater confusion in the beleaguered garrison. At last Ma Su decided to make a dash for safety toward the west.

Ssŭma allowed him to pass, but Chang Ho was sent to pursue and chased him for thirty *li*. But then there came an unexpected roll of drums. Chang Ho was stopped by Wei Yen while Ma Su got past. Whirling up his sword, Wei Yen dashed toward Chang, who retired within his ranks and fled. Wei followed and drove Chang backward toward Chieht'ing.

The pursuit continued for fifty *li*, and then Wang found himself in an ambush, Ssŭma I on one side and his son on the other. They closed in behind Wei Yen, and he was surrounded. Chang Ho then turned back, and the attack was now on three sides. Wei Yen lost many men, and all his efforts failed to get him clear of the press. Then help appeared in the person of Wang P'ing.

"This is life for me," said Wei Yen as he saw Wang coming up, and the two forces joined in a new attack on the men of Wei. So the men of Wei drew off, while Wei Yen and Wang P'ing made all haste back to their own camps—only to find them in the hands of the enemy.

Shên I and Shên Tan then rushed out and drove Wei and Wang toward Liehliuch'êng. There they were received by Kao Hsiang, who had come out to meet his unfortunate colleagues.

When Kao Hsiang heard their story, he at once proposed a night attack on the Wei camp and the recovery of Chieht'ing. They talked this over on the hillside and arranged their plans, after which they set themselves to wait till it was dark enough to start.

They set out along three roads; and Wei Yen was the first to reach Chieht'ing. Not a soldier was visible, which looked suspicious. He decided to await the arrival of Kao Hsiang and they both speculated as to the whereabouts of their enemy. They could find no trace, and the third army had not yet come up.

Suddenly a bomb exploded, and a brilliant flash lit up the sky; drums rolled as though the earth was rending, and the enemy appeared. In a trice the armies of Shu found themselves hemmed in. Both leaders pushed here and shoved there, but could find no way out. Then most opportunely from behind a hill rolled out a thunder of drums, and there was Wang P'ing coming to their rescue. Then the three forced their way to Liehliuch'êng. But just as they drew near to the rampart another body of men came up, which, from the writing on their flags, they recognised as Kuo Huai's army.

Now Kuo was here from unworthy motives. He had talked over Ssǔma's recall with his colleague Ts'ao Chên, and, fearing lest the recalled general should acquire too great glory, Kuo had set out to anticipate him in the capture of Chieht'ing. Disappointed when he heard of his rival's success there, he had decided to try a similar exploit at Liehliuch'êng. So he had diverted his march thither.

He engaged the three Shu armies at once and slew so many of them that at Wei Yen's suggestion they all left for Yang-p'ing Pass, which might be in danger.

Kuo Huai, pleased with his success, gathered in his army after the victory and said to his officers, "I was disappointed at Chieht'ing, but we have taken this place, and that is merit of high order."

Thereupon he proceeded to the city gates. Just as he arrived, a bomb exploded on the wall, and, looking up, he saw

the rampart bedecked with flags. On the largest banner he
read the name of the general, Ssŭma I. At that moment
Ssŭma himself lifted a board that hung in front of him and
looked over the breast-high rail. He looked down and smiled,
saying, "How late you are, friend Kuo!"

Kuo was amazed. "He is too much for me," said he. So
he resignedly entered the city and went to pay his respects to
his successful rival.

Ssŭma was gracious, and said, "K'ung-ming must retire now
that Chieht'ing is lost. You join forces with Ts'ao Chen and
follow up quickly."

Ssŭma called to him his van-leader, and said, "Those two
thought we should win too great merit, so they tried to get
ahead of us here. We are not the only ones who desire to
achieve good service and acquire merit, but we had the good
fortune to succeed. I thought the enemy would first try to
occupy Yangp'ing Pass, and if I went to take it then Chuko
would fall on our rear. It says in the books on war that one
should crush a retreating enemy not pursue broken rebels,
so you may go along the by-roads and smite those withdrawing
down the Chi Valley, while I oppose the Hsieh Valley army.
If they flee, do not fight, but just hold them up on the road and
capture the baggage train."

Chang marched away with half the force to carry out his
part of this plan, while Ssŭma gave orders to go to Hsieh
Valley by way of Hsich'êng, which though a small place, was
important as a dépôt of stores for the Shu army, beside
commanding the road to the three districts of Nanan, T'ienshui
and Anting. If this place could be captured the other three
could be recaptured.

Ssŭma left Shên Tan and Shên I to guard Liehliuch'êng and
marched his army toward the Hsieh Valley.

After K'ung-ming had sent Ma Su to guard Chieht'ing he
was undecided what to do next. Then arrived the messenger
with the plan prepared by Wang P'ing. K'ung-ming went
over to his table and opened the letter. As he read it he smote
the table in wrath.

"Ma Su's foolishness has destroyed the army," he cried.

"Why are you so disturbed, O Minister?" asked those near.

"By this plan I see that we have lost command of an
important road. The camp has been made on the hill, and
if the Wei men come in force our army will be surrounded
and their water supply interrupted. In two days the men
will be in a state of mutiny, and if Chieht'ing shall be lost
how shall we be able to retire?"

Here the *Chang-shih* Yang I said, "I am none too clever I
know, but let me go to replace Ma Su."

K'ung-ming explained to him how and where to camp, but
before he could start a horseman brought the news of the loss

of Chieht'ing and Liehliuch'êng. This made K'ung-ming very sad, and he sighed, saying, "The whole scheme has come to nought, and it is my fault."

He sent for Kuan and Chang, and said, "You two take three companies of good men and go along the road to Wukungshan. If you fall in with the enemy do not fight, but beat drums and raise a hubbub and make them hesitate and be doubtful, so that they may retire. Do not pursue, but when they retire make for Yangp'ing Pass."

He also sent Chang I to put Chienko in order for retreat and issued instructions for making ready to march. Ma Tai and Chiang Wei were told to guard the rear, but they were to go into ambush in the valleys till the army was on the march. Trusty men were sent with the news to T'ienshui, Nanan and Anting that the officers, army and people might go away into Hanchung. He also sent to remove to a place of safety the aged mother of Chiang Wei.

All these arrangements made, K'ung-ming took five companies and set out for Hsich'êng to remove the stores. But messenger after messenger came to say that Ssŭma I was advancing rapidly on Hsich'êng with a large army. No leader of rank was left to K'ung-ming; he had only the civil officials and the five companies, and as half this force had started to remove the stores, he had only two and a half companies left.

His officers were all frightened at the news of near approach of the enemy. K'ung-ming himself went up on the rampart to look around. He saw clouds of dust rising into the sky. The Wei armies were nearing Hsich'êng along two roads. Then he ordered all the banners to be removed and concealed, and said if any officer in command of soldiers in the city moved or made any noise he would be instantly put to death. Next he threw open all the gates and set a score of soldiers dressed as ordinary people cleaning the streets at each gate. When all these preparations were complete, he donned the simple Taoist dress he affected on occasions and, attended by a couple of lads, sat down on the wall by one of the towers with his lute before him and a stick of incense burning.

Ssŭma's scouts came near the city gate and saw all this. They did not enter the city, but went back and reported what they had seen. Ssŭma I smiled incredulously. But he halted his army and rode ahead himself. Lo! it was exactly as the scouts had reported; K'ung-ming sat there, his face all smiles. A lad stood on one side of him bearing a sword and on the other a boy with the ordinary symbol of authority, a yak's tail. Just inside the gates a score of persons with their heads down were sweeping as if no one was about.

Ssŭma hardly believed his eyes and thought this meant some peculiarly subtle ruse. So he went back to his armies, faced them about and moved toward the hills on the north.

"I am certain there are no soldiers behind this foolery," said his second son. "What do you retire for, father?"

"Chuko is always most careful and runs no risks. Those open gates undoubtedly mean an ambush, and if our men enter the city they will fall victims to his guile. How can you know? No; our course is to retire."

Thus were the two armies turned back from the city, much to the joy of K'ung-ming, who laughed and clapped his hands as he saw them hastening away. The officials gasped with astonishment, and they asked K'ung-ming to explain the phenomenon of a great army marching off at the sight of a single man. So he told them.

"He knows my reputation for carefulness and that I play not with danger. Seeing things as they were made him suspect an ambush, and so he turned away. I do not run risks, but this time there was no help for it. Now he will meet with Kuan and Chang, whom I sent away into the hills to wait for him."

They were still in the grip of fear, but they praised the depth of insight of their chief and his mysterious schemes and unfathomable plans.

"We should simply have run away," said they.

"What could we have done with two companies and a half even if we had run? We should not have gone far before being caught," said K'ung-ming.

> Quite open lay the city to the foe,
> But Chuko's lute of jasper wonders wrought;
> It turned aside the legions' onward march
> For both the leaders guessed the other's thought.

"But if I had been in his place I should not have turned away," said K'ung-ming, smiling and clapping his hands.

He gave orders that the people of the place should follow the army into Hanchung, for Ssŭma would assuredly return.

They abandoned Hsich'êng and returned into Hanchung. In due course the officials and soldiers and people out of the three districts also came in.

It has been said that Ssŭma I turned aside from the city. He went to Wukungshan. Presently there came the sounds of an army from behind the hills. The leader turned to his sons, saying, "If we do not retire we shall yet somehow fall victims to this Chuko Liang."

Then appeared a force advancing rapidly, the banners bearing the name of Chang Pao. The men of Wei were seized with sudden panic and ran, flinging off their armour and throwing away their weapons. But before they had fled very far they heard other terrible sounds in the valley and soon saw another force, with banners inscribed "Kuan Hsing." The roar of armed men echoing up and down the valley was terrifying, and as no one could tell how many men there were bearing down on them the panic increased. The Wei army abandoned all the baggage and took to flight. But having orders not to pursue, the two Shu generals let their enemies run in peace, while they gathered up the spoils. Then they returned.

Seeing the valley apparently full of men of Shu, Ssǔma dared not leave the main road. He hurried back to Chieht'ing.

At this time Ts'ao Chên, hearing that the army of Shu was retreating, went in pursuit. But at a certain point he encountered a strong force under Ma Tai and Chiang Wei. Valley and hill seemed to swarm with enemies, and Ts'ao became alarmed. Then his van-leader was slain by Ma Tai, and the soldiers were panic-sticken and fled in disorder.

Meanwhile the men of Shu were hastening night and day along the road into Hanchung. Chao Yün and Têng Chi, who had been lying in ambush in Chi Valley, heard that their comrades were retreating. Then said Chao Yün, "The men of Wei will surely come to smite us while we are retreating. Wherefore let me first take up a position in their rear, and then you lead off your men and part of mine, showing my ensigns. I will follow, keeping at the same distance behind you, and thus I shall be able to protect the retreat."

Now Kuo Huai was leading his army through the Chi Valley. He called up his van-leader Su Yung and said to him, "Chao Yün is a warrior whom no one can withstand. You must keep a most careful guard lest you fall into some trap while they are retreating."

Su Yung replied, smiling, "If you will help me, O Commander, we shall be able to capture this Chao Yün.

So Su Yung, with three companies, hastened on ahead and entered the valley in the wake of the Shu army. He saw upon a slope in the distance a large red banner bearing the name of Chao Yün. This frightened him, and he retired. But before he had gone far a great uproar arose about him, and a mighty warrior came bounding forth on a swift steed, crying, "Do you recognise Chao Yün?"

Su Yung was terrified. "Whence came you?" he cried. "Is there another Chao Yün here."

He could make no stand, and soon fell victim to the spear of the veteran. His men scattered, and Chao Yün hurried on after the main body.

But soon another company came in pursuit, this time led by one Wan Chêng. As they came along Chao Yün halted in the middle of the road. By the time Wan had come close the other Shu soldiers had gone about thirty *li* along the road. However, when Wan drew nearer still and saw who it was standing in his path, he hesitated and finally halted. Presently he turned back and retired altogether, confessing on his return that he had not dared to face the old warrior, who seemed as terrible as ever.

However, Kuo Huai was not content and ordered him to return to the pursuit of the retreating army. This time he had many horsemen with him. Presently they came to a wood, and, as they entered, a loud shout arose in the rear, "Chao Yün is here!"

Terror seized upon the pursuers, and many fell from their horses. The others scattered among the hills. Wan Chêng braced himself for the encounter and went on. Chao shot an arrow which struck the plume on his helmet. Startled, he tumbled into a water-course. Then Chao pointed his spear at him and said, "Be off! I will not kill you. Go and tell your chief to come quickly, if he is coming."

Wan fled for his life, while Chao continued his march as rear-guard, and the retreat into Hanchung steadily continued. There were no other episodes by the way. Ts'ao Chen and Kuo Huai took to themselves all the credit of having recovered the three districts.

Before the cautious Ssŭma was ready to pursue the army of Shu it had already reached Hanchung. He took a troop of horse and rode to Hsich'êng and there heard from the few people who had formerly sought refuge in the hills, and now returned, that K'ung-ming really had had no men in the city, with the exception of the two and a half companies, that he had not a single military commander, but only a few civil officers. He also heard that Kuan and Chang had had only a few men whom they led about among the hills making as much noise as they could. Ssŭma felt sad at having been tricked. "K'ung-ming is a cleverer man than I am," said he with a sigh of resignation.

He set about restoring order, and presently marched back to Ch'angan. He saw his master Ts'ao Jui, who was pleased with his success and said, "It is by your good service that Shênsi is again mine."

Ssŭma replied, "But the army of Shu is in Hanchung undestroyed; wherefore I pray for authority to go against them that you may recover Shu also."

Ts'ao Jui rejoiced and approved, and authorised the raising of an army.

But then one of the courtiers suddenly said, "Your servant can propose a plan by which Shu will be overcome and Wu submit."

> The captains lead their beaten soldiers home,
> The victors plan new deeds for days to come.

Who offered this plan? Succeeding chapters will tell.

CHAPTER IVC.

K'ung-ming Weeps, But Puts Ma Su to Death:
Chou Fang Cuts Off His Hair and Beguiles Ts'ao Hsiu.

The proposer of the great plan that was to reunite the empire was a President of a Board, named Sun Tzŭ.

"Noble Sir, expound your excellent scheme," said King Jui of Wei.

And Sun Tzŭ said, "When your great progenitor, the Emperor Wu (Ts'ao Ts'ao), first got Chang Lu he was at a critical stage in his career, but thenceforward all went well. He used to say 'Nanchêng is really a natural hell. In the Hsieh Valley there are five hundred *li* of rocks and caves, so that it is an impossible country for an army.' If the country be denuded of soldiers in order to conquer Shu, then for sure we shall be invaded by Wu on the east. My advice is to divide the army among the various generals and appoint each a place of strategic value to hold, and let them train their forces. In a few years the Central Land will be prosperous and wealthy, while the other two, Shu and Wu, will have been reduced by mutual quarrels and will fall an easy prey. I hope Your Majesty will consider whether this is not a superior plan."

"What does the great General think? said Ts'ao Jui to Ssŭma.

He replied, "President Sun says well."

So Jui bade Ssŭma I draw up a scheme of defence and station the soldiers, leaving Kuo Huai and Chang Ho to guard Ch'angan. And having rewarded the army, he the returned to Loyang.

When K'ung-ming got back to Hanchung and missed Chao Yün and Têng Chih, the only two captains who had not arrived, he was sad at heart and bade Kuan and Chang go back to afford them assistance. However, before the reinforcing parties could leave, the missing men arrived. Furthermore, they came with their men in excellent condition and not a man short, nor a horse nor any of their equipment. As they drew near, K'ung-ming went out to welcome them. Thereupon Chao Yün hastily dismounted and bowed to the earth, saying, "The Prime Minister should not have come forth to welcome a defeated general."

But K'ung-ming lifted him up and took his hand and said, "Mine was the fault, mine were the ignorance and unwisdom

that caused all this. But how is it that amid all the defeat
and loss you have come through unscathed?"

And Têng Chih replied, "It was because friend Chao sent
me ahead, while he guarded the rear and warded off every
attack. One leader he slew, and this frightened the others.
Thus nothing was lost or left by the way."

"A really great captain!" said K'ung-ming.

He sent Chao Yün a gift of much gold and many rolls of
silk for his army. But these were returned, Chao Yün saying
that the army deserved punishment rather than reward, since
they had accomplished nothing, and the rules for reward and
punishment must be strictly kept. He prayed that these
things be kept in store till the winter, when they could be
distributed among the men."

"When His late Majesty lived he never tired of extolling
Chao Yün's virtues; lo! he was perfectly right," said K'ung-
ming.

And his respect for the veteran was doubled. Then came
the turn of the four unfortunate leaders Ma, Wang, Wei and
Kao to render account. Wang P'ing was called to the general's tent and rebuked.

"I ordered you and Ma Su to guard Chieht'ing; why did you
not remonstrate with him and prevent this great loss?"

"I did remonstrate many times. I wished to build a rampart down in the road and construct a solid camp, but the
assistant general would not agree and showed ill temper. So
I led half a legion and camped some ten *li* off, and when the
men of Wei came in crowds and surrounded my colleague,
I led my army to attack them a score of times. But I could
not penetrate, and the catastrophe came quickly. Many of
the men surrendered, and mine were too few to stand.
Wherefore I went to friend Wei for help, but I was intercepted
and imprisoned in a valley and only got out by fighting most
desperately. I got back to my camp to find the enemy in
possession, and so I set out for Liehliuch'êng. On the road
I met Kao Hsiang, and we three tried to raid the enemy's
camp, hoping to recover Chieht'ing, but as there was no one
of our side there I grew suspicious. From a hill I saw my
colleagues had been stopped by the men of Wei, so I went to
rescue them. Thence we hastened to Yangp'ing Pass to try
to prevent that from falling. It was not that I failed to
remonstrate. And you, O Minister, can get confirmation of
my words from any of the officers."

K'ung-ming bade him retire, and sent for Ma Su. He came,
bound, and threw himself on the earth at the tent door.

"You have filled yourself with the study of the books on
war ever since you were a boy; you know them thoroughly.
I enjoined upon you that Chieht'ing was most important, and
you pledged yourself and all your family to do pour best in

the enterprise; yet you would not listen to Wang P'ing, and thus you caused this misfortune. The army is defeated, generals have been slain and cities and territory lost, all through you. If I do not make you an example and vindicate the law, how shall I maintain a proper state of discipline? You have offended and you must pay the penalty. After your death the little ones of your family shall be my care, and I will see that they get a monthly allowance. Do not let their fate cause you anxiety."

He told the executioners to take him away.

Ma Su wept bitterly, saying, "Pity me, O Minister, you have looked upon me as a son; I have looked up to you as a father. I know my fault is worthy of death, but I pray you to remember how Shun dealt with Kun, the father of Yu and with Yu himself. Though I die I will harbour no resentment down in the dark depths of the Nine Springs."

K'ung-ming brushed aside his tears and said, "We have been as brothers, and your children shall be as my own. It is useless to say more."

They led the doomed man away. Without the main gate, just as they were going to deal the fatal blow, Chiang Yuan, an officer of rank, who had just arrived from the capital, was passing in. He bade the executioners wait a while, and he went in and interceded for Ma Su.

"Formerly the King of Ch'u put his minister to death and Duke Wên rejoiced. There is great confusion in the land, and yet you would slay a man of admitted ability. Can you not spare him?"

K'ung-ming's tears fell, but he said, "Sun and Wu maintain that the one way to obtain success is to make the law supreme. Now confusion and actual war are in every quarter, and if the law be not observed, how may rebels be made away with? He must die."

Soon after they bore in the head as proof, and K'ung-ming wailed for the victim.

"Why do you weep for him now that he has met the just penalty for his fault?" said Chiang.

"I was not weeping then because of Ma Su, but because I remembered the words of our late Emperor. When in great stress at Paitch'êng, he said that Ma Su's words exceeded the truth, and he was incapable of great deeds. It has come true, and I greatly regret my want of insight. That is why I weep."

Every officer wept. Ma Su was but thirty-nine, and he met his end in the fifth month of the sixth year of *Chien-Hsing*.

A poet wrote about him thus:—

'Twas pitiful that he who talked so glib
Of war, should lose a city, fault most grave,
With death as expiation. At the gate
He paid stern law's extremest penalty.
Deep grieved, his chief recalled the late king's words.

The head of the victim was paraded round the camps. Then it was sewn again to the body and buried with it. K'ung-ming conducted the sacrifices for the dead and read the oration. A monthly allowance was made for the family and they were consoled as much as possible. Next K'ung-ming made his memorial to the Throne and bade Chiang Wan bear it to the king. Therein he proposed his own degradation from his high office.

"Naturally a man of mediocre abilities, I have enjoyed your confidence undeservedly. Having led out an expedition, I have proved my inability to perform the high office of leader. Over solicitude was my undoing. Hence happened disobedience at Chieht'ing and the failure to guard Chiku. The fault is mine in that I erred in the use of men. In my anxiety I was too secretive. The 'Spring and Autumn' has pronounced such as I am to be blameworthy, and whither may I flee from my fault? I pray that I may be degraded three degrees as punishment. I cannot express my mortification. I humbly await your command."

"Why does the Prime Minister speak thus?" said the king. "It is but the ordinary fortune of war."

The courtier Fei I said, "The Ruler must enhance the majesty of the law, for without law how can men support him? It is right that the minister should be degraded in rank."

Thereupon an edict was issued reducing K'ung-ming to the rank of a *Chiang-chün*, Generalissimo, but retaining him in the same position in the direction of state affairs and command of the military forces. Fei I was directed to communicate the decision.

Fei bore the edict into Hanchung and gave it to K'ung-ming, who bowed to the decree. The envoy thought K'ung-ming might be mortified, so he ventured to felicitate him in other matters.

"It was a great joy to the people when the four districts were captured," said he.

"What sort of language is this?" said K'ung-ming, annoyed. "Success followed by failure is no success. It shames me indeed to hear such a compliment."

"His Majesty will be very pleased to hear of the acquisition of Chiang Wei."

This remark also angered K'ung-ming, who replied, "It is my fault that a defeated army has returned without any gain of territory. What injury to the enemy was the loss of this man?"

Fei I tried again. "But with an army of ten legions of bold men you can attack Wei again."

"When we were at Ch'ishan and Chi Valley we outnumbered the enemy, but we could not conquer them. On the contrary, they beat us. The defect was not in the number of soldiers, but in the leadership. Now we must reduce the army, discover our faults, reflect on our errors and mend our ways against the future. Unless this is so, what is the use of a numerous army? Hereafter every man will have to look to the future of his country. But most diligently we must fight against our shortcomings and blame our inefficiencies; then we may succeed. Rebellion can be exterminated and merit can be set up."

Fei I and the officers acknowledged the aptness of these remarks. Fei went back to the capital, leaving K'ung-ming in Hanchung resting his soldiers and doing what he could for the people, training and heartening his men and turning special attention to the construction of apparatus for assaults on cities and crossing rivers. He also collected grain and fodder and built battle rafts, all for future use.

The spies of Wei got to know of these doings, and the king called Ssŭma I to council and asked how Shu might be annexed.

"Shu cannot be attacked," was the reply. "In this present hot weather they will not come out, but, if we invade, they will only garrison and defend their strategic points, which we should find it hard to overcome."

"What shall we do if they invade us again?"

"I have prepared for that. Just now Chuko Liang is imitating Han Hsin when he secretly crossed the river into Ch'ênts'ang. I can recommend a man to guard the place by building a rampart there and rendering it absolutely secure. He is a tall man, round shouldered and powerful, a good archer and prudent strategist. He would be quite equal to dealing with an invasion. His name is Hao Chao, and he is in command at Hohsi."

The king accepted the recommendation, and an edict went forth promoting this man and sending him to command in the Ch'ênts'ang district.

Soon after this edict was issued, a memorial was received from Ts'ao Hsiu, Minister of War and Commandant of Yangchou, saying that Chou Fang, Prefect of Yehyang, wished to tender his submission and transfer his allegiance, and had sent a man to present a memorandum under seven headings showing how the power of East Wu could be broken and to ask that an army be despatched soon. Ts'ao Jui spread the document out on the couch that he and Ssŭma might read it.

"It seems very reasonable," said Ssŭma. "Wu could be quite destroyed. Let me go with an army to help Ts'ao Hsiu."

But from among the courtiers stepped out Chia K'uei, who said, "What this man of Wu says may be understood in two ways; do not trust it. Chou Fang is a wise and crafty man and very unlikely to desert. In this is some ruse to decoy our soldiers into danger."

"Such words also must be listened to," said Ssŭma. "Yet such a chance must not be missed."

"You and he might both go to the help of Ts'ao Hsiu," said the king.

They went; and a large army, led by Ts'ao Hsiu, moved to Wanch'êng (Anking, another to Yangch'êng, just toward the East Pass, and a third under Ssŭma I to Chiangling.

Now the King of Wu, Sun Ch'üan, was at the East Pass in Wuchang, and there he assembled his officers and said, "The Prefect of Yehyang, Chou Fang, has sent up a secret memorial saying that Ts'ao Hsiu, of Wei, intends to invade. He has therefore set out a trap for him and has drawn up a document giving seven plausible circumstances, hoping thereby to cajole the Wei army into his power. The armies of Wei are on the move in three divisions, and I need your advice."

Ku Yung stood forth, saying, "There is only one man fit to cope with the present need; he is Lu Hsün."

So Lu Hsün was summoned and made "Upholder of State" General, Master of the Forces and Commander-in-chief of all the State Armies, including the Royal Corps of Guards, and Associate Assistant in the Royal Duties. He was given the White Banners and the Golden Axes, which denoted imperial rank in the days of Chou, and all officers, civil and military, were placed under his orders. Moreover, Sun Ch'üan personally stood beside him and held his whip while he mounted his steed.

Having received all these marks of confidence and favour, Lu Hsün named as his two immediate assistants Chu Huan and Ch'üan Ts'ung, who were approved by the king. Their titles were Right and Left Commander-in-chief respectively.

Then the grand army, comprising all the forces of the eighty one districts of Chiangnan and the levies of Chingchou and Hu, seventy-one legions, was assembled and marched out in three divisions, Lu Hsün in the centre, with his two lieutenants supporting him right and left with the other two columns.

Then said Chu Huan, "Ts'ao Jên is neither able nor bold; he holds office because he is of the blood. He has fallen into the trap laid by Chou Fang and marched too far to be able to withdraw. If the Master of the Forces will smite he must be defeated. Defeated, he must flee along two roads, one Chia-shih, the other Kueich'e, both of which are precipitous and narrow. Let me and my colleague go to prepare an ambush in these roads. We will block them and so cut off their escape. If this Ts'ao Hsiu could be captured, and a hasty advance made, success would be easy and sure. We should get Shouch'un, whence Hsüch'ang and Loyang can be seen. This is the one chance in the thousand."

"I do not think the plan good," said Lu Hsün. "I have a better one."

Chu Huan resented the rejection of his scheme and went away angry. Lu Hsün ordered Chuko Chin and certain others to garrison Chiangling and oppose Ssŭma I and made all other dispositions of forces.

Ts'ao Hsiu neared Huanch'êng, and Chou Fang came out of the city to welcome him and went to the general's tent. Ts'ao Hsiu said, "I received your letter and the memorandum, which was most logical, and sent it to His Majesty. He has set in motion accordingly three armies. It will be a great merit for you, Sir, if Chiangtung can be added to his dominions. Men say you are insufficient in craft, but I do not believe what they say, for I think you will be true to me and not fail."

Chou Fang wept. He seized a sword from one of his escort and was about to kill himself, but Ts'ao Hsiu stopped him. Still leaning on the sword, Chou Fang said, "As to the seven things I mentioned, my regret is that I cannot show you all. You doubt me because some persons from Wu have been poisoning your mind against me. If you heed them the only course for me is to die. Heaven only can make manifest my loyal heart."

Again he made to slay himself. But Ts'ao Hsiu in trepidation threw his arms about him, saying, "I did not mean it; the words were uttered in jest. Why do you act thus?"

Upon this, Chou Fang, with his sword, cut off his hair and threw it on the ground, saying, "I have dealt with you with sincerity, Sir, and you joke about it. Now I have cut off the hair, which I inherited from my parents, in order to prove my sincerity."

Then Ts'ao Hsiu doubted no more, but trusted him fully and prepared a banquet for him, and when the feast was over Chou Fang returned to his own.

The General Chia K'uei came to Ts'ao Hsiu, and when asked whether there was any special reason for the visit, he said, "I have come to warn you, Commander, to be cautious and wait till you and I can attack the enemy together. The whole army of Wu is encamped at Wanch'êng."

"You mean you want to share in my victory," sneered Ts'ao Hsiu.

"It is said Chou Fang cut off his hair as a pledge of sincerity; that is only another bit of deceit. According to the 'Spring and Autumn' Yao Li cut off his arm as a pledge that he meant to assassinate Ch'ing Chi; mutilation is no guarantee. Do not trust him."

"Why do you come to utter ill-omened words just as I am opening the campaign? You destroy the spirit of the army," said Ts'ao.

In his wrath he told the lictors to put Chia to death. However, the officers interceded, and Chia was reprieved; but he was not assigned any part in the campaign, and his men were left in reserve. He himself went away to Tung Kuan. When Chou Fang heard that Chia had been broken, he rejoiced in his heart, saying, "If Ts'ao Hsiu had attended to his words then Wu would have lost. Heaven is good to me and is giving me the means of achieving great things."

Then he sent a secret messenger to Wanch'êng, and Lu Hsün knew that the time had come. He assembled the officers for orders.

Lu said, "Shiht'ing, lying over against us, is a hilly country fit for preparing an ambush. It will be occupied as suitable to array our army and await the coming of Wei. Hsü Shêng is to be leader of the van, and the army will move."

Now Ts'ao Hsiu told Chou Fang to lead the way for his attack. He asked Chou the name of the place lying ahead, and was told Shiht'ing.

"It is a suitable place to camp in," said Chou Fang.

So a great camp was made there. But soon after the scouts reported that a very large number of soldiers of Wu had occupied the hills. Ts'ao Hsiu began to feel alarmed. "Chou Fang said there were no soldiers; why these preparations?"

He hastily sought Chou Fang to ask him, and was told he had gone away, no one knew whither.

"I have been deceived and am in a trap," said Ts'ao Hsiu, now very repentant of his easy confidence. "However, there is nothing to fear."

Then he made his arrangements to march against the enemy, and when they were complete and the array drawn up, Chang P'u, the leader of the van, rode out and began to rail at the men of Wu.

"Rebel leader, come and surrender!" cried Chang.

Then rode out Hsü Shêng and fought with him. But Chang was no match for the men of Wu, as was soon evident, wherefore he led his men to retire.

"Hsü Shêng is too strong," said he when he saw Ts'ao Hsiu.

"Then will we defeat him by a surprise," said Ts'ao Hsiu.

He sent Chang with two legions to hide in the south of Shiht'ing, while another equal party was sent north. And they arranged that on the morrow Ts'ao Hsiu, by pretended defeat, should lead the men of Wei into the ambush thus prepared.

On the other side Lu Hsün called his two lieutenants Chu and Ch'üan and said, "Each of you is to lead three legions and take a cross cut from Shiht'ing to the enemy's camp. Give a signal on arrival, and then the main army will advance between you."

As evening fell these two moved out their men, and by the middle of the second watch both had got close to the camp of

Wei. Chang P'u, of Wei, who was there in ambush, as has been said, did not recognise that the men who approached him were enemies, but went as to meet friends and was at once slain by Chu Huan of Wu. The men of Wei then fled, and Chu lit his signal fires. Ch'üan Ts'ung, marching up, came across the southern ambush under Hsüeh Ch'iao. Ch'üan began a battle at once, and the men of Wei were soon put to flight. Both the armies of Wu pursued, and confusion reigned in Ts'ao Hsiu's camp, men fighting with others of their own side and slaying each other.

Ts'ao Hsiu despaired and fled toward Chiashih. Hsü Shêng, with a strong force, came along the high road and attacked. And the men of Wei killed were very many. Those who escaped did so by abandoning all their armour.

Ts'ao Hsiu was in straits, but he struggled along the Chiashih Road. Here came a cohort into the road from the side. It was led by Chia K'uei. Ts'ao Hsiu's alarm gave place to shame on meeting Chia K'uei.

"I took no notice of what you said, and so this evil came upon me," said he.

Chia K'uei replied, "Sir, you should quickly get out of this road, for if the men of Wu block it we shall be in grave danger."

So Ts'ao Hsiu hastened, while Chia K'uei protected his retreat. And he behaved cunningly, setting flags and banners up among trees and in thickets and along by-paths, so as to give an impression of having many men posted all round. Wherefore when Hsü Shêng came in pursuit he thought the country was full of ambushed men and dared not proceed far. So he gave up the pursuit and retired.

By these means Ts'ao Hsiu was rescued, and finally Ssŭma arrived and drove the enemy off.

In the meantime, Lu Hsün was awaiting news of victory. Soon his various captains came and reported their successes, and they brought great spoil of carts and bullocks, horses and mules and military material and weapons. And they had also many prisoners. There was great rejoicing, and Lu Hsün with Chou Fang led the army home into Wu. On their return Sun Ch'üan came out with a numerous cortège of officers to welcome the victors, and an imperial umbrella was borne over the head of Lu Hsün as they wended their way homeward.

When the officers presented their felicitations Sun Ch'üan noticed that Chou Fang had no hair, and he was very gracious to him, saying, "This deed of yours, and the sacrifice you made to attain it, will surely be written in the histories."

He created Chou Marquis of the "Gate Within." Then there were great feastings and greetings and much revelry.

Lu Hsün said, "Ts'ao Hsiu has been thoroughly beaten, and the men of Wei are cowed. I think now is an occasion to send letters into Shu to advise Chuko Liang to attack Wei."

Sun Ch'üan agreed, and letters were sent.

> The east, successful in one fight,
> Would unto war the west incite.

The next chapter will say if K'ung-ming once more tried to overcome Wei.

CHAPTER IIIC.

K'UNG-MING PROPOSES TO RENEW THE ATTACK ON WEI: CHIANG WEI DEFEATS AN ARMY BY MEANS OF A FORGED LETTER.

It was in the autumn of the sixth year that the Wei army was defeated, with very great loss, by Lu Hsün of Wu. Ts'ao Hsiu's mortification brought on an illness from which he died in Loyang. By command of the king he received most honourable burial.

Then Ssŭma I brought the army home again. The other officers went to welcome him and asked why he hurried home after a defeat, which affected him also as Master of the Forces. He replied that he came for reasons of strategy, because of K'ung-ming's probable intentions. They listened and smiled; for they thought he was afraid.

Letters from Wu came to Shu proposing a joint attack on Wei and detailing their recent victory. In these letters two feelings were gratified—that of telling the story of their own grandeur and prowess, and furthering the design of a treaty of peace. The king was pleased and sent the letters to K'ung-ming in Hanchung.

At that time the army was in excellent state, the men hardy, the horses strong. There were plentiful supplies of all kinds. K'ung-ming was just going to propose a new war.

On receipt of the letter he made a great banquet to discuss an expedition. A severe gale came on from the north-east and brought down a fir tree in front of the general's shelter. It was an inauspicious omen to all the officers, and they were troubled. K'ung-ming cast lots to know what portent was intended, and announced the loss of a great leader. They hardly believed him. But before the banquet ended two sons of Chao Yün came and wished to see K'ung-ming.

K'ung-ming, deeply affected, threw aside his wine cup and cried, "That is it; Chao Yün is gone."

When the two young men came in they prostrated themselves and wept; their father had died the night before at the third watch. K'ung-ming staggered and burst into lamentation.

"My friend is gone; the country has lost its great beam and I my right arm."

Those about him joined in, wiping away their tears. K'ung-ming bade the two young men go in person to Ch'êngtu to bear the sad tidings to the king. And the king also wept.

"Tzŭ-lung was my saviour and friend; he saved my life when I was a child in the time of great confusion," cried the king.

An edict was issued creating the late general "Marquis of Shun-p'ing" and permitting burial on the east of Chinp'ing Hill. A temple was ordered to his memory and sacrifices.

> From Ch'angshan came a captain, tiger-bold,
> In wit and valour he was fitting mate
> For Kuan and Chang, his exploits rivalling
> E'en theirs. Han Waters and Tangyang recall
> His name. Twice in his stalwart arms he bore
> The prince, his well-loved leader's son and heir.
> In storied page his name stands out, writ large,
> Fair record of most brave and loyal deeds.

The king showed his affectionate gratitude to the late leader, not only in according him most honourable burial, but in kindness to his sons, the elder, T'ung, being made a "Fiercely-energetic" *Chunglang* General and the younger *Kuang Ya-mên* General. He also set guards over the tomb.

When the two sons had left, the ministers reported to the king that the dispositions of the army were complete, and the leader proposed to march against Wei without delay. Talking this over with one and another, the king found the courtiers much inclined to a cautious policy and somewhat fearful. And the doubts entered into the king's mind so that he could not decide. Then came a memorial from K'ung-ming, and the messenger, Yang I, was called into the presence and gave it to the king. He spread it on the imperial table and read: "The late Emperor was anxious lest the rebels should set up a rival empire and the legitimate Ruler's domain be restricted. Wherefore he laid upon me, thy minister, to destroy them. Measuring my powers by his perspicacity he knew that I should attack and oppose my talents, inadequate as they might be, to their strength, for, if I did not, the royal domain would be destroyed. It was a question whether to await destruction without effort, or to attack? Wherefore he assigned me the task confidently. Thenceforward this task occupied all my thoughts.

"Considering that the south should be made secure before the north could be attacked, I braved the heat of summer and plunged deep into the wilds. Sparing not myself nor regarding privation, urged by the one consideration, that the royal domain should not be confined to the capital of Shu, I faced dangers in obedience to the late Emperor's behest. But there are critics who may say that I failed. Now the rebels have been weakened in the west and have become involved in the east. The rule of war is to take advantage of the enemy's weakness, and so now is the time to attack. I shall discuss the various circumstances in order.

"The enlightenment of the Founder of the Hans rivalled the glory of the sun and moon; his counsellors were profound as the ocean abyss. Nevertheless, he trod a hazardous path and suffered losses, only attaining repose after passing through great dangers. Your Majesty does not reach his level, nor do your counsellors equal Chang Liang and Ch'ên P'ing, yet, while they desire victory, they would sit idle, waiting till the empire should become settled. This attitude is beyond my comprehension.

"Liu Yu and Wang Lang each occupied a district. They passed their time in talking of tranquillity and discussing plans, quoting the sayings of the sages till they were filled with doubts and obsessed with difficulties. So this year was not the time to fight, nor next year the season to punish, and, thus talking, it came about that Sun Ts'ê grew powerful and possessed himself of all Chiangtung. This sort of behaviour I cannot understand.

"In craft Ts'ao Ts'ao surpassed all men. He could wield armies like the great strategists of old, Sun Wu and Wu Ch'i. Yet he was hemmed in in Nanyang, was in danger at Wuch'ao, was in difficulties at Ch'ilien, was hard pressed in Liyang, was nearly defeated at Peishan and nearly killed at Ch'angkuan. Yet, after all these experiences, there was a temporary and artificial state of equilibrium. How much less can I, a man of feeble powers, bring about a decision without running risks? I fail to understand.

"Ts'ao Ts'ao failed in five attacks on Changpa, and four times crossed the Ch'aohu without success. He employed Li Fu, who betrayed him, and put his trust in Hsiahou, who was defeated and died. His late Majesty always regarded Ts'ao Ts'ao as an able man, and yet he made such mistakes. How then can I, in my worn-out condition, necessarily conquer? I do not understand why.

"Only one year has elapsed since I went into Hanchung, yet we have lost Chao Yün, Yang Chün, Ma Yü, Yen Chih, Ting Li, Pai Shou, Liu Ho, Têng T'ung, and others, and leaders of rank and captains of stations, to the number of near four score, all men unsurpassed in dash and valour, and more than a thousand of the irregular horse and trained cavalry of the *Sou* (aborigines) of Ts'ung and the Tanguts of Tsinghai (Gobi Desert), whose martial spirit we have fostered these ten years all about us, and not only in one district. If we delay much longer, two-thirds of this will have dissipated, and how then shall we meet the situation? I do not understand delay.

"The people are poor and the army exhausted indeed, and confusion does not cease. If confusion does not cease, then, whether we go on or stand still the drain is the same. Yet it seems that attack should not be made yet! Is it that the rebels

are to be allowed to obtain a permanent hold on some province?
I do not understand the arguments.

"A stable condition of affairs is indeed difficult to obtain.
Once, when the late Emperor was defeated in Ch'u, Ts'ao
Ts'ao patted himself on the back and said that the empire
was settled. Yet, after that, the late Emperor obtained the
support of Wu and Yüeh on the east, took Pa and Shu on the
west and undertook an expedition to the north, wherein Hsiahou lost his life. So Ts'ao Ts'ao's calculations proved erron-
eous, and the affairs of Han seemed about to prosper. But, still
later, Wu proved false to pledges, our Kuan was defeated, we
sustained a check at Tzŭkuei—and Ts'ao P'ei assumed the
imperial style. Such events prove the difficulty of forecast.
I shall strive on to the end, but the final result, whether success
or failure, whether gain or loss, is beyond my powers to
foresee."

The king was convinced, and by edict directed K'ung-ming
to start on the expedition. He marched out with thirty legions
of well-trained men, Wei Yen leading the first division, and
made all haste to Ch'ênts'ang.

The news soon reached Loyang, and Ssŭma I informed the
King of Wei, who called his council. Then Ts'ao Chên stepped
forth and said, "I failed to hold Shênsi, and my disgrace is
terrible to bear. But now I beg to be given another command
that I may capture Chuko Liang. Lately I have found a
stalwart soldier for a leader, a man who wields a sixty catty
sword, rides a swift and savage steed, bends the two hundred
catty bow and carries hidden about him when he goes into
battle three meteor maces with which his aim is certain. So
valorous is he that none dare stand against him. He comes
from Shênsi and is named Wang Shuang. I would recommend
him for my leader of the van."

Ts'ao Jui approved at once and summoned this marvel to
the hall. There came a tall man with a dusky complexion,
hazel eyes, strong as a bear in the hips and with a back
supple as a tiger's.

"No need to fear anything with such a man," said Ts'ao Jui,
laughing.

He gave the new hero rich presents, a silken robe and golden
breastplate, and gave him the title "Tiger-majesty" General.
And he became leader of the van of the new army.

Ts'ao Chên took leave of his master and left the court. He
collected his fifteen legions of veterans and, in consultation
with Kuo Huai and Chang Ho, decided upon the districts and
the points to be guarded.

The first companies of the army of Shu sent out their scouts
as far as Ch'ênts'ang. They came back and reported that a
rampart had been built and behind it was a captain named
Hao Chao in command. The rampart was very strong and

was further defended by "deerhorns." And they thought it would be well to give up all thought of taking it and go out to Ch'ishan by T'aipailing, where was a practicable, though winding, road.

But K'ung-ming said, "Due north of Ch'ênts'ang is Chieht'ing, so that I must get this city in order to advance."

Wei Yen was sent to surround the city and take it. He went, but days passed without success. Therefore he returned and told his chief the place was impregnable. In his anger, K'ung-ming was going to put his general to death, but a certain Yin Hsiang, who said he was a close friend of Hao's, suddenly asked to be allowed to try the effect of persuasion.

"How do you think you will persuade him?" said K'ung-ming. "What will you say?"

"We are both from Shensi and pledged friends from boyhood. If I can get to see him I will so lay matters before him that he must surrender."

He got permission to try, and rode quickly to the wall. Then he called out, "Friend Hao, your old chum Yin has come to see you."

A sentry on the wall told Hao Chao, who bade them let the visitor enter and bring him up on the wall.

"Friend, why have you come?" asked Hao.

"I am in the service of Shu, serving under K'ung-ming as an assistant in the tactical department. I am treated exceedingly well, and my chief has sent me to say something to you."

Hao was rather annoyed, and said, "Chuko is our enemy. I serve Wei while you serve Shu. Each serves his own lord. We were brothers once, but now we are enemies; so do not say any more."

And the visitor was requested to take his leave. He tried to reopen the conversation, but his friend left him and went up on the tower. The Wei soldiers hurried him on to his horse and led him to the gate. As he passed out he looked up and saw his friend leaning on the guard rail. He pulled up his horse, pointed with his whip at Hao, and said, "My friend and worthy brother, why has your friendship become so thin?"

"Brother, you know the laws of Wei," replied Hao. "I have accepted their bounty, and if that leads to death, so be it. Say no more, but return quickly to your master and tell him to come and attack. I am not afraid."

So the abashed Yin had to return and report failure.

"He would not let me begin to explain," said he.

"Try again," said K'ung-ming. "Go and really talk to him."

So the go-between soon found himself once more at the foot of the wall. Hao presently appeared on the tower, and Yin shouted to him, "My worthy brother, please listen to my words while I explain clearly. Here you are holding one single city; how can you think of opposing ten legions? If you do not yield, you will be sorry when it is too late. Instead of serving the great Hans, you are serving a depraved country called Wei. Why do you not recognise the decree of Heaven? Why do you not distinguish between the pure and the foul? Think over it."

Then Hao began to get really angry. He fitted an arrow to his bow and he called out, "Go! or I will shoot. I meant what I said at first, and I will say no more."

Again Yin returned and reported failure to K'ung-ming.

"The fool is very ill-mannered," said K'ung-ming. "Does he think he can beguile me into sparing the city?"

He called up some of the local people and asked about the forces in the city. They told him about three companies.

"I do not think such a small place can beat me," said K'ung-ming. "Attack quickly before any reinforcements can arrive."

Thereupon the assailants brought up scaling ladders, upon the platforms of which a half score men could stand. These were surrounded by planks as protection. The other soldiers had short ladders and ropes, and, at the beat of the drum, they attempted to scale the walls.

But when Hao saw the ladders being brought up he made his men shoot fire-arrows at them. K'ung-ming did not expect this. He knew the city was not well prepared for defence, and he had had the great ladders brought up and bade the soldiers take the wall with a rush. He was greatly chagrined when the fire arrows set his ladders on fire and so many of his men were burned. And as the arrows and stones rained down from the wall, the men of Shu were forced to retire.

K'ung-ming angrily said, "So you burn my ladders; then I will use battering rams" ("battering carts").

So the rams were brought and placed against the walls and again the signal given for assault. But the defenders brought up great stones suspended by ropes, which they swung down at the battering rams and so broke them to pieces. Next the besiegers set to work to bring up earth and fill the moat, and three companies were set to excavating a tunnel under the ramparts. But Hao Chao cut a counter-trench within the city and turned that device.

So the struggle went on for near a month, and still the city was not taken. K'ung-ming was very depressed.

That was not all. The scouts reported the coming of a relief force, the flags of which bore the name of Wang Shuang. Some one had to try to turn him back, and Wei Yen offered himself.

"No," said K'ung-ming; "you are too valuable as leader of the van."

Hsieh Hsiung offered his services; they were accepted, and he was given three companies. After he had gone, K'ung-ming decided to send a second force, and for command of this one Kung Ch'i volunteered and was accepted. He also had three companies. Then K'ung-ming feared lest there would be a sortie from the city to aid the relief force just arriving, so he led off the army twenty *li* and made a camp.

The first body sent against Wang Shuang had no success; its leader fell almost immediately under Wang's great sword. The men fled and Wang pursued, and so came upon Kung, who had come to support his colleague. He met a similar fate, being slain in the third bout.

When the defeated parties returned, K'ung-ming was anxious and called up three leaders to go out to check this Wang. They went and drew up in formal array, and then Chang I rode to the front. Wang Shuang rode to meet him, and they two fought several bouts. Then Wang Shuang ran away and Chang I followed. His colleague, Wang P'ing, suspected this flight was but a ruse, so he called to Chang to stop. Wang Shuang then turned and hurled one of his meteor hammers, which hit Chang I in the back, so that he fell forward and lay over the saddle. Wang Shuang rode on to follow up this advantage, but the two colleagues of Chang I interfered and checked him. Wang Shuang's whole force then came on and slew many of the men of Shu.

Chang I was hurt internally and vomited blood at times. He came back and told K'ung-ming that Wang Shuang was very terrible and no one could stand up to him. Beside there was a strong camp at the city with double walls and a deep moat.

Having lost two captains, and a third being wounded, K'ung-ming called up Chiang Wei and said, "We are stopped this way; can you suggest another road?"

"Yes," said Chiang, "The place is too well protected and, with this Wang as defender, cannot be taken. I would propose to move away to some suitable place and make a strong camp. Then try to hold the roads so that the attack on Chieht'ing may be prevented. Then if you will send a strong force against Ch'ishan I can do something which will give us success."

K'ung-ming agreed. He sent Wang P'ing and Li K'uei to hold the side road to Chieht'ing, and Wei Yen was sent to guard the way from Ch'ênts'ang. And then the army marched out of Hsieh Valley by a small road and made for Ch'ishan.

Now Ts'ao Chên still remembered bitterly that in the last campaign Ssŭma I had filched from him the credit he hoped to obtain. So when he reached Lok'ou he detached Kuo Huai and Sun Li and sent them to hold positions east and west. Then he had heard that Ch'ênts'ang was threatened, so had sent Wang Shuang to its relief, and now to his joy he heard of his henchman's success. He placed Fei Yao in command of the van and stationed other captains at strategic and commanding points.

Then they caught a spy. He was taken into the presence of the general to be questioned. The man knelt down and said, "I am not really a spy in the bad sense. I was bringing a secret communication for you, Sir, but I was captured by one of the parties in ambush. Pray send away your attendants."

The man's bonds were loosed and the tent cleared. The captive said, "I am a confidant of Chiang Wei, who has entrusted me with a secret letter."

"Where is the letter?"

The man took it from among his garments and presented it to Ts'ao Chên, who read:—"I, Chiang Wei, your guilty captain, make a hundred prostrations to the great leader Ts'ao, now in the field. I have never forgotten that I was in the employ of Wei and disgraced myself; having enjoyed favours, I never repaid them. Lately I have been an unhappy victim of Chuko Liang's wiles and so fell into the depths. But I never forgot my old allegiance; how could I forget? Now happily the army of Shu has gone west, and Chuko Liang trusts me. I rely upon your leading an army this way. If resistance be met, then you may simulate defeat and retire, but I shall be behind and will make a blaze as signal. Then I shall set fire to their stores, whereupon you will face about and attack. Chuko Liang ought to fall into your hands. If it be that I cannot render service and repay my debt to the state, then punish me for my former crime.

"If this should be deemed worthy of your attention, then without delay communicate your commands."

The letter pleased Ts'ao Chên, and he said, "This is heaven-sent help to aid me in an achievement."

He rewarded the man and bade him return to say that it was accepted. Then he called Fei Yao to his councils and said, "I have just had a secret letter from Chiang Wei telling me to act in a certain fashion."

But Fei Yao replied, "Chuko Liang is very crafty and Chiang Wei is very knowing. If by chance Chuko has planned all this and sent this man we may fall into a snare."

"But Chiang Wei is really a man of Wei; he was forced into surrender. Why are you suspicious?"

"My advice is not to go, but to remain here on guard. Let me go to meet this man, and any service I can accomplish will redound to your credit. And if there be any craft I can meet it for you."

Ts'ao Chên approved this and bade Fei Yao take five legions by way of Hsieh Valley. He told him to halt after the second or third stage and send out scouts. This was done, and the scouts reported that the Shu army was coming through the valley. Fei Yao at once advanced, but before the men of Shu got into contact with him they retired. Fei Yao pursued. Then the men of Shu came on again. Just as Fei Yao was forming up for battle the Shu army retreated again. And these manœuvres were repeated thrice, and a day and a night passed without any repose for the Wei army.

At length rest was imperative, and they were on the point of entrenching themselves to prepare food when a great hubbub arose all around, and with beating of drums and blaring of trumpets the whole country was filled with the men of Shu. Suddenly there was a stir near by the great standard, and out came a small four-wheeled chariot in which sat K'ung-ming. He bade a herald call the leader of the Wei army to a parley.

Fei Yao rode out and, seeing K'ung-ming, he secretly rejoiced. Turning to those about him, he bade them retire if the men of Shu came on and look out for a signal. If they saw a blaze they were to turn and attack, for they would be reinforced.

Then he rode to the front and shouted, "You rebel leader in front there; how dare you come here again?"

K'ung-ming replied, "Go and call Ts'ao Chên to a parley."

"My chief, Ts'ao Chên, is of the royal stock; think you that he will come to parley with rebels?"

K'ung-ming angrily waved his fan, and there came forth Ma Tai and Chang I and their men with a rush. The Wei army retired. But ere they had gone far they saw a blaze in the rear of the advancing host of Shu and heard a great shouting. Fei Yao could only conclude that this was the signal he was looking for, and so he faced about to attack.

But the enemy also turned about and retired. Fei Yao led the pursuit, sword in hand, hastening to the point whence the shouting came. Nearing the signal fire, the drums beat louder than ever, and then out came two armies, one under Kuan Hsing and the other under Chang Pao, while arrows and stones rained from the hill-tops. The Wei men could not stand it and knew not only they were beaten, but beaten by a ruse. Fei Yao tried to withdraw his men into the shelter of the valley to rest, but the enemy pressed on him, and the army of Wei fell into confusion. Pressing upon each other, many fell into the streams and were drowned.

Fei Yao could do nothing but flee for his life. Just as he was passing by a steep hill there appeared a cohort, and the leader was Chiang Wei. Fei Yao began to upbraid him for his treachery and craftiness.

Wei replied, "You are the wrong victim; we meant to capture Ts'ao Chên not you. You would do well to yield."

But Fei only galloped away toward a ravine. Suddenly the ravine filled with flame. Then he lost all hope. The pursuers were close behind, so he put an end to his own life.

Of the men of Wei many surrendered. The Shu army pressed home their advantage and, hastening forward, reached Ch'ishan and made a camp. There the army was mustered and put in order.

Chiang Wei received a reward, but he was chagrined that Ts'ao Chên had not been taken.

"My regret is that I did not slay Ts'ao Chên," said he.

"Indeed, yes," replied K'ung-ming. "It is a pity that a great scheme should have had so poor a result."

Ts'ao Chên was very sad when he heard of the loss of his captain. He consulted Kuo Huai as to a new plan to drive back the enemy.

Meanwhile, flying messengers had gone to the capital with news of K'ung-ming's arrival at Ch'ishan and the defeat. Ts'ao Jui called Ssŭma I to ask for a plan to meet these new conditions.

"I have a scheme all ready, not only to turn back K'ung-ming, but to do so without any exertion on our part. They will retire of their own will."

> Ts'ao Chên's wits are dull; so he
> Fights on Ssŭma's strategy.

The strategy will appear in the next chapter.

CHAPTER IIC.

DEATH OF WANG SHUANG;
K'UNG-MING'S VICTORY AT CH'ÊNTS'ANG.

Now Ssŭma I spoke to the king, saying, "I have said repeatedly that K'ung-ming would come against us by way of Ch'ênts'ang; wherefore I set Hao Chao to guard it. If an enemy did invade, he could easily obtain his supplies by that road; but with Hao and Wang on guard there he will not dare to come that way. It is very difficult to get supplies any other way. Therefore I can give the invaders a month to exhaust their food. Hence their advantage lies in forcing a battle; ours is postponing it as long as possible. Wherefore I pray Your Majesty to order Ts'ao Chên to hold passes and positions tenaciously and on no account to seek battle. In a month the enemy will have to retreat, and that will be our opportunity."

Jui was pleased to hear so succinct a statement, but he said, "Since, Noble Sir, you foresaw all this so plainly, why did you not lead an army to prevent it?"

"It is not because I grudged the effort, but I had to keep the army here to guard against Lu Hsün of Wu. Sun Chüan will declare himself 'Emperor' before long. If he does, I think Your Majesty will attack him, and I shall be ready to cross over the frontier. The army is prepared."

Just then one of the courtiers announced despatches from Ts'ao Chên on military affairs, and Ssŭma closed his speech, saying, "Your Majesty should send someone especially to caution the general to be careful not to be tricked by K'ungming, not to pursue rashly and never to penetrate deeply into the enemy country."

The king gave the order, and he sent the command by the hand of the *T'ai-ch'ang* Han Chi and gave him authority to warn Ts'ao Chên against giving battle. Ssŭma escorted the royal messenger out of the city and, at parting, said "I am giving this magnificent opportunity to obtain glory to Ts'ao Chên, but do not tell him the suggestion was mine; only quote the royal command. Tell him that defence is the best, pursuit is to be most cautious, and he is not to send any impetuous man to follow up the enemy."

Ts'ao Chên was deep in affairs connected with his army when they brought news of a royal messenger, but he went forth to bid him welcome, and when the ceremonial receipt of the edict had come to an end, he retired to discuss matters with Kuo Huai and Sun Li.

"Ssŭma's idea," said Kuo with a laugh.

"But what of the idea?" asked Ts'ao.

"It means that the man who perfectly understands Chuko Liang's plans and who will eventually have to be called in to defeat them is our friend Ssŭma."

"But if the Shu army holds its ground?"

"We will send Wang Shuang to reconnoitre and keep on the move along the by-roads so that they dare not attempt to bring up supplies. They must retreat when they have no more to eat, and we shall be able to beat them."

Then said Sun Li, "Let me go out to Ch'ishan as if to escort a convoy, only the carts shall be laden with combustibles instead of grain. We will sprinkle sulphur and nitre over wood and reeds. The men of Shu will surely seize the convoy and take it to their own camp, when we will set fire to the carts. When they are blazing, our hidden men can attack."

"It seems an excellent plan," said Ts'ao Chên, and he issued the requisite orders: Sun to pretend to escort a convoy; Wang to prowl about the by-roads; Kuo to command in the Chi Valley. Also Chang Hu, son of Chang Liao, was made leader of the van, and Yo Lin, son of Yo Chin, was his second. These two were to remain on guard in the outermost camp.

Now at Ch'ishan K'ung-ming sought to bring on a battle, and daily sent champions to provoke a combat. But the men of Wei would not come out.

Then K'ung-ming called Chiang Wei and certain others to him and said, "I do not know what to do. The enemy refuse battle, because they know we are short of food. We can get none by way of Ch'ênts'ang, and all other roads are very difficult. I reckon the grain we brought with us will not last a month."

While thus perplexed, they heard that many carts of provisions for Wei were in the west and the convoy was commanded by Sun Li.

"What is known of this Sun?" asked K'ung-ming.

A certain man of Wei replied, "He is a bold man. Once he was out hunting on Great Rock Hill, and a tiger suddenly appeared in front of his master's chariot. He jumped off his horse and despatched the beast with his sword. He was rewarded with a leadership. He is an intimate friend of Ts'ao Chên."

"This is a ruse," said K'ung-ming. "They know we are short of food, and those carts are only a temptation. They are laden with combustibles. How can they imagine that I shall be deceived by this sort of thing when I have fought them with fire so many times? If we go to seize the convoy they will come and raid our camp. But I will meet ruse with ruse."

Then he sent Ma Tai, with three companies, to make his way to the enemy's store camp and, when the wind served, to start a fire. When the stores were burning, the soldiers of Wei would come to surround the camp of Shu. He also sent Ma Chung and Chang I to halt near the camp so that they might attack. These having gone, he called Kuan Hsing and Chang Pao, and said, "The outermost camp of Wei is on the main road. This night, when the enemy see a blaze, our camp will be attacked, so you two are to lie in wait on the two sides of the Wei camp and seize it when they have left."

Calling Wu Pan and Wu I, he said, "You are to lie in wait outside the camp to cut off the retreat of the men of Wei."

All these arrangements made, K'ung-ming betook himself to the summit of Ch'ishan to watch the results.

The men of Wei heard that their enemies were coming to seize the grain convoy and ran to tell Sun Li, who sent on a message to Ts'ao Chên. Ts'ao sent to the chief camp to the officers on guard and told them to look out for a signal blaze. That would mean the coming of the men of Shu, and then they were to issue forth and carry out certain instructions.

Watchers were sent on the tower to look out for the promised blaze. Meanwhile Sun Li marched over and hid in the west hills to await the coming of the men of Shu. That night, at the second watch, Ma Tai came with his three companies all silent, the men with gags, the horses with a lashing round their muzzles. They saw tier after tier of carts on the hills, making an enclosure like a walled camp, and on the carts were planted many flags.

They waited. Presently the south-west wind came up, and then the fire was started. Soon all the carts were in a blaze that lit up the sky. Sun saw the blaze and could only conclude that the men of Shu had arrived and his own side were giving the signal, so he dashed out to attack. But soon two parties of soldiers were heard behind him closing in. These were Ma Chung and Chang I, who soon had Sun as in a net. Then he heard a third ominous roll of drums, which heralded the approach of Ma Tai from the direction of the blaze.

Under these several attacks the men of Wei quailed and gave way. The fire grew more and more fierce. Men ran and horses stampeded, and the dead were too many to count. Sun Li made a dash through the smoke and fire of the battle and got away.

When Chang Hu and Yo Lin saw the fire they threw open the gates of their camp and sallied forth to help defeat the men of Shu by seizing their camp. But when they reached the camp they found it empty. So they set out to return. That was the moment for Wu Pan and Wu I to appear and cut off their retreat. However, they fought bravely and got through. But when at length they reached their own camp they were met by arrows flying thick as locusts. For Kuan and Chang had taken possession in their absence.

They could only set out for headquarters to report their mishap. As they neared Ts'ao Chên's camp they met another remnant marching up. They were Sun Li's men, and the two parties went into camp together and told the tale of their victimisation. Ts'ao Chên thereafter looked to his defences and attacked no more.

Thus victorious, the men of Shu went to K'ung-ming, who at once despatched secret directions to Wei Yen. Then he gave orders to break camp and retreat. This move was not understood, and Yang I asked the leader why he retired after a victory so damaging to the enemy.

"Because we are short of food," said K'ung-ming. "Our success lay in swift victory, but the enemy will not fight, and thus they weaken us day by day. Though we have worsted them now they will soon be reinforced, and their light horse can cut off our provisions. Then we could not retreat at all. For a time they will not dare look at us, and we must take the occasion to do what they do not expect, and retreat. But I am solicitous about Wei Yen, who is on the Ch'ênts'ang road to keep off Wang Shuang. I fear he cannot get away. I have sent him certain orders to slay Wang, and then the men of Wei will not dare to pursue."

So the retreat began, but to deceive the enemy the watchmen were left in the empty camp to beat the watches through the night.

Ts'ao Chên was depressed at his recent misfortune. Then they told him Chang Ho had come. Chang came up to the gate, dismounted and entered. When he saw Ts'ao Chên he said, "I have received a royal command to come and enquire into your arrangements."

"Did you take leave of friend Ssŭma?" asked Ts'ao.

Chang said, "His instructions to me were to stay away if you were victor, to come if you were not. It seems that our side has missed success. Have you since found out what the men of Shu are doing?"

"Not yet."

So he sent out some scouts, and they found empty camps. There were flags flying, but the men had been gone two days. Ts'ao Chên was disgusted.

When Wei Yen received his secret orders he broke up camp that night and hastened toward Hanchung. Wang Shuang's scouts heard this and told their chief, who hurried in pursuit. After about twenty *li* he came in sight of Wei Yen's ensigns. As soon as he got within hailing distance he shouted, "Do not flee, Wei Yen."

But no one looked back, so he again pressed forward. Then he heard one of his men behind him shouting, "There is a blaze in the camp outside the wall; I think it is some wile of the enemy."

Wang Shuang pulled up and, turning, saw the fire. He
therefore tried to draw off his men. Just as he passed a hill,
a horseman sudenly came out of a wood.

"Here is Wei Yen," shouted the horseman.

Wang Shuang was too startled to defend himself and fell
at the first stroke of Wei Yen's sword. His men thought this
was only the beginning of an ambush and serious attack, so
they scattered; but really Wei Yen only had thirty men with
him, and they moved off leisurely toward Hanchung.

> No man could better K'ung-ming's foresight keen;
> Brilliant as a comet where it flashed:
> Back and forth at will his soldiers dashed,
> And Wang's dead body marked where they had been.

Now we may tell the secret orders sent to Wei Yen. He
was to keep back thirty men and hide beside Wang Shuang's
camp till that warrior left. Then the camp was to be set on
fire. After that the thirty were to wait till Wang's return
to fall upon him. The plan being successfully carried out,
Wei Yen followed the retreating army into Hanchung and
handed over his command.

Here nothing will be said of the feastings that took place
in Hanchung, but the story will return to Chang Ho, who,
failing to come up with the retiring enemy, presently returned
to camp.

Hao Chao sent a letter to say that Wang Shuang had met
his end. This loss caused Ts'ao Chên deep grief, so that he
became ill and had to return to Loyang. He left Chang Ho,
Sun Li and Kuo Huai to guard the approaches to Ch'angan.

At a court held by Sun Ch'üan, King of Wu, a certain spy
reported the doings in the west and the results of Chuko
Liang's expeditions. Thereupon certain ministers urged on
Sun Ch'üan that he should attack Wei and try to gain the
capital. However, Sun Ch'üan could not make up his mind,
and Chang Chao endeavoured to prove to him that his hour
was come by this memorial:—

"I have heard that a phœnix has lately appeared in the hills
east of Wuch'ang and bowed; that a yellow dragon has been
seen in the Great River. My lord, your virtue matches that
of Tang and Yü and your understanding is on a level with
that of Kings Wên and Wu. Wherefore you should now
proceed to the imperial style and then raise an army to
maintain your authority."

And many other officers supported Chang Chao's proposal.
They finally persuaded Sun Ch'üan to decide upon a day.
They prepared an altar on the south of Wuch'ang, and on that
day his courtiers formally requested him to ascend to the high
place and assume the style of "Emperor."

Huang-Lung was chosen as the style of the reign. Sun Chien, the deceased father of the new Emperor, was given the title of Emperor *Wu-lieh*, his mother a corresponding title, his elder brother, Sun T'sê, was made posthumously Prince Huan of Ch'angsha, and his son, Sun Têng, was styled Heir Apparent. A high rank, Companion of the Heir Apparent, was conferred upon the eldest son of Chuko Chin and the second son of Chang Chao.

This son of Chuko Chin was a person below middle height, but very clever, and especially apt at capping verses. Sun Ch'üan liked him much. When he was six he went with his father to a banquet. Sun Ch'üan noticed that Chuko Chin had a long face, so he bade a man lead in a donkey, and he wrote on it with chalk, "My friend Chuko." Every one roared. But the youngster ran up and added a few strokes making it read, "My friend Chuko's donkey." The guests were astonished at his ready wit, and praised him. Sun Ch'üan was also pleased and made him a present of the donkey.

Another day, at a large official banquet, Sun Ch'üan sent the boy with a goblet of wine to Chang Chao. The old man declined it, saying, "This is not the proper treatment for old age."

"Can you not make him drink?" said the host.

Then said K'o to the old gentleman, "You remember Father Chiang Shang; he was ninety and yet 'gripped the signalling flags and wielded the axes' of an army commander in the field. He never spoke of age. Nowadays in battle we put seniors behind, but at the banquet board we give them a front place. How can you say we do not treat old age properly?"

Chang Chao had no reply ready, and so had to drink. This sort of precocity endeared the boy to Sun Ch'üan, and now he made him an officer, "Companion to the Heir Apparent."

Chang Chao's son was chosen for honour on account of the eminent services of his father. Then Ku Yung became Prime Minister and Lu Hsün, Generalissimo. And he assisted the Heir Apparent in the custody of Wuch'ang.

As Sun Ch'üan seemed powerful and well established, the whole of his court turned their thoughts toward the suppression of Wei. Only Chang Chao opposed it and tendered counsels of internal reform.

"It is not well to begin Your Majesty's new reign with fighting; rather improve learning and hide the sword; establish schools and so give the people the blessings of peace. Make a treaty with Shu to share the empire, and lay your plans slowly and carefully."

Sun Ch'üan, by nature peaceful and cautious, saw the wisdom of the advice. He sent an envoy into Shu to lay the scheme of an alliance before the king. The king called his courtiers to discuss it. Many were opposed to Sun Ch'üan as an upstart usurper and advised rejection of any friendly proposals from him. Then Chiang Wan said they might get the opinion of K'ung-ming.

So they sent and put the matter before him. He said, "Send an envoy with presents and felicitations and ask Sun Ch'üan to send Lu Hsün against Wei. Then Ssǔma I will be engaged, and I may once more attempt the capital."

Wherefore Ch'ên Chên was sent with presents of horses, and a jewelled belt, and gold and pearls and precious things into Wu to congratulate the ruler on his newly assumed dignity. And the presents were accepted, and the bearer thereof honoured and allowed to return.

When this was all over, Sun Ch'üan called in Lu Hsün and asked his opinion about the compact with Shu. Lu saw through the scheme at once.

"We owe this to K'ung-ming's fear of Ssǔma I," said he. "However, we must consent since they ask it. We will make a show of raising an army and in a measure support them. When K'ung-ming has actually attacked Wei we will make for the capital ourselves."

Orders went forth for enlisting and training soldiers ready for an expedition to start presently.

When Ch'ên Chên returned from Hanchung, he reported that K'ung-ming was grieving that he could not take Ch'êntsang. Soon after this, however, he was cheered by the news that the able defender of the city, Hao Chao, was very ill.

"That means success for me," cried he.

He called in Wei Yen and Chiang Wei, and said, "Take half a legion and hasten to Ch'êntsang. If you see a blaze, then attack."

They could hardly believe the order was meant, and came again to see their chief and asked the exact date of departure.

"In three days you should be ready to march. Do not come to take leave of me, but set out as soon as possible."

After they had left his tent he summoned Kuan and Chang and gave them secret instructions.

Now when Kuo Huai heard that the commander of Ch'êntsang was ill, he and Chang Ho talked over the matter.

Kuo Huai said, "Hao Chao is very ill; you had better go and relieve him. I will report to the capital what we have done that they may arrange."

So Chang Ho started with his three companies to relieve the sick man. Hao was indeed at the point of death, and suddenly they told him that the men of Shu had reached the walls. Hao roused himself and bade them go on the ramparts. But then fire broke out at each gate, a panic spread in the city and the noise of the confusion startled the dying man so that he passed away just as the men of Shu were bursting in.

When Wei Yen and his colleague reached the walls they were perplexed to find no sign of life. No flags were flying and no watchmen struck the hours. They delayed their attack for a time. Then they heard a bomb, and suddenly the wall was thick with flags, and there appeared the well-known figure of the minister.

"You have come too late," cried he.

Both dropped out of the saddle and prostrated themselves.

"Really, you are supernatural, O Minister!" they cried.

They entered the city, and then he explained to them that they had been sent as a blind so that his real plan should be a secret. He had hidden himself in the ranks of another force, which had come by double marches. He had sent spies into the city to start the fires and throw the defenders into confusion.

"This is an instance of the rule of war. Do the unexpected; attack the unprepared," said he at the end.

They bowed. In commiseration K'ung-ming sent all the family of Hao Chao, and his coffin, over to Wei, thus showing his sense of the dead man's loyalty.

Turning once more to the two generals, he said, "But do not divest yourself of your armour. Go and attack San Pass and drive away the guards while they are in a state of surprise. If you delay, Wei will have sent reinforcements."

They went. Surely enough the capture was easy. But when they went up to look around they saw a great cloud of dust moving toward them; the reinforcements were already near.

They remarked to each other how exceedingly keen was the foresight of their leader. When they had looked a little longer they saw the leader of the Wei army then approaching was Chang Ho.

They then divided their men to hold the approaches. When Chang Ho saw that all was prepared, he retired. Wei Yen followed and fought a battle, defeating Chang with only slight loss to himself.

He sent to report his success, but K'ung-ming had already left Ch'ênts'ang and had gone into Hsieh Valley to capture Chienwei.

Other armies from Shu followed. Moreover, the king sent Ch'ên Shih to assist in the campaign. K'ung-ming hurried his main force out by Ch'ishan and there made a camp. Then he called an assembly of officers.

"Twice have I gone out by Ch'ishan without success, but at last I am here. I think Wei will resume the former battle ground and oppose us. If so, they will assume that I shall attack Yung and Mei and send armies to defend them. But I see Yinp'ing and Wutu are connected with Hanchung, and if I can win these I can drive a wedge into the Wei force. Who will go to take these places?"

Chiang Wei and Wang P'ing offered themselves. The former was sent with one legion to capture Wutu; the latter, with an equal force, went to Yinp'ing.

Chang Ho went back to Ch'angan and saw his colleagues, to whom he said, "Ch'ênts'ang is lost, Hao Chao is dead, San Pass is taken and K'ung-ming is again at Ch'ishan; and thence has sent out two armies."

Kuo Huai was frightened. "In that case, Yung and Mei are in danger," said he.

Leaving Chang Ho to guard Ch'angan, he sent Sun Li to Yungch'êng, and he himself set out at once for Meich'êng. He sent an urgent report to Loyang.

At Wei's next court the king was informed of all the misfortunes in the west and the threats in the east. Ts'ao Jui was embarrassed and frightened. Ts'ao Chên, being ill, could not be consulted, and Ssŭma I was called. He was ready with a proposal.

"In my humble opinion, Wu will not attack us," said he.

"What makes you think so?" asked the king.

"Because K'ung-ming still resents, and wishes to avenge, the event at Hsiaot'ing. He never ceases to desire to absorb Wu. His only fear is that we may swoop down upon Shu. That is why there is an alliance with Wu. Lu Hsün knows it also quite well, and he is only making a show of raising an army as they arranged. The truth is he is sitting on the fence. Hence Your Majesty may disregard the menace on the east and only protect yourself against Shu," said he.

"Your insight is very profound," said the king.

Ssŭma I was created Commander-in-chief of all the forces in the east, and the king directed a courtier to go to Ts'ao Chên for the seal.

"I would rather go myself," said Ssŭma I. So he left the audience and went to the palace of Ts'ao Chên, where presently he saw the invalid. First he asked after his health and then gradually opened his errand.

"Shu and Wu have made an alliance to invade us, and K'ung-ming is at Ch'ishan. Have you heard, Illustrious Sir?"

"My people have kept back all news as I am ill," said he, startled. "But if this is true the country is in danger. Why have they not made you Commander-in-chief to stop this invasion?"

"I am unequal to the post," said Ssŭma.

"Bring the seal and give it to him," said Ts'ao.

"You are anxious on my account; really I am only come to lend you an arm. I dare not accept the seal."

Ts'ao started up, saying, "If you do not take it I shall have to go to see the king, ill as I am. The country is in danger."

"Really the king has already shown his kindness, but I dare not accept his offer."

"If you have been appointed then Shu will be driven off."

Thrice Ssŭma declined the seal, but eventually he received it into his hands. Then he took leave of the king and marched to Ch'angan.

> The seal of office changes hands,
> Two armies now one force become.

Ssŭma's success or failure will be told in the next chapter.

CHAPTER IC.

CHUKO LIANG WINS A GREAT VICTORY;
SSŬMA I INVADES SHU.

The fourth month of *Chien-An*, seventh year, found Chuko Liang camped at Ch'ishan in three camps, waiting for the army of Wei.

When Ssŭma I reached Ch'angan, the officer in command, Chang Ho, told him all that had happened. He gave Chang Ho the post of leader of the van, with Tai Ling as his second, and then marched out toward the enemy, camping on the Wei River's south bank. When the local commanders Kuo Huai and Sun Li went to see the new Commander-in-Chief, he asked if they had fought any battle.

"Not yet," said they.

Ssŭma said, "The enemy had a long march; their chance lay in attacking quickly. As they have not attacked they have some deep laid scheme to work out. What news have you from the west?"

Kuo replied, "The scouts say that the greatest care is being taken in every district. But there is no news from Wutu and Yinp'ing."

"I must send someone to fight a battle with them. You get away as quickly and privily as you can to the rescue of those two towns, and then attack the rear of the Shu army so as to throw them into disorder."

They set out to obey these orders, and on the way they fell to discussing Ssŭma.

"How does Ssŭma compare with Chuko?" said Kuo.

"Chuko is by far the better," replied Sun.

"Though Chuko may be the cleverer, yet this scheme of our leader's shows him to be superior to most men. The enemy may have got those two cities yet; when we unexpectedly fall upon their rear, they will certainly be disordered."

Soon after this a scout came in to say that the two cities were in possession of the enemy, and, further, that the Shu army was not far in front.

Said Sun, "There is some crafty scheme afoot. Why are they prepared for battle in the open when they hold two cities? We had better retire."

His companion agreed, and they issued orders to face about and retreat. Just then a bomb exploded, and, at the same time, there suddenly appeared from the cover of some hills a

small body of men. On the flag that came forward they read
the name Chuko Liang, and in the midst of the company they
saw him, seated in a small chariot. On his left was Kuan
Hsing, and on his right Chang Pao.

They were quite taken aback. K'ung-ming laughed and
said, "Do not run away. Did you think that your leader's
ruse would take me in? Sending a challenge to fight every
day, indeed, while you were to slip round behind my army and
attack! I have the two cities, and if you have not come to
surrender, then hurry up and fight a battle with me."

By now they were really frightened. Then behind them
there rose a shout as of battle, and Wang P'ing and Chiang
Wei began to smite them in the rear, while Kuan and Chang
bore down upon them in front. They were soon utterly
broken, and the two leaders escaped by scrambling up the
hillside.

Chang Pao saw them, and was urging his steed forward to
catch them, when unhappily he and his horse went over
together into a gully. When they picked him up they found
that he had been kicked in the head and was badly hurt.
K'ung-ming sent him back to Ch'êngtu.

It has been said that the two leaders escaped. They got
back to Ssŭma's camp and said, "Wutu and Yinp'ing were
both in the enemy's possession, and K'ung-ming had prepared
an ambush, so that we were attacked front and rear. We lost
the day and only escaped on foot."

"It is no fault of yours," said the general. "The fact is he
is sharper than I. Now go to defend Yung and Mei and
remain on the defensive; do not go out to give battle. I have
a plan to defeat them."

These two having left, Ssŭma called in Chang Ho and Tai
Ling and said, "K'ung-ming has captured Wutu and Yinp'ing.
He must restore order and confidence among the people of
these places, and so will be absent from his camp. You two
will take a legion each, start to-night and make your way
quietly to the rear of the Shu army. Then you will attack
vigorously. When you have done that I shall lead out the
army in front of them and array ready for battle. While they
are in disorder I shall make my attack. Their camp ought to
be captured. If I can win the advantage of these hills their
defeat will be easy."

These two left, marching one right the other left. They
took by-roads and got well to the rear of the Shu army. In
the third watch they struck the high road and joined forces.
Then they marched toward the enemy. After about thirty *li*
there was a halt in front. The two leaders galloped up to see
what had caused it and found many straw-carts drawn across
the road.

"This has been prepared," said Chang. "We should return."

Just as they ordered the men to turn about, torches broke into flame all over the hills, the drums rolled, trumpets blared and soldiers sprang out on every side. At the same time K'ung-ming shouted from the hill-top, "Tai Ling and Chang Ho, listen to my words. Your master reckoned that I should be busy restoring order in the two towns and so should not be in my camp. Wherefore he sent you to take the camp, and you have just fallen into my snare. As you are leaders of no great importance I shall not harm you. Dismount and yield."

Chang's wrath blazed forth at this, and he pointed at K'ung-ming, crying, "You peasant out of the woods, invader of our great country! How dare you use such words to me? Wait till I catch you; I will tear you to shreds."

He galloped forward to ascend the hill, his spear ready for the thrust. But the arrows and stones pelted too quickly. Then he turned and dashed in among the soldiers, scattering them right and left. He got clear, but he saw his colleague was not with him. At once he turned back, fought his way to his comrade and brought him out safely.

K'ung-ming on the hill-top watched this warrior and saw he was a right doughty fighting man.

"I have heard that men stood aghast when Chang Fei fought his great fight with Chang Ho. Now I can judge his valour for myself. He will do harm to Shu one day if I spare him. He will have to be removed."

Then he returned to his camp. By this time Ssŭma had completed his battle line and was waiting the moment of disorder to attack. Then he saw his two captains come limping back dejected and crestfallen. They said, "K'ung-ming forestalled us; he was well prepared, and so we were quite defeated."

"He is more than human!" exclaimed Ssŭma. "We must retreat."

So the whole army retired into the fortified camps and would not come out.

Thus a great victory fell to Shu, and their booty was immense; weapons and horses innumerable. K'ung-ming led his army back to camp.

Thereafter he sent parties to offer a challenge at the gate of the Wei camp every day, but the soldiers remained obstinately behind their shelters and would not appear. When this had continued half a month K'ung-ming grew sad.

Then came a messenger from the capital. He was received with all respect, and incense was burnt as propriety demanded. This done, the command was unsealed, and K'ung-ming read:—

"The failure at Chieht'ing was really due to the fault of Ma Su. However, you held yourself responsible and blamed yourself very severely. It would have been a serious matter for me to have withstood your intentions, and so I did what you insisted on. However, that was a glorious exploit last year when Wang Shuang was slain. This year, Kuo Huai has been driven back and the *Ch'iang* have been reduced; the two districts have been recovered; you have driven fear into the hearts of all evil doers and thus rendered magnificent services.

"But the land is in confusion, and the original evil has not been destroyed. You fill a great office, for you direct the affairs of the state. It is not well for you to remain under a cloud for any length of time and cloak your grand virtue, wherefore I restore you to the rank of Prime Minister and pray you not to decline the honour."

K'ung-ming heard the edict to the end and then said, "My task is not yet accomplished; how can I return to my duties as Prime Minister? I must really decline to accept this."

Fei I said, "If you decline this you flout the desires of the king and also show contempt for the feelings of the army. At any rate accept for the moment."

Then K'ung-ming humbly bowed acquiescence.

Fei I went away. Seeing that Ssŭma remained obstinately on the defensive, K'ung-ming thought of a plan by which to draw him. He gave orders to break camp and retire.

When the scouts told Ssŭma, he said, "We may not move; certainly there is some deep craftiness in this move."

Chang said, "It must mean that their food is exhausted. Why not pursue?"

"I reckon that K'ung-ming laid up ample supplies last year. Now the wheat is ripe, and he has plenty of every sort. Transport might be difficult, but yet he could hold out half a year. Why should he run away? He sees that we resolutely refuse battle, and he is trying some ruse to inveigle us into fighting. Send out spies to a distance to see what is going on."

They reconnoitred a long way round, and the scouts returned to say that a camp had been formed thirty *li* away.

"Ah; then he is not running away," said Ssŭma. "Remain on the defensive still more strictly and do not advance."

Ten days passed without further news; nor did the men of Shu offer the usual challenge. Again spies were sent far afield, and they reported a further retreat of thirty *li* and a new encampment.

"K'ung-ming is certainly working some scheme," said Ssŭma. "Do not pursue."

Another ten days passed and spies went out. The enemy had gone thirty *li* farther and encamped.

Chang Ho said, "What makes you so over-suspicious? I can see that K'ung-ming is retreating into Hanchung, only he is doing it gradually. Why not pursue before it is too late. Let me go and fight one battle."

"No," said the general. "A defeat would destroy the morale of our men, and I will not risk it. K'ung-ming's vile tricks are innumerable."

"If I go and get beaten I will stand the full rigour of military punishment," said Chang.

"Well, if you are set on going, we will divide the army. You take your wing and go, but you will have to fight your best. I will follow to help in case of need."

So Chang got independent command of three legions and took Tai Ling as his second in command, and he had a few score of captains of lower rank. Halfway they camped. Then Ssŭma, leaving a substantial guard for his camp, set out along the same road with five legions.

K'ung-ming knew the movements of the army of Wei and when Chang's army camped to rest. In the night he summoned his captains and told them.

"The enemy are coming in pursuit and will fight desperately. You will have to fight every one of you like ten, but I will set an ambush to attack their rear. Only a wise and bold leader is fit for this task."

As he closed this speech he glanced at Wei Yen, but this captain hung his head without response. Then Wang P'ing stepped forth and said he was willing to go on this expedition.

"But if you fail, what then?" said K'ung-ming.

"Then there is the military rule."

K'ung-ming sighed. "Wang P'ing is most loyal. He is willing to risk wounds and death in his country's service. However, the enemy are in two divisions, one coming in front, the other trying to get round to the rear. Wang P'ing is crafty and bold, but he cannot be in two places at once, so I must have yet another captain. Is it that among you there is no other willing to devote himself to death?"

He did not wait long for a reply; Chang I stepped to the front.

"Chang Ho is a most famous leader in Wei and valorous beyond all compare. You are not a match for him," said K'ung-ming.

"If I fail may my head fall at the tent door," said he.

"Since you wish to go, I accept you. Each of you shall have a legion of veterans. You will hide in the valleys till the enemy come up, and you will let them pass. Then you will fall upon their rear. If Ssŭma comes you must divide the men, Chang to hold the rear and Wang to check the advance. But they will fight desperately, and I must find a way to aid you."

When they had gone, Chiang Wei and Liao Hua were called, and K'ung-ming said, "I am going to give you a silken bag. You are to proceed secretly into those mountains in front. When you see that your two colleagues are in great straits with the enemy, then open the bag and you will find a plan of escape."

After this he gave secret instructions to four other captains to observe the enemy and, if they seemed confident of victory, to retire, fighting at intervals, till they saw Kuan Hsing and Chang Pao come up, when they could turn and fight their best.

Then calling Kuan and Chang, he said to them, "Hide in the valleys with half a legion till you see a red flag flutter out, and then fall on the enemy."

Chang Ho and Tai Ling hurried along like a rain squall till they were suddenly confronted by the men of Shu. Chang dashed toward his enemy, and then they retired, stopping at intervals to fight. The Wei army pursued for about twenty *li*.

It was the sixth moon and very hot, so that men and horses sweated profusely. When they had gone thirty *li* farther the men and horses were panting and nearly spent. Then K'ung-ming, who had watched the fighting from a hill, gave the signal for Kuan Hsing to emerge and join battle. The four other leaders all led on their men. Chang and Tai fought well, but they could not extricate themselves and retire.

Presently, with a roll of drums, Wang P'ing and Chang I came out and made for the rear to cut the retreat. "Why do you not fight?" shouted Chang Ho when he saw their move.

The men of Wei dashed this way and that, but were stayed at every attempt. Then there was heard another roll of drums, and Ssŭma came up in the rear. He at once signalled to his captains to surround Wang P'ing and Chang I.

"Our minister is truly wonderful. The battle goes just as he foretold," cried Chang I. "He will surely send help now, and we will fight to the death."

Thereupon the men were divided into parties Wang P'ing led one army to hold up Chang Ho and Tai Ling; Chang I led the other division to oppose Ssŭma. On both sides the fighting was keen and continued all the day.

From their station on a hill, Chiang Wei and Miao Hua watched the battle. They saw that the Wei force was very strong and their side was in danger and slowly giving way.

"Now surely is the moment to open the bag," said Chiang Wei.

So the bag was opened, and they read the letter. It said that if Ssŭma came and Wang P'ing and Chang I seemed hard pressed, they were to divide forces and go off to attack Ssŭma's camp, which would cause him to retire, and then they could attack him. The actual capture of the camp was not of great moment.

So they divided the force and started for the enemy's camp. Now Ssŭma had really feared that he would fall victim to some ruse of K'ung-ming, so he had arranged for news to meet him at intervals along the road. He was pressing his men to fight when a messenger galloped up to say that the men of Shu were making for his camp.

Ssŭma was frightened and changed colour. He turned on his captains, saying, "I knew K'ung-ming would plan some trick, but you did not believe me. You forced me to pursue, and now the whole scheme has gone agley."

Thereupon he gathered in his men and turned to retire. The men went hurriedly and got into disorder. Chang I came up behind, and they were routed. Chang Ho and Tai Ling, having but few men left, sought refuge among the hills. The victory was to Shu, and Kuan Hsing came up helping in the rout wherever there appeared a chance to strike.

Ssŭma, defeated, hurried to the camp. But when he reached it the men of Shu had already left. He gathered in his broken army and abused his captains as the cause of his failure.

"You are all ignorant of the proper way to wage war, and think it simply a matter of valour and rude strength. This is the result of your unbridled desire to go out and give battle. For the future no one of you will move without definite orders, and I will apply strict military law to any who disobey."

They were all greatly ashamed and retired to their quarters. In this fight the losses of Wei were very heavy, not only in men, but in horses and weapons.

K'ung-ming led his victorious army to their camp. He intended to advance still farther, when a messenger arrived from the capital with the sad news that Chang Pao had died. When they told K'ung-ming he uttered a great cry, blood gushed from his mouth and he fell in a swoon. He was raised and taken to his tent, but he was too ill to march and had to keep his bed. His captains were much grieved.

A later poet sang:—

> Fierce and valiant was Chang Pao,
> Striving hard to make a name;
> Sad the gods should interfere
> And withhold a hero's fame!
> K'ung-ming wept his end untimely,
> For he knew a warrior gone,
> And he needed every helper;
> His own strength was nearly done.

K'ung-ming's illness continued. Ten days later he summoned to his tent Tung Chüeh and Fan Chien, and said, "I feel dizzy and am too ill to carry on, and the best thing for me is to return into Hanchung and get well. You are to keep my absence perfectly secret, for Ssŭma will certainly attack if he hears."

He issued orders to break up the camp that night, and the army retired into Hanchung forthwith. Ssŭma only heard of it five days later, and he knew that again he had been outwitted.

"The man appears like a god and disappears like a demon; he is too much for me," sighed he.

Ssŭma set certain captains over the camp and placed others to guard the commanding positions, and he also marched homeward.

As soon as the Shu army was settled in Hanchung, K'ungming went to Ch'êngtu for treatment. The officials of all ranks came to greet him and escort him to his palace. The king also came to enquire after his condition and sent his own physicians to treat him. So gradually he recovered.

In *Chien-Hsing*, eighth year and seventh month, Ts'ao Chên, the Commander-in-chief in Wei, had recovered, and he sent a memorial to his master, saying, "Shu has invaded more than once and threatened the capital. If this state be not destroyed it will ultimately be our ruin. The autumn coolth is now here. The army is in good form, and it is the time most favourable for an attack on Shu. I desire to take Ssŭma as colleague and march into Hanchung to exterminate this wretched horde and free the borders from trouble."

Personally, King Jui approved, but he consulted Liu Hua, who replied, "The Commander-in-chief speaks well. If that state be not destroyed it will be to our hurt. Your Majesty should give effect to his desire."

When he came out, a crowd of officers flocked to enquire, saying, "We heard the king has consulted you about an expedition against Shu: what think you?"

"No such thing," said Liu. "Shu is too difficult a country to invade; it would be a mere waste of men and weapons."

They left him. Then Yang Chi went into the king and said, "It is said that yesterday Liu Hua advised Your Majesty to fall upon Shu; to-day when we talked with him he said Shu could not be attacked. This is treating Your Majesty with indignity, and you should issue a command to punish him."

Wherefore the king called in Liu Hua and asked him to explain.

Liu Hua replied, "I have studied the details; Shu cannot be attacked."

The king laughed. In a short time Yang Chi left, and then Liu Hua said, "Yesterday I advised Your Majesty to attack Shu; that being a matter of state policy should be divulged to no person. The essential of a military move is secrecy."

Then the king understood, and thereafter Liu Hua was held in greater consideration. Ten days later Ssŭma came to court, and Ts'ao Chên's memorial was shown him.

Ssŭma replied, "The moment is opportune; I do not think there is any danger from Wu."

Ts'ao Chên was created Minister of War and Commander-in-chief of the Western Expedition, and Ssŭma I was made General and was second in command. Liu Hua was made

Master of the Army. These three then left the court, and the army marched to Ch'angan, intending to dash to Chienko and attack Hanchung.

The men of Hanchung told K'ung-ming, then quite recovered and engaged in training his army and elaborating the "Eight Arrays." All was in an efficient state and ready for an attack on the capital.

When he heard of the intended attack, he called up Chang I and Wang P'ing and sent them to garrison the old road to Ch'ênts'ang so as to check the Wei army. The two replied, "It is said the Wei army numbers forty legions, though they pretend to have eighty legions. But they are very numerous, and a thousand men is a very small force to meet them."

K'ung-ming replied, "I would give you more, but I fear to make it hard for the soldiers."

The two captains stood looking at each other, not daring to undertake such a task with such a force.

"If there be a failure I shall not hold you responsible," said K'ung-ming. "Do not say any more, but get off quickly."

The two officers pleaded with him, saying that if he desired to kill them he had better do it, but they dared not go.

K'ung-ming laughed. "How silly you are!" said he. "If I send you, you may be sure there is a meaning in it. I observed the stars yesterday, and I see there will be a tremendous rain this month. The army of Wei may consist of any number of legions, but they will be unable to penetrate into a mountainous country. So there is no need to send a large force. You will come to no harm, and I shall lead the main body into Hanchung and rest for a month while the enemy retreats. Then I shall smite them. My army will be able to account for their four times as many."

This satisfied them, and they left, while the main body went out toward Hanchung. Moreover, every station was ordered to lay in a stock of wood and straw and grain enough for a whole month's use, ready against the autumn rains. A month's holiday was given, and food and clothing were issued in advance. The expedition was postponed for the present.

When Ts'ao Chên and Ssǔma I approached Ch'ênts'ang and entered the city, they could not find a single house. They questioned some of the people near, who said that K'ung-ming had burned everything before he left. Then Ts'ao proposed to advance along the road, but Ssǔma opposed, saying that the stars foretold much rain.

"If we get deep in a difficult country and are always victorious it is all very well. But if we lose, we shall not get out again. Better remain in this city and build what shelter we can against the rain."

Ts'ao Chên followed his advice. In the middle of the month the rain began, and came down in a deluge so that the sur-

415

rounding country was three feet under water. The equipment of the men was soaked, and the men themselves could get no place to sleep. For a whole month the rain continued. The horses could not be fed, and the men grumbled incessantly. They sent to Loyang, and the king himself prayed for fine weather, but with no effect.

An officer, Wang Su, sent up a memorial:—"The histories say that when supplies have to be conveyed a long distance the soldiers are starved; if they have to gather brushwood before they can cook then the army is not full fed. This applies to ordinary expeditions in an ordinary country. If, in addition, the army has to march through a difficult country and roads have to be cut, the labour is doubled. Now this expedition is hindered by rain and steep and slippery hills; movement is cramped and supplies can only be maintained with difficulty. All is most unpropitious to the army.

"Ts'ao Chên has been gone over a month and has only got half through the valley. Road making is monopolising all energies, and the fighting men have to work on them. The state of affairs is the opposite to ideal, and the fighting men dislike it. I may quote certain parallels. King Wu attacked Chou; he went through the pass, but returned. In recent times your father and grandfather, attacking Sun Ch'üan, reached the river, and went no farther. Did they not recognise limitations and act accordingly? I pray Your Majesty to remember the grave difficulties caused by the rain and put an end to this expedition. By and by another occasion will arise for using men, and in the joy of overcoming difficulties the people will forget death."

The king could not make up his mind, but two other memorials followed, and then he issued the command to return, which was sent to the two generals. They had already discussed the abandonment of the expedition. Ts'ao Chên had said, "We have had rain for a whole month, and the men are downhearted and think only of getting home again. How can we stop them?"

Ssŭma replied, "Return is best."

"If K'ung-ming pursue, how shall we repulse him?"

"We can leave an ambush."

While they were discussing this matter the king's command arrived. Whereupon they faced about and marched homeward.

Now K'ung-ming had reckoned upon this month of rain and so had had his men camped in a safe place. Then he ordered the main army to assemble at Ch'ihp'i and camp there. He summoned his officers to his tent and said, "In my opinion the enemy must retire, for the king will issue such an order. To pursue needs preparation, and so we will let them retire without molestation. Some other plan must be evolved."

So when Wang P'ing sent news of the retreat of the enemy the messenger carried back the order not to pursue.

It is only lost labour to cover retreat
When your enemy does not pursue.

By what means K'ung-ming intended to defeat Wei will be told in the next chapter.

CHAPTER C.

When the officers got to know that the Wei army had gone but they were not to pursue, they were inclined to discontent and went in a body to the general's tent and said, "The rain has driven the enemy away; surely it is the moment to pursue."

K'ung-ming replied, "Ssŭma I is an able leader who would not retreat without leaving an ambush to cover it. If we pursue we shall fall victims. Let him go in peace, and I shall then get through Hsieh Valley and take Ch'ishan, making use of the enemy's lack of defence."

"But there are other ways of taking Ch'angan," said they; "why only take this one?"

"Because Ch'ishan is the first step to Ch'angan, and I want to gain the advantage of position. Any attack on Shênsi must come this way. It rests on the rivers Wei and Pin in front and is backed by Hsieh Valley. It gives the greatest freedom of movement and is a natural manœuvring ground. That is why I want it."

They bowed to his wisdom. Then he despatched four captains for Chi Valley and four others for Hsieh Valley, all to meet at Ch'ishan. He led the main army himself, with Kuan Hsing and Miao Hua in the van.

When the Wei army retreated, the Commander-in-chief and his second remained in the rear superintending the movement. They sent a reconnoitring party along the old road to Ch'ênts'ang, and they returned saying no enemy was to be seen. Ten days later the leaders, who had commanded in the ambush, joined the main body saying that they had seen no sign of the enemy.

Ts'ao Chên said, "This continuous autumn rain has rendered all the ways impassable; how could the men of Shu know of our retreat?"

"They will appear later," said Ssŭma.

"How can you know?"

"These late five days they have not pursued because they think we shall have left a rear-guard in ambush. Therefore they have let us get well away. But after we have gone they will occupy Ch'ishan."

Ts'ao Chên was not convinced.

"Why do you doubt?" asked Ssŭma. "I think K'ung-ming will certainly advance by way of the two valleys, and you and I should guard the entrances. I give them ten days, and if they do not appear, I will come to your camp painted and powdered and dressed as a woman to own my mistake."

"If the men of Shu do appear I will give you the girdle and the steed that the king gave me," replied Ts'ao.

But they split their force, Ts'ao Chên taking up his station on the west of Ch'ishan in the Hsieh Valley, and Ssŭma going to the east in the Chi Valley.

As soon as the camp was settled, Ssŭma I led a cohort into hiding in the valley. The remainder of the force was placed in detachments on the chief roads.

Ssŭma disguised himself and went among the soldiers to get a private survey of all the camps. In one of them he happened upon a junior officer who was complaining, saying, "The rain has drenched us for days and they would not retire. Now they have camped here for a wager. They have no pity for us or the men."

Ssŭma returned to his tent and assembled his officers. Hauling out the grumbler, he said to him, angrily, "The state maintains soldiers a thousand days for one hour's service. How dare you give vent to your spleen to the detriment of discipline?"

The man would not confess, so his comrades were called to bear witness. Still he would not own up.

"I am not here for a wager, but to overcome Shu," said Ssŭma. "Now you all have done well and are going home, but only this fellow complains and is guilty of mutinous conduct."

He ordered the lictors to put him to death, and in a short time they produced his head. The others were terrified, but Ssŭma said, "All you must do your utmost to guard against the enemy. When you hear a bomb explode rush out on all sides and attack."

With this order they retired.

Now Wei Yen and his three comrades, with two legions, entered the Chi Valley. As they were marching, the Assistant Adviser Têng Chih came.

"I bear an order from the minister. As you go out of the valley beware of the enemy," said he.

Ch'ên Shih said, "Why is the minister so full of doubts? We know the men of Wei have suffered severely from the rain and must hasten home. They will not lay any ambush. We are doing double marches and shall gain a great victory. Why are we to delay?"

Têng Chih replied, "You know the minister's plans always succeed. How dare you disobey his orders?"

Ch'ên Shih smiled, saying, "If he was really so resourceful we should not have lost Chieht'ing."

Wei Yen, recalling that K'ung-ming had rejected his plan, also laughed, and said, "If he had listened to me and gone out through Tzŭwu Valley, not only Ch'angan but Loyang too would be ours. Now he is bent on taking Ch'ishan; what is the good of it? He gave us the order to advance and now he stops us. Truly the orders are confusing."

Then said Ch'ên Shih, "I will tell you what I will do. I shall take my men, get through the valley and camp at Ch'ishan. Then you will see how ashamed the minister will look."

Têng Chih argued and persuaded, but to no avail; the wilful leader hurried on to get out of the valley. Têng could only return as quickly as possible and report.

Ch'ên Shih proceeded. He had not gone far when he heard a bomb, and he was in an ambush. He tried to withdraw, but the valley was full of the enemy, and he was surrounded as in an iron cask. All his efforts to get out failed. Then there was a shout, and Wei Yen came to the rescue. He saved his comrade, but his half legion was reduced to about a half company, and these wounded. Two other divisions coming up prevented pursuit, and finally the men of Wei retired. The two who had criticised K'ung-ming's powers of prevision no longer doubted that he saw very clearly. They regretted their own shortsightedness.

When Têng Chih told his chief of the bad behaviour of Ch'ên and Wei he only laughed. "That fellow Wei has never been quite true; he has always been disposed to disobey and is unsteady. However, he is valiant, and so I have used him, but he will do real harm some day."

Then came a messenger with news of Ch'ên's defeat and loss of men. K'ung-ming sent Têng Chih back again to console with him and so keep him from actual mutiny. Then he called to his tent Ma Tai and Wang P'ing, and said, "If there are any of the men of Wei in Hsieh Valley you are to go across the Yüehshan range, marching by night and concealing yourselves by day, and make for the east of Ch'ishan. When you arrive, make a fire as a signal. Ma Chung and Chang I were told to go in similar fashion to the west and join up with the other two. Then they were to make a joint attack on Ts'ao Chên's camp. The chief would also attack in the centre. Kuan Hsing and Miao Hua received secret orders, which are not recorded here.

The armies marched rapidly. Not long after starting, two other detachments led by Wu Pan and Wu I received secret orders and left the main body.

The doubts about the coming of the Shu army made Ts'ao Chên careless, and he allowed his men to become slack and rest. He only thought of getting through the allotted ten days, when he would have the laugh against his colleague.

Seven of the days had passed, when a scout reported a few odd men of Shu in the valley. Ts'ao sent to reconnoitre and keep them at a distance. Ch'in Liang was in command, and he led his men to the entrance of the valley. As soon as he arrived the enemy retired. Ch'in Liang went after them, but they had disappeared. He was perplexed and puzzled, and while trying to decide, he told the men to dismount and rest.

But almost immediately he heard a shout, and ambushed men appeared in front of him. He jumped on his horse to look about him, and saw a great cloud of dust rising among the hills. He disposed his men for defence, but the shouting quickly came nearer, and then Wu Pan and Wu I appeared advancing towards him. Retreat was impossible, as the hills were on both sides, and from the hill-tops came shouts of "Dismount and yield!"

More than half did surrender. Ch'in Liang was killed. K'ung-ming put the men who had come over to his side in one of the rear divisions. With their dress and arms he disguised half a legion of his own men so that they looked like his enemies, and then he sent this division, under four trusty leaders, to raid Ts'ao Chên's camp. Before they reached the camp they sent one of their number ahead as a galloper to tell Ts'ao Chên that there had been only a few men of Shu and they had all been chased out of sight, and so lull him into security.

This news satisfied Ts'ao Chên. But just then a trusty messenger from Ssŭma came with a message, "Our men have fallen into an ambush and many have been killed. Do not think any more about the wager: that is cancelled. But take most careful precautions."

"But there is not a single man of Shu near," said Ts'ao Chên.

He told the messenger to go back. Just then they told him Ch'in Liang's men had returned, and he went out to meet them. Just as he got near, someone remarked that some torches had flared up in the rear of his camp. He hastened thither to see. As soon as he was out of sight the four leaders waved on their men and dashed up to the camp. At the same time Ma Tai and Wang P'ing came up behind and two other troops came out.

The men of Wei were trapped and helpless; they scattered and fled for life. His officers got Ts'ao Chên away to the eastward. The enemy chased them. As Ts'ao fled there arose a great shouting, and up came a troop at full speed. Ts'ao thought all was lost, and his heart sank, but it was Ssŭma, who drove off the pursuers.

Though Ts'ao was saved he was almost too ashamed to show his face. Then said Ssŭma, "Chuko Liang has seized Ch'ishan, and we cannot remain here; let us go to Weipin, whence we may try to recover our lost ground."

"How did you know I was in danger of defeat?" asked Ts'ao Chên.

"My messenger told me what you had said, and I knew K'ung-ming would try to seize your camp. So I came to your help. The enemy's plan succeeded, but we will say no more about that wager. We must both do our best for the country."

But the fright and excitement made Ts'ao Chên ill, and he took to his bed. And while the men were in such a state of disorder Ssŭma was afraid to advise a return. They camped at Weipin.

After this adventure K'ung-ming hastened back to Ch'ishan. After the soldiers had been feasted and services recognised, the four discontented leaders, headed by Wei Yen, came to the tent to apologise.

"Who caused the loss?" said K'ung-ming.

Wei Yen said, "Ch'ên Shih disobeyed orders and rushed into the valley."

"Wei Yen told me to," said Ch'ên.

"Would you still try to drag him down after he rescued you?" said K'ung-ming. "However, when orders have been disobeyed it is useless to try and gloze it over."

He sentenced Ch'ên to death, and he was led away. Soon they brought his head into the presence of the assembled captains. Wei Yen was spared as there was yet work for him to accomplish.

After this, K'ung-ming prepared to advance. The scouts reported that Ts'ao Chên was ill, but was being treated by doctors in his tent. The news pleased K'ung-ming, and he said to his officers, "If he dies they will surely return to Ch'angan. They must be delayed by his sickness. He stays on so that his men may not lose heart. Now I will write him such a letter that he will die."

Then he called up the men of Wei who had yielded, and said to them, "You are Wei men and your families are all over there: it is wrong for you to serve me. Suppose I let you go home?"

They thanked him, falling prostrate and weeping. Then K'ung-ming continued, "Friend Ts'ao and I have a compact, and I have a letter for him which you shall take. The bearer will be well rewarded."

They received the letter and ran home to their own tents, where they gave their general the letter. Ts'ao Chên was too ill to rise, but he opened the cover and read:—"The Prime Minister of Han, Chuko Liang, to the Minister of War, Ts'ao Tzŭ-tan:

"You will permit me to say that a leader of an army should be able to go and come, to be facile and obdurate, to advance and retire, to show himself weak or strong, to be immovable as mountains, to be inscrutable as the operations of nature, to be infinite as the universe, to be everlasting as the blue void, to be vast as the ocean, to be dazzling as the lights of heaven, to foresee droughts and floods, to know the nature of the ground, to understand the possibilities of battle arrays, to conjecture the excellences and defects of the enemy.

"Alas! one of your sort, ignorant and inferior, rising impudently in heaven's vault, has had the presumption to assist a rebel to assume the imperial style and state at Loyang, to send some miserable soldiers into Hsiehku. There they happened upon drenching rain. The difficult roads wearied both men and horses, driving them frantic. Weapons and armour littered the countryside, swords and spears covered the ground. You, the Commander-in-chief, were heart-broken and cowed, your captains fled like rats. You dare not show your faces at home, nor can you enter the halls of state. The historians' pens will record your—salaries; the people will recount your —infamies. Chung-ta (Ssŭma I) is frightened when he hears of battle fronts, you are alarmed at mere rumours. My men are fierce and their steeds strong; my great captains are eager as tigers and majestic as dragons. I shall sweep Ts'inchüan bare and make Wei desolate."

Ts'ao Chên's wrath rose as he read; at the end it filled his breast. He died that evening. His colleague sent his coffin to Loyang on a waggon.

When King Jui heard of the death, he issued an edict urging Ssŭma to prosecute the war, to raise a great army and fight with Chuko Liang.

A declaration of war was sent one day in advance, and K'ung-ming replied that he would fight on the morrow. After the envoy had left, K'ung-ming called Chiang Wei by night to receive secret orders. He also summoned Kuan Hsing and told him what to do.

Next morning the whole force marched to the bank of the Wei River and took up a position in a wide plain with the river on one flank and hills on the other. The two armies saluted each other's appearance with heavy flights of arrows. After the drums had rolled thrice the Wei centre opened at the great standard and Ssŭma appeared, followed by his officers. Opposite was K'ung-ming, in a four-horse chariot, waving his feather fan.

Ssŭma addressed him, "Our master's ascension of the throne was after the manner of Yao, who abdicated in favour of Shun. Two emperors have succeeded and have their seat in the capital district. Because of his liberality and graciousness, my lord has suffered the rule of Shu and Wu lest the people should suffer in a struggle. You, who are but a peasant from Nanyang, ignorant of the ways of Heaven, wish to invade us, and you should be destroyed, but if you will examine your heart and repent of your fault and retire, then each may maintain his own borders, and a settled state will be attained. Thus the people may be spared distress, and you will all save your lives."

K'ung-ming smiled and replied, "Our late Emperor entrusted to me the custody of his orphan son: think you that I shall fail to exert myself to the uttermost to destroy rebels against his authority? Your soldiers of the Ts'ao family will soon be exterminated by Han. Your ancestors were servants of Han and for generations ate of their bounty. Yet, instead of giving grateful service, you assist usurpers. Are you not ashamed?"

The flush of shame spread over Ssŭma's face, but he replied, "We will try the test of battle. If you can conquer, I pledge myself to be no longer a leader of armies; but if you are defeated, then you will retire at once to your own village and I will not harm you."

"Do you desire a contest of captains, or of weapons, or of battle array?" asked K'ung-ming.

"Let us try a contest of battle array," replied Ssŭma.

"Then draw up your array that I may see," said K'ung-ming.

Ssŭma withdrew within the line and signalled to his officers with a yellow flag to draw up their men. When he had finished, he rode again to the front, saying, "Do you recognise my formation?"

"The least of my captains can do as well," said K'ung-ming, smiling. "This is called the 'Hung-yüan-i-ch'i' formation."

"Now you try while I look on," said Ssŭma.

K'ung-ming entered the lines and waved his fan. Then he came out and said, "Do you recognise that?"

"Of course; this is the pa-kua."

"Yes; you seem to know it. But dare you attack?"

"Why not, since I know it?" replied Ssŭma.

"Then you need only try."

Ssŭma entered the ranks and called to him three captains, Tai Ling, Chang Hu and Yüeh Lin, to whom he said, "That formation consists of eight gates of well-known names. You will go in from the east at the Gate of Life, turn to the south-west and make your way out by the Gate of Destruction. Then enter at the north, at the Open Gate, and the formation will be broken up. But be cautious."

They started with Chang Hu leading, Tai Ling next and Yüeh Lin in rear, each with thirty horsemen. They made their way in at the Gate of Life amid the applause of both sides. But when they had got within they found themselves facing a wall of troops and could not find a way out. They hastily led their men round by the base of the line toward the south-west to rush out there. But they were stopped by a flight of arrows. They became confused and saw many gates, but they had lost their bearings. Nor could they aid each other. They dashed hither and thither in disorder, lost as in gathering clouds and rolling mists. Then a shout arose, and each one was seized and bound.

They were taken to the centre, where K'ung-ming sat in his tent, and the three leaders with their ninety men were ranged in front.

"Indeed you are prisoners; are you surprised?" said K'ung-ming, smiling. "But I will set you free to return to your leader, and tell him to read his books again, and study his tactics, before he comes to try conclusions with me. You are pardoned, but leave your weapons and horses."

So they were stripped of their arms and armour and their faces blackened. Thus were they led on foot out of the array. Ssŭma lost his temper at sight of his men thus put to shame.

Said he, "After this disgrace, how can I face the other officers in the capital?"

He gave the signal for the army to fall on and attack the enemy, and, grasping his sword, led his brave captains into the fray and commanded the attack. But just as the two sides came to blows, Kuan Hsing came up, his drums rolling and men shouting, and attacked. Ssŭma told off a division from the rear to oppose him, and again turned to urge on his main body.

Then the army of Wei was thrown into confusion by another attack from Chiang Wei, who came up silently and joined in the battle. Thus three sides of the Wei army were engaged by three different divisions of the enemy, and Ssŭma decided to retire. However, this was difficult. The men of Shu hemmed him in and came closer every moment. At last, by a desperate push, he made an opening toward the south and freed his army. But he had lost six or seven out of every ten of his soldiers.

The Wei army withdrew to the south bank of the Wei River and camped. They strengthened their position and remained entirely on the defensive.

K'ung-ming mustered his victorious army and returned to Ch'ishan.

Now Li Yen sent an officer, a *Tu-yu*, named Kou An, from Jungan with a convoy of grain. This man was a drunkard and loitered on the road so that he arrived ten days late. K'ung-ming, angry at the delay, upbraided him, saying, "This grain is of the utmost importance to the army and you delay it. Three days' delay ought to mean the death penalty; what can you say to this delay of ten?"

Kou was sentenced to death and hustled out. But two officers ventured to intervene. They said, "Kou An is a servant of Li Yen's, and Li has sent large supplies of all sorts from the west. If you put this man to death perhaps others will not undertake escort duty."

K'ung-ming then bade the executioners loose the offender, give him eighty blows and let him go.

This punishment filled Kou An's heart with bitter resentment, and, in the night, he deserted to the enemy, he and his half dozen personal staff. He was taken before Ssŭma and told the tale of his wrongs.

"Your tale may be true, but it is hard to trust it," said Ssŭma. "K'ung-ming is full of guile. However, you may render me a service, and if you do, I will ask the king that you may be allowed to serve him and obtain a post for you."

"Whatever you ask I will do the best I can," replied the deserter.

"Then go to Ch'êngtu and spread a lying report that K'ung-ming is angry with the powers there and means to make himself emperor. This will get him recalled, and that will be a merit to you."

Kou An accepted the treacherous mission. In Ch'êngtu he got hold of the eunuchs and told them his lying tale. They became alarmed for their own safety and told the Emperor all these things.

"In such a case what am I to do?" asked the Later Ruler.

"Recall him to the capital," said the eunuchs; "and take away his military powers so that he cannot rebel."

The Later Ruler issued an edict recalling the army.

"The minister has rendered many and great services since he led out the army; wherefore is he recalled?" said Chiang Wan.

"I have a private matter to consult him about," said the king. "I must see him personally."

So the edict was issued and sent to K'ung-ming. The messenger was at once received as soon as he reached Ch'ishan.

"My king is young, and there is some jealous person by his side," said K'ung-ming sadly. "I was just going to achieve some solid success; why am I recalled? If I go not, I shall insult my king; if I retire, I shall never get such a chance again."

"If the army retire, Ssŭma will attack," said Chiang Wei.

"I will retire in five divisions. Thus to-day this camp goes. Supposing that there are a thousand men in the camp, then I shall have two thousand cooking places prepared, or if there are three thousand men, then four thousand cooking places shall be got ready; and so on, increasing the cooking arrangements as the men are sent away."

Yang I said, "In the days of old, when Sun Pin was attacking P'ang Chüan, the cooking arrangements were decreased as the men were increased. Why do you reverse this, O Minister?"

"Because Ssŭma is an able leader and would pursue if he knew we were retreating. But he would recognise the probability of an ambush, and if he sees an increase in the cooking

426

arrangements in a camp he will be unable to conclude whether the men have gone or not, and he will not pursue. Thus I shall gradually withdraw without/loss."

The order for retreat was given.

Confident of the effect that Kou An's lying report would produce, Ssŭma waited for the retreat of the Shu army to begin. He was still waiting when the scouts told him the enemy's camps were empty. Wishing to make sure, he rode out himself with a small reconnoitring party and inspected the empty camps. Then he bade them count the stoves. Soon after he paid a second visit, and again the cooking stoves were counted. The count showed an increase of a tenth.

"I felt sure that K'ung-ming would have some ruse ready. He has increased the cooking arrangements, and so, if we pursue, he will be ready for us. No; we also will retire and await another opportunity."

So there was no pursuit, and K'ung-ming did not lose a man. By and by, men came in from Ch'uank'ou to say that the retreat was a fact and that only the cooking arrangements had been increased, not the men. Ssŭma knew that he had been tricked, and once more acknowledged sadly his rival's superior guile. And he set out for Loyang.

> When players of equal skill are matched,
> Then victory hovers between;
> Perhaps your opponent's a genius,
> So put on your lowliest mien.

What happened when K'ung-ming reached Ch'êngtu will be told next.

CHAPTER CI.

By means of the artifice just described, Chuko withdrew his army safely into Hanchung, while Ssŭma retreated upon Ch'angan. K'ung-ming distributed the rewards for success and then went to the capital for audience.

"Your Majesty recalled me just as I was about to advance upon Ch'angan; what is the important matter?" said the minister.

For a long time the king made no reply. Presently he said, "I longed to see your face once more, that is the only reason."

K'ung-ming replied, "I think my recall was not on your own initiative; some slanderous person has hinted that I cherished ulterior objects."

The king, who indeed felt guilty and ill at ease, made no reply, and K'ung-ming continued, "Your late father laid me under an obligation which I am pledged to fulfil to the death. But if vile influences are permitted to work at home, how can I destroy the rebels without?"

"The fact is I recalled you because of the talk of the eunuchs. But I understand now and am unutterably sorry."

K'ung-ming interrogated the eunuchs and thus found out the base rumours that had been spread abroad by Kou An. He sent to arrest this man, but he had already fled and gone over to Wei. The eunuchs who had influenced the king were put to death, and all the others were expelled from the palace. The Prime Minister also upbraided Chiang Wan and Fei I for not having looked into the matter and set the king right.

K'ung-ming then took leave of the king and returned to the army. He wrote to Li Yen to see to the necessary supplies and began preparations for a new expedition.

Yang I said, "The soldiers are wearied by the many expeditions, and the supplies are not regular. I think a better plan would be to send half the army to Ch'ishan for three months, and at the end of that time exchange them for the other half; and so on alternately. For example, if you have twenty legions, let ten legions go into the field and ten remain. In this way, using ten and ten, their energies will be conserved and you can gradually work toward the metropolis."

"I agree with you," said K'ung-ming. "Our attack is not a matter to be achieved in haste. The suggestion for an extended campaign is excellent."

Wherefore the army was divided, and each half went out for one hundred days' service at a time, when it was relieved by the other half. Full penalties were provided for any laxity and failure to maintain the periods of active service.

In the spring of the ninth year of *Chien-Hsing* the army once more took the field against Wei. In Wei it was the fifth year of *T'ai-Ho*.

When the King of Wei heard of this new expedition he called Ssŭma and asked his advice.

"Now that my friend Ts'ao Chên is no more, I am willing to do all that one man can to destroy the rebels against Your Majesty's authority."

The king was gratified by this ready offer, and honoured Ssŭma with a banquet. Soon after came the news of actual attack and an edict issued for the army to move. The king, riding in his state chariot, escorted Ssŭma I out of the city, and, after the farewells, the general took the road to Ch'angan, where the force was gathering. There was assembled a council of war.

Chang Ho offered to guard Yung and Mei, but Ssŭma said, "Our leading army is not strong enough to face the enemy's whole force. Moreover, to divide an army is not generally a successful scheme. The better plan will be to leave a guard in Shangk'uei and send all the others to Ch'ishan. Will you undertake the leadership of the van?"

Chang Ho consented, saying, "I have always been most loyal and will devote my energies entirely to the service of the state. So far I have not had an adequate opportunity to prove my sincerity, but now that you confer upon me a post of such responsibility I can only say that no sacrifice can be too great for me, and I will do my utmost."

So Chang was appointed van-leader, and then Kuo Huai was set over Shênsi. Other captains were distributed to other posts, and the march began. The spies ascertained that the main force of Shu was directed toward Ch'ishan, and the leaders of the van were Wang P'ing and Chang I. The route chosen for their march was from Ch'ênts'ang across Chienko, through Sankuan and the Hsieh Valley.

Hearing this, Ssŭma said, "K'ung-ming is advancing in great force and certainly intends to reap the wheat in Shênsi for his supply. You get sufficient men to hold Ch'ishan, while I and Kuo Huai go over and foil the enemy's plan to gather the wheat."

So Cang Ho took four legions to hold Ch'ishan, and Ssŭma set out westwards.

When K'ung-ming reached Ch'ishan and had settled his men in camp, he saw that the bank of the River Wei had been fortified by his enemy.

"That must be the work of Ssŭma I," remarked he to his captains. "But we have not enough food in camp. I have written to Li Yen to send grain, but it has not yet arrived. The wheat in Shênsi is now just ripe, and we will go and reap it."

Leaving a guard for the camps, K'ung-ming, with several captains, went over to Luch'êng. The Prefect of that city knew he could not offer any real defence, so he opened the gates and yielded. Then K'ung-ming asked him where the ripe wheat was to be found, and Shênshang was named. So a few men were left in the city, and the remainder of the army went to Shênshang.

But soon the leading body returned to say that Ssŭma had already occupied that city.

"He guessed what I intended to do," said K'ung-ming, taken aback.

K'ung-ming then retired, bathed and put on another dress. Next he bade them bring out three four-wheeled chariots, all exactly alike, that were among the impedimenta of the army. They had been built in Shu some time before.

Chiang Wei was told off to lead a company as escort for one chariot, and a half company of drummers were appointed to accompany it. The chariot with its escort and drummers was sent away behind the city. In like manner two other chariots were equipped and sent east and west of the city. Each chariot was propelled by a team of twenty men, all dressed in black, barefooted and with loosened hair. Each one of the team also had a sword or a black seven-starred bannerol.

While the chariots were taking up their positions the remaining men were ordered to prepare ropes and sickles to cut and carry away the grain.

Next K'ung-ming selected twenty-four handsome soldiers, whom he dressed and armed like those sent away with the three chariots, save that all carried swords instead of some swords and some bannerols. These were to push his own chariot. Kuan Hsing was told to dress up as a sort of angel and to walk in front of K'ung-ming's chariot holding a black seven-starred bannerol. These preparations complete, K'ung-ming mounted, and the chariot took the road toward the Wei camp.

The appearance of a chariot with such attendants more than startled the enemy's scouts, who did not know whether the apparition was that of a man or a demon. They hastened to their general and told him. Ssŭma came out himself and saw the cavalcade, and its central figure dressed as a Taoist mystic, with head-dress, white robe and a feather fan.

"Some of K'ung-ming's odd doings," said he, and he ordered a couple of companies to go out and bring in the chariot, escort and the seated figure.

The soldiers went out to do their bidding, but as soon as they appeared, the chariot retired and took a road leading to the rear of the Shu camp. Although the Wei soldiers were mounted, they could not come up with the cavalcade. What they did meet with was a chilly breeze and a cold mist that rolled about them.

They found it uncanny and halted, saying one to another, "How extraordinary it is that we have been pressing on and yet we got no nearer. What does it mean?"

When K'ung-ming saw that the pursuit had ceased, he had his chariot pushed out again to the front and passed within sight of the halted men. At first they hesitated, but presently took up the pursuit once more. Whereupon the chariot again retired, proceeding slowly, but always keeping out of reach. And thus more than twenty *li* were covered and the chariot was still not captured.

Again the soldiers halted, puzzled and perplexed at this incomprehensible chase. But as soon as they stopped, the chariot came again toward them and they retook pursuit.

Ssŭma now came up with a strong force. But he also halted, and said to his men, "This K'ung-ming is a past master in the arts of necromancy and juggling and knows how to call up spirits to his aid. I know this trick of his; it is one of the 'Six *Chia*,' and it is vain to pursue."

So they ceased following. But then a roll of drums came from the side of the enemy as if a body of men were approaching. Ssŭma told off some companies to repel them, but there only came into view a small force, and in their midst was a party of men dressed in black, the exact counterpart of the cavalcade he had first sent to pursue. In the chariot sat another K'ung-ming just like the one that had just disappeared.

"But just now he was sitting in that other chariot; how can he be here? It is most wonderful," said Ssŭma.

Shortly after they heard another roll of the drums, and as the sound died away there appeared another body of men, with a chariot in the midst, exactly like the last and also carrying a sitting figure of K'ung-ming.

"They must be magic soldiers," said Ssŭma.

The men were now feeling the strain of these weird appearances and began to get out of hand. They dared not stay to fight such beings, and some ran away. But before they had gone far, lo! another roll of drums, another cohort and another chariot with a similar figure seated therein.

The men of Wei were now thoroughly frightened, and even Ssŭma himself began to feel doubtful whether these appearances should be ascribed to men or devils. He realised, however, that he was in the midst of dangers, and he and his men ran away helter-skelter, never stopping till they reached Shangk'ui. They entered the city and closed the gates.

Having thus driven off the Wei soldiers, K'ung-ming proceeded to reap and gather the wheat, which was carried into Luch'êng and laid out to dry.

Ssŭma remained shut up within the walls for three days. Then, as he saw his enemies retiring, he sent out some scouts, who presently returned with a Shu soldier they had captured. The prisoner was questioned.

"I was of the reaping party," said the man. "They caught me when I was looking for some horses that had strayed."

"What wonderful soldiers were they of yours that one saw here lately?" asked the general.

The man replied, "K'ung-ming was with one party of them, the others were led by Chiang Wei, Ma Tai and Wei Yen. There was a company of fighting men with each chariot and half a company of drummers. K'ung-ming was with the first party."

"His comings and goings are not human," said Ssŭma sadly.

He sent for Kuo Huai to talk over plans. Said Kuo, "I hear the men of Shu are very few and they are occupied with gathering the grain; why not smite them?"

Ssŭma told him his last experience of his opponent's wiles.

"He threw dust in your eyes that time," said Kuo with a smile. "However, now you know. What is the good of more talk? Let me attack the rear, while you lead against the front, and we shall take the city and K'ung-ming too."

An attack was decided upon.

While the men were still busy with the wheat, K'ung-ming called up his captains, and said, "The enemy will attack tonight. There is a suitable place for an ambush in the newly reaped fields, but who will lead for me?"

Four captains offered themselves, and he posted them, each with two companies, outside the four corners of the city. They were to await the signal and then converge. When these had gone, K'ung-ming led out a small party of men and hid in the newly reaped fields.

In the meantime Ssŭma was drawing near. It was dusk when he stood beneath the walls of Luch'êng.

Said he to his officers, "If we attacked by daylight we should find the city well prepard, so we will take advantage of the darkness The moat is shallow here, and there will be no difficulty in crossing it."

The men bivouacked till the time should come to attack. About the middle of the first watch Kuo Huai arrived, and his force joined up with the others. This done, the drums began to beat, and the city was quickly surrounded. However, the defenders maintained such a heavy discharge of arrows, bolts and stones from the walls that the besiegers dared not close in.

Suddenly from the midst of the Wei army came the roar of a bomb, soon followed by others from different places. The soldiers were startled, but no one could say whence the sounds had proceeded. Kuo Huai went to search the wheat fields, and then the four armies from the corners of the city converged upon the Wei army. At the same time the defenders burst out of the city gates, and a great battle began. Wei lost many men.

After heavy fighting Ssŭma extricated his army from the battle and made his way to a hill, which he set about holding and fortifying, while Kuo Huai got round to the rear of the city and called a halt.

K‘ung-ming entered the city and sent his men to camp again at the four corners of the walls.

Kuo Huai went to see his chief, and said, "We have long been at grips with these men and are unable to drive them off. We have now lost another fight, and unless something is done we shall not get away at all."

"What can we do?" asked Ssŭma.

"You might write to Yung and Liang to send their forces to our help. I will try my fortune against Chienko and cut off Chuko's retreat and supplies. That should bring about discontent and mutiny, and we can attack when we see the enemy in confusion."

The letters were sent, and soon Sun Li came leading the men, foot and horse, of the two districts. The new arrivals were sent to help Kuo in the attack on Chienko.

After many days had passed without sight of the enemy, K‘ung-ming thought it was time to make another move. Calling up Chiang Wei and Ma Tai, he said, "The men of Wei are well posted on the hills and refuse battle because, firstly, they think that we are short of food, and, secondly, they have sent an army against Chienko to cut off our supplies. Now each of you will take a legion and garrison the important points about here to show them that we are well prepared to defend ourselves. Then they will retire."

After these two had gone, Chang Shih and Chang I came to see the general about the change of troops then due. They told him the reliefs had alredy left Hanchung and that despatches from the leading divisions had come in. Four legions were due for relief.

"There is the order; carry it out," replied K‘ung-ming.

So the home-going legions prepared to withdraw. Just then came the news of reinforcements for the enemy from Yung and Liang and a report of actual attacks on Luch‘êng and Chienko. In the face of such important news, Yang I went to ask if the change of forces was to take place or be postponed for a time.

K‘ung-ming replied, "I must keep faith with the men. Since the order for the periodical exchange of men has been issued it must be carried out. Beside, the men due for relief are all prepared to start, their expectations have been roused and their relatives await them. In the face of yet greater difficulties I would let them go."

So orders were given for the time-expired men to march that day. But when the legionaries heard it a sudden movement of generosity spread among them, and they said they did not wish to go, but would prefer to remain to fight.

"But you are due for home; you cannot stay here," said the general.

They reiterated that they all wished to stay instead of going home.

"Since you wish to stay and fight with me you can go out of the city and camp ready to encounter the men of Wei as soon as they arrive. Do not give them time to rest or recover breath, but attack vigorously at once. You will be fresh and fit, waiting for those fagged with a long march."

So they gripped their weapons and joyfully went out of the city to array themselves in readiness.

Now the Hsiliang men had travelled by double marches, and so were worn out and needed rest. But while they were pitching their tents the men of Shu fell upon them lustily, leaders full of spirit, men full of energy. The weary soldiers could make no proper stand, and retired. The men of Shu followed, pressing on them till corpses littered the whole plain and blood flowed in runnels.

It was a victory for K'ung-ming, and he came out to welcome the victors and led them into the city and distributed rewards.

Just then arrived an urgent letter from Li Yen, then at Jungp'ing, and when K'ung-ming had torn it open he read:—
"News has just come that Wu has sent an envoy to Loyang and entered into an alliance with Wei whereby Wu is to attack us. The army of Wu has not yet set out, but I am anxiously awaiting your plans."

Doubts and fears crowded in upon K'ung-ming's mind as he read. He summoned his officers:

"As Wu is coming to invade our land, we shall have to retire quickly," said he. "If I issue orders for the Ch'ishan force to withdraw, Ssǔma will not dare to pursue while we are camped here."

The Ch'ishan force broke camp and marched in two divisions. Chang Ho watched them go, but was too fearful of the movement being some ruse to attempt to follow. He went to see Ssǔma.

"The enemy have retired, but I know not for what reason."

"K'ung-ming is very crafty, and you will do well to remain where you are and keep a careful look-out. Do nothing till their grain has given out, when they must retire for good."

Here Wei Yen stepped forward, saying, "But we should seize the occasion of their retreat to smite them. Are they tigers that you fear to move? How the world will laugh at us."

But Ssŭma was obstinate and ignored the protest.

When K'ung-ming knew that the Ch'ishan men had got away safely, he called Yang I and Ma Chung and gave them secret orders to lead a legion of bowmen and crossbowmen out by the Wooden Gate of Chienko and place them in ambush on both sides of the road.

"If the men of Wei pursue, wait till you hear a bomb. When you hear the bomb, at once barricade the road with timber and stones so as to impede them. When they halt, shoot at them with the bows and the crossbows."

Wei Yen and Kuan Hsing were told to attack the rear of the enemy.

These orders given, the walls of the city were decorated lavishly with flags, and at various points within the city were piled straw and kindling wood ready to raise a blaze as though the city was on fire. The soldiers were sent out along the road from the Wooden Gate.

The spies of Wei returned to headquarters to say that most of the Shu soldiers had left, only a few being in the city. In doubt, Ssŭma went himself to look, and when he saw the smoke rising from within the walls and the fluttering flags he said, "The city is deserted." He sent men in to confirm this, and they said the place was empty.

"Then K'ung-ming is really gone; who will pursue?"

"Let me," replied Chang Ho.

"You are too impulsive," said Ssŭma.

"I have been leader of the van from the first day of this expedition; why not use me to-day, when there is work to be done and glory to be gained?"

"Because the utmost caution is necessary. They are retreating, and they will leave an ambush at every possible point."

"I know that, and you need not be afraid."

"Well; you wish to go and may, but whatever happens you must be prepared for."

"A really noble man is prepared to sacrifice self for country; never mind what happens."

"Then take half a legion and start; Wei P'ing shall follow with two legions of horse and foot to deal with any ambush that may discover itself. I will follow later with three companies to help where need be."

So Chang Ho set out and advanced quickly. Thirty li out he heard a roll of drums, and suddenly appeared from a wood a cohort led by a captain of high rank, who galloped to the front crying, "Whither would you go, O rebel leader?"

Chang Ho swiftly turned and engaged Wei Yen, for it was he who led, but after a few passes Wei fled. Chang rode after him along the road he had come by and then stopped and turned again. All went well till he came to a slope, when there arose shouts and yells and another body of soldiers came out.

"Chang Ho, do not run away!" cried this leader, who was Kuan Hsing.

Kuan galloped close, and Chang did not flee. They fought, and after half a score of passes Kuan seemed to have the worst of the encounter and fled. Chang Ho followed. Presently they neared a dense wood. Chang was fearful of entering in, so he sent forward men to search the thickets. They could find no danger, and Chang again pursued.

But quite unexpectedly Wei Yen, who had formerly fled, got round ahead of Chang and now appeared again. The two fought a half score bouts and again Wei ran. Chang followed, but Kuan also got round to the front by a side road and so stopped the pursuit of Wei. Chang attacked furiously as soon as he was checked, this time so successfully that the men of Shu threw away their war-gear and ran. The road was thus littered with spoil, and the Wei men could not resist the temptation to gather it. They slipped from their horses and began to collect the arms.

The manœuvres just described continued, Yen and Kuan one after the other engaging Chang and Chang pressing on after each one, but achieving nothing. And as evening fell the running fight had led both sides close to the Wooden Gate Road.

Then suddenly Wei's men made a real stand, and he rode to the front yelling, "Yield, rebel! I have not fought yet and you have had it all your own way so far. Now we will fight to the death."

Chang was furious and nothing loth, so he came on with his spear to meet Wei, who was flourishing his sword. They met; yet again, after a few bouts, Wei threw aside weapons, armour, helmet and all his gear, and even left his horse and went away along the Wooden Gate Road.

Chang Ho was filled with the lust to kill, and he could not let Wei escape. So he set out after him, although it was already dark. But suddenly lights appeared, and the sky became aglow, and at the same time huge boulders and great baulks of timber came rolling down the slopes and blocked the way.

Fear gripped Chang, for he saw he had blundered into an ambush. The road was blocked in front and behind and bordered by craggy precipices. Then, rat-tat-tat! came the sound of a rattle, and therewith flew clouds of arrows and showers of bolts. Chang Ho and many of his officers were killed.

With myriad shining bolts the air was filled,
The road was littered with brave soldiers killed;
The force to Chienko faring perished here;
The tale of valour grows from year to year.

Soon the second army of Wei came up, but too late to help. From the signs they knew that their comrades had been victims of a cruel trick, and they turned back. But as they faced about a shout was heard, and from the hill-tops came, "I, Chuko Liang, am here!"

Looking up they saw his figure outlined against a fire. Pointing to the slain, he cried, "I have been hunting, as you see; only instead of slaying a horse (Ma, for Ssǔma) I have killed a deer (Chang). But you may go in peace, and when you see your general, tell him that he will be my quarry one day."

The soldiers told this to Ssǔma when they returned, and he was deeply mortified, and blamed himself as the cause of the death of his colleague Chang Ho. And when he returned to Loyang the king wept at the death of his brave leader and had his body honourably buried.

K'ung-ming had no sooner reached Hanchung than he prepared to go on to the capital and see his lord.

But Li Yen, who was in charge of the capital beside being responsible for supplying the army, said to the king, "Why does the Prime Minister return, for I have kept him fully supplied with all things needed for the army?"

Then the king sent Fei I into Hanchung to enquire why the army had retired. And when he had arrived and showed the cause of his coming, K'ung-ming was greatly surprised and showed the letter from Li telling of the alliance and threatened invasion from Wu. Then Fei related the gist of Li's memorial to the Throne. So K'ung-ming enquired carefully, and then it came out that Li had failed to find sufficient grain to keep the army supplied and so had sent the first lying letter to the army that it might retire before the shortage showed itself. His memorial to the Throne was designed to cover the former fault.

"The fool has ruined the great design of the state just to save his own skin," cried K'ung-ming bitterly.

He called in the offender and sentenced him to death. But Fei I interceded, saying that the late Emperor had loved and trusted Li Yen, and so his life was spared. However, when Fei made his report the king was wroth and ordered Li Yen to suffer death.

But this time Chiang Wan intervened, saying, "Your late father named Li Yen as one of the guardians of your youth." And the king relented. However, Li was stripped of all rank and exiled. But K'ung-ming gave Li's sons employment.

Preparations then began for an expedition to start in three years. Plans were discussed, provisions were accumulated, weapons put in order and officers and men kept fit and trained. By his kindness to all men K'ung-ming won great popularity, and the time passed quickly.

In the second month of the thirteenth year K'ung-ming presented a memorial saying, "I have been training the army for three years; supplies are ample and all is in order for an expedition. We may now attack Wei. If I cannot destroy these rebels, sweep away the evil hordes and bring about a glorious entry into the capital, then may I never again enter your Majesty's presence."

The king replied, "Our state is now firmly established, and Wei troubles us not at all; why not enjoy the present tranquillity, O Father-Minister?"

"Because of the mission left me by your father. I am ever scheming to destroy Wei, even in my dreams. I must strive my best and do my utmost to restore you to the ancient capital of your race and replace the Hans in their old palace."

As he said this a voice cried, "An army may not go forth, O Minister!"

Ch'iao Chou had raised a last protest.

> K'ung-ming's sole thought was service,
> Himself he would not spare;
> But Ch'iao had watched the starry sky,
> And read misfortune there.

The next chapter will give the arguments against fighting.

CHAPTER CII.

SSŬMA OCCUPIES THE RIVER BANKS;
CHUKO CONSTRUCTS "BULLOCKS" AND "HORSES."

Ch'iao Chou, who protested against the war, was Grand Historian. He was also a student of astrology. He opposed the war, saying, "My present office involves the direction of the observations on the Astrological Terrace, and I am bound to report whether the aspect forebodes misfortune or promises happiness. Not long since, several flights of orioles came from the south, plunged into the Han Waters and were drowned. This is an evil augury. Moreover, I have studied the aspect of the sky, and the 'Wolf' constellation is influencing the aspect of the planet Venus. An aura of prosperity pervades the north. To attack Wei will not be to our profit. Again, the people say that the cypress trees moan in the night. With so many evil omens, I would that the Prime Minister should not go forth to war, but remain at home to guard what we have."

"How can I?" said K'ung-ming. "His late Majesty laid upon me a heavy responsibility, and I must exert myself to the utmost in the endeavour to destroy these rebels. The policy of a state cannot be changed because of vain and irresponsible talk of inauspicious signs."

K'ung-ming was not to be deterred. He instructed the officials to prepare the Great Bovine Sacrifice in the Dynastic Temple. Then, weeping, he prostrated himself and made this declaration: "Thy servant Liang has made five expeditions to Ch'ishan without gaining any extension of territory. His fault weighs heavily upon him. Now once again he is about to march, pledged to use every effort of body and mind to exterminate the rebels against the Han House, and to restore to the Dynasty its ancient glory in its old capital. To achieve this end he would use the last remnant of his strength and could die content."

The sacrifice ended, he took leave of the king and set out for Hanchung to make the final arrangements for his march. While so engaged, he received the unexpected news of the death of Kuan Hsing. He was greatly shocked, and fainted. When he had recovered consciousness his officers did their utmost to console him.

"How pitiful! Why does Heaven deny long life to the loyal and good? I have lost a most able captain just as I am setting out and need him most."

As all are born, so all must die;
Men are as gnats against the sky;
But loyalty or piety
May give them immortality.

The armies of Shu numbered thirty-four legions, and they marched in five divisions, with Chiang Wei and Wei Yen in the van, and when they had reached Ch'ishan, Li K'uei, the Commissary General, was instructed to convey stores into Hsieh Valley in readiness.

In Wei they had recently changed the style of the year-period to *Ch'ing-Lung*, Black Dragon, because a black dragon had been seen to issue from Mop'o Well. The year of the fighting was the second year.

The courtiers said to King Jui, "The wardens of the marches report thirty or so legions advancing in five divisions from Shu upon Ch'ishan."

The news distressed the king, who at once called in Ssŭma I and told him of the invasion.

Ssŭma replied, "The aspect of the sky is very auspicious for the capital. The *K'uei* star has encroached upon the planet Venus, which bodes ill for Hsich'üan. Thus K'ung-ming is pitting his powers against the heavens and will meet defeat and suffer death. And I, by virtue of Your Majesty's good fortune, am to be the instrument of destruction. I request leave to name four men to go with me."

"Who are they? Name them," said the king.

"They are the four sons of Hsiahou Yüan, Pa, Wei, Hui and Ho. The first two trained archers and cavaliers, the other two are deep strategists. All four desire to avenge the death of their father. Pa and Wei should be leaders of the van; Hui and Ho Expeditionary Ministers of War to discuss and arrange plans for the repulse of our enemy."

"You remember the evil results of employing the 'Dynastic Son-in-Law,' Hsiahou Mou; he lost his army and is still too ashamed to return to court. You are sure these are not of the same kidney?"

"They are not like him in the least."

The king granted the request and named Ssŭma I as Commander-in-chief with the fullest authority. When Ssŭma took leave of the king he received a command in the king's own writing:—

"When you, Noble Sir, reach the banks of the Wei River and have well fortified that position, you are not to give battle. The men of Shu, disappointed of their desire, will pretend to retire and so entice you on, but you will not pursue. You will wait till their supplies are consumed and they are compelled to retreat, when you may smite them. Then you will obtain the victory without distressing the army unduly. This is the best plan of campaign."

Ssŭma took it with bowed head. He proceeded forthwith to Ch'angan. When he had mustered the forces assembled from all districts they numbered forty legions, and they were all camped on the river. In addition, five legions were farther up the stream preparing nine floating bridges. The two leaders of the van were ordered to cross the river and camp, and in rear of the main camp on the east a solid earth rampart was raised to guard against any surprises from the rear.

While these preparations were in progress, Kuo Huai and Sun Li came to the new camp, and the former said, "With the men of Shu at Ch'ishan there is a possibility of their dominating the Wei River, going up on the plain and pushing out a line to the north hills whereby to cut off Shensi."

"You say well," said Ssŭma. "See to it. Take command of all the Shênsi forces, occupy Peiyüan and make a fortified camp there. But adopt a fabian policy; wait till the enemy's food supplies get exhausted before you think of attack."

So they left to carry out these orders.

In this expedition K'ung-ming made five main camps at Ch'ishan, and between Hsieh Valley and Chienko he established a line of fourteen large camps. He distributed the men among these camps as for a long campaign. He appointed inspecting officers to make daily visits to see that all was in readiness. When he heard that the men of Wei had camped in Peiyüan, he said to his officers, "They camp there fearing that our holding this district will sever connection with Shênsi. I am pretending to look toward Peiyüan, but really my objective is the Wei River. I am going to build several large rafts and pile them with straw, and I have five companies of watermen to manage them. In the darkness of the night I shall attack Peiyüan; Ssŭma will come to the rescue; if he is only a little worsted I shall cross the river with the rear divisions. Then the leading divisions will embark on the rafts, drop down the river, set fire to the bridges and attack the rear of the enemy. I shall lead an army to take the gates of the first camp. If we can get the south bank of the river the campaign will become simple."

The spies carried information of the doings of the men of Shu to Ssŭma, who said to his men, "K'ung-ming has some crafty scheme, but I think I know it. He proposes to make a show of taking Peiyüan, and then, dropping down the river, he will try to burn our bridges, throw our rear into confusion and then attack."

So he ordered Hsiahou Pa and his brother to listen for the sounds of battle about Peiyüan; if they heard the shouting they were to march down to the river, to the hills on the south, and attack the men of Shu as they arrived. Two other forces, of two companies of bowmen each, were to lie in hiding on the north bank near the bridges to keep off the rafts that might come down on the current and keep them from touching the bridges.

Then he sent for Kuo Huai and Sun Li, and said, "K'ung-ming is coming to Peiyüan to cross the river secretly. Your force is small, and you can hide half way along the road. If the enemy come in the afternoon, that will mean an attack on us in the evening. Then you are to simulate defeat and run. They will pursue. You can shoot with all your energy, and our marines will attack. If the attack is in great force, look out for orders."

All these orders given, Ssŭma sent his two sons Shih and Chao to reinforce the front camp while he led his own men to relieve Peiyüan.

K'ung-ming sent Wei Yen and Ma Tai to cross the Wei River and attack Peiyüan, while the attempt to set fire to the bridges was confided to Wu Pan and Wu I. The general attack was to be made by three divisions. The various divisions started at noon and crossed the river, where they slowly formed up in battle order.

The armies sent against Peiyüan arrived about dusk. The scouts having informed the defenders of their approach, Sun Li abandoned his camp and fled. This told Wei Yen that his attack was expected, and he turned to retire. At this moment a great shouting was heard, and there appeared two bodies of the enemy bearing down upon the attackers. Desperate efforts were made to extricate themselves, but many of the men of Shu fell into the river. The others scattered. However, Wu I came up and rescued the force from entire destruction.

Wu Pan set half his men to navigate the rafts down the river to the bridges. But the men of Wei stationed near the bridges shot clouds of arrows at them, and the Shu leader, Wu Pan, was wounded. He fell into the river and was drowned. The crews of the rafts jumped into the water and got away. The rafts fell into the hands of the men of Wei.

At this time Wang P'ing and Chang I were ignorant of the defeat of their Peiyüan army, and they went straight for the camps of Wei. They arrived in the second watch. They heard loud shouting, and Wang P'ing said to his colleague, "We do not know whether the cavalry sent to Peiyüan has been successful or not. It is strange that we do not see a single soldier of the enemy. Surely Ssŭma has found out the plan and prepared to frustrate the attack. Let us wait here till the bridges have been set on fire and we see the flames."

So they halted. Soon after, a mounted messenger came up with orders for them to retire, as the attack on the bridges had failed. They attempted to withdraw, but the men of Wei had taken a by-road to their rear, and they were at once attacked. A great fire started also. A disorderly battle ensued, from which the two leaders eventually got out, but only with great loss. And when K'ung-ming collected his army at Ch'ishan once more he found, to his sorrow, that he had lost more than the equivalent of a legion.

Just at this time Fei I arrived from Ch'êngtu. K'ung-ming received him and, after the ceremonies were over, said, "I would trouble you, Sir, to carry a letter for me into Wu; will you undertake the mission?"

"Could I possibly decline any task you laid upon me?"

So K'ung-ming wrote a letter and sent it to Sun Ch'üan. Fei I took it and hastened to Chienyeh, where he saw Sun and presented this letter:—"The Hans have been unfortunate, and the line of rulers has been broken. The Ts'ao party have usurped the seat of government and still hold the command. My late master confided a great task to me, and I must exhaust every effort to achieve it. Now my army is at Ch'ishan and the rebels are on the verge of destruction on the River Wei. I hope Your Majesty, in accordance with your oath of alliance, will send a leader against the north to assist by taking the capital, and the empire can be shared. The full circumstances cannot be told, but I hope you will understand and act."

Sun Ch'üan was pleased at the news and said to the envoy, "I have long desired to set my army in motion, but have not been able to arrange with K'ung-ming. After this letter I will lead an expedition myself and go to occupy Ch'aomên and capture the new city of Wei. Moreover, I will send Lu Hsün with an army to camp at Mienk'ou and take Hsiangyang. I will also send an army into Huaiyang. The total number will be thirty legions, and they shall start at once."

Fei I thanked him and said, "In such a case the capital will fall forthwith."

A banquet was prepared. At this, Sun Ch'üan said, "Whom did the minister send to lead the battle?"

Fei replied, "Wei Yen was the chief leader."

"A man brave enough, but crooked. One day he will work a mischief unless K'ung-ming is very wary. But surely he knows."

"Your Majesty's words are to the point," said the envoy; "I will return at once and lay them before K'ung-ming."

Fei quickly took leave and hastened to Ch'ishan with his news of the intended expedition."

"Did the King of Wu say nothing else?" asked K'ung-ming.

Then Fei told him what had been said about Wei Yen.

"Truly a comprehending ruler," said K'ung-ming, appreciatively. "But I could not be ignorant of this. However, I use him because he is very bold."

"Then, Sir, you ought to decide soon what to do with him."

"I have a scheme of my own."

Fei returned to Ch'êngtu, and K'ung-ming resumed the ordinary camp duties of a leader.

Then suddenly a certain Wei leader came and begged to be allowed to surrender. Kung-ming had the man brought in and questioned him.

"I am a supplementary leader, Chêng Wên by name. A certain Ch'in Lang and I are old colleagues. Recently Ssŭma transferred us and, showing great partiality for my colleague, gave him high rank and threw me out like a weed. I was disgusted and left, and I wish to join your ranks if you will accept my service."

Just at that moment a man came in to say that Ch'in Lang, the very man whose promotion had sent the deserter to the other side, had appeared in front of the tents and was challenging Chêng Wên.

Said K'ung-ming, "How does this man stand with you in fighting skill?"

"I should just kill him," said Chêng.

"If you were to slay him that would remove my doubts."

Chêng accepted the proposal with alacrity, mounted his horse and away he went. K'ung-ming went out to see the fight. There was the challenger shaking his spear and reviling his late friend as rebel and brigand and horse-thief.

"Give me back my horse you stole!" cried he, galloping toward Chêng as soon as he appeared. Chêng whipped up his horse, waved his sword and went to meet the attack. In the first bout he cut down Ch'in Lang.

The Wei soldiers then ran away; the victor hacked off the head of his victim and returned to lay it at K'ung-ming's feet. Seated in his tent, he summoned the victor and burst out:—

"Take him away and behead him!"

"I have done nothing wrong," cried Chêng.

"As if I do not know Ch'in Lang! The man you have just killed was not Ch'in Lang. How dare you try to deceive me?"

Chêng said, "I will own up; but this was his brother Ming."

K'ung-ming smiled. "Ssŭma sent you to try this on for some reason of his own, but he could not throw dust in my eyes. If you do not tell the truth I will put you to death."

Thus caught, the false deserter confessed and begged his life.

K'ung-ming said, "You can save your life by writing a letter to Ssŭma telling him to come to raid our camp. I will spare you on this condition. And if I capture Ssŭma, I will give you all the credit and reward you handsomely."

There was nothing for it but to agree, and the letter was written. Then the writer was placed in confinement.

"How did you know this was only a pretended desertion?" said Fan Chien.

"Ssŭma looks to his men," replied K'ung-ming. "If he made Ch'in Lang a leading general, he was certainly a man of great military skill and not the sort of man to be overcome by this fellow Chêng in the first encounter. So his opponent certainly was not Ch'in Lang. That is how I knew."

They congratulated him on his perspicacity. Then K'ung-ming selected a certain persuasive speaker from among his officers and whispered certain instructions in his ear. The officer at once left and carried the letter just written to the Wei camp, where he asked to see the general. He was admitted, and the letter was read.

"Who are you?" said Ssŭma.

"I am a man from the capital, a poor fellow stranded in Shu. Chêng Wên and I are fellow villagers. K'ung-ming has given Chêng a van-leadership as a reward for what he has done, and he got me to bring this letter to you and to say that he will show a light to-morrow evening as a signal, and he hopes you will lead the attack yourself. Chêng will work from the inside in your favour."

Ssŭma took great pains to test the reliability of these statements, and he examined the letter minutely to see if it bore any signs of fabrication. Presently he ordered in refreshments for the bearer of the letter, and then he said, "We will fix to-day at the second watch for the raid, and I will lead in person. If it succeeds I will give you a good appointment as a reward."

Taking leave, the soldier retraced his steps to his own camp and reported the whole interview to K'ung-ming.

K'ung-ming held his sword aloft, took the proper paces for an incantation, and prayed. This done, he summoned six of his most able and trusty leaders, to whom he gave certain instructions. When they had gone to carry them out he ascended a hill, taking with him a few score men only.

Ssŭma had been taken in by Chêng Wên's letter and intended to lead the night raid. But the elder of his sons, whom he had selected to help him, expostulated with his father.

"Father, you are going on a dangerous expedition on the faith of a mere scrap of paper," said his son. "I think it imprudent. What if something goes unexpectedly wrong? Let some captain go in your place, and you come up in rear as a reserve."

Ssŭma saw there was reason in this proposal, and he finally decided to send Ch'in Lang, with a legion, and he himself would command the reserve.

The night was fine with a bright moon. But about the middle of the second watch the sky clouded over, and it became very black, so that a man could not see his next neighbour.

"This is providential," chuckled Ssŭma.

The expedition duly started, men with gags, and horses with cords round their muzzles. They moved swiftly and silently, and Ch'in Lang made straight for the camp of Shu.

But when he reached it, and entered, and saw not a man, he knew he had been tricked. He yelled to his men to retire, but lights sprang up all round, and attacks began from four sides. Fight as he would, Ch'in Lang could not free himself.

From behind the battle area Ssŭma saw flames rising from the camp of Shu and heard continuous shouting, but he knew not whether it meant victory for his own men or to his enemy. He pressed forward toward the fire. Suddenly, a shout, a roll of drums and a blare of trumpets close at hand, a bomb that seemed to rend the earth, and Wei Yen and Chiang Wei bore down upon Ssŭma, one on each flank.

This was the final blow to him. Of every ten men of Wei eight or nine were killed or wounded and the few others scattered to the four winds. Meanwhile Ch'in Lang's men were falling under arrows that came in locust-flights, and their leader was killed. Ssŭma and the remnant of his army ran away to their own camp.

After the third watch the sky cleared. K'ung-ming from the hill-top sounded the gong of retreat. This obscurity in the third watch was due to an incantation called *tun-chia* of "The concealing *chia*." The sky became clear, but K'ung-ming performed another incantation of the sixth of the *ting* and the *chia* in order to sweep away the few floating clouds that still persisted.

The victory was complete. The first order on K'ung-ming's return to camp was to put Chêng to death.

Next he considered new plans for capturing the south bank. Every day he sent a party to offer a challenge before the camps of the enemy, but no one accepted.

One day K'ung-ming rode in his small chariot to the front of Ch'ishan, keenly scanned the course of the Wei River and carefully surveyed the lie of the land. Presently he came to a valley shaped like a bottle-gourd, large enough to form a hiding place for a whole company of soldiers in the inner recess, while half as many more could hide in the outer. In rear the mountains were so close that they left passage only for a single horseman. The discovery pleased the great captain mightily, and he asked the guides what the place was called.

They replied, "It is called Shangfang Valley, or Hulu Valley."

Returning to his camp, he called up two leaders named Tu Jui and Hu Chung and whispered into their ears certain secret orders. Next he called up a company of the artizan camp followers and sent them into the valley to construct some "wooden oxen and running horses" for the use of the

troops. Finally he set Ma Tâi with half a company to guard
the mouth of the valley and prevent all entrance and exit.
He added that he would visit the valley at irregular intervals
to inspect the work.

"A plan for the defeat of Ssŭma is being prepared here and
must be kept a profound secret," said he.

Ma Tai left to take up the position. The two captains, Tu
Jui and Hu Chung, were superintendents of the work in the
valley. K'ung-ming came every day to give instructions.

One day Yang I went to K'ung-ming and said, "The stores
of grain are all at Chienko, and the labour of transport is
very heavy. What can be done?"

K'ung-ming replied, smiling, "I have had a scheme ready for a
long time. The timber that I collected and bought in Hsich'üan was for the construction of wooden transport animals
to convey grain. It will be very advantageous, as they will
require neither food nor water and they can keep on the move
day and night without resting."

All those within hearing said, "From old days till now no
one has ever heard of such a device. What excellent plan
have you, O Minister, to make such marvellous creatures?"

"They are being made now after my plans, but they are not
yet ready. Here I have the plans for these 'oxen and horses,'
with all their dimensions written out in full. You may see
the details."

K'ung-ming then produced a paper, and all the captains
crowded round to look at it.

[*Here follows a specification which appears incomprehensible, and is omitted.*]

They were all greatly astonished and lauded K'ung-ming's
cleverness. A few days later the new transport animals were
complete and began work. They were quite life-like and went
over the hills in any desired direction. The whole army saw
them with delight. They were put in charge of Kao Hsiang
and a company to guide them. They kept going constantly
between Chienko and the front carrying grain for the use of
the soldiers.

> Along the Chienko mountain roads
> The running horses bore their loads,
> And through Hsieh Valley's narrow way
> The wooden oxen paced each day.
> O generals, use these means to-day,
> And transport troubles take away.

Ssŭma was already sad enough at his defeat when the spies
told him of these "bullocks and horses" of new design which
the men of Shu were using to convey their grain. This
troubled him still more. With this device they might never
be compelled to retreat for want of food. What was the use
for him to shut his gates and remain on the defensive waiting
for the enemy to be starved when they never would be starved?

Then he called up two captains and bade them lurk beside the track of the "bullocks and horses" and capture four or five of them.

So a half company went on this service disguised as men of Shu. They made their way along the by-ways by night and hid. Presently the "wooden" convoy came along under the escort of Kao Hsiang. Just as the end of it was passing they made a sudden rush, and captured a few of the "animals" which the men of Shu abandoned. In high glee they took them to their own camp.

When Ssŭma saw them he had to confess they were very life-like. But what pleased him most was that he could imitate them now that he had models.

"If you can use this sort of thing it would be strange if I could not," said he.

He called to him many clever artizans and made them then and there take the machines to pieces and make some exactly like them. In less than half a month they had completed a couple of thousand after K'ung-ming's model, and they could move. Then he placed Ts'ên Wei, an officer of high rank, in charge of this new means of transport, and the "animals" began to ply between the camp and Shênsi.

Kao Hsiang returned to camp and reported the loss of a few of his "oxen and horses."

"I wished him to capture some of them," said K'ung-ming, much pleased. "I am just laying out these few, and before long I shall get some very solid help in exchange."

"How do you know, O Minister," said his officers.

"Because Ssŭma will certainly copy them, and when he has done that I have another trick ready to play on him."

Some days later K'ung-ming received a report that the enemy were using the same sort of "bullocks and horses" to bring up supplies from Shênsi.

"Exactly as I thought," said he.

Calling Wang P'ing, he said, "Dress up a company as men of Wei and find your way quickly and secretly to Peiyüan. Pretend you are escort men, for the convoy, and mingle with the real escort. Then suddenly turn on them so that they scatter. Then you will turn the "animals" this way. By and by you will be pursued. When that occurs you will give a turn to the tongues of the wooden animals, and they will not move. Leave them where they are and run away. When the men of Wei come up they will be unable to drag the creatures and equally unable to carry them. I shall have men ready, and you will go back with them, give the tongues a backward turn and bring the convoy here. The enemy will be greatly astonished."

Next he called Chang I and said, "Dress up half a company in the costume of the 'six *ting*' and the 'six *chia*' so that they appear

supernatural. Fit them with demon heads and wild beast
shapes, and let them stain their faces various colours so as
to look as strange as possible. Give them flags and swords
and bottle-gourds with smoke issuing from combustibles
inside. Let these men hide among the hills till the convoy
approaches, when they will start the smoke, rush out suddenly
and drive off the 'animals.' No one will dare pursue such
uncanny creatures."

When he had left, Wei Yen and Chiang Wei were called.

"You will take one legion, go to the border of Peiyüan to
receive the wooden transport creatures and defend them
against attack."

Then another half legion was sent to check Ssŭma if he
should come, while a small force was sent to bid defiance to
the enemy near their camp on the south bank.

So one day when a convoy was on its way from Shênsi, the
scouts in front suddenly reported some soldiers ahead who
said they were escort men for the grain. The Commander
Ts'ên Wei halted and sent to enquire. It appeared they were
really men of Wei, however, and so he started once more.

The new comers joined up with his own men. But before
they had gone much farther there was a yell, and the men of
Shu began to kill, while a voice shouted "Wang P'ing is here!"
The convoy guard were taken aback. Many were killed, but
the others rallied round Ts'ên Wei and made some defence.
However, Wang P'ing slew the leader, and the others ran
this way and that, while the convoy was turned toward the
Shu camp.

The fugitives ran off to Peiyüan and reported the mishap
to Kuo Huai, who set out hot foot to rescue the convoy.
When he appeared, Wang P'ing gave the order to turn
tongues, left the "animals" in the road and ran away. Kuo
Huai made no attempt to pursue, but tried to put the
"animals" in motion toward their proper destination. But
could he move them?

He was greatly perplexed. Then suddenly there arose the
roll of drums all round, and out burst two parties of soldiers.
These were Wei Yen and Chiang Wei's men, and when they
appeared Wang P'ing's men faced about and came to the
attack as well. These three being too much for Kuo Huai,
he retreated before them. Thereupon the tongues were
turned back again and the "animals" set in motion.

Seeing this, Kuo Huai came on again. But just then he
saw smoke curling up among the hills and a lot of extraordinary
creatures burst out upon him. Some held swords and some
flags and all were terrible to look at. They rushed at the
"animals" and urged them away.

"Truly these are supernatural helpers," cried Kuo, quite
frightened.

The soldiers also were terror-stricken and stood still.

Hearing that his Peiyüan men had been driven off, Ssŭma came out to the rescue. Midway along the road, just where it was most precipitous, a cohort burst out upon him with fierce yells and bursting bombs. Upon the leading banner he read "Chang I and Liao Hua, Generals of Han."

Panic seized upon his men, and they ran like rats.

> In the field the craftier leader on the convoy makes a raid,
> And his rival's life endangers by an ambush subtly laid.

If you would know the upshot, read the next chapter.

CHAPTER CIII.

SSUMA SURROUNDED IN SHANGFANG VALLEY;
CHUKO INVOKES THE STARS IN THE WUCHANG PLAIN.

Sorely smitten in the battle, Ssŭma fled from the field a lonely horseman, a single spear. Seeing a thick wood in the distance he made for its shelter.

Chang I halted the rear division while Miao Hua pressed forward after the fugitive, whom he could see threading his way among the trees. And Ssŭma indeed was soon in fear of his life, dodging from tree to tree as his pursuer neared. Once Miao Hua was actually close enough to slash at his enemy, but he struck a tree instead of his man, and before he could pull his sword out of the wood Ssŭma had got clear away. When Miao got through into the open country he did not know which way to go. Presently he noticed a helmet lying on the ground, just lately thrown aside. He picked it up, hung it on his saddle and went away eastward.

But the crafty fugitive, having flung away his helmet thus on the east side of the wood, had gone away west, so that Miao was going away from his quarry. After some time Miao fell in with Chiang Wei, when he abandoned the pursuit and rode with him back to camp.

The "wooden oxen and running horses" having been driven into camp, their loads were put into the storehouse. The grain that fell to the victors amounted to a myriad "stone" or more.

Miao Hua presented the enemy's helmet as proof of his prowess in the field and received a reward of the first grade of merit. But Wei Yen had nothing to offer, and so was overlooked. He went away angry and discontented, muttering that the general pretended to be ignorant of his services.

Very sadly Ssŭma returned to his own camp. Bad news followed, for a messenger brought letters telling of an invasion by three armies of Wu. The letters said that forces had been sent against them, and the king again enjoined upon his general a waiting and defensive policy. So Ssŭma deepened his moats and raised his ramparts.

King Ts'ao Jui had sent three armies against the invaders; Liu Shao led that to save Changhsia, T'ien Yu led the Hsiangyang force. The king, with Man Ch'ung, went into Hofei. This last was the main army.

Man Ch'ung led the leading division toward Ch'aohuk'ou. Thence, looking across to the eastern shore, he saw only a few ships, but a large number of flags and banners. So he returned to the main army and proposed an attack without loss of time.

"The enemy think we shall be fatigued after a long march and have not troubled to prepare any defence; we should attack this night, and we shall overcome them."

"What you say accords with my own ideas," said the king, and he told off the cavalry leader, Chang Ch'iu, to take five companies and try to burn out the enemy. Man Ch'ung was also to attack from the eastern bank.

In the second watch of that night the two forces set out and gradually approached the entrance to the lake. They reached the marine camp unobserved, burst upon it with a yell, and the men of Wu fled without striking a blow. The men of Wei set fires going in every direction and thus destroyed all the ships together with much grain and many weapons.

Chuko Chin, who was in command, led his beaten men to Mienk'ou, and the attackers returned to their camp much elated.

When the report come to Lu Hsün he called together his officers and said, "I must write to the king to abandon the siege of Hsinch'êng, that the men may be employed to cut off the retreat of the Wei army, while I will attack them in front. They will be harassed by the double danger, and we shall break them."

All agreed that this was a good plan, and the memorial was drafted. It was sent by the hand of a junior officer, who was told to convey it secretly. But this messenger was captured at the ferry and taken before King Jui, who read the despatch, saying, with a sigh, "This Lu Hsün is really very resourceful."

The captive was put into prison, and Liu Shao was told off to defend the rear and keep off Sun's army.

Now Chuko's defeated men were suffering from hot weather illnesses, and at length he was compelled to write and tell Lu Hsün, and ask that his army be relieved and sent home. Having read this despatch, Lu said to the messenger, "Make my obeisance to the Great General and say that I will decide."

When the messenger returned with this reply Chuko asked what was doing in the Commander-in-chief's camp. He replied that the men were all outside planting beans, and the officers were amusing themselves at the gates. They were playing a game of skill, throwing arrows into narrow-necked vases.

Then Chuko himself went to his chief's camp and asked how the pressing danger was to be met.

Lu Hsün replied, "My messenger to the king was captured, and thus my plans were discovered. Now it is useless to prepare to fight, and so we had better retreat. I have sent in a memorial to engage the king to retire gradually."

Chuko replied, "Why delay? If you think it best to retire, it had better be done quickly."

"My army must retreat slowly, or the enemy will come in pursuit, which will mean defeat and loss. Now you must first prepare your ships as if you meant to resist, while I make a semblance of an attack toward Hsiangyang. Under cover of these operations I shall withdraw into Chiangtung, and the enemy will not dare to follow."

So Chuko returned to his own camp and began to fit out his ships as if for an immediate expedition, while Lu made all preparations to march, giving out that he intended to advance upon Hsiangyang. The news of these movements were duly reported in the Wei camps, and when the leaders heard it they wished to go out and fight. But the king knew his opponent better than they and would not bring about a battle. So he called his officers together and said to them, "This Lu Hsün is very crafty; keep careful guard, but do not risk a battle."

The officers obeyed, but a few days later the scouts brought in news that the armies of Wu had retired. The king doubted and sent out some of his own spies, who confirmed the report. When he thus knew it was true he consoled himself with the words, "Lu Hsün knows the rat of war even as did Sun Wu and Wu P'ing; they were no whit his superior. The subjugation of the south-east is not for me this time."

Thereupon he distributed his captains among the various vantage points and led the main army back into Hofei, where he camped ready to take advantage of any change of conditions that might promise success.

Meanwhile K'ung-ming was at Ch'ishan, where, to all appearances, he intended to make a long sojourn. He made his soldiers mix with the people and share in the labour of the fields. He gave strict orders against any encroachment on the property of the farmers, and so they and the soldiers lived together very amicably.

Then Ssŭma's son, Shih, went to his father and said, "These men of Shu have despoiled us of much grain, and now they are mingling with the people of Ch'ishan and tilling the fields along the banks of the Wei River as if they intended to remain there. This would be a calamity for us. Why do you not appoint a time to fight a decisive battle with K'ung-ming?"

His father replied, "I have the king's orders to act on the defensive and may not do as you suggest."

While they were thus talking, one reported that Wei Yen had come near and was insulting the army and reminding them that they had the helmet of its leader. And he was challenging them. The captains were greatly incensed and desired to accept the challenge, but the Commander-in-chief was immovable in his decision to obey his orders.

"The Holy One says if we cannot suffer small things, great matters are imperilled. Our plan is to defend."

So the challenge was not accepted, and there was no battle. After reviling them for some time, Wei Yen went away.

Seeing that his enemy was not to be provoked into fighting, K'ung-ming gave orders to build a strong stockade and therein to excavate pits and to collect large quantities of inflammables. So on the hill they piled wood and straw in the shape of sheds, and all about they digged pits and buried mines. When these preparations were complete Ma Tai received instructions to block the road in rear of Hulu Valley and to lay an ambush at the entrance.

"If Ssŭma comes, let him enter the valley, and then explode the mines and set fire to the straw and the wood," said K'ung-ming.

K'ung-ming set up a seven-star signal at the mouth of the valley and also arranged a night signal of seven lamps on the hill. After Ma Tai had gone, Wei Yen was called in, and K'ung-ming said to him, "Go to the camp of Wei with half a company and provoke them to battle. The important matter is to entice Ssŭma out of his stronghold. You will be unable to obtain a victory, so retreat that he may pursue; and you are to make for the signal, the seven stars by day or the seven lamps at night. Thus you will lead him into the Hulu Valley, where I have a plan prepared for him.'

When he had gone; Kao Hsiang was summoned.

"Take small herds, two or three score at a time, of the 'wooden oxen and running horses,' load them up with grain and lead them to and fro on the mountains. If you can succeed in getting the enemy to capture them you will render a service."

So the transport "cattle" were sent forth to play their part in the scheme, and the remainder of the Ch'ishan soldiers were sent to work in the fields, with orders to join in the battle only if Ssŭma came in person. In that case they were to attack the south bank of the river and cut off the retreat. Then K'ung-ming led his army away to camp in the Shangfang Valley.

Hsiahou Hui and Hsiahou Ho went to their chief, Ssŭma I, and said, "The enemy have set out camps and are engaged in field work as though they intended to remain. If they are not destroyed now, but are allowed to consolidate their position, they will be hard to dislodge."

"This certainly is one of K'ung-ming's ruses," said the chief.

"You seem very afraid of him, General," retorted they. "When do you think you can destroy him? At least let us two brothers fight one battle that we may prove our gratitude for the king's kindness."

"If it must be so, then you may go in two divisions," said Ssŭma.

As the two divisions were marching along they saw coming toward them a number of the transport "animals" of the enemy. They attacked at once, drove off the escort, captured them and sent them back to camp. Next day they captured more, with men and horses as well, and sent them also to camp.

Ssŭma called up the prisoners and questioned them. They told him that K'ung-ming quite understood that he would not fight and so had told off the soldiers to various places to work in the fields and thus provide for future needs. They had been unwittingly captured.

Ssŭma set them free and bade them begone.

"Why spare them?" asked Hsiahou Ho.

"There is nothing to be gained by the slaughter of a few common soldiers. Let them go back to their own and praise the kindliness of the Wei leaders. That will slacken the desire of their comrades to fight against us. That was the plan by which Lü Mêng captured Chingchou."

Then he issued general orders that all Shu prisoners should be well treated and sent away free, and he rewarded those of his army who had done well.

As has been said, Kao Hsiang was ordered to keep pretended convoys on the move, and the soldiers of Wei attacked and captured them whenever they saw them. In half a month they had scored many successes of this sort, and Ssŭma's heart was cheered. One day, when he had made new captures of men, he sent for them and questioned them again.

"Where is K'ung-ming now?"

"He is no longer at Ch'ishan, but in camp about ten *li* from Shangfang Valley. He is gathering great store of grain there."

After he had questioned them fully, he set the prisoners free. Calling together his officers, he said, "K'ung-ming is not camped on Ch'ishan, but near Shangfang Valley. To-morrow you shall attack the Ch'ishan camp, and I will command the reserve."

The promise cheered them, and they went away to prepare.

"Father, why do you intend to attack the enemy's rear?" asked Ssŭma Shih.

"Ch'ishan is their main position, and they will certainly hasten to its rescue. Then I shall make for the valley and burn the stores. That will render them helpless and will be a victory."

The son dutifully agreed with his father and set out, while his father followed with the reserves.

From the top of a hill K'ung-ming watched the Wei soldiers march and noticed that they moved carelessly, not even keeping their ranks. He guessed that their object was the Ch'ishan camp and sent strict orders to his captains that if Ssŭma led in person they were to go off and capture the camp on the south bank.

When the men of Wei had got near and made their rush toward the camp of Shu, the men of Shu ran up also, yelling and pretending to reinforce the defenders. Ssŭma, seeing this, suddenly changed his direction and turned off for the Shangfang Valley. Here Wei Yen was expecting him, and as soon as he appeared Wei Yen galloped up and soon recognised Ssŭma as the leader.

"Ssŭma I, stay!" shouted he as he came near. He flourished his sword, and Ssŭma set his spear. The two warriors exchanged a few passes, and then Wei Yen suddenly turned his steed and bolted. As he had been ordered, he made direct for the seven-starred flag, and Ssŭma followed, the more readily as he saw the fugitive had but a small force. The two sons of Ssŭma rode with him, one on either hand.

Presently Wei Yen and his men entered the mouth of the valley. Ssŭma halted a time while he sent forward a few scouts, but when they returned and reported nothing to be seen but a few straw houses on the hills, he rode in, saying, "This must be the store valley."

But when he had got well within, Ssŭma noticed that kindling wood was piled over the straw huts, and as he saw no sign of Wei Yen he began to feel uneasy.

"Supposing soldiers seize the entrance; what then?" said he to his sons.

As he spoke there arose a great shout, and from the hillside came many torches, which fell all around them and set fire to the straw, so that soon the entrance to the valley was lost in smoke and flame. They tried to get away from the fire, but no road led up the hillside. Then fire-arrows came shooting down, and the earth-mines exploded, and the straw and firewood blazed high as the heavens. Ssŭma I, scared and helpless, dismounted, clasped his arms about his two sons and wept, saying, "My sons, we three are doomed."

But suddenly a fierce gale sprang up, black clouds gathered, a peal of thunder followed and rain poured down in torrents, speedily extinguishing the fire all through the valley. The mines no longer exploded and all the fiery contrivances ceased to work mischief.

"If we do not break out now, what better chance shall we have?" cried the father, and he and his two sons made a dash for the outlet. As they broke out of the valley they came upon reinforcements under Chang Hu and Yüeh Lin, and so were once more safe. Ma Tai was not strong enough to pursue, and the men of Wei got safely to the river.

But there they found their camp in the possession of the enemy, while Chiang Huai and his colleague were on the floating bridge struggling with the men of Shu. However, as Ssŭma neared, the men of Shu retreated, whereupon the bridges were burned and the north bank occupied.

The Wei army attacking the Ch'ishan camp were greatly disturbed when they heard of the defeat of their general and the loss of the camp on the Wei River. The men of Shu took the occasion to strike with greater vigour, and so gained a great victory. The beaten army suffered great loss. Those who escaped fled across the river.

When K'ung-ming from the hill-top saw that his enemy had been inveigled into the trap he had so carefully prepared, he rejoiced exceedingly, and when he saw the flames burst forth he thought surely his rival was done for. Then, unhappily for him, Heaven thought it well to send down torrents of rain, which quenched the fire and upset all his calculations.

Soon after, the scouts reported the escape of his victims, and he sighed, saying, "Man proposes; God disposes. We cannot wrest events to our will."

> Fierce fires roared in the valley,
> But the rain quenched them.
> Had Chuko's plan but succeeded,
> Where had been the Chins?

From the new camp on the north bank of the river Ssŭma issued an order that he would put to death any officer who proposed going out to battle. The final result of the late ill-advised expedition had been the loss of the south bank of the river. Accordingly no one spoke of attacking, but all turned their energies toward defence.

Kuo Huai went to the general to talk over plans. He said, "The enemy have been carefully spying out the country and are certainly selecting a new position for a camp. If K'ung-ming go out to Wukung, and thence eastward, we shall be in grave danger; if he go out by Huainan and halts on the Wuchang Plain, we need feel no anxiety."

They decided to send scouts to find out the movements of their enemy. Presently the scouts returned to say that he had chosen the plain.

"Our great Emperor of Wei has remarkable fortune," said Ssŭma, clapping his hand to his forehead. Then he confirmed the order to remain strictly on the defensive till some change of circumstances on the part of the enemy should promise advantage.

After his army had settled into camp on the plain, K'ung-ming continued his attempts to provoke a battle. Day after day, parties went to challenge the men of Wei, but they resisted all provocation.

One day K'ung-ming packed a woman's head-dress and a robe of white silk in a box, which he sent, with a letter, to his rival. The insult could not be concealed, so the captains led the bearer of the box to their chief. He opened the box and saw the dress of a woman. Then he opened the letter, which read something like this:—

"Friend Ssŭma, although you are a General and lead the troops of the capital, you seem but little disposed to display the firmness and valour that would render a contest decisive. Instead, you have prepared a comfortable lair where you are safe from the keen edge of the sword. Are you not very like a woman? Wherefore I send the bearer with a suitable gift, and you will humbly accept it and the humiliation, unless, indeed, you finally decide to come out and fight like a man. If you are not entirely indifferent to shame, if you retain any of the feelings of a man, you will send this back to me and come out and give battle."

Ssŭma I, although inwardly raging, pretended to take it all as a joke and smiled.

"So he regards me as a woman," said he.

He accepted the gift and treated the messenger well. Before he left, Ssŭma asked him a few questions about his master's eating and sleeping and hours of labour.

"He works very hard," said the messenger. "He rises early and retires to bed late. He attends personally to all cases requiring punishment of over a score of strokes. As for food, he does not eat more than a few *hsing* (pints) of grain."

"That is, he eats little and works much," remarked Ssŭma. "Can he last long?".

The messenger returned to his own side and reported that the general had taken the whole episode in good part and shown no sign of anger. He had only asked about K'ung-ming's hours of rest, and food and such things. He had said no word about military matters. "I told him that you ate little and worked long hours, and then he said, ' Can he last long?' That was all."

"He knows," said K'ung-ming, pensively.

The Accountant Yang Yung presently ventured to remonstrate with his chief.

"I notice," said Yang, "that you check the books personally. I think that is needless labour for a Prime Minister to undertake. In every administration the higher and subordinate ranks have their especial fields of activity, and each should confine his labours to his own field. In a household, for example, the male servants plough and the female cook, and thus operations are carried on without waste of energy, and all needs are supplied. The master of the house has ample leisure and tranquillity. If one individual strives to attend personally to every matter he only wearies himself and fails to accomplish his end. How can he possibly hope to perform all the various tasks so well as the maids or the hinds?

He fails in his own part, that of playing the master. And, indeed, the ancients held this same opinion, for they said that the high officers should attend to the discussion of ways and means and the lower should carry out details. Of old, Ping Chi was moved to deep thought by the panting of an ox, which showed the seasons untimely, but enquired not about the corpses—of certain brawlers—which lay about the road, for this matter concerned the magistrate. Ch'ên P'ing was ignorant of the figures relating to taxes, for he said these were the concern of the controllers of taxes.

"O Minister, you weary yourself with minor details and sweat yourself every day. You are wearing yourself out, and Ssŭma I has good reason for what he said."

"I know; I cannot but know," replied K'ung-ming. "But this heavy responsibility was laid upon me, and I fear no other will be so devoted as I am."

Those who heard him wept. Thereafter K'ung-ming appeared more and more harassed, and military operations did not speed.

On the other side the officers of Wei resented bitterly the insult that had been put upon them when their leader had been presented with a woman's dress. They wished to avenge the taunt, and went to their general, saying, "We are reputable captains of the army of a great state; how can we put up with such insults from these men of Shu? We pray you to let us fight them."

"It is not that I fear to go out," said Ssŭma, "nor that I relish the insults, but I have the king's command to hold on and may not disobey."

The officers were not in the least appeased. Wherefore he said, "I will send your request to the Throne in a memorial; what think you of that?"

They consented to await the king's reply, and a messenger bore to King Jui, in Hofei, this memorial:—

"I have small ability and high office. Your Majesty laid on me the command to defend and not fight till the men of Shu had suffered by the efflux of time. But Chuko Liang has now sent me a gift of a woman's dress, and my shame is very deep. Wherefore I advise Your Majesty that one day I shall have to fight in order to justify your kindness to me and to remove the shameful stigma that now rests upon my army. I cannot express the degree to which I am urged to this course."

The king read it and turned questioningly to his courtiers seeking an explanation. Hsin P'i supplied it.

"Ssŭma has no desire to give battle; this memorial is because of the shame put upon the officers by K'ung-ming's gift. They are all in a rage. He wishes for an edict to pacify them."

The king understood and gave to Hsin P'i a *chieh* (formal authority) and sent him to the river camp to make known that it was the king's command not to fight. Ssŭma received the messenger with all respect, and it was given out that any future reference to offering battle would be taken as disobedience to the king's especial command in the edict.

The officers could but obey, but their general told the king's messenger that he had interpreted his own desire correctly.

It was thenceforward understood that the general was forbidden to give battle. When it was told to K'ung-ming, he said, "This is only Ssŭma's method of pacifying his army. He has never had any intention of fighting and requested the edict to justify his strategy. It is well known that a general in the field takes no command from any person, not even his own king. Is it likely that he would send a thousand *li* to ask permission to fight if that was all he needed? The officers were bitter, and so Ssŭma got the king to assist him in maintaining discipline. All this is meant to slacken our men."

Just at this time Fei I came. He was called in to see the general, and K'ung-ming asked the reason for his coming. He replied, "King Jui, of Wei, hearing that Wu has invaded his country at three points, has led a great army to Hofei and sent three other armies to oppose the invaders. The stores and fight-material of Wu have been burned, and the men of Wu have fallen victims to sickness. A letter from Lu Hsün containing a scheme of attack fell into the hands of the enemy, and the lord of Wu has marched back into his own country."

K'ung-ming listened to the end; then, without a word, he fell in a swoon. He recovered after a time, but he was broken.

He said, "My mind is all in confusion. This is a return of my old complaint, and I am doomed."

Ill as he was, K'ung-ming that night went forth from his tent to scan the heavens and study the stars. They filled him with fear. He returned and said to Chiang Wei, "My life may end at any moment."

"Why do you say such a thing?"

"Just now in the *San-t'ai* constellation the roving star was twice as bright as usual, while the fixed stars were darkened; the supporting stars were also obscure. With such an aspect I know my fate."

"If the aspect be as malignant as you say, why not pray in order to avert it?" replied Chiang.

"I am in the habit of praying," replied K'ung-ming, "but I know not the will of God. However, prepare me forty-nine men and let each have a black flag. Dress them in black and place them outside my tent. Then will I from within my tent invoke the Seven Stars of the North. If my master-lamp remain alight for seven days, then is my life to be prolonged. If the lamp go out, then I am to die. Keep all idlers away from the tent and let a couple of youths bring me what is necessary."

Chiang prepared as directed. It was then the eighth month, mid-autumn, and the Silver River (Milky Way) was brilliant with scattered jade. The air was perfectly calm, and no sound was heard.

The forty-nine men were brought up and spaced out to guard the tent, while within K'ung-ming prepared incense and offerings. On the floor of the tent he arranged seven lamps, and, outside these, forty-nine smaller lamps. In the midst he placed the lamp of his own fate.

This done, he prayed, saying, "Liang, born into an age of trouble, would willingly have grown old in retirement. But His Majesty Chao-Lieh sought him thrice and confided to him the heavy responsibility of guarding his son. He dared not do less than spend himself to the utmost in such a task and he pledged himself to destroy the rebels. Suddenly the star of his leadership has declined, and his life now nears its close. He has humbly indited a declaration to the Great Unknowable and now hopes that He will graciously listen and extend the number of his days that he may prove his gratitude to his prince and be the saviour of the people, restore the old state of the empire and establish eternally the Han sacrifices. He dares not make a vain prayer; this is from his heart."

This prayer ended, in the solitude of his tent he awaited the dawn.

Next day, ill as he was, he did not neglect his duties, although he spat blood continually. All day he laboured at his plans, and at night he paced the magic steps, the steps of "the four" and "the seven" stars of Ursa Major.

Ssŭma I remained still. on the defensive. One night as he sat gazing up at the sky and studying its aspect he suddenly turned to Hsiahou Pa, saying, "A leadership star has just lost position; surely K'ung-ming is ill and will soon die. Take a reconnoitring party to the Wuchang Plain and find out. If you see signs of confusion do not attack; it means that K'ung-ming is ill. I shall take the occasion to smite hard."

Hsiahou Pa left. It was the sixth night of K'ung-ming's prayers, and the lamp of his fate still burned brightly. He began to feel a secret joy. Presently Chiang Wei entered and watched the ceremonies.

Suddenly a great shouting was heard outside, and immediately Wei Yen dashed in, crying, "The Wei soldiers are upon us!"

In his haste he had knocked over and extinguished the Lamp of Fate.

K'ung-ming threw down the sword and sighed, saying, "Life and death are foreordained; no prayers can alter them."

Wei Yen fell to the earth and craved forgiveness. Chiang drew his sword to slay the unhappy soldier.

> Nought is under man's control,
> Nor can he with fate contend.

Did Chiang kill the blundering warrior? The next chapter will unfold.

CHAPTER CIV.

A STAR FALLS AS CHUKO LIANG ASCENDS TO HEAVEN;
A WOODEN IMAGE AFFRIGHTS SSŬMA I.

The unhappy Wei did not suffer the edge of the sword, for Chuko stayed the stroke, saying, "It is my fate; not his fault."

So Chiang put up his sword, and K'ung-ming sank wearily upon his couch.

"Ssŭma I thinks I am dead, and he sent these few men to make sure. Go ye and drive them off," said he.

Wei Yen left the tent and led out a small party to drive away the men of Wei, who fled as they appeared. He chased them to a distance and returned. Then K'ung-ming sent him to his own camp and bade him keep a vigilant look-out.

Presently Chiang Wei came in, went up to the sick man's couch and asked how he felt.

He replied, "My death is very near. My chief desire has been to spend myself to the utmost to restore the Hans and lead a glorious return of the Hans to their capital, but Heaven decrees it otherwise. I have never ceased from my studies. I have written a book in twenty chapters, one hundred and four thousand, one hundred and twelve words, treating 'The eight Needfuls,' 'The seven Cautions,' 'The six Fears' and 'The five Dreads' of war. But among all those about me there is no one fit to receive it and carry on my work save you. I pray you not to despise it."

He gave the treatise to Chiang Wei, who received it sobbing.

"I have also a plan for a multiple crossbow, which I have been unable to execute. The weapon shoots ten bolts of eight inches length at every discharge. The plans are quite ready and the weapons can be made according to them."

Chiang took the papers with a deep bow.

The dying man continued, "There is no part of Shu that causes anxiety, save Yenp'ing. That must be carefully guarded. It is protected naturally by its lofty precipices, but it will surely be lost by and by."

Next K'ung-ming sent for Ma Tai, to whom he gave certain whispered instructions, and then said aloud, "You are to follow out my instructions after my death."

Soon after, Yang I entered the tent and went to the couch. He received a silken bag containing certain secret orders. As K'ung-ming gave it him, he said, "After my death Wei Yen will turn traitor. When that happens you will find herein who is to slay him."

Just as these arrangements were finished K'ung-ming fell into a swoon, from which he did not revive till the evening. Then he set himself to compose a memorial to the king. When this reached the king he was greatly alarmed and at once sent Li Fu to visit and confer with the dying minister.

Li travelled quickly to the camp and was led to the tent of the Commander-in-chief. He delivered the king's command and enquired after the sick man's welfare. K'ung-ming wept, and he replied, "Unhappily I am dying and leaving my task incomplete. I am injuring my country's policy and am in fault to the world. After my death you must aid the king in perfect loyalty and see that the old policy is continued, and the rules of government maintained. Do not lightly cast out the men I have employed. My plans of campaign have been confided to Chiang Wei, who can continue my policy for the service of the state. But my hour draws near, and I must write my testament."

Li Fu listened, and then took his leave. K'ung-ming made one final effort to carry out his duties. He rose from his couch, was helped into a small carriage and thus made a round of inspection of all the camps and posts. But the cold autumn wind chilled him to the bone.

"I shall never again lead the army against the rebels," said he. "O distant and azure Heaven, when will this end?"

K'ung-ming returned to his tent. He became rapidly weaker and called Yang I to his bedside.

Said he, "Wang P'ing and the others with him may be depended on to the death. They have fought many campaigns and borne many hardships; they should be retained in the public service. After my death let everything go on as before, but the army is to be gradually withdrawn. You know the tactics to be followed, and I need say little. My friend Chiang Wei is wise and brave; set him to guard the retreat."

Yang received these orders weeping. Next, writing materials were brought in and the dying minister set himself to write his testament. It is here given in substance:—

"Life and death are the common lot, and fate cannot be evaded. Death is at hand, and I desire to prove my loyalty to the end. I, thy servant Liang, dull of parts, was born into a difficult age, and it fell to my lot to guide military operations. I led a northern expedition, but failed to win complete success. Now sickness has laid hold upon me and death approaches, so that I shall be unable to accomplish my task. My sorrow is inexpressible.

"I desire Your Majesty to cleanse your heart and limit your desires, to practise self-control and to love the people, to maintain a perfectly filial attitude toward your late father and to be benevolent to all the world. Seek out the recluse scholars that you may obtain the services of the wise and good;

repel the wicked and depraved that your moral standard may be exalted.

"To my household belong eight hundred mulberry trees and five thousand *mou** of land; thus there is ample provision for my family. While I have been employed in the service of the state my needs have been supplied from official sources, but I have not contrived to make any additions to the family estate. At my death I shall not leave any increased possessions that may cause Your Majesty to suspect that I have wronged you."

Having composed this document, the dying man turned again to Yang I, saying, "Do not wear mourning for me, but make a large coffer and therein place my body, with seven grains of rice in my mouth. Place a lamp at my feet and let my body move with the army as I was wont to do. If you refrain from mourning, then my leadership star will not fall, for my inmost soul will ascend and hold it in place. So long as my star retains its place Ssŭma I will be fearsome and suspicious. Let the army retreat, beginning with the rearmost division; send it away slowly, one camp at a time. If Ssŭma pursue, array the army and offer battle, turn to meet him and beat the attack. Let him approach till he is very near and then suddenly display the image of myself that I have had carven, seated in my chariot in the midst of the army, with the captains right and left as usual. And you will frighten Ssŭma away."

Yang listened to these words intently and without remark. That night K'ung-ming was carried into the open and gazed up at the sky.

"That is my star," said he, pointing to one that seemed to be losing its brilliancy and to be tottering in its place. K'ung-ming's lips moved as if he muttered a spell. Presently he was borne into his tent and for a time was oblivious of all about him.

When the anxiety caused by this state of coma was at its height Li Fu arrived. He wept when he saw the condition of the great leader, crying that he had foiled the great designs of the state.

However, presently K'ung-ming's eyes reopened and fell upon Li Fu standing near his couch.

"I know your mission," said he.

"I came with the royal command to ask also who should control the destinies of the state for the next century," replied Li. "In my agitation I forgot to ask that."

"After me, Chiang Wan is the most fitting man to deal with great matters."

"And after him?"

"After him, Fei I."

"Who next after him?"

*Six *mou* equal one acre, roughly.

No reply came, and when they looked more carefully they perceived that the soul of the Great Minister had passed.

Thus died Chuko Liang, on the twenty-third day of the eighth month in the twelfth year of the period *Chien-Hsing,* at the age of fifty and two

The poet Tu Fu wrote some verses on his death.

> A bright star last night falling from the sky
> This message gave, "The Master is no more."
> No more in camps shall bold men tramp at his command,
> At court no statesman e'er will fill the place he held.
> At home, his clients miss their patron kind.
> Calm was his bosom, full of strategy.
> But lately fared we to the wood's green shade
> To hail him victor; hushed that song for him.

And Po Chü-i also wrote a poem:—

> Within the forest dim the Master lived obscure,
> Till, thrice returning, there the king his mentor met.
> As when a fish the ocean gains, desire was filled
> Wholly; the dragon freed could soar aloft at will.
> As king's son's guardian none more zealous was;
> As minister, most loyally he wrought at court.
> His war memorials still to us are left
> And, reading them, the tears unconscious fall.

Now in past days a certain officer named Liao Li had a high opinion of his own abilities and thought himself perfectly fitted to be K'ung-ming's second. So he neglected the duties of his proper post, showed discontent and indiscipline and was constantly slandering the minister. Thereupon he was degraded and exiled by K'ung-ming. When he heard of his death he shed tears and said, "Then, after all, I am but a barbarian."

Li Yen also grieved deeply at the sad tidings, for he had always hoped that K'ung-ming would restore him to office and so give him the opportunity of repairing his former faults. After K'ung-ming had died he thought there was no hope of re-employment, and so he died.

Another poet, Yüan Wei-chih, also wrote in praise of the great adviser.

> He fought disorder, helped a failing king;
> Most zealously he kept his master's son.
> In state-craft he o'erpassed both Kuan and Yo,
> In war-craft he excelled both Sun and Wu.
> With awe the court his war memorial heard,
> With majesty his "Eight Arrays" were planned.
> Good reader, an there's virtue in your heart
> You'll sigh to think that he has had no peer.

Heaven grieved and earth mourned on the night of K'ung-ming's death. Even the moon was dimmed. And K'ung-ming returned to Heaven.

As the late commander had directed, no one wailed his death. His body was placed in the coffer as he had wished, and three hundred of his near comrades were appointed to watch it.

Secret orders were given to Wei Yen to command the rear-guard, and then, one by one, the camps were broken up and the army began its homeward march.

Ssŭma I watched the skies. One night a large red star with bright rays passed from the north-east to the south-west and dropped over the camps of Shu. It dipped thrice and rose again. Ssŭma heard also a low rumbling in the distance. He was pleased and excited, and said to those about him, "K'ung-ming is dead."

At once he ordered pursuit with a strong force. But just as he passed the camp gates doubts filled his mind and he gave up the plan.

"K'ung-ming is a master of mysteries, and it may be that this is but a ruse to get us to take the field. We may fall victims to his guile."

So he halted. But he sent Hsiahou Pa with a few scouts to reconnoitre the enemy's camps.

One night as Wei Yen lay asleep in his tent he dreamed a dream. In his vision two horns grew out of his head. When he awoke he was much perplexed to explain his dream. A certain Expeditionary Ssŭ-ma, Chao Chih, came to see him, and Wei Yen said, "You are versed in mysteries. I have dreamed that two horns grew upon my head, and would trouble you to expound the dream and tell me its portent."

His visitor thought a moment and replied, "It is an auspicious dream. There are horns on the head of the *chilin* and the dragon. It augurs transformation into an ascending creature."

Wei Yen, much pleased, thanked the interpreter of his dream and promised him gifts when the dream proved true.

Chao Chih left and presently met Fei I, who asked whence he came.

"From the camp of our friend Wei Yen. He dreamed that he grew horns upon his head, and I have given him an auspicious interpretation. But really it is inauspicious. However, I did not wish to annoy him."

"How do you know it is inauspicious?"

"The word for horn is composed of two parts, 'knife' above and 'use' below, and so means that there is a knife upon his head. It is a terrible omen."

"Keep it secret," said Fei.

Then Fei I went to the camp of Wei Yen, and when they were alone, he said, "The minister died last night in the third watch. He left certain final orders, and among them, that you are to command the rear-guard to keep Ssŭma at bay while the army retreats. No mourning is to be worn. Here is your authority, so you can march forthwith.

"Who is acting in place of the late minister?" asked Wei.

"The chief command has been delegated to Yang I, but the secret plans of campaign have been entrusted to Chiang Wei. This authority issues from him."

Wei replied, "Though the minister is dead, I am yet alive. Yang is only a civil officer and unequal to this post. He ought to conduct the coffin home while I lead the army against Ssŭma I. I shall achieve success, and it is wrong to abandon a whole plan of campaign because of the death of one man, even if that be the Prime Minister.'

"His orders were to retire, and these orders are to be obeyed."

"If the late minister had listened to me we should now have been at Ch'angan. I am the senior general and of high rank. I am not going to act as rear-guard for any civil official."

"It may be as you say, General, but you must not do anything to make us ridiculous. Let me go back to Yang I and explain, and I may be able to persuade him to pass on to you the supreme military authority he holds."

Wei Yen agreed, and the visitor went back to the main camp and told Yang I what had passed.

Yang replied, "When near death the minister confided to me that Wei would turn traitor. I sent him the authority to test him, and now he has discovered himself as the minister foretold. So I will direct Chiang Wei to command the rear-guard."

The coffer containing the remains of K'ung-ming was sent on in advance, and Chiang Wei took up his post to cover the retreat. Meanwhile Wei Yen sat in his tent waiting for the return of Fei I and was perplexed at the delay. When the suspense became unbearable he sent Ma Tai to find out the reason. Ma returned and told him that Chiang Wei was covering the retreat and that most of the army had already gone.

Wei Yen was furious. "How dare he play with me, the pedantic blockhead?" cried he. "But he shall die for this. Will you help me?" said he, turning to Ma Tai.

Ma replied, "I have long hated him; certainly I am ready to attack him."

So Wei Yen broke camp and marched southward.

By the time Hsiahou Pa had reached the Shu camps they were all empty, and he hastened back with this news.

"Then he is really dead; let us pursue," said Ssŭma I, much irritated at being misled.

"Be cautious," said Hsiahou. "Send an inferior leader first."

"No; I must go myself this time."

So Ssŭma and his two lieutenants hastened to the Wuchang Plain. With shouts and waving flags, they rushed into the camps, only to find them quite deserted. Telling his lieutenants to bring up the remaining force with all speed, Ssŭma hastened in the wake of the retreating army. Coming to some hills, he saw them in the distance and pressed on still harder. Then suddenly a bomb exploded, a great shout broke the stillness, and the retiring army turned about and came toward him, ready for battle. In their midst fluttered a great banner bearing the words, "Prime Minister of Han, Marquis of Wuhsiang, Chuko Liang."

Ssŭma I stopped, pale with fear. Then out from the army came some score of captains of rank, and they were escorting a small carriage, in which sat K'ung-ming as he had always appeared, in his hand the feather fan.

"Then he is still alive!" gasped Ssŭma. "And I have rashly placed myself in his power."

As he pulled round his horse to flee, Chiang Wei shouted, "Do not try to run away, O rebel; you have fallen into one of the minister's traps and had better stay."

The soldiers, seized with panic, fled, throwing off all their gear. They trampled each other down, and many perished. Their leader galloped fifty *li* without pulling rein. When at last two of his captains came up with him, and had stopped his flying steed by catching at the bridle, Ssŭma clapped his hand to his head, crying, "Have I still a head?"

"Do not fear, General, the soldiers of Shu are now far away," they replied.

But he still panted with fear, and only after some time did he recognise that his two companions were Hsiahou Pa and Hsiahou Hui.

The three found their way by by-roads to their own camp, whence scouts were sent out in all directions. In a few days the natives brought news that the Shu army had really gone, and they said further that as soon as the retiring army had entered the valley they had raised a wailing for the dead and hoisted white flags. They also said that K'ung-ming was really dead, and Chiang Wei's rear-guard consisted of only one company. The figure in the carriage was only a wooden image of the minister.

"While he lived I could guess what he would do; dead, I was helpless," said Ssŭma.

The people had a saying that a dead Chuko was enough to scare off a live Ssŭma.

> In the depth of night a brilliant star
> Fell from the northern sky;
> Doubts stayed Ssŭma when he would pursue
> His dead, but fearsome enemy.

> And even now the western men,
> With scornful smile, will say,
> "Oh, is my head on my shoulder still?
> It was nearly lost to-day."

Now indeed Ssŭma knew that his great rival was no more, so he retook the pursuit. But he never came up with the Shu army. As he took the homeward road he said to his officers, "We can now sleep in comfort."

As they marched back they saw the camps of their enemies, and were amazed at their skilful arrangement.

"Truly a wonderful genius?" sighed Ssŭma.

The armies of Wei returned to Ch'angan; leaving officers to guard the various strategical points. Ssŭma himself went cn to the capital.

Yang I and Chiang Wei retired slowly and in good order till they neared the Tsanko road, when they donned mourning garb and began to wail for their dead. The soldiers threw themselves on the ground and wailed in sorrow. Some even wailed themselves to death.

But as the leading companies entered upon the Tsanko road they saw a great blaze in front, and, with a great shout, a cohort came out barring the way. The leaders were taken aback and sent to inform the general.

> The regiments of Wei are nowhere near,
> Then who are these soldiers that now appear?

The next chapter will tell who they were.

CHAPTER CV.

The Plan of the Silken Bag;
The Bronze Statue With the Dew Bowl.

Yang I sent forward a man to find out what force this was that stood in his way, and the scout returned to say they were soldiers of Shu led by Wei Yen. Wei had burned the wooden roads and now barred the way.

Then said Yang, "Just before his death the late minister foretold that this man would one day turn traitor, and here it has come to pass. I did not expect to meet it thus, but now our road of retreat is cut, and what is to be done?"

Then replied Fei I, "He certainly has slandered us to the Emperor and said that we were rebelling, and therefore he has destroyed the wooden roads in order to prevent our progress. First, therefore, we must memorialise the truth about him and then plan his destruction."

Chiang Wei said, "I know a by-way hereabout that will lead us round to the rear of these covered roads. True it is precipitous and dangerous, but it will take us to our destination. It is called the Ch'ashan Path."

So they prepared a memorial and turned off in order to follow the narrow mountain road.

Meanwhile the King of Shu was troubled; he lost his appetite and was sleepless. Then he dreamed that the hill that protected his capital was riven and fell. This dream troubled him till morning, when he called in his officers of all ranks to ask them to interpret his vision.

When he had related his dream, Ch'iao Chou stood forth and said, "I saw a large red star fall yesternight; surely it forebodes a misfortune to the king or to his First Minister. Your Majesty's dream corresponds to what I saw."

The king's anxiety increased. Presently Li Fu returned and was summoned into the king's presence. He bowed his head and wept, saying, "The Prime Minister is dead."

He repeated Chuko's last messages and told all that he knew. The king was overcome with great sorrow, and wailed, crying, "Heaven smites me!" and he fell over and lay upon his couch. They led him within to the inner chambers, and when his Consort heard the sad tidings she also wailed without ceasing. And all the officers were distressed and wept, and the common people showed their grief.

The king was deeply affected, and for many days could hold no Court. And while thus prostrate with grief they told him that Wei Yen had sent up a memorial charging Yang I with rebellion. The astounded courtiers went to the king's chamber to talk over this thing, and his Consort was also there. The memorial was read aloud. It was much like this:—

"I, thy Minister and General, Wei Yen, 'Corrector of the West' and Marquis Chêng, humbly and with bowed head write that Yang I has assumed command of the army and is in rebellion. He has made off with the coffin of the late Prime Minister and wishes to lead enemies within our borders. As a precaution, and to hinder his progress, I have burned the covered ways and now report these matters."

The Latter Ruler said, "Wei Yen is a valiant warrior and could easily have overcome Yang I; why then did he destroy the covered ways?"

Wu, the *T'ai-hou,* said, "The late Emperor used to say that K'ung-ming knew that treachery lurked in the heart of Wei Yen, and he wished to put him to death; he only spared him because of his valour. We should not believe too readily this tale of his that Yang I has rebelled. Yang I is a scholar, and the late Prime Minister placed him in a position of great responsibility, thereby proving that he trusted him and valued him. If this statement is true, surely Yang would have gone over to Wei. Nothing should be done without due meditation."

As they were discussing this matter, an urgent memorial came from Yang I, and opening it, they read:—

"I, Yang I, leader of the retreating army, humbly and with trepidation, present this memorial. In his last moments the late Prime Minister made over to me the charge of the great emprise, and bade me carry out his plan without change. I have respected his charge. I ordered Wei Yen to command the rear-guard with Chiang Wei as his second. But Wei Yen refused obedience and led away his own army into Hanchung. Then he burned the covered ways, tried to steal away the body of the late Commander-in-chief and behaved altogether unseemly. His rebellion came upon me suddenly and unexpectedly. I send this memorial in haste."

The Empress Dowager listened to the end. Then, turning to the nobles, she said, "What is your opinion now?"

Chiang Wan replied, "Yang I is hasty and intolerant, but he has rendered great services in supplying the army. He has long been a trusted colleague of the late Prime Minister, who, being near his end, entrusted to him the conduct of affairs. Certainly he is no rebel. On the other hand, Wei Yen is bold and ambitious and thinks himself everybody's superior. Yang I is the only one who has openly been of different opinion, and hence Wei hates him. When he saw Yang placed over his head in command of the army he refused his support. Then he burned the covered ways in order to cut off Yang's retreat, and maligned him, hoping to bring about his fall. I am ready to guarantee Yang's fealty to the extent of my whole house, but I would not answer for Wei Yen."

Tung Yün followed, "Wei Yen has always been conceited and discontented. His mouth was full of hate and resentment, and only fear of the late Prime Minister held him in check. The minister's death gave him his opportunity, and he turned traitor. This is certainly the true state of the case. Yang I is able, and his employment by the late minister is proof of his loyalty."

"If this is true and Wei is really a rebel, what should be done?" asked the king.

"I think the late minister has framed some scheme by which to get rid of Wei Yen. If Yang had not felt secure he would scarcely have set out to return through the valleys. Your Majesty may feel sure that Wei will fall into some trap. We have received, almost at the same time, two memorials from two men, each bringing against the other a charge of rebellion. Let us wait."

Just then Fei I arrived. He was summoned into the royal presence and told the story of Wei Yen's revolt.

The king replied, "In that case I should do well to send Tung Yün with temporary authority to clear up the situation and attempt to persuade Wei with kind words."

So Tung Yün left on this mission. At this time Wei Yen was camped at Nanku, which was a commanding position. He thought his plan was succeeding well. It had not occurred to him that Yang and Chiang could get past him by any by-way. On the other hand, Yang, thinking that Hanchung was lost, sent Ho P'ing with three companies on in front while he followed with the coffin.

When this little army had got to the rear of Wei's position they announced their presence with rolling drums. The scouts quickly told Wei, who at once armed himself, took his sword and rode out to confront Ho P'ing. When both sides were arrayed Ho rode to the front and began to revile his opponent.

"Where is that rebel Wei Yen?" cried Ho.

"You aided that traitor Yang," cried Wei, no way backward with his tongue; "how dare you abuse me?"

Ho waxed more indignant. "You rebelled immediately after the late chief's death, before even his body was cold. How could you?"

Then shaking his whip at the followers of Wei, he cried, "And you soldiers are Hsich'uan men. Your fathers and mothers, wives and children and your friends are still in the land. Were you treated unkindly that you have joined a traitor and aid his wicked schemes? You ought to have returned home and waited quietly the rewards that would have been yours."

The soldiers were touched by his words; they cheered, and more than a half ran away.

Wei was now raging. He whirled up his sword and galloped forward straight for Ho P'ing, who went to meet him with his spear ready. They fought several bouts, and then Ho rode away as if defeated. Wei followed, but Ho's men began to shoot and Wei was driven backward. As he got near his own men he saw many captains leaving their companies and going away. He rode after them and cut some of them down. But this did not stay the movement; they continued to go. The only steady portion of his own army was that commanded by Ma Tai. They stood their ground.

"Will you really help me?" said Wei Yen. "I will surely remember you in the day of success."

The two then went in pursuit of Ho P'ing, who fled before them. However, it was soon evident that Ho was not to be overtaken, and the pursuers halted. Wei mustered his now small force

"What if we go over to Wei?" said he.

"I think your words unwise," said Ma. "Why should we join anyone? A really strong man would try to carve out his own fortune and not be ready to crook the knee to another. You are able enough and brave enough to be more than a match for any man in the west. No one would care to stand up to you. I pledge myself to go with you to the seizure of Hanchung, and thence we will attack the west."

So they marched together toward Nanchêng, where was Chiang Wei. From the bridge he saw their approach and marked their proud, martial look. He ordered the drawbridge to be raised and sent to tell his colleague, Yang I.

As they drew near, both Wei and Ma shouted out, "Surrender!"

In spite of the smallness of their following, Chiang Wei felt that Ma Tai acting with Wei Yen was a dangerous combination, and he wanted the advice of Yang.

"How shall we repel them?" asked he.

Yang replied, "Just before his death the minister gave me a silken bag, which he said I was to open when Wei's mutiny reached a critical point. It contains a plan to rid ourselves of this traitor, and it seems that now is the moment to see what should be done."

So he opened the bag and drew forth the letter it held. On the cover he read, "To be opened when Wei Yen is actually arrayed opposite you."

Said Chiang, "As this has all been arranged for I had better go out, and when his line is formed then you can come forth."

Chiang donned his armour, took his spear and rode out, with three companies. They marched out of the city gates with the drums beating. The array completed, Chiang took his place under the great standard and opened with a volley of abuse.

"Rebel Wei, the late minister never harmed you; why have you turned traitor?"

Wei Yen reined up, lowered his sword and replied, "Friend Chiang, this is no concern of yours; tell Yang I to come."

Now Yang was also beneath the standard, but hidden. He opened the letter, and the words therein seemed to please him, for he rode forward blithely. Presently he reined in, pointed to Wei and said, "The minister foresaw your mutiny and bade me be on my guard. Now if you are able thrice to shout, 'Who dares kill me will be a real noble!' I will yield to you the whole of Hanchung."

Wei Yen laughed. "Listen, you old fool! While K'ung-ming lived I feared him somewhat. But he is dead and no one dares stand before me. I will not only shout the words thrice, but a myriad times. Why not?"

He raised his sword, shook his bridle and shouted, "Who dares kill me——"

He never finished. Behind him someone shouted savagely, "I dare kill you!" and at the same moment Wei fell dead, cut down by Ma Tai.

This was the dénouement, and was the secret entrusted to Ma Tai just before K'ung-ming's death. Wei was to be made to shout these words and slain when he least expected it. Yang knew what was to happen, as it was written in the letter in the silken bag.

A poem says:—

> Chuko foresaw when freed from his restraint
> Wei Yen would traitor prove. The silken bag
> Contained the plan for his undoing. We see
> How it succeeded when the moment came.

So before Tung Yün had reached Nanchêng Wei was dead. Ma Tai joined his men to Chiang's, and Yang wrote another memorial, which he sent to the king. The king issued an edict that as the guilty officer had paid the penalty of his crime he should be honourably buried in consideration of his former services.

Then Yang I continued his journey and in due time arrived at Ch'êngtu with the coffin of the late minister. The king led out a large cavalcade of officers to meet the body at a point twenty *li* from the walls, and he lifted up his voice and wailed for the dead, and with him wailed all the officers and the common people, so that the sound of mourning filled the whole earth.

By royal command the body was borne into the city to the dead man's residence, and his son Chuko Chan was chief mourner.

When next the king held a Court Yang I appeared thereat bound, and confessed he had been in fault. The king bade them loose his bonds and said, "Noble Sir, the coffin would never have reached home but for you. You carried out the orders of the late minister, whereby Wei Yen was destroyed and all was made secure. This was all your doing."

Yang I was promoted to be the Master of the Centre Army, and Ma Tai was rewarded with the rank that Wei Yen had forfeited.

Yang I presented K'ung-ming's testament, which the king read, weeping. By a special edict it was commanded that soothsayers should cast lots and select the site for the tomb of the great servant of the state.

Then Fei said to the king, "When nearing his end the Prime Minister commanded that he should be buried on Tingchün Hill, in open ground, without sacrifice or monument."

This wish was respected, and they chose a propitious day in the tenth month for the interment, and the king followed in the funeral procession to the grave on the Tingchün Hill. The posthumous title conferred upon Chuko Liang was *Chung-wu,* "Loyally Martial," and a temple was built in Mienyang wherein were offered sacrifices at the four seasons.

The poet Tu Fu wrote a poem:—

> To Chuko stands a great memorial hall,
> In cypress shade, without the Chukuan Wall,
> The steps thereto are bright with new grass springing,
> Hid 'mongst the branches orioles are singing.
> Devotion patient met reward; upon
> The throne, built for the father, sat the son.
> But ere was compassed all his plans conceived
> He died; and heroes since for him have ever grieved.

Another poem by the same author says:—

> Chuko's fair fame stands clear to all the world;
> Among king's ministers he surely takes
> Exalted rank; for when the empire cleft
> In three, a kingdom for his lord he won
> By subtle craft. Throughout all time he stands
> A shining figure, clear against the sky.
> Akin was he to famous I and Lü,
> Yet stands with chiefs who failed, like Hsiao and Ts'ao;
> The fates forbade that Han should be restored,
> War-worn and weary, yet he steadfast stood.

Evil tidings came to the king on his return to his capital. He heard that Ch'üan Tsung had marched out with a large army from Eastern Wu and camped at the entrance to Pach'iu. No one knew the object of this expedition.

"Here is Wu breaking their oath just as the Prime Minister has died," cried the king. "What can we do?"

Then said Chiang Wan, "My advice is to send Wang P'ing and Chang I to camp at Yungan as a measure of precaution, while you send an envoy to Wu to announce the death and period of mourning. He can there observe the signs of the times."

"The envoy must have a ready tongue," said the king.

One stepped from the ranks of courtiers and offered himself. He was Tsung Yu, a man of Nanyang, an officer in the army. So he was appointed as envoy—and spy.

He set out for Chinling, arrived and was taken in to the king's presence. When the ceremony of introduction was over and the envoy looked about him, he saw that all were dressed in mourning. But Sun Ch'üan's countenance wore a look of anger, and he said, "Wu and Shu are one house; why has your master increased the guard at Poti?"

Tsung replied, "It seemed as necessary for the west to increase the garrison there as for the east to have a force at Pach'iu. Neither is worth asking about."

"As an envoy you seem no way inferior to Têng Chih," said the king, smiling. He continued, "When I heard that your Minister Chuko had gone to heaven I wept daily and ordered my officers to wear mourning. I feared that Wei might take the occasion to attack Shu, and so I increased the garrison at Pach'iu by a legion that I might be able to help you in case of need. That was my sole reason."

The envoy bowed and thanked the king.

"I would not go back upon the pledge between us," said the king.

The envoy said, "I have been sent to inform you of the mourning for the late Prime Minister."

Sun Ch'üan took up a silver barbed arrow and snapped it in twain, saying, "If I betray my oath may my posterity be cut off!"

Then he despatched an envoy with incense and silk and other gifts to be offered in sacrifice to the dead in the land of Shu.

The two envoys took leave of the King of Wu and journeyed to Ch'êngtu, where they went to the King of Shu, and Tsung Yü made a memorial saying, "The King of Wu has wept for our K'ung-ming and put his court into mourning. The increased garrison at Pach'iu is intended to safeguard us from Wei, lest they take the occasion of a public sorrow to attack. And in token of his pledge King Sun Ch'üan broke an arrow in twain."

The king was pleased and rewarded Tsung Yü; moreover, the envoy of Wu was generously treated.

According to the advice in K'ung-ming's testament, the Latter Ruler made Chiang Wan Prime Minister, and Chief of the Presidents and General, while Fei I became President

of a Board, and associate in the Prime Minister's office. Many
other promotions were made, and among them Wu I was made
Governor of Hanchung, to keep Wei in check.

Now as Yang I was senior in service to Chiang Wan, who had
thus been promoted over his head, and as he considered his
services had been inadequately rewarded, he was discontented
and spoke resentfully.

He said to Fei I, "If when the minister died I had gone
over to Wei, with the whole army, I should not have been
thus left out in the cold."

Fei secretly reported this speech to the king, who was
angered and threw Yang into prison. He intended putting
him to death, but Chiang Wan reminded him of his services,
and he was reprieved. However, he was degraded and sent
into Hanchung, where he committed suicide through shame.

In the thirteenth year of the period *Chien-Hsing* of Shu,
the same year being the third year of *Ching-Lung* of Wu, and
the fourth year of *Chia-Ho* of Wei, there were no military
expeditions. However, it is recorded that Ssŭma I was
created a *Tai-yü*, with command over all the forces of Wei,
and he departed for Loyang.

King Jui, of Wei, at Hsüch'ang, made preparations to build
himself a palace. At Loyang also he built the *Ch'ao-yang Tien*,
or "Hall of Sunrise," and the *T'ai-chi Tien*, or "Hall of the
Firmament," both lofty and of beautiful design. He also
raised a "Hall Beautiful" and a storeyed building called the
"Pavilion of the Pair of Phœnixes." He also digged a Pool
of the Nine Dragons. Over all these works he placed the
scholar Ma Chün as superintendent of their building.

Nothing was spared that would contribute to the beauty of
these buildings. The beams were carved, the rafters were
painted, the walls were of golden bricks and the roofs of green
tiles. They glittered and glowed in the sunlight. The most
cunning artizans in the world were sought, many thousands
of them, and myriads of ordinary workmen laboured day and
night on these works for the king's glory and pleasure. But
the strength of the people was spent in this toil, and they
cried aloud and complained unceasingly.

Moreover, King Jui issued an edict to carry earth and
bring trees for the Garden of the Fragrant Forest, and he
employed officers of state in these labours, carrying earth
and transporting trees.

The Minister of Education, Tung Hsün, ventured upon a
remonstrance, saying, "From the beginning of the period
Chien-An, a generation ago, wars have been continuous and
destruction rife. Those who have escaped death are few, and
these are old and weak. Now indeed it may be that the
palaces are too small and enlargement is desired, but would it
not be more fitting to choose the building season so as not to

interfere with cultivation? Your Majesty has many honourable officers wearing beautiful head-dresses, clad in handsome
robes, and riding in decorated chariots to distinguish them
from the common people. Now these officers are being made
to carry timber and bear earth, to sweat and soil their feet.
To destroy the glory of the state in order to raise a useless
edifice is indescribable folly. The Great Teacher said that
princes should treat ministers with polite consideration,
ministers should serve princes with loyalty. Without loyalty,
without propriety, can a state endure?

"I recognise that these words of mine mean death, but I
am of no value, a mere bullock's hair, and my life is of no
importance, as my death would be no loss. I write with tears,
bidding the world farewell.

"Thy servant has eight sons, who will be a burden to Your
Majesty after his death. I cannot say with what trepidation
I await my fate."

"Has the man no fear of death?" said King Jui, greatly
angered.

The courtiers requested the king to put him to death, but
he remembered his rectitude and proven loyalty and only
degraded him, adding a warning to him to curb his tongue.

A certain Chang Mou, in the service of the Heir Apparent,
also ventured upon a remonstrance; he suffered death.

King Jui summoned his Master of Works, Ma Chün, and
said, "I have builded high terraces and lofty towers with
intent to hold intercourse with *shên* and *hsien*, gods and
djinn, that I may obtain from them the elixir of life."

Then Ma replied, "Of the four and twenty emperors of the
line of Han only the Emperor Wu enjoyed the throne very
long and really attained to old age. That was because he
drank of the essence of the brilliancy of the sun and the
brightness of the moon. In the palace at Ch'angan is the
Terrace of Cyprus Beams, upon which stands the bronze
figure of a man holding up a Dew Bowl, whereinto distils, in
the third watch of the night, the vapour from the great
constellation of the north. This liquid is called 'Celestial
Elixir, or ' Gentle Dew.' If mingled with powdered jade and
swallowed it restores youth to the aged."

"Take men to Ch'angan immediately and bring hither the
bronze figure to set up in the new garden," said the
king.

As the king commanded, they took a multitude of men to
Ch'angan, and they built a scaffold around the figure. Then
they attached ropes to haul it down. The terrace being two
hundred feet high and the pedestal ten cubits in circumference,
Ma Chün bade his men first detach the bronze image. They
did so and brought it down. Its eyes were moist as with
tears, and the workmen were affrighted.

Then suddenly beside the terrace sprang up a whirlwind, with dust and pebbles flying thick as a shower of rain, and there was a tempestuous roar as of an earthquake. Down fell the pedestal, and the platform crumbled, crushing many men to death.

However, the bronze figure and the golden bowl were conveyed to Loyang and presented to the king.

"Where is the pedestal?" asked the king.

"It is too heavy to transport," replied the Master Workman.

"It weighs a million catties."

Wherefore the king ordered it to be broken up and the metal brought, and from this he caused to be cast two figures which he named *Wêng*, Grandfather, and *Chung*, Uncle. They were placed outside the gate of the Board of War. A pair of dragons and a pair of phœnixes were also cast, the dragons forty feet high and the birds thirty. These were placed in front of the Hall of Audience.

Moreover, in the Upper Forest Garden the king planted wonderful flowers and rare trees, and he also established a menagerie of strange animals.

Yang Fou remonstrated with the king on these extravagances.

"As is well known, Yao preferred his humble thatched cottage, and all the world enjoyed tranquillity; Yü contented himself with a small modest palace, and all the empire rejoiced. In the days of Yin and Chou the Hall of the ruler stood three feet above the usual height and its area was nine 'mats.' The sage emperors and illustrious kings had no decorated chambers in lofty palaces built with the wealth, and by the strength, of a worn-out and despoiled people. Chieh built a jade chamber and elephant stables; Chou erected a surpassingly beautiful palace and a Deer Terrace. But these lost the empire. Duke Ling, of Ch'u, built beautiful palaces, but he came to an evil end. The 'First Emperor,' of Ts'in, made the Afang Palace, but calamity fell upon his son, for the empire rebelled and his house was exterminated in the second generation. All those who have failed to consider the means of the people and given way to sensuous pleasures have perished. Your Majesty has the examples of Yao and Shun, of Yü and T'ang on the one hand, and the warnings of Chieh and Chou, Ch'u and Ts'in on the other. To seek only self-indulgence and think only of fine palaces will surely end in calamity.

"The prince is the first and the head; his ministers are his limbs; they live or die together, they are involved in the same destruction. Though I am timorous, yet if I dared forget my duty, or failed to speak firmly, I should be unable to move Your Majesty. Now I have prepared my coffin and bathed my body ready for the most condign punishment."

But the king disregarded this memorial and only urged on the rapid completion of the terrace. Thereon he set up the bronze figure with the golden bowl. Moreover, he sent forth a command to select the most beautiful women in the empire for his garden of delight. Many memorials were presented, but the king heeded them not.

Now the Consort of King Jui was of the Mao family of Honan. In earlier days, when he was a prince, he had loved her exceedingly, and when he succeeded to the throne she became Empress. Later he favoured the Lady Kuo, and his Consort was neglected. The Lady Kuo was beautiful and clever, and the king delighted in her. He neglected state affairs for her society and often spent a month at a time in retirement with her. Every day there was some new gaiety.

In the spring, when the plants in the Fragrant Forest Garden were in flower, the king and his favourite came to the garden to enjoy them and to feast.

"Why not invite the Empress?" asked the Lady Kuo.

"If she came nothing would pass my lips," replied the king.

He gave orders that his Consort should be kept in ignorance of these rejoicings. But when a month passed without the appearance of the king, his Consort and her ladies went to the Blue Flower Pavilion to find out what was the reason. Hearing music, she asked who was providing it, and they told her that the king and the Lady Kuo were feasting in the grounds.

That day she returned to her palace filled with rage. Next day she went out in her carriage and saw the king on a verandah.

"Yesterday Your Majesty was walking in the north garden, and you had plenty of music too," said she, laughing.

The king was wroth and sent for all the attendants. He upbraided them with disobedience and put them all to death. The Empress feared and returned to her palace.

Then an edict appeared condemning the Empress to death and raising the Lady Kuo to be Empress in her place. And no officer dared to utter a remonstrance.

Just after this the Governor of Yuchou, Much'iu Ch'ien, sent in a memorial saying that Kungsun Yüan of Liaotung had risen in revolt, had assumed the style of "King" and adopted a *nien-hao*. He had built himself a palace, established an administration of his own and was disturbing the whole north with plundering.

A council met to consider this memorial.

> Within, officials labour at ignoble tasks, and mean,
> Without, the glint of weapons on the border may be seen.

How the insurgents were attacked will be related in the next chapter.

CHAPTER CVI.

DEFEAT AND DEATH OF KUNGSUN YÜAN;
PRETENDED ILLNESS OF SSŬMA I.

This Kungsun Yüan was of a family long settled in Liaotung. When Ts'ao Ts'ao was pursuing Yüan Shang, who had fled eastward, Kungsun K'ang, the father of the present rebel, had captured him, beheaded him and sent his head to Ts'ao. For this service Kungsun received the title of "Marquis of Hsiangp'ing." After Kungsun K'ang's death, as his two sons were young, his brother took the chiefship, and Ts'ao P'ei, beside confirming the marquisate, gave him the rank of General. A few years later, the second son, Yüan, being now grown up, well-educated and trained in military exercises, obstinate and fond of fighting, took away his uncle's power and ruled the heritage of his father. Ts'ao Jui conferred upon him the title of *Yang-lieh*, "Wielder of Ferocity," and made him Prefect.

Then Sun Ch'üan, anxious to secure his support, sent two envoys with gifts and offered Kungsun Yüan the title of "Prince Yen." Fearing that the capital would resent any dallying with Wu, the Prefect slew the envoys. For this proof of lealty Ts'ao Jui gave him the title of Minister of War and the Dukedom of Yüehlang. However, he was dissatisfied, and his thoughts turned toward independence. He took council with his officers and proposed to style himself "King Yen" and to adopt a reign-title of his own.

One officer, Chia Fan, opposed this and said, "My lord, the central authorities have treated you well and honoured you. I fear that Ssŭma I is too skilful a leader for rebellion to succeed. You see even Chuko Liang cannot defeat him; how much less can you?"

Kungsun's reply was to condemn Chia Fan to death. However, General Lun Chih ventured upon further remonstrance.

"Chia Fan spoke well. The Sacred One says that extra-ordinary phenomena presage the destruction of a state. Now this time portents are not wanting, and wonders have been seen. A dog, dressed in red and wearing a turban, went up the length of a room walking like a man. Moreover, while a certain person living in a village south of the city was cooking his food, he saw a child in the pan, boiled to death. A great cave opened near the market-place and threw out a large, fleshy body completely human save that it lacked limbs.

Swords could not cut it; arrows could not penetrate it. No one knew what to call it, and when they consulted the *sortes* they obtained the reply, 'Incomplete shape, silent mouth: a state is near destruction.' These prodigies are all inauspicious. Flee from evil and strive to walk in fair fortune's way. Make no move without most careful thought."

This second remonstrance enraged the rebel still more, and he sent Lun to death with Chia. Both were executed in the public place.

Kungsun then prepared to make a bid for empire. He raised an army of fifteen legions, appointed a general, Pei Yen, and a leader of the van, Yang Tsu. This army set out for the capital.

King Jui was alarmed at the report of this rising, and sent for Ssŭma I. Ssŭma was not greatly perturbed, and said, "My four legions will be equal to the task."

The king replied, "The task is heavy, for your men are few and the road is long."

"The strength of an army is not in numbers, but in strategy. Aided by Your Majesty's good fortune I shall certainly be able to bring this fellow a captive to your feet."

"What do you think will be the rebel's plan?" asked the king.

"His best plan would be flight before our army can arrive; his second best is defending his position; his third, and worst, would be to try to hold Hsiangp'ing. In the last case I shall certainly capture him."

"How long will the expedition take?"

"We have to cover four thousand *li*, which will take a hundred days. Attack will consume another hundred. The return will need a hundred, and with sixty days to rest we shall take a year."

"Suppose during that year we are attacked by Wu or Shu."

"My plans provide for that; Your Majesty need have no anxiety."

The king being thus reassured, formally ordered Ssŭma to undertake the expedition.

Hu Tsun was appointed to lead the van. He went and camped in Liaotung. The scouts hasted to tell Kungsun, who sent his general and van-leader to camp at Liaochui. They surrounded their camp with a wall twenty *li* in circumference and placed "deer-horns" outside the rampart. It seemed very secure. Hu Tsun saw these preparations and sent to tell his chief. Ssŭma smiled.

"So the rebel does not want to fight, but thinks to weary my men," said Ssŭma. "Now I am disposed to think that most of his army is within that wall, so that his stronghold is empty and undefended. I will make a dash at Hsiangp'ing. He will have to go to its rescue and I will smite him on the way. I should score a great success."

So he hastened to Hsiangp'ing along unfrequented ways.

Meanwhile the two captains within the walled camp discussed their plans.

Yang Tsu said, "When the Wei army comes near we will not fight. They will have come a long march and their supplies will be short, so that they cannot hold out long. When they retreat we shall find our opportunity. These were the tactics Ssŭma I used against Chuko on the Wei River, and Chuko died before the end of the expedition. We will try similar means."

Presently the scouts reported that the Wei army had marched south. Pei Yen at once saw the danger and said, "They are going to attack Hsiangp'ing, which they know is defenceless. If that be lost this position is useless."

So they broke up their camp and followed the enemy. When Ssŭma heard it he rejoiced, saying, "Now they will fall into the snare I have laid for them."

He sent the two Hsiahous to take up position on the Chi River. They were to attack if the men of Liao came near them. They had not long to wait. As soon as Pei Yen and his army approached they exploded a bomb, beat the drums, waved their flags and came out, one force on each side. The Liao leaders made but a feeble fight and soon fled to Shoushan, where they joined the main army under Kungsun Yüan. Then they turned to give battle to the Wei army.

Pei Yen rode to the front and reviled the enemy, taunted them with trickery and challenged to a fight in the open. Hsiahou Pa rode out to accept the challenge, and after a few bouts Pei fell. In the confusion caused by the death of their leader, Hsiahou urged on his men and drove Kungsun back to Hsiangp'ing. He took refuge in the city.

The city was surrounded. It was autumn, and the rain fell day after day without ceasing. At the end of the month the plain was under three feet of water, so that the grain boats sailed straight from Liaohok'ou to the city walls. The besiegers suffered much from the floods.

The Commander of the Left went to Ssŭma and asked that the army might be moved to camp on the higher ground, out of the mud and water. But Ssŭma flouted the suggestion.

"How can the army move away just when success is in sight? The rebels will be conquered now any day, and if any other speaks about drawing off he will be put to death."

Pei went away muttering angrily to himself. Soon after, his colleague in command of the right wing repeated the suggestion and was put to death. His head was suspended at the camp gate as a warning to others. The soldiers were much depressed.

Then the south camp was abandoned, and the men marched twenty *li* south. This side of the city being thus left clear, the soldiers and people came out to gather fuel and pasture their cattle. The attacking army could not understand this move, and Ch'ên Chün spoke about it.

"When you besieged Shangyung, O *T'aiyü*, you attacked all round at eight points, and the city fell in as many days. Mêng Ta was taken, and you won a great success. Now your four legions have borne their armour many days over long marches and you do not press the attack, but keep the men in the mud and mire and let the enemy gather supplies and feed their cattle. I do not know what your intention may be."

"Sir," replied the Commander-in-chief, "I see you are ignorant of war after all. You do not understand the different conditions. Mêng Ta then had ample supplies and few men; we were under exactly opposite conditions, and so we had to attack vigorously and at once. The suddenness of the attack defeated the enemy. But look at present conditions. The Liao men are many and we few; they are on the verge of starvation, and we are full fed. Why should we force the attack? Our line is to let them flee and smite them as they run. Therefore I leave a gate open and the road free that they may run away."

Ch'ên then understood and acknowledged the correctness of the strategy. Ssŭma sent to Loyang to hasten supplies, that there should be no shortage.

However, the war was not supported in the capital, for when the messenger arrived and the king summoned his courtiers, they said, "In Liaotung the rain has been continuous for a month, and the men are in misery. Ssŭma ought to be recalled and the war renewed at a more convenient season."

The king replied, "The leader of our army is most capable and best able to decide upon what should be done. He understands the conditions and is teeming with magnificent plans. He will certainly succeed. Wherefore, O Nobles, wait a few days and let us not be anxious about the result."

So the king heeded not the voice of the dissentients, but took care that provisions were sent. After a few days the rain ceased, and fine, clear weather followed. Ssŭma went out of his tent that he might study the sky. Suddenly he saw a very large and bright star start from a point over Shoushan and travel over toward Hsiangp'ing, where it fell. The soldiers were rather frightened at this apparition, but the leader rejoiced.

"Five days from now Kungsun Yüan will be slain where that star fell," said he. "Therefore attack with vigour."

They opened the attack the next morning at dawn, throwing up banks and sapping the walls, setting up ballistæ and rearing ladders. When night came the attack did not cease. Arrows fell in the city like pelting rain.

Within the city, grain began to run short, and soon there was none. They slaughtered bullocks and horses for food. The soldiers began to be mutinous and no longer fought with any spirit. There was talk of slaying Kungsun and yielding the city.

Kungsun was disheartened and frightened, and decided to sue for peace. He sent a minister and a censor out of the city to beg Ssŭma to allow him to submit. These two had to be let down from the walls by ropes, as no other means of exit were possible. They found their way to Ssŭma and said, "We pray you, O T'ai-yü, to retire twenty li and allow the officers to come forth and surrender."

"Why did not Kungsun himself come?" said Ssŭma. "He is rude."

He put the two envoys to death and sent their heads back into the city.

Kungsun was still more alarmed, but he resolved to make one more attempt. This time he sent Wei Yen, a *Shih-chung*, as his envoy. Ssŭma received this messenger sitting in state in his tent with his officers standing right and left. The envoy approached on his knees, and when he reached the door of the tent recited his petition."

"I pray you, O T'ai-yü, to turn your thundrous wrath from us; we will send the son of our leader as hostage and all the officers shall appear before you bound with cords."

Ssŭma replied. "There are five possible operations for any army. If you can fight, fight; if you cannot fight, defend; if you cannot defend, flee; if you cannot flee, surrender; if you cannot surrender, die. These five courses are open to you, and a hostage would be useless. Now return and tell your master."

Wei Yen put his hands over his head and fled like a rat. He went into the city and related what had happened to him.

The Kungsuns, father and son, resolved to flee. They chose a company of mounted men, and in the dead of night opened the south gate and got out. They took the road to the east and were rejoiced to find it clear.

All went well for a distance of ten li, when a bomb exploded. This was followed by a roll of drums and the blare of trumpets; and a cohort stood in the way. The leader was Ssŭma I, supported by his two sons.

"Stop, O rebel!" cried they.

But Kungsun lashed his steed to a gallop. Then Hu Tsun and the two Hsiahous, with their men, came up and quickly surrounded them so that they were helpless. Kungsun saw that escape was impossible, so he came with his sons, dismounted and offered surrender. Ssŭma hardly looked at the two men, but he turned to his officers and pointed out that the two Kungsuns stood where the star had fallen just five nights previously. They all felicitated him and praised his superhuman skill. The two helpless men were slain where they stood.

Ssŭma turned to resume the siege of the city, but before he had reached the walls Hu Tsun's men had entered. Ssŭma went in and was received with great respect, the people burning incense as he passed. He went to the residence, and then the whole of the Kungsun clan, and all who had assisted in his rising, were beheaded. They counted heads to the number of three score and ten.

The city taken and the rebels destroyed, the victor issued a proclamation in order to restore confidence among the people. Certain persons told him that Chia Fan and Lun Chih had been against the revolt and had therefore suffered death, so he honoured their tombs and conferred ranks upon their children. The contents of the treasury were distributed among the soldiers as rewards, and then the army marched back to Loyang.

One night the King of Wei was suddenly awakened by a chill blast that extinguished all the lights, but he saw the form of his late Consort, with a score or two of others, coming toward the seat whereon he sat, and as they approached they demanded his life. He was very frightened and fell ill so that he was like to die.

So the two officers Liu Fang and Sun Tzŭ were set over the privy council, and he summoned his brother Yü to the capital to make him *Ta-Chiang-Chün*, and assistant to the regent, Ts'ao Fang, the Heir Apparent. However, his brother being modest and retiring by nature, declined these high offices and their responsibilities.

The king then turned to his two confidants and enquired of them who of the family was a suitable person to support the Heir Apparent. As they had both received many favours from Ts'ao Chên, they replied that none was so fit as Ts'ao Shuang, the son of their patron. The king approved their choice, and thus Shuang became a great person. Then they memorialised, saying that as Ts'ao Shuang had been chosen, the king's broher Ts'ao Yü, Prince Yen, should be ordered to leave the capital and return to his own place.

The king consented and issued an edict, which these two bore to the prince, saying, "The edict in the King's own hand bids you return to your own domain at once, and you are not to return to court without a special command."

The prince wept, but he left forthwith. Thereupon Ts'ao Shuang was created *Ta-Chiang-chün*, and administered the government.

But the king's illness advanced rapidly, and he called Ssŭma into the palace. As soon as he arrived he was led to the king's chamber.

"I feared lest I should not see you again," said the king; "but now I can die content."

The general bowed and said, "On the road they told me the sacred person was not perfectly well; I grieved that I had not wings to hasten hither. But I am happy in that I now behold the 'dragon' countenance."

The heir was summoned to the king's bedside and also Ts'ao Shuang, Liu Fang, Sun Tzŭ, and certain others. Taking Ssŭma by the hand, the dying king said, "When Liu Yüan-tê lay dying at Paitich'êng he confided his son, so soon to be an orphan, to the care of Chuko K'ung-ming, who laboured in this task to the very end and whose devotion only ceased with death. If such conduct is possible in the mere remnant of a dying dynasty continued in a small state, how much more may I hope for it in a great country! My son is only eight years of age, and incapable of sustaining the burden of rulership. Happily for him he has ample merit and experience around him in the persons of yourself and his relatives. He will never lack friends for my sake." Turning to the young prince, he continued, "My friend Chung-ta is as myself, and you are to treat him with the same respect and deference."

The king bade Ssŭma lead the young prince forward. The boy threw his arms around his new guardian's neck and clung to him.

"Never forget the affection he has just shown," said the king, weeping. And Ssŭma wept also.

The dying man swooned; although he could not speak, his hand still pointed to his son, and soon after he died. He had reigned thirteen years and was thirty-six years of age. His death took place in the last decade of the first month of the third year of Ch'u-Ching.

No time was lost in enthroning the new king, the supporters being Ssŭma and Ts'ao Shuang. The new ruler's name was Ts'ao Fang, his other name being Lan-ching. However, he was the King's son only by adoption. He had been brought up in the palace as a son, and no one knew his real origin.

The posthumous title of "Emperor Ming" was conferred upon the late ruler, and he was buried in the Kaop'ing Tombs.

The late Empress Kuo was given the title of "T'ai-hou."

The new reign was styled Chêng-Shih. Ssŭma I and Ts'ao Shuang conducted the government, and in all matters the latter treated his colleague with deference and took no steps without his knowledge.

Ts'ao Shuang was no stranger at court. The late king had respected him for his diligence and care and had been very fond of him, He had had the freedom of the palace all his life. He had a host of clients and retainers. Among them were five wholly light and foppish. Their family names were Ho, Têng, Li, Ting and Pi. Beside these five there was another named Huan Fan, a man of good parts, who had the sobriquet of "Bag o' Wisdom". These six were Ts'ao Shuang's most trusted companions and confidants.

Now that they saw their patron in such an exalted position they began to think how to exploit it. One day Ho Yen said, "Ts'ao Shuang, you should not let your great powers slip into the hands of any other, or you will repent it."

Ts'ao replied, "Ssŭma I as well as I received the king's sacred trust, and I mean to be true."

Ho said, "When your father and this Ssŭma were winning their victories in the east, your father suffered much from this man's temper, which ultimately brought about his death. Why do you not look into that?"

Ts'ao seemed suddenly to wake up. Having entered into an intrigue with the majority of the officers about the court, then one day he presented to the king a memorial proposing that Ssŭma should be promoted to the rank of T'aifu for his great merits and services.

The promotion was made, and, consequently, Ssŭma disappeared from the administration, and the whole military authority fell into the hands of Ts'ao Shuang.

Having thus far succeeded, Ts'ao next appointed his brothers to high military posts, so that each commanded three companies of the guards, with right to go in and out of the palace at will. Moreover, three of his friends were created Presidents, and the two others received powerful offices, one of which was the governorship of Honan. These five and their patron were close associates in all concerns of state.

Ts'ao Shuang gathered about him larger and still larger numbers of supporters, till Ssŭma gave out that he was ill and remained in seclusion. His two sons also resigned their offices.

Ts'ao Shuang and his friends now gave themselves up to dissipation, spending days and nights in drinking and music. In their dress and the furniture of their table they copied the palace patterns. Tribute in the shape of jewels and curios went to the residence of Ts'ao before it entered the palace, and his courts swarmed with beautiful damsels.

The eunuch Chang Fang toadied to Ts'ao Shuang so far as to select a few of the late emperor's handmaids and send them to the now powerful minister; he also chose for him a chorus of two score well-born ladies who were skilled in music and dancing. Ts'ao Shuang also built for himself beautiful towers and pavilions and made to himself vessels of gold and silver, the work of the most expert craftsmen, whom he kept constantly employed.

Now Ho Yen heard of Kuan Lu's great skill in divination and sent to him in P'ingyuan to invite him to take the *sortes* on his account. When the soothsayer arrived, Têng Yang was of the company to meet him, and he said to Kuan, "You call yourself a skilful diviner, but your speech does not resemble the language of the Book of Changes. How is that?"

Kuan replied, "An interpreter does not use the language of the original."

Ho laughed, saying, "Certainly good words are not wearisome. But cast a lot for me, and tell me whether I shall ever arrive at the highest dignity or not, for I have dreamed repeatedly that many black flies settled on my nose."

Kuan replied, "Yüan K'ai aided Shun; Duke Chou assisted Chou; both these were kindly and modest and enjoyed great happiness. You, Sir, have come to high honours and wield great powers, but those who esteem you are few and those who fear you, many. You are not careful to walk in the way of good fortune. Now the nose is an eminence. If an eminence retains its characteristic, thereby it remains in honour. But is it not that black flies gather to foul objects and the lofty fears a fall? I would wish you to give of your abundance for the good of the poor and avoid walking in the wrong road. Then indeed may you reach the highest dignity, and the black flies will disperse."

"This is mere senile gossip," said Têng.

"The gift of age is to see that which is yet to come; the gift of gossip is to perceive what is not said," replied Kuan.

Thereupon he shook out his sleeves and went away.

"He is very mad, really," said his two hosts.

Kuan Lu went home. When he saw his uncle he gave him an account of the interview. His uncle was alarmed at the probable consequences, and said, "Why did you anger them? They are too powerful for you to offend."

"What is there to fear? I have been talking to two dead men."

"What do you mean?"

"Têng Yang's gait is that of one whose sinews are loosed from his bones, and his pulse is unsteady. When he would stand he totters as a man without limbs. This is the aspect of a disembodied soul. Ho Yen looks as if his soul was about to quit its habitation. He is bloodless, and what should be solid in him is mere vapour. He looks like rotten wood. This is the aspect of a soul even now in the dark valley. Both these men will certainly soon die a violent death, and none need fear them."

His uncle left, cursing him for a madman.

Ts'ao Shuang and his five friends were devoted to the chase and were often out of the city. Ts'ao Hsi. a brother of Shuang's, remonstrated with him about this and pointed out the dangers of such frequent absence on these excursions. "You are in an exalted position and yet you are constantly going out hunting. If anyone took advantage of this to work you evil you might have cause to be exceedingly regretful."

Ts'ao Shuang only showed anger, and replied, "The whole military authority is in my hands and what is there to fear?"

Huan Fan, then Minister of Agriculture, also reasoned with him, but he would not listen.

About this time the style of the reign was changed to *Chia-P'ing*.

Now ever since Ts'ao had enjoyed the monopoly of military authority he had never heard the truth about the state of health of the man he had manœuvred out of power. But when a certain Li Shêng was appointed to the governorship of Ch'ingchou he bade him go to take leave of Ssŭma I, at the same time to find out the true state of his rival's health.

So Li proceeded to the residence of the *T'ai-fu* and was announced. Ssŭma saw through the device at once and told his sons the real reason of this visit, and bade them play their parts in the scene he arranged before the visitor was admitted.

He threw aside his head-dress, so letting his hair fall in disorder, stretched himself upon his couch, tumbled the bedding into confusion, got a couple of slave girls to support him, and then told his servants to lead in the visitor.

Li came in and went up to the sick man, saying, "It is a long time since I have seen you, and I did not know you were so seriously ill. His Majesty is sending me to Ch'ingchou, and I have come to pay my respects to you and bid you farewell."

"Ah; Pingchou is in the north; you will have to be very careful there," said Ssŭma feigning that he had not heard.

"I am going as Governor of Ch'ingchou, not Pingchou," said Li.

"Oh, you have just come from Pingchou."

"Ch'ingchou, in Shantung."

"Just back from Ch'ingchou, eh?" said Ssŭma, smiling.

"How very ill the *T'ai-fu* is!" said Li Shêng to the servants.

"The *T'ai-fu* is deaf," said they.

"Give me paper and a pen," said Li.

Writing materials were brought, when Li wrote what he wished to say and put it before his host.

"My illness has made me very deaf; take care of yourself on the way," said Ssŭma.

Looking up, he pointed to his mouth. One of the girls brought some broth and held the cup for him to drink. He put his lips to the cup, but spilled the broth all over his dress.

"I am very weak and ill," said he, "and may die at any moment. My sons are but poor things, but you will instruct them, and when you see the general you will remember them, will you not?"

At this point he fell back on the couch, panting, and Li took his leave. He told his patron what he had seen, and Ts'ao Shuang rejoiced, thinking his rival could not last long.

"If the old man died, I should not be the one to grieve," said he.

But no sooner had Li gone than Ssŭma rose from his couch and said to his sons, "Li Shêng will take a full account of this to his patron, who will not fear me any more. But wait till he goes on his next hunting trip, and we will see what can be done."

Soon after this, Ts'ao Shuang proposed to the king to visit the tomb of his father and perform the filial sacrifices in person. So they went, a goodly company in the train of the imperial chariot, and Ts'ao Shuang with all his brothers and his friends went with the guards. Ts'ao's friend Huan entreated him to remain in the city for fear of plots and risings, but Ts'ao asked angrily and rudely who would dare make trouble, and bade him hold his tongue. And he went with the king.

His departure rejoiced the heart of Ssŭma, who at once began quietly to muster his trusty friends and henchmen and put the finishing touches to the plot for the overthrow of his rival.

> Now terminates his forced inaction,
> He must destroy the hostile faction.

Ts'ao Shung's fate will appear in the next chapter.

CHAPTER CVII.

Ssŭma I Recovers Political Power;
Chiang Wei is Defeated at Niut'ou Hills.

The Ssŭmas were very pleased to hear that their rival and his party were to follow the king on a visit to the tombs combined with a hunt, for it meant that the whole enemy faction left the city. As soon as they left, Ssŭma entered, gave the minister Kao Jou provisional command of the army and sent him to seize the camp of Ts'ao Shuang. His brother's camp was also occupied. Having secured his position thus, he and his supporters went to the palace of the Empress Dowager and said to her, "Ts'ao Shuang has betrayed the trust placed in him by the late Emperor and has ruined the government. His fault must be expiated."

She replied, "What can be done in the absence of His Majesty?"

"I have prepared plans for the destruction of these base ministers and will see to it that no trouble happens to yourself."

The Empress was much alarmed, but could only act as she was directed and agree. So two of Ssŭma's supporters copied out the memorial he had prepared and it was sent to the king by the hand of an eunuch. Then the arsenals were seized.

Soon the news of the rising came to the knowledge of the family of Ts'ao Shuang, and his wife came out from the inner apartments and summoned the captain of the guard to enquire into the truth of the rumours. He told her that she need feel no alarm and he would go and see. Thereupon the captain P'an Chü, at the head of a few bowmen, went up on the wall and looked around. At that moment Ssŭma was crossing the court, and P'an bade his men shoot. But one of his officers reminded him that the *T'ai-fu* was one of the highest officers of state.

"You must not shoot at the *T'ai-fu;* he is on public service."

Thrice he urged his chief not to let the men shoot, and so P'an desisted. Ssŭma went across guarded by his son Shao. Then he went out of the city and camped on the Lo River at the floating bridge.

When the revolution began, one of Ts'ao Shuang's officers, Ssŭma Lu-chih by name, took counsel with his subordinate Hsin Ch'ang.

"Now that this revolt has begun, what should we do?"

"Let us go to the king with what troops we have," replied Hsin.

"Perhaps the best course," replied Lu-chih, and he went to his own house to get ready to start. There he met his sister, Hsien-ying, who asked the meaning of all this haste.

"His Majesty is out on a hunt and the *T'ai-fu* has closed the gates of the city. This is rebellion."

"I do not think so. He only means to slay Ts'ao Shuang, his rival," replied she.

"Why should he desire to do that?" asked her brother, sharply.

"Ts'ao Shuang is no match for the *T'ai-fu*," replied she.

"If Ssŭma asks us to join him, should we?" asked Hsin.

Hsien-ying replied, "You know what a true man should do. When a man is in danger there is the greater need for sympathy. To be of his men and desert in an emergency is the greatest of evils."

This speech decided Hsin, who went with Ssŭma Lu-chih. At the head of a few horsemen they forced the gate and got out of the city. When their escape was reported to Ssŭma I he thought that Huan Fan would surely try to follow their example, so he sent to call him. However, on the advice of his son, Huan did not answer the summons, but decided to flee. He got into his carriage and drove hastily to the P'ingch'ang Gate.

But the gate was barred. The warden was an old dependant of Huan's. Huan pulled out from his sleeve a slip of bamboo and said, "The Empress's command; open the gate for me."

"Let me look," said the warden.

"What! How dare you, an old servant of mine, behave thus?"

The warden let him pass. As soon as he had got outside he shouted to the warden, "Ssŭma I has raised a revolt, and you had better follow me."

The warden realised that he had made a mistake, and ran after Huan, but failed to come up with him.

"So Bag o' Wisdom has got away too; that is a pity, but what can we do?" said Ssŭma, when they reported the escape.

"The old horse always hankers after the old stable and manger, and he would have been useless to us," replied Chiang Chi.

Then Ssŭma called to him Hsü Yün and Ch'ên T'ai and said, "Go ye to Ts'ao Shuang and say that I have no other intention than to take away the military power from him and his brother."

As soon as they had left, he called Yin Ta-mu and ordered Chiang Chi prepare a letter to be taken to Ts'ao Shuang.

Said Ssŭma, "You are on good terms with the man and are the fittest person for this mission. Tell him that Chiang Chi and I are concerned solely with the military powers in the hands of himself and his brother, as we have sworn pointing to the Lo River."

So Yin Ta-mu went his way.

Out in the country Ts'ao Shuang was enjoying the hunting, flying his falcons and coursing his hounds. Suddenly came the news of the rising in the city and the memorial against him. He almost fell out of the saddle when they told him. The eunuch handed in the memorial to the king in the presence of Ts'ao, who took it and opened it. A minister in attendance was ordered to read it. It said:—

"On my return from the expedition into Liaotung His late Majesty summoned Your Majesty with Prince Ts'in, myself and certain others to his bedside, took me by the arm and impressed upon us all our duty in the years to be. Now Ts'ao Shuang has betrayed the trust placed in him, has disordered the kingdom, usurped power at court and seized upon power in the provinces. He has appointed the eunuch Chang Tang Commandant of the City to control the court and spy upon Your Majesty. He is surely lying in wait to seize the empire. He has sown dissension in the royal family and injured his own flesh and blood. The whole land is in confusion, and men's hearts are full of fear. All this is opposed to the injunctions of His late Majesty and his commands to me. Stupid and worthless as I am, yet I dare not forget his words. My colleagues, *T'ai-yu* Chiang Chi and *Shang-shu* Ssŭma Fu agree that Ts'ao Shuang is disloyal at heart. Great military powers should not be entrusted to brothers.

"I have memorialised Her Majesty and obtained her authority to act.

"All military powers have been wrested from the hands of the Ts'ao family, leaving them only the simple title of Marquis, so that hereafter they may be unable to hinder or control Your Majesty's actions. If there be any obstruction, the matter shall be summarily dealt with.

"Although in ill health, as a precautionary measure I have camped at the Floating Bridge, whence I write this."

When they had made an end of reading, the king turned to Ts'ao Shuang and said, "In the face of such words what mean you to do?"

Shuang was at a loss and turned to his younger brother, saying, "What now?"

Ts'ao Hsi replied, "I remonstrated with you, but you were obstinate and listened not. So it has come to this. Ssŭma I is false and cunning beyond measure. If K'ung-ming could not get the better of him, could we hope to do so? I see nothing but to yield that haply we may live."

Just at this moment arrived Hsin Ch'ang and Ssŭma Lu-chih. Ts'ao Shuang asked what tidings they brought.

They replied, "The city is completely and closely surrounded, the *T'ai-fu* is camped on the river at the Floating Bridge, and you cannot return. You must decide how to act at once."

Then galloped up Huan Fan, who said, "This is really rebellion; why not request His Majesty to proceed to Hsütu till provincial troops can arrive and deal with Ssŭma?"

Ts'ao Shuang replied, "How can we go to another place when all our families are in the city?"

"Fool! Even in this crisis you think only of life. You have the Son of Heaven with you here and command all the forces of the empire. None would dare disobey you, and yet you march quietly to death."

The unhappy man could not decide to strike a blow for safety; he did nothing but snivel.

Huan continued, "The stay in Hsütu would be but brief, and there are ample supplies for years. You have forces at your call at Nankuan. You hold the seal of Minister of War, and I have brought it with me. Everything is in your favour. Act! Act at once! Delay is death."

"Do not hurry me," said Ts'ao. "Let me think it over carefully."

Then came the two messengers of Ssŭma I, to say that he desired only to strip the Ts'aos of their military power. If they yielded they might return peacefully to the city.

Still the Ts'aos hesitated. Next arrived Yin Ta-mu with Ssŭma's second message that he had sworn by the Lo River to the singleness of his aim. He tendered the letter of Chiang Chi to the effect that if the conditions were complied with the Ts'aos might return to their palace in peace.

When Ts'ao Shuang seemed disposed to accept the assurance of Ssŭma, Huan inveighed against it, saying, "You are a dead man if you listen to the voice of these men."

Night found Ts'ao Shuang still vacillating. As twilight faded into darkness he stood, sword in hand, sad, sighing and weeping. And morning found him still trying to make up his mind.

Huan again urged him to decide upon some course. "You have had a whole day and a whole night for reflection and must decide," said he.

"I will not fight; I will yield all and save my house," said Ts'ao, throwing down his sword.

Huan left the tent wailing. "Ts'ao Chên might boast of his abilities, but his brothers are mere cattle," said he. He wept copiously.

The two messengers bade Ts'ao offer his seal of office to Ssŭma, and it was brought. Its custodian clung to it and would not give it up, saying, "Alas! that you, my lord, should resign your powers and make such a pitiful surrender. For surely you will not escape death in the eastern market-place."

"The *T'ai-fu* will surely keep faith with me," said Ts'ao.

The seal was borne away, and the captains, thus released from the bonds of discipline, dispersed and the hosts melted away. When the brothers reached the Floating Bridge, they were ordered to go to their dwellings, and they went. Their supporters were imprisoned to await the pleasure of the Emperor.

Ts'ao Shuang and his friends, so lately all-powerful, entered the city alone, without even a servant following. As Huan approached the bridge, Ssŭma, from horseback, pointed his whip disdainfully at him and said, "What brought you to this?" Huan made no reply, but with head bent followed the others.

It was decided to request the Emperor to declare the hunt at an end and order a return to the city. The three Ts'aos were confined in their own house, the gate whereof was fastened with a huge lock, and soldiers were set to guard it round about. They were sad and anxious, not knowing what would be their fate. Then Ts'ao Hsi said, "We have but little food left. Let us write and ask for supplies. If he send us food we may be sure he does not intend harm."

They wrote, and ample supplies were sent. This cheered them, and they thought their lives were safe.

The eunuch Chang Fang was arrested and put to the question. He said he was not the only one who had tried to subvert the government, and he named the five friends of Ts'ao Shuang. So they were arrested and, when interrogated, confessed that a revolt had been arranged for the third month. All were locked in one long wooden collar. The Warden of the Gate testified that Huan Fan had imposed upon him with a pretended command from Her Majesty and so had escaped out of the city. Beside he had said the *T'ai-fu* was a rebel.

Then said Ssŭma I, "When a man maligns another and is false, the punishment for such a crime as he imputes falls upon his own head."

Huan and those with him were thrown into prison.

Presently Ts'ao Shuang and his brothers, and all persons connected with them, were put to death in the market-place. All the treasure of their houses was sent to the public treasury.

Now there was a certain woman of the Hsiahou family who had been wife to a second cousin of Ts'ao Shuang's. Early left a childless widow, her father wished her to marry again. She refused and cut off one ear as a pledge of constancy. However, when the Ts'aos were all put to death her father arranged another marriage for her; whereupon she cut off her nose. Her own people were chagrined at her obstinate determination.

"For whom are you keeping your vow?" said they. "Man is but as the light dust upon the tender grass, and what is the good of mutilating your body?"

The woman replied, weeping, "The honourable woman does not break a vow of chastity for the sake of wealth, and the heart of a righteous woman is constant unto death. While the house of Ts'ao enjoyed prosperity I remained faithful; how much more should I be true now that it has fallen upon evil days? Can I act like a mere beast of the field?"

The story of her devotion came to the ears of Ssŭma, who praised her conduct and allowed her to adopt a son to rear as her own and so continue the family.

A poem says:—

> What is a man to be mindful of?
> A grain of dust on a blade of grass;
> Such virtue as Hsiahou's daughter had
> Stands out sublime as the ages pass.
> This fair young wife of gentle mien
> Dared all to maintain her purpose high.
> What man though strong in the flush of life
> Has equalled her in constancy?

After Ts'ao Shuang had suffered death, Chiang Chi recalled certain others who had been of his party and were still alive, notably Yang Tsung, who had opposed the surrender of the seal of the late minister. However, no action was taken against them.

"He is a righteous man who serves his master faithfully," said Ssŭma, and he even confirmed these men in their offices.

Hsin Ch'ang remembered that it had been on the advice of his sister that he had decided to stand by his lord, and thus had saved his reputation.

A poet has praised his sister's conduct.

> "You call him lord and take his pay,
> Then stand by him when danger nears."
> Thus to her brother spake Hsien-ying,
> And won fair fame though endless years.

A general amnesty was extended to all Ts'ao's partizans, and no officer was removed or dismissed for having supported the late order of things. All were left in possession of their property, and soon all was tranquillity.

However, it is to be noted that Ho and Têng met the unhappy end that Kuan Lu had foretold for them.

> The seer Kuan Lu was deeply read
> In all the lore of th' ancient sages.
> Thus he could see events to come
> As clear as those of former ages.
> And he perceived the soul of Ho,
> Already in the vale of gloom,
> And knew the outer shell of Têng
> Was hastening to an early tomb.

After his recovery of power, Ssŭma was made Prime Minister and received the Nine Gifts. Ssŭma refused these honours, but the king insisted and would take no denial. His two sons were made assistants to their father, and all state affairs fell under the control of these three.

However, Ssŭma remembered that one man, Hsiahou Pa, a member of the Ts'ao clan, still commanded at Yungchou. In his position he might be a real danger, and he must be removed. So an edict was issued calling him to the capital to discuss affairs. But instead of obeying this call, Hsiahou declared himself a rebel, although he had but a small force to support him. As soon as this was known, Kuo Huai marched to suppress the malcontent. The two armies were soon face to face, and Kuo went to the front and began to revile his opponent.

"How could you rebel against the ruling house, you who are of the same clan as our great founder, and who have always been treated generously?"

Hsiahou Pa replied, "My forefathers served the state right well, but who is this Ssŭma that he has put to death my kinsmen and would now destroy me? What is his aim, if it be not to usurp the Throne? If I can cut him off and so frustrate his design I shall at least be no traitor to the state."

Kuo Huai rode forward to attack, and Hsiahou advanced to the encounter. They fought a half score of bouts, and then Kuo turned and fled. But this was only a feint to lead on his enemy, for ere Hsiahou had gone far he heard a shout behind him and turned to see Ch'ên T'ai about to attack. At the same moment Kuo turned again, and thus Hsiahou was between two fires. He could effect nothing, so he fled, losing many men. Soon he decided that his only course was to desert to Shu.

Wherefore he went into Hanchung to see if haply the Later Ruler would accept his services. When Chiang Wei heard of his desire to surrender, he had doubts of his sincerity. However, after due enquiry Chiang was satisfied and allowed the renegade from Wei to enter the city. After making his obeisance, Hsiahou, with many tears, told the story of his wrongs. Chiang expressed sympathy.

Said he, "A thousand years ago Wei Tsŭ left the court of Chou in disgust, and this act has assured to him everlasting honour. You may be able now to assist in the restoration of the House of Han, and you will then stand no whit inferior to any man of antiquity."

A banquet was ordered, and while it was being prepared the host talked of affairs in the capital.

"The Ssŭma family is now most powerful and in a position to carry out any scheme they planned. Think you that they have any intentions against us?"

"The old traitor has enough to do with his rebellion; he has no leisure to trouble about any outside matters. However, two other men in Wei have lately come to the front, and if he sent them against your country and Wu it might go ill with you both."

"And who are these two?"

"One is named Chung Hui, a man of Ch'angsha; he is a descendant of the *T'ai-fu* Chung Yu. As a mere boy he was noted for being bold and smart. His father used to take him and his brother to court. Chung Hui was seven and his brother a year older. The Emperor Ts'ao P'ei noticed one day that the elder boy was sweating and asked him the reason.

" 'Whenever I am frightened the sweat pours out and I cannot help it,' " replied the boy.

" 'You do not seem frightened,' said the Emperor to the other.

" 'I am so frightened that the sweat cannot come out,' replied he.

"The Emperor was the only one who discerned the extraordinary ability of the boy. A little later the lad was always studying books on war and tactics, and became an able strategist, so that he won admiration from both Ssŭma and Chiang Chi.

"The second man is Têng Ai. He was left an orphan very early, but he was ambitious and enterprising. If he saw lofty mountains or wide marshes he always looked for those points where soldiers might be stationed or dépôts of provisions made or combustibles laid. People ridiculed him, but Ssŭma saw there was much to admire and employed the young man on his staff.

"Têng Ai had an impediment in his speech, so that he called himself 'Ai-Ai,' and Ssŭma used to make fun of him and asked him one day how many there were of him since he called himself 'Ai-Ai.'

"Têng at once replied, 'There was only one Fêng in the *Lun-yü* when Chieh Yu cried 'O Fêng.'

"This ready repartee shows the quickness of his intellect, and you may well be on your guard against him and the other, for they are to be feared."

"I do not think them worth even talking about," replied Chiang Wei.

Chiang Wei took Hsiahou Pa to Ch'êngtu and presented him to the king, telling the story of events in Loyang, the overthrow of Ts'ao Shuang, the rise of the Ssŭma family to supreme power, the weakness of Ts'ao Fang, the king, and then proposed that another attempt be made to re-establish the House of Han in its old capital.

But Fei I opposed any expedition, saying, "We have lately lost by death two trusty counsellors, and there is no one left fit to take care of the government. The attempt should be postponed."

"Not so," replied Chiang. "Life is short. Our days flash by as the glint of a white horse across a chink in the door. We are waiting and waiting. Are we never to try to restore Han to its old glory?"

"Remember the saying of the wise Sun: 'Know thyself and know thine enemy. Then is victory sure.' We are not the equals of the late Prime Minister, and where he failed, are we likely to succeed?"

Chiang said, "I would enlist the aid of the *Ch'iang*. I have lived near them in Shênsi and know them well. With their help, even if we do not gain the capital and the whole empire, we can at least conquer and hold all west of Shênsi."

The king here closed the discussion, saying, "Sir, as you desire to conquer Wei, do your best. I will not damp your enthusiasm."

Thus the king's consent was given. Then Chiang Wei left the court and betook himself, with Hsiahou Pa, into Hanchung to prepare for a new expedition.

"We will first send an envoy to the *Ch'iang* to make a league with them," said Chiang. "Then we will march out by Hsip'ing to Yungchou, where we will throw up two ramparts near the Ch'ü Hills and garrison them. The position is a point of vantage. Then we will send supplies to Ch'uank'ou, and advance gradually, according to the plan devised by the great strategist."

In the autumn of the year they sent the two Shu generals Chü An and Li Hsin, with a large force, to construct the two ramparts, of which Chü was to hold the eastern and Li the western.

When the news reached Yungchou, the Governor, Kuo Huai, sent a report to Loyang and also despatched a force to oppose the men of Shu. When that army arrived both the Shu captains led their men to meet it, but their armies were too weak and they once more retired into the city. The army of Wei laid siege and occupied the road that led to Hanchung, so that supplies were cut off. After some days, and when the men of Shu began to feel the pinch of hunger, Kuo Huai came to see what progress his two lieutenants were making. At sight of the position he rejoiced exceedingly, and when he returned to camp he said to Ch'ên T'ai, "In this high country the city must be short of water, which means that the besieged must come out for supplies. Let us cut off the streams that supply them, and they will perish of thirst."

So the soldiers were set to work to divert the streams above the city, and the besieged were soon distressed. Li Hsin led out a strong force to try to seize the water sources and fought stubbornly, but was at length worsted and driven back within the walls.

Meanwhile the soldiers were parched with thirst. They could not account for the delay of Chiang Wei's reinforcements and finally decided that Li Hsin should try to fight his way out and get help.

So the gates were opened, and Li rode out with a score or so of horsemen. These were opposed and had to fight every inch of the way, but eventually the leader won though severely wounded. All his men had fallen.

That night a strong north wind brought a heavy fall of snow, and the besieged were thus temporarily relieved from the water famine. They melted the snow and prepared food.

Li Hsin, sorely wounded, made his way west along the hill paths. After two days he fell in with Chiang Wei. He dismounted, prostrated himself and told his story.

"The delay is not due to my slackness; the allies we depended upon have not come," said Chiang.

Chiang sent an escort with the wounded officer to conduct him to Ch'êngtu, where his wounds could be treated. Turning to his colleague, Hsiahou Pa, he asked if he had any plan to propose.

Hsiahou replied, "If we wait for the coming of the *Ch'iang* it looks as if we shall be too late to relieve Ch'üshan. It is very probable that Yungchou has been left undefended, wherefore I propose that you go toward Niut'ou Hills and work round to the rear of Yungchou, which will cause the Wei armies to fall back to relieve Yungchou and so relieve our force."

"The plan appears excellent," replied Chiang. And he set out.

When Ch'ên T'ai knew that Li Hsin had escaped, he said to his chief. "Now that this man has got out he will tell Chiang Wei of the danger, and he will conclude that our efforts are concentrated on the ramparts and will endeavour to attack our rear. Therefore I suggest, General, that you go to the T'ao River and stop the supplies of our enemies, while I go to the Niut'ou Hills and smite them. They will retreat as soon as they know their supplies are threatened."

So Kuo Huai marched secretly to the T'ao River, while his colleague went to the hills.

When the Shu army led by Chiang Wei came near they heard a great shouting, and the scouts came in to report that the road was barred. Chiang Wei himself rode out to look.

"So you intended to attack Yungchou, did you?" shouted Ch'ên T'ai. "But we know it and have been watching for you a long time."

Chiang Wei rode forth to attack. His opponent advanced with a flourish of his sword, and they engaged. Ch'ên T'ai soon ran away. Then the men of Shu came forward and fell on, driving the men of Wei back to the summit of the hills.

But they halted there, and Chiang encamped at the foot of the hills, whence he challenged the enemy every day. But he could gain no victory.

Seeing no result after some days of this, Hsiahou said, "This is no place to remain in. We can get no victory and are tempting fate by remaining open to a surprise. I think we should retire till some better plan can be tried."

Just then it was reported that the supplies road was in the hands of the enemy, and it was imperative to retreat. Hsiahou marched away first, and Chiang covered the retreat. Ch'ên T'ai pursued in five divisions along five different roads, but Chiang got possession of the meeting point and held them all in check, finally forcing them back on the hills. But from this position such a heavy discharge of arrows and stones was maintained that the Wei armies were forced to abandon their position. Chiang went to the T'ao River, where the men of Wei attacked. Chiang went to and fro smiting where he could, but he was surrounded and only got out by a desperate effort and after suffering great loss.

Chiang hastened toward Yangp'ing Pass, but fell in with another body of the enemy, at the head of which he saw a fierce, youthful leader, who at once rode out furiously to attack.

This leader had a round face, long ears and a square mouth with thick lips. Below his left eye was a large hairy mole. It was the elder son of Ssŭma I. He was a General of Cavalry.

"Simpleton, how dare you stand in my way?" yelled Chiang, as he rode forward with his spear set.

Ssŭma Shih met the attack, and three bouts were fought. Chiang Wei came off victor and so was free to continue his way. Presently he reached the pass and was welcomed within its sheltering walls. Ssŭma attacked soon after his arrival, but those within the ramparts replied with the multiple crossbows which threw ten bolts at each discharge. For the men of Shu had made these engines of war after the design left by Chuko Liang.

> Owing to superior weapons, Shu defeated Wei,
> Wei will ne'er recover what was lost that day.

What befell Ssŭma Shih will be told in the next chapter.

CHAPTER CVIII.

As has been said, Chiang Wei, in his retreat, fell in with a force under Ssŭma Shih, barring his road. It came about thus. After the capture of Yungchou, Kuo Huai had sent a flying messenger to the capital and the king summoned Ssŭma I for advice. It had then been decided to send reinforcements to Yungchou, and five legions had marched, led by the son of the Prime Minister. On the march Ssŭma Shih had heard that the Shu army had been beaten back and had concluded they were weak. So he decided to meet them on the road and give battle. Near the Yangp'ing Pass, however, the roads had been lined with men armed with the multiple crossbows designed by Chuko Liang. Since his death large numbers of these weapons had been made, and the bolts from them, which went in flights of ten, were poisoned. Consequently the Wei losses were very heavy, and Shih himself barely escaped with life. However, eventually he returned to Loyang.

From the walls of Ch'üshan the Shu captain Chü An, watched anxiously for the expected help. As it came not, he ultimately surrendered. And Chiang Wei, with a greatly reduced army, marched back into Hanchung.

In the third year of *Chia-P'ing*, in the eighth month, Ssŭma I fell ill. His sickness increased rapidly, and, feeling that his end was near, he called his two sons to his bedside to hear his last words.

"I have served Wei many years and reached the highest rank possible among ministers. People have suspected me of ulterior aims, but I have always felt afraid to take the final step. After my death the government will be in your hands, and you must be doubly careful."

He passed away even as he said these last words. The sons informed the king, who conferred high honours upon the dead and advanced his sons, the elder to the rank of General with the leadership of the Presidents, and the younger to the rank of General of Cavalry.

It is here necessary to return and survey events in Wu. Sun Ch'üan had named his son Têng as his heir. His mother was the Lady Hsü. But Têng died, and the second son was chosen his successor. His mother was the Lady Wang. A quarrel arose between the new Heir Apparent and Princess

Chin, who maligned him and intrigued against him, so that he was set aside. He died of mortification. Then the third son was named; his mother's name was P'an.

At this time Lu Hsün and Chuko Chin were both dead, and the business of the government, great and small, was in the hands of Chuko Ch'üo.

In the first year of *T'ai-Ho*, on the first of the eighth month, a great gale passed over Wu. The waves rose to a great height, and the water stood eight feet deep over the low-lying lands. The pines and cypresses, which grew at the cemetery of the kings of Wu, were uprooted and carried to the gates of Chienyehch'êng, where they stuck, roots upward, in the road.

Sun Ch'üan was frightened and fell ill. In the early days of the next year his illness became serious, whereupon he called in Chuko Ch'üo and Lü Tai to hear the declaration of his last wishes. Soon after he died, at the age of seventy-one. He had ruled in Wu for twenty-four years.

> A hero, grey-eyed and red-bearded,
> He called forth devotion from all.
> He lorded the east without challenge
> Till death's one imperative call.

Chuko immediately placed his late lord's son Liang on the throne, and the opening of the new reign was marked by the adoption of the style *Ta-Hsing*. A general amnesty was proclaimed. The late ruler received the posthumous style of "Great Emperor" and was buried in Chiangling.

When these things were reported in the Wei capital, Ssŭma Shih's first thought was to attack the east. But his plans were opposed by Fu Ku, saying, "Remember what a strong defence to Wu is the Great River. The country has been many times attacked, but never conquered. Rather let us all hold what we have till the time be expedient to possess the whole empire."

Shih replied, "The way of Heaven changes thrice in a century, and no emperor is permanent. I wish to attack Wu."

Ssŭma Chao, his brother, was in favour of attack, saying "The occasion is most opportune. Sun Ch'üan is newly dead and the present ruler is a child."

An expedition was decided upon. There was a certain general named Wang Ch'ung, whose title was "Conqueror of the South," and it was settled that he should command. He led away ten legions with orders to attack Tunghsing. Another leader, Wuch'iu Chien, was given ten legions to go against Wuch'ang. They marched in three divisions. Ssŭma Chao went in chief command.

The armies drew near to the Wu frontiers in the tenth month and camped. Chao called together the various commanders to decide upon plans. He said, "This Tunghsing district is most important to Wu. They have built a great rampart, with walls right and left to defend Ch'aohu from an attack in the rear. You gentlemen will have to exercise extreme care."

Then he bade Wang Ch'ung and Wuch'iu Chien each to take a legion and place themselves right and left, but not to advance till Tunghsing had been captured. When that city had fallen, these two were to go forward at the same time. Hu Tsun was to lead the van.

The first step was to construct a floating bridge to storm the rampart. The two walls should then be captured.

News of the danger soon came to Wu, and Chuko Ch'üo called a council to take measures.

Then said Ting Fêng, whose title was "Pacificator of the North, "Tunghsing is of the utmost importance as its loss would endanger Wuch'ang."

"I agree with you," said Chuko. "You say just what I think. You should lead three thousand marines up the river in thirty ships while I follow on land."

Three other legions were sent out along different roads to help where needed. The signal for the general advance was to be three bombs.

Hu Tsun, of Wei, crossed on the floating bridge, took and camped on the rampart. He then sent Huan Chia and Han Tsung to assault the flanking forts, which were held by Ch'uan I and Liu Lüeh. These forts had high walls and strong, and made a good resistance, but the garrison dared not venture out to attack so strong a force as was attacking them.

Hu Tsun made a camp at Hsüchou. It was then the depth of winter and intensely cold. Heavy snow fell. Thinking that no warlike operations were possible in such weather, Hu and his officers made a great feast.

In the midst of the feasting came one to report that thirty ships had come up river. The general went out to look and saw them come into the bank. He made out a hundred men on each. As they were so few, he returned to the feast and told his officers that there was nothing to be alarmed at. Giving orders to keep a careful watch, they all returned to enjoy themselves.

Ting Fêng's ships were all drawn up in line. Then he said to his officers, "To-day there is indeed a grand opportunity for a brave man to distinguish himself. We shall need the utmost freedom of movement, so throw off your armour, leave your helmets, cast aside your long spears and reject your heavy halberds. Short swords are the weapons for to-day."

From the shore the men of Wei watched them with amusement, taking no trouble to prepare against an attack. But suddenly bombs exploded, and simultaneously with the roar of the third Ting Fêng sprang ashore at the head of his men. They dashed up the bank and made straight for the camp.

The men of Wei were taken completely by surprise and were helpless. Han Tsung grasped one of the halberds that stood by the door of the commander's tent, but Ting Fêng stabbed him in the breast, and he rolled over. Huan Chia went round and came up on the left. Just as he poised his spear to thrust, Ting gripped it under his arm. Huan let go and turned to flee, but Ting sent his sword flying after him and caught him in the shoulder. He turned and was thrust through.

The three companies of Wu marines went to and fro in the camp of Wei slaying as they would. Hu Tsun fled. His men ran away across the floating bridge, but that gave way and many were thrown into the water and drowned. Dead bodies lay about on the snow in large numbers. The spoil of military gear that fell to Wu was immense. The other Wei leaders retreated.

When Chuko had finished the feastings and distribution of rewards in celebration of victory, he thought he could push on and capture the capital. So he told his officers that this was his intention, and also sent away letters to Shu to engage the aid of Chiang Wei, promising that the empire should be divided between them when they had taken it.

An army of twenty legions was told off to march on the capital. Just as it was starting, a stream of white vapour was seen emerging from the earth, and as it spread it gradually enveloped the whole army so that men could not see each other.

"It is a white rainbow," said Chiang Yen, "and it bodes ill to the army. I advise you, O *T'ai-fu*, to return and not march against Wei."

"How dare you utter such ill-omened words and blunt the keenness of my army?" cried Chuko, angrily.

He bade the lictors take him out and put him to death. Chiang's colleagues interceded for him, and he was spared, but he was stripped of all rank. Orders were issued to march quickly.

Then Ting offered a suggestion, saying, "Wei's chief defence is Hsinch'êng; it would be a sore blow to Ssŭma Chao to capture it."

Chuko welcomed this suggestion and gave orders to march on Hsinch'êng. They came up and found the city gates closed, wherefore they began to besiege the city.

A hasty messenger was sent to Loyang, and one Yü Sung told the Prime Minister, Ssŭma Shih.

Yü said, "Wu is laying siege to Hsinch'êng; the city should not try to repulse the attack, but simply hold out as long as possible. When the besiegers have exhausted their provisions they will be compelled to retire. As they retreat we can smite them. However, it is necessary to provide against any invasion from Shu."

Accordingly Ssŭma Chao was sent to reinforce Kuo Huai so as to keep off Chiang Wei, while Wuch'iu Chien and Hu Tsun kept the army of Wu at bay.

For months the army of Chuko battered at Hsinch'êng without success. He urged his captains to strenuous efforts, threatening to put to death anyone who was dilatory. At last his attacks looked like succeeding, for one of the corners of the wall seemed shaken.

Then the commander of Hsinch'êng thought of a device. He sent a messenger to the commander of the attack to say that it was a rule in Wei that if a city held out against attack for a hundred days its commandant might surrender without penalty. "Now the city has held out for over ninety days, and my master hopes you will allow him to withstand the few days necessary to complete the hundred, when he will yield."

The messenger also presented a letter to the same effect, and Chuko had no doubts that the story was genuine. The attack therefore slackened, and the defenders enjoyed a rest. But all that was really desired was time wherein to strengthen the weak angle of the wall. As soon as the attacks ceased the defenders pulled down the houses near the corner and repaired the wall with the material. As soon as the repairs were complete, the commandant threw off all pretence and cried from the wall, "I have half a year's provisions yet and will not surrender to any curs of Wu."

The defence became as vigorous as before the truce. Chuko was enraged at being so tricked, and urged on the attack. But one day one of the thousands of arrows that flew from the rampart struck him in the forehead, and he fell. He was borne to his tent, but the wound inflamed, and he became very ill.

Their leader's illness disheartened the men, and, moreover, the weather became very hot. Sickness invaded the camp, so that when Chuko had recovered sufficiently to resume command the men were unfit. An officer who told him the men were too ill to give battle met with an outburst of fierce anger, and Chuko said he would behead the next man who mentioned illness.

When the report of this threat got abroad, the men began to desert freely. Presently one Ts'ai Lin, with his whole company, went over to the enemy. Chuko began to be alarmed and rode through the camps to see for himself. Surely enough, the men all looked sickly, with pale and puffy faces.

The siege had to be raised, and Chuko retired into his own country. The enemy harassed his march and inflicted a severe defeat. Mortified by the course of events, he did not report his return, but pretended illness.

King Liang went to the camp to see his general, and the officers came to call. In order to silence comment, Chuko assumed an attitude of extreme severity, investigating every one's conduct very minutely, punishing rigourously any fault or shortcoming and meting out sentences of banishment, or death with exposure, till every one walked in teror. He also placed two of his own clique over the royal guards, making them the teeth and claws of his vengeance.

Now Sun Hsün was a great grandson of Sun Ching, brother of Sun Chien. Sun Ch'üan loved him and had put him in command of the guards. He was enraged at being superseded by the two creatures of Chuko Ch'üo, and intrigued with one T'eng Yin, who had an old quarrel with Chuko.

Taking advantage of this rift, T'êng said to Sun Hsün, "This Chuko is as cruel as he is powerful. He abuses his authority and no one is safe against him. I also think he is aiming at something yet higher, and you, Sir, as one of the ruling family ought to put a stop to it."

"I agree with you, and I want to get rid of him," replied Sun. "Now I will obtain an edict condemning him to death."

Both went in to see King Liang, and they laid the matter before him.

"I am afraid of him, too," replied the king. "I have wanted to remove him for some time, but have found no opportunity. If you would prove your loyalty you would do it for me."

Then said T'êng, "Your Majesty can give a banquet and invite him, and let a few bravos be ready hidden behind the arras. At a signal, as the dropping of a wine cup, they might slay him, and all further trouble would be avoided."

Chuko Ch'üo had never been to court since his return from the unfortunate expedition. Under a plea of indisposition he had remained moping at home. One day he was going out of his reception room when he suddenly saw coming in a person dressed in the hempen garb of mourning.

"Who are you?" said he, rather roughly.

The person seemed too terror-stricken to reply or resist when he was seized. They questioned him, and he said he was in mourning for his father newly dead, and had come into the city to seek a priest to read the liturgy. He had entered by mistake, thinking it was a temple.

The gate wardens were questioned. They said, "There are scores of us at the gate, which is never unwatched. We have not seen a man enter."

Chuko raged and had the whole lot put to death. But that night he was restless and sleepless. By and by he heard a rending sound that seemed to come from the reception hall, so he arose and went to see what it was. The great main beam had broken in two.

Chuko, much disturbed, returned to his chamber to try once more to sleep. But a cold wind blew, and, shivering in the chilly air, he saw the figures of the hempen-clad mourner and the gate wardens he had put to death. They advanced toward him holding their heads in their hands and seemed to threaten him. He was frightened, and fell in a swoon.

Next morning, when washing his face, the water seemed tainted with the smell of blood. He bade the maid throw it away and bring more; it made no difference, the odour was still there.

He was perplexed and distressed. Then came a messenger with an invitation to a royal banquet. He had his carriage prepared. As he was passing through the gate a yellow dog jumped up and caught hold of his garment and then howled lugubriously.

"The dog even mocks me," said he, annoyed, and he bade his attendants take it away. Then he set out for the palace. Before he had gone far, he saw a white rainbow rise out of the earth and reach up to the sky. While he was wondering what this might portend, his friend Chang Yüeh came up and spake a word of warning.

"I feel doubtful about the real purpose of this banquet," said Chang, "and advise you not to go."

Chuko gave orders to drive home again, but before he had reached his own gate the two conspirators rode up and asked why he was turning back.

"I feel unwell and cannot see the king to-day," replied Chuko.

They replied, "This court is appointed to be held especially to do honour to you and the army. You have not yet reported, and there is a banquet for you. You may be ill, but you really must go to court."

Chuko yielded, and once more set his face toward the palace. The two conspirators went with him, and his friend Chang followed. The banquet was spread when he arrived, and after he had made his obeisance he went to his place.

When the wine was brought in Chuko, thinking it might be poisoned, excused himself from drinking on account of his state of health.

"Will you have some of the medicated wine brought from your own residence?" said Sun Hsün.

"Yes; I could drink that," replied he.

So a servant was sent for a supply that he might drink with the other guests.

After several courses, the king made an excuse and left the banquet hall. Sun went to the foot of the hall and changed his garments of ceremony for more homely garb, but underneath these he put on armour. Then suddenly he raised his keen sword and ran up the hall, shouting, "The king has issued an edict to slay a rebel."

Chuko, startled so that he dropped his cup, laid his hand upon his sword. But he was too late; his head rolled to the floor. His friend Chang drew his sword and rushed at the assassin, but Sun evaded the full force of the blow and was only wounded in the finger. Sun slashed back at Chang and wounded him in the right arm. Then the bravos dashed in and finished him.

The ruffians were then sent to murder the Chuko family, while the bodies of the two victims were hastily rolled in matting, thrown into a cart, taken to the outside of the south gate and tossed into a rubbish pit.

While Chuko was absent in the palace, his wife sat in the women's quarters at home feeling strangely unquiet. Presently a maid came in and, when she drew near her mistress, said, "Why does your clothing smell of blood?"

To her horror the maid suddenly transformed into a weird creature with rolling eyes and gritting teeth, that went dancing about the room and leaping till it touched the roof-beams, shrieking all the time, "I am Chuko Ch'üo, and I have been slain by that dastard Sun Hsün."

By this time the whole family were frightened and began wailing. And a few minutes later the residence was surrounded by a crowd of armed men sent to murder the inmates, whom they bound, carried off to the market-place and put to the sword.

These things occurred in the second year of the period *Ta-Hsing*. Before Chuko Chin, father of the murdered minister, died he had a premonition that his son's ability would lead him into trouble and that he would not safeguard his family. Others had also predicted an early death. A certain officer in Wei said Chuko would die soon, and when asked why, replied, "Can a man live long when his dignity endangers that of his lord?"

Sun Hsün, the chief conspirator and real murderer, became Prime Minister in place of his victim. He was also placed in command of all the military forces, and became very powerful. The control of all matters was in his hands.

When the letter asking help from Chiang Wei arrived in Shu, Chiang had audience with the king and requested authority to raise an army against the north.

> The army fought, but fought in vain,
> Success may crown a new campaign.

Who were victorious will appear in the next chapter.

CHAPTER CIX.

Ssŭma Surrounded; a Han Leader Employs an Unexpected Ruse;
The King Dethroned; Retribution for the Wei Family.

It was in the sixteenth year of *Yen-Hsi* that Chiang Wei's army of twenty legions was ready to march against the House of Wei. Miao Hua and Chang I were leaders of the van; Hsiahou Pa was strategist; Chang Ni was in command of the commissariat. The army marched out by the Yangp'ing Pass.

Discussing the plan of campaign with Hsiahou Pa, Chiang Wei said, "Our former attack on Yungchou failed, so this time they will doubtless be even better prepared to resist. What do you suggest?"

The strategist replied, "Nanan is the only well-provided place in all Shênsi; if we take that it will serve as an excellent base. Our former ill-success was due to the non-arrival of the *Ch'iang*. Let us therefore send early to tell them to assemble, after which we will move out at Shihying and march to Nanan by way of Tungt'ing."

Chiang approved the plan and at once sent Ch'i Chêng as his envoy, bearing gifts of gold and pearls and Ssuch'uan silk to win the help of the Prince of the *Ch'iang*, whose name was Mitang. The mission was successful; the prince accepted the presents and sent five legions to Nanan under the leadership of Ohoshaoko.

When Kuo Huai heard of the threatened attack, he sent a hasty memorial to Loyang. Ssŭma Shih at once asked who of his captains would go out to meet the army from the west. Hsü Chih volunteered, and as the Prime Minister had a high opinion of his capacity, he was appointed leader of the van. The brother of the Prime Minister, Ssŭma Chao, went as Commander-in-chief.

The Wei army set out for Shênsi, reached Tungt'ing and there fell in with Chiang Wei. When both sides were arrayed Hsü Chih, who wielded a mighty axe called "Splitter of Mountains" as his weapon, rode out and challenged. Miao Hua went forth to accept, but after a few bouts he took advantage of a feint and fled.

Then Chang I set his spear and rode forth to continue the fight. He also soon fled and returned within his own ranks. Thereupon Hsü Chih gave the signal to fall on in force, and the army of Shu lost the day. They retired thirty *li*; Ssŭma also drew off his men, and both sides encamped.

"Hsü Chih is very formidable; how can we overcome him?" asked Chiang Wei.

"To-morrow make pretence of defeat and so draw them into an ambush," was the reply.

"But remember whose son this Ssŭma Chao is," said Chiang. "He cannot be a novice in war, and if he sees a likely spot for an ambush he will halt. Now the men of Wei have cut our communications many times; let us do the same to them, and we may slay this Hsü."

He called in the two leaders of his van and gave them secret orders, sending them in different directions. Then he laid iron caltrops along all the approaches and planted *chevaux de frise* ("deer-horns") as if making a permanent defence. When the men of Wei came up and challenged, the men of Shu refused battle.

The scouts discovered that the Shu supplies were coming up along the rear of T'iehlung Mountains, and they were using the wooden oxen and running horses as transport. They also reported the look of permanency in the defences and said they were evidently awaiting the arrival of their allies the barbarian tribes.

Then said Ssŭma, "We formerly defeated the army of Shu by cutting off supplies, and we can do that again. Let half a legion go out to-night and occupy the road."

About the middle of the first watch Hsü Chih marched across the hills, and when he came to the other side he saw a couple of hundred men driving a hundred or so head of mechanical animals laden with grain and forage. His men rushed down upon them with shouts, and the men of Shu, seeing that their road was impassable, abandoned their supplies and ran away. Hsü took possession of the supply train, which he sent back to his own camp under the escort of half his men. With the other half he set out in pursuit.

About ten *li* away, the road was found blocked with carts set across the track. Some of his men dismounted to clear the way, but as they did so the brushwood on both sides burst into a blaze. Hsü at once drew off his men and turned to retire, but coming to a defile he found the road again blocked with waggons, and again the brushwood began to burn. He made a dash to escape, but before he could get clear a bomb roared, and he saw the men of Shu coming down on him from two directions. Both fell on Hsü with great fury, and the men of Wei were wholly defeated. Hsü Chih himself got clear, but without any following.

He struggled on till he and his steed were almost spent with fatigue. Presently he saw another company of the enemy in his way, and the leader was Chiang Wei. He could make no resistance. His horse fell from a spear thrust, and as Hsü Chih lay on the ground he was cut to pieces.

Meanwhile those men of Wei who had been sent to escort to camp the convoy of supplies which they had seized were captured by Hsiahou Pa. They surrendered. Hsiahou then stripped them of their weapons and clothing and therein disguised some of his own men. Holding aloft banners of Wei, these disguised men made for the Wei camp. When they arrived they were mistaken by those in the camp for comrades, and the gates were thrown open.

They rushed in and began to slay. Taken wholly by surprise, Ssŭma Chao leaped upon his steed and fled. But Miao Hua met him and drove him back. Then appeared Chiang Wei in the path of retreat, so that no road lay open. Ssŭma made off for the hills, hoping to be able to hold out on the T'iehlung Hill.

Now there was but one road up the hill, which rose steeply on all sides. There was but one small spring of water, enough to serve a hundred men or so, while Ssŭma's force numbered six thousand. Their enemies had blocked the only road. This one fountain was unequal to supplying the needs of the beleaguered army, and soon they were tormented with thirst. In despair, Ssŭma looked up to heaven and sighed, saying, "Death will surely come to me here."

> The host of Wei on T'iehlung Hill
> Were once fast held by Chiang Wei's skill;
> When P'ang first crossed the Maling line
> His strategy was reckoned fine
> As Hsiang Yü's at the Nine Mile Hill;
> Both bent opponents to their will.

In this critical situation a certain civil officer, Wang T'ao by name, reminded his leader of what Kêng Kung had done, saying, "O General, why do you not imitate Kêng Kung, who, being in great need, prostrated himself and prayed at a well, wherefrom he afterwards was supplied with sweet water?"

So the leader went to the summit of the hill and knelt beside the spring and prayed thus:—"The humble Chao received a command to repulse the army of Shu. If he is to die here, then may this spring cease its flow, when he will end his own life and let his soldiers yield to the enemy. But if his allotted span of life be not reached, then, O Blue Vault, increase the flow of water and save the lives of this multitude."

Thus he prayed; and the waters gushed forth in plenty, so that they all quenched their thirst and lived.

Chiang Wei had surrounded the hill, holding the army thereon as in a prison. He said to his officers, "I have always regretted that our great minister was unable to capture Ssŭma I in the Shangfang Valley, but now I think his son is doomed to fall into our hands."

However, news of the dangerous position of Ssŭma Chao had come to Kuo Huai, who set about a rescue.

Ch'ên T'ai said to him, "Chiang Wei has made a league with the *Ch'iang*, and they are helping him. They will first take Nanan. If they have arrived, and you go away to rescue Ssŭma, leaving this city weak, they will attack from the rear. Therefore I would propose to send some one to the barbarians to try to create a diversion and get them to retire. If they are disposed of, you may go to the rescue of Ssŭma.

Kuo saw there was much reason in this and told Ch'ên to take a small force and go himself to the camp of the Prince of the *Ch'iang*. When he reached the camp he threw off his armour and entered weeping and crying that he was in danger of death.

He said, "Kuo Huai sets himself up as superior to everyone and is trying to slay me. Therefore I have come to offer my services to you. I know all the secrets of the Wei army, and, if you will, this very night I can lead you to their camp. I have friends in the camp to help, and you can destroy it."

Prince Mitang was taken with the scheme, and sent his lieutenant Ohoshaoko to go with Ch'ên. The deserters from Wei were placed in the rear, but Ch'ên himself rode with the leading body of *Ch'iang*. They set out at the second watch and soon arrived. They found the gates open, and Ch'ên rode in boldly.

But when the *Ch'iang* galloped in, there suddenly arose a great cry as men and horses went tumbling into great pits. At the same time Ch'ên came round in the rear and attacked, while Kuo appeared on the flank. The barbarians trampled each other down, and many were killed. Those who escaped death surrendered, and the leader, Ohoshaoko, committed suicide.

Kuo and Ch'ên then hastened back into the camp of the *Ch'iang*. Mitang, taken unprepared, rushed out of his tent to get to horse, but was made prisoner. He was taken before Kuo Huai, who hastily dismounted, loosed the prisoner's bonds and soothed him with kindly words.

"Our government has always regarded you as a loyal and true friend," said Kuo. "Why then are you helping our enemies?"

Mitang sank to the ground in confusion, while Kuo continued, "If you will now raise the siege of T'iehlung Hill and drive off the men of Shu, I will memorialise and obtain a substantial reward for you."

Mitang agreed. He set out forthwith, his own men leading and the men of Wei in the rear. At the third watch he sent on a messenger to tell Chiang Wei of his coming. And the Shu leader was glad. Mitang was invited to enter, leaving the greater portion of his men outside.

On the march the men of Wei had mingled with the *Ch'iang*, and many of them were in the forefront of the army. Mitang went up toward the gate with a small company, and Chiang Wei with Hsiahou Pa went to welcome him. Just as they met, before Mitang could say a word, the Wei captains dashed on past him and set on to slay. Chiang was taken aback, leaped on his steed and fled, while the mixed force of men of Shu and barbarians drove the camp defenders before them and sent them flying.

When Chiang leaped upon his steed at the gate he had no weapon in his hand, only his bow and quiver hung at his shoulder. In his hasty flight the arrows fell out and the quiver was empty, so when he set off for the hills with Kuo Huai in pursuit, Chiang had nothing to oppose to the spears of his pursuers. As they came near he laid hands upon his bow and made as if to shoot. The string twanged and Kuo Huai blenched. But as no arrow went flying by he knew Chiang had none to shoot. Kuo therefore hung his spear, took his bow and shot. Chiang caught the arrow as it flew by and fitted it to his bowstring. He waited till his enemy came quite near, when he pulled the string with all his force and sent the arrow flying straight at Kuo's face. Kuo fell even as the bowstring sang.

Chiang pulled up and turned to finish his fallen enemy, but the men of Wei were nearly upon him, and he had only time to snatch up his spear and ride off. Now that Chiang Wei was armed and their own leader wounded, the soldiers of Wei had no more desire to fight. They picked up their general and carried him to camp. There the arrow-head was pulled out, but the flow of blood could not be staunched, and Kuo Huai died.

Ssŭma descended from the hill as soon as Chiang moved away, and pursued some distance.

Hsiahou Pa rejoined his colleague as soon as he could, and they marched together. The losses of Shu in this defeat were very heavy. On the road they dared not halt to muster or reform, but went helter-skelter into Hanchung. The leaders said to themselves that, though they had been defeated, they had killed two generals on the other side and had damaged the prestige of Wei.

After rewarding the *Ch'iang* for their help, Ssŭma led his army back to Loyang, where he joined his brother in administering the government. They were too strong for any of the officers to dare opposition, and they terrorised King Fang so that he shook with fright whenever he saw Ssŭma Shih at court, and felt as if needles were being stuck into his back.

One day, when the king was holding a Court, Ssŭma Shih came into the hall wearing his sword. The king hastily left his place to receive him.

"What does this mean? Is this the correct etiquette for a prince when his minister approaches?" said Ssŭma, smiling. "I pray Your Majesty remember your dignity and listen while the ministers address the Throne."

Court business then proceeded. Ssŭma decided every question without reference to the king, and when he retired he stalked haughtily down the hall and went home, followed by his escort, which numbered thousands of horse and foot.

When the king left the court only three followed him to the private apartments. They were Hsiahou Hsien, Li Fêng and Chang Ch'i, all ministers. The last was the father of his Consort. Sending away the servants, the king and these three went into a private chamber.

Seizing his father-in-law's hand, the king began to weep, saying, "That man Ssŭma Shih treats me as a child and regards the officers of state as if they were so many straws. I am sure the throne will be his one day."

And he wept bitterly. Said Li, "Do not be so sad, Sire. I am but a poor sort of person, but if Your Majesty will give me authority, I will call together all the bold men in the country and slay this man."

"It was from fear of this man that my brother was forced to go over to Shu," said Hsiahou Hsien. "If he were destroyed, my brother could return. I belong to a family related to the rulers of the state for many generations, and I cannot sit still while a wretch ruins the government. Put my name in the command as well as Li's, and we will work together to remove him."

"But I am afraid," said the king.

They wept. The three ministers pledged themselves to work together for the destruction of the tyrant. The king them stripped himself of his innermost garment, gnawed his finger till the blood flowed and with his finger-tip traced a command in blood. He gave it to his father-in-law, saying, "My ancestor the Emperor Wu (Ts'ao Ts'ao) put to death Tung Ch'êng for just such a matter as this, so you must be exceedingly careful and maintain the greatest secrecy."

"Oh, why use such ill-omened words?" cried Li Fêng. "We are not like Tung any more than Ssŭma Shih resembles your great ancestor. Have no doubts."

The three conspirators took leave and went out carrying the edict with them. Beside the Tunghua Gate of the palace they saw their enemy coming to meet them wearing a sword. Following him were many armed men. They took the side of the road to let the party go by.

"Why are you three so late in leaving the palace?" asked Ssŭma.

"His Majesty was reading, and we stayed with him," said Li.

"What was he reading?"

"The histories of the Hsia, Shang and Chou dynasties."

"What questions did the king ask as he read those books?"

"He asked about I Yin and how he upheld the Shangs; and Duke Chou, how he acted when he was regent. And we told His Majesty that you were both I Yin and Duke Chou to him."

Ssŭma smiled grimly. "Why did you compare me with those two? You made him think me a rebel like Wang Chieh or Tung Cho."

"How should we dare when we are your subordinates?"

"You are a lot of flatterers," said Ssŭma, angrily. "And what were you crying about in that private chamber with the king?"

"We did no such thing."

"Your eyes are still red; you cannot deny that."

Hsiahou Hsien then knew that they had been betrayed already, so he broke out into a volley of abuse, crying, "Well, we were crying because of your conduct, because you terrorise over the king and are scheming to usurp the Throne."

"Seize him!" roared Ssŭma.

Hsiahou threw back his sleeves and struck at Ssŭma with his fists, but the lictors pulled him back. Then the three were searched, and on Chang was found the blood-stained garment of the king. They handed it to their chief, who recognised the object of his search, the secret edict.

It said:—"The two brothers Ssŭma have stolen away all my authority and are plotting to take the Throne. The edicts I have been forced to issue do not represent my wishes, and hereby all officers, civil and military, may unite to destroy these two and restore the authority of the Throne. These ends achieved, I will reward those who help to accomplish them."

Ssŭma, more angry than ever, said, "So you wish to destroy me and my brother. This is too much."

He ordered his followers to cut the three to pieces on the public execution ground and to destroy their whole clans.

The three reviled without ceasing. On the way to the place of execution they ground their teeth with rage, spitting out the pieces they broke off. They died muttering curses.

Ssŭma then went to the rear apartments of the palace, where he found the Emperor talking with his Consort. Just as he entered she was saying, "The palace is full of spies, and if this comes out it will mean trouble for me."

Ssŭma strode in, sword in hand.

"My father placed Your Majesty on the throne, a service no less worthy than that of Duke Chou; I have served Your Majesty as I Yin served his master. Now is kindness met by enmity and service regarded as a fault. Your Majesty has plotted with two or three insignificant officials to slay me and my brother. Why is this?"

"I had no such intention," said the king.

In reply, Ssŭma drew the garment from his sleeve and threw it on the ground.

"Who did this?"

The king was overwhelmed; his soul flew beyond the skies, his spirit fled to the ninth heaven. Shaking with fear, he said, "I was forced into it. How could I think of such a thing?"

"To slander ministers by charging them with rebellion is an aggravated crime," said Ssŭma.

The king knelt at his feet, saying, "Yes; I am guilty; forgive me."

"I beg Your Majesty to rise; the laws must be respected."

Pointing to the Empress, he said, "She is of the Chang house and must die."

"Spare her," cried the king, weeping bitterly.

But Ssŭma was obdurate. He bade the lictors lead her away, and she was strangled with a white silk cord at the palace gate.

Now I recall another year; and lo!
An empress borne away to shameful death.
Barefooted, weeping bitterly, she shrieks
"Farewell," torn from her consort's arms. To-day
History repeats itself; time's instrument,
Ssŭma, avenges this on Ts'ao Ts'ao's heirs.

The day after these events Ssŭma Shih assembled all the officers and addressed them thus:—"Our present lord is profligate and devoid of principle; familiar with the vile and friendly with the impure. He lends a ready ear to slander and keeps good men at a distance. His faults exceed those of Chang I of Han, and he has proved himself unfit to rule. Wherefore, following the precedents of I Yin and Ho Kuang, I have decided to put him aside and to set up another, thereby to maintain the sanctity of the ruler and ensure tranquillity. What think you, Sirs?"

They all agreed, saying, "General you are right to play the same part as I Yin and Ho Kuang, thereby acting in accordance with Heaven and fulfilling the desire of mankind. Who dares dispute it?"

Then Ssŭma, followed by the whole of the officials, went to the Palace of Eternal Peace and informed the Empress Dowager of his intention.

"Whom do you propose to place on the throne, General?" she asked.

"I have observed that Ts'ao Chü, Prince P'êngch'êng, is intelligent, benevolent and filial; he is fit to rule the empire."

She replied, "He is my uncle and cannot become Emperor. However, there is Ts'ao Mao, Duke of Kaokueihsiang, and grandson of the Emperor Wên. He is of mild temperament, respectful and deferential, and may be set up. You, Sir, and the high officers of state might favourably consider this.".

Then spake one, saying, "Her Majesty speaks well; he should be raised to the throne."

All eyes turned toward the speaker, who was Ssŭma Fu, uncle of Ssŭma Shih.

The duke was summoned to the capital. The Empress called King Ts'ao Fang into her presence in the Hall of Eternity and blamed him, saying, "You are vicious beyond measure, a companion of lewd men and a friend of vile women. You are unfitted to rule. Therefore resign the imperial seal and revert to your status of Prince Ch'i. You are forbidden to present yourself at court without special command."

Ts'ao Fang, weeping, threw himself at her feet. He gave up the seal, got into his carriage and went away. Only a few faithful ministers restrained their tears and bade him farewell.

> Ts'ao Ts'ao, the mighty minister of Han
> Oppressed the helpless; little then thought he
> That only two score swiftly passing years
> Would bring like fate to his posterity.

The Emperor-elect Ts'ao Mao, who also bore the name Yen-shih, was the grandson of the Emperor Wên, and son of Ts'ao Lin, Prince Ting of Tunghai. When he was nearing the capital all the officers attended to receive him at the Nanyeh Gate, where an imperial carriage awaited him. He hastily returned their salutations.

"The ruler ought not to return these salutations," said Wang Shu, one of the officers.

"I also am a minister and must respond," replied he.

They conducted him to the carriage to ride into the palace, but he refused to mount it, saying, "Her Majesty has commanded my presence, I know not for what reason. How dare I enter the palace in such a carriage?"

He went on foot to the Hall, where Ssŭma Shih awaited him. He prostrated himself before the minister. Ssŭma hastily raised him and led him into the presence.

The Empress-Dowager said, "In your youth I noticed that you bore the impress of majesty. Now you are to be the Ruler of the Empire. You must be respectful and moderate, diffusing virtue and benevolence. You must do honour to your ancestors the former emperors."

Ts'ao Mao modestly declined the proposed honour, but he was compelled to accept it. He was led out of the presence of the Empress-Dowager and placed in the seat of empire.

The style of the reign was proclaimed as *Chêng-Yüan.* An amnesty was granted. Honours were heaped upon Ssŭma Shih, who also received the golden axes, with the right to proceed leisurely within the precincts, to address the Throne without using his prænom and to wear arms at court.

520

But in the spring it was reported at court that the General Wuch'iu Chien and the Governor of Yangchou, Wên Ch'in, were raising armies with the declared design of restoring the deposed emperor.

Ssŭma Shih was disconcerted.

> If ministers of Han have always faithful been,
> Wei leaders, too, to prove their loyalty are keen.

How this new menace was met will appear in the next chapter.

CHAPTER CX.

WÊN YANG REPULSES THE ENEMY;
CHIANG WEI DEFEATS HIS OPPONENT.

It has been said that in the second year of *Chêng-Yüan*, Wên Ch'in, Governor of Yangchou, and General Wuch'iu Chien, a distinguished officer who commanded the forces in Huainan, were reported to be raising armies to avenge the deposition of Ts'ao Fang.

Wuch'iu Chien was a native of Wênhsi in Honan. He was moved to great anger against the minister who had deposed the king, and his son Tien fomented his father's wrath, saying, "Father, you are chief of all this district. With this Ssŭma Shih in such a position the country is in danger, and you cannot sit still and look on."

"My son, you speak well," replied he.

Whereupon he requested Governor Wên to come and consult with him. This Wên Ch'in had been a client of Ts'ao Shuang's, and he hastened at the call of the general. When he arrived he was led into the private apartments, and, the salutations at an end, the two began to talk over the situation. Presently the host began to weep, and his visitor asked the cause of his tears.

"Think you that this conduct of Ssŭma Shih does not tear my heart? He has deposed the king and now holds in his grip all the authority of the state. Things are all upside down."

Wên replied, "You are a Warden of the Marches. If you are willing to play the part, you ought to take arms and slay this rebel. I will help you, regardless of consequences. My second son, Shu, is a good soldier and a man of great valour, Moreover, he hates Ssŭma Shih and wishes to avenge on him and his brother the death of Ts'ao Shuang. He would make an excellent leader of the van."

Wuch'iu was delighted to get such ready and willing support, and the two poured a libation in pledge of mutual good faith. Then, pretending that they held an edict from the Empress-Dowager, they summoned all the officers to Shouch'un, where they built an altar on the west side and sacrificed a white horse, smearing their lips with its blood in token of their oath.

They made this declaration:—"Ssŭma Shih is a rebel and devoid of rectitude. We have a secret edict commanding us to muster the forces of Huainan and put down this rebellion."

Thus supported, Wuch'iu led six legions to Hsiangch'êng, where he camped, while his fellow-conspirator Wên Ch'in took two legions to the front to go to and fro lending help where it was needed. Letters were sent all through the district calling for assistance.

Now that mole below the left eye of Ssŭma Shih used to pain at times, and he decided to have it removed. The surgeon excised it, closed and dressed the wound, and the patient rested quietly in his palace till it should heal.

It was at this time that he received the disquieting news of opposition to his authority. Whereupon he called in the *T'ai-yü* Wang Su to discuss the matter.

Said Wang, quoting Kuan Yü as an example, "When Kuan Yü was most famous, Sun Ch'üan sent Lü Mêng to capture Chingchou. What did he do? He first won over the officers by taking care of their families and thus broke the power of his enemy like a tile. Now the families of all the officers of Huainan are here in your hands. Treat them well, at the same time taking care that they do not get away, and you will be irresistible."

"Your words are good," said Ssŭma. "However, I cannot go out to war till I have recovered. Yet, to send another is to take great risks, and I shall feel insecure."

There was also present Chung Hui, who here interposed, saying, "The forces of Huai and Ch'u are very formidable. If you send another there is danger whatever happens, and if your lieutenant make a serious mistake your whole policy will fail."

"No one but myself can succeed," cried Ssŭma, starting from his couch. "I must go."

So, in spite of illness, he resolved to lead in person. He left his brother in charge of affairs at Loyang and set out, travelling in a padded carriage.

Chuko Tan was given command over all the forces of Yüchou and ordered to take possession of Shouch'un, while Hu Tsun, with the Chingchou forces, was sent to bar any retreat. The Governor of Yüchou, Wang Chi, was sent to capture Chênnan and the district south.

To his camp at Hsiangyang, Ssŭma summoned all his officers to a council. Chêng Pao spoke first, saying, "Wuch'iu Chien is fond of laying plans, but slow to come to any decision. His fellow-conspirator Wên Ch'in is bold, but imprudent. Now this scheme of theirs is too large for their minds, but as their men are full of spirit they should not be engaged lightly. We should remain on the defensive till their ardour has burned out. This is what Ya Fu did."

But Wang Chi objected, saying, "This is not a rising of the people, nor of the soldiers, but is the work of Wuch'iu Chien. The people are merely his tools and cannot help themselves.

The rebellion will go to pieces as soon as an army approaches the district."

"I agree with you," replied Ssŭma.

Then he advanced upon the Yinshui River and camped by the bridge.

Wang Chi said, "Nant'un is an excellent camping ground; occupy it at once, for if not the enemy will do so."

He was sent to carry out his own plan.

Reports of these movements of the enemy came to Wuch'iu in Hsiangch'êng, and an assembly of officers was called. The leader of the van, Ho Yung, said, "Nant'un is an excellent site for a camp, with a river beside it and hills at the rear. If the Wei armies camp there we shall be unable to dislodge them. Let us occupy it."

So the army set out. But before they drew near, the scouts reported a camp already there. It was incredible, and the leader rode to the front to reconnoitre. He was convinced by the sight of flags and banners over all the plain, fluttering above an orderly array of tents and huts. The sight disconcerted him, and he rode back to the main body not knowing what to do. Just then a scout came in to say that Sun Hsün of Wu had crossed the river to attack Shouch'un.

"If we lose that city we shall have no base," cried Wuch'iu.

That same night he retreated upon Hsiangch'êng. Seeing the enemy retreat, Ssŭma called together his officers to talk it over. Fu Ku, a President, who was of the expedition, said the retirement was obviously due to Wu's threatened attack upon Shouch'un, and he advised their own attack upon Hsiangch'êng, another on Lochia and sending an army to capture Shouch'un. He also proposed that Têng Ai, the Governor of Yenchou, should attack Lochia jointly with their own army.

His plan was acceptable to Ssŭma, who sent letters to Yenchou telling Têng Ai to march against Lochia, where Ssŭma himself would soon meet him.

Camped at Hsiangch'êng, Wuch'iu sent spies to Lochia to see what might be happening there, for he feared it would be attacked. When he spoke of his fears to Wên Ch'in, the latter said, "General, you need not be anxious. I and my son will answer for its safety. Give us but half a legion."

Father and son, with the half legion, went to Lochia. Before the main body arrived it was seen that Wei banners were flying on the west of the city. By and by they made out that the leader was no other than Ssŭma himself. His camp was forming rapidly, but was not yet complete.

When this was reported to Wên Ch'in, his son Yang, bearing his famous whip of steel, was by his father's side.

"We should attack before they have settled down in camp, father," said he. "Let us go quickly and attack on two sides."

"When can we start?" said the father.

"To-night at dusk. You lead half the force round by the south, and I will march the other half round by the north, and we will meet in the third watch at the Wei camp."

The youth who propounded this plan was then eighteen, tall and strong. He wore complete armour and carried at his waist a steel whip. When the hour came to start he took his spear, swung himself into the saddle and set out.

That night Ssŭma Shih, who had arrived and had at once set about settling into camp, lay on a couch in his tent, for he was still suffering pain from the wound beneath his eye. The tent was surrounded by a numerous guard. Têng Ai had not arrived.

About the third watch he heard a great shouting and asked what it was. One replied that an army had come round from the north and burst into the lines. The leader was too bold for anyone to face.

Ssŭma became much troubled. His heart burned within him, and the excitement caused the wound to open, so that the eyeball protruded and blood flowed freely. The pain became intense, nearly unbearable. In his agony and alarm lest his army should be thrown into confusion, he lay gnawing the bedclothes till they were in rags.

Wên Yang's force lost no time, but attacked as soon as it arrived. He dashed into the camp, slashing and thrusting right and left, and everyone gave way before him. If anyone stayed to oppose, the sharp spear or the terrible whip did its work, and he fell. But after a time, seeing no sign of his father, he grew anxious. And he had to retire several times before the fierce flights of arrows and crossbow bolts.

About daylight he heard shouts and thought they must mean the arrival of his father with help. But the shouting came from the north, and his father was to arrive by the south road. He galloped out to get a clearer view, and saw a force sweeping down like a gale of wind.

It was not his father, but a body of the enemy, and the leader was Têng Ai. Têng rode forward shouting, "Rebel, flee not!"

Wên Yang had no intention to flee. Setting his spear, he rode savagely toward his opponent. They engaged and fought half a hundred bouts without either gaining the advantage. Then, the duel still raging, the Wei army attacked, and Wên's men began to give way and run, so that soon he found himself alone.

However, he got clear of the fight and went away south. But he was pursued, for many captains plucked up courage to follow when he ran away. They pressed on his heels till near the Lochia Bridge it seemed that they must catch him. Then he suddenly pulled up his steed, turned and rode in among them, flogging with the terrible steel whip, and wherever it struck there lay men and horses in confused heaps. So they left him, and he retook his way in peace.

Then the Wei captains met and said, "Lo! here is a man who has driven us all backward. But we are many and may not suffer that."

Wherefore they re-formed and once again took up pursuit.

"You fools?" cried Wên, as he saw them coming on. "Have you then no regard for your lives?"

Again he fell upon them with the steel whip and slew many, so that the survivors retreated. But yet again they found courage to come on, and yet again, but they had to fall back before the lash of that terrible whip.

> Defiance hurled at Ts'ao Ts'ao's mighty host
> Arrayed near Ch'angan Slope proclaimed Chao Yün
> A valiant man; and peerless stood he till,
> At Lochiach'êng another hero faced,
> Alone, another host, and Wên Yang's name
> Was added to the roll of famous men.

Wên Ch'in never reached the appointed rendezvous. In the darkness he lost his way among the precipices and gullies, whence he only got out as day dawned. He saw all the signs of a fight and a victory for Wei, but could not discover whither his son had gone. So he returned without fighting, and in spite of pursuit, made his way safely to Shouch'un.

Now Yin Ta-mu was an officer of the court and had accompanied Ssŭma on his expedition, but was no friend of his. He had been of the Ts'ao Shuang party and bitterly resented the death of his patron. He was watching for a chance to avenge him. Seeing that Ssŭma was ill, he thought to secure his end by making friends with Wên Ch'in. So he went in to see the sick general, and said, "Wên Ch'in had no sincere intention to rebel, but was led astray by Wuch'iu. If you will let me go and speak with him he will come over to you at once."

Ssŭma said he might go to try, and Yin put on his armour and rode after Wên Ch'in. By and by he got near enough to shout.

"Do you not recognise me? I am Yin Ta-mu."

Wên Ch'in stopped and looked back. Yin removed his helmet that his face might be clearly seen, and said, "O Governor Wên, why can you not bear up for a few days? I know that Ssŭma Shih is very near death, and I wish you to remain at hand."

But Wên did not understand. He abused Yin and even threatened that the bowmen should shoot, and Yin could only sorrowfully turn away.

When Wên reached Shouch'un and found it occupied he tried for Hsiangch'êng, but three armies of the enemy lay near by and it seemed impossible that it could hold out long. So he decided to desert to Wu and serve Sun Hsün.

Wuch'iu Chien, then behind the walls of Hsiangch'êng, heard that Shouch'un had fallen, that his fellow-conspirator Wên had failed and, with three armies against his city, knew that his case was desperate. He mustered all the forces in the city and marched out to try his fortune.

As he went forth he fell in with Têng Ai. He bade Ko Yung go out to fight, but he fell in the first encounter, cut down by Têng himself. The enemy came on in force. Wuch'iu fought gallantly, but his army fell into confusion. Then two other armies came up, and he was completely surrounded. Nothing could be done, and he fled from the field and made for Shênhsien City. Here the governor received him kindly and comforted him with a feast. At the banquet the fugitive drowned his sorrows in the wine cup till he was helpless, when he was slain by his host. His head was sent to the Wei army as proof of his death, and the rising came to an end. Peace was restored in Huainan.

Ssŭma Shih grew worse. Recovery being hopeless, he called Chuko Tan to his tent and gave him a seal and conferred upon him the title of "Conqueror of the East," with command of all the forces in Yangchou, and soon after the army marched back to Hsüch'ang.

The sick man began to have visions. Night after night he was troubled by the apparitions of the three courtiers he had put to death, and he knew that his end was near. He sent for his brother, who came and wept by his couch while he listened to his elder brother's last commands.

"The responsibility of power is heavy, but we must bear it; there is no relief. You must continue my plans and maintain my policy yourself, and you must be exceedingly careful how you entrust any other with power, lest you bring about the destruction of our whole clan."

Then he handed the seal of office to Ssŭma Chao, weeping the while. Chao would ask some questions still, but with a deep groan his brother died. It was the second month of the second year of *Cheng-Yüan*.

Ssŭma Chao put on mourning for his brother and informed King Ts'ao Mao of the death. By special edict Ssŭma Chao was ordered to remain at Hsüch'ang so as to guard against any attack from Wu. This order was unpleasing to its recipient, but he felt doubtful what to do. He took counsel with Chung Hui, who said, "The death of your brother has disturbed the country, and if you remain here some shifting of power at the capital will surely work to your disadvantage. It will be too late for regrets then."

Wherefore Ssŭma left Hsüch'ang and camped on the Lo River. This move alarmed the king. Then Wang Su advised him to placate the powerful minister with a new title. So Wang Su went, bearing an edict creating Ssŭma Chao *Ta Chiang-chun,* or Generalissimo, with control of the Presidents of Boards. He came to Loyang to thank the king for these honours and stayed. Henceforward all matters and the whole government were under his hand.

When news of these things came to Ch'êngtu, Chiang Wei thought the time had come to make another bid for the empire, so he wrote a memorial to the king.

"Ssŭma Shih having just died, his brother, who succeeds, will be unable to leave Loyang until he has consolidated his position. Wherefore I crave permission to attack Wei."

The king agreed and bade him raise an army. So he went into Hanchung to prepare for the expedition.

However, General Chang I was opposed to the expedition and said the state policy should rather be the improvement of conditions at home. He endeavoured to win over Chiang Wei to his views.

"You are mistaken," said Chiang. "Before our great Minister Chuko emerged from his reed hut in the wilds and undertook the affairs of a state, the three kingdoms were already a fact. Six times he led armies to try to gain the northern portion of the empire, but failed to attain his desire. Unhappily he died leaving his design unaccomplished. But he bequeathed to me the legacy of his intention, and I must be a loyal and worthy executor. If I die in the attempt I will perish without regret. Now is our opportunity, and if we miss it, shall we find a better?"

"What you say is the real truth," said Hsiahou Pa. "Let us send first some light horse out by Paokan to capture Nanan and thereby settle that district."

Then said Chang I, "Procrastination and delay have been hitherto the causes of our failure. We ought to obey the precepts of the books of war, strike where the enemy is unprepared and appear where he does not expect us. A rapid march and a sudden blow will find Wei unready, and we shall succeed."

So Chiang Wei led a huge army out by Paokan. When he reached the T'ao Waters the spies reported his arrival to the Governor of Yungchou, who led out seven legions against him. Chiang gave certain orders to his subordinates, and after they had marched, he drew up the main body by the T'ao River.

Wang Ching, the Governor of Yungchou, rode out to parley.

"The three states are now actually established; why then have you invaded our borders these many times?"

Chiang replied, "Because Ssŭma deposed your late king without cause, and it behoves the neighbouring countries to punish such a crime. Moreover, yours is a rival state."

Then Wang turned and said to four of his captains, "You see that the enemy is drawn up with a river at his back so that his men must conquer or drown. Chiang Wei is bold, but you will fight him and pursue if he retire."

The four rode out two and two. Chiang stood through a few encounters, but then moved backward toward his camp. At this, Wang led on his main body to smite. Chiang fled toward the river. As he drew near he shouted, "Danger, O captains! Now do your utmost."

His captains turned on the foe and fought with such vigour that the Wei army was defeated, and, as they turned away, Chang I and Hsiahou Pa fell upon their rear. Soon the Wei army was hemmed in and the bold Chiang Wei rushed in among the host of Wei and threw them into utter confusion. They trod each other down in the press, and many fell into the river. Dead bodies lay about over many *li*.

Wang Ching and a few horsemen got clear and fled to Titaoch'êng, where they entered within the walls and barred the gates.

After Chiang Wei had rewarded and feasted his army he was for attacking the city, but Chang I was against this.

"General, you have won a great victory, which will bring you fame. If you attempt more things may go agley, and you will only add legs to your sketch of a serpent."

"I disagree," said Chiang. "Our opponents have been overcome, and if we press forward we may overrun the whole north. This defeat has broken the spirit of the army, and this city can be easily captured. Do not damp the spirit of my men."

So it was decided to attack Titaoch'êng.

Ch'ên T'ai, who was also of Yungchou, was just about to set out to avenge the defeat of Wang Ching when Têng Ai, the Governor of Yenchou, arrived with his army. Ch'ên welcomed him, and when Têng had said he had come to assist to defeat the men of Shu, Ch'ên asked his plans.

Têng Ai replied, "They are victors on the T'ao Waters. If they enlist the aid of the *Ch'iang* to cause a diversion in Shênsi and also obtain the support of the four districts, it will be a misfortune for us. If they do not think of that, but try to take Titaoch'êng, they will only fritter away their energies against a place too strongly fortified for them to capture. Let us now array our force along Hsiangling, and then we can advance and smite them. We shall get a victory."

"That is well said!" cried Ch'ên.

Then twenty cohorts were told off to find their way secretly to the south east of Titaoch'êng and there hide in the valleys. They were then to display many ensigns and sound trumpets as if they were a very large force, and make huge fires at night, so as to cause anxiety among the enemy. And thus they waited for the men of Shu to come, while Ch'ên T'ai and Têng Ai marched against them.

The army of Shu had marched to Titaoch'êng and begun the siege around the whole circuit of the walls. At the end of many days the fall of the city seemed no nearer, and Chiang Wei began to fret. He could think of no plan likely to succeed. One eventide a horseman came in to report the approach of two armies, and the names on the banners were Ch'ên and Têng.

Chiang called in his colleague Hsiahou and said, "I have spoken to you of Têng Ai many times. He is perspicacious, valiant, resourceful and has always delighted in the study of military topography. As he is coming we shall have to put forth all our energies."

Hsiahou replied, "We will attack before he can get a foothold and while his men are fatigued with the march."

So Chang I was left to carry on the siege while the two leaders went out to meet the new armies. Chiang went against Têng, and his colleague against Ch'ên.

Before Chiang had marched far the stillness was broken by the roar of a bomb, and at once all about the Shu army arose the rolling of drums and the blare of trumpets, soon followed by flames that shot up to the very sky. Chiang rode to the front and saw the ensigns of Wei all about him.

"I have fallen into a trap set by Têng Ai," cried he.

He sent orders to Hsiahou and Chang to withdraw immediately while he would cover their retreat. When they had retired, he followed them into Hanchung, harassed all along the road by the sounds of marching men and glimpses of enemy banners. But these enemies never attacked, and it was only when too late that Chiang knew that all this was make-believe.

He camped in Chungti. For his services and success on the T'ao River Chiang was rewarded with the rank of *Ta Chiang-chün*.

As soon as the ceremonies connected with his promotion were ended, he began again to talk of an expedition against Wei.

> Remember enough is as good as a feast,
> Having sketched a good snake don't add legs to the beast;
> And in fighting remember that others are bold,
> And tigers have claws though their teeth may be old.

The result of the new expedition will be told in the next chapter.

CHAPTER CXI.

TÊNG AI OUTWITS CHIANG WEI;
CHUKO TAN THINKS IT HIS DUTY TO DESTROY SSŬMA CHAO.

Chiang Wei camped at Chungti; the army of Wei camped outside Titaoch'êng. Wên Ching, the Governor, welcomed his deliverers and prepared a banquet to celebrate the raising of the siege and also rewarded the army with gifts. Then he sent up a memorial to King Ts'ao Mao, of Wei, eulogising the magnificent services of Têng Ai, who was rewarded with the title, "Pacificator of the West." For the time, Têng was left in the west as *T'ai-yü* of the *Ch'iang* tribes. He and Ch'ên T'ai placed their men in cantonments in Yung, Liang and the districts round about.

After Têng Ai had rendered his thanks to the king, Ch'ên T'ai spread a great feast in his honour, and in congratulating his guest, said, "Chiang Wei slipped off in the night because he was broken, and he will never dare to return."

"I think he will," replied Têng, smiling. "I can give five reasons why he should."

"What are they?"

"Although the men of Shu have retired, they have the self-possessed and confident look of holding the mastery; our men are really weak and broken. The men of Shu were trained and inspirited by K'ung-ming and are mobile; our men are all of different periods of service and indifferently trained. The Shu soldiers often use boats for travelling; ours do all their journeys on land, so that while one army moves at leisure and the men arrive fresh, those of the other arrive fatigued with marching. Again, Titaoch'êng, Shênsi, Nanan and Ch'ishan are all places suitable for defence or use as battle fields, and thus the men of Shu can conceal their intentions and strike where they will; we have to remain on guard at many points, thus dividing our forces. When they concentrate they have only to reckon with a part of our force. If they come out by way of Shênsi and Nanan, they have the grain of the *Ch'iang* to depend upon, and if they choose Ch'ishan, they have the wheat there. These are the five reasons why they should make another expedition."

Ch'ên T'ai was overcome with the clear vision of his new colleague. "Sir, your foresight is godlike. I think we need feel no anxiety about what the enemy can achieve."

The two soldiers became the best of friends in spite of the difference of age. Têng spent his time in training the army, and garrisons were placed at all points where surprise attacks seemed possible.

There was feasting also at Chungti, and the occasion was taken to discuss a new attack on Wei. But Fan Chien opposed. "General, your expeditions have partly failed many times; you have never scored a complete victory. But now on the T'ao River the men of Wei recognise your superiority, and why should you try again? There is small chance of success, and you risk all you have gained."

The general replied, "You all regard only the extent and population of Wei and the time necessary for conquest, but you do not see five reasons for victory."

The assembly asked what these were.

"The fighting spirit of the men of Wei has been badly broken on the T'ao River, while that of our men, although we retired, is unimpaired. If we attack we shall certainly succeed. Our men can travel in boats and so will not be wearied with marching; their men have to march to meet us. Our men are thoroughly trained; theirs are recruits, a mere flock of crows, quite undisciplined. When we go out by Ch'ishan we can seize upon the autumn wheat for food. Finally they are scattered, having to defend various points, while we can concentrate on any point we wish and they will find it difficult to bring up reinforcements. If we miss this chance, can we hope for a better?"

Hsiahou Pa said, "Têng Ai is young, but he is deep and crafty. He has certainly taken great pains to secure the district under his charge as 'Pacificator of the West.' Victory will not be so easy as it was before."

"Why should I fear him?" cried Chiang, angrily. "You should not laud the spirit of the enemy and belittle that of our own men. But in any case I have made up my mind and shall take Shênsi."

No one dared to offer any further opposition. Chiang himself led the first army; the others followed in due order, and thus the men of Shu marched out.

Before they could reach Ch'ishan the scouts reported the hills already occupied by the armies of Wei. Chiang rode forward to verify this, and, surely enough, he saw the Wei camps, nine in number, stretching over the hills like a huge serpent, and all arranged to give each other support.

"Hsiahou Pa spoke only too well," said he. "The plan of those camps is excellent and only our K'ung-ming could have laid them out with equal skill."

Returning to his own army, he said to his officers, "They must have known of my coming, and I think Têng Ai is here too. Now from this as base you are to send out daily small reconnoitring parties showing my banner, but different flags and uniforms, blue, yellow, red, white and black, in turns. While you are thus distracting attention, I will lead the main army by a détour to attack Nanan."

Pao Su was sent to camp at the mouth of the Ch'ishan Valley while the main army marched.

As soon as Têng had heard that the enemy would come out at Ch'ishan he had camped there with his colleague Ch'ên T'ai. But when days had passed without anyone coming to fling a challenge he sent out spies to find out where the Shu army was lurking. They could find nothing, and so Têng went to the summit of a high hill to look around. He came to the conclusion that some other vulnerable point was threatened. Finally he thought it must be Nanan. In the daily reconnaissances he saw nothing but a feint, accentuated by the daily change of uniform. He returned to camp and spoke with his colleague.

"These men have been going to and fro for days and must be tired, and their leaders are certainly none of the ablest. Therefore, General, I advise an attack here. If that succeeds the Tungt'ing road can be occupied, and Chiang Wei will be unable to retreat. I think I ought to try to relieve Nanan. I will go by Wuch'êngshan, and if I occupy that, the enemy will try to take Shangkuei. Near that place is a narrow and precipitous valley called Tuan Valley, just the place for an ambush, where I shall lie in wait till they come to take Wuch'êngshan."

Ch'ên replied, "I have been here over a score of years and have never known so much of the military possibilities of the place. You are very wonderful and had better carry out your plan."

So Têng marched toward Nanan by double marches. Soon they came to the hill, where they camped without opposition. He sent his son Chung and Shih Tsuan, each leading half a legion, to lie in wait in the Tuan Valley and not to betray their presence.

In the meantime Chiang Wei was marching between Tungt'ing and Nanan. Near Wuch'êngshan he turned to Hsiahou Pa and said, "That hill is our point, and Nanan is close. I fear lest the artful Têng Ai may seize and fortify it."

They hastened, anxious to reach the hill before the enemy. But it was not to be. Presently they heard the roar of bombs and the beating of drums, and then flags and banners appeared, all of Wei. And among them fluttered the leader's standard, bearing the name Têng.

This was a sad disappointment. The men of Shu halted, and veteran soldiers of Wei came rushing down from various points on the hill, too many for the men of Shu to drive back. So the advance guard was defeated. Chiang went to their help with his central body, but when he got near the soldiers of Wei were nowhere to be seen.

Chiang went on to the foot of the hill and challenged, but no one came out to accept. The men of Shu began to shout abuse, and kept it up till late in the day, but they failed to provoke a fight. As the men of Shu began to retire, the drums beat furiously, yet no one appeared. Chiang turned about to ascend the hill, but its defenders prevented that by stones thrown from cannon (p'ao). He hung on till the third watch, when he tried again. But he failed.

Thereupon he went down the hill and halted, bidding his men build a barricade of wood and boulders. The men of Wei came on again and stopped the work.

Next day Chiang brought up many transport waggons and placed them on the slope as the nucleus of a camp. But in the night a number of men came down with torches and set fire to them. A fight ensued, which lasted till dawn.

Seeing that a camp could not be made there Chiang retired to consider new plans with Hsiahou Pa.

"Since we cannot take Nanan, our next best plan is to try for Shangkuei, which is the storehouse of Nanan."

Leaving Hsiahou Pa on the hill, Chiang led a force of veteran soldiers and bold officers along the road toward Shangkuei. They marched all night, and dawn found them in a deep valley, which the guides said was Tuan Valley.

"That sounds too much like 'Cut-off Valley,'" said Chiang. "And if a force held the mouth we should be in sorry straits."

While hesitating whether to advance farther or not, the leading men came back to say they had seen a cloud of dust beyond the hills, which seemed to indicate a body of men in hiding. So the order was given to retire.

At that moment the armies under Shih Tsuan and Têng Chung came out and attacked. Chiang Wei, alternately fighting and retreating, tried to get away. Then Têng himself appeared, and the Shu army had enemies on three sides. They were in grave danger, but Hsiahou Pa came to their rescue, and so Chiang escaped.

Chiang proposed to return to Ch'ishan, but his rescuer said, "We cannot go thither, for Ch'ên T'ai has destroyed the force under Pao Su, and he himself was killed. All that was left of that army has gone back into Hanchung."

It was no longer a question of taking Tungt'ing. Chiang sought out by-roads to march along. Têng came in pursuit, and as he pressed hard on the rear, Chiang sent the others on ahead while he covered the retreat.

Soon Ch'ên T'ai came out from the hills, and Chiang was surrounded by a shouting body of the enemy. He was very weary when Chang I, who had heard of his straits, came to his rescue with a body of cavalry. Chang saved his general, but lost his own life. Finally Chiang Wei got back into Hanchung.

From Hanchung the death of Chang I in battle was reported to the king and suitable honours requested. And seeing that there had been serious loss of life in the military operations that had just failed, Chiang, following the precedent of the late Marquis of Wu, asked that he himself should be degraded in rank, retaining, however, the command. He was put back to Junior Generalissimo.

The country being now cleared of the enemy, Ch'ên T'ai and Têng Ai prepared a banquet in honour of victory and gave rewards to the men who had fought. A memorial was sent to the capital upon the services of Têng, and a special commission brought him higher rank; the title of "Marquis" was given to his son.

At this time the style of the reign in Wei was changed to *Kan-Lu* (Gentle Dew). Ssŭma Chao commanded all the military forces. He assumed great pomp, and whenever he moved outside his palace he was escorted by a guard of three thousand mail-clad men, beside squadrons of cavalry. All power lay in his hands, and he decided all questions so that the court was rather in his palace than in that of the king.

Plans for taking the final step constantly occupied his thoughts. The question of mounting the throne was openly mooted by one Chia Yün, a confidant, who was descended from a family that had long held rank at court.

He said, "Sir, all real authority is in your hands, and the country is not tranquil. The only remedy is for you to become actual ruler, and you should find out who are your supporters."

Ssŭma replied, "This has been in my thoughts a long time. You might be my emissary to the east to find out the feeling there. You can pretend you go to thank the soldiers who took part in the late campaign. That would be a good pretext."

Accordingly Chia travelled into Huainan, where he saw Chuko Tan, the "Guardian of the East." This officer was of the same family as the late Marquis of Wu, Chuko Liang. He had gone to Wei for employment, but had received no office while his brother lived. On his brother's death his promotion was rapid. He was also titular marquis.

As he was in command of all the Huainan forces, Chia Yün went to him to ask him to convey to the army the appreciation of the soldiers' services. He was received courteously, and at a banquet, when host and guest were both mellow with wine, Chia set himself to discover Chuko's feelings.

He said, "Lately in Loyang there has been much talk of the weakness and lack of ability of the king and his unfitness to rule. Now General Ssŭma comes of a family noted for state service for several generations. His own services and virtues are high as the heavens, and he is the man best fitted to take the rulership of Wei. Is this not your opinion?"

But Chuko did not favour the suggestion. On the contrary, he broke out angrily, "If the state is in difficulty, then one ought to stand up for it even to the death."

Chia said no more. He soon returned and told his patron what had been said.

"The rat!" cried Ssǔma, angrily. "He is exceedingly popular there in Huainan, but if he is left too long he will do harm."

Ssǔma began to take measures. He wrote privately to Yüeh Lin, Governor of Yangchou, and sent a messenger to Chuko Tan with an edict making him President of the Board of Works. This meant that he had to come to the capital.

But Chuko knew that his late guest had done him mischief, and he interrogated the messenger, who told him that Yüeh Lin knew all about the matter.

"How does he know?"

"General Ssǔma sent him a private letter."

The messenger was condemned to death. Then Chuko placed himself at the head of his personal guard and marched to Yangchou. The city gates were closed and the drawbridge raised. He summoned the gate, but no one answered.

"How dare this fellow treat me thus?" cried he.

He ordered his men to force the gate. A few dismounted, crossed the moat and climbed the ramparts, where they slew all who opposed them and opened the gate. The others entered, set fire to the houses and began to fight their way toward the residence. The Governor sought refuge in a tower, but Chuko made his way up and, after reproaching his enemy for dishonouring his father, slew him.

Then Chuko sent up a memorial detailing Ssǔma's many faults, and made preparations for war. He called up all the militia and took over the four legions who had surrendered on the fall of Yüeh Lin and gathered supplies. He also sent to Wu for aid, offering his son Chuko Ching as a hostage for his good faith.

At this time Sun Hsün was dead and his brother, Sun Ch'ên, was Prime Minister. He was a man of cruel and violent temper and had put many officers to death on his way to power. The King of Wu, although no fool, was helpless in his hands.

The messenger, Wu Kang, conducted the proposed hostage to the residence of this monster, who asked what he had come for. Wu Kang explained and asked for help. His request was received favourably, and Sun sent seven legions with a full complement of officers. They marched, and Chuko returned to report success. Chuko thought all was going well.

Chuko's memorial angered Ssǔma, who wished to set out to revenge the attack at once, but Chia Yün preached caution.

"My lord, you derived your power from your father and brother, and people have not had time to discover your own virtue. If you leave the court and there be a revulsion of feeling against you, you will lose all. Rather request the Empress Dowager and the Son of Heaven to go with you, and nothing is to be feared."

The plan was accepted as excellent. He went into the palace and proposed it to Her Majesty, saying, "Chuko Tan is in revolt, and I and my colleagues intend to punish him. I beg that you will accompany the expedition as the late Emperor would have done."

She was afraid, but dared not refuse, and the next day was requested to set out with the king.

The king said, "General, you command all the armies and dispose them as you will; why do you ask me to go?"

Ssŭma replied, "Your Majesty is wrong to hesitate. Your ancestors travelled over the empire and wished to unite the whole under one ruler. Wherever there was a worthy opponent they went to face him. Your Majesty should follow their example and sweep the land clean. Why fear?"

The king, fearing his minister's terrible power, consented, and an edict was issued for the commands to march. Wang Chi, a distinguished general, was in command of the van, while Shih Pao and Chou T'ai led the imperial escort. The army moved into Huainan like a great flood.

The van-leader of Wu encountered them, and both sides drew up for battle. Chu I, the leader on the Wu side, rode out and took the challenge, but was overcome in the third bout. P'ang Tzŭ also followed, but was also beaten in the third encounter.

Wang Chi ordered the Wei army to pursue. The men of Wu retired fifty *li* and camped. Thence they sent tidings of their ill-success to Shouch'un and Chuko Tan; Wên Ch'in and the two sons of Chuko set out with reinforcements.

Thus Ssŭma was faced by many legions of valiant men.

> Now here is a check to the armies of Wu,
> And Wei's gallant men advance.

The next chapter will tell how went victory.

CHAPTER CXII.

YU CH'UAN DIES NOBLY AT SHOUCH'UN;
CHIANG WEI FIGHTS FIERCELY AT CH'ANGCH'ENG.

Hearing of this threatened attack, Ssŭma sought advice from two of his officers, P'ei Hsiu, a Leader of Irregular Cavalry, and Chung Hui, a civil official.

The latter said, "The Wu army is helping our enemies for the sake of profit, and hence we can seduce them with an offer of greater profit."

Ssŭma agreed in this opinion and resolved accordingly. As part of his plan, he sent to lay ambushes in different places near Shiht'ouch'êng.

As ordered by Ssŭma, Ch'êng Ts'ui led several legions out to bring on a battle, while Ch'ên Chün got together many waggons, herds of oxen, droves of horses, donkeys and mules, and heaps of military supplies, all of which he crowded together in the midst of the army. This stuff was meant to be abandoned as soon as the fight began, so that the enemy might be tempted to plunder.

The armies being drawn up, Chuko Tan looked across at his opponents and saw that the centre of the Wei army was taken up by a disorderly mass of transport. Presently he led on his men to attack, and Ch'êng Ts'ui, as bidden to do gave way and fled, leaving a large amount of spoil. When the men of Wu saw such huge quantities of booty, theirs for the taking, they lost all desire to fight and scattered to gather the spoil.

While thus occupied, suddenly a bomb exploded and down came the men of Wei upon the spoilers. Chuko Tan attempted to draw off, but other forces appeared, and he was sore smitten. Then came on Ssŭma with his army, and Chuko fled to Shouch'un, where he entered and shut the gates. The army of Wei sat down to the siege of the city, and the army of Wu retired into camp at Anfêng. The King of Wei was lodging at this time in Hsiang-ch'êng.

Then said Chung Hui, "Chuko Tan has been worsted, but the city wherein he has taken refuge is well supplied, and his allies, the men of Wu, are not distant. His position is strong. Our soldiers are besieging the city all round, which means that those within will hold out for a long time, or they will make a desperate sortie. Their allies also may fall upon us at the same time, and it would go hard with us. Therefore I advise that the attack be made only on three sides, leaving the south gate open for them if they wish to flee. If they flee, we can fall on the fugitives. The men of Wu cannot have supplies for very long, and if we sent some light cavalry round by their rear we might stay their fighting power without a battle."

"You are my Tzŭ-fang (Chang Liang)", said Ssŭma, stroking the back of his adviser. Your advice is excellent."

So Wang Chi, who was on the south of the city, was ordered to withdraw.

But in the Wu camp at Anfêng was much sadness at the want of success. The General Sun Ch'ên said to his captain Chu I, "I have given up all hope of succouring Shouch'un, and overrunning the north is out of the question. Now and here you have to win a victory or die, for another defeat will mean death."

The threatened leader went back to his camp and talked with Yü Ch'üan. Yü said, "The south gate is free, and I will lead therein some of our men to help Chuko. Then you challenge the Wei army, and we will come out from the city and attack."

Chu I thought the plan good, and many captains were willing to go into the city and share in the attack. They were allowed to march in without hindrance as the Wei captains had no orders to stop them.

When this was reported to Ssŭma, he said, "This is a plan to defeat our army by making a front and rear attack."

So he called Wang Chi and Ch'ên Chên and told them to take half a legion to keep the road along which Chu I would come and strike him in rear.

Chu I was advancing toward the city when he heard a shouting in the rear, and soon the attack began from two sides. His army was worsted and returned to Anfêng.

When Sun Ch'ên heard of this new defeat he was very angry. "What is the use of leaders who always lose?" cried he.

He sentenced the unfortunate general to death and upbraided Ch'üan I, son of Ch'üan Tuan, and said, "If you do not drive off this army of Wei let me never again see your face, nor that of your father.

Then Sun Ch'ên returned to Chienyeh.

When this was known in the Wei camp Chung Hui said to his chief, "Now the city may be attacked, for Sun Ch'ên has gone away, and there is no hope of succour for the besieged."

A vigorous assault began. Ch'üan I tried to cut his way through and get into the city, but when he saw Shouch'un quite surrounded by the enemy and no hope of success he gave in and went over to Ssŭma Chao, by whom he was well received and given office.

Deeply affected by this kindness, he wrote to his father and uncle advising them to follow his example. He tied the letter to an arrow and shot it over the walls. So his father and uncle, with their companies, came out and yielded.

Within the city Chuko Tan was very sad. Two advisers came to him to urge him to fight, since the food in the city was short. He turned on them angrily.

"Why do you tell me to fight when I am set on holding out to the very last? If you say that again you shall die as traitors."

"He is lost," said they, going away. "We can do no other than surrender or we shall die too."

That night they slipped over the wall and surrendered. Both were given employment. Of those left in the city some were for fighting, but no one dared say so."

Meanwhile the besieged saw the defenders making a wall against the expected floods of the River Huai. This flood had been the only hope of the besieged, who had trusted to be able to smite the besiegers when it came. However, the autumn was dry any and the river did not swell.

Within the besieged city the food diminished rapidly, and soon starvation stared them in the face. Wên Ch'in and his sons were defending the citadel, and they saw their men sinking one by one for lack of food till the sight became unbearable.

Wên went to Chuko to propose that the northern men should be sent away in order to save food. His suggestion called forth an outburst of fierce wrath.

"Do you want me to kill you that you propose to send them away?"

Wên suffered death. His two sons ran amok with rage. Armed with short swords they attacked all they met and slew many score in their desperate anger. The fit over, they dropped down the wall and deserted to the Wei camp.

However, Ssŭma Chao had not forgotten that one of the two, Wên Ying, had defied and held at bay his whole army. At first he refused to receive the deserter; he even thought to put him to death, but his advisers interposed.

"The real offender was his father," said Chung Hui, "but he is dead, and these two come to you in desperation, and if you slay those who surrender you will strengthen the obstinacy of those who remain in the city."

There was reason in this, and so their submission was accepted. They were led to Ssŭma's tent, and he soothed them with kind words and gave them gifts and employment. After expressing their gratitude they rode about the city on the horses he had given them, shouting, "We have received great kindness at the hands of Ssŭma Chao, who not only has pardoned us but given us gifts. Why do you not all yield?"

When their companions heard this they said one to another. "This Wên Ying was an enemy, and yet he has been well received; how much more may we expect generous treatment!"

The desire to surrender possessed them all. When Chuko heard it, he was incensed and went round the posts night and day on the watch for any who seemed inclined to go. He put many to death in these efforts to retain his authority.

Chung Hui heard how things were going in the city and went in to the general to say the moment to attack had come. Ssŭma was only too pleased. He stimulated his men, and they flocked to the ramparts and assaulted vigorously. Then a certain captain treacherously opened the north gate and let in the Wei soldiers.

When Chuko heard that the enemy were in the city he called his guards and tried to escape. He took his way along the smaller streets to the gate, but on the drawbridge he met Hu Tsun, who cut him down. His followers were made prisoners.

Wang Chi fought his way to the west gate, where he fell in with the Wu captain, Yü Ch'üan.

"Why do you not yield?" shouted Wang.

"It would be treachery to yield instead of obeying my orders to seek help." Throwing off his helmet, he cried, "The happiest death a man can die is on the battle-field."

Whirling his sword about he dashed among his enemies and fought till he fell under many wounds.

> Many were they who yielded at Shouch'un
> Bowing their heads in the dust before Ssŭma.
> Wu has produced its heroes,
> Yet none were faithful to the death like Yü Ch'üan.

When the victor entered the city he put to death the whole family of Chuko. Some of his guards fell into the hands of Ssŭma alive, and he offered them their lives if they would yield. They all refused, saying they would rather share the fate of their leader.

They were sent out of the city to be beheaded, but orders were given to offer each one his life at the last moment. Not one accepted, and they all died. In admiration for their fortitude they were honourably interred.

> The loyal servant flees not in the day of disaster;
> Such were they who followed Chuko to the shades.
> Ever and again begins the Song of Life's Brevity.
> Faithful unto death were they, even as T'ien Kêng's men.

As has been said, many of the men of Wu surrendered. Then said P'ei Hsiu, "The parents and children of these men are scattered all over the east, and if you spare them and they return home they will foment rebellion by and by. The best way is to bury them."

But Chung Hui said, "No; When the ancients made war their policy was to maintain the state as a whole, and so they only put to death the originators of trouble. It would be inhumane to slay all. Rather let them return home as witnesses to your liberal policy."

"That is better advice," said Ssŭma. So the men of Wu were released and allowed to return home.

"T'ang Tzŭ dared not return to his own place for fear of the cruel Sun Ch'ên, so he went over to Wei, taking his company with him. He was well received, and his men spread over the district of the three rivers.

The country about the Huai River being now quiet, Ssŭma decided to march homeward. Just then the news came that Chiang Wei, the Shu General, had taken Ch'angch'êng and was interfering with the supplies, and so a council was called to discuss this matter.

At this time the period-style in Shu, which had been *Yen-Hsi* for a score of years, was changed to *Ching-Yao*. Chiang Wei chose two officers, Chuan Ch'ien and Chiang Shu, both of whom he loved greatly, and set them to train the army, horse and foot. When again came news that Chuko Tan had set out to destroy Ssŭma Chao and had obtained the support and help of Wu, he said that the great opportunity had come at last, so he asked the king's authority to make another expedition.

But Ch'iao Chou heard this with grief, for internal affairs were not well.

Said he, "The court is sunk in dissipation and the king's confidence is given to that eunuch, Huang Hao; state affairs are neglected for pleasure; which is the king's sole aim. Chiang Wei has led many expeditions and wasted the lives of many men, so that the state is falling."

He then wrote an essay on "State Injuries," which he sent to Chiang Wei.

"When one asks by what means the weak overcame the strong in past times, the answer is that those responsible for the strong state made no struggle against general laxity, while those in power in a weak state took careful steps for improvement. Confusion followed upon laxity and efficiency grew out of diligence, as is the universal rule. King Wên devoted himself to the welfare of his people, and with a small number achieved great results; Kou Chien sympathised with all, and with a weak force overcame a powerful opponent. These were their methods. One may recall that in the past Ch'u was strong and Han weak when the country was divided by agreement at Hungkou. Then, seeing that his people were satisfied and settled in their minds, Chang Liang went in pursuit of Hsiang Yü and destroyed him.

"But is it necessary to act like King Wên and Kou Chien? Listen to the reply. In the days of Shang and Chou, when ranks had long existed and the relations between prince and minister were firmly established, even such as the Founder of the Hans could not have carved his way to a throne. But when the dynasty of Ts'in had suppressed the feudal nobles and set up mere representatives of its own power, and the people were weak and enslaved, the empire was riven asunder and there succeeded a time of contention, when every bold man strove with his neighbour.

"But we are now in other times. Since there is not the state of confusion that waited on the end of Ts'in, but a state of things more nearly like that of the period of the Six States, therefore one may play the part of King Wên. If one would found a dynasty, then must he wait upon time and favourable destiny. With these in his favour, the consummation will follow forthwith, as the armies of T'ang and Wu fought but one battle. Therefore have real compassion for the people and wait on opportunity. If wars are constant, and a mishap come, even the wisest will be unable to show the way of safety."

"An effusion from the pen of a rotten pedant?" cried Chiang wrathfully as he finished reading, and he dashed the essay on the ground in contempt.

The protest was disregarded, and the army marched.

"In your opinion where should we begin?" asked he of Fu Ch'ien.

Fu replied, "The great storehouse of Wei is at Ch'angch'êng and we ought to burn their grain and forage. Let us go out by Lo Valley and cross the Shên Ridge. After the capture of Ch'angch'êng we can go on to Ch'inch'uan and the conquest of the capital will be near."

"What you say just fits in with my secret plans," replied Chiang.

So the army marched. The Commander in Ch'angch'êng was Ssŭma Wang, of the same clan as the Prime Minister. Huge stores of grain were in the city, but its defences were weak. So a camp was made twenty *li* from the walls to keep any attack at a distance. Wang Chên and Li P'êng were Ssŭma's two captains.

When the enemy came up, Ssŭma and his two captains went forth from the ranks to meet them; Chiang Wei stood in the front of his army and said, "Ssŭma Chao, you have forced the King to go with you to war, which plainly indicates that you intend to emulate the deeds of Li Ts'ui and Kuo Ssŭ. My government has commanded me to punish this fault. Wherefore I say to you yield at once, for if you persist in the way of error you and yours shall all be put to death."

Ssŭma Wang shouted back, "You and yours are wholly strangers to any feeling of rectitude. You have repeatedly invaded a superior state's territory, and if you do not at once retire I will see to it that not even a breastplate returns."

With these words the Captain Wang rode out, his spear set ready to thrust. From the host of Shu came Fu Ch'ien to take the challenge, and the two champions engaged. After a few encounters Fu tempted his opponent by feigning weakness. Wang thrust at the opening he gave. Fu evaded the blow, snatched Wang out of the saddle and bore him off.

Seeing this, his colleague Li whirled up his sword and went pounding down toward the captor. Fu went but slowly, thus luring Li into rash pursuit. When Li was near enough, Fu dashed his prisoner with all his strength to the earth, took a firm grip on his four-edged brand, and smote his pursuer full in the face. The blow knocked out an eye, and Li fell dead. Wang had been already killed as he lay on the ground. Both captains being dead, the men of Wei fled into the city and barred the gates.

Orders were given for the men to rest that night and take the city on the morrow.

Next day, at dawn, the assault began. The men, fresh from their rest, vied with each other who should be first on the wall. They shot over the ramparts fire-arrows and fire-bombs and burned all the buildings on the wall. They next brought up brushwood and piled it against the rampart and set it alight, so that the flames rose high.

When the city seemed about to fall, the defenders set up a howling and a lamentation that could be heard all around. But suddenly a great rolling of drums diverted the attention of the assailants from the city, and they turned their faces to see a great host of Wei soldiers marching up in all the glory of waving banners. Chiang Wei faced about to meet this attack and took his place beneath the great standard.

Presently he made out a youthful-looking leader riding in advance with his spear ready to thrust. He looked scarcely more than twenty years of age, his face was smooth as if powdered, and his lips were crimson. But from them came fierce words.

"Do you recognise General Têng?" cried he.

"So this is Têng Ai," thought Chiang.

Thereupon Chiang set his spear and rode out. Both were adepts in arms and neither gave the other an opening, so that at the end of near half a hundred bouts neither could claim advantage. The youth wielded his spear with perfect skill.

"If I cannot gain the advantage by some ruse, how shall I win?" thought Chiang.

So he turned aside his steed and dashed along a certain road that led to the hills. The youth followed. Presently Chiang slung his spear, laid hands upon his carven bow, chose with care a feathered arrow and laid it on the string. But the youth was quick of eye, and as the bowstring sang he bent his head over the saddle and the arrow passed harmlessly by.

The next time Chiang turned he saw his pursuer close upon him, and already the spear was threatening his life. But as the youth thrust, Chiang evaded the blow and caught the shaft under his arm. Thus deprived of his weapon, the young man made for his own array.

"What a pity! What a great pity!" cried Chiang, turning to pursue.

He followed Têng close up to the standard, but just as he came near, a warrior came to the front, saying, "Chiang Wei, you fool, do not pursue my son when I am here."

Chiang Wei was taken aback; so he had only been contending with the son of his real opponent. Although he was astonished at the skill and vigour of the youth, he now knew that a heavier task lay before him and feared lest his steed was then too far spent for the contest.

So he said to Têng Ai, "Seeing things are so, let us both hold off our men till the morrow, when we will fight."

Têng Ai, glancing around, saw that the place was ill-suited for him, so he agreed to wait, saying "Let us lead off our men then, and whoever shall take any secret advantage is a base fellow."

Both sides retired into camp, Têng on the bank of the Wei River and Chiang on the hills.

Têng saw that the men of Shu had the advantage of position, so he wrote off at once to Ssŭma Wang not to give battle, but to wait for reinforcements. Meanwhile the men of Shu would be consuming their supply of grain, and he reckoned upon striking his blow when they began to be hungry. He also wrote to Ssŭma Chao for further help.

A messenger was sent to the Wei camp to deliver a letter of battle, the contest to take place the next day. Têng Ai openly accepted, but when morning came and Chiang Wei had arrayed his men, his enemy had not appeared on the field. Nor was there any sign of giving battle, no display of flags or rolling of drums all day.

At nightfall the army of Shu returned to camp and Chiang sent a letter reproaching his opponent with his failure to keep his word. Têng Ai treated the bearer of the letter with great courtesy and explained that he had been indisposed that day, but would certainly fight on the morrow.

But the next day passed also without any move on the part of Wei; and the same thing went on for five days.

Then said Fu Ch'ien to his chief, "There is some knavery afoot, and we must be on our guard."

"They must be waiting for reinforcements that they may attack on three sides," said Chiang. "But now will I send into Wu and get Sun Ch'ên to strike at the same time as I.

Just then came news of the rout of the army of Wu, of the fall of Shouch'un and the death of Chuko Tan. Moreover, that an army was going to attack Ch'angch'êng.

"So our attack on Wei is but a sham!" said Chiang, bitterly. "It is only a picture of a Cake."

> Four times he missed! he hailed
> The fifth occasion joyfully,—and failed.

The next chapter will tell the story of the retreat.

CHAPTER CXIII.

Ting Fêng's Plan to Slay Sun Ch'ên;
Chiang Wei Defeats Têng Ai.

Fearing lest reinforcements would strengthen his enemy beyond his own power of resistance, Chiang decided to retreat while he could. He sent all his stores and baggage away first with the footmen, and kept the cavalry to cover the retirement.

The spies reported his movements to Têng Ai, who said, "He has gone because he knew that the main army would soon be upon him. Let him go, and do not follow. If we pursue he will play us some evil trick."

Scouts were sent to keep in touch with the retreating army, and when they returned they reported that preparations had been made in the Lo Valley to check any pursuit with fire. The officers praised the prescience of their leader. When Têng reported these matters he was commended, and the Prime Minister requested the king to confer a reward.

The Prime Minister of Wu was greatly angered by the desertion of so many of his men and officers to Wei, and revenged himself by putting their families to death. King Liang disapproved of these acts of cruelty, but he was powerless.

The young king was of an ingenious turn of mind, as will be seen from the following story. One day he went to the West Park to eat of the newly ripened plums. He bade one of the eunuchs bring some honey. It was brought, but there were lumps of dirt in it. The young king called the store-keeper and blamed him for carelessness. The storekeeper said he was very careful to keep his stores in good order, and the honey could not possibly have been fouled in the store-house.

"Has any one asked you for honey lately?" asked the king.

"One of the eunuchs asked for some a few days ago. I refused him."

"You defiled the honey out of spite," said the king to the eunuch named.

The man denied it.

"It is very easy to tell," said the king. "If the dirt has been lying in the honey for some time it will be soft all through."

He broke one of the lumps, and it was quite dry inside. The eunuch then confessed.

This shows the king was quick-witted. But clever as he was, he could not control his Prime Minister, whose relatives were in command of all the garrisons and armies, so that he was unassailable.

One day the young king, musing over his sorrows and feeling very miserable, began to weep. The officer in charge of the eunuchs, who was a "State Uncle," stood by.

"Sun Ch'ên holds all real power and does as he wishes, while I am despised," said the king. "Something must be done."

Ch'üan Chi said, "I would think no sacrifice too great if Your Majesty would make use of me."

"If you could muster the guards and help General Liu to keep the gates, I would go and murder that ruffian. But you must not let anyone know, for if you tell your noble mother she will tell her brother, and that would be very serious for me."

Now Ch'üan's mother was the Prime Minister's sister.

"Will Your Majesty give me a command that I may have authority to act when the time comes?" said Ch'üan. "At the critical moment I could show the edict and hold back Sun's supporters."

The command was given, and Ch'üan went home. But he could not keep his secret, and confided the plan to his father, Shang. His father told his wife that Sun would be got rid of in a few days.

"Oh, you are going to kill him then," said she.

Although she seemed to approve with her tongue, she sent a secret messenger with a letter to the proposed victim.

That same night Sun Ch'ên called in his four soldier brothers, and the palace was surrounded. The conspirators were seized, with Liu Ch'eng and Ch'üan Shang and all their families. About dawn the young king was disturbed by a commotion at the gates, and a servant told him that the palace was surrounded.

The king knew that he had been betrayed. He turned on the Empress, who was of the Ch'üan house, and reproached her.

"Your father and brother have upset all my plans."

Drawing his sword, he was dashing out when his Consort and her people clung to his clothing and held him back.

After putting to death Liu Ch'êng and Ch'üan Shang, the Prime Minister Sun Ch'ên assembled the officers in the court and addressed them thus:—"The king is vicious and weak, depraved and foolish and unfit for his high office. Wherefore he must be deposed. Any of you who oppose will be punished as for conspiracy."

Only one of those present dared to say a word of protest. It was an officer named Hêng I, who said, "How dare you utter such words? Our king is very intelligent, and I will not support you. I had rather die."

Death was his portion. Then Sun went into the palace and said to the king, "O unrighteous and unenlightened King, your death would be the only fitting reparation to make to the empire, but out of consideration for your ancestors you are only deposed and degraded to princely rank as Prince Hui-chi. I will select a worthy successor."

Li Tsung, the *Chung-shu-lang*, was ordered to bring in the the royal seal, which was delivered to Têng Ch'êng. The deposed ruler retired weeping.

> The sage example of the wise I Yin
> Perverted now to traitor's use we see;
> And Ho Kuang's faithful services are made
> A cloak to cover vilest treachery.
> Even able princes are but toys of fate,
> And need our pity, fall'n from high estate.

Then two officers of the court, Sun K'ai and Tung Chao, went as envoys to Hulin to request Sun Hsiu, Prince of Langya, to ascend the throne.

The King-elect had had some premonition of the high honour to which he was now called, for in a dream he ascended into the skies seated on a dragon. Only the dragon seemed to have no tail. He woke up in a fright, and the next day brought the messengers.

He set out. At Ch'üa his carriage was stopped by a venerable old man who offered felicitations.

"Changes are inevitable, and I wish you a prosperous journey," said the aged one.

At Pusait'ing awaited an officer with a chariot, but Sun Hsiu's modesty would not allow him to mount it. He remained in his own simple carriage and therein travelled to the capital. Officials lined the road to salute him, and he dismounted to return their salutations. Then the Prime Minister stood forth and bade them take the newly-elected king by the arm and lead him into the Great Hall, where, after thrice refusing the honour, he at last took his seat and received the jade seal passed from one ruler to another.

When all the officers had made obeisance, there were the usual amnesties, promotions, honours and change of reign-style. *Jun-An*, "Eternal Tranquillity," was the name of the new reign. Sun Ch'ên was confirmed as Prime Minister, with the governorship of Chingchou. Moreover, Sun Hao, the son of his elder brother, was created Marquis of Wuch'êng.

Sun Ch'ên, with five marquisates in his family and the whole army under their command, was immensely powerful, able to set up and pull down at will. The new king secretly feared him, and although outwardly he showed him great favour, yet he kept careful watch over his Prime Minister, whose arrogance knew no bounds.

In the autumn Sun Ch'ên sent into the palace presents of oxen and wine as birthday gifts. The king declined them. The Minister was very annoyed and took the presents to General Pu's residence, where they two dined together. When warmed with wine, Sun said, "When I deposed the present Prince Hui-chi many people urged me to take the throne myself. But I acted magnanimously and set up this present king. Now I suffer the mortification of seeing my presents rejected. You will see what will come of this slight."

Chang sympathised, but the next day he secretly told the king, and the king's fears increased so that he could not rest. Shortly after this, Sun sent a large body of troops under the command of Mêng Tsung into camp at Wuch'ang, and he armed them from the state arsenals. Whereupon Wei Miao and Shih Shuo secretly memorialised the Throne that Sun's action pointed to rebellion.

Then the king called in Chang Pu to consult, and he recommended Ting Fêng as an able and trustworthy officer. So Ting was called and taken into the king's confidence.

"Have no anxiety," said Ting. "I will find some way of ridding the state of this evil."

"What do you propose?"

"When the winter Court is held, and all the officers are assembled, spread a great banquet and invite Sun. I shall be ready to act."

Wei Miao and Shih Shuo were taken into the plot and were to do what was possible outside the palace, and Chang Pu saw to arrangements within.

One night a heavy gale came on to blow, which tore up great trees by the roots. However, by daylight it had abated, and that morning a king's messenger arrived bearing an invitation to a banquet in the royal palace. Sun rose from his couch, and, as he did so, fell flat on the ground as though he had been pushed from behind. This accident troubled him, and he felt apprehensive, so he called half a score of his trusty men to act as his escort to the palace.

As he was leaving home his family besought him not to go out, for they feared the omens of the gale in the night and the fall that morning. However, he made light of their fears and said no one would dare come near him since the family was so strong.

"But if there is anything amiss I will signal."

So he took his seat, and the carriage set out. When he reached the palace the king rose from his place to welcome him, and at table he sat in the seat of honour. The banquet proceeded.

"There is a fire outside; what does that mean?" said a guest presently.

Sun rose to go out, but the king said, "There is no danger, and there are plenty of soldiers outside."

Just at that moment General Chang entered at the head of a couple of score of armed men. He rushed up the banquet chamber shouting, "I hold a command to slay the rebel Sun."

Instantly the Prime Minister was seized. He fell prostrate before the king, knocking his head on the ground and crying, "Spare my life! Exile me to my own place, but let me live."

"Did you exile any of your victims?" said the king, angrily.

The order went forth to carry out the execution, and Sun was hustled out and put to death. No single person raised a hand to help him. Then it was proclaimed that Sun was the only culprit and no other would be questioned.

Then at Chang's request the king went up on the Tower of the Five Phœnixes. The brothers of the Prime Minister were brought before him and also condemned to death. After this their families were slain, so that many hundreds suffered death. Not content with all these things, the tomb of Sun Hsün was broken open and his corpse beheaded.

Magnificent tombs were raised to his victims, Chuko Ch'üo, Têng Yin and others. Thus at last loyalty was rewarded, and the banished were permitted to return home with full pardon. The conpirators were rewarded.

News of this revolution was sent into Shu, and King Liu Ch'an sent an envoy into Wu with felicitations. The envoy, Hsüeh Hsü by name, at his audience was questioned about affairs in the west, and he told King Sun Hsiu, saying, "All affairs of state are in the hands of a certain eunuch named Huang Hao, and all the courtiers look up to him as to a father. At Court plain truth is never heard, and the country people look sallow and starved. The whole country appears on the verge of destruction. The birds on the roof do not know that the building is about to be burned."

"Ah! If only Chuko Liang, The Warlike, was still alive; how different all would be!" said King Hsui, with a sigh.

Letters were prepared saying that beyond doubt Ssŭma Chao intended usurpation, and when that came about in Wei, both Wu and Shu would be invaded. Wherefore both should be ready.

On the arrival of these letters Chiang Wei hastened to seek permission to attempt another expedition. Consent being given, a large army marched into Hanchung, with Liao Hua and Chang I as van-leaders. Wang Han, Chiang Pin, Chiang Shu and Hu Chi were on the wings, while Chiang Wei and Hsiahou Pa led the main column.

Asked what he thought should be the first objective, Hsiahou Pa replied, "There is no better fighting ground than Ch'ishan, as the tactics of the late minister made evident, and it is the only good exit."

So thither the armies marched, and they camped at the entrance to the valley. At this time Têng Ai had a training camp at Ch'ishan drilling the Shênsi troops. The scouts told him of the coming of the western men, and he ascended a hill to see and verify their reports. He seemed pleased when he saw the enemy camp.

"They have just done as I foresaw," said he.

Now Têng Ai had carefully considered the "pulse" of the countryside and so had not interfered with the Shu army when it was on the march or settling into camp. Moreover, he had excavated a subterranean road to the spot where he had thought they would halt, and their "left" camp had been pitched just on it. Wang and Chiang Chi commanded in that camp.

Têng Ai called his son and Shih Tsuan and sent them to attack, one on each flank. He sent men into the underground road, which opened in rear of the threatened camp.

As the newly made camp was not yet well fortified, its two commanders exercised great care and kept their men under arms all night, watching with vigilance. So when the alarm was given they had but to seize their weapons and go out. But as the two leaders were mounting their steeds Têng Ai also attacked, and two faces had to be defended. Soon they found the position untenable and fled.

When Chiang Wei saw that his left camp had been attacked on two sides he mounted and took his position in front of the centre camp.

"Let no one move on pain of death!" he shouted. "Stand still, and when the enemy approaches shoot."

The right camp was ordered to stand fast. His defence was effective. Half a score of times the men of Wei came forward, only to be driven back before the arrows and bolts of the defenders. Daylight found the Shu camps still firm, and Têng Ai drew off.

"Chiang Wei has indeed learned of K'ung-ming," said Têng. "His men stood the night attack without flinching, and the leaders took the chances of battle quite calmly. He is able."

When the two commanders of the camp that had been attacked went to confess their fault, Chiang said, "It was less your fault than mine, for I did not clearly recognise the nature of the terrain."

So no penalty was inflicted. The camp was made stronger, and the subterranean passage was filled with the bodies of the slain.

A challenge to battle for the following day was sent to Têng, who accepted it joyfully.

Next day the two armies were arrayed in front of Ch'ishan, the men of Shu according to the "Eight Formations" designed by Chuko Liang, which are called Heaven, Earth, Wind, Cloud, Bird, Serpent, Dragon and Tiger. While the manœuvre was in progress, Têng recognised it as the *pa-kua* and placed his men accordingly. Chiang Wei then gripped his spear and rode out, saying, "You have made a good imitation of my eight, but can you work variations?"

"You call these yours! Did you think that you alone held the secret? Since I have made it, of course I know the variations."

Têng re-entered his ranks, gave the signal officers certain orders, and the "eight eights" of the variations were evolved in rapid succession. Then he rode to the front again.

"What of my evolutions?" asked he.

"Not so bad; would you like to try a surrounding move with me?" replied Chiang.

"Why not?"

The two armies moved in orderly ranks. Têng stood in the midst of his army giving the necessary orders. Then the clash came, but his tactics did not grip. Then Chiang waved a certain signal flag, and his force suddenly assumed the form of a serpent coiled on the ground with Têng in the centre. Shouts arose all about him. He could not understand what had happened and began to feel afraid. Gradually the men of Shu closed in upon him, and he saw no way of escape.

"Têng Ai, you must surrender," cried the soldiers.

"Indeed I am in the toils," he replied.

Suddenly from the north-west a cohort dashed in. To Têng's great joy they were soldiers of Wei, and they crossed over and released him. The leader was Ssŭma Wang.

But although Têng had been rescued, his nine camps were seized by his enemy and he had to retire. He led his army to the south of the River Wei and halted.

"How did you know exactly where to strike?" asked Têng of his rescuer.

Ssŭma replied, "In my youth I studied tactics and was friendly with Kuang Yüan of P'ingshih. He explained that formation to me. Chiang Wei used what is known as "The Serpent Coil," and the only way to break it is to attack the head, which I saw was in the north west."

Têng replied, "Although I have studied formations, I do not know all the modifications. But since you know about this we may be able to recover our camps."

"I fear the little I have learned will not be enough to overcome Chiang Wei."

"To-morrow you shall contend with him, and while his attention is engaged I will attack the rear of Ch'ishan, and we will recover our camps."

So a force was prepared to attack on the morrow, and he sent a challenge to a contest in tactics for the same day. Chiang accepted.

Chiang Wei said to his officers, "In the secret book that I received from the marquis the variations are three hundred and sixty-five, corresponding to the circuit of the heavens. This challenge from them is as one going to teach hewing to the God of Carpenters. I think some ruse lies behind this. Can you guess what it is?"

Liao replied, "While they engage your attention in this competition they intend to attack our rear."

"Just so; that is my opinion." replied Chiang.

So he prepared a counter-stroke by sending Liao and Chang, two of his captains, to lie in wait at the back of the hills.

Next day the men from the nine camps were led out and drawn up in front of the hills. Ssŭma Wang came out on the other side and presently rode to the front to parley.

"You have challenged me to a contest; now draw up your men for me to see," said Chiang.

Ssŭma did so and arrayed the eight diagrams, *pa-kua*.

"That is what we know as the eight diagrams," said Chiang. "But it is nothing wonderful, only a sort of array fit for a brigand's raid."

"You also have only stolen another man's tactics," replied his adversary.

"How many modifications of this are there?" asked Chiang.

"Since I have arranged this, naturally I know the variations, of which there are nine nines, making eighty-one."

"Try them."

Ssŭma returned to his array and evolved many, finally riding out and asking his opponent if he recognised them.

"My formation admits of three hundred and sixty-five variations. You are but a frog in a well and know nothing of the deeper mysteries."

Now Ssŭma knew that so many variations were possible, but had not studied them. However, he put on a bold air and said contemptuously that he did not believe it. And he challenged Chiang to show them.

"Go and call Têng Ai," raplied he. "I will display them to him."

"General Têng has excellent plans and does not think much of such tactics."

"What plans? I suppose you mean a plan to keep me here while he tries a surprise attack in the rear."

Ssŭma was aghast. He made a sudden dash forward, and a mêlée began. Chiang Wei made a signal with his whip, and his men poured in from both wings. The men of Wei were seized with sudden panic, threw down their weapons· and fled.

Now Têng had hurried on Chêng Lun to make the first attack. As Chêng turned the corner of the hill a bomb exploded. At once the drums rolled and an ambush discovered itself. Liao was in command. Neither side stayed to parley, and the leaders engaged in single combat. In the first encounter Chêng fell.

Têng had not expected such preparation, and he hastened to withdraw. Then Chang came forth and attacked on the other side. The army of Wei was worsted. Têng fought his way clear, but he bore four arrow wounds upon his body. He got to the river, where he found Ssŭma Wang, and they discussed how to get away.

But Ssŭma proposed another form of attack.

"The King of Shu has a favourite, the eunuch Huang Hao, in whom he places all his trust and with whom he spends his time in one round of pleasure. Let us use the eunuch to sow distrust between the king and his general and so get Chiang Wei recalled. In that way we shall retrieve our defeat."

So Têng assembled his advisers and asked who could go into Shu and get into communication with the eunuch, the king's favourite.

A certain Tang Chün volunteered at once. To him was entrusted gold and pearls and precious things, and he was sent into Shu to win the treacherous alliance of the eunuch. As he went he also disseminated reports that Chiang Wei was angry and intended to desert.

These rumours became the common talk in Ch'êngtu, and everyone believed them. Huang Hao carried them to the king, and a messenger was sent to call the general to the capital.

Meanwhile Chiang tried every day to bring the enemy to give battle, but they remained obstinately behind their defences. Chiang began to think some evil scheme was afoot, when suddenly he was recalled. Although ignorant of the reason, he could not disobey, and when he retired the Wei leader knew that their plot had succeeded.

They broke camp and set out to attack the retreating army.

> Because of Court intrigues
> Yo I and Yo Fei failed.

How matters went will be told in the next chapter.

CHAPTER CXIV.

KING MAO DRIVES TO HIS DEATH;
CHIANG WEI ABANDONS STORES AND CONQUERS.

When the order to retreat was given, Liao Hua reminded his general of the standing precept that a leader in the field is independent and need not obey even the command of his prince, but Chiang was not inclined to disobey, and beside he recognised that the people, tired of war and disappointed with unfulfilled hopes, would be glad to rest.

Chang I said, "The country begins to resent these many years of war; rather take the occasion of the victory you have just won to return and pacify the people."

"It is good," said Chiang Wei.

A systematic and orderly retirement began. The army of Wei, loth to forgo an opportunity, followed, but the absence of the least confusion gave them no chance, and as he saw his enemy disappearing in perfect order Têng Ai had to confess that Chiang Wei was a worthy inheritor of the warlike methods of Chuko. He returned to his camp on Ch'ishan.

On his return to Ch'êngtu, Chiang Wei had audience with the king whereat he inquired why he had been commanded to return.

The king replied, "Because you have been so long on the frontier, noble Sir; I thought the soldiers must be weary. There was no other reason."

"O King, thy servant had got his camps on Ch'ishan and was on the eve of complete success. To leave off thus in the middle just played into the hands of our enemies. Surely Têng Ai found means of sowing distrust in me." The king sat lost in thought, and silent.

Chiang Wei continued, "I am pledged to destroy those rebels and prove my devotion to my country. Your Majesty should not listen to the babble of mean persons till distrust grows in your heart."

"I do not distrust you," said the king after a long pause. "You may return into Hanchung and await the next favourable opportunity."

Chiang Wei left the court and betook himself into Hanchung to the army.

Tang Chün went back to the Ch'ishan camp and reported his success. The two leaders rejoiced, knowing that trouble was not far off when the king had lost confidence in his servants. They sent Tang to Loyang to tell his own story to Ssŭma Chao, who also rejoiced, for he ardently desired to subdue Shu.

On this matter he consulted the military officer Chia Ch'ung. "What do you think of an attack upon Shu?"

"Not to be considered," said Chia. "The Emperor does not trust you, and your departure would be the beginning of trouble for you. When the yellow dragon was seen in the well and all the officers were felicitating the king upon such a very auspicious occurrence the Emperor said, 'It is not auspicious; just the reverse. The dragon symbolises the ruler. To be neither in heaven, nor on earth among the people, but to be in a well, is a dark portent and bodes evil.' He wrote some verses, and one stanza undoubtedly points to you, my lord."

> The dragon scotched a prisoner is,
> No longer leaps he in th' abyss,
> He soars not to the Milky Way,
> Nor can he in the meadows play;
> But coiled within a dismal well,
> With slimy creatures he must dwell,
> Must close his jaws, his claws retract,
> Alas! quite like myself in fact.

The recital of the poem annoyed Ssŭma Chao. "This fellow is very like Ts'ao Fang, and if I do not remove him he will hurt me," said he.

"I will see to it for you," said Chia.

In the fifth year, during the fourth month, Ssŭma Chao had the effrontery to go to Court armed. However, the king received him with exaggerated courtesy, and the courtiers began to praise and magnify his services and say that he had been inadequately rewarded with the title "Duke of Chin" and the Nine Gifts.

And Ssŭma himself said discontentedly, "My father and my brother have all given great services to Wei, and yet I am a mere duke; something seems wrong."

"Should I dare not do what you requested?" said the king.

"That poem about the Lurking Dragon called us slimy creatures; what sort of politeness is that?" said Ssŭma Chao.

The king had nothing to say, and the haughty minister left the chamber, smiling cruelly as he strode past the shivering courtiers.

The king retired, taking with him Wang Shên, Wang Ching and Wang Yeh, and they went to a privy chamber to consult. The king was very sad. He said, "There is no doubt that he intends to usurp the throne; everybody knows that. But I will not sit thereon patiently awaiting the indignity of being pushed off. Cannot you gentlemen help me to kill him?"

"He may not be slain," said Wang Ching. "That will not do. In the old state of Lu, Duke Shao could not bear with the Ch'i family, and ran away, thus losing his country. But this man and his family have been in power very long and have innumerable supporters, many of whom are quite independent of any act of his whether loyal or disloyal. They support him under any conditions. Your Majesty's guards are few and weak and incapable; not the men for any desperate effort. It would be most lamentable if Your Majesty could not bear this trial. The correct course is to wait and not act hastily."

"If I can bear this, what cannot I bear?" said the king. "But I will do something, and if I die, what matters?"

He went into the private apartments and spoke to his Consort. The three men sat outside talking.

"This matter is coming to a head, and unless we want to be put to death and all our loved ones with us, we had better go and warn Ssŭma Chao," said Wang Shên.

This advice angered Wang Ching, whose nature was more noble, and he said, "The king's sorrow is the minister's shame, and a shamed minister dies. Dare you contemplate treachery?"

Wang Ching would have nothing to do with this visit to Ssŭma Chao, but the other two went to the Ssŭma palace to betray their king.

Shortly after, King Mao appeared, called the officer of the guard, Chiao Po, and bade him muster his men, grey-heads and lads, as many as he could. He got together about three hundred, and this little force marched out to the beating of a drum as escort to a small carriage, in which sat the king gripping his sword. They proceeded south. Wang Ching stepped to the front and prayed the king to stay his steps and not go.

"To go against Ssŭma with such a force is driving the sheep into the tiger's jaws. To die such a death is a vain sacrifice. You can do nothing," said Wang.

"Do not hinder me. I have made up my mind," replied the king, heading toward the Dragon Gate.

Presently Chia Ch'ung came in sight. He was armed and mounted on a fine horse. Beside him rode two officers, and behind him followed a body of mail-clad men, who shouted one to another as they rode.

Then Mao held up his sword and cried, "I am the Emperor. Who are you thus breaking into the forbidden precincts? Are you come to murder your lawful ruler?"

The soldiers suddenly stopped, for they were palace guards. Then Chia shouted to one of the officers, Ch'êng Chi, saying, "What did the general train you for if not for this day's work?"

Ch'êng took his halberd and turned to Chia, saying, "Death or capture?" "Ssŭma said he had to die," replied Chia.

Ch'êng rushed toward the carriage.

"Fool! How dare you?" cried the king.

But the shout was cut short by a thrust from the halberd full in the breast; another thrust, and the point came out at the back, so that the king lay there dead beside his carriage. Chiao Po coming up to strike a blow in defence was also slain, and the little escort scattered.

Wang Ching, who had followed, upbraided Chia Ch'ung, calling him traitor and regicide till Chia bade his lictors arrest him and stop his tongue.

When they told Ssŭma, he went into the palace, but the king was dead. He assumed an air of being greatly shocked and beat his head against the carriage, weeping and lamenting the while. He sent to tell all the officials of high rank.

When the *T'ai-fu* Ssŭma Fu saw the dead body of the king he threw himself beside it, his head resting thereon, and wept, saying, "It is my fault that they slew Your Majesty."

He had a coffin brought, and the remains were laid therein and borne to the side hall. Therein Ssŭma Chao entered and summoned the chief officers to a council. They came, all but the President Ch'ên T'ai. Ssŭma noticed his absence and sent Hsün Chuan, his uncle and colleague, to call him. Ch'ên T'ai wept aloud, saying, "Gossips will class me and my uncle together. Yet is my uncle less virtuous than I."

However, he obeyed the summons and came, dressed in the coarse hempen cloth of mourning, and prostrated himself before the bier. Ssŭma Chao feigned to be grieved also.

"How can this day's work be judged?" said he.

"If only Chia Ch'ung be put to death, that will scarce be an atonement to satisfy the empire," replied Ch'ên T'ai.

Ssŭma was silent and thought long before he spoke. Then he said, "What next, think you?"

"That is only the beginning; I know not the sequel."

"Ch'êng Chi is the ungodly rebel and actual criminal; he should suffer the death of shame; and his family," said Ssŭma Chao.

Thereupon Ch'êng broke out into abuse of Ssŭma and reviled him, saying, "It was not my crime; it was Chia Ch'ung who passed on your own orders."

Ssŭma bade them cut out his tongue and put him to death. They did so; and he and his brother were both put to death in the market place, and their families were exterminated.

> "The king must die," thus spoke Ssŭma full plain
> In Chia Ch'ung's hearing; and the king was slain.
> Although they killed Ch'êng Chi, who dealt the blow,
> The author of the crime we all well know.

Wang Ching's whole household were imprisoned. He himself was standing by the *T'ing-yü* Pavilion when he saw his mother being brought up a prisoner. He knocked his head on the ground and wept, saying, "O unfilial son to bring distress upon a gentle mother!"

But his mother laughed.

"Who does not die?" cried she. "The only thing to be feared is not dying the proper death. Who would regret dying like this?"

When next day the family were led out to execution, both mother and son smiled as they went past. But the whole city wept tears of sorrow.

> Fu Chien was famous at the rise of Han,
> When Han declined, Wang Ching was proved a man
> Of purest virtue and unfaltering heart;
> With resolution stern he played his part.
> His fortitude was great as T'aihua Mount,
> His life but as the floating down did count,
> The fame of son and mother n'er will die,
> So long as shall endure the earth and sky.

Ssŭma Fu proposed that the body of the late king should receive a royal funeral, and the minister consented. Chia Ch'ung and those of his party urged Ssŭma Chao to put Wei Ch'an on the throne in place of Ts'ao Mao, but he refused.

"Formerly King Wên had two-thirds of the state, and yet he supported and served Yin. Wherefore the Holy One called him 'Complete of Virtue.' Emperor Wu of Wei would not take Ch'an into the Hans, nor will I receive a Ch'an into Wei."

Those who heard this felt that in these words was an implication that he intended to place his own son Ssŭma Yen on the throne, and they ceased to urge him to act.

In the sixth year Ts'ao Huang, Duke of Ch'angtaohsiang, was raised to the throne as Emperor, the period-style being changed to *Ching-Yüan*. The personal name of the Emperor was also changed to Huan. He was a grandson of Ts'ao Ts'ao. Ssŭma was still Prime Minister and Duke of Chin. Beside, he received rich gifts, and all the officers were promoted or received honours.

When these doings in Wei were told in Shu, Chiang Wei seized upon them as pretext for another war, to punish Wei for the deposition of its ruler. So letters were written calling upon Wu to help, and a memorial was sent to the Throne. The army raised was fifteen legions, and there were many carts with boxes made to fit them. The two van-leaders went by Tzŭwu and Lo Valleys, while Chiang Wei took the Hsieh Valley road. They marched at the same time and hastened toward Ch'ishan.

Têng Ai was still on the mountain training the Wei soldiers when he heard that the Shu armies were once more on the war path. He called his officers together. And Wang Kuan said he had a plan to propose, but he would not tell it openly. However, he agreed to write it, and he placed it before the leader.

"Though excellent, I fear it is not enough to beguile the leader of Shu," said Têng Ai as he finished reading.

"I am willing to stake my life on it," said Wang, "and I will lead the way."

"Since you have such confidence you may try. You ought certainly to succeed."

So half a legion of men were put under the leadership of Wang, and they set out for Hsieh Valley, where they fell in with the scouts of Chiang Wei's force. Seeing these, their leader, Wang, shouted, "We are deserters: tell your leader."

So the scouts told Chiang Wei, who replied, "Hold up the soldiers, letting their leader only come to me."

Wang Kuan went forward and kneeled before him, saying, "I am a nephew of Wang Ching, and I hate Ssŭma Chao for what he has done to the king, and my uncle and I wish to join you and my men with me. I also desire to be sent against the rebel crew that I may avenge my uncle."

Then said Chiang Wei, "Since you are sincere in your desertion, I must be sincere in my treatment of you. The one thing my army needs is grain. There is plenty at Ch'uank'ou, and if you can transport it to Ch'ishan I can go straightway and take the Ch'ishan camps."

This reply rejoiced Wang Kuan, who saw that Chiang Wei was just going to walk into the trap. So he agreed at once.

"But you will not want half a legion to see after the transport. Take three companies and leave two as guides for me."

Wang Kuan, thinking that suspicions would be raised by a refusal, took the three companies, and the other two were attached to the army of Shu.

Then Hsiahou Pa was announced, and, when he was come in, he said, "O Commander, why have you believed the tale of this Wang? I never heard that he was related to Wang Ching, though it is true I never made particular enquiries. You should look to it, for there is much pretence in his story."

"I know he is false," said Chiang Wei, with a smile. "That is why I have taken away many of his men. I am meeting trick with trick."

"How do you know for certain?"

"Ssŭma Chao is as wicked as Ts'ao Ts'ao. If he slew all Wang Ching's family, would he have left a nephew on the male side, and sent him beyond his own reach with soldiers? You saw this, as did I."

So Chiang Wei did not go out by the Hsieh Valley, but he set an ambush there ready for any move of the so-called deserters. And indeed, within ten days, the ambush caught a man with a letter from Wang to Têng telling him what had come about, and from the letter and the bearer thereof they learned that a convoy was to be diverted to the Wei camps on the twentieth and Têng Ai was to send men to Yünshan to help. Another letter was sent to Têng Ai by a man dressed as a Wei soldier, the date being made the fifteenth instead of the twentieth.

As a preparation, many waggons were emptied of their grain and laden with inflammables, covered with green cloth. The two companies of Wei soldiers were ordered to show flags belonging to the transport corps. Then Chiang Wei and his colleague went into the valleys in ambush, while three bodies of men were sent to attack Ch'ishan.

The letter, apparently from Wang Kuan, was sufficient for Têng Ai, and he wrote back to say it was agreed. So on the fifteenth day five legions hove in sight near Yünshan. And the scouts saw endless carts of grain and fodder in the distance coming from the mountains. When Têng Ai got closer, he distinguished the uniforms of Wei. His staff urged him to hurry as it was getting dark, but Têng was more cautious.

"It is gloomy and dark over there," said the general. "If by any chance an ambush has been laid we could hardly escape. We will wait here."

But just then two horsemen came up at a gallop and said, "Just as General Wang was crossing the frontier with the convoy he was pursued, and reinforcements are urgently needed."

Têng Ai, realising the importance of the request, gave orders to press onward. It was the first watch, and a full moon was shining as bright as day. The shouting heard behind the hills he could only conclude was the noise of the battle in which his colleague was engaged.

So he dashed over the hills. But suddenly a body of men came out from the shelter of a grove of trees, and at their head rode the Shu leader, Fu Ch'ien.

"Têng Ai, you are stupid! You have just fallen into the trap set for you by our general. Dismount and prepare for death!"

Têng Ai halted and turned to flee. Then the waggons burst into flame. That flame was a signal, and down came the men of Shu. Têng Ai heard shouts all round him, "A thousand taels for anyone who captures Têng Ai, and a marquisate as well!"

Terrified, Têng dropped his arms, threw aside his armour, slipped from his steed, mingled with the footmen, and with them scrambled up the hills. The captains of Shu only looked

562

for him among the mounted leaders, never guessing that he
had got away among the common soldiers. So he was not
captured.

Chiang Wei gathered in his victorious men and went to
meet Wang Kuan with his convoy.

Having made all arrangements, as he thought, complete,
Wang Kuan was patiently awaiting the development of his
scheme, when a trusted friend came and told him that the
ruse had been discovered and Têng Ai had already suffered
defeat. Wang sent out some scouts, and the report was
confirmed, with the addition that armies were coming against
him. Moreover, clouds of dust were rising. There was no
way of escape, so he ordered his men to set fire to the convoy,
and soon huge flames were rising high into the air.

"The case is desperate," cried Wang. "It is a fight to the
death."

He led his men westward, but the men of Shu came in
pursuit. Chiang Wei thought his enemy would try at all costs
to get back to his own, but instead, Wang Kuan went on
toward Hanchung, and as his men were too few to risk a
battle he destroyed the military stations and covered ways
as he went. Fearing the loss of Hanchung, Chiang Wei
abandoned all thought of pursuing Têng Ai, but made all
haste along the by-roads after Wang Kuan. Surrounded on
all sides, Wang Kuan jumped into the Black Dragon River
and so died. Those of his men who survived were slain by
Chiang Wei.

A victory had been won, but it was costly. Many men had
been killed, much grain had been lost and the covered roads
had been destroyed. Chiang led his men into Hanchung.

Têng Ai made his way back to Ch'ishan. From there he
reported his defeat to the King of Wei and asked for degradation as a penalty. However, in view of his victories, he was
not degraded, but, on the other hand, was consoled with
magnificent gifts, which he distributed to the families of the
men who had been killed. Ssŭma Chao also sent him five
legions as reinforcement lest Shu should attack again.

Chiang Wei set about the restoration of the covered roads
ready for the next expedition.

Repair the roads for marching feet to tread,
The strife will only cease when all are dead.

The next chapter will tell who won.

CHAPTER CXV.

THE KING LISTENS TO SLANDER AND RECALLS HIS ARMY; CHIANG WEI TAKES COMMAND OF THE CANTONMENTS AND ESCAPES DEATH.

In the autumn of the fifth year of *Ching-Yao*, Chiang Wei was occupied with preparations for the renewal of an attack; mending the hill roads, gathering stores and mobilising his boats on the waterways of Hanchung. These things done, he asked permission to go again to the attack, saying, "Although I have not been wholly victorious nor accomplished great things, yet I have put fear into the hearts of the Wei armies. Our men have been long under training, and they must now be used, or the army will go to pieces for lack of employment. The men are ready to die, the officers prepared for all risks and I am determined to conquer or perish."

The king did not consent at once. As he was hesitating, Chiao Chou stood forth and said, "I have observed the heavens. I have seen the men of Shu scattered over the wilds and the leader stars dull and obscured. This expedition will be disastrous, and I hope Your Majesty will not approve."

The king replied, "Let us see the results of this campaign; if it fail, then the war shall cease."

Chiao resented the rejection of his advice, withdrew to his home and retired on the pretext of illness.

As the final preparations were being made, Chiang Wei said to Liao Hua, "We are pledged to get through to the capital this time: what do you advise to start with?"

"I dare not presume to advise you, General. For years we have been fighting and giving the people no rest. In Têng Ai we find a most formidable and resourceful opponent and an extraordinarily capable man, so that you must exert yourself to the very utmost."

Chiang Wei was annoyed. Said he, "The late minister made six attempts, all for the state. I have attacked eight times. Was any one of those attacks to serve my private ends? This time I go to attack T'aoyang, and no one shall say me nay. I will punish opposition with death."

He left Liao Hua in charge of the base in Hanchung and marched with thirty legions. His movements were reported in the Ch'ishan camps, and Têng's spies confirmed the news.

It happened that Ssŭma Wang was with Têng Ai discussing military matters, and the former, when he heard it, said, "That move is a blind; he does not mean it. What he really intends is an attack on Ch'ishan."

"However, he has really gone to T'aoyang," said Têng.

"How can you know?"

"Formerly he has always opened with a march to that part of the country where we have stored supplies. T'aoyang has no stores, so he thinks we shall not have taken care for its defence as we shall concentrate our efforts on Ch'ishan. But if he can take that place he can collect stores there, and get into touch with the *Ch'iang* and finally work out some grand plan."

"Supposing this true, what should we do?"

"I advise the abandonment of this place and a march in two bodies toward T'aoyang. I know a small town on the Hou River, not far from T'aoyang, which is the throat of the place. You go to T'aoyang, secrete your force and open the gates. Then act as I shall tell you presently. I will lie in wait at Hou River. We shall score a victory."

An officer of low rank was left in charge of Ch'ishan station when the main body left.

Meanwhile Hsiahou Pa led the van of the army toward T'aoyang. As he drew near he noticed the place seemed to have no defences; not a flagstaff reared its head. The gates stood wide open. He was too wary to go straight in however, though his captains agreed that the city looked empty. A few people were running away along the southern road.

Hsiahou rode south and saw there that the north-west road, at a little distance from the city, was crowded with fugitives.

"The city is really empty," said Hsiahou.

He led the way in all ready to fight, and the men followed. As they came near to the curtain wall, however, a bomb exploded. At this sound the drums beat, trumpets blared, and flags suddenly appeared. At the same moment the drawbridge rose.

"Caught!" said Hsiahou.

As he turned to retire, the arrows and stones flew down in clouds, and under these Hsiahou and many of his men lost their lives.

> Most able strategist and brave,
> Hsiahou, outwitted here
> By Têng, more prudent still, and slain,
> Deserves a pitying tear.

The flights of arrows from the ramparts was followed by a sortie, which broke up the force of Shu entirely, and the men fled. However, Chiang Wei came up and drove off Ssŭma

Wang, and the men of Shu camped beside the walls. He was very grieved at the loss of his able colleague.

That night Têng Ai came up secretly and attacked the camp. At the same time the men within the city made a sortie. Chiang Wei could not resist the double attack, and left the field. He marched some twenty *li* and camped.

Twice beaten, the men of Shu were very downcast. The general tried to console them with the truisms and platitudes of war, the need to bear misfortune as well as enjoy good fortune, and such sayings; but he wound up his speech with severity:

"But remember, no mutiny! He who talks ot retreat will suffer death."

Then Chang I said, "With so many men of Wei here, their camp at Ch'ishan must be undefended. I propose, General, that while you continue the contest here I go to try to capture the nine camps. If I succeed, Ch'angan will be at our mercy."

The second division of the army was detached to march on Ch'ishan, and Chiang Wei went down to the river to provoke Têng Ai into fighting. The challenge this time was accepted forthwith, but after several bouts without a decision, both retired to their camps.

For days after this, Chiang challenged again and again, but Têng declined and would not fight. The Shu soldiers howled abuse and hurled insults at their opponents, but all without effect.

Then Têng thought within him, "There must be some reason for this persistence. I think they have sent an army to try to seize Ch'ishan while they hold me here. The force there is insufficient, and I shall have to go to the rescue."

Têng called his son Chung, and said, "Hold this place most carefully. Let them challenge as they may, do not go out. To-night I go to the help of Ch'ishan."

It was night, and Chiang Wei was in his tent, intent upon his plans, when he was disturbed by a great shouting and drumming. They told him Têng Ai had suddenly appeared. The captains asked leave to go out to fight.

"Let no one move!" said Chiang Wei.

The fact was Têng Ai had only made a demonstration at the camp of Shu on his way to reinforce Ch'ishan.

Then Chiang Wei said to his officers, "The attack of Têng Ai was a feint; he has certainly gone to relieve Ch'ishan."

So Chiang decided to go to the aid of Chang I. He left Fu Ch'ien to guard the city.

Chang I was then actually attacking the Wei position on Ch'ishan. The defenders were few, and it looked as though they must soon give in, when the sudden appearance of Têng Ai made all the difference. The onslaught of Têng's force drove off Chang I, and he was forced to take refuge behind

the hills. No road was open to him. When things looked
worst he saw the Wei soldiers suddenly falling back in
confusion.

"General Chiang has come!" they told him.

Chang I took the opportunity to return to the attack, and
the tables were turned. Têng Ai lost the game and retired
into his camp, which Chiang Wei surrounded.

Here a digression is necessary. In Ch'êngtu the king fell
daily more and more under the malign influence of Huang Hao,
who encouraged him in every form of self-indulgence and
ministered to every desire for luxury and dissipation.
Government was left to look after itself.

A certain minister, Liu Yen, had a very beautiful wife.
One day she went into the palace to visit the Empress, who
kept her there a whole month. Liu Yen was not without
suspecting an intrigue with the Latter Ruler and took a brutal
revenge. He bound the lady, and made five hundred of his
soldiers shame her to the last degree by beating her on the
face with their boots. She swooned many times.

The story got to the ears of the king, and he ordered the
officials concerned to investigate and decide the crime and its
punishment. The judges found that 'soldiers were not proper
persons to administer a punishment to a woman, and the face
was not a portion of the body to be mortified; the author of
this crime ought to be put to death.' Wherefore Liu Yen was
beheaded.

Thereafter women were forbidden to go to Court. As time
went on the king indulged in unbridled sensuality, and
gradually all good men left the government, giving place to
the meanest, who soon swarmed there.

Among the sycophants of Huang Hao was a certain incapable
and worthless general named Yen Yü, whose lack of merit
had not stood in the way of preferment. Hearing of Chiang's
defeats at Ch'ishan, he got his friend the eunuch to propose
to the king that Chiang should be recalled and he himself sent
in command. The king agreed, and the edict was issued.

One day, as Chiang Wei was working out his plan of attack
on the camps of Wei, three edicts came, all to the same effect,
recalling him to the capital. Disobedience being out of the
question, Chiang Wei ceased all operations and sent the
T'aoyang force back first. Then gradually he withdrew the
others.

Têng Ai in his camp wondered at the rolling of drums one
night, but next day he heard that the Shu camps were empty.
However, he suspected some ruse and did not pursue.

Arrived in Hanchung, the army halted, and its leader went
on to the capital in company with the messenger who had
brought his orders. Here he waited ten days, and still the
king held no Court. He began to suspect mischief.

One day near the palace gate he met a secretary, Ch'i Chêng, whom he knew, and asked whether he knew the reason for his recall.

"What General! Do you not know? Huang Hao wanted to push Yen Yü into favour, so he intrigued for your récall. Now they have found out Têng Ai is too clever to be tackled, and so they are not fighting any more."

"I shall certainly have to put this eunuch fellow out of the way," said Chiang Wei.

"Hush! You are the successor of the great minister, the man to whom he bequeathed his unfinished task. You are too important to act hastily or indiscreetly. If the Emperor withdrew his support, it would go ill with you."

"Sir, what you say is true," replied Chiang.

However, soon after this Chiang, with a small party, got into the palace. The king was enjoying himself with the eunuch in the gardens. They told Huang Hao, who at once hid himself. Chiang approached his master and prostrated himself, saying, "Why did Your Majesty recall me? I had the enemy in my power at Ch'ishan when the triple edict came."

The king hummed and hawed, but made no reply. Then Chiang Wei began his real grievance.

"This Huang Hao is wicked and artful and seems to have the last say in everything. The times of the Emperor Ling and The Ten have returned. Your Majesty may recall Chang Jang or Chao Kao, but if you will only slay this man the Court will be purified and you may return gloriously to the home of your fathers."

The king smiled. "Huang Hao is but a minor servant, one who runs errands for me. If he tried to do as you say, he could not. I always wondered why Tung Yün seemed to hate poor Hao so much. I pray you, noble Sir, to take no notice of him."

"Unless Your Majesty gets rid of him, evil is very close," said Chiang, beating his head upon the ground.

The king replied, "If you love anyone, you want him to live; if you dislike him, you desire his death; can you not bear with my one poor eunuch?"

He bade one of the attendants go and call Huang Hao. When he approached the pavilion, the king told him to ask pardon of Chiang Wei.

Huang Hao prostrated himself and wept, saying, "I am always in attendance upon the Sacred One; that is all I do. I never meddle in state affairs. I pray you, General, to pay no heed to what people say. If you desire my death, I am in your hands, but pity me."

And tears ran down his cheeks. Chiang Wei went away in ill humour. Outside he sought his friend Ch'i Chêng and told him what had happened.

"General, you are in grave danger," said Ch'i. "And if you fall, the country falls with you."

"Can you advise me?" said Chiang. "How can I secure the state and myself?"

Ch'i replied, "There is a place of refuge for you in Shênsi, and that is Miaochung. It is a rich country, and you can make a cantonment there like the Marquis of Wu did. Request the Emperor to let you go thither. You can gather in corn for your armies, you can secure all the west of Shênsi, you can keep Wei from troubling Hanchung, you will retain your military authority, so that no one will dare intrigue against you, and you will be safe. Thus you can ensure the safety of the state and yourself. You should lose no time."

"Your speech is gold and jewels," said Chiang Wei, gratefully.

Without loss of time, Chiang memorialised the throne and obtained the king's consent. Then he returned to Hanchung, assembled his officers and told them his plans.

"Our many expeditions have failed to achieve success owing to lack of supplies. Now I am about to take eight legions to Miaochung to form a cantonment and grow corn ready for the next expedition. You are spent with much fighting and may now repose while collecting grain and guarding Hanchung. The armies of Wei are from home and have to drag their grain over the mountains. They will be worn out with the labour and must soon retire. That will be the time to smite them, and success must be ours."

Hu Chi was set over Hanshouch'êng, Wang Han over Yoch'êng, Chiang Pin over Hanch'êng and Chiang Shu with Fu Ch'ien went to guard the passes. After these arrangements had been made, Chiang Wei went off to Miaochung to grow grain and mature his plans.

Têng Ai heard of these dispositions and discovered that the armies of Shu were distributed in two score camps, each connected with the next like the joints of a huge serpent. He sent out his spies to survey the country, and they made a map which was sent to the capital.

But when the Duke of Chin saw the memorial and the map, he was very angry.

"This Chiang Wei has invaded our country many times, and we have been unable to destroy him. He is the one sorrow of my heart."

Said Chia Ch'ung, "He has carried on the work of K'ungming only too thoroughly, and it is hard to force him back. What you need is some crafty bravo to assassinate him, so remove this constant menace of war."

But Hsün Hsü said, "That is not the way. Liu Ch'an, the King of Shu, is steeped in dissipation and has given all his confidence to one favourite, the eunuch Huang Hao. The higher officers of state are concerned solely with their own safety and Chiang Wei has gone to Miaochung only that he may save his life. If you send an able leader, victory is certain. Where is the need for an assassin's dagger?"

"These are excellent words," said Ssŭma Chao, with a laugh, "but if I would attack Shu where is the leader?"

"Têng Ai is the ablest leader of the day," said Hsün. "Give him Chung Hui as his second, and the thing is done."

"Exactly what I think," said Ssŭma. So he summoned Chung Hui and said to him, "I desire to send you as leader against Wu; can you go?"

"My lord's design is not against Wu, but Shu," was his reply.

"How well you know my inmost thought!" said Ssŭma. "But how would you conduct an expedition against Shu?"

"Thinking that my lord would desire to attack Shu, I have already prepared plans. Here they are."

He laid out his maps, and thereon were shown the camps, and storehouses and roads all complete.

Ssŭma was highly pleased. "You are an excellent leader," said he. "What say you to going with Têng Ai?"

"Ssŭch'uan is large, and there is space for more than one set of operations. Têng Ai can be sent along another line."

Chung Hui was given the title of "Conqueror of the West" and the insignia of a Commander-in-chief over the forces within the pass and control of the armies of Ch'ing, Hsü, Yen, Yü, Ching and Yang. At the same time a commission was sent to Têng Ai giving him command of the forces without the pass, with the title of "Conqueror of the West." And the time for an attack on Shu was settled.

When Ssŭma Chao was settling the plans in the court, the General Têng Tun said, "Why are you sending our armies into a distant and dangerous country and thus inviting trouble? Chiang Wei has invaded this country many times, and the wars have cost us many lives. We should rather seek safety in defence.

"I am sending a righteous army against an unrighteous king; how dare you oppose my designs?"

He ordered the executioners to put Têng Tun to death forthwith, and they soon returned to lay his head at the foot of the steps. This frightened all those present, and they turned pale.

Ssŭma said, "It is six years since I conquered the east, and the six years have been spent in preparation. I have long intended to reduce both Wu and Shu. Now I will destroy Shu, and then like a flood I will descend upon Wu and conquer that. Thus will I destroy both Kuo and Yü. I can tell very nearly what forces they have in Shu. There are eight or nine legions in the garrison of the capital, four or five on the frontier, while Chiang Wei has about six in his cantonments.

Against them we can pit ten legions under Têng Ai, enough to hold Chiang Wei and keep him from moving east, and Chung Hui has twenty or thirty legions of veterans. And they will go in three divisions straight into Hanchung. The King of Shu is a blind fool with his frontier cities in ruins, his courtiers and women quaking with fear. He will not last long."

The assembly praised this perspicacity.

Chung Hui marched as soon as he received his seal of office. Lest his real object should be known, he gave out that his force was directed against Wu, and to give colour to the pretence he had many large ships put in hand. He also sent T'ang Tzŭ to Tênglai and along the sea coast to collect vessels.

Even his chief, Ssŭma, was deceived and called him to ask why he was collecting ships.

He replied, "If Shu hears that we intend to attack the west they will ask assistance from Wu. So I pretend to attack Wu, and they will not dare to move under a year. When Shu is beaten, the ships will be ready and useful for an expedition into the east."

Ssŭma was pleased. The day chosen for the march was the third day of the seventh mouth. Ssŭma escorted his leader out of the city for ten *li* and then took his leave.

A certain Shao T'i, the *"Western Ts'ao-chüan,"* whispered a word of warning.

"My lord has sent Chung Hui with a large army against Shu. I think he is too ambitious to be trusted with such powers?"

"Think you I do not know?" said Ssŭma.

"Then why have you sent him alone and without a colleague?"

Ssŭma said a few words to Shao T'i which put his doubts at rest.

> Chung went alone, although his master knew,
> Occasion serving, he would be untrue.

The next chapter will tell the reader what Shao T'i heard.

CHAPTER CXVI.

CHUNG HUI DIVIDES HIS ARMY;
APPARITION OF WU HOU.

The words whispered in the ear of Shao T'i proved Ssŭma's subtlety. Said he, "This morning they all maintained that Shu should not be attacked, because they are timid. But a determined attack will defeat them. You saw Chung Hui was set upon his plan, and he is not afraid. Shu must therefore be beaten, and then the people's hearts will be torn. Beaten leaders cannot boast, and the officers of a broken state are no fit guardians of its welfare. When Chung turns against us, the men of Shu will not support him, and our men being victors they will wish to return home and will not follow their leader into revolt. Hence there is nothing to be feared. I know this, as you do, but it must remain our secret."

Shao T'i understood.

In his camp, just prior to his march, Chung Hui assembled his officers, four score of them and many bearing well-known names, to receive orders.

"Firstly I want a leader of the van," said he. "He must be skilled in making roads and repairing bridges."

"I will take that post," said a voice, and the speaker was Hsü I, son of the "Tiger Leader" Hsü Chu.

"Nobody is fitter," cried all present.

"You shall have the seal," said Chung. "You are lithe and strong and have the renown of your father to maintain. Beside, all your colleagues recommend you. Your force shall be half a legion of cavalry and a company of footmen. You are to march into Hanchung in three divisions, the centre one going through Hsieh Valley, the other two passing through Lo and Tzǔwu Valleys. You must level and repair the roads, put the bridges in order, bore tunnels and break away rocks. Use all diligence, for any delay will entail punishment."

Hsü I was told to set out immediately, and his chief would start as soon as possible.

As soon as Têng Ai received his orders to attack Shu he sent Ssŭma Wang to enlist the aid of the *Ch'iang*. Next he summoned the Prefects of the various districts, and soon soldiers gathered in Shênsi like clouds.

One night Têng dreamed a dream wherein he was climbing a lofty mountain on the way into Hanchung. Suddenly a spring of water gushed out at his feet and boiled up with great force so that he was alarmed.

He awoke all in a sweat and did not sleep again, but sat awaiting the dawn. At daybreak he summoned Shao Huan, who was skilled in the Book of Changes, told him the dream and asked the interpretation.

He replied, "According to the book, 'water on a mountain' signifies the diagram Ch'ien, whereunder we find that the south-west augurs well, but the north-east is unpropitious. The Sage said of Ch'ien that it meant advantage in the south-west, i.e., success; but the north-east spelt failure, i.e., there was no road. In this expedition, General, you will overcome but you will be checked before you can proceed far."

Têng listened, growing more and more sad as the interpretation of his dream was unfolded. Just then came despatches from Chung Hui asking him to advance into Hanchung and take Ch'i. He at once sent Chuko Hsü, Governor of Yungchou, to cut off Chiang Wei's retreat, and sent other bodies against the various cantonments. Têng Ai took command of a force to go to and fro and reinforce whatever body needed help.

All the officials came out to see Chung depart. It was a grand sight, the gay banners shutting out the sun, breastplates and helmets glittering. The men were fit and the horses in good condition. They all felicitated the leader.

All save one; for Liu Shih was silent. He smiled grimly. Then Wang Hsiang made his way through the crowd and said, "Do you think these two will overcome Shu?"

"They will overcome Shu certainly, only I think neither will ever come back."

"Why do you say that?"

But Liu did not reply; he only smiled. And the question was not repeated.

The armies of Wei were on the march before Chiang Wei heard of the intended attack. He at once sent up a memorial asking that certain defensive arrangements be made. Chang I and Liao Hua were to command at the two most important points, upon which depended the security of Hanchung. He also sent to engage the help of Wu, and gathered soldiers in Miaochung ready for defence.

That year in Shu the reign-style had been changed to the first year of Yen-Hsing. When the memorial came to the king it found him as usual amusing himself with his favourite Huang Hao. He read the document and said to the eunuch, "Here Chiang Wei says that the Wei armies under Têng Ai and Chung Hui are on the way against us. What shall we do?"

"There is nothing of the sort. Chiang Wei only wants to get a name for himself, and so he says this. Your Majesty need feel no alarm, for we can find out the truth from a certain wise woman I know. She is a real prophetess. May I call her?"

The king consented, and a room was fitted up for the séance. They prepared therein incense, flowers, paper, candles, sacrificial articles and so on, and then the eunuch went with a carriage to beg the wise woman to attend upon the king.

She came and was seated on a dragon couch. After the king had kindled the incense and repeated the prayer, the wise woman suddenly let down her hair, dropped her slippers and capered about barefoot. After several rounds of this she coiled herself up on a table.

The eunuch then said, "The spirit has now descended. Send everyone away and pray to her."

So the attendants were dismissed, and the king entreated the wise woman.

Suddenly she cried out, "I am the guardian spirit of Hsi-ch'uan. Your Majesty rejoices in tranquillity; why do you enquire about other matters? Within a few years the land of Wei shall come under you, wherefore you need not be sorrowful."

She then fell to the ground as in a swoon, and it was some time before she revived. The king was well satisfied with her prophesy and gave her large presents. Further, he thereafter believed all she told him. The immediate result was that Chiang's memorial remained unanswered, and as the king was wholly given to pleasure it was easy for the eunuch to intercept all urgent memorials from the general.

Meanwhile Chung Hui was hastening toward Hanchung. The van-leader Hsü I was anxious to perform some startling exploit, and so he led his force to Nanchêng Pass.

He said to his officers, "If we can take this pass then we can march directly into Hanchung; the defence is weak."

A dash was made for the fort, each one vying with the rest to be first. But the commander was Lu Hsün, and he had had early information of the coming of his enemies. So on both sides of the bridge he posted men armed with multiple bows and crossbows. As soon as the attacking force appeared, the signal was given by a clapper and a terrific discharge of arrows and bolts opened. Many men fell, and the army of Wei was defeated.

Hsün I returned and reported his misfortune. Chung Hui himself went with a few horse to see the conditions. Again the machine bows let fly clouds of missiles, and Chung turned to flee.

But a sortie was made, and as Chung crossed the bridge at a gallop the roadway gave, and his horse's hoof went through so that he was nearly thrown. The horse could not free his hoof, and Chung slipped from his back and fled on foot. As he ran down the slope of the bridge Lu Hsün came at him with a spear, but one of Chung's followers, Hsün K'ai by name, shot an arrow at him and brought him to the earth. Seeing this lucky hit, Chung turned back and signalled to his men to make an attack. They came on with a dash, the defenders were afraid to shoot, as their men were mingled with the enemy, and soon the pass was in the hands of the Wei men. The defenders scattered.

The pass being captured, Hsün K'ai was well rewarded for the shot that had saved his general's life. He was promoted to the guards and received presents of a horse and a suit of armour.

Hsün I was called to the tent, and the general blamed him for the lack of care in his task. "You were appointed leader of the van to see that the roads were put in repair, and your special duty was to see that the bridges were in good condition. Yet on the bridge just now my horse's hoof was caught, and I nearly fell. Happily Hsün K'ai was by, or I had been slain. You have been disobedient and must bear the penalty."

The delinquent was sentenced to death. The other captains tried to beg him off, but the general was obdurate, rejecting even the plea of the good services rendered by Hsün's father.

"How can discipline be maintained if the laws are not enforced?" said he.

The sentence was carried out, and the unhappy man's head was exposed as a warning. This severity put fear into the hearts of the officers.

On the side of Shu, Wang Han commanded at Loch'êng and Chiang Pin was in Hanchung. As the enemy came in great force, they dared not go out to meet them, but stood on the defensive with the gates of the cities closed.

Chung Hui issued an order, "Speed is the soul of war; no halts."

Li Fu was ordered to lay siege to Loch'êng, and Hsün K'ai was to surround Hanch'êng. The main army would capture Yangp'ing Pass.

Fu Ch'ien commanded at the pass. He discussed plans with his second in command, and this latter was wholly in favour of defence, saying that the enemy was too strong to think of any other course.

"I do not agree," replied Fu. "They are now fatigued with marching, and we need not fear them. Unless we go out and attack, the two cities will fall."

The lieutenant, Chiang Shu, made no reply. Soon the enemy arrived, and both officers went up to the wall and looked out. As soon as Chung Hui saw them he shouted, "We have here a host of ten legions. If you yield you shall have higher rank than you hold now, but if you persist in holding out then, when we take the pass, you shall all perish. Jewels and pebbles will share the same destruction."

This threat angered Fu. He bade his lieutenant guard the walls, and he went down to give battle, taking three companies. He attacked, and Chung fled; Fu pursued. But soon the army of Wei closed up their ranks and stood. Fu turned to retire, but when he reached his own defences he saw they flew the flags of Wei; the banners of Shu had gone.

"I have yielded," cried Chiang Shu from the ramparts.

Fu reviled him as ungrateful and treacherous, but that did no good. He turned to go once more into the battle. He was soon surrounded. He fought desperately, but could not win clear. His men fell one by one, and when they were reduced to about half a score he cried, "Alive I have been a servant of Shu; dead I will be one of their spirits."

He forced his way into the thickest of the fight. Then his steed fell, and as he was grievously wounded he put an end to his own life.

> The loyalty Fu showed in stressful days
> Won him a thousand autumns' noble praise;
> The base Chiang Shu lived on, a life disgraced,
> I would prefer the death that Fu Ch'ien faced.

With the pass fell into the hands of Chung great booty of grain and weapons. He feasted the army, and that night they rested in Yangan City. However, the night was disturbed by sounds as of men shouting, so that the leader got up and went out thinking there must be an attack. But the sounds ceased, and he returned to his couch. However, he slept no more.

Next night the same thing happened, shoutings in the southwest. As soon as day dawned scouts went out to search, but they came back to say they had gone ten *li* and found no sign of any person. Chung did not feel satisfied, so he took a few cavalrymen and rode in the same direction to explore. Presently they happened upon a hill of sinister aspect overhung by a dismal cloud, while the summit was wreathed in mist.

"What hill is that?" asked Chung, pulling up to question the guides.

"It is known as Tingchünshan, 'The hill of the Halted Army,'" was the reply. "It is where Hsiahou Yüan met his death."

This did not sound cheering at all, and Chung turned back to camp greatly depressed. Rounding the curve of a hill, he came full into a violent gust of wind and there suddenly appeared a large body of horse coming down the wind as if to attack.

The whole party galloped off panic-stricken, Chung leading the way. Many captains fell from their steeds. Yet when they arrived at the pass not a man was missing, although there were many with bruises and cuts from the falls and many had lost helmets. Everyone had seen phantom horsemen, who did no harm when they came near, but melted away in the wind.

Chung Hui called Chiang Shu and asked if there was any temple to any supernatural being on Tingchünshan.

"No," replied he; "there is nothing but the tomb of Chuko Liang."

"Then this must have been a manifestation of the noble Chuko," said Chung. "I ought to sacrifice to him."

So he prepared presents and slew an ox and offered sacrifice at the tomb, and when the sacrifice had been completed the wind calmed, and the dark clouds dispersed. There followed a cool breeze and a gentle shower, and the sky cleared. Pleased with the evidence of the acceptance of their offerings, the sacrificial party returned to camp.

That night Chung fell asleep in his tent with his head resting on a small table. Suddenly a cool breeze began to blow, and he saw a figure approaching clad in Taoist garb, turban, feather fan, white robe of Taoist cut bound with a black girdle. The countenance of the figure was pale and refined, the lips a deep red and the eyes clear. The figure moved with the calm serenity of a god.

"Who are you, Sir?" asked Chung, rising.

"Out of gratitude for your kindly visit this morning, I would make a communication. Though the Hans have declined and the mandate of the Eternal cannot be disobeyed, yet the people of the west, exposed to the inevitable miseries of war, are to be pitied. After you have passed the frontier do not slay ruthlessly."

Then the figure disappeared with a flick of the sleeves of its robe, nor would it stay to answer any questions.

Chung awoke and knew that he had been dreaming, but he felt that the spirit of the great Marquis of War had visited him, and he was astonished.

He issued an order that the leading division of his army should bear a white flag with four words plainly written thereon, "Secure state, comfort people," so that all might know that no violence was to be feared. If anyone was slain wantonly, then the offender should pay with his own life. This tender care was greatly appreciated, so that the invaders were welcomed. Chung Hui soothed the people, and they suffered no injury.

> Those phantom armies circling in the gloom
> Moved Chung to sacrifice at Chuko's tomb;
> For Liu had Chuko wrought unto the end,
> Though dead, he would Liu's people still defend.

Chiang Wei at Miaochung heard of the invasion and wrote to his three Captains to march against the enemy, while he prepared to repulse them if they came to his station.

Soon they came, and he went out to encounter them. Their leader was the Prefect of T'ienshui, Wang Ch'i by name. When near enough, Wang shouted, "Our forces are numbered by millions, our captains by thousands. Twenty legions are marching against you, and Ch'êngtu has already fallen. In spite of this you do not yield, wherefore it is evident you do not recognise the divine command."

Chiang Wei cut short this tirade by galloping out with his spear set. Wang stood three bouts and then fled. Chiang pursued, but a score of *li* away he met a cohort drawn up across the road. On the banner he read that the leader was Ch'ien Hung, Prefect of Shênsi.

Despising this antagonist, he led his men straight on, and the enemy fell back. He drove them before him for some distance, and then came upon Têng Ai. A battle at once began, and the lust of battle held out in the breast of Chiang for a score of bouts.

But neither could overbear the other. Then in the rear arose the clang of gongs and other signs of coming foes. Chiang retired the way he had come, and presently one came to report the destruction of his camps at Kansung.

This was evil tidings. He bade his lieutenants keep his own standard flying and hold Têng while he went to try to recover the camps. On the way he met Yang Hsin, the worker of mischief, but Yang had no stomach for a fight with Chiang and made for the hills. Chiang followed till he came to a precipice down which the enemy were hurling boulders and logs of wood so that he could not pass.

He turned to go back to the battle-field he had just left, but on the way he met the army of Wei, for Têng had overcome his lieutenants. He was surrounded, but presently got clear with a sudden rush and hastened to the great camp.

Next came news of the loss of Yangp'ing Pass and the treachery of Chiang Shu and the death of Fu Ch'ien. The messenger added that Hanchung was now in the possession of Wei, and Loch'êng and Hanch'êng had also opened their gates and yielded to the invaders. Hu Ch'i had gone to the capital for help.

This greatly troubled Chiang, so he broke camp and set out for the frontier. An army barred his way, and again he was forced to fight, this time with Yang Hsin. Chiang rode out in a great rage, and as Yang fled he shot at him thrice, but his arrows missed.

Throwing aside his bow, he gripped his spear and set off in pursuit, but his horse tripped and fell, and Chiang lay on the ground. Yang turned to slay his enemy now that he was on foot, but Chiang wounded Yang's horse in the head. Others coming up rescued Yang.

Mounting another steed, Chiang was just setting out again in pursuit when they reported that Têng Ai was coming against his rear. Realising that he could not cope with this new force, Chiang collected his men in order to retreat into Hanchung. However, the scouts reported another army in the way holding Yinp'ing Bridge, so he halted and made a camp in the mountains. Advance and retreat seemed equally impossible, and he cried in anguish, "Heaven is destroying me!"

Then said Ning Sui, one of his captains, "If our enemies are guarding Yinp'ing Bridge they can only have left a weak force in Yungchou. We can make believe to be going thither through the K'unghan Valley and so force them to abandon the bridge in order to protect the city. When the bridge is clear, you can make a dash for Chienko and hold out there while the army retires into Hanchung."

This plan seemed to promise success, so they marched into the valley, making as though they would go to Yungchou.

When Chuko Hsü, who was at the bridge, heard this he was afraid that his own city, and his headquarters, would be lost and that he would be punished, so he set off to its relief by the south road. He left only a small force at the bridge.

Chiang marched along the north road till he guessed that Chuko Hsün had abandoned the bridge, when he retraced his steps. He dispersed the small force left at the bridge head and burned their camp. Chuko, as he marched, saw the flames, and he turned back to the bridge, but he arrived too late. The army of Shu had already crossed, and he dared not pursue.

Soon after Chiang crossed the bridge he saw another force, but this was led by his own captains, Chang and Liao. They told him that Huang Hao, firm in his faith in the wise woman, would not send help to defend the frontiers. They had come on their own initiative. They also reported the capture of Yangp'ing Pass.

The two armies amalgamated and marched together.

Liao Hua said, "We are attacked all round, and it seems to me wisest to retire on Chienko."

But Chiang Wei was doubtful. Then they heard that enemies were approaching in ten divisions. Chiang was disposed to stand, but Liao Hua said the country was too difficult to fight in with any hope of success, and again urged the wisdom of falling back on Chienko.

At last Chiang Wei consented, and the march began. But as they neared the town they heard drums rolling and saw flags fluttering, which told them that the pass was held.

> Hanchung, that strong defence is lost,
> And storm clouds gather round Chienko.

What force was at the pass will be told in the next chapter.

CHAPTER CXVII.

Tếng Gets Through Yinp'ing Pass;
Chuko Dies at Mienchu.

The soldiers, whose coming had at first alarmed Chiang Wei, were, however, from his own country, part of a force brought to the frontier by Tung Chüeh when he heard of the invasion from Wei. Two legions had been sent to Chienko, and when the dust showed an approaching army he thought it wise to go to the Pass lest the coming men should be enemies to be stopped.

When Tung found that the newcomers were friends, he let them pass through and gave them the news from the capital, bad news of the deeds of both the king and the eunuch-favourite.

"But do not grieve," said Chiang Wei, "so long as I live I will not allow Wei to come and conquer Shu."

They kept good guard at Chienko while they discussed future plans.

"Though we are holding this pass, yet Ch'êngtu is well-nigh empty of soldiers," said Tung Chüeh. "If it was attacked it would go crack!"

Chiang Wei replied, "The natural defences are excellent; it is hard to cross over the mountains and climb the steep roads. No one need fear."

Soon after this, Chuko Hsü appeared at the pass challenging the defenders. Chiáng Wei forthwith placed himself at the head of a half legion and went down to meet him. He gained an easy victory, slaying many of the enemy and taking much spoil in horses and weapons.

While Chiang went back to the pass, the defeated general made his way to Chung Hui's camp to confess his failure. His general was very angry.

"My orders to you were to hold Yinp'ing Bridge so as to stop Chiang Wei, and you lost it. Now without any orders you attack and are defeated."

"Chiang Wei played so many deceitful tricks. He pretended to be going to take Yungchou, and I thought that was very important, so I sent troops to rescue it. Then he meanly got away. I followed to the pass, but never thought he would come out and defeat my men."

Chuko pleaded thus, but he was sentenced to die. Now Chuko was really a subordinate of Têng Ai and, admitting that he was in fault, his punishment should not have been pronounced by Chung Hui. But when Wei Kuan mentioned that as a reason for reprieve, Chung Hui swaggeringly replied, "I have a command from the Emperor and orders from the Prime Minister to attack Shu; if Têng Ai himself offended I would behead him."

However, in spite of these big words, he did not put Chuko to death, but sent him a prisoner to the capital to be judged. The surviving men were added to Chung Hui's army.

This insolent speeech of Chung Hui was duly repeated to Têng Ai, who was angry in his turn and said, "His rank and mine are the same. I have held a frontier post for years and sustained many fatigues in the country's service. Who is he that he gives himself such airs?"

His son Chung endeavoured to appease his wrath. "Father, if you cannot suffer small things you may upset the grand policy of the state. Unfriendliness with him may do great harm, so I hope you will bear with him."

Têng Ai saw he was right, and said no more; but he nourished anger in his heart. With a small escort he went to call upon his colleague. When his coming was announced, Chung Hui asked his staff how many men were following Têng Ai.

"He has only half a score of horsemen," they replied.

Chung Hui had a large body of men drawn up about his tent, and then gave orders that his visitor should be led in. Têng Ai dismounted, and the two men saluted each other. But the visitor did not like the look on the faces of his host's guard. He decided to find out what Chung Hui was thinking.

"The capture of Hanchung is a piece of excellent fortune for the state," said he. "The capture of Chienko can now be accomplished easily."

"What is your own idea, General?" asked Chung Hui.

Têng Ai tried to evade answering the question, but could not. Chung Hui pressed him to reply. Finally he said, "In my simple opinion one might proceed by by-roads from the pass through Hanchung to Yangt'ing, and thence make a surprise march. Chiang Wei must go to its defence, and you, General, can take Chienko."

"A very good plan," said Chung Hui. "You may start forthwith, and I will wait here till I hear news of your success."

They drank, and Têng took his leave. Chung Hui went back to his own tent filled with contempt for Têng's plan, which he thought impracticable.

"They say Têng Ai is able; I think he is of most ordinary capacity," said he to his officers.

"But why?" said they.

"Because the by-roads by Yinp'ing are impassable, nothing but lofty mountains and steep hills. A hundred defenders at a critical point could cut all communications, and Têng Ai's men would starve to death. I shall go by the direct road, and there is no fear about the result. I shall overcome Shu."

So he prepared scaling ladders and ballistæ and set himself to besiege Chienko.

Têng Ai went out to the main gate of the court. While mounting, he said to his followers, "What did Chung Hui think of me?"

"He looked as though he held a poor opinion of what you had said, General, and disagreed with you, although his words were fair enough."

"He thinks I cannot take Ch'êngtu; and so I will take it."

He was received at his own camp by Shih Tsuan and his son, and a party of others of his captains, and they asked what the conversation had been about.

"I told him simple truth, but he thinks I am just a common person of no ability to speak of. He regards the capture of Hanchung as an incomparable feat of arms. Where would he have been if I had not held up Chiang Wei? But I think the capture of Ch'êngtu will beat that of Hanchung."

That night camp was broken up, and they set out upon a march of seven hundred *li* along the hill paths. At that distance from Chienko they were to make a permanent camp. Chung Hui laughed at the attempt.

From his camp Têng Ai sent a secret letter to Ssŭma Chao. Then he called his officers to his tent and asked them, saying, "I am going to make a dash for Ch'êngtu while it is still undefended, and success will mean unfading glory for us all. Will you follow me?"

"We will follow you and obey your orders," cried they all.

So the final dispositions were made. Têng Chung went first to improve the road. His men wore no armour, but they had axes and boring tools. They were to level roads and build bridges.

Next went three legions furnished with dry grain and ropes. At every three hundred *li* they were to make a post of three companies.

In the autumn they left Yinp'ing, and in the tenth month they were in most precipitous country. They had taken twenty-seven days to travel seven hundred *li*. They were in an uninhabited country. After garrisoning the various posts on the way, they had only two companies left. Before them stood a range named Mot'ien Ling, which no horse could ascend. Têng Ai climbed up on foot to see his son and the men with him opening up a road. They were exhausted with fatigue and weeping.

Têng Ai asked why they were so sad, and his son replied, "We have found an impassable precipice away to the northwest which we cannot get through. All our labour has been in vain."

Têng Ai said, "We have got over seven hundred *li* and just beyond is Chiangyu: we cannot go back. How can one get tiger cubs except by going into tiger caves? Here we are, and it will be a very great feat to capture Ch'êngtu."

They all said they would go on. So they came to the precipice. First they threw over their weapons; then the leader wrapped himself in blankets and rolled over the edge, next the captains followed him, also wrapped in blankets. Those who had not blankets were let down by cords round the waist and others clinging to trees followed one after another till all had descended and the Mot'ien Ling was passed. Then they retook their armour and weapons and went on their way.

They came across a stone by the roadside. It bore a mysterious inscription composed by Chuko Liang. Translated literally it read:—

> "Two fires first set out,
> Men pass by here,
> Two soldiers compete
> Both soon die."

Têng Ai was perplexed. Presently he bowed before the stone and prayed to the spirit of Chuko Liang.

"O Marquis, immortal. I grieve that I am not thy worthy disciple."

> The rugged lofty mountain peaks
>   Of Yinp'ing, pierce the sky,
> The sombre crane with wearied wing
>   Can scarcely o'er them fly.
> Intrepid Têng in blankets wrapped
>   Rolled down the craggy steep,
> His feat great Chuko prophesied
>   By insight wondrous deep.

Note.—The interpretation of the inscription is as follows:—
"Two fires" form the ideograph *yen*; "set out" is *hsing*; "first," refers to the year. Thus the first line gives the date, "Yen-Hsing, first year." The two men were Têng Ai and Chung Hui, rivals for glory.

Having crossed this great range of mountains without discovery, Têng Ai marched forward. Presently he came to a roomy camp, empty and deserted. He was told that while Chuko Liang lived two companies had been kept in garrison at this point of danger, but King Ch'an had withdrawn them. Têng Ai sighed at the thought.

He said to his men, "Now retreat is impossible, there is no road back. Before you lies Chiangyu with stores in abundance. Advance and you live, retreat and you die. You must fight with all your strength."

"We will fight to the death," they cried.

The leader was now afoot, doing double marches with his two companies toward Chiangyu.

The commander at Chiangyu was Ma Yao. He heard the east had fallen into the hands of the enemy. Though something prepared for defence, yet his post had a wide area to cover and guard, and he trusted Chiang Wei would defend Chienko. So he did not take his military duties very seriously, just maintaining the daily drills and then going home to his wife to cuddle up to the stove and drink.

His wife was of the Li family. When she heard of the state of things on the frontier she said to her husband, "If there is so great danger on the borders, how is it you are so unaffected?"

"The affair is in Chiang Wei's hands and is not my concern," replied he.

"Nevertheless, the general finally has to guard the capital, and that is a heavy responsibility."

"O, well! The king trusts his favourite entirely and is sunk in vice and pleasure. Disaster is very near, and if the Wei armies get here I shall yield. It is no good taking it seriously."

"You call yourself a man! Have you such a disloyal and treacherous heart? Is it nothing to have held office and taken pay for years? How can I bear to look upon your face?"

Ma Yao was too ashamed to attempt to reply. Just then his house servants came to tell him that Têng Ai, with his two companies, had found their way along some road and had already broken into the city.

Ma was now frightened and hastily went out to find the leader and offer his formal submission. He went to the Town Hall and bowed on the steps, crying, "I have long desired to come over to Wei. Now I yield myself and my army and all the town."

Têng Ai accepted his surrender and incorporated his men with his own force. He took Ma into his service as guide.

In the meantime Ma's wife had hanged herself, overcome with shame and mortification. Ma told Têng Ai why she had done it, and Têng, admiring her rectitude, gave orders for an honourable burial. He also went in person to sacrifice. Everyone extolled her conduct.

> When the King of Shu had wandered from the way,
> And the House of Han fell lower,
> The Lord sent Têng Ai to smite the land.
> Then did a woman show herself most noble,
> So noble in conduct,
> That no leader equalled her.

As soon as Chiangyu was taken, the posts along the road by which the army had come were withdrawn, and there was a general rendezvous at this point. This done, they marched toward Fouch'êng.

T'ien Hsü, a captain, remonstrated, saying, "We have just finished a long and perilous march and are weary and worn out. We ought to repose for a few days to recover."

Têng Ai angrily replied, "Speed is the one important matter in war: do not encourage any discontent. I will not have it."

He was sentenced to death, but as many officers interceded for him he was pardoned.

The army pressed on toward Fouch'êng. As soon as they arrived, the officers yielded as if they thought Têng Ai had fallen from the heavens. Some took the news to the capital, and the king began to feel alarmed. He hastily called for his favourite, who at once denied the report.

"The spirits would not deceive Your Majesty," said Huang Hao.

The king summoned the wise woman to the palace, but the messengers said she had gone no one knew whither. And now urgent memorials and letters fell in from every side like a snow storm, and messengers went to and fro in constant streams. The king called a Court to discuss the danger, but no one had any plan or suggestion to offer. The courtiers just looked blankly into each other's faces.

Finally Ch'i Chêng spoke out, "In this extremity Your Majesty should call in the help of the son of Marquis Wu."

This son of Chuko Liang, known as the Marquis of Wu after his father's death, was named Chan. His mother was born of the Huang family. She was singularly plain and extraordinarily talented. She had studied everything, even books of strategy and magic. Chuko had married her because of her goodness, and she had shared his studies. She had survived her husband but a short time, and her last words to her son had been to be loyal.

Chan had been known as a clever lad and had married a daughter of the king, so that he was a "Fu-ma." His father's rank had descended to him, and he had received general's rank in the guards as well. But he had retired when Huang Hao, the eunuch, as first favourite, began to direct state affairs.

As suggested, the king summoned Chuko Chan to court, told him the troubles that threatened the country and asked for some plan to save his throne.

"My father and I owe too much to the late Emperor's kindness for me to think any sacrifice too great to make for Your Majesty. I pray that you give me command of the troops in the capital, and I will fight a decisive battle."

So the soldiers, seven legions, were placed under his command. When he had gathered all together, he called the officers and asked for a volunteer for the vanguard. His son, Shang, then nineteen, offered himself. He had studied military books and made himself an adept in the various exercises.

So he was appointed, and the army marched to find the enemy. In the meantime the traitor, Ma Yao, had given Têng Ai very complete plans of the country showing the whole one hundred and sixty *li* of road he had to traverse. However, Têng was dismayed when he saw the difficulties ahead of him.

"If they defend the hills in front I shall fail, for if I am delayed Chiang Wei will come up, and my army will be in great danger."

"The army must press on." He called his son and Shih Tsuan and said, "Lead one army straight to Mienchu to keep back any Shu soldiers sent to stop our march. I will follow as soon as I can. But hasten; for if you let the enemy forestall you I will put you to death."

They went. Nearing Mienchu they met the army under Chuko Chan. Both sides prepared for battle, the Shu armies adopted the *pa-kua*, or "Eight Diagrams" formation and presently, after the usual triple roll of drums, Shih and Têng saw their opponents' ranks open in the centre, and therefrom emerge a light carriage in which sat a figure looking exactly as K'ung-ming used to look when he appeared on the battle-field. Everybody knew the Taoist robes and the feather fan. The standard bore his name and titles too.

The sight was too much for the two leaders. The cold sweat of terror poured down them, and they stammered out, "If K'ung-ming is still alive, that is the end of us."

They retreated. The men of Shu came on, and the army of Wei was driven away in defeat and chased a distance of twenty *li*. Then the pursuers sighted Têng Ai and they turned and retired.

When Têng Ai had camped, he called the two leaders before him and reproached them for retreating without fighting.

"We saw K'ung-ming leading the enemy," said Têng Chung, "so we ran away."

"Why should we fear, even if they bring K'ung-ming to life again? You ran away without cause, and we have lost. You ought both to be put to death."

However, they did not die. Their fellows pleaded for them, and Têng's wrath was mollified. Then the scouts came in to say that the leader of the army was a son of K'ung-ming, and they had set up on the carriage an image of the great strategist.

Têng Ai, however, said to the two, "This is the critical stage, and if you lose the next battle you will certainly lose your lives with it."

At the head of one legion they went out to battle once more. This time they met the vanguard led by Chuko Shang, who rode out alone, boldly offering to repulse the invaders. At Chuko Chan's signal the two wings advanced and threw themselves against the line of Wei. The centre portion of the line met them and the battle went to and fro many times, till at length the men of Wei, after great losses, had to give way. Both the leaders being badly wounded, they fled and the army of Shu pursued and drove the invaders into their camp.

Shih and Têng had to acknowledge a new defeat, but when Têng Ai saw both were sorely wounded he forbore to blame them or decree any penalty.

To his officers he said, "This Chuko Chan well continues the paternal tradition. Twice they have beaten us and slain great numbers. We must defeat them, and that quickly, or we are lost."

Then Ch'iu Pên said, "Why not persuade their leader with a letter?"

Têng Ai agreed and wrote a letter, which he sent by the hand of a messenger. The warden of the camp gate led the messenger in to see Chuko Chan, who opened the letter and read:—"General Têng, 'Conqueror of the West,' writes to General Chuko of the Guard, leader of the army in the field.

"Now having carefully observed your talent in attack, I see you are not equal to your most honoured father. From the moment of his emergence from his retreat he said that the country was to be in three divisions. He conquered Chiang-chou and Yichou and thus established a position. Few have been his equal in all history. He made six expeditions from Ch'ishan, and, if he failed, it was not that he lacked skill; it was the will of Heaven. But now this Latter Ruler is dull and weak, and his kingly aura is already exhausted. I have a command from the Son of Heaven to smite Shu with severity, and I already possess the land. Your capital must quickly fall. Why then do you not bow to the will of Heaven and fall in with the desires of men by acting rightly and coming over to our side? I will obtain the rank of Prince of Langya for you, whereby your ancestors will be rendered illustrious. These are no vain words if happily you will consider them."

The letter made Chuko Chan furiously angry. He tore it to fragments and ordered the bearer thereof to be put to death immediately. He also ordered the escort to bear the head of their chief to the camp of Wei and lay it before Têng Ai.

Têng Ai was very angry at this insult and wished to go forth at once to battle. But Ch'iu Pên dissuaded him.

"Do not go out to battle," said he, "rather overcome him by some unexpected stroke."

So Têng Ai laid his plans. He sent Wang Ch'i, Prefect of T'ienshui, and Ch'ien Hung, Prefect of Shênsi, to lie in wait in the rear while he led the main body.

Chuko Chan happened to be close at hand seeking battle, and when he heard the enemy was near he led out his army eagerly and rushed into the midst of the invaders. Then Têng

Ai fled as though worsted, so luring on Chuko. But when the pursuit had lasted some time the pursuers were attacked by those who lay in wait and they were defeated. They ran away into Mienchu.

Therefore Têng Ai besieged Mienchu, and the men of Wei shouted about the city and watched the ramparts, thus keeping the defenders close shut in as if held in an iron barrel.

Chuko Chan was desperate, seeing no way of escape without help from outside. Wherefore he wrote a letter to East Wu begging for assistance, and he gave this letter to one P'êng Ho to bear through the besiegers.

P'êng fought his way through and reached Wu, where he saw King Hsiu. And he presented the letter showing the wretched plight of Chuko and his urgent need.

Then the king assembled his officers and said to them, "The land of Shu being in danger, I cannot sit and look on unconcerned."

He therefore decided to send five legions, over whom he set the veteran captain Ting Fêng, with two able lieutenants. Having received his edict, the general sent away his lieutenants with two legions to Mienchung, and he himself went with three legions toward Shouch'un. The army marched in three divisions.

In the city Chuko Chan waited for the rescue which never came. Weary of the hopeless delay, he said to his captains, "This long defence is useless; I will fight."

Leaving his son and another officer in the city, Chan put on his armour and led out three companies through three gates to fight in the open. Seeing the defenders making a sortie, Têng Ai drew off and Chuko Chan pursued him vigorously, thinking he really fled before his men. But there was an ambush, and falling therein he was quickly surrounded as is the kernel of a nut by the shell. In vain he thrust right and shoved left, he only lost his men. When he halted, the men of Wei poured in flights of arrows, so that his men ran hither and thither to escape. Before long, Chuko Chan was wounded and fell.

"I am done," cried he. "But in my death I will do my duty."

He drew his sword and slew himself.

From the city walls his son Shang saw the death of his father. Girding on his armour he made to go out to fight. A colleague told him the sacrifice would be vain, but he was obstinate.

Cried he, "My father and I and all our family have received favours from the state. My father has died in battle against our enemies, and can I live?"

He whipped his horse and dashed out into the thick of the fight, where he died. A poem has been written extolling the conduct of both father and son.

In skill he was found wanting, not in loyalty;
But the Lord's word had gone forth,
That the King of Shu was to be cut off.
Vàin were the efforts of Chuko's noble descendants,
Though they died at the call of duty.

In commiseration of their loyalty, Têng Ai had both father
and son buried fittingly.

Then he seemed as if he relaxed the closeness of the siege,
and the defenders made a sortie. However, the numbers
being small it availed nothing, and the leaders were slain.
This was the end of the defence, and Têng Ai then entered as
conqueror. Having rewarded his men, he set out for
Ch'êngtu.

The closing days of the Latter Ruler were full of pain and sorrow,
As had been those of Liu Chang.

The next chapter will tell of the defence of Ch'êngtu.

CHAPTER CXVIII.

A Filial Prince Dies;
Jealousy Between Leaders.

The news of the fall of Mienchou and the death in battle of the two Chukos, father and son, brought home to King Ch'an that danger was very near, and he summoned a council. Then he heard that panic had seized upon the people, and they were leaving the city in crowds. Sorely he felt his helplessness. Soon they reported the enemy actually in the city, and many courtiers advised flight.

"Leave the city and flee south to Nanchung," said they. "The country is difficult and easily defended. We can get the *Mans* to come and help us."

But Ch'iào Chou opposed. "No, no; that will not do. The *Mans* are old rebels, ungentle; to go to them would be a calamity."

Then some proposed seeking refuge in Wu. "The men of Wu are our sworn allies, and this is a moment of extreme danger; let us go thither."

But Ch'iao Chou also opposed this. "In the whole course of past ages no Emperor has ever gone to another state. So far as I can see, Wei will presently absorb Wu, and certainly Wu will never overcome Wei. Imagine the disgrace of becoming a minister of Wu and then having to style yourself minister of Wei. It would double the mortification. Do neither. Wei will give Your Majesty a strip of land where the ancestral temple can be preserved, and the people will be saved from suffering. I desire Your Majesty to reflect well upon this."

The distracted ruler retired from the council without having come to any decision. Next day confusion had become still worse. Ch'iao Chou saw that matters were very urgent and presented a written memorial. The king accepted it and decided to yield.

But from behind a screen stepped out one of the king's sons, Liu Shên, Prince of Peiti, who shouted at Ch'iao, "You corrupt pedant, unfit to live among men! How dare you offer such mad advice in a matter concerning the existence of a dynasty? Has any Emperor ever yielded to the enemy?"

The Latter Ruler had seven sons in all, but the ablest, and the only one above the common level of men, was this Liu Shên.

The king turned feebly to his son and said, "The ministers have decided otherwise; they advise surrender. You are the only one who thinks that boldness may avail, and would you drench the city in blood?"

The prince said, "While the late Emperor lived, this Ch'iao had no voice in state affairs. Now he gives this wild advice and talks the most subversive language. There is no reason at all in what he says, for we have in the city many legions of soldiers, and Chiang Wei is undefeated. He will come to our rescue as soon as he knows our straits, and we can help him to fight. We shall surely succeed. Why listen to the words of this dryasdust? Why abandon thus lightly the work of our great forerunner?"

The king became angry at this harangue and turned to his son, saying, "Be silent! You are too young to understand."

The prince beat his head upon the ground and implored his father to make an effort. "If we have done our best and defeat yet comes; if father and son, prince and minister have set their backs to the wall and died in one final effort to preserve the dynasty, then in the shades we shall be able to look the Former Ruler in the face, unashamed. But what if we surrender?"

The appeal left the king unmoved. The prince cried, "Is it not shameful in one day to throw down all that our ancestors built up with so great labour? I would rather die."

The king, now very angry, bade the courtiers thrust the young man out of the palace. Then he ordered Ch'iao Chou to prepare the formal Act of Surrender. When it was written, two officers, with Ch'iao Chou, were sent with it and the hereditary seal to the camp of Têng Ai to offer submission.

Every day Têng's horsemen rode to the city to see what was afoot. It was a glad day when they returned reporting the hoisting of the flag of surrender. The general had not long to wait. The three messengers soon arrived and presented the letter announcing surrender and the seal therewith. Têng read the letter with great exultation, and took possession of the seal. He treated the envoys courteously and by their hands sent back a letter to allay any anxiety among the people. In due time they re-entered the city and bore this missive to the king, who read it with much satisfaction. Then he sent Chang Hsien to order Chiang Wei to surrender.

The President Li Hu carried to the victorious general a statistical statement of the resources of the kingdom: 280,000 households, 914,000 souls, 102,000 armed men of all ranks and 40,000 civil employés. Besides, there were granaries with much grain, gold and silver, silks of many qualities and many unenumerated but precious things in the various storehouses. The same officer arranged that the ceremony of surrender should take place on the first day of the twelfth month.

The wrath of Prince Peiti swelled high as heaven when he heard that his father had actually arranged the date of his abdication. Girding on his sword, he was setting out for the palace when his Consort, the Lady Ts'u, stopped him, saying, "My Prince, why does your face bear this look of terrible anger?"

He replied, "The army of Wei is at the gates, and my father has made his Act of Surrender. To-morrow he and all his ministers are going out of the city to submit formally, and the dynasty will end. But rather than bow the knee to another I will die and go into the presence of the late Emperor in the realms below."

"How worthy; how worthy!" replied she. "And if my lord must die, I, thy handmaid, prays that she may die first. Then may my Prince depart."

"But why should you die?"

"The Prince dies for his father and the handmaid for her husband. One eternal principle guides us all. When the husband dies the wife follows without question."

Thereupon she dashed herself against a pillar, and so she died. Then the prince slew his three sons and cut off the head of his Consort that he might sever all ties to life lest he be tempted to live. Bearing the head of the princess in his hand, he went to the Temple of the Former Ruler, where he bowed his head, saying, "Thy servant is ashamed at seeing the kingdom pass to another. Therefore has he slain his Consort and his sons that nothing should induce him to live and forego death."

This announcement recited, he made yet another to his ancestors. "My ancestors, if you have spiritual intelligence yon know the feelings of your descendant."

Then he wept sore till his eyes ran blood, and he committed suicide. The men of Shu grieved deeply for him, and a poet has praised his noble deed.

> Both king and courtiers, willing, bowed the knee,
> One son alone was grieved and would not live.
> The western kingdom fell to rise no more,
> A noble prince stood forth, for aye renowned
> As one who died to save his forbears' shame.
> With grievous mien and falling tears he bowed
> His head, declaring his intent to die.
> While such a memory lingers none may say
> That Han has perished.

When the king knew of the death of his son, he sent men to bury him.

Soon the main body of the Wei army came. The king and all his courtiers to the number of three score went out at the north gate to bow their heads in submission, the king with his face covered as far as the grave, taking a coffin with him. But Têng Ai with his own hands raised Liu Ch'an from the ground and took off the napkin from his face. The coffin was burned. Then the victorious leader and the vanquished king returned into the city side by side.

> Wei's legions entered Shu,
> And the ruler thereof saved his life
> At the price of his honour and his throne.
> Huang Hao's vicious counsels had brought disaster
> Against which Chiang Wei's efforts were vain.
> How bright shone the loyalty of the faithful one!
> How noble was the fortitude of the prince, grandson of the
>   First Ruler!
> Alas! it led him into the way of sorrow.
> And the plans of the Former Ruler,
> Excellent and far-reaching,
> Whereby he laid the foundations of a mighty state,
> Were brought to nought in one day.

The common people rejoiced at the magnanimity of the victor and met the returning cavalcade with burning incense and flowers. The title of General of Cavalry was given to the late king and other ranks were given to the ministers who had surrendered.

Têng Ai requested the king to issue one more proclamation from the palace to reassure the people, and then the conquerors took formal possession of the state and its granaries and storehouses. Two officers were sent into the provinces to explain the new situation and pacify malcontents, and another was sent to exhort Chiang Wei to yield peaceably. A report of the success was sent to Loyang.

Huang Hao, the eunuch whose evil counsels had wrought such ruin to his master, was looked upon as a danger, and Têng decided to put him to death. However, he was rich and by means of bribes he escaped the death penalty.

Thus perished the House of Han. Reflecting on its end a poet recalled the exploits of Chuko Liang, Marquis of War, and he wrote a poem.

> The denizens of tree-tops, apes and birds,
> Most lawless of created things, yet knew
> And feared his mordant pen. The clouds and winds
> Conspired to aid him to defend his lord.
> But nought awaited the leader's precepts, wise
> To save; with base content the erstwhile king
> Too soon surrendered, yielding all but life.
> In gifts Chuko was peer with Kuan and Yo,
> His hapless death compared with Kuan and Chang's;
> Sad sight, his temple on the river's brink!
> It wrings the heart more than the tearful verse
> Of Liang Fu-yin, the poet he most loved.

In due time Chiang Hsien reached Chienko, and gave the general the king's command to surrender to the invaders. Chiang Wei was dumb with amazement at the order; his officers ground their teeth with rage and mortification. Their hair stood on end with anger: they drew their swords and slashed at stones in their wrath, shouting they would rather die than yield thus. The roar of their angry lamentation was heard for miles.

But Chiang Wei soothed them with kindly words, saying, "Captains, grieve not; even yet I can restore the House of Han."

"How?" cried they.

And he whispered low in their ears.

The flag of surrender fluttered over the ramparts of Chienko, and a messenger went to Chung Hui's camp. When Chiang Wei and his captains drew near, Chung Hui went out to meet them. "Why have you been so long in coming?" was his greeting.

Chiang Wei looked him straight in the face and said, without a tremor, but through falling tears, "The whole armies of the state are under me, and I am here far too soon."

Chung wondered what this cryptic remark might mean, but said nothing more. The two saluted each other and took their seats, Chiang being placed in the seat of honour.

Chiang Wei said, "I hear that every detail of your plans, from the time you left Huainan till now, has been accomplished. The good fortune of the Ssŭma family is owing to you, and so I am the more content to bow my head and yield to you. Had it been Têng Ai I should have fought to the death, for I would not have surrendered to him."

Then Chung Hui broke an arrow in twain, and they two swore close brotherhood. Their friendship became close-knit. Chiang Wei was continued in command of his own army, at which he secretly rejoiced. Chiang Hsien went back to Ch'êngtu.

As conqueror, Têng Ai arranged for the administration of the newly-gained territory. He made Shih Tsuan Governor of Ichou and appointed many others to various posts. He also built a tower in Mienchu in commemoration of his conquest.

At a great banquet, where most of the guests were men of the newly-conquered province, Têng Ai drank too freely and in his cups became garrulous. With a patronising wave of his hand, he said to his guests, "You are lucky in that you have had to do with me. Things might well have been otherwise, and you might all have been put to death."

The guests rose in a body and expressed their gratitude. Just at that moment Chiang Hsien arrived from his visit to Chiang Wei to say that he and his army had surrendered to Chung Hui. Têng Ai thereupon conceived a great hatred for

Chung, and soon after he wrote to Loyang a letter something like this:—

"I would venture to remark that misleading rumours of war should precede actual attack. Now that Shu has been overcome, the manifest next move is against Wu, and in present circumstances victory would easily follow an attack. But after a great effort, both leaders and led are weary and unfit for immediate service. Therefore of this army two legions should be left west of Shênsi and with them two legions of the men of Shu, to be employed in boiling salt so as to improve the finances. Moreover, ships should be built ready for an expedition down the river. When these preparations shall be complete, then send an envoy into Wu to lay before its rulers the truth about its position. It is possible that matters may be settled without any fighting. Further, generous treatment of Liu Ch'an will tend to weaken Sun Hsiu, but if Liu Ch'an be removed to the capital, the men of Wu will be perplexed and doubtful about what may happen to them, and they will not be amenable. Therefore it seems the most fitting to leave the late King of Shu here. Next year, in the winter season, he might be removed to the capital. For the present I would recommend that he be created Prince of Fufêng, and granted a sufficient revenue and suitable attendants. His sons also should receive ducal rank. In this way would be demonstrated that favourable treatment follows upon submission. Such a course would inspire fear of the might of Wei and respect for its virtue, and the result will be all that could be desired."

Reading this memorial, the thought entered the mind of Ssŭma Chao that Têng Ai was exaggerating his own importance, wherefore he first wrote a private letter to Wei Kuan and then caused the king to issue an edict concerning the successful general. The edict ran thus:—

"General Têng has performed a glorious exploit, penetrating deeply into a hostile country and reducing to submission a usurping potentate. This task has been quickly performed; the clouds of war have already rolled away and peace reigns throughout Pa and Shu.

"The merits of Têng Ai surpass those of Po Ch'i, who subdued the mighty state of Ch'u and Han Hsin, who conquered Chao. Têng Ai is created *T'ai-yü*, and We confer upon him a fief of 20,000 homesteads, and his two sons are ennobled, each with a fief of 1,000 homesteads."

After the edict had been received with full ceremonies, the Inspector of the Forces, Wei Kuan, produced the private letter, which said that Têng's proposals would have suitable consideration in due time.

Then said Têng, "A general in the field may decline to obey even the orders of his prince. My commission was to conquer the west; why are my plans hindered?"

So he wrote a reply and sent it to the capital by the hand of the envoy. At that time it was common talk at court that Têng Ai intended to rebel, and when Ssǔma Chao read the letter his suspicions turned to certainty, and he feared. This was the letter:—

"General Têng, 'Conqueror of the West,' has reduced the chief of the revolt to submission and must have authority to act according as he sees best in order to settle the early stages of administration of the new territory. To await government orders for every step means long delays. According to the 'Spring and Autumn' Annals a high officer, when abroad, has authority to follow his own judgment for the safety of the Throne and the advantage of the state.

"Now seeing that Wu is still unsubdued, all interest centres upon this country, and schemes of settlement should not be nullified by strict adherence to rules and formalities. In war advances are made without thought of reputation, retreats without consideration of avoiding punishment. Though I do not possess the fortitude of the ancients, I shall not be deterred from acting for the benefit of the state by craven and selfish fears for my own reputation."

In his perplexity Ssǔma Chao turned to Chia Ch'ung for advice. Said he, "Têng Ai presumes upon his services to be haughty and imperious: his recalcitrancy is very evident. What shall I do?"

"Why not order Chung Hui to reduce him to obedience?" replied Chia.

Ssǔma Chao accepted the suggestion and issued an edict raising Chung Hui to presidential rank. After this the Inspector of the Forces, Wei Kuan, was set over both, with special orders to keep a watch upon Têng and guard against any attempt at insubordination.

The edict sent to Chung Hui ran as follows:—"General Chung, 'Conqueror of the West,' against whose might none can stand, before whom no one is strong, whose virtue conquers every city, whose wide net no one escapes, to whom the valiant army of Shu humbly submitted, whose plans never fail, whose every undertaking succeeds, is hereby made President of the Board of Revenue and raised to the rank of Marquis of a fief of 10,000 families. His two sons also have similar rank with a fief of 1,000 families."

When this edict reached Chung Hui, he called in Chiang Wei and said to him, "Têng Ai has been rewarded more richly than I and is a *T'ai-yü*. But Ssǔma suspects him of rebellion and has ordered Wei Kuan and myself to keep him in order. What does my friend Po-Yüeh think ought to be done?"

Chiang Wei replied, "They say Têng's origin was ignoble and in his youth he was a farmer and breeder of cattle. However, he had good luck and has won a great reputation in this expedition. But this is due not to his able plans, but to the good fortune of the state. If you had not been compelled to hold me in check at Chienko he could not have succeeded. Now he wishes the late king to be created Prince Fufêng, whereby he hopes to win the goodwill of the men of Shu. But to me it seems that perfidy lies therein. The duke suspects him, it is evident."

Chung complimented him. Chiang Wei continued, "If you will send away your people I have something to say to you in private."

When this had been done and they two were alone, Chiang drew a map from his sleeve and spread it before Chung, saying, "Long ago, before he had left his humble eot, K'ung-ming gave this to the Former Ruler and told him of the riches of Ichou and how well it was fitted for an independent state. Whereupon Ch'êngtu was seized as a first step towards attaining it. Now that Têng Ai has got to the same point it is small wonder that he has lost his balance."

Chung asked many questions about the details of the features of the map, and Chiang explained in full. Toward the end, he asked how Têng could be got rid of.

"By making use of Duke Chin's suspicions," replied Chiang. "Send up a memorial to say that it looks as if Têng Ai really contemplated rebellion. You will receive direct orders to check the revolt.

So a memorial was sent to Loyang. It said that Têng Ai aimed at independence, nourished base designs, was making friends with the vanquished and was about to revolt.

At this news the court was much disturbed. Then to support his charges, Chung's men intercepted Têng's letters and re-wrote them in arrogant and rebellious terms. Ssŭma Chao was greatly angered and ordered an expedition into the Hsieh Valley to arrest Têng, he himself directing it under the leadership of the King of Wei, whom he compelled to go with him.

Then said Shao T'i, "Chung Hui's army outnumbers that of Têng Ai by six to one. You need not go; you need only order Chung to arrest Têng."

"Have you forgotten?" said Ssŭma, smiling. "You said Chung Hui was a danger; I am not really going against Têng Ai, but against the other."

"I feared lest you had forgotten," said Shao. "I ventured to remind you, but the matter must be kept secret."

The expedition set out. By this time Chung's attitude had aroused Chia Chung's suspicions, and he spoke of it to Ssŭma Chao, who replied, "If I sent you should I feel doubts? However, come to Ch'angan and you will understand."

The despatch of the army was reported to Chung Hui, who wondered what it might mean. He at once called in Chiang Wei to consult about the seizure of Têng Ai.

598

Lo! he is victor here, a king must yield;
And there a threatening army takes the field.

The next chapter will relate the plan to arrest Têng Ai.

CHAPTER CXIX.

FALSE DESERTION; A SUBTLE SCHEME;
A SECOND ABDICATION RESEMBLES THE FIRST.

Asked to say what was the best plan to secure the arrest of Têng Ai, Chiang Wei said, "Send Wei Kuan: Têng will try to kill him and so manifest the desire of his heart. Then you can destroy him as a traitor."

Hence Wei was sent, with a score or so of men, to effect the arrest. Wei's own men saw the danger of the enterprise and urged him not to go, but he felt confident and heeded them not.

Wei Kuan first wrote a score or two of letters, all in the same terms, saying that he had orders to arrest Têng Ai, but no other persons would be dealt with providing they submitted quickly. On the contrary, they might hope for rewards. However, the laggards and those who were contumacious would be dealt with severely. He sent these letters to various officers who were serving under Têng. He also prepared two cage carts.

Wei and his small party reached the capital about cock-crow and found waiting for him most of the officers to whom he had written. They at once yielded. Têng Ai was still asleep when the party reached his palace, but Wei entered and forced his way into Têng's chamber. He roared out that he had orders to arrest father and son, and the noise awakened the sleeper, who tumbled off his couch in alarm. But before he could do anything to defend himself he was seized, securely bound and huddled into one of the carts. Têng's son rushed in at the noise, but was also made prisoner and thrust into the other cart. Many captains and attendants were in the palace, but before they had recovered from their fright a cry arose that Chung Hui was close at hand, and they scattered.

Chung Hui and Chiang Wei dismounted at the palace gates and entered. The former, seeing both the Têngs prisoners, struck the elder about the head and face with his whip and insulted him, calling him a vile cattle breeder and so on. Nor was Chiang Wei backward.

"You fool! See what your good luck has brought you to-day!" cried he.

And Têng Ai replied in kind. Chung Hui at once sent off both the prisoners to Loyang, and then entered the capital in state. He added all Têng's army to his own forces, so that he became very formidable.

"To-day I have attained the one desire of my life," cried Chung.

Chiang replied, "Han Hsin hearkened not to K'uai T'ung and so blundered into trouble at the Weiyang Palace; the *T'ai-fu* Wên Chung would not follow Fan Li into retirement and fell victim to a sword on the lakes. No one would say these two were not brilliant, but they did not scent danger early enough. Now, Sir, your merit is great and your prestige overwhelming, but why do you risk future dangers? Why not sail off in a boat leaving no trace of your going? Why not go to Mount Omi and wander free with Chih Sung-tzǔ?"

Chung smiled. "I do not think your advice much to the point. I am a young man, not forty yet, and think rather of going on than halting. I could not take up a do-nothing hermit's life."

"If you do not, then take heed and prepare for dangers. Think out a careful course, as you are well able to do. You need not trouble any old fool for advice."

Chung Hui laughed loud and rubbed his hands together with glee.

"How well you know my thoughts, my friend!" said he.

They two became absorbed in the plans for their grand scheme. But Chiang wrote a secret letter to his late lord praying him to be patient and put up with humiliations for a season, for he would be restored in good time. The sun and moon were all the more glorious when they burst through the dark clouds. The House of Han was not yet done.

While these two were planning how best to outwit each other, but both being against Wei, there suddenly arrived a letter from Ssǔma Chao saying he was at Ch'angan with an army lest there should be any difficulty in disposing of Têng Ai. Chung Hui divined the real purport at once.

"He suspects," said Chung. "He knows quite well that my army outnumbers that of Têng many times and I could do what he wishes easily. There is more than that in his coming."

He consulted his fellow-conspirator, who said, "When the prince suspects a minister, that minister dies. Have we not seen Têng Ai?"

"This decides me," replied Chung. "Success, and the empire is mine; failure, and I go west into Shu to be another Liu Pei, but without his mistakes."

Chiang said, "The Empress Kuo has just died. You can pretend she left you a command to destroy Ssǔma Chao, the real murderer of the Emperor. Your talents are quite sufficient to conquer the empire."

"Will you lead the van?" said Chung. "When success is ours we will share the spoil."

"The little I can do I will do most willingly," said Chiang. "But I am not sure of the support of all our subordinates."

"To-morrow is the Feast of Lanterns, and we can gather in the palace for the congratulations. There will be grand illuminations, and we will prepare a banquet for the officers, whereat we can kill all those who will not follow us."

At this the heart of Chiang Wei leapt with joy. Invitations were sent out in the joint names of the two conspirators, and the feast began. After several courses, suddenly Chung Wei lifted his cup and broke into wailing.

Everyone asked what was the cause of this grief, and Chung replied. "The Empress has just died, but before her death she gave me an edict, which is here, recounting the crimes of Ssŭma Chao and charging him with aiming at the Throne. I am commissioned to destroy him, and you all must join me in the task."

The guests stared at each other in amazement, but no one uttered a word. Then the host suddenly drew his sword, crying, "Here is death for those who oppose!"

Not one was bold enough to refuse, and, one by one, they all signed a promise to help. As further security, they were all kept prisoners in the palace under careful guard.

"They are not really with us," said Chiang Wei. "I venture to request you to 'bury' them."

"A great pit has been already dug," replied his brother host. "And I have a lot of clubs ready. We can easily club those who disagree and bury them in the pit."

A certain officer named Ch'iu Chien, a man in the confidence of the conspirators, was present. He had once served under Hu Lieh, who was one of the imprisoned guests, and he found means to warn his former chief.

Hu Lieh wept and said, "My son is in command of a force outside the city. He will never suspect Chung capable of such a crime, and I pray you to tell him. If I am to die it will be with less regret if my son can be told."

"Kind master, have no anxiety; only leave it to me," replied Ch'iu.

He went to Chung Hui, and said, "Sir, you are holding in captivity a large number of officers, and they are suffering from lack of food and water. Will you not appoint an officer to supply their needs?"

Chung Hui was accustomed to yield to the wishes of Ch'iu, and he made no difficulty about this. He told him to see to it himself. Only saying, "I am placing great trust in you, and you must be loyal."

"My lord, you may be quite content. I know how to keep a strict watch when necessary."

But he allowed to enter into the place of confinement a trusty confidant of Hu Lieh, who gave him a letter to his son Yüan. It told him the whole story.

Hu Yüan told his subordinates, and they were greatly enraged. They came to their commander's tent to say they would rather die than follow a rebel. So Hu Yüan fixed upon the eighteenth day of the month to attempt the rescue. He enlisted the sympathy of Wei Kuan and got his men ready. He bade Ch'iu tell his father what was afoot. Hu Lieh told his fellow-captives.

Now Chung Hui dreamed a dream, that he was bitten by many serpents, and he asked Chiang Wei to expound the vision. Chiang replied that dreams of dragons and snakes and scaly creatures were exceedingly auspicious. Chung was only too ready to accept this interpretation. Then he told Chiang that all was ready and they would put the crucial question to each captive.

"I know they are opposed to us, and you would do well to slay them all, and that right quickly," replied Chiang.

"Good," replied Chung.

He bade Chiang turn in some ruffians among the captives. But just as Chiang was starting to carry out these instructions he was seized with a sudden spasm of the heart, so severe that he fainted. He was raised from the earth and in time revived. Just as he came to, a tremendous hubbub arose outside the palace. Chung at once sent to enquire what was afoot, but the noise waxed louder and louder, sounding like the rush of a multitude.

"The officers must be raging," said Chung. "We had best slay them at once."

But they told him that soldiers were in the palace. Chung bade them close the doors of the Hall of Audience, and he sent his own men upon the roof to pelt the incoming soldiers with tiles. A few were slain on either side.

Then a fire broke out. The assailants broke open the doors. Chung Hui faced them and slew a few, but others shot at him with arrows, and he fell and died. They hacked off his head.

Chiang Wei ran to and fro slaying all he met till another heart spasm seized him.

"Failed!" he shrieked, "But it is the will of Heaven." He put an end to his own life. He was fifty-nine.

Many hundreds were slain within the precincts of the palace. Wei Kuan presently ordered that the soldiers were to be led back to their various camps to await the orders of the king. The soldiers of Wei, burning for revenge, hacked the dead body of Chiang Wei to pieces. They found his gall bladder extraordinarily large, as large as a hen's egg. They also seized and slew all the family of the dead leader.

Seeing that Têng Ai's two enemies on the spot were both dead, his old soldiers bethought themselves of trying to rescue him. When Wei Kuan, who had actually arrested Têng, heard this he feared for his life. Further, he was unwilling to forgo his revenge.

"If he gets free it means my death," said Wei.

Then T'ien Hsü spoke out, saying, "When Têng Ai took Chiangyu he wished to put me to death. It was only at the prayer of my friends that he let me off. May I not have my revenge now?"

So at the head of half a company T'ien went in pursuit of the cage-carts. He came up with them at Mienchu and found that the two prisoners had just been released from the carts in which they were being carried to Loyang. When Têng saw that those coming up were men of his own late command, he took no thought for defence. Nor did T'ien waste time in preliminaries. He went up to where Têng was standing and cut him down. His men fell upon the son, Têng Chung, and slew him also, and thus father and son met death in the same place.

A poem, pitying Têng Ai, was written:—

> While yet a boy, Têng loved to sketch and plan;
> He was an able leader as a man.
> The earth could hide no secrets from his eye,
> With equal skill he read the starry sky.
> Past every obstacle his way he won,
> And onward pressed until his task was done.
> But foulest murder closed a great career,
> His spirit ranges now a larger sphere.

A poem was also composed in pity for Chung Hui:—

> Of mother-wit Chung had no scanty share,
> And in due time at court did office bear;
> His subtle plans shook Ssŭma's hold on power,
> He was well named the *Tzŭ-fang* of the hour.
> Chouch'un and Chienko ramparts straight fell down,
> When he attacked, and he won great renown.
> Ambition beckoned, he would forward press—
> His spirit homeward wandered, bodiless.

Another poem, in pity of Chiang Wei, runs:—

> Tiensui boasts of a hero, talent came forth from
>   Liangchou,
> Chang Liang fathered his spirit, Chuko tutored his
>   mind,
> Valiant he ever pressed forward, nor had a thought
>   of returning,
> Grieved were the soldiers of Han when death rapt
>   his soul from his body.

And thus died all three of the great leaders in Shu. Many
other captains also perished, and with them died Liu Jui, the
heir-apparent. Followed a time of great confusion, which
endured till Chia Ch'ung arrived and restored confidence and
order. He set Wei Kuan over the city of Ch'êngtu and sent
the captive king to Loyang. Few officers accompanied the
deposed king on this degrading journey. Liao Hua and Tung
Chüeh made illness an excuse not to go. They died of grief
soon after.

At this time the year-style of Wei was changed to *Hsien-
K'ang*. In the third month of this year, since nothing could
be done to assist Shu to recover its independence, the troops of
Wu were withdrawn and returned to their own land.

Now the officer Hua Ho sent up a memorial to Sun Hsiu,
King of Wu, saying, "Wu and Shu were as close as are one's
lips to one's teeth, and when the lips are gone the teeth are
cold. Without doubt Ssŭma Chao will now turn his thoughts
to attacking us, and Your Majesty must realise the danger and
prepare to meet it."

The king knew that he spoke truly, so he set Lu K'ang, son
of the late able leader Lu Hsün, over the army of Chingchou
and the river ports with the title "Guardian of the East," and
Sun I was sent to Nanhsü to control the camps along the river
banks. Over all he set the veteran Ting Fêng.

When Ho Ko, Prefect of Chienning, heard that Ch'êngtu had
been taken, he dressed himself in white and wailed during
three days, facing toward the capital.

"Now that the capital has fallen and the king is a captive,
it would be well to surrender," said his officers.

Ho replied, "There is a hindrance. I know not how fares
our lord, whether he is in comfort or in misery. If his captors
treat him generously, then will I yield. But perhaps they will
put him to shame, and when his prince is shamed the minister
dies."

So certain persons were sent to Loyang to find out how fared
the late king.

Soon after Liu Ch'an reached the capital of Wei, Ssŭma
Chao returned. Seeing Liu Ch'an at court, he upbraided him,
saying that he deserved death for his vicious courses, which
had brought misfortune upon him. Hearing this, the face of
the late king turned to the colour of clay with fear, and he was
speechless.

But certain of the courtiers said, "He has lost his kingdom,
he has surrendered without a struggle, and he now deserves
pardon."

Liu Ch'an suffered no injury, but was created Duke of Anlô.
Moreover, he was assigned a residence and a revenue, and he
received presents of silk, and servants were sent to wait upon
him, male and female. The officers of Shu, who had accom-

panied him into exile, were given ranks of nobility. But Huang Hao, whose evil influence had brought the kingdom to nought, and who had oppressed the people, was put to death with ignominy in the public place.

When Ho Ko heard all these things he came with his officers and yielded submission.

Liu Ch'an went to the residence of Ssŭma Chao to thank him for his bounty, and a banquet was prepared. At the banquet they performed the music of Wei, with the dances, and the hearts of the men of Shu were sad; only Liu Ch'an appeared merry. Half way through the feast, Ssŭma said to Chia Ch'ung, "The man lacks feeling; that is what has ruined him. Even if Chuko Liang had lived, he could not have maintained such a man. It is not wonderful that Chiang Wei failed."

Turning to his guest, Ssŭma said, "Do you never think of Shu?"

"With such music as this I forget Shu," replied Liu Ch'an.

Presently Liu Ch'an rose and left the table. Ch'i Chêng went over to him and said, "If you are questioned again, weep and say that in Shu are the tombs of your forefathers and no day passes that you do not grieve to be so far away. The duke may let you return."

The late king promised he would. When the wine had gone round several more times Ssŭma put the same question a second time; the king replied as he had been told. He also tried to weep, but failed to shed a tear. So he shut his eyes.

"Is not that just what Ch'i Chêng told you to say?" asked his host.

"It is just as you say," was the reply.

They all laughed. But really Ssŭma was pleased with the frank answer and felt that nothing was to be feared from him.

> Laughter loving, pleasure pursuing,
>   Rippling smiles o'er a merry face,
> Never a thought of his former glory
>   In his callous heart finds place.
> Childish joy in a change of dwelling,
>   That he feels, and that alone;
> Manifest now that he was never
>   Worthy to sit on his father's throne.

The courtiers thought that so grand an exploit as the conquest of the west was worthy of high honour, so they memorialised the King of Wei to confer princedom on Ssŭma Chao. At that time, Ts'ao Huan ruled in name only, for he had no authority. The whole land was under Ssŭma, whose will the king himself dared not cross. And so, in due course, the duke became Prince of Chin. To match the new honour to the son, his father, Ssŭma I, was posthumously created Prince Hsüan and his late elder brother Prince Ching.

The wife of Ssŭma Chao was the daughter of Wang Su. She bore to him two sons, the elder of whom was named Yen. Yen was huge of frame, his flowing hair reached to the ground when he stood up, and both hands hung down below his knees. He was clever, brave and skilled in the use of arms.

The second son, Yu, was mild of disposition, a filial son and a dutiful brother. His father loved him dearly. As Ssŭma Shih had died without leaving sons, this youth, Yu, was regarded as his son, to continue that line of the family. Ssŭma Chao used to say that the empire was really his brother's.

Becoming a prince, it was necessary for Ssŭma Chao to choose his heir, and he wished to name his younger son. Shan T'ao remonstrated.

"It is improper and infelicitous to prefer the younger," said Shan, and Chia Ch'ung followed in the same strain.

"The elder is clever, able in war, one of the most talented men in the state and popular. With such natural advantages he has a great destiny; and was not born to serve."

Ssŭma hesitated, for he was still unwilling to abandon his desire. But two other officers of rank also remonstrated, saying, "Certain former dynasties have preferred the younger before the elder and rebellion has generally followed. We pray you reflect upon these cases."

Finally Ssŭma Chao yielded and named his son Yen as his successor.

Certain officers memorialised that a gigantic figure of a man had descended from heaven in Hsiangwuhsien. They gave his height as twenty feet and said that his foot-print measured over three feet two inches. He had white hair and a hoary beard. He wore an unlined yellow robe and a yellow cape. He walked leaning on a black-handled staff.

This extraordinary man preached, saying, "I am the king of men now come to tell you of a change of ruler and the coming of peace."

He wandered about for three days and then disappeared.

They continued, "Evidently this portent refers to yourself, Noble Sir, and now you should assume the imperial head-dress with twelve strings of pearls, set up the imperial standard and have the roads cleared when you make a progress. You should ride in the golden-shafted carriage with six coursers. Your Consort should be styled ' Empress ' and your heir the ' Heir Apparent.' "

Ssŭma Chao was greatly pleased. He returned to his palace, but just as he was sitting down he was suddenly seized with paralysis and lost the use of his tongue. He quickly grew worse. His three chief confidants, Wang Hsiang, Ho Tsêng and Hsün I, together with many court officials, came to enquire after his health, but he could not speak to them. He pointed toward the heir apparent, Ssǔma Yen, and died. It was the *hsin-mao* day of the eighth month.

Then said Ho Tsêng, "The care of the empire devolves upon the Prince of Chin; let us induct the heir. Then we can perform the sacrifices to the late prince."

Thereupon Ssǔma Yen was set up in his father's place. He gave Ho the title of Prime Minister and conferred many other titles and ranks. The posthumous title of "Prince Wên" was conferred upon his late father.

When the obsequies were finished, Ssǔma Yen summoned Chia Ch'ung and P'ei Hsiu into the palace, and said, "Ts'ao Ts'ao said that if the celestial mandate rested upon him he could be such as was King Wên of Chou; is this really so?"

Chia replied, "Ts'ao Ts'ao was in the service of Han and feared lest posterity should reproach him with usurpation. Wherefore he spoke thus. Nevertheless he cause Ts'ao P'ei to become Emperor."

"How did my father compare with Ts'ao Ts'ao?" asked Ssǔma Yen.

"Although Ts'ao was universally successful, yet the people feared him and credited him with no virtue. His son differed from him greatly, and his rule was marked by strife and lack of tranquillity. No single year was peaceful. Later Prince Hsüan and Prince Ching of your line rendered great services and disseminated compassion and virtue, so that they were beloved. Your late father overcame Shu in the west and was universally renowned. Comparison with Ts'ao is impossible."

"Still Ts'ao P'ei continued the rule of Han; can I not in like manner continue that of Wei?"

The two counsellors bowed low and said, "Ts'ao P'ei's action may be taken as a precedent to continue an older dynasty. Wherefore prepare a terrace to make the great declaration."

Ssǔma Yen resolved to act promptly. Next day he entered the palace armed with a sword. No Court had been held for many days, for Ts'ao Huan was ill at ease and full of dread. When Yen appeared, the king left his place and advanced to met him. Ssǔma Yen sat down.

"By whose merits did Wei succeed to empire?" he asked suddenly.

"Certainly success was due to your forefathers," replied the king.

Yen smiled, saying, "Your Majesty is unskilled in debate, inept in war and unfit to rule. Why not give place to another more able and virtuous?"

The king's lips refused a reply. But one of the ministers cried, "You are wrong to speak thus, O Prince. His Majesty's ancestor conquered east and west, north and south, and won the empire by strenuous effort. The present Emperor is virtuous and without fault. Why should he yield place to another?"

Ssŭma Yen replied angrily, "The imperial right lay with the Hans, and Ts'ao Ts'ao coerced them as he did the nobles. In making himself the King of Wei he usurped the throne of Han. Three generations of my forefathers upheld the House of Wei, so that their power is not the result of their own abilities, but of the labour of my house. This is known to all the world, and am I not equal to carrying on the rule of Wei?"

"If you do this thing you will be a rebel and an usurper," said Chang Chieh.

"And what shall I be if I avenge the wrongs of Han?"

He bade the lictors take Chang outside and beat him to death, while the king wept and besought pardon for his faithful counsellor.

Ssŭma rose and left. The king turned to Chia Ch'ung and P'ei Hsiu, saying, "What should I do? Some decision must be taken."

They replied, "Truth to tell, the measure of your fate is accomplished and you cannot oppose the will of Heaven. You must prepare to abdicate as did Hsien of the Hans. Resign the throne to the prince and thereby accord with the design of Heaven and the will of the people. Your personal safety need not cause you anxiety."

Huan could only accept this advice, and the terrace was built. The day *chia-tzŭ* of the twelfth month was chosen for the ceremony. On that day the king, dressed in full robes of ceremony, and bearing the seal in his hand, ascended the terrace in the presence of a great assembly.

> The House of Wei displaced the House of Han
> And Chin succeeded Wei; so turns fate's wheel
> And none escape its grinding. Chang the true
> Stood in the way and died. We pity him.
> Vain hope with one small hand to hide Mount T'ai!

The Emperor-elect was requested to ascend the high place, and there received the great salute. Huan then descended, robed himself as a duke and took his place as the first of subjects.

Ssŭma Yen now stood upon the terrace, supported by Chia and P'ei. Ts'ao Huan was ordered to prostrate himself, while the command was recited, and Chia Chung read:—

"Forty-five years have elapsed since, in the twenty-fifth year of *Chien-An*, the House of Han gave place to the House of Wei. But the favour of Heaven has now left the latter House and reverts to Chin. The merits and services of the family of Ssŭma reach to the high heavens and pervade the earth. The Prince of Chin is fitted for the high office and to continue the rule. Now His Majesty the Emperor confers upon you the title of Prince Ch'ênliu; you are to proceed to Chinchingchung, where you will reside; you are forbidden to come to Court unless summoned."

Sadly Ts'ao Huan withdrew. The *T'ai-fu* Ssŭma Fu wept before the deposed king and promised eternal devotion. "I have been a servant of Wei and will never turn my back upon the House," said he.

Ssŭma Yen did not take this amiss, but offered him a princedom. He declined the offer.

The new Emperor was now seated in his place, and all the officers made their salutations and felicitated him. The very hills rang with *"Wan shui!* O King, live for ever!"

Thus succeeded Ssŭma Yen, and the state was called Ta Chin and a new year-style was chosen, *T'ai-Shih,* or the *"Great Beginning."* An amnesty was declared.

The kingdom of Wei had ended.

> The Founder of the Dynasty of Chin
> Took Wei as model; thus the displaced king
> Was named a prince, when on the terrace high
> His throne he had renounced.
> We grieve when we recall these deeds.

The new Emperor conferred posthumous rank upon his late father, Ssŭma I, his uncle and his grandfather. He built seven temples in honour of his ancestors, dedicated to Ssŭma Chun, Ssŭma Liang, Ssŭma Chien, Ssŭma Fang, Ssŭma I, Ssŭma Shih and Ssŭma Chao. All these, except his uncle, were in his own direct line of ancestry.

All these things being accomplished, Courts were held daily, and the one subject of discussion was the subjugation of Wu.

> The House of Han has gone for aye,
> And Wu will quickly follow.

The story of the attack upon Wu will be told next.

CHAPTER CXX.

A Veteran Offers New Plans;
Sun Hao Surrenders and the Three States Re-Unite.

When the King of Wu knew that the House of Wei had fallen before the Chins he also knew that the usurper's next thought would be the conquest of his own land. The anxiety made him ill, so that he took to his bed and was like to die. He then summoned to his bedside Puyang Hsing, his First Minister, and his heir Sun Ling. But they two came almost too late. The dying ruler, with his last effort, took the minister by the hand, but could only point to his son. Then he died.

Puyang left the couch and called a meeting of the officers, whereat he proposed to place the heir on his father's throne. Then one Wan Yü rose and said the young prince was too youthful to rule in such troublous times, and he suggested instead Sun Hao, who stood in the direct line from Sun Ch'üan. He was then Marquis of Wuch'êng. The General Chang Pu supported his election, saying he was able and prompt in decision. However, Puyang was doubtful and consulted the Empress Dowager.

"Settle this with the nobles," she replied; "I am a widow and know nothing of such matters."

Finally Sun Hao won the day, and in the seventh month he was enthroned as Emperor in Wu, and the first year of his reign was *Yüan-Hsing* (264 A.D.). The excluded prince was consoled with the title of Prince Yüchang. Posthumous rank was given to the late Emperor's father and mother. The veteran leader Ting Fêng was made Minister of War.

However, the year-style was changed to *Kan-Lu* the very next year.

The new ruler soon proved himself cruel and oppressive and day by day grew more so. He indulged in every form of vice and chose an eunuch as his confidant and favourite. When the Prime Minister and Chang Pu ventured upon remonstrance, both, with all their family, were put to death. Thereafter none dared to speak; the mouth of every courtier was "sewn up."

Another year-style, *Pao-Ting*, was adopted the next year, and the responsibility of the Prime Minister's office was shared by two officers, "the left" and "the right."

At this time the imperial residence was in Wuch'ang. The people of Yangchow refused tribute and suffered exceedingly. There was no limit to the ruler's extravagance; the treasury was swept clean and the income of the royal domain exhausted.

At length Lu K'ai, "left," or senior, Prime Minister, ventured a memorial, saying, "No natural calamity has fallen upon the people, yet they starve; no public work is in progress, yet the treasury is empty. I am distressed. The country under the Hans has fallen apart and three states have arisen therefrom. Those ruled by the Ts'aos and the Lius, as the result of their own folly, have been lost in Chin. Foolish I may be, but I would protect the state for Your Majesty against the evils we have seen in the other divisions. This city of Wuch'ang is not safe as a royal residence. There is a rhyme concerning it, the gist of which is that it is better to drink the water of Chienyeh than eat the fish of Wuch'ang, better to die in Chienyeh than to live in Wuch'ang. This shows the regard of the people as well as the will of Heaven. Now the public storehouses are nearly empty; they contain insufficient for a year's use. The officers of all grades vex and distress the people and none pity them.

"In former times the palace women numbered less than a hundred; for years past they have exceeded a thousand. This is an extravagant waste of treasure. The courtiers render no disinterested service, but are split into cliques and cabals. The honest are injured and the good driven away. All these things undermine the state and weaken the people. I beg Your Majesty to reduce the number of officers and remove grievances, to dismiss the palace women and select honest officers, to the joy of the people and the tranquillity of the state."

But the king was displeased, and showed his contempt for the minister's remonstrance by beginning to collect material for the building of a new palace to be called the "Chaoming Palace." He even made the officers of the court go into the forest to fell trees for the work.

The king called in the soothsayer Shang Kuang and bade him take the *sortes* and enquire as to the attainment of empire. The soothsayer replied that all was propitious and in the year *kêng-tzu* a black umbrella would enter Loyang. And the king was pleased.

He said to Hua Fu, "The former rulers listened to your words and sent captains to various points and placed defensive camps along the rivers. And over all these was set Ting Fêng. Now my desire is to conquer Han and avenge the wrongs of my brother, the ruler of Shu. What place should be first conquered?"

Hua Fu replied, "Now that Ch'êngtu has fallen and the Throne there been overturned, Ssŭma Yen will assuredly desire to absorb this land. Your Majesty should display virtue and restore confidence to your people. That would be the best plan. If you engage in war it will be like throwing on hemp to put out a fire; the hemp only adds to the blaze. This is worthy of careful consideration."

But Sun Hao grew angry and said, "I desire to take this opportunity to return to my real heritage. Why do you employ this ill-omened language? Were it not for your long service, now would I slay you and expose your head as a warning."

He bade the lictors hustle the faithful minister from his presence, and Hua Fu left the court.

"It is pitiful," said he, "Ere long our beautiful country will pass to another."

So he retired. And the king ordered Lu K'ang, "Guardian of the East," to camp his army at Chiangk'ou in order to attack Hsiangyang.

Spies reported this in Loyang and it was told the King of Wei. When he heard that the army of Wu threatened to invade Hsiangyang he called a council, and Chia Ch'ung stood forth, saying, "I hear the government of Wu, under its present king, is devoid of virtue and the king has turned aside out of the road. Your Majesty should send Yang Hu to oppose this army, and when internal trouble shall arise let him attack, and victory will then be easy."

The king issued an edict ordering Yang Hu to prepare, and so he mustered his men and set himself to guard the district.

Yang was very popular. Any of the men of Wu who desired to desert to the other side were allowed to come over. He employed only the fewest possible men on patrol duty. Instead he set his men to till the soil, and they cultivated an extensive area, whereby the hundred days' supplies with which they set out were soon increased to enough for ten years.

Yang maintained great simplicity, wearing the lightest of garments and no armour. His personal escort numbered only about a score.

One day his officers came to his tent to say that the spies reported great laxity in the enemy's camp, and they wished to attack.

But Yang replied, "You must not depise Lu K'ang, for he is able and crafty. Formerly his master sent him to attack Hsiling, and he slew Pu Shan and many of his captains. I could not save them. So long as he remains in command I shall remain on the defensive. I shall not attack till there be trouble and confusion among our enemies. To be rash and not await the proper moment to attack is to invite defeat."

They found him wise and said no more. They only kept the boundaries. One day Yang and his officers went out to hunt, and it happened that Lu had chosen the same day to hunt.

Yang gave strict orders not to cross the boundary, and so each hunted only on his own side. Lu was astonished at the enemy's scrupulous propriety. In the evening, after both parties had returned, Yang ordered an inspection of the slaughtered game and sent over to the other side any that seemed to have been first struck by the men of Wu.

Lu K'ang was greatly pleased and sent for the bearers of the game. "Does your leader drink wine?" asked he.

They replied, "Only on ceremonial occasions does he drink."

"I have some very old wine," replied Lu, smiling, "and I will give of it to you to bear to your general as a gift. It is the wine I myself drink on ceremonial occasions, and he shall have half in return for to-day's courtesy."

They took the wine and left.

"Why do you give him wine?" asked Lu's officers.

"Because he has shown kindness, and I must return courtesy for courtesy."

When the gift of wine arrived and the bearers told Yang the story of their reception he laughed.

"So he knows I can drink," said he.

He had the jar opened, and the wine was poured out. One of his captains begged him to drink moderately lest there should be some harm come of it.

"Lu K'ang is no poisoner," replied the general.

And he drank. The friendly intercourse thus begun continued, and messengers frequently passed from one camp to the other.

One day the messengers said that Lu K'ang was unwell and had been ailing for several days.

"I think he suffers from the same complaint as I," said Yang, "I have some remedies ready prepared and will send him some."

The drugs were taken over to the other camp. But the sick man's officers were suspicious and said, "This medicine is surely harmful; it comes from the enemy."

Lu K'ang cried, "What! Think you that old Uncle Yang would poison a man? Do not doubt."

He drank the decoction. Next day he was much better, and when his staff came to congratulate him he said, "If he takes his stand upon virtue and we take ours upon violence, he will drag us after him without fighting. See to it that the boundaries be well kept and that we seek not to gain any unfair advantage."

Soon after came a special envoy from the King of Wu to urge upon his general prompt activity.

"Our Emperor sends orders for you to press forward," said the envoy. "You are not to await invasion."

"You may return and I will send up a memorial," replied the leader.

So a memorial was written and soon followed the envoy to Chienyeh. When the king read it he found therein many arguments against attacking Chin and exhortations to exercise a virtuous rule instead of engaging in hostilities. It angered him.

"They say he has come to an understanding with the enemy, and now I believe it," said the king.

Thereupon he deprived Lu of his command and took away his commission and degraded him in rank. Another general, Sun Chi, was sent to supersede Lu. And none dared to intervene.

King Hao became still more arbitrary and of his own will changed the year-style once more. Day by day his life became more wanton and vicious.

The soldiers in every camp murmured with anger and resentment, and at last three high officers, led by the senior Prime Minister, boldly and earnestly remonstrated with the king for his many irregularities. They suffered death. Within ten years more than two score ministers were put to death for doing their duty.

King Hao maintained an extravagantly large guard of five legions of heavy cavalry, and these men were the terror of everyone.

Now when Yang Hu, on the Chin side of the frontier, heard that his opponent had been removed from his command and that the conduct of the king had become wholly unreasonable he knew that the time was near for him to overcome Wu. Wherefore he presented a memorial.

"Although fate is superior to man, yet success depends upon human effort. Now as the danger of Chiang and Huai are not as those of Chienko, while the ferocity of Sun Hao exceeds that of Liu Ch'an, the misery of the men of Wu exceeds that of the dwellers in the west. Our armies are stronger than ever before, and if we miss this opportunity to bring the whole land under one rule, but continue to weary our men with continual watching and cause the world to groan under the burden of militarism, then our efficiency will decline and we shall not endure."

When Ssŭma Yen read this he gave orders for the army to move. But three officers, led by Chia Ch'ung, opposed it, and the orders were withdrawn. Yang Hu was disappointed and said, "What a pity it is that of ten possible vexations one always meets with eight or nine!"

In the fourth year of the period Yang Hu went to court and asked leave to retire on account of ill health. Before granting him leave to go, the king asked him what means he would propose to settle the state.

He replied, "'Sun Hao is a very cruel ruler and could be conquered without fighting. If he were to die and a wise successor sat upon his throne, Your Majesty would never be able to gain possession of Wu."

"Suppose your army attacked now; what then?" asked the king.

"I am now too old and too ill for the task," replied Yang. "Some other bold and capable leader must be found."

He left the court and retired to his home. Toward the end of the year he was nigh unto death, and the king went to visit him. The sight of his king at his bedside brought tears to the eyes of the faithful old soldier. "If I died a myriad times, I could never requite Your Majesty," said he.

The king also wept, saying, "My great grief is that I could not take advantage of your abilities to attack Wu. Who now is there to carry out your design?"

Hesitatingly the sick man replied, "I am dying and must be wholly sincere. The General Tu Yü is equal to the task, and is the one man to attack Wu."

The King said, "How beautiful it is to bring good men into prominence! But why did you write a memorial recommending certain men and then burn the draft so that no one knew?"

The dying man answered, "I bowed before the officials in open court, I besought the kindness of the private attendants, but all in vain."

So he died, and Ssŭma Yen wailed for him and then returned to his palace. He conferred on the dead leader the posthumous rank of *T'ai-fu* and the title of Marquis. The traders closed their shops out of respect to his memory, and all the frontier camps were filled with wailing. The people of Hsiangyang, recalling that he loved to wander on the Hsien Hills, built there a temple to him and set up a stone and sacrificed regularly at the seasons. The passers-by were moved to tears when they read Yang's name on the tablet, so that it came to be called "The Stone of Tears."

> I saw the fragments of a shattered stone
> One spring time on the hillside, when, alone,
> I walked to greet the sun. The pines distilled
> Big drops of dew unceasing; sadness filled
> My heart. I knew this was the Stone of Tears,
> The stone of memory sad of long-past years.

On the strength of Yang's recommendation Tu Yü was placed over Chingchou, and the title of "Guardian of the South" was conferred upon him. He was a man of great experience, untiring in study and devoted to the Tso Chuan, the book of history composed by Tso Ch'iu-ming upon the record "Spring and Autumn." In hours of leisure a copy was never out of his hand and when he went abroad an attendant rode in front with the beloved book. He was said to be "Tso Chuan mad."

Tu went to Hsiangyang and began by being kind to the people and caring for his soldiers. By this time Wu had lost by death both Ting Fêng and Lu K'ang, its two most famous leaders.

The conduct of the King of Wu waxed worse and worse. He used to give great banquets whereat intoxication was universal. He appointed Rectors of Feasts to observe all the faults committed by guests, and after these banquets all offenders were punished, some by flaying the face, others by gouging out the eyes. Every one went in terror of these Rectors.

Wang Chün, Governor of Yichou, sent in a memorial advising an attack upon Wu. He said, "Sun Hao is steeped in vice and should be attacked at once. Should he die and be succeeded by a good ruler we might meet with serious opposition. The ships I built seven years ago lie idle and rotting; why not use them? I am seventy years of age and must soon die. If any one of three events happen, the death of Sun Hao, the destruction of these ships, or my death, then success will be difficult to ensure. I pray Your Majesty not to miss the tide."

At the next assembly of officers King Ssŭma Yen said to them, "I have decided to act; I have received similar advice from two officers."

At this arose Wang Hun and said, "I hear Sun Hao intends to march north and has his army ready. Report says it is formidable and would be hard to defeat. I counsel to await another year till that army has lost its first vigour."

A command to cease warlike preparations was the result of this counsel. The king betook himself to his private chamber where he engaged in a game of *wei-ch'i*, with Chang Hua as opponent. While at the game, another memorial arrived; it was from Tu Yü. It read:—

"Formerly Yang Hu explained his plans confidentially to Your Majesty, but did not lay them before the court. The result has been much debate and conflict of opinion. In every project there are *pros and cons*, but in this the arguments are mostly in favour. The worst that can happen is failure. Since last autumn the proposed attack has become generally known, and, if we stop now, Sun Hao will be frightened and remove the capital to Wuch'ang, repair his fortifications in Chiangnan and move his threatened people out of danger. Then the capital cannot be assaulted, nor is there anything left in the countryside to rob. Hence next year's attack will also fail."

Just as the King finished reading, Chang Hua pushed back the board, rose and drew his hands into his sleeves, saying, "Your Majesty's skill in war is almost divine, your state is prosperous and the army strong; the King of Wu is a tyrant, his people are miserable and his country mean. Now you can easily conquer him, and I pray that there be no further hesitation."

"How could I hesitate after your discourse?" said the king.

Thereupon he returned to the council chamber and issued his commands. Tu Yü was given chief command and was to attack Chiangling; Wang Yu, of Langya, to attack Ch'uchung; Wang Hun to go up against Hêngchiang; Yang Jung to move against Wuch'ang; Hu Fên to attack Hsiak'ou. And all divisions were under the orders of Tu Yü. In addition to the land forces, two large fleets were to operate on the river. A separate force was sent away to Hsiangyang.

The King of Wu was greatly alarmed at the news of such armies and fleets, and he called to him quickly his Prime Minister Chang T'i and two others, Ho Chih and Hsi Hsiu, to consult how to defend his land. The Prime Minister proposed to send Wu Yen to meet the enemy at Chiangling, Sun Hsin to Hsiak'ou, while he himself took command of a camp at Niuchu, ready to lend help at any point.

The King approved his dispositions and felt satisfied that he was safe by land. But in the privacy of his own apartment he felt miserable, for he realised that no preparations had been made against an attack by water. Then Ts'ên Hun asked the king why he bore a sad countenance and King Sun Hao told him of his dread of the enemy navy.

"But I have a scheme that will smash all their ships," cried Ts'en.

"What is it?" asked the King, pleased to hear this.

"Iron is plentiful. Make great chains with heavy links and stretch them across the river at various points. Also forge many massive hammers and arrange them in the stream so that when the enemy's ships sail down before the wind they will collide with the hammers and be wrecked. Then they will sail no more."

Blacksmiths were soon at work on the river bank welding the links and forging the hammers. Work went on day and night, and soon all were in place.

As has been said Tu Yü was to attack Chiangling, and he sent Chou Chih with eight hundred sailors to sail secretly along the river to Lohsiang. There they were to make a great show of flags along the bank and among the trees. Drums were to be beaten and bombs exploded during the day and many fires lighted at night to give the appearance of a great army.

So Chou sailed to Pashan. Soon after the army and the marine forces made a simultaneous advance, but the navy of Wu, under Sun Hsin, came up, and at the first encounter Tu Yü's army retired. Sun Hsin landed his men and pursued. But in the midst of the pursuit a signal bomb sounded and Sun Hsin was attacked on all sides. He tried to retire, but the army he had been pursuing, Tu's force, turned back too and joined in the attack.

Wu's losses were very heavy, and Sun Hsin hastened back to the city. At the ramparts the men of Chin mingled with his own and so entered the gates. They raised signal fires on the walls. This manœuvre amazed Sun, and he said that the northern men had surely flown into the city. He made an effort to escape, but the leader of Chin, Chou Chih, unexpectedly appeared and slew him.

A fleet of the ships of Wu had accompanied Sun Hsin. The admiral, Lu Ching, saw on the south shore a great standard bearing the name of Tu Yü. He became alarmed and landed to try to escape, but was soon found and slain.

At his position at Chiangling Wu Yen heard of these defeats and knew his position was untenable, so he fled. However, he was soon captured and led into the presence of the victorious general.

"No use sparing you," said Tu Yü, and he sentenced the prisoner to death.

Thus Chiangling was captured and all the districts along the Hsiang and Yüan rivers as far as Huangchou, which surrendered at the first summons.

Tu Yü sent out officers to soothe the people of the conquered districts, and they suffered nothing from the soldiery. Next he marched toward Wuch'ang, and that city also yielded. So the glory of Tu Yü was very great.

Tu summoned his officers to a council to decide upon attacking Chienyeh. Hu Fu said, "A whole century's raiding will not reduce it completedly. The time of the spring rise of waters is near and our position is precarious. We should do well to await the coming spring."

Tu Yü replied, "In the days of old, Yo I obtained the aid of the west and overcame Ch'i in one battle. Our prestige is now high and success certain, easy as the splitting of a bamboo, which seems to welcome the knife after the first few joints have been overcome. We shall meet no great opposition."

So he gave orders to the various leaders to move in concert against the city.

Now Wang Chün had gone down the river with his naval force. From his scouts he heard of the chains and the hammers that had been laid in the river to hinder his progress. But he only smiled. He constructed great rafts of timber and placed on them straw effigies of men in armour and sent them down river with the current. The defenders of Wu took them for real men and, alarmed by their numbers, fled in panic. Then the great hammers were lifted out of the stream and the rafts drifted on.

Moreover, on the rafts they laid great torches many fathoms long, and very thick, made of straw soaked in linseed oil.

When the raft was checked by a chain the torches were lighted and the chains exposed to the heat till they melted and broke asunder. Thus the rafts went down stream conquering wherever they came.

Then the Prime Minister of Wu sent two generals, Shên Jung and Chuko Ching, to try to check the advance of the armies. Shên Jung said to his colleague, "The forces above have failed to stop the enemy, and they will surely come here. We shall have to put forth all our strength. If haply we can succeed, the safety of our country is assured. But suppose we fight and lose the battle, then is our country lost."

"Sir, you only say what is too true," said his colleague.

Just as they talked of these matters came reports of the approach of their enemies in irrestible force. The two leaders were seized with panic and went back to see the Prime Minister.

"Our country is lost," cried Chuko. "Why not run?"

"We all know that the land is doomed," replied the Prime Minister, "but if we make no defence, and no one dies for his country, shall we not be shamed?"

Chuko Ching left, weeping, and the Prime Minister went with Shên Jung to the army. The invaders soon arrived, and Chou Chih was the first to break into the camp. Chang T'i, the Prime Minister, resisted stubbornly, but was soon slain in a mêlée, and Shên was killed by Chou Chih. The army of Wu was defeated and scattered.

> Chin's army banners waved on Pashan mount
> And trusty Chang in Chiangling fighting died;
> He recked not that the kingly grace was spent,
> He rather chose to die than shame his side.

The armies of Chin conquered at Niuchu and penetrated deeply into the country of Wu. From his camp Wang Chün sent a report of his victory to Loyang, and Ssŭma Yen was pleased.

But Chia Ch'ung again opposed further fighting, saying, "The armies have been long absent and the men will suffer from the unhealthiness of the country. It would be well to call them home."

Chang Hua spoke against this course, saying, "The army has reached the very home and centre of the enemy. Soon their courage will fail and the king himself will be our prisoner. To recall the army now would be to waste the efforts already made."

The king inclined to neither side. Chia turned upon his opponent savagely, saying, "You are wholly ignorant and understand nothing; you are bent upon winning some sort of glory at the expense of our soldiers' lives. Death would be too good for you."

"Why wrangle?" said the king. "Chang Hua agrees with me, and he knows my wishes."

Just at this moment came a memorial from the leader Tu Yü also recommending advance, whereupon the king decided that the army should go on.

The royal mandate duly reached the camp and the Chin navy went out to the attack in great pomp. The men of Wu made no defence, but surrendered at once.

When the King of Wu heard his men had surrendered thus, he turned pale, and his courtiers said, "What is to be done? Here the northern army comes nearer every day and our men just give in."

"But why do they not fight?" said the king.

The courtiers replied, "The one evil of to-day is the eunuch Ts'ên Hun. Slay him, and we ourselves will go out and fight to the death."

"How can a eunuch harm a state?" cried the king.

"Have we not seen what Huang Hao did in Shu?" shouted the courtiers in chorus.

Moved by sudden fury, the courtiers rushed into the palace, found the wretched object of their hate and slew him, some even tasting of his palpitating flesh.

Then T'ao Chün said, "All my ships are small, but give me large vessels and I will place thereon two legions and go forth to fight. I can defeat the enemy."

His request was granted, and the royal guards were sent up the river to join battle, while another naval force went down stream. But a heavy gale came on. The flags were blown down and lay over in the ships, and the men would not embark. They scattered leaving their leader with only a few score men.

Wang Chün, the leader of Chin, set sail and went down the river. After passing Three Hills, the sailing master of his ship said the gale was too strong for him to go on. He wished to anchor till the storm had moderated. But Wang would not listen. "I wish to capture Shiht'ouch'êng (now Nanking)," said he, "and will not hear of anchoring."

So he compelled the sailing master to continue. On the way Chang Hsiang, one of the leaders of Wu, came to offer surrender.

"If you are in earnest, you will lead the way and help me," said Wang.

Chang consented, returned to his own ship and led the squadron. When he reached the walls he called to the defenders to open the gates and allow the Chin army to enter. The gates were opened.

When the King heard that his enemies had actually entered the city he wished to put an end to his life, but his officers prevented this.

They said, "Your Majesty, why not imitate the conduct of Liu Ch'an, now Duke of Anlô?"

So the king no longer thought of death, but went to offer submission, his face covered and taking a coffin with him. His officers followed him. He was graciously received, General Wang himself removing the cloth from his face, and the coffin was burned. The vanquished ruler was treated with the ceremony due to a prince.

A poet of the T'ang Dynasty wrote a few lines on this surrender:—

> Adown the stream ride storeyed warships tall;
>   With massive chains some seek to stop their way.
>   But Chinling's independence fades away
> And soon "We yield" is signalled from the wall.
>
> Full oft I think of bygone days and sigh,
>   Along the stream, unmoved, the old hills rest,
>   While I am homeless on the earth's broad breast,
> Where grim old forts stand grey beneath the sky.

So Wu was subdued and ceased to exist as a state; its four provinces, eighty-three districts, three hundred and ten departments, five hundred and twenty-three thousand families, thirty-two thousand military officers, two hundred and thirteen thousand soldiers, two million three hundred thousand inhabitants, its stores of grain and over five thousand ships, all fell booty to the victorious Chin Dynasty. In the women's quarters of the palace were found more than five thousand persons.

Proclamations were issued; treasuries and storehouses were sealed. T'ao Chün's army soon melted away without striking a blow. Wan Yu and Wang Jung submitted quietly. Wang Chün was greatly elated at his success.

When the Commander-in-chief arrived there were great feastings and rewards for the soldiers. The granaries were opened and doles of grain issued to the people, so that they also were glad of peace.

One city only stood out; Chienp'ing, under the Prefect Wu Yen. However, he too surrendered when he heard the capital had fallen.

The tidings of all these successes reached Loyang just at the celebration of the birthday of the Chin Emperor, and the rejoicings and congratulations were redoubled. At one of the banquets the Emperor did honour to the memory of the late Yang Hu. Raising his wine cup, and in a voice broken by emotion, he said, "To-day's success is the merit of Yang *T'ai-fu*. I regret that he is not here to share our rejoicings."

Sun Hsiu, a General of Cavalry in Wu, went away from the court and wailed, facing the south.

"Alas, ye blue heavens! What manner of man is this Sun Hao to yield thus the heritage of his family, won by the sword of his forbears in the brave days that are past?"

Meantime the victors marched homeward, and Sun Hao went to Loyang to present himself at court, and in his capacity of minister he prostrated himself at the feet of the Emperor of the Chin Dynasty in the Hall of Audience. He was allowed a seat.

"I set that seat for you long since," said the Emperor.

"Thy servant also set a seat for Your Majesty in the south," retorted Sun Hao.

The Emperor laughed loudly. Then Chia Ch'ung turned to Sun Hao and said, "I hear, Sir, that when you were in the south they gouged out people's eyes and flayed their faces; what crimes were so punished?

"Murders of princes, and malicious speech and disloyal conduct were so punished."

Chia was silenced, for he was greatly ashamed.

Sun Hao was created Marquis of Kueiming. His sons and grandsons received minor ranks and other grades were conferred upon his ministers who had followed him in his surrender. The sons and grandsons of the late Prime Minister of Wu, Chang T'i, who had perished in battle, were given ranks, and the victorious leader, Wang Chün, was rewarded with the title "Pillar of the State." And many other ranks were conferred.

The tale is told. The Three States have been rewelded into one empire under the rule of Ssŭma Yen of the Chin Dynasty. And here we may say as in the beginning:—"States fall asunder and re-unite; empires wax and wane."

A poet has summed up the history of these stirring years in a poem.

It was the dawning of a glorious day
When first the Founder of the House of Han
Hsienyang's proud palace entered. Noontide came
When Kuang-Wu the imperial rule restored.
Alas, that Hsien succeeded in full time
And saw the setting of the sun of power!
Ho Chin, the feeble, fell beneath the blows
Of palace minions. Tung Cho, vile though bold,
Then ruled the court. The plot Wang Yün devised
To oust him, failed, recoiled on his own head.
The Li and Kuo lit up the flame of war
And brigands swarmed like ants through all the land.
Then rose the valiant and deployed their might.
The Suns carved out a kingdom in the east,
Honan the Yüans strove to make their own.
The Lius went west and seized on Pa and Shu,
Another Liu laid hold on Ching and Hsiang,
Chang Miao, Chang Lu, in turn held Chêng by force.
Each of three others seized upon a fief;
T'ao Chien, Han Hsiu and Kungsun Ts'an, the bold.

But overtopping all Ts'ao Ts'ao the strong
Became first minister, and to his side,
Drew many able men. He swayed the court,
Without, he held the nobles in his hand;
By force of arms he held the capital
Against all rivals. Of imperial stock
Was born Yüan-tê, who with sworn brothers twain
Made oath the dynasty should be restored.
These wandered homeless east and west for years,
A petty force. But Destiny was kind
And led Liu Pei to Nanyang's rustic cot,
Where lay Reposing Dragon, he who knew
Already that the empire must be rent.
Twice Liu essayed in vain to see the sage;
Once more he went, and then his fortune turned.
Chingchou fell to him, followed Ssŭch'uan.
A fitting base to build an empire on.
Alas! He ruled there only three short years,
Then left his only son to K'ung-ming's care.
Full nobly K'ung-ming played protector's part,
Unceasing strove to win first place for Shu;
But Fate forbade; one night for aye his star
Went down behind the rampart of the hills.
Chiang Wei the strong inherited his task
And struggled on for years. But Chung and Têng
Attacked the Hans' last stronghold, and it fell.
Five sons of Ts'ao sat on the dragon throne,
And Ssŭma snatched the sceptre from Ts'ao Huan.
Before him bowed the kings of Shu and Wu,
Content to forfeit kingly power for life.
All down the ages rings the note of change,
For fate so rules it; none escapes its sway.
The kingdoms three have vanished as a dream,
The useless misery is ours to grieve.

THE END